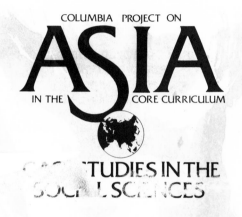

COLUMBIA PROJECT ON

ASIA

IN THE   CORE CURRICULUM

CASE STUDIES IN THE
SOCIAL SCIENCES

Columbia Project on Asia in the Core Curriculum

ASIA: CASE STUDIES IN THE SOCIAL SCIENCES
A GUIDE FOR TEACHING
Myron L. Cohen, editor

MASTERWORKS OF ASIAN LITERATURE IN COMPARATIVE PERSPECTIVE
A GUIDE FOR TEACHING
Barbara Stoler Miller, editor

ASIA IN WESTERN AND WORLD HISTORY
A GUIDE FOR TEACHING
Ainslie T. Embree and Carol Gluck, editors

Roberta Martin
Project Director

Wm. Theodore de Bary, Ainslie T. Embree, Carol Gluck
Project Chairmen

COLUMBIA PROJECT ON

ASIA

IN THE   CORE CURRICULUM

CASE STUDIES IN THE SOCIAL SCIENCES

A Guide for Teaching

Edited by Myron L. Cohen

An East Gate Book

M. E. Sharpe
Armonk, New York
London, England

JUL 0 6 1994

An East Gate Book

Library of Congress Cataloging-in-Publication Data

Asia, case studies in the social sciences : a guide for teaching /
Myron L. Cohen, editor
p.   cm.
Includes bibliographical references and index.
ISBN 1-56324-156-0 (cloth) — ISBN 1-56324-157-9 (pbk.)
1. Social sciences— Study and teaching (Higher)— United States.
2. Social sciences— Asia— Case studies.
3. Asia— Social conditions— Case studies.
4. Asia— Economic conditions— Case studies.
5. Asia— Politics and government— Case studies.
I. Cohen, Myron L.
H62.5.U5A83   1992
306′.095— dc20
92-31585
CIP

Printed in the United States of America
The paper used in this publication meets the minimum
requirements of American National Standard for
Information Sciences— Permanence of Paper for
Printed Library Materials, ANSI Z 39.48-1984.

∞

BM (c)   10   9   8   7   6   5   4   3   2

BM (p)   10   9   8   7   6   5   4   3   2

Contents

Japan

Korea

Philippines

Thailand

IV. Sociology

China

Comparative/Interarea

India

Japan

Vietnam

Contents by Discipline and Subdiscipline

Anthropology

See also SOCIOLOGY paper by Hardacre on Japan (p. 526)

Economics

Political Science

THE MILITARY

RELIGION

Japan

*See also ANTHROPOLOGY papers by Cohen on China (p. 17),
Bowen on Indonesia (p. 91), and Babb on India (p. 32)*

SOCIOLOGY OF WORK/INDUSTRIAL SOCIETY

China

India

Japan

Japan-U.S.

STRATIFICATION, HIERARCHY, AND MOBILITY

Japan

*See also ANTHROPOLOGY papers by Hefner on Indonesia
(p. 105) and Lynch on India (p. 67)*

URBAN SOCIETY

India

See also ANTHROPOLOGY paper by Bestor on Japan (p. 116)

Contents by Country
and Discipline

Thailand

Political Science

Vietnam

Sociology

Comparative/Interarea

Preface

The Project on Asia in the Core Curriculum began in 1984 to support the introduction of material on Asia into the core curricula of undergraduate institutions throughout the country. Three "Guides for Teaching" are the result of dialogue between Asian specialists and colleagues specializing in the Western tradition who most often teach the introductory, general education courses in the various academic disciplines. No attempt has been made to stress Asia at the expense of the West. The purpose of the project is to identify themes, texts, and comparative concepts that provide avenues of entry for Asian material into core courses in history, literature, and the social sciences. We asked: "How can core courses focusing primarily on Western culture, tradition, and canon be enhanced by reference to Asian traditions?" and "Which aspects of the rich and varied Asian traditions should be brought to the attention of students?"

The guides are entitled: **Asia in Western and World History**, **Masterworks of Asian Literature in Comparative Perspective**, and **Asia: Case Studies in the Social Sciences**. The approximately forty essays by leading specialists in each volume suggest a range of possibilities for introducing material on Asia. The essays are arranged to provide the widest choice of approaches to meet the reader's pedagogical needs. While each of the guides is a discrete publication, together they form a series that facilitates interdisciplinary teaching: in a course on anthropology, for example, the instructor who chooses to draw upon Lawrence Babb's overview of religion in India (in **Asia: Case Studies in the Social Sciences**) will also find much of interest in Ainslie Embree's review of South Asian history (in **Asia in Western and World History**) and in Barbara Stoler Miller's introduction to the imaginative universe of Indian literature (in **Masterworks of Asian Literature in Comparative Perspective**).

The Project on Asia in the Core Curriculum has involved over one hundred scholars from seventy-five public and private undergraduate institutions throughout the United States. It is chaired at Columbia University by a panel composed of Wm. Theodore de Bary, Ainslie T. Embree, and Carol Gluck.

The National Endowment for the Humanities, the Henry Luce Foundation, the Panasonic Foundation, and the U.S. Department of Education sponsored the project. We are deeply indebted to them for their continuing support.

We welcome any and all contributions to this curricular effort. The dialogue has just begun.

Roberta Martin
Project Director

Guide to the Reader

ASIA: *Case Studies in the Social Sciences* includes three tables of contents that provide the reader access to the material by discipline, subdiscipline, or country. For example, a political scientist offering a course on the military and seeking a comparative case from Asia can look under "Political Science: The Military" and select one of the case studies listed. Similarly, a sociologist encouraged to include some reference to Japan in an introductory course can look under "Sociology: Japan" and choose from among several different topics on which case studies are offered. The first page of each entry provides a list of the topics covered within the essay as well as an overview of central theoretical points that can be included in lectures. The remainder of the essay elaborates these central points and concludes with a list of suggested Issues for Discussion to raise with students. The Selected Readings at the end of each essay include titles appropriate for a student syllabus and those recommended for faculty background.

Each entry is a discrete essay, but entries for several disciplines on any given country provide complementary approaches to the same society. The reader may wish to peruse them all in order to gain a better understanding of the functioning of that society. Similarly, a course that includes a comparison of two or more different examples of "religion in society," "the family," or "the military in politics" will deepen the student's appreciation of the variety of cultures and social, political, and economic systems in Asia.

Principles of Transliteration

For non-English words used in this volume, those words which appear in **Webster's 3rd International Dictionary** are written with Webster's spelling.

For proper names of persons and places and some religious texts (the Qur'an, for example), no diacritics or italics are used.

Italics are used for all other non-English words, with diacritics as appropriate.

The pinyin system of romanization is used for Chinese words, except in essays dealing with Taiwan where the names of organizations and individuals are rendered in the Wade-Giles system of romanization that is preferred in Taiwan.

Asia: Case Studies in the Social Sciences

Introduction

Myron L. Cohen

The purpose of this book is to provide teachers in the social sciences with Asian materials for inclusion in general introductory undergraduate courses and in more advanced courses dealing with a particular theme. Within the limits posed by restriction to one volume the attempt has been made to have the different social science disciplines as well as Asia's cultural and social diversity reasonably well represented. The case-study format has been adapted so as to provide treatment of particular subjects in sufficient detail to enable their inclusion in classroom lectures without requiring additional background preparation by the instructor. To further enhance the integration of the material into the overall curriculum, a brief outline of the major themes and ideas it addresses is presented at the beginning of each case study. We expect that this arrangement will provide a convenient overview, suggesting where the material can be fitted into an established teaching plan; we hope that some teachers will find within these outlines of basic themes and the essays that follow them materials of sufficient interest to warrant modification or expansion of the plan itself.

The problems encountered in achieving greater representation of different cultures and societies in introductory or topical courses relate in part to the particular historical development of each social science discipline. In social and cultural anthropology courses, the earlier bias toward the "exotic" and "primitive" has been corrected in recent years precisely by the inclusion of material pertaining to the United States and other industrialized societies, while for the other social sciences there is the increasingly felt need to go beyond the United States and Western Europe.

There are also practical problems to be confronted. It is hardly to be expected that an instructor in the social sciences will have control over material pertaining to his or her own discipline for cultures in all parts of the world. Neither is it to be expected that this college teacher will have the time to prepare to include a particular world area in course curricula by examining the scholarly monographs and articles pertaining to it. Asia, a vast area with tremendous cultural diversity, presents just such problems, and this book represents an effort to provide a solution.

This volume is not meant to serve as an introductory textbook. It intends to be of aid to instructors not by providing a general narrative, but rather by making available in a convenient format discussions by specialists of specific issues. At the same time, issues of major interest only to a particular community of Asian specialists are avoided, as in each essay the discussion is presented within the framework of the relevant discipline's broader theoretical, methodological, and comparative concerns. With its treatment of different countries and regions of Asia, this book can serve as a self-contained source for cross-cultural comparisons within a variety of disciplinary or thematic contexts. Furthermore, instructors using the case studies written by his or her disciplinary colleagues may find it useful to refer for background information to the essays in this book by Asia specialists in other areas of the social sciences. Although it is our intention that each essay serve on its own or in combination with others as a resource for the college teacher, we also recognize that instructors may be interested in further exploring certain topics, or in assigning their students supplementary readings. We therefore have included at the end of each essay a brief list of additional books or articles and have indicated whether they are more suitable for the instructor's own reference or for students.

The social sciences are by definition concerned with different areas of human behavior. On purely scholarly grounds, current debate over the place of multicultural studies in the college curriculum is irrelevant to the social sciences precisely because these disciplines assert that their domain is pan-cultural. There is nothing in the intellectual foundation of any social science that places Western culture or Western societies in a privileged position as object of analysis or source of example, for the theories and methodologies of a social science discipline found to be inappropriate or indeed disproven when applied to either a Western or a non-Western cultural setting will require modification or outright rejection. Ideally speaking, courses in the social sciences which focus on basic concepts or on a more advanced treatment of specific subjects will not be confined to a particular culture or world area for purposes of providing examples or illustrating the application of theory or methodology.

Discussion regarding the desirability of greater multicultural content in social science courses therefore really hinges on the issue of the non-disciplinary relevance of different societies and world areas to students. While it is obvious that undergraduates taking a sociology course on family and marriage, or an introductory course in economics, will benefit from analysis that incorporates material drawn from a familiar cultural setting, it is hardly self-evident that the student stands to gain even more when the focus is exclusively on American data. If the assertion that we now live in a "global community" has been made often enough to be trite, the fact remains that multicultural comparisons play a vital role in social science courses not only when the goal is to provide exposure to a particular discipline's intellectual foundations but also when the intent additionally is to enhance a student's self-understanding and his or her appreciation of circumstances encountered in daily life. The growing presence and impact in this country of products, people, ideas, and lifestyles from world areas whose significance for American culture previously had been far less evident, or at least far less noted, is so obvious as to require no further comment. Within the United States, it is hardly a new development for people to assert their particular cultural heritage precisely in the context of claiming their rights or demanding their acceptance within the larger society. That such assertions involve an increasingly large number of cultural and national traditions is of course a reflection of changes in this country's population; but it also represents the growing determination of people of diverse origins to have their heritage be a marker of cultural parity rather than merely an attribute of minority status.

Asia certainly looms large in all of these developments which are linked to the increasing significance of cultural differences for and in American society. In addition to such obvious factors as the substantial growth in the economic impact of many Asian countries on the United States, or the increase of the Asian-American component of our population, there is the cultural diversity of Asia itself. Asia in fact is nothing more and nothing less than a massive geographic area, but one with a formidable historical and contemporary impact on the rest of the globe. In terms of economy, society, culture, religion, and political arrangements its peoples are heterogeneous to the extent that generalizations pitched at the level of Asia as a whole cannot differ from those regarding the human condition as such. If there is an Asian "essence" it can only be one that people everywhere share. Except in terms of a disciplinary or topical focus, there can be no textbook on all of Asia united by a theme other than geography. This circumstance makes the case-study approach employed in this book all the more appropriate for an instructor seeking to expose students to such an important part of the world.

The preparation of this book would have been impossible without the cooperation of many scholars at all stages of its development. Specialists contributed their time and expertise in helping to determine the topics to be covered and suggesting who might write on them. While many of the experts involved in the earlier discussions also contributed essays of their own, we wish here to express our thanks to all who so enthusiastically gave us advice. That this book has seen the light of day is due most of all to the efforts of Roberta Martin, the executive director of the Columbia Project on Asia in the Core Curriculum under whose auspices this book has been produced. Whether in terms of administration, organization, or energy, the greatest contribution has been hers, and those of us who have contributed to this volume owe her a great debt of gratitude. The essays were skillfully edited by Winifred Olsen and each phase of production most ably managed by Madge Huntington. They were assisted by Wang Xi, Paul Grunewald, Sarah Lindsay, and Ann Marie Murphy, who spent long hours generating the final copy of the manuscript. Project support from the National Endowment for the Humanities, the Henry Luce Foundation, the Panasonic Foundation, and the U.S. Department of Education is gratefully acknowledged.

I
Anthropology

Anthropology: China

Family Organization in China

Myron L. Cohen

I. INTRODUCTION: CENTRAL POINTS

The Chinese family provides an excellent illustrative case for the study of several central issues of concern to anthropologists: the role of the family in traditional agrarian (i.e., peasant) societies; differential social change and its impact on the family; rural-urban distinctions in traditional peasant societies; political factors affecting social change.

Role of the Family in Traditional Agrarian Societies. Three interrelated characteristics of late imperial Chinese society all point to the family's significance, making the Chinese case an excellent illustrative example of the family's role in a traditional peasant society:

• the family indeed was the **basic working unit of the Chinese economy**, both rural and urban;

• there was in late traditional China a **deemphasis of the**

hereditary status relationships so common in other peasant societies (e.g., India's caste system, medieval Europe's hereditary serfs and nobility), and rather a far more "fluid" social system with **considerable upward and downward mobility, in terms not of individuals but of families**;

• there was in Chinese **state ideology**, including Confucianism, a concern and preoccupation with familial relationships and ethics far more pronounced than in most other known peasant societies. Indeed, it was commonly held by traditional Chinese thinkers that harmonious families, organized on the basis of "proper" relations, were fundamental to the maintenance of the country's social and political order. **In other words, in China, the world's largest premodern state, attention was singularly focused on society's smallest unit**.

Differential Social Change: Impact on the Family. The Chinese case also furnishes an important example of the impact of modern political, economic, and cultural factors on family organization. Differential social change is shown by the fact that the traditional Chinese family system of late imperial times largely continued unchanged among the peasantry during the latter portion of the nineteenth and the first half of the twentieth centuries, when the country otherwise was experiencing penetration by the Western powers and undergoing a series of rapid, violent, and remarkable social and economic transformations, culminating in the establishment of the People's Republic in 1949.

Rural-Urban Distinctions in Traditional Peasant Societies. The case of the Chinese family can be used to challenge the common generalization that traditional peasant societies are characterized by severe rural-urban distinctions, for in China the emergence of such distinctions was precisely a symptom of the traditional system's breakdown. Prior to the mid-nineteenth century onset of Western attacks and penetration, there was a pattern of family organization common to rural and urban society and to different socioeconomic strata. Later, with growing industrialization, especially in the port cities, and with the emergence of a wage-earning working class and Western-oriented or radical elites, new family patterns also began to appear, so that there was the beginning of true contrasts, as between rural and urban or modern and traditional.

Political Factors Affecting Social Change in the Family. Discussions of the family and social change rarely take into account political influences, and here again the Chinese case is useful for introducing the political dimension. Indeed, only after the coming to power of the Communist government were there forces set in motion of general significance to Chinese family patterns in city and countryside alike. Through collectivization, families throughout rural and urban China were transformed from self-managing economic units into groups deriving their income from outside work. Linked to this, and to government education and family planning programs, was the emergence of a pronounced trend toward simplification of family structure and reduction in family size. During the past decade, government policy has been to foster decollectivization, especially in the countryside, so that many economic functions have once again devolved to the family level.

The discussion below deals first with the traditional family, then turns to pre-Communist changes, and finally to developments in the People's Republic.

II. MAJOR TOPICS

TRADITIONAL FAMILY ORGANIZATION

In traditional China during late imperial times the family was the basic unit of economic organization. It obtained its livelihood through the coordinated efforts of its members, who usually would eat together and otherwise be supported by the common family fund. The vast majority of families were farmers, yet as economic and social groups they were organized along the same lines as families whose members might be engaged in any combination of agricultural, commercial, or handicraft activities, or even as those families with wealth, learning, and elite status.

Peasant and Town Families. The overwhelmingly rural economy had as its foundation the family farm: as tenants or as owner-cultivators, farm families both worked their plots and also were directly responsible for the management of their farm as an enterprise. In the cities and towns of China, non-agricultural production and distribution largely was based upon the family firm or shop. In both city and countryside alike, family management was combined with family labor to as great an extent as possible, so that the family can be seen as an integrated economic unit for the organization and carrying out of productive labor, and also for its management. Under such circumstances, most wealthier families with surplus land found it both easier and more profitable to rent plots to tenant families rather than directly supervise field workers. While their tenants would assume the burdens of such tasks as daily field management, or crop planning, the landlord families would profit from the rent at the same time that they would be able to devote family managerial efforts to a variety of additional entrepreneurial undertakings.

Family Property and Social Stratification. The close connection between family organization and economic management was reflected in the traditional criteria for status evaluation. On top were those richer and more educated families whose members could avoid physical labor and instead devote their efforts exclusively to the management of their property; in the middle was the largest group, consisting of respected community members who were mainly farmers but also artisans and shopkeepers, who owned and managed land and other property, but had to do physical labor in deriving an income from their holdings; at the bottom of the social ladder were the poor propertyless with no managerial responsibilities, the hired field hands in the countryside or the paid manual laborers in the cities.

Gender Stratification. The Chinese family was male-centered, most emphatically with respect to the distribution of authority, patterns of residence, patterns of inheritance, and a pronounced preference for male offspring. While women could find ways of expressing their opinions and influencing events, it was mainly the men who directed family affairs, especially these pertaining to farm management or other major economic activities, and the family's overall relationships with the outside world. The father's position of authority was assured from the moment he began to head an independent family unit, but his wife would obtain a degree of authority in her own right only after the passage of many years. Her position was weakest when she was still childless (sonless); it improved when she bore a son; it grew even stronger when a daughter-in-law came under her direction; and by the time she entered into advanced age her authority began to approximate that of her husband, especially in peasant families; if his was the earlier death, full power within the family might sometimes then be in her hands.

The Collective Family Economy. The family was a group of kin related through marriage, birth, or adoption. The economic foundation of the family was its estate, owned jointly by male members and worked in common by the family as a whole. While the most significant property in the estate was land (owned outright or tenanted under a permanent or near-permanent arrangement), the family could also own residences, farm buildings, tools, livestock, etc. If the family was engaged in commerce, the shop and other assets likewise were family holdings. Associated with joint ownership of the estate was the common budget kept by family members. Persons working family fields or managing the family shop would contribute the earnings to a common fund managed by the family head, who was usually the father, on behalf of the family as a whole. Those working outside for wages were expected to do likewise if they earned a surplus above agreed-upon requirements for subsistence and personal expenses. The family was thus a cohesive unit economically as well as socially, but one strengthened to the extent that it owned property. Once again, there can be seen the tie between the internal economic forces making for family unity and the family's social standing in the community: the property relationships fostering familial solidarity also provided it with status in society at large.

Family Division and the Family Cycle. In China, marriage as such did not lead to the creation of a new family; rather, it usually meant that the bride moved into her husband's family unit (in a family in which there were no sons, a daughter might be joined by her husband). New families were created through partition of the family estate; with the division of family holdings there was the termination of many of the social and economic obligations and residential arrangements which previously had held the family together. Family partition brought into sharp focus the dominance of males within the family system. It was the men who shared in the division of the estate, and in most cases married brothers obtained equal portions. Each would use his share as the economic foundation for the new, smaller family he now headed, while it was common for an unmarried brother temporarily to continue to maintain a joint estate with one of his married siblings or with his father. There was, therefore, a cyclical process whereby family formation through division was followed by expansion and then division again.

Variations in Family Size and Complexity. Families large by contemporary Western standards and including more than one married couple most closely approximated the Confucian ideal of numerous male offspring for the perpetuation of the family line and the maintenance of family unity across several generations. Actually, the large family ideal was achieved only in a minority of cases, and in any event it was inevitable that most larger families would split into smaller units at one point or another. In a village, at any given time most families were small; some included both parents (or one surviving parent), one son, his wife, and their children; others were limited to parents and unmarried children and would thus be similar to many present-day Western families in size and composition.

Demographic Factors. Especially among the less well-to-do, family size was restricted not only because of divisive tendencies within the family organization but also because of high infant mortality rates. To carry on the ancestral line was a major tenet of Chinese kinship ideology, and male infant mortality was one of the factors leading many families to bring males in through adoption or through "calling in a son-in-law," a form of marriage looked down upon by society at large but often the only option available to a family without sons or to a man without property. One reason for the larger size of richer families was that they were more successful in raising their children to maturity; infant mortality was especially prevalent among the less well-to-do. Family size also could be increased through the practice of polygyny (i.e., a man's having two or more wives at the same time), and the presence of the additional women would greatly increase the likelihood of more children; although polygyny generally was acceptable in China, richer families were far better able to afford it.

Economic Factors. Yet another reason for bigger families among the wealthy was the tendency for brothers in such families to postpone division of family holdings; if through the effective coordination of family members the family improved its economic condition, the brothers would be less inclined to risk striking out on their own, while in families that were declining, the brothers might be encouraged to demand division relatively early. Thus the forces keeping a family together also illustrate the close connection between greater adherence to large family ideals on the one hand, and achievement of higher social and economic status on the other. It is not surprising, therefore, that the large "joint" or "extended" family was especially common among China's elite.

Ideological and Religious Factors. The Chinese imperial state attempted to give strong ideological support to the maintenance of family unity. A family where there were "five generations living together" could receive a special placard from the local magistrate, and for a widow refusing to remarry there might finally be erected a large memorial arch testifying to her virtue. All such official endorsements of behavior reflected the Confucian and state concern with maintaining social harmony on the basis of the proper acting out of particular social relationships. The three most crucial of these relationships were ruler-minister, father-son, and husband-wife, representing the equation of political and familial values, and also the state's focus on social ties involving pronounced super- and subordination. Given less emphasis were two other relationships that classically had received attention along with those already noted, the ties between brothers and between friends, for by late imperial times these implied equality between the parties involved and were less attractive to a state firmly committed to patterns of domination.

The ideological foundation of the subordination of children to their parents was filiality, the idea that the younger generation was ethically bound to support, love, and be obedient to their seniors. Ancestor worship gave powerful support to filiality, for when expressed religiously it was shown to be uninterrupted by death.

Thus family division, especially while the parents were still alive, was considered to go against Confucian ethics, for it was widely understood that most parents would want their families to remain intact. Nevertheless, early family division was common, especially among the nonelite. However, even after division sons would continue to support their parents, and it is therefore important to distinguish family division as a structural factor from the unending obligations of the young toward the old.

NEW SOCIAL FORCES AND FAMILY CHANGE IN MODERN TIMES

In the late nineteenth century there began the development of a new intellectual elite that was the product of Western-style schooling either in China or abroad, a new business class, especially in the Western-dominated treaty ports, and in these same cities a new working class, defined as wage earners in the modern sector characterized by large-scale firms and factories. For all of these social groups, the family had reduced significance with respect to economic management and production. One way or another, they increasingly obtained their income through participation in much larger organizations or arrangements. These new economic circumstances weakened the forces that traditionally had encouraged brothers to remain together and wives to accept subordination. Furthermore, it was precisely these social groups that were most exposed and receptive to the new cultural and intellectual forces entering China from Japan and the West.

Among these groups, therefore, new family patterns began to emerge at the same time that the younger generation, especially, began to agitate for legal and cultural reforms that would sanction and encourage the changes in family life that in fact already were under way. For all of the new groups, among actual changes was the increasing trend toward smaller conjugal (husband and wife) family units, and a growing freedom of choice for men and women with respect to marriage. Among members of both the modern-sector bourgeoisie and the increasingly radical new intelligentsia, the reform of the family system focused on the ideals of marriage based upon free and romantic attachments, and the equality of women with respect to marriage, property, and inheritance. But many members of the bourgeoisie took family reform as a goal quite independent of economic and social change in other areas; for the radical intellectuals and especially the growing numbers of Communist party members, however, significant and nationwide family reform could only occur in the context of total revolution.

In fact, the changes in family organization that did occur prior to the Communist victory were indeed largely restricted to precisely those groups which had been agitating for them. Among the vast rural majority, and even in the non-modern sectors of urban China, families continued to be organized along traditional lines. This is not surprising, given that the rural Chinese economy on the very eve of the Communist triumph was overwhelmingly still based on the same forms of technology, cultivation, and organization that had characterized it during imperial times.

THE FAMILY IN CONTEMPORARY CHINA

In countryside and city alike the family has remained a basic social unit in China throughout the period of Communist rule. Since the establishment of the People's Republic in 1949, the family's continuing viability is attested to by its providing the framework for reproduction, residence (in its own household), food preparation, consumption and expenditure, and child rearing. However, Communist programs of education, collectivization, agricultural modernization, industrialization, and urbanization have led to important changes in family patterns.

In the countryside, Communist-initiated land reform in the early 1950s did not as such appreciably change the family-based organization of production. However, the subsequent long period of collectivization (1955–1980) did lead to important changes in family life; some reflected the direct impact of collectivization, while others resulted from government policies which, while not directly involved with collectivization, could be applied more readily due to the much tighter connection between state and society that collectivization facilitated.

The Impact of Collectivization on Family Organization. Due to collectivization, which transformed rural China's population into wage earners, the farming family largely lost its status as a production enterprise; the old relationship between family size and family wealth no longer applied, for there was no longer the possibility that larger family holdings would encourage brothers to stay together under their father's authority as one family. Brothers therefore tended to separate from their parents shortly after marriage, often being constrained (usually for a relatively short period) only by the cost and availability of new housing, although it is true that the parents frequently continued to live with one of their married sons (or, if they had none, with a daughter). Collectivization by no means created economic equality among families; rather, the source of inequality was no longer importantly linked to differential wealth in the form of land or other private holdings, but to the differing ratios of wage earners to consumers in different families; the per capita income of families with fewer workers and many children or other dependents to feed tended to be considerably lower than for those where the worker/dependent ratio was reversed.

Changing Family Pattern. Several factors linked to collectivization led to changes in the pattern of family relationships. The father's authority—which in the past had been reinforced by his management of family property, farm work, and dealings with the outside world—was weakened (as was his wife's authority, especially her control over her daughters-in-law). Rather than depending on the holdings and output of the family farm and other properties, the family's well-being was now based far more on the earnings of individual family members working for their collective unit or in other ways outside the family context. This, plus the fact that working in a collective gave young people an opportunity for daily contact that they did not have in the past, led to a substantial increase in their freedom to marry someone of their own choosing. The old system—whereby parents negotiated the marriage of their son or daughter as an agreement between the two families, so that bride and groom frequently were strangers until their wedding day—was replaced by a variety of arrangements, all of which give young people greater freedom of choice. At one extreme, the marriage still was arranged by the parents, but the son and daughter had to be given the opportunity to meet and agree to the match, while at the other, the young couple became acquainted on their own and asked their parents to prepare the wedding; the latter arrangement presently appears to be increasing in popularity.

The trend towards growing freedom of choice in marriage was in fact given its first major encouragement through the promulgation of the 1950 code concerning family and marriage. In order to meet the novel requirement that a marriage license be obtained, young couples had to confirm their consent to the match. However, it was collectivization that only a few years later provided an enduring context which encouraged the very developments called for by the new code.

Thus during the period of collectivization the weakening of family bonds was linked to the transfer on a major scale of the individual's sources of security and livelihood from his family to his collective unit. However, most parents remained deeply involved in the marriages of their children, even if they had become acquainted on their own. Although now illegal, it was common for a man's parents to give his bride's family a large cash gift, viewed as compensation for their having lost her earning power in the collective (in the past, this gift usually would be matched or exceeded by the dowry the bride brought to her new family; with collectivization, dowry in much of the country had been reduced to a few token items, perhaps because the bride no longer obtained access via marriage to family holdings of which her husband would have been part owner). Also, the bride usually moved into her husband's house where, for a period at least, she lived with her parents-in-law and, during her free time, helped her mother-in-law with housework. Likewise, the mother-in-law commonly helped raise her grandchildren, thus freeing the wife to contribute to family income through full-time work in the fields of the collective. Interestingly, the traditional practice of the bride moving into her husband's home or village was reinforced informally by local authorities during this period. Because some collectives were wealthier than others, with better land and a more favorable land/population ratio, freedom for either husband or wife to change residence upon marriage would result in an undesirable flow of persons from poorer to richer collectives, where individual earnings were higher. By enforcing the traditional pattern, a more balanced movement between collectives was obtained.

Decollectivization: The Reestablishment of the Family Economy. In a truly dramatic policy shift, there was initiated in the late 1970s a process of decollectivization, with a result that by the early 1980s agriculture in China became once again overwhelmingly an undertaking of individual families, which now rent land on a long-term basis (fifteen-year or even twenty-five-year contracts are common) from the collectives which previously had been the units of agricultural production. On the basis of recent fieldwork and other reports it is clear that this shift has had implications for family organization. Wealthier families are now reappearing in the countryside; some are larger than average and contain married brothers. In some case, therefore, brothers by postponing division, are in fact reestablishing the kinds of family relationships that traditionally were diagnostic of family unity, especially the solidarity of brothers and the overall authority of the father over family affairs. Such strong and enduring "joint" families are once again associated with successful management of the family as an enterprise. These entrepreneurial families are all the more interesting because they survive and flourish in the face of new forces encouraging earlier family division. If collectivization has been eliminated as a force weakening extended family ties, the desirability of conjugal independence nevertheless has been strengthened, for this is now seen as one element of lifestyle enhancement by young people at a time when China is beginning an uncertain entry into an era of mass communications and a new popular culture. Under these circumstances successful family managers must be concerned not only with family enterprises but also with the satisfaction of the demands of the younger generation, such that the conjugal units within the larger family now commonly have far more financial autonomy than they did in the past. For most families, however, the new economic and social circumstances encourage continuation of the pattern that took hold during the collective era, whereby sons separate from their parents shortly after marriage. In any event, since decollectivization the Chinese rural economy has rapidly expanded, and it may be that China's leadership has come to understand that the Chinese family is a remarkable asset that ought to be given freedom of economic expression.

Education and Birth Control. Agricultural policy aside, the strong impact of government on family life is notable especially with regard to education and birth control. The widespread availability of at least a primary school education means that some of the socialization and educational functions previously undertaken by the family (often out of necessity—many families simply were unable to provide their children with formal schooling) have now been assumed by the state, which is able to teach basic skills and also inculcate Communist political and social ideology. Since the establishment of Communist rule there has been a marked increase in the prevalence of literacy; this is especially true for girls, who traditionally were denied the educational opportunities available to boys. In recent years, however, there have been reports of decreasing enrollments and attendance at basic-level schools. This may reflect the growing economic importance of family labor (even the labor of children) since decollectivization, together with the fact that only a minority of students are able to gain admittance to senior high schools while even far fewer pass the examinations for college entrance. In other words, there may be a perception that education generally provides little in terms of future economic advantages.

Birth control is a major and generally successful effort of the Chinese government today; in addition to the widespread dissemination of information about birth control, and the means to achieve it, the government attempts to enforce legally stipulated late marriages (no earlier than age twenty-five for men, twenty-three for women) and forcefully employs measures to limit the number of children per couple (one in the cities, or two in the countryside, if the first child is a daughter). All other things being equal, the successful continuation of government family policy will pose obvious limits on the development of extended families.

Continuity and Innovation in Urban Life. It is important to stress both continuities and innovations in Chinese cities because many changes in family life linked to collectivization in the countryside had already been anticipated among workers in the modern urban areas prior to the Communist victory. As indicated above, workers in the modern occupational groups, like those in the rural collectives, were not members of families having farms or other enterprises; thus their families similarly were characterized by weaker parental authority and greater freedom of marriage (some city workers in fact were members of rural families with land or other commercial holdings; for them, traditional family organization might still have retained much of its strength). Thus with increasing urbanization and industrialization since the establishment of the People's Republic, the preexisting forces making for the greater independence of the husband-wife unit and the simplification of family organization have been given vastly greater expression, and this has been further reinforced by the strict implementation in the cities of the policy of one child per family.

However, even in the cities the process of family change must be viewed relative to China's own past; in comparison with many Western societies, the Chinese family still plays a more important role in the lives of its members. The elderly in China generally continue to live with one of their children, a situation encouraged by the survival of traditional views concerning children's responsibilities, and also because such views have been reinforced by modern Chinese law, which stipulates that as parents must care for their young children, so must their adult offspring care for them. Also, it is especially true in the cities that housing problems frequently encourage parents to remain together with at least one of their married children. Thus while the old arrangement of married brothers opting to maintain common family membership is now especially rare in urban settings, three-generation families are still common. The contemporary Chinese family thus represents both the continuity of tradition and adjustment to new forces.

III. ISSUES FOR DISCUSSION

1. In light of the economic organization of the traditional Chinese family, consider the proposition that property relationships will vary from one culture to another.

2. How did the cycle of family development influence family size and organization in China?

3. Does the Chinese case confirm or deny the common assumption that modernization leads to similarities in family form and organization throughout the world?

IV. SELECTED READINGS

Baker, Hugh D. R. *Chinese Family and Kinship.* New York: Columbia University Press, 1979 (student reading). A very good general introduction; available in paperback for class assignment.

Cohen, Myron L. *House United, House Divided: The Chinese Family in Taiwan.* New York: Columbia University Press, 1976 (faculty background). A detailed and somewhat technical analysis of family organization and development in a Taiwan village where traditional elements still characterized family patterns.

Freedman, Maurice, ed. *Family and Kinship in Chinese Society.* Stanford: Stanford University Press, 1970 (faculty background). An excellent collection of scholarly articles.

Watson, Rubie S., and Patricia Buckley Ebrey, eds. *Marriage and Inequality in Chinese Society.* Berkeley: University of California Press, 1991 (faculty background). Another fine set of articles reflecting contemporary scholarly concern.

Wolf, Margery. *The House of Lim: A Study of a Chinese Farm Family.* New York: Prentice-Hall, 1968 (student reading). A well-written and fascinating account of life in a large and undivided Chinese family in Taiwan. In paperback and most suitable as a student assignment.

Wolf, Margery. *Revolution Postponed: Women in Contemporary China.* Stanford: Stanford University Press, 1985 (student reading). A discussion of the position of women in the family life and society of the People's Republic of China. Available in paperback and can be assigned to advanced undergraduates.

Yang, Martin. *A Chinese Village: Taitou, Shantung Province.* New York: Columbia University Press, New York, 1946 (student reading). Good chapters on still largely traditional rural family structure. Available in paperback.

Anthropology: China

Religion in a State Society: China

Myron L. Cohen

I. INTRODUCTION: CENTRAL POINTS

China, the world's largest society both now and in preindustrial times, provides an excellent case for consideration of the multifaceted role of religion in the expression of social and political relationships.

• China, because of its size and complexity, furnishes an especially important illustration of **religion's role in the political and social integration of a traditional agrarian state**.

• China also is an excellent example for consideration of **how religion was involved in the manifestation of the village and family autonomy characteristic of peasant populations in pre-**

17

modern state settings. In addition to reinforcing links between state and society and at the same time expressing the interests of local kinship and community groups, religion also was very importantly involved in expressions of hostility by some groups both to the state and to the larger social status quo.

• Because within one society there was this variety in religious expression, China provides an especially good example for considering religion in terms of social context and function.

• In modern times China has undergone a painful and tumultuous process of social, political, and economic change. Given religion's deep penetration into its traditional social fabric, China can be used as an equally important case study of **the relationship between traditional religions and the modern transformation of society**.

II. MAJOR TOPICS

INTRODUCTION

For purposes of the following discussion, traditional China refers to the period when the last of the imperial dynasties, the Qing or Manchu, held sway. Following the Manchu conquest in 1644, Qing rule was not significantly threatened until the onset of incursions by the modern Western powers in the mid-nineteenth century; this was followed in 1912 by the collapse of the Qing and the establishment of the Republic of China, and then by the formation of the People's Republic of China with the Communist triumph in 1949. This sequence of political events was linked to important changes in culture and society and provides the framework for consideration below of traditional religion, pre-Communist change, and religion in the People's Republic.

Diffuse and Institutional Religion. Religion was deeply involved in all aspects of social life in traditional China, and there can be distinguished a "diffuse" or popular religion looming largest in the daily lives of the people, and the major formal "institutional" religions of Buddhism, Taoism, and the State Cult. The religious beliefs and behavior of the vast majority of the Chinese are characterized as diffuse because they were expressed largely in family and community contexts, and not conditioned by acceptance of a specific doctrine or through affiliation with a particular church. Daily ritual and worship typically was a family affair, and lineages or territorial communities also would manage their own periodic rites. On the other hand, the Buddhist or Taoist clergy of institutional religion usually lived in temples away from villages, which they entered purely as hired ritual specialists for weddings or funerals and during community and other special observances.

CHINESE RELIGIOUS TRADITIONS

The historical development of Chinese religion in both its institutional and diffuse aspects involved several traditions, including folk or popular beliefs in gods, spirits, and ghosts; ancestor worship; the imperial or state ritual; divination and geomancy; Confucianism; Taoism; and Buddhism. Buddhism, imported from India, underwent important changes as it developed in China in conjunction with the other traditions that were almost entirely Chinese in origin. Even before the Qing period, elements from these traditions had already combined into the diffuse religion that was a coherent set of practices and beliefs for the individual, the family, and the community. In China, therefore, diffuse religion and popular religion for all intents and purposes were the same, a situation unlike that in many other premodern societies where popular and institutional religion were far more tightly linked. Thus, it is most useful to focus not on these separate traditions, but on how they contributed to Chinese popular religion as a whole. Because this popular religion framed much of social life, it will be viewed first in conjunction with the official rites that emphasized links between state and society, and then in contrast to the salvationistic traditions that rejected state, society, and the "orthodox" religion that supported both.

THE OFFICIAL RELIGION

The official religion or State Cult gave powerful ritual emphasis to key elements of state ideology and to the basic political organization of the state. Participants in the official rites were the emperor, his bureaucracy, and also other degree-holders (those passing the imperial examinations, which served to create a national elite and a smaller pool of high-ranking degree-holders for recruitment to the bureaucracy). There was no independent priesthood, for worship, guided by bureaucrats according to government regulations, was considered an official duty. The emperor, as the Son of Heaven with the Mandate of Heaven to rule over human society, worshipped Heaven and Earth as his symbolic parents and in expression of the anciently established Chinese state ideology which held that the emperor was not divine but rather divinely appointed; his duty was to insure that society expressed its natural order, which was but an aspect of the cosmic order of humanity (society), heaven, and earth. The emperor also worshipped his own ancestors, expressing the Confucian ethic of filial loyalty. Among other objects of imperial worship were the sun, the moon, Confucius, the emperors of earlier dynasties, the god of agriculture (in a ritual which included the symbolic plowing by the emperor of the first furrow of the new farming season), and other divinities representing important natural or social forces (e.g., the god of learning).

The arrangement of state ritual below the emperor was coordinated exactly with the national administrative system. At each administrative level— province, prefecture, and county— there was a city or town serving as the administrative seat, where in addition to the government compound (*yamen*) which was the officiating magistrate's headquarters, there were several official religious establishments: among the most important were the Confucian or civil temple (*wen miao*), and the military temple (*wu-miao*), which were the ritual foci of the two major divisions in the Chinese bureaucracy; and also the City God temple (*cheng huang miao*). A city serving as both prefectural seat and county seat would have two *yamen* and two sets of state temples. In the civil temples were tablets bearing the names of Confucius, his disciples, and certain later eminent scholars and officials, while military temple tablets were dedicated to the god of war (*Guan Yu*), historically a military leader, and to other military leaders of the past renowned especially for their patriotism and loyalty. Rites at these temples were held by and for government officials, and for the vastly larger number of degree-holders not in office.

Ritual and Belief in the State Cult. In considering the State Cult, a question is whether emphasis should be on ritual or on religion, on the symbolic expression of those social and political values given emphasis in state ideology, or on the worship of the supernatural. For many Chinese thinkers in the Confucian tradition, there was a natural order linking humanity to the rest of the cosmos, which, as a totality, operated on moral principle. Humans are endowed with a nature that is good, and only selfish desires and passions place them in conflict with the (or their) natural order. Confucius himself stressed the use of ritual and sacrifice as means to inculcate values of ethical and social importance for the living; rituals thus were used to encourage greater conformity to this natural order, rather than to express dependence on the supernatural. The arrangement of state ritual largely was compatible with such Confucian views; the focus of sacrifice and reverence was on natural forces or historical sages represented as inscribed tablets and not personified by images. Whether these beliefs were "religious" has been a matter of some debate; however they may be characterized, these elite convictions did contrast with the beliefs in the supernatural held by the masses and indeed by many if not most officials and degree-holders.

Popular Religion and the State. While a high-ranking Confucian scholar-official and the average person might interpret rituals in different ways, the state did make an effort to control popular religion. The imperial government actively manipulated its own pantheon of deities into which the more important gods of popular religion were incorporated. An important religious link between state and society was the City God, whose temple was found at every administrative seat. The City God was popularly considered the magistrate's supernatural or divine counterpart. Both held sway over the same administrative area, the magistrate attending to this-worldly affairs and the City God to the supernatural. The magistrate, depending on one's interpretation, either paid formal reverence to the City God or worshipped him, and was expected to appeal to the City God for supernatural assistance during droughts, floods, or other crises beyond direct human control.

POPULAR RELIGION

Projection of State and Society in the Cosmos of Popular Religion. The state encouraged the belief of most people that the City God occupied an important position in a pantheon of gods organized in a supernatural hierarchy paralleling that of the imperial government. This divine hierarchy was arranged into the three major divisions of heaven, earth, and the underworld; it comprised gods and spirits represented in temples and at shrines or domestic alters by carved images or woodblock prints. The belief was that the gods, although having supernatural powers, closely resembled in their desires and behavior living government officials. On earth, each household was kept under scrutiny by its own Stove God (*zao chun*). Also in close contact with the living were the Earth Gods (*tu di*) of local territorial communities, be they rural or urban neighborhoods, entire villages, towns, or other settlements. Each Earth God was believed to protect the area under its juris-

diction as a subordinate of the City God. Thus the local arrangement of communities within an administrative district was given a
religious dimension.

The City God was also linked to the second major division of
the cosmos of popular religion: the underworld of the dead. A
person's death was announced by surviving family members to
the local Earth God, who was quite familiar with all residents of
his domain. The Earth God in turn reported to the City God, who
arranged for the soul's delivery to the underworld. Although partially derived from Buddhism, the underworld in its Chinese form
had long been assimilated into the hierarchical framework of popular religion and was seen as the domain of ten judges or magis-
trates. The soul of the dead passed through each magistrate's
department for judgment and, if appropriate, submission to sometimes horrible punishments. While those who had led exemplary
lives might obtain early or even immediate release, prayers and rites
for the soul in the underworld loomed large during funeral ritual.

The third major division of popular religion's cosmos was the
heavenly court of the Jade Emperor, thought to be the supreme
ruler of all the supernatural domains described so far. The Jade
Emperor was the analogue in popular religion of the more ab-
stractly conceived Heaven of the State Cult. Likewise, he was the
divine parallel of the living emperor. Attending the Jade Emperor
in the heavenly court were many other gods, some the spirits of
historical figures who had led lives of merit, others representing
the forces of nature, and yet others adopted from Buddhism.
Generally, a local temple's major god (often together with other
deities), worshipped both by individuals and during community
rites, was considered by local residents to be a member of this
heavenly pantheon.

Kinship Solidarity and the Worship of Ancestors. Like other aspects of Chinese religion, rites for the ancestors could have differing elite and popular interpretations. Scholars and officials could
see these rites as expressions of principles governing human relationships. People owed their parents obedience, respect, and gratitude for having been given life and sustenance; and they had the
responsibility to support them in their old age. Such obligations
were expressions of filiality (*xiao*), a fundamental ethical concept
of Confucianism. *Xiao* was to be manifested even after the
parents' death through sacrifices and obeisances in front of tablets or scrolls bearing their names. Because among the Chinese
descent was through the male line, women married into the family

were expected to honor their husband's ancestors. Likewise, when a woman died her sons honored her and her husband. Ancestral rites also expressed the idea of an unbroken line of descent, whose preservation was another important duty of filiality. Thus the ancestral rites could unite, in life and in death, not only parents and children, but also a larger group of kinsmen who traced their descent from more remote ancestors. In many parts of China, especially in the south, such large lineages tended to remain together in the same village or neighborhood. In addition to tablets for nearer ancestors kept in their separate homes, the lineage would build in common a larger ancestral hall, often an impressive edifice with row upon row of tablets placed in the main room and arranged by generation. The achievements of prominent ancestors were recorded in such halls, and sometimes their tablets were arranged separately and given pride of place; these ancestors were meant to be sources of both pride and inspiration for their descendants.

Ancestors held in common could bring together the rich and the poor, the Confucian scholar and the ordinary farmer. They could all articulate, though in different ways, the moral and ethical obligations underlying the ancestral rites. But for the majority, once again, there was a religious and supernatural component; for them, it was ancestor worship. The spirit of the ancestor resided in the tablet; the ancestors were nourished by sacrifices, and if the line of descent were broken, or if for any other reason worship was discontinued, these ancestral spirits would turn into "hungry ghosts," malicious and feared by the living, and doomed to wander about the earth.

Ghosts and Ancestors in Popular Religion: The Religious Expressions of Kinship and Community Solidarity in a Dangerous World. The contrast between ancestors and ghosts was crucial to popular belief. Ancestors and hungry ghosts were in that domain of the supernatural closest to the world of the living, and there were also the masses of ghosts in the underworld. The ancestors were spirits who were socially intimate with the living; they took great interest in the affairs of their descendants, drew sustenance from their good fortune, and might at times render them assistance. Ancestors, in fact, were analogous to living kinsmen and, by extension, to all those with whom one had important social ties based upon familiarity and propinquity, that is, with the members of one's own community. Because ghosts, the spirits of the unworshipped dead, were cut off from living kin (or had none) they were readily identified with beggars, bandits, and others among the living who lacked kin and community roots and were thus not controlled in their behavior by a network of social ties and obligations. More generally, ghosts were viewed as the supernatural analogues of strangers, always potentially dangerous because they did not belong to one's own community. The correspondence of ghosts to strangers helps explain why some of the most important religious activities undertaken by the community as a whole involved special prayers for the otherwise unworshipped dead. Although communities in many ways were linked to each other and to Chinese society as a whole, community religion emphasized a desire for community security and prosperity which because of traditional China's scarce resources might be obtained only at the expense of others. By propitiating ghosts, Chinese community religion expressed local solidarity.

Popular Religion in Daily Life. Popular religious activity included a family's offerings to the ancestors and to other household and local spirits, and also series of festivals and feasts, some celebrated throughout the country (such as the lunar new year), some by particular local communities (e.g., the birthday of the village god), and some linked to important events in the lives of individuals and their families (weddings, birthdays of the elderly, and even funeral banquets). Popular religion also involved communication with the gods and the dead in the underworld through spirit mediums, shamans, the casting of wooden blocks, and a variety of other means. Geomantic and horoscopic prognostications also loomed large in popular belief, and implied direct interaction with the forces of the cosmos unmediated by the gods or other supernatural entities. Geomancy or "wind and water" (*feng-shui*) was most significant with respect to the siting of graves and structures; experts were hired to determine the proper placing of such edifices, so as to ensure, for example, good fortune for those entombing their ancestor or for a family building a new home. Experts, or the commonly available farmer's almanacs, were also consulted for horoscopic guidelines regarding "good" or "bad" days for marriage, travel, and a variety of other activities.

Salvation in Popular Religious Belief. In popular religion the idea of salvation involved belief in a Pure Land, Western Heaven, or Western Paradise which formed yet another domain of the supernatural universe; unlike earth, heaven, and the underworld, however, paradise was not a projection of the arrangements among the living but rather represented joyful release from the human situation. The popular conception of paradise also was obvious evidence of the strong influence on the masses of the dominant Pure Land sect of orthodox Chinese Buddhism. However, religious thinkers firmly linked to institutional and canonic Buddhism could view ultimate salvation as enlightenment, or release from the cycle of birth and rebirth (reincarnation) through the higher understanding that existence is but a manifestation of the suffering of egoism. In popular religion the focus was squarely on salvation as taken to mean entrance into a true paradise and the enjoyment of blissful immortality.

Deemphasis of Salvation in Popular Religion. Under most circumstances, concern for salvation did not loom large in religious activities, which usually focused on gods and other supernatural beings and reflected the this-worldly hopes, needs, and anxieties of individuals, families, and communities. Salvation also was deemphasized due to the popular belief in multiple souls: one in the grave, one represented by the ancestral tablet, and one in the underworld. The soul in the underworld might hope for release to paradise, but far more probably would be reincarnated. Although the deceased's family and relatives prayed for such release during the funeral and on other occasions, the deceased had additional religious significance as an ancestor and as the spirit in the grave, which, if properly sited according the principles of geomancy, could bring good fortune to his descendants. Most of the time, therefore, salvation was a religious concern of persons having to confront their own mortality, especially the elderly and the ill. When so limited, salvation as a religious concept coexisted with the larger body of religious beliefs, which reflected the society of the living and was concerned with its needs. Indeed, these beliefs, as described so far, were basically supportive of the social and political status quo.

"HETERODOXY": THE EXPRESSION OF DISSENT IN CHINESE RELIGION

In reaction to famine, drought, increasing poverty, or other conditions giving rise to large-scale social distress, salvational concerns might loom larger and form the basis of religious movements that called into question the validity of the existing social and political order and met with the state's bitter opposition. Such movements, which sometimes developed into full-scale insurrections (e.g., the White Lotus and Eight Trigrams rebellions in the late eighteenth and early nineteenth centuries) were manifestations of dissenting religious traditions with deep roots in China, traditions involving particular synthesis of elements drawn from other areas of religious life, including popular religion, Taoism, and Buddhism. Yet the dissenting traditions stood in opposition to the other religious beliefs and practices and also challenged the legitimacy of traditional Chinese political and social arrangements.

Some of the religious traditions labelled "heterodox" (*xie*) by officials of the Chinese imperial state in fact denied major tenets of the religious system, both official and popular, that have been described above. If the state cult expressed the idea of humanity's place in an integrated and enduring cosmos, the White Lotus heterodoxy proclaimed the coming destruction of the universe. Instead of seeing the emperor as the nondivine mediator between heaven, society, and earth, White Lotus movements focused on a divine Buddha-savior who would save from destruction those believing in his mission. By distinguishing believers from nonbelievers, such movements denied both the efficacy of the gods and spirits of popular religion and also the community and other social arrangements validated by these supernatural entities. White Lotus heterodoxy rejected the this-worldly concerns of popular religion at the same time that it promised believers immortality and paradise on earth. In other heterodox traditions the Western Paradise familiar in ordinary popular religion became the sole focus; for the poor and uprooted attracted to heterodox sects, the aim was to obtain release from the cosmos which humans inhabited together with gods, ghosts, and ancestors.

Although small numbers of heterodox believers were found in different parts of China during the Qing period (and earlier), the emergence of large-scale heterodox movements and insurrections was symptomatic of the inability of growing numbers of people to derive minimum security from traditional economic and social arrangements. Although within the heterodox tradition there was an emphasis on greater economic and sexual equality, such movements never succeeded in conquering state or society. Heterodoxy, a religion of opposition, was unable to provide a workable alternative to the orthodox social and religious order.

RELIGION IN MODERN CHINA

The British defeat of China which concluded the Opium War

(1839–41) marked the onset of a succession of encroachments by the Western powers (later joined by Japan), which posed military, political, and ideological threats that China's traditional ruling elite were unable to resist. The onslaught of the industrialized nations coincided with a deepening internal crisis largely resulting from the traditional agrarian economy's inability to keep up with population growth. Neither the Western penetration nor the economic crisis had substantial direct effect on religious practices in China as a whole during the remainder of the nineteenth century. This period did mark the intensified penetration of China's interior by Western Protestant and Catholic missionaries, but they failed to gain many converts in the countryside or even in those cities that were made treaty ports and partially placed under foreign control.

The Taiping Rebellion: From Revitalization Movement to Civil War. One early, devastating, but largely indirect Western contribution to religious ferment was the Taiping Rebellion (1850–65), led by Hong Xiuquan, a man who proclaimed himself to be the younger brother of Jesus Christ, sent by his heavenly father to destroy the Manchus, as well as the traditional religion and learning, and establish a new heavenly kingdom where the Christian holy scriptures would replace the classical texts of Confucian orthodoxy. The founder of this movement was from a village near Canton, where he had taken and repeatedly failed the traditional examinations, both before and after that city came under British attack and occupation during Opium War battles. His first information about Christianity was also obtained in Canton from a Chinese missionary. These events obviously had an enormous impact on this one individual, and in his syntheses and propagation of a new religion there could be seen in China an example of a syncretic revitalization movement of the kind associated in many parts of the world with culture contact, especially in the context of Western expansion. Thus the Taiping religion differed from traditional heterodox messianism, which had a long history of development in China itself. Unlike the traditional White Lotus movements, the Taiping followers linked their religious goals to a concrete program for radical social and economic change. Like earlier heterodoxies, however, many initial recruits to the Taiping cause had been uprooted from their communities. To the imperial government, the Taipings represented total cultural confrontation; they were crushed only after a bloody fifteen-year civil war, during which Taiping iconoclasm was manifested by the large-scale destruction of the temples and other religious structures of institutional, popular, and official religion alike. After their defeat, little if anything remained of Taiping religion; their most enduring legacy may indeed be their iconoclasm, which at least anticipated later developments.

The Emergence of Iconoclastic Nationalism and the Assault on Popular Religion. By the end of the nineteenth century, a new school system based upon Western models and curricula was forming in China, and increasing numbers of Chinese students were abroad, in Japan, especially, but also in Europe and the United States. The emerging educated class was both ideologically and structurally in conflict with the old elite which had studied for the traditional examinations. The new elite possessed skills appropriate for the developing modern sectors of China's cities, while those with only the classical education could best preserve their elite standing in communities and settings where traditional standards were not threatened by the new developments. The new elite were passionately nationalistic, and linked China's frequently demonstrated military weakness to the nation's "backwardness," which they defined as China's old culture, including the country's religious and social traditions. There thus emerged a link between nationalism and rejection of tradition that became increasingly characteristic especially of China's urban intelligentsia. With the fall of the dynasty and the establishment of the Republic, the assault on "superstitious" and "backward" customs intensified; taking the country as a whole, however, the traditional practices of popular religion tended to be maintained, although in some areas temples were converted to schools or other nonreligious uses. It is important to note that during the period of the Republic hostility to traditional elite and popular religious practices and institutions was shared across a broad political spectrum. Nationalists, liberals, socialists, and even warlords might violently oppose each other politically and ideologically, but they could share common hostility to and contempt for traditional religion and other "backward" customs. Thus Marxism-Leninism was not the sole source of the anti-religious attitudes and policies of the founders and later members of the Communist party, although the party expresses opposition to religion in Marxist terms.

Post-1949 China. Since the establishment of the People's Republic in 1949, freedom of religion, as well as freedom to propagate atheism, has been guaranteed in the Chinese Constitution. Yet

the Communist party has consistently maintained a negative attitude; active suppression was greatest during the Cultural Revolution (1966–1976), and more recently has considerably abated.
Although diffuse religion played a much larger role in daily life
than did institutional forms, the government now only grants
official recognition as religious groups to the major organized
churches of Islam, Christianity, Taoism, and Buddhism. All but
the last two had been significant for only a minority of the population, and institutional Buddhism and Taoism had only a specialized and limited role in the religious life of most people. Under the
Communists, the number of believers affiliated at least publicly
with the institutional religions had decreased significantly, but in
the more permissive atmosphere of recent times, especially since
the several national religious associations were reactivated in
1979, Buddhism and Christianity in particular have shown signs
of revival.

Pressure against popular religion, considered to be "feudal superstition," has always been greatest, and even to the present this
religious system continues to be most disfavored. Since popular
beliefs constituted a religious framework for traditional social organization they were viewed by the Communists as a major obstacle to the goal of radical reorganization. The Communist attack on
popular religion thus was greatest during the periods of land
reform (1950–1954) and collectivization (1954–1979), for popular
religion reinforced traditional social alignments by emphasizing
community solidarity and autonomy, values the Communists
wished to replace with class consciousness and the integration of
collectivized communities into a socialist economy and polity.
Thus while popular religion as a whole was denounced and suppressed, community religion came under the strongest attack.
Throughout China village temples, local Earth God shrines, ancestral halls and other such structures were dismantled or converted to nonreligious uses.

Important elements of popular religion have survived, however,
to varying degrees in different parts of the country. During periods
of greater repression, almost all such religious practices were carried out within the family, thus offering testimony to the continuing vitality and autonomy of family organization. Ancestor worship
remains widespread, especially in the countryside, although even
today it is sometimes practiced covertly; in some villages the objects of worship are tablets, scrolls or photographs kept at home;
in others, tablets destroyed during the Cultural Revolution have
not been replaced, but the rituals of ancestor worship are main-

tained. The joint worship by several families of a common ancestor is practiced far less frequently, for this involves organization above the family level. Within the family there continues the worship of other gods and spirits, at least in some parts of the country. It is not surprising that funerals appear to have consistently retained more of their religious content than other rituals. This presumably reflects concerns about mortality that cannot be satisfied by more contemporary world-views.

The reform of the rural economy beginning in the late 1970s has led to large-scale decollectivization, such that almost everywhere in China the basic unit of agricultural production once again is the individual family, which now rents land on a long-term basis from the collectives which previously had also been the key units of agricultural organization. With this development there also has been considerable lessening of state pressure against popular religion, the renewal of which is increasingly apparent. Although the government continues to most strongly oppose community religion, instances of large-scale community religious celebrations are now reported. As far as religion is concerned, it is safe to say that the political atmosphere in China following decollectivization has been more relaxed than at any other time since the establishment of the People's Republic. Even the heightened political suppression following the 1989 Tiananmen killings does not appear to have significantly involved an intensification of the Communist government's anti-religious activities. However, it remains to be seen how traditional religion ultimately will fare under circumstances so vastly different from those which nurtured its development.

III. ISSUES FOR DISCUSSION

1. Compare the roles of institutional and diffuse religion in China with circumstances in the United States or any other culture which you are familiar with.

2. Compare the attitude of the state toward popular religion in traditional China with the current situation in that country.

3. What were the circumstances encouraging people to focus on religious salvation in traditional China, and what were those that tended to deflect interest in such religious beliefs?

IV. SELECTED READINGS

Luo Zhufeng, ed. *Religion Under Socialism in China.* Translated by Donald E. MacInnis and Zheng Xi'an. Armonk, NY: M. E. Sharpe,

1991 (faculty background). Chinese Communist views, including their distinction between "religion" and "feudal superstition."

Naquin, Susan. *Millenarian Rebellion in China: The Eight Trigrams Uprising of 1813.* New Haven: Yale University Press, 1976 (faculty background). Contains the best account of White Lotus "heterodox" beliefs.

Overmyer, Daniel L. *Religions of China.* New York: Harper & Row, 1986 (student reading). A short and basic survey appropriate for assignment.

Thompson, Laurence G. *Chinese Religion: An Introduction.* 4th ed., Belmont, CA: Wadsworth, 1989 (student reading). A very readable short book, available in paperback. Although not written strictly from a sociological or anthropological point of view, nevertheless an appropriate text to assign.

Watson, James L., and Rawski, Evelyn S., eds. *Death Ritual in Late Imperial and Modern China.* Berkeley: University of California Press, 1988 (faculty background). Anthropologists and historians deal with a key area of religion and ritual in China.

Wolf, Arthur P., ed. *Religion and Ritual in Chinese Society.* Stanford: Stanford University Press, 1974 (faculty background). An excellent collection of mainly anthropological papers, focusing on aspects of popular religion.

Yang, C. K. *Religion in Chinese Society: A Study of Contemporary Social Functions of Religion and Some of Their Historical Factors.* 1961. Reprint: Prospect Heights, IL: Waveland Press, 1991 (faculty background; advanced student reading). Still the best general treatment, by a sociologist. Develops the analysis of "institutional" and "diffuse" religion.

Anthropology: India

Religion in a State Society: India

Lawrence A. Babb

I. INTRODUCTION: CENTRAL POINTS

Traditional India is an excellent case for considering the structure of religious tradition in a highly stratified and culturally pluralistic preindustrial social order. A religious tradition of immense complexity, Hinduism reflects the cultural layering and regional differentiation of this complex civilization.

• Because of the diversity of its sources, the Hindu tradition illustrates well the role of **syncretism in the growth of a complex religious system**.

• Given the immense differences between the sophisticated theologies and philosophies of textual Hinduism and the unsystematized beliefs and practices of most villagers, India provides a good illustration of the **integration of a multi-leveled religious tradition**.

• Because of the manifold and intimate connections between Hinduism and the social structures that provide its context, especially the caste system, India is an excellent case for showing how **religious symbols express and support crucial features of a social order**.

- Because of its religious diversity and the vitality of its religious traditions, modern India illustrates potential **conflicts between religious traditionalism and secular modernism and the
dangers of religious communalism for a multi-cultural state**.

II. MAJOR TOPICS

India can refer to the modern Indian Republic (which came into
existence in 1950) or, in a broader sense, to the South Asian
cultural region. The dominant religious tradition in South Asia is
Hinduism, although Pakistan and Bangladesh are overwhelmingly
Muslim, and Hindus are a minority in predominantly Buddhist
Sri Lanka. Hindus constitute about 83 percent of the population
of the Republic of India; at 11 percent, Muslims are the largest
religious minority. Also present are Sikhs, Jains, Buddhists, Parsis and Christians. This discussion will focus on Hinduism.

RELIGIOUS HETEROGENEITY

The Hindu tradition is a highly complex and internally variegated
amalgam of beliefs and practices drawn from quite various
sources. Its historical dynamic has been a process of interaction
and dialogue between religious specialists— priests and salvation-
seeking virtuosi— and the mostly rural masses. It encompasses
highly diverse philosophies and sectarian theologies together with
the largely unsystematized religious customs and usages of ordinary people. Supplying diffuse sanction to the whole is a "high"
religious culture, present in Sanskrit texts and associated with
Brahman priests and scholars who are the principal custodians
and transmitters of the textual tradition. No single belief system
commands a consensus in the texts, but the soteriologies, mythol-
ogies, ethical systems, and ritual idioms present in the texts define a general religious praxis and outlook that enjoys high
prestige throughout the Hindu world and that supplies a pan-
Hindu frame of reference for more parochial traditions. The various linguistic regions of India have produced their own distinctive
forms of Hinduism which have been expressed in rich regional
literatures; in effect, these are regional "high" religious cultures.
Both pan-Hindu and regional traditions affect the religious patterns of villages and other local communities, but at this level
local customs and beliefs loom large. Brahman priests and other
specialists act as agencies for the transmission of pan-Hindu traditions at the local level, but much ordinary ritual life is con-

ducted by the participants themselves or by purely local religious specialists. The links between popular religion and textual Hinduism are complex, often indirect, and sometimes very tenuous.

It is important to note that the concept of Hinduism as a distinct "religion" is not indigenous to South Asia. The word "Hindu," derived from Persian, was originally used by Muslims to describe the native peoples of South Asia whose religious identities were in fact highly differentiated by sect, caste and community. **The notion of Hindus as coconfessionals is a purely modern idea, a joint product of British administrative convenience, Orientalist scholarship, and the responses of Indian intellectuals in the nineteenth century to the cultural challenges of colonial rule.**

THE VEDIC HERITAGE

Although the sources of the Hindu tradition are quite diverse, an important strand consists of religious ideas created and elaborated by Indo-Europeans, the Aryans, who entered India from the northwest beginning around 1500 B.C.E. or possibly earlier. Our knowledge of this tradition and its development is based on the Vedas, a body of originally orally transmitted Sanskrit hymns, composed after the Aryans had arrived in India, to which ritual manuals and philosophical treatises were later appended. The early Vedic religion focused on the fire sacrifice, a rite designed to induce deities to grant boons, and the centrality of the sacrifice greatly accentuated the importance of the priest, the Brahman. Doctrines of salvation were not present; the emphasis was on obtaining wealth, health and power from the gods. The life of world renunciation, which was to become central to later soteriologies, was not a part of the Vedic tradition, although priests did utilize ascetic techniques to prepare for performing certain sacrifices. There is evidence, however, of the existence of wandering ascetics beyond the fringes of Aryan society.

By roughly the tenth to seventh centuries B.C.E. the sacrifice began to assume expanded significance. The rite came to be attributed with greater power than the deities it was originally supposed to supplicate, and ultimately this power was seen as a single force or principle that lay behind the cosmos and its creation and that was inherent in man as well. This paved the way for the doctrine, originally announced in the Upanishads (dating from around 600 B.C.E. and after and the latest of the Vedic materials), that the self (atman) within, conceived as pure consciousness, is identical with the ground of all reality (*brahman*, [Absolute]). The idea of the transmigration of the self through an endless cycle of rebirth (and death) also came into prominence in the Upanishads, as did the notion that one's destiny in future rebirths is shaped by one's actions (karma). The supreme goal of the Upanishadic thinkers was liberation from the cycle of rebirth. This could be achieved by means of an inward realization, likened to an intuitive "knowing," of one's true self, which is identical with the ultimate reality of the cosmos and beyond all change and death. Such disciplined introspection required a life of austerity, free of all desire, and thus world renunciation entered the orthodox tradition. These soteriological themes represented a considerable change from the rather practical boon-oriented early sacrificial tradition. The notions of transmigration and karmic destiny, and the goal of escape from the cycle of rebirth, remained— in varying formulations— central to virtually all later indigenous Indian theological systems.

NON-ORTHODOX TRADITIONS

A number of anti-Vedic religious movements appeared in the sixth and fifth centuries B.C.E., of which two remain in existence today: Jainism and Buddhism. These systems emerged in the context of rapid social change and dislocation in the central Gangetic plain; centralized monarchies were replacing what have been called "tribal republics," and rapid urbanization was bringing new forms of social and economic life into existence. All this created disenchantment with Brahmanical orthodoxy, which was associated with an older and more rigid social order. It is significant that both Jainism and Buddhism were founded, not by Brahmans, but by members of the warrior and kingly class (the Kshatriyas), and that both found substantial support among merchants and other urban groups.

Although it had much earlier (and probably non-Aryan) roots, Jainism assumed final shape in the teachings of Vardhamāna Mahāvira (c. 540–468 B.C.E.), who is sometimes considered Jainism's founder. The Jains teach that the universe contains an infinity of "souls" (jivas) present in human beings, deities, animals and plants, and even in apparently non-living things. The soul is held in the cycle of rebirth by an accumulation of karmic "matter," and liberation requires absolute non-violence and rigorous asceticism. The extreme emphasis on non-harm (ahimsa) created a special affinity between Jainism and merchant communities whose occupations do not require physical violence.

More than Jainism, Buddhism was closely associated with the personality of a single founder, Siddhārtha Gautama (c. 563–483 B.C.E.), who became a Buddha (an enlightened one) after he achieved his insight into the nature and causes of suffering. In contrast to Jainism (and other ascetic paths), he taught a "middle way," rejecting extremes of worldliness and asceticism alike. And in contrast to Jainism and the Upanishadic systems, he taught a doctrine of no-self; with the end of the false idea of the permanent self, which is fueled by ignorance and desire, comes the cessation of suffering.

Alike in their rejection of Brahmanical pretensions and Vedic orthodoxy, Jainism and Buddhism had quite different destinies. Jainism survives to the present day in India, but never spread beyond its borders. Buddhism became a major religious and political force in India and was exported to other Asian countries. Greatly weakened by a resurgent devotional Hinduism, however, Buddhism was eliminated from the Indian scene by the Muslim invasions of the early second millennium C.E.

THE HINDU TRADITION

It is sometimes said that acceptance of the authority of the Vedas is a test of who is a Hindu. In fact, however, the Vedic heritage is only one strand in the tradition, and sometimes hardly visible at all. Hinduism also drew heavily from the non-orthodox systems, but much of what is known as Hinduism had its roots in religious traditions that predated the coming of Indo-Europeans to the subcontinent and that continued to exist as a historically invisible substrate during the Vedic period. There is some evidence of continuity between elements of Hinduism and the Harappan civilization that flourished in the Indus valley between c. 2400 and 1750 B.C.E. It is clear that from the very start Vedic culture was in constant interaction with indigenous cultures, and that this resulted in changes on both sides of the dialogue. In the end, Vedic orthodoxy was virtually swamped in a new and sprawling synthesis— Hinduism— that emerged in its classic form in North India during the Gupta era (fourth to sixth centuries C.E.). New forms of worship came into prominence, new non-Aryan deities came to the fore, and a new religious attitude, devotionalism, became central to religious belief and practice. The scriptural basis of Hinduism is a vast body of texts postdating the Vedas and distinguished from them as smriti (remembered) as opposed to shruti (heard, revealed).

Hindu devotionalism (bhakti) emphasized personal devotion to a deity, and this tendency has remained at the core of Hinduism to the present day. The ideas of transmigration and karmic destiny remained, as did (for virtuosi) the overarching goal of attaining release from the cycle of rebirth. Added to this were theologies of deliverance that focused on devotion to particular deities, through whose grace release (or more worldly boons) could be obtained. Image worship and temples were unknown to the Vedic tradition: the physical focus of sacrifice was the fire which consumed offerings and conveyed them to the gods. In the emerging Hindu tradition, worship of divine images in temples and shrines became the dominant ritual form, although Vedic-style sacrifices continued to be important in some contexts. Brahmans retained their role as priests and transmitters of the tradition. Many of the later devotional sects, however, rejected Brahmanical authority and employed vernacular languages instead of Sanskrit.

HINDUISM AND THE STATE

The Hindu king was seen as a divine being, a deity on earth. His role, however, was decisively separated from that of the Brahman priest. According to an ancient Vedic paradigm, the king is the sponsor of sacrifices which the Brahman performs; king and priest are thus bound together in a tight symbiosis. The Brahman was the key to the king's legitimacy: the rituals he performed and the genealogies he authored lent plausibility to the king's claims to divine authority. The king, in his turn, supported the Brahmans by means of lavish gifting, most significantly grants of land. Kings were also builders and endowers of temples. In South India, particularly, temples became an integral feature of state authority. The ruler was the protector and supporter of the temple, and was identified with the temple deity; god and ruler were seen as sharing sovereignty, which created a conflation of political communities and communities of worship. Despite his divine status, however, the classical lawbooks circumscribed the king's authority. He was seen as the protector of the sacred moral order (dharma) that underlay the proper functioning of society, but he was not seen as a lawmaker. In theory, at least, castes and other groups in society were governed by their own normative systems (that is, their own separate dharmas); the state's function was to preserve order, but not to promulgate any particular normative code. This notion fit well with the cultural pluralism that has always been characteristic of Indian society.

THE HINDU PANTHEON

The Hindu pantheon is as complex as the Hindu social world and in some respects mirrors it. According to an influential view, divinity is ultimately one, but is manifested as distinct deities, male and female, whose characters differ and who play different roles in the cosmic drama. From a soteriological standpoint, these deities and the traditions of their worship represent different paths to the same ultimate goal, which is the Absolute. Most worshippers, however, do not engage in such recondite rationalizations. At the apex of the pantheon, as represented in texts, are Brahm, Vishnu and Shiva (known together as the *trimūrti* or triform) who are responsible, respectively, for the periodic creation, preservation, and destruction of the cosmos. Vishnu and Shiva are the most important of the three, and the two predominant sectarian traditions in Hinduism are the Vaishnavas (worshippers of Vishnu) and Shaivas (worshippers of Shiva). Vishnu is said to appear in the world periodically in the form of avataras (descents) to restore dharma (the moral order) in times of trouble. The deities Krishna and Rāma are the best known of Vishnu's avataras. Shiva, usually worshipped in the form of the phallic linga, is a highly complex figure: his character combines asceticism and eroticism; he is associated with death and destruction, but also with creative energy. The Hindu goddesses embody shakti, the divine energy that drives the cosmos through its unending cycles of creation and destruction. Some of the goddesses preside over such positive features of life as fertility, growth, and abundance; other more sinister goddesses are associated with disease, destruction, and death. Worshippers of the goddess, known as Shaktas, constitute a major cultic subdivision of the tradition.

Regional and local pantheons include these pan-Hindu deities, but sometimes under local names and with local modulations of their character. Also present are deities of regional or purely local renown who are frequently associated with the welfare of territorial units or particular social groups. Some lesser deities preside over specific kinds of troubles or afflictions (such as the smallpox goddess); they are worshipped for protection from, or amelioration of, the misfortune in question. Paternal ancestors are venerated by families, but this pattern is not as strong as in other parts of Asia. Malevolent spirits and ghosts constitute yet another layer of supernaturals; they are dealt with by avoidance and exorcism.

CONTEXTS OF RITUAL ACTION

For most Hindus living in villages the religious life is less a matter of systematized belief than of ritual and ceremony, and the content of an individual's ritual life is determined by a great variety of factors, including place of birth, caste and family custom, and to some degree personal choice. In each locality there is typically a rich array of calendrical festivals and periodic rites of other kinds which most Hindus observe. Many of these rites are presided over by particular deities, pan-Hindu or local. Life-cycle rituals, of which the rites of birth, marriage and death are the most important, constitute another major focus of popular religion. Worship of caste and lineage deities and family ancestors is interwoven into the wider system of periodic rites. In times of misfortune specific deities may be propitiated or exorcised, often on the advice of a local diviner/exorcist. Individuals can also propitiate, or make special vows to, particular deities to get rid of troubles or achieve success in some endeavor. Pilgrimage to important temple centers or sacred sites is often undertaken as a spiritually meritorious act or to obtain divine boons. One may also have a special relationship with one's personally "chosen deity" (iṣṭa-devatā), from whom one may seek worldly help or salvation, or possibly both. It should be understood, however, that seeking salvation in the classical sense has little to do with the ritual life of most Hindus. For the most part, ritual observances are embedded in a web of socially obligatory behavior, and to the degree that they are rationalized at all, they are associated with worldly welfare. For some, however, salvation is indeed a goal of religious life.

Hindu ritual patterns are linked with social identities at multiple levels. At the uppermost reaches of the system great pilgrimage centers such as Banaras have subcontinental constituencies, and while the question of "Hindu identity" is extremely complex, it can be said that these great sacred centers belong to a sacred landscape that is, for some, definitive of a Hindu world as such. Much denser are such symbolisms at the regional level, where important temples and pilgrimages are often associated with regional identity and impart distinctive emphases to regional variants of Hinduism. Castes and descent groups often have tutelary deities that are sometimes represented by temples and shrines supported by the groups in question. Different castes often have special ritual roles in temple ceremonies or other important rites, thus symbolizing their distinctive identities and hierarchical standings in the wider community. The household shrine is a sacred-symbolic expression of family solidarity. Much of the apparent clutter of Hindu ritualism resolves into order when seen in relation to the social structures that provide its context.

THE STRUCTURE OF HINDU WORSHIP

The core ritual of Hinduism is puja (homage), a form of devotional worship usually directed toward a physical representation of a deity. Most deities are represented by anthropomorphic or theriomorphic icons, but this is not always the case. Shiva is usually worshipped in the form of the linga (a rounded upright shaft), and deities are frequently represented by unaltered stones or other objects, especially in village shrines. Trees, plants and features of the physical landscape can also be treated as deities. Temporary images of deities are often fabricated for worship during festivals; afterwards they are disposed of by immersion in water. Permanent images are installed in temples and shrines, which are places of protected ritual purity and thus fir habitations for deities. A consecrated image is regarded as an embodiment of the deity it represents and is to be treated as an actual divine presence.

A minimal act of worship is to see and be seen by the deity, an act known as taking darshan. The worshipper enters the temple and makes a gesture of obeisance in the deity's presence. In more elaborate forms of worship the deity is honored with various attentions appropriate for a highly esteemed person. A nearly invariant feature of worship is feeding the deity. After being presented to the deity, food offerings become *prasād*, the deity's "grace" or "blessing." Charged with divine power, *prasād* is distributed to worshippers at the end of the ceremony. Another important feature of Hindu worship is *arati*: a flame is moved in a circular fashion before the deity while a bell is rung and appropriate *arati* hymns are sung. Brahman priests may or may not function as intermediaries in worship. They usually do in more important temples and in some of the domestic ceremonies of higher castes.

The Hindu tradition does not radically separate the human and divine worlds. Brahmans, for example, are said to be "deities" to lower castes, as are husbands to their wives. The acts by which deities are worshipped are not fundamentally different from gestures of homage that may be made in the presence of august or powerful human beings. Implicit in the structure of worship, and consistent with the continuity of divine and human spheres, is an intimacy of substance between worshippers and worshipped.

When, for example, the worshippers consume a deity's leftover food they are internalizing and sharing in the deity's powers and virtues, which inhere in the recovered offering. But the intimacy is hierarchical; the worshipper consumes the deity's leavings, and not the other way around.

RELIGION AND THE CASTE HIERARCHY

The system of castes, which is generally regarded as Hindu society's most distinctive feature, must not be confused with the system of varnas. The varna system, which first emerged in the Vedic period and was elaborated in the classical lawbooks, was an idealized scheme by which society was divided into four ranked classes or estates: the Brahmans (priests), Kshatriyas (rulers and warriors), Vaishyas (husbandmen and traders) and Shudras (servants). The texts also mention a fifth, excluded class, the chandalas, who are equivalent to the so-called Untouchables. These ideal categories classify castes on an all-India basis, but actual caste hierarchies are essentially local phenomena.

The Indic term most properly translated as "caste" is *jāti*, meaning "birth" or "type." A typical village contains a number of different *jātis*, most of which have occupational specialties. Membership is by birth and is a crucial determinant of an individual's access to the society's resources and rewards. These groups are endogamous and often have customs and social usages distinctive to themselves. They are also ranked in local hierarchies.

The caste hierarchy receives general sanction from the Hindu textual tradition. The prevailing view is that members of each caste should perform the duties pertaining thereto to the best of their ability; the performance of the caste duties of others is condemned. Low caste status is often said to be a consequence of sins in past lives, and high status a product of past virtues. One's adherence to the system's norms in the present, moreover, will affect one's status and destiny in future lives.

The criteria of ranking in local systems are relative purity and pollution: lower castes are seen as more polluted than higher ones. Perceptions of the ranking of *jātis* are based on general estimations of the relative purity or pollution of their traditional occupations, food habits, and so on. Also important is the degree to which the group's customs seem to exemplify norms set forth in Sanskrit texts. Restrictions on commensality are an important expression of difference in relative rank. Although there is usually considerable dissensus about the relative ranking of groups in the middle of the hierarchy, there tends to be consensus concerning the high and low extremes. At the bottom are groups whose traditional occupations (such as removing waste) and diets mire them in a condition of severe and permanent hereditary pollution. Brahman *jātis* tend to be at the apex of local systems. They are the purest of men, which indeed they must be to mediate (as priests, though most Brahmans are not priests) between the community and the highest gods. Purity and pollution (as the opposite of purity) are thus ritual concepts, having to do essentially with the appropriateness for given groups or individuals to enter defined spheres of ritual activity. In this sense, status in the caste hierarchy is "ritual status."

Caste identity and relative standing are therefore powerfully expressed in the ritual life of communities. The lowest castes are (or were traditionally) barred from entering some temples. Different castes often have distinctive ritual functions in village-wide ceremonies or in life-cycle rites (such as marriages) requiring multi-caste participation. The village system as a whole, moreover, draws upon ritual imagery of deep antiquity in the Indic world. The traditional but now rapidly eroding system of patronage in Indian villages is the jajmani system. The jajman ("sacrificer") occupies the ancient role of sovereign/sacrificial sponsor who, in partnership with the Brahman priest, presided over the state. The wealthy and powerful, the landholders, are styled jajman; they are served by members of other castes in the capacities of their various traditional occupations. The village order thus becomes the sacred state in miniature; the local lord is ritually supported by the priest (who performs his domestic ceremonies), and the other castes are linked to him as ritual servants whose standing is reckoned in ritual terms. The village hierarchy is actually rooted in fundamental disparities of wealth and power, but in Hindu India such disparities are, to an extraordinary degree, expressed in a religio-ritual idiom. [*Readers are referred to the essay on "Stratification, Inequality, Caste System: India," by Owen M. Lynch, for additional discussion of the definition of caste.*]

CONTEMPORARY INDIA

Older forms of Hinduism continue to flourish in modern India with apparently undiminished vitality. Traditional festival and ceremonial cycles remain highly salient features of village life, and Hindu ritualism has adapted easily to the vicissitudes of urban life. There is little evidence of a secularizing trend in modern

India, save possibly among the most cosmopolitan (and perhaps culturally deracinated) elites. Modern communications technologies have had a profound effect on religion, though not on its essential content. With the development of a vernacular printing industry in the late nineteenth century, cheaply printed ritual manuals, didactic tracts, and religious literature of other kinds became available, which accelerated the dissemination of textual Hinduism into geographic and cultural hinterlands. With lithography came religious poster art, which seems to be generating new iconographic conventions. Films on religious themes have enjoyed enormous popularity, and at least one has generated its own cult (of the goddess Santoṣī Mā). Recent years have witnessed the sensational popularity of television serializations of the great Hindu epics, the *Rāmāyaṇa* and the *Mahābhārata*. There are reports of television sets being treated as sacred objects during the presentation of these shows.

A conspicuous presence on the contemporary Hindu scene are various religious movements catering largely to members of the urban middle class; in fact, the rise of middle-class cults and sects, often focused on particular holy men, seems to be an emerging trend in modern India. Many of these movements have drawn inspiration from the Hindu reformist and revivalist movements of the nineteenth century. They have tended to project an image of the Hindu tradition as belief-oriented (as opposed to ritualistic) and decoupled from features of Hindu society, such as caste, that are seen as unmodern. Some of these movements have become socially disembedded to a remarkable degree, crosscutting older boundaries of caste and region. And because of the English-speaking urban milieu in which they grew, many such movements have found it easy to internationalize; they have become Hinduism in its "export" version.

The modern Republic of India is a secular state, which means that citizens are constitutionally guaranteed the right to profess and propagate their religions, and that the state does not favor any religion. However, the recent presentation of religious material (the Hindu epics) on state-run television raises awkward questions about the religious neutrality of the state. The issue of the limits of religious freedom was pushed to the fore in the recent (1987) case of a sati (the burning of a widow on her husband's funeral pyre) in the state of Rajasthan. This practice, outlawed in India and anathema to secular modernists and many others, is regarded as a legitimate religious act by some religious conservatives. Government attempts to suppress ceremonies stemming from the event provoked vigorous reaction from the religious Right, and the passage of a more stringent law against sati in Rajasthan led to massive pro-sati demonstrations.

Conflict between religious communities remains one of India's most vexing problems. This has mainly been a problem of Hindu-Muslim relations. Although Hindus and Muslims can and do live peacefully together, the two communities have often found themselves violently at odds, especially when mistrust is fanned by politicians playing at religious politics. It was such mistrust that lay behind the partition of the subcontinent between India and Pakistan at the time of Independence, and Hindu-Muslim tension continues to be a potentially explosive problem in India today. A recent manifestation of tension has been the controversy surrounding a mosque in the city of Ayodhya, built by the Muslim Emperor Babar in the sixteenth century on what is believed to be the exact birthplace of the Hindu deity Rāma. In 1949 an icon of Rāma "appeared" (to many Hindus miraculously) in the mosque, which resulted in communal rioting; as a result the Government closed the building to both Muslims and Hindus. The building was re-opened in 1986, and within the month there was serious rioting in North Indian cities. The issue has continued to simmer, and at the time of this writing (1989) the VMP (a Hindu right-wing organization) is campaigning vigorously to have the mosque demolished and a Hindu temple built in its place. It seems likely that the violence is not over.

Recent years have also seen an upsurge in Sikh nationalism. Founded in the fifteenth century and rooted in the Hindu tradition, Sikhism developed a distinctive identity as a religious community. It is professed by about two percent of the Indian population. Since the early 1980s Sikh revivalists have waged a campaign of terror in Punjab, the Sikh heartland, resulting in great carnage and the 1984 assassination of Prime Minister Indira Gandhi. The current goal of the extremists is a Sikh homeland in Punjab. The apparent waxing of Hindu, Muslim and Sikh revivalism suggests that India will face ongoing problems of communal harmony in years to come.

III. ISSUES FOR DISCUSSION

1. Compare the gap between textual and popular levels in Hinduism with other religions with which you are familiar.

Hinduism with other religions with which you are familiar.

2. Compare the religious sanctioning of hierarchy in India with the role of religion in other systems of social stratification.

3. Discuss religious conflict in India in comparison with similar situations in other countries.

IV. SELECTED READINGS

Babb, Lawrence A. *Redemptive Encounters: Three Modern Styles in the Hindu Tradition.* Berkeley: University of California Press, 1986 (faculty background/student reading). A discussion of modern sectarian movements in Hinduism emphasizing common Hindu themes.

Brockington, J.L. *The Sacred Thread: Hinduism in Its Continuity and Diversity.* Edinburgh: Edinburgh University Press, 1981 (faculty background). A compact but comprehensive account of the historical development of Hinduism. Its approach is not anthropological, but the material it presents is essential to an understanding of the Hindu tradition.

Eck, Diana L. *Banaras: City of Light.* New York: Alfred A. Knopf, 1982 (student reading). An account of Hinduism's most sacred city that also provides a superb introduction to Hindu belief and practice.

Gold, Ann G. *Fruitful Journeys: The Ways of Rajasthani Pilgrims.* Berkeley: University of California Press, 1988 (faculty background). An anthropological analysis of village Hinduism emphasizing pilgrimage.

Srinivas, M.N. *The Remembered Village.* Berkeley: University of California Press, 1976 (student reading). An anthropological account of village life in South India with good material on caste and some discussion of popular religion.

Anthropology:
India

Gender Relations: Changing Patterns in India

Doranne Jacobson

I. INTRODUCTION: CENTRAL POINTS

Women in India, the world's second most populous country, have not yet been accorded a status equal to that of men. According to a 1988 study of ninety-nine countries by the Population Crisis Committee, India ranks in the bottom quarter of the world's nations with regard to women's status.[1] The ratings considered the areas of health, marriage and children, education, employment, and social equality as these affect the majority of the people. Although equality of the sexes, along with a few special rights and privileges for women, is mandated by law, Indian women continue to suffer severe constraints and discrimination. Even today, one hears reports from India of female infanticide and of widows who have sacrificed themselves upon the funeral pyres of their husbands. And yet India, whose pantheon of deities includes omnipotent, sword wielding female goddesses, was recently ruled by a woman head of state, the world's most powerful woman during her fifteen-year tenure. Gender roles in India thus provide an excellent case study of interwoven contradictions and contrasts in both ideology and actuality.

• In Indian society, an inherent superiority of males over females has traditionally been accepted by both men and women as morally correct and part of the divine plan. Still, the power of goddesses to control human life is acknowledged by Hindu worshippers of both sexes.

• The Indian Constitution grants equal rights to men and women, and even provides for elective offices reserved exclusively for women. Many women, primarily of elite backgrounds, have attained high-ranking positions in government, business, and the professions. However, the vast majority of Indian women suffer conspicuous disadvantages relative to men in virtually every aspect of health care, work and social life.

• Changes are occurring rapidly, and an expanding women's rights movement seeks to bring real equity to relations between the sexes. Indian feminists are critical of Indian traditions, yet, wishing to retain some time-honored values, they reject certain key aspects of the feminist movement in the West.

• While the problems of gender relations in India are of a different scope and nature from problems in the West, there are important similarities. An examination of gender relations in the Indian context can sharpen our perceptions and enhance our understanding of the issues as experienced in the West.

II. MAJOR TOPICS

Approximately one-sixth of the world's women live in India, a nation undergoing dramatic social, economic, and political change. Between 1966 and 1977 and again from 1980 until her assassination in 1984, Prime Minister Indira Gandhi determined policies that affected the lives of hundreds of millions of people. Yet her life, as well as the lives of numerous other well-placed women, contrasts sharply with the lives of the vast majority of Indian women. Many cannot make even minor purchases or step outside their neighborhoods without the permission of family males, and most are engaged in endless domestic duties. With limited access to educational opportunities, many are forced by economic circumstances to labor at demanding menial tasks. While many disadvantaged men also face similar difficulties, women's problems are often more daunting. Many women, especially in North India, are still subject to stringent purdah restrictions involving the veiling of the body and face as well as severe limitations on physical mobility.

Restricted though they are, in the contexts of Hindu ritual and common parlance, women are often likened to the many powerful goddesses worshipped by some 700 million Hindus of both sexes in tacit acknowledgement that the health and continuance of families largely lie in female hands. After all, it is only through a women's ability to bring children into a family, as well as her willingness to carry out essential tasks, that her family can prosper. India's 100 million Muslims also acknowledge the importance of women as a source of strength for both the family and society.

TRADITIONAL ROLES AND IDEALS

Regional variations as well as socioeconomic, cultural, and religious differences render problematic generalizations about the lives of women in India. Although, for example, the roles of women in North India differ from those of women in South India, and those of urban women differ from those of rural women (nearly 80 percent of India's population is rural), certain key norms are pervasive.

Subordination. The sexes are seen as very different, existing in essential complementarity. While interdependence is noted, women are widely regarded as subordinate to and dependent upon men. Often quoted are the ancient Hindu Laws of Manu with regard to women (ca. second or third century, C.E.):

> She should do nothing independently, even in her own house.
> In childhood subject to her father, in youth to her husband,
> And when her husband is dead, to her sons; she should never
>   enjoy independence . . .
> Though he be uncouth and prone to pleasure, though he
>   have no good points at all,
> The virtuous wife should ever worship her lord as a god.

Today such ideals remain strong among most Indians and are reiterated in popular pulp guides on ideal wifehood frequently presented to brides. Similar ideals among Muslims are expounded in conservative marriage manuals. Extrapolating well beyond Qur'anic injunctions, such works admonish women to carry out unquestioningly their husbands' commands and never to utter a word of complaint, no matter how grave a husband's faults. These tomes insist that economic pursuits are solely the domain of men, whose duty it is to protect and provide for the basic needs of women.

Contemporary Indians acknowledge these ideals, even when they deviate from them. In one Central Indian village, a young wife recently said, "Why should a woman obey her husband all the time? I do what I want most of the time." Another added, "Oh, everyone says a husband is a god, but no one's a god." But another village woman summarized the situation succinctly: "Men are high and women low. This is the rule of the world." In village society, and among some urban groups, a woman walks behind her husband and sits on the ground in the presence of her father-in-law. She asks permission from father or husband before traveling far from home. During her menstrual period she is considered polluted and segregated from others. She eats after her husband does and may consume his leavings: he would be defiled were he to eat her leavings. Even if of the priestly Brahman caste, she cannot conduct ceremonies as male priests do. If she is of a high-status group, she may marry only once, but a widowed or divorced man of any status may remarry if he can find a bride. While she can have but one husband at a time, her mate may take another wife or wives.

Traditionally, it was expected that all women would marry, and if economically feasible, confine their activities to the home sphere. Outside employment for women was associated with low socioeconomic status, and until recent decades, formal education for girls was not valued, since it was considered irrelevant or even contrary to domestic concerns. Politics and other public activity were ideally the domain of males.

Inheritance. Most significantly, by traditional Hindu custom, a woman does not inherit real estate from either parents or husband: such property is inherited patrilineally only by sons. A widow can use her dead husband's property but cannot alienate it. Only a portion of a woman's jewelry is hers to pawn in case of adversity. Modern Indian law assures women the right to inherit and own property outright, but few village women risk alienating kinsmen by challenging tradition. Only occasionally does a Hindu man without male issue formally will his property to his daughter. Among Muslims, customary law grants women inheritance rights to property, including real estate (usually half that of a similarly related male), but many women waive these rights in the face of opposition from male kin.

Chastity and Women's Value. Chastity is expected of all women. If a woman has a sexual liaison with any man other than her husband she risks bringing devastating shame upon herself and her kin group and in rare cases, death at the hands of her own kinsmen. Men have much greater sexual freedom. On the other hand, a woman's control of her sexuality is seen as virtuous and even empowering. According to widely held Indian ideals, a chaste women is given respect, and her actions enhance her family's honor. The honor, or *izzat*, of a family or kin group, is an important component of its social and economic strength.

Women are revered through many cultural symbols. Another ancient text, the *Mahābhārata*, says, "Even a man in the grip of rage will not be harsh to a woman, remembering that on her depend the joys of love, happiness, and virtue . . . ." Throughout India, the concept of motherhood is revered. A child is taught to honor his mother, and the very terms for mother (*mātā, mā*) connote warmth, protection, and life-giving power. The cow, sacred to Hindus because of her usefulness as a producer of milk, dung, and hardworking bullocks, is called "Mother Cow." The Ganges River, sacred source and sustainer of life, is called "Mother Ganges," and other sacred rivers are similarly named. The most powerful local goddesses, responsible for the care and protection of whole villages and regions, are known as Mother (*mātā*). Yet it is these very mother goddesses who, if angered, can bring death and destruction to their charges.

A mother goddess is believed to gain power through controlled sexuality. As one Central Indian village priest explained of Mātābāī, the goddess most revered locally, "Mātābāī is not married. She is the mother of us all, the mother of the world. She creates everyone and also destroys them." The priest explained that in years past, Mātābāī had been angered by villagers who had failed to honor her properly. In response, Mātābāī sent a cholera epidemic to scourge the village. It is believed that at any time, Mātābāī may elect to save—or kill—a particular child or adult. Thus chaste womanhood is powerful and worthy of adulation—but can also be extremely dangerous.

The most powerful goddesses, such as Kālī and Durgā, are unmarried, while some less powerful divinities such as Sītā and Pārvatī are married and very much under the control of male deities. Such goddesses are considered the shakti, the strength or potency of their male counterparts. Clearly, both men and women share an ambivalent view of femininity. On a daily basis, however, women are neither idealized nor despised, but are treated as ordinary mortals with normal human strengths and weaknesses.

Daughters. The birth of a daughter is met with much less acclaim and joy than the birth of a son. In this overwhelmingly patrilineal, patrilocal, agrarian-based society, parents depend on their sons for cooperation in agricultural and other family work as well as for support in old age. A daughter is expected to marry and reside in the patrilineal joint family of the husband, with her natal kin subsequently having limited access to her labors.

Actually, young girls are often treasured by their families, and in certain Hindu rituals worshipped as representatives of the local mother goddess. Their departure after marriage can be heart-wrenching for their natal kin. Nevertheless, the preference for males is revealed in statistics showing a disproportionate number of female deaths among young girls as well as adult women. Since the turn of the century—when the census of India began its tabulations—the Indian population has become increasingly male, with the number of females for every 1000 males dropping from 972 in 1901 to 930 in 1971. In some parts of North India, girls suffer blatant discrimination and are more likely than boys to die of malnutrition and general neglect. In certain small communities in both North and South India, female infanticide is practiced even today, although it is illegal. A recent study shows that in some villages, the disparity between male and female child mortality is growing, despite improvements in child mortality rates as a whole. These trends have been linked, among the poor, to decreasing availability of employment for poor women, and among the wealthy, to population limitation within specific caste groups and the consequent consolidation of wealth in the hands of a limited number of prosperous families.

Increasingly popular is the use of amniocentesis to detect female fetuses, which are subsequently aborted. Between 1978 and 1983, about 78,000 female fetuses were aborted after sex-determination tests. Female feticide is under strong attack from feminists, and legislation to ban it has been passed in Maharashtra and is under consideration in three other states. In contrast, in the southwestern state of Kerala, where matrilineal groups such as the Nayar form a significant component of the population, sex ratios slightly favor females.

Throughout most of India, the increasingly skewed sex ratio and higher mortality rates for females in virtually every age group show that women are exposed to greater health risks and suffer disproportionately from deficient medical care throughout their lives.

Marriage, Family, and Fertility. Parents usually arrange marriages for their offspring. North Indian Hindus favor marriages with un-related members of the same caste (*jāti*), while some South Indian Hindus seek links with cross-cousins and other relatives. [*Readers are referred to the discussion of the definition of caste in the essays on "Stratification, Inequality, Caste System: India," by Owen M. Lynch, and "Religion in a State Society: India," by Lawrence Babb.*] Muslims often prefer marriage between cousins and other more distantly related kin. Village girls are frequently married about the time of puberty, while educated urban girls may not be wed until after college. The groom is almost always older than the bride, thus facilitating her subordination to him, as well as to his relatives.

As a daughter, a girl usually enjoys some freedom of movement within her natal settlement, as well as affectionate treatment from natal kin. At her wedding, the Hindu bride is likened to Lakṣmī, the Goddess of Wealth, in symbolic recognition of the fact that the groom's patrilineage can increase and prosper only through the fertility and labors of the new bride. Despite this simile, stated in elegant language in the Brahmanical nuptial ritual, the new wife is pressed into service as the most subordinate member of her husband's joint family. Only by producing much-desired sons and, ultimately, becoming a mother-in-law herself does she grad-ually improve her position within her conjugal household.

It is through bearing children, especially sons, that the married woman finds social approval, economic security, and emotional satisfaction. Her contributions bring strength to the patrilineal joint family, the key social and economic unit in rural India. (Despite many variations in actual family structure, the joint fam-ily is the ideal, and a high proportion of couples live with the husband's kin for at least some period of time.) Because she herself receives acclaim for giving birth to sons, she typically joins in the traditional disparagement of females when she bears a daughter.

Purdah. In traditional households of North and Central India, young wives are expected to observe purdah— veiling and seclu-sion. The secluded Muslim woman shields herself from men outside the trusted family circle by remaining in the inner rooms of the house and by wearing an all-covering veil when escorted on sanctioned outings. The Hindu wife veils her face with the end of her sari in the presence of elder affines, male and female, both of her actual marital kin group, and a wide range of fictive affines. She also strictly limits her movements outside the house in her marital village or town. Social gatherings are segregated by sex. Strict purdah is associated with high family status and enhanced family honor as well as with an image of women as being in need of male shelter and protection. Indeed, in some prosperous families it is the men who provide economic necessities for women, while women tend to domestic duties. But women of poorer groups work long hours in the fields, on construction gangs, and at myriad other tasks, often veiling their faces as they work.

Among the urban elite, purdah practices are rapidly disappearing, while lower-status groups are increasing purdah observances in an attempt to raise their status. For most villagers of northern India, however, purdah limitations on female independence remain an integral aspect of male-dominated family hierarchy and valued household harmony.

Dowry. In most communities throughout India, a dowry has traditionally been given by a bride's parents and other kin upon her marriage. In ancient times seen as a woman's wealth— property due a beloved daughter who had no claim upon her natal family's real estate— the dowry typically included portable valuables such as jewelry and household goods that a bride could control throughout her life. In fact, over time, the larger proportion of the dowry has come to consist of goods and cash payments that go straight into the hands of the groom's family. In recent years, dowry payments have escalated, with a groom's parents sometimes insisting on compensation for their son's education and even for his future earnings, to which the bride will have some access. Among some lower-status groups large dowries are currently replacing traditional bride price payments. The dowry is becoming an increasingly onerous burden for a girl's family, contributing to the distress with which an infant girl is greeted and reflecting and perpetuating women's inferior status.

Extant anti-dowry legislation is largely ignored, and a bride's treatment in her marital home is often affected by the value of her dowry. Of increasing frequency are incidents, particularly in urban areas, where a groom's family makes exorbitant demands on the bride's family even after marriage, and when these are not met, kills the bride, typically by setting her clothes on fire in a cooking "accident." The groom is then free to remarry and collect another sumptuous dowry. Female as well as male affines have been implicated in these murders, which are rarely punished. Fears of impoverishing their parents have recently led some urban middle-class young women, married and unmarried, to commit suicide.

On the other hand, the newly wealthy are often able to marry their treasured daughters up the status hierarchy by giving large dowries.

Wifehood and Widowhood. A married woman is referred to as a *suhāgan* (a woman with a living husband), an auspicious term embodying the concept that not as individuals, but only in union are men and women complete. The *suhāgan* wears colorful clothing, beautiful jewelry, including tinkling bangles on her wrists, luscious red designs on palms and feet and red mark or spangle upon her forehead as well as red powder in the parting of her long, lustrous hair, all indicating happy wifehood, fertility, and well-being. Ideally faithful, self-sacrificing, and attentive to her husband, she is the very embodiment of wifely virtue. The auspiciousness and power of the male-female union is idealized in lingam-yoni representations (a phallic shape protruding from a female symbol) seen in Shiva temples, and in numerous temple sculptures of gods and goddesses in the act of love, as well as the image of the divine *ardhāngini*, half-man, half-woman.

While some goddesses are unmarried, few male gods are conceptualized without consorts, who are considered a key source of their vital powers. For Muslims, Allah is purely male, and mosques contain no sexual representations, but Muhammad is known to have benefitted from supportive and devoted wives, and all Muslims are expected to marry. Virtually all Hindu women marry, and men who fail to find wives are believed to become ghosts after death, eternally distressed at having been deprived of the pleasures of marriage. A small number of Hindu males elect asceticism, and through controlling their sexuality are thought to accrue spiritual power. In some communities it is believed that the allure of women and consequent male loss of semen leads to temporary physical weakness for men. Thus, again, women are viewed ambivalently, as both sources of and threats to male power.

Upon the death of the husband, the venerable state of wifehood ends, and a woman is plunged into inauspicious widowhood. There is suspicion that her misconduct in a past life has resulted in her husband's premature death. The very word "widow" is an epithet. With shorn hair, naked wrists, and plain white or dark clothing, the widow's appearance announces her undesirable status. Her presence can bring bad luck to brides and new mothers; she avoids social events and eats meager rations. Widows of lower-ranking groups have always been allowed to remarry, but widows of high rank have been expected to remain unmarried and chaste until death. In the case of child brides married to older men and widowed at a young age, this rule was especially difficult to follow.

In past centuries, the ultimate rejection of widowhood occurred in the burning of the widow on her husband's funeral pyre, a practice known as sati (meaning, literally, true or virtuous one). Women who so perished in the funeral flames were posthumously adulated and are even today worshipped at memorial tablets and temples erected in their honor. In western India, Rajput lineages point proudly to satis in their history. Although never widespread, and illegal since 1829, even today several instances of sati are known to occur annually. In choosing to die with her husband, a woman evinces great merit and power, and is able to bring boons to her husband's patriline and to others. Thus, through her ostensibiy voluntary death does a widow avoid disdain and achieve glory.

An alternative model to wifely devotion is provided by Mīrābāī, a sixteenth-century Rajput mystic who, according to legend, rejected the traditional female role and became a wandering devotee of Lord Krishna, to whom she considered herself married. Songs attributed to her stress her independence from convention and her devotion to Krishna. According to one legend, when a holy man tried to pressure her into sleeping with him, she publicly spread her bed beside his and loudly told him to enjoy himself. Shamed, he fell at her feet, asking her to guide him in the path of devotion. Today, traditional villagers and urban educated feminists alike admire Mīrābāī as an example of honorable feminine independence.

Threads of Indian culture are woven into a multiplicity of complex patterns, some emphasizing women's power, virtue, and spiritual superiority, while others stress women's subordination, weakness, dangerousness, and inferiority.

LEGAL EQUALITY, POLICIES, AND DE FACTO DISCRIMINATION

During the centuries of British involvement in Indian affairs, foreign and Indian reformers worked in a variety of ways to alter the position of women. Targeted issues were female infanticide, child marriage, enforced harsh widowhood, sati, strict purdah, lack of female education, and lack of women's involvement in politics and public life. Indian reformers particularly stressed that they wished merely to restore to women the rights and status they had enjoyed in much earlier times, before the arrival of Muslim and European invaders. Classical Hindu texts as well as unwritten indigenous ideals exalting womanhood were used as justification for these efforts, which were apparently inspired to some extent by foreign criticism of Indian customs.

The great Indian leader Mohandas Gandhi urged women to emerge from their homes and become actively involved in the independence movement against the British. He also strongly supported reforms benefiting women.

The 1950 Constitution of independent India, a parliamentary democracy, granted universal suffrage and included an equal rights provision forbidding discrimination on the basis of sex. Further, elective seats for women were set aside in the state and national legislatures. Women stepped forward to achieve international distinction. Prime Minister Nehru's sister, Mrs. Vijayalakshmi Pandit, served as ambassador to three nations, while other women attained high political office within India. Two years after Nehru's death, following the subsequent death of his successor, Nehru's daughter, Indira Gandhi, was chosen leader of the world's largest democracy. Membership of women in legislative bodies has been about 5 percent, which compares well with figures in many other countries. Further, an increasingly well-educated group of elite and middle-class women have found employment in the professions, public service, and business. Have India's women, then, achieved equality with men? Hardly.

There have certainly been important changes in women's roles among some classes of Indians, yet today most Indian women are in no more advantageous positions than their forebears were, and in many cases they are worse off. In 1975, the Government of India released the lengthy official report of the Committee on the Status of Women in India, *Towards Equality*, providing detailed statistics documenting systematic discrimination against women. Since then, important strides toward progress have been made, yet the essential findings of the report remain valid.

Economic Participation. Virtually all women are responsible for domestic tasks, in addition to whatever other work they engage in. Village women rise before dawn to begin their duties, which include fetching water and firewood, cleaning and grinding grain, cooking over smokey fires in dark kitchens, preparing cow dung fuel cakes, plastering their houses with mud, washing clothes, and caring for demanding children and husbands. City women likewise spend many hours daily at what Gandhi called "domestic slavery." As in many societies, such arduous and continuous labors are undervalued and omitted from work statistics, even though the society could not continue without them.

Of the 12 percent of Indian women officially recognized as "workers," more than 80 percent labor in agriculture, both on their own family lands and on the lands of others as sharecroppers or day laborers. Women's participation is vital to virtually every agricultural endeavor—sowing, weeding, harvesting, and hauling—save plowing (a male preserve). Especially arduous is the women's task of transplanting and weeding rice, which requires standing long hours in muddy water. Such employment—while sought after by poor women as the only alternative to destitution—heightens the risk of miscarriage and many other health problems.

Women agricultural laborers are 92 percent illiterate and endure low pay, wage discrimination, and seasonal unemployment. The introduction of new agricultural technology has favored men. While males monopolize new methods and machinery, women continue to use laborious manual methods—or suffer unemployment. The proportion of landless women laborers to women who work on family lands is increasing, a strong indicator of increasing poverty.

Many women follow occupational specialties traditional to their caste, including delivering babies, making baskets, painting earthen pots, cleaning latrines, sewing, washing clothes, etc. Juggling their domestic duties, others work at cottage industries, making cigarettes, matches, incense sticks, embroideries, and the like, earning meager returns on their labors. Even very young children toil at these jobs. Uneducated, poor, and generally isolated from each other, these workers are virtually without bargaining power. Some work as street vendors, others as domestic servants, and a large number as manual laborers; many are migrants, dwelling in gunny-sack huts on the sites of the great dams and luxury apartment buildings they construct, while their unschooled children play at the edge of excavations or are themselves put to work. After work, male laborers relax while women laborers fetch water, cook, and clean. Studies have shown that women are paid at half the rate that men are, even though their work is often more arduous.

Fewer than three percent of women working outside their homes are employed in organized industry—factories, mines, plantations, etc. In such employment, female participation relative to that of males has declined. The Constitution advocates protection for women workers, and special labor laws provide for women's welfare as well as for wage parity. Nonetheless, these provisions are widely evaded, resulting in unequal opportunity and remuneration for women. As new technology is introduced, management and unions tend to train men in the newly necessary skills, while jobs allocated to women disappear.

For urban working class women, new organizations have begun to bring benefits. Most famous is the Self Employed Women's Association (SEWA) of Ahmedabad, founded by Ela Bhatt, now internationally renowned for her accomplishments. SEWA is a trade union of some 14,000 self-employed women engaged in such jobs as pulling heavy handcarts, picking through wastepaper, making baskets, printing cloth, etc. Making decisions jointly, SEWA's members benefit from low-cost loans and efforts to raise income. Similarly, the Working Women's Forum and other grassroots organizations attempt to improve working conditions for women, creating conditions in which working women can come together, discuss problems, identify solutions, and build unity.

Numerous government-sponsored schemes also aim at benefiting women. Many of these are inefficient and fail to adequately address the real problems women face.

Education. Nearly three-quarters of Indian women are illiterate — vs. 55 percent of men— and fewer than five percent of women are college graduates.[2] There are many hindrances to women's education. In North and Central India, where purdah is practiced extensively, fewer than a third of all girls attend primary school, and rural girls are less likely to attend classes than urban girls. Many parents view education outside the home as useless and even jeopardizing their daughters' chastity. Further, they are needed at home for domestic duties. (Again, heavily matrilineal Kerala provides a contrast: there school attendance by girls is almost one hundred percent.) Limits on education have important implications for a woman's ability to earn an independent living, take initiatives outside the home, participate in informed political activity, and contribute to national development.

Currently, the number of female students is increasing, and higher education for girls has expanded dramatically. For some women, education has merely been a means of enhancing traditional roles— for example, educated brides are in increased demand as ornaments to a high-status household, and "home science" remains a popular college subject. For other women, higher education has helped provide entree to desirable white-collar employment.

As higher education for women expands, there has been an increase in opportunities for women as teachers. In the medical field, the modesty of women and their reluctance to visit male doctors has greatly encouraged women to enter the medical profession. Even as employment opportunities for unskilled and semi-skilled women are dwindling, the range of jobs open to educated women is growing (although unemployment is high for them as well). Stepping beyond the protective circle of domesticity and dominance by male kin, women, especially those of the privileged classes, are enjoying opportunities in every field. Their new earning ability has encouraged some women to be less submissive to abuse and even to live independently of men.

Politics. Since independence, women have remained active in politics. As noted earlier, a few upper-class women have achieved great prominence and many more women have been involved in advocating and agitating for political change. Several prominent women politicians seem to have attained their positions in part because of their ties to eminent male politicians (e.g., Mrs. Indira Gandhi), and most are members of elite groups. (Similarly, in Pakistan, former Prime Minister Z. A. Bhutto's daughter Benazir Bhutto has served as prime minister, the modern Islamic world's first female leader.) Their elite status allows them special privileges of authority, despite their gender (and in Mrs. Gandhi's case, widowhood).

About half of eligible women vote in national elections, reflecting a lack of political awareness or interest, or a cynical view of politicians and the political process.

Legal Rights. Since independence, several laws have been framed with the specific intent of improving the social and economic position of women. Their rights to property were expanded, and some independence of action in divorce proceedings, remarriage, and other personal concerns sanctioned. Unfortunately, many of these laws are extremely difficult to enforce, and have not succeeded in altering the cultural and social structures that maintain women's subordinate position. Further, the majority of women are ignorant of their rights, and even when they are not, find it almost impossible to assert their rights in the face of opposition from their male kin. Of particular concern are laws applying to women of different religious groups, especially Muslims, Christians, and Sikhs, which take precedence over secular legislation. Traditional Muslim family laws, for example, disallow female adherents some rights that other women legally enjoy. A recent case in which Shah Bano, an aged Muslim divorcee was granted a small maintenance from her wealthy ex-husband by the Supreme Court, contrary to Muslim customary law, led to an outcry from Muslim fundamentalists demanding non-interference in their affairs. Eventually rather than alienate herself from her religious community, Shah Bano withdrew her claim and accepted a life of penury.

Like women the world over, most Indian women encounter prejudice and disadvantages, both gross and subtle, in virtually every field of endeavor, despite genuine efforts which have been made to create equality between the sexes.

THE MODERN INDIAN WOMEN'S MOVEMENT

Inspired by international feminism and by *Towards Equality*, the report of the Committee on the Status of Women in India, a strong modern Indian feminist movement arose in the mid-1970s. The movement has grown and spread throughout the country, into both urban and rural areas, involving women both wealthy and poor, communist and socialist, conservative and apolitical. The Indian women's movement includes numerous loosely allied and highly diverse organizations focusing on issues of rights and equality, and empowerment and "liberation" of women. They include consciousness-raising groups, mass-based organizations including trade unions and caste and tribal associations, groups providing services to needy women, professional women's organizations, women's wings of political parties, and research networks including both scholars and activists documenting data on women's issues. Strategies for improving conditions for women include promotion of legislation and grass-roots organization to raise awareness and encourage struggle against discrimination among the mass of Indian women.

There remains, however, a gap between the privileged and the poor, and true solidarity between upper- and lower-class women has yet to emerge on a wide scale (a problem for women's movements throughout the world). Many upper-class women fail to realize or acknowledge that their ability to hold prestigious positions in private and public life depends to a great extent upon the labors of servant women, struggling to make a living even as they raise their own families in difficult circumstances.

Since the late 1970s, a new journal, *Manushi* (Woman), published in English and in Hindi, has served as a forum for the discussion of women's issues. Letters to the journal often include poignant firsthand accounts of outrage and brutality against women, and articles analyze instances of unequal treatment of women in the context of Indian values and political realities.

The escalating issues of dowry-related murder and suicide have galvanized Indian feminists. Some groups, e.g., *Saheli* (Woman Friend) in New Delhi, help enable troubled women to leave threatening in-laws. Women's groups have laid blame for these horrors not only on the greed of the families of grooms but on the pervasive societal devaluing of women. Many are demanding more stringent enforcement of existing anti-dowry legislation and are encouraging men and women to refuse to take part in marriages involving dowry.

The 1987 sati of eighteen-year-old Roop Kanwar excited tremendous feminist protest. Her businessman father and teacher father-in-law, among others, explained that the young woman was extremely religious and possessed an unshakable intent to die in her husband's cremation flames. The hundreds of witnesses declared that she sat upon the pyre calmly and smilingly, and that to attempt to stop her would have invited the feared sati *shräp*, a curse believed to destroy families and villages. Her memory is glorified by flocks of pilgrims who visit the sacred site. Women activists, however, say that sati is but one more form of glorifying crimes against women and that women are driven to sati because life as a widow is so difficult. As a leading newsmagazine, *India Today*, stated, "Whether she was forced or went voluntarily, the stark and brutal reality is that a woman barely out of adolescence was burnt alive before cheering, applauding, frenzied crowds in 20th century India and has now become the basis of a highly profitable religious worship."[3]

There have been reports of militant young men (mostly outsiders) shouting slogans, posturing and dancing at the sati site—in a progressive village, as if part of a victory celebration. Far from being a manifestation of superstitious village ignorance, the present glorification of the sati is seen by feminists as a modern predominantly male statement of what men regard as a "woman's place." In a public speech, Rani Chuhrawat, a well-known public figure, pointed out that since few women had the right to make any significant decisions about their lives, how could it be that a young bride suddenly had the right to make the major decision to die as a sati? For a powerless young woman, surely such a momentous decision cannot be considered voluntary, she said.

Another feminist issue is "eve-teasing," sexual harassment of women in public places, usually manifested as fondling and bumping of educated urban women by middle-class young men on crowded buses and sidewalks. There have also been a large number of cases of women who were raped by policemen while in police custody. Many of these assaulted women were not accused criminals but were plaintiffs.

Feminism and Indian Values. Despite their efforts to restructure society and gender relations in certain basic ways, most Indian feminists shrink from being too strongly linked with Western feminists. After centuries of colonial criticism and exploitation, there is a great reluctance among educated Indians to criticize their own nation. Indian women activists do not want to be viewed as similar to the early British and American reformers who so harshly attacked the place of women in India and additionally vilified much of Indian culture and character. While Indian feminists reject female infanticide, dowry abuse, child marriage, purdah restrictions, polygyny, and sati, all decried by foreign reformers of the past, they clearly want to retain key Indian institutions and values.

For example, instead of abolishing dowry, the suggestion is made to return to ancient dowry practices in which the woman, presumably, retained control of her dowry wealth. The family, idealized so highly in India, is seldom attacked, and some groups downplay conflicts between men and women. There is uneasiness about separating women from their families and home duties, as is often advocated in the West. Indeed, it is within the family that women have found their greatest strength, and like all Indians, women depend on their families for support. Even professional women depend on their family members and upon family servants to care for their children and help run their households while they hold demanding positions outside the home.

Indian women have not found appealing the image of the autonomous Western woman, single or divorced, living apart from relatives, her children placed in day-care centers. Even less attractive has been the Western advocacy of sexual liberation for women, which is rather seen as demeaning and dishonorable promiscuity, in contrast to the ideal of chastity. Indian feminists may want equality and equity, but they do not want to be like Western women.

In a land of polygyny, former royal harems, "eve-teasing," and other clear manifestations of sexual exploitation of women, chastity has special virtue. Indians socialized to traditional values consider it an act of independence for a woman to withhold sex if she so desires, and thus control sexuality. Carried to a logical extreme, some believe that complete male-female equality can only be achieved through total asexuality. The Brahma Kumari sect, a small but growing movement primarily of women but also including men, requires complete celibacy of its members and views sexual activity as "wallowing in a sewer," the source of women's subordination to men. Drawing on ancient Hindu ideals, the group advocates ceibacy as a method of concentrating and storing power, especially for women, who would otherwise be dominated by sexually exploitative men. The Brahma Kumaris wish to emulate the great powerful and chaste goddesses, worthy of worship like the maidens of Hindu festivals.

Concerned Indian women, however, are no longer satisfied with the adulation of goddesses, maidens, and virtuous woman saints, nor are they satisfied with the accomplishments of a relatively small number of well-placed women. Their goal is real opportunity and empowerment for all women of every class. For the Indian women's movement, achieving true gender equality while retaining treasured Indian ideals will be a major challenge for the future.

III. ISSUES FOR DISCUSSION

In some ways, gender issues in India seem very different from those in the West. However, certain key similarities exist, and consideration of these issues in the Indian context may heighten awareness of related issues in the United States.

1. Indian ideologies and laws suggest that women are entitled to equal and even preferential treatment, yet, in fact, women face multiple disadvantages in comparison to men. Outline and discuss similar contradictions in the United States.

2. What would true equality between men and women be like? In India? In the United States?

3. In a society espousing gender equality, such as India or the United States, what place should complementarity of sex roles have? What about separation of the sexes? How do complementarity and separation of the sexes compare with notions of "separate but equal" in race relations in the United States?

4. In India a certain number of seats in legislative bodies are reserved for women and for members of low-ranking castes, thus ensuring representation for these groups. Would reserved seats in state legislatures and in Congress be advantageous for women in the United States? Would the existence of reserved seats suggest the idea that women are inferior to men and require special treatment in order to be elected? What about reserved seats for mem-

bers of disadvantaged minority groups? Discuss existing forms of protective discrimination in the United States.

5. Women have been chosen as political leaders in India, Pakistan, Sri Lanka, and the Philippines, yet no woman has come close to being elected U.S. president. Why might this be? How does class membership relate to the political success of Asian women leaders? What about Margaret Thatcher?

6. Professional women in India often depend on family members and servants to help care for children and run their households. To what extent is this true in the United States? Must the advancement of privileged women depend on the exploitation of less privileged women? How does this issue relate to men's unwillingness to take responsibility for child care and domestic tasks?

7. Indian feminists object to amniocentesis being used for the destruction of female fetuses, yet feminist goals usually include a woman's right to control her reproductive capacities. How do female feticide and the notion of "woman's place" in India relate to pro-choice and right-to-life issues now current in the United States?

8. While the Western feminist agenda frequently stresses sexual "liberation" for women, most Indian feminists consider traditional female chastity a virtue and source of female power. There are religious orders in the United States which also have advocated chastity as a means of achieving a measure of female independence in a male-dominated society. The celibate Brahma Kumaris are even finding new members in the United States. Consider the relationships between asceticism, asexuality, and male domination of women in both the United States and India.

NOTES

1. Population Crisis Committee, "Poor, Powerless, and Pregnant," Washington, DC, 1988, report and chart. (Available from the Population Crisis Committee, 1120 19th St., N.W., Washington, D.C. 20036.)

2. United Nations, The Situation of Women, 1990. UN Publication Sales No. E.90.XVIII.3A.

3. India Today, October 15, 1987, p. 61.

IV. SELECTED READINGS

Babb, Lawrence A. *Redemptive Encounters: Three Modern Styles in the Hindu Tradition.* Berkeley: University of California Press, 1986 (faculty and student reading). Includes insightful study of the Brahma Kumari movement.

Bennett, Lynn. *Dangerous Wives and Sacred Sisters: Social and Symbolic Roles of High-Caste Women in Nepal.* New York: Columbia University

Press, 1983 (faculty background/advanced student reading). Ethnography focusing on women's roles and rituals among Nepali Hindus.

Bumiller, Elisabeth. *May You Be The Mother of a Hundred Sons*. New York: Random House, 1900. An exploration of various aspects of women's lives in India, by a sensitive journalist. Somewhat controversial and widely read; instructors should be aware that students may be familiar with the book.

Calman, Leslie. *Toward Empowerment: Women in Movement Politics in India*. Boulder, CO: Westview Press, 1992 (faculty and student reading). A new study of the women's movement.

Gross, Susan Hill, and Mary Hill Rojas. *Contemporary Issues for Women in South Asia: India, Pakistan, Bangladesh, Sri Lanka, Nepal, and Bhutan*. St. Louis Park, MN: The Upper Midwest Women's History Center Collection, 1989. A fine resource for teaching about South Asian women, intended for teachers, with classroom participation exercises. Funded by U.S.A.I.D.'s Development Education Program for secondary school use, it is also appropriate for college use.

India Today, a fortnightly illustrated news magazine similar to *Time*, frequently includes articles on social and economic issues, including female infanticide, sati, and discrimination against widows. Available through Living Media India, Limited, 404 Park Avenue South, New York, NY 10016, for $39 per year (faculty background/student reading).

Jacobson, Doranne. "Indian Women in Processes of Development." *Journal of International Affairs*. (Special Issue on Women and Change in the Developing World), Vol. 30, No. 2, Fall/Winter 1976–77: 211–242. (Published by Columbia University, School of International Affairs.) Summarizes some key points in *Towards Equality* as well as other issues salient to women's status and activities relevant to development in India. Suitable for instructor and students particularly interested in the subject.

Jacobson, Doranne. "The Women of North and Central India: Goddesses and Wives." In *Many Sisters: Women in Cross-Cultural Perspective*, edited by Carolyn Matthiasson, pp. 99–175. New York: The Free Press, 1974 (student reading). An overview of women's roles and status in northern India throughout different stages of life. Illustrated.*

Lebra, Joyce, Joy Paulson, and Jane Everett, eds. *Women and Work in India: Continuity and Change*. New Delhi: Promilla & Co., 1984 (student reading). (Available through South Asia Books, Columbia, MO.) Includes good case study material on women working in a variety of fields.

Mandelbaum, David G. *Society in India*. 2 vols. Berkeley: University of California Press, 1970 (faculty background/student reading). Readable summary chapters on women and family life. Although not recent, basic cultural patterns are well-described.

Mandelbaum, David G. *Women's Seclusion and Men's Honor: Sex Roles in North India, Bangladesh and Pakistan*. Tucson: University of Arizona Press, 1988 (student reading). Nicely written summary of concepts and practices relating to the seclusion of women in cultural context.

Manushi, the pioneering Indian feminist journal, edited by Madhu Kishwar, provides an up-to-date chronicle of Indian feminism as it is developing. The immediacy of contributions from disadvantaged women is most instructive. Available for $25 per year through Esther Jantzen, 5008 Erringer Place, Philadelphia, PA 19144, or *Manushi*, C/202 Lajpat Nagar 1, New Delhi 110024 (faculty background/student reading).

Ramusack, Barbara. "Women in South and Southeast Asia." In *Restoring Women to History*, Teaching Packets for Integrating Women's History into Courses on Africa, Asia, Latin America, the Caribbean, and the Middle East. Bloomington, IN: Organization of American Historians, 1988 (faculty background). (May be obtained by writing to the Organization at 112 N. Bryan St., Bloomington, IN 47408–4199.) Excellent 62-page summary of women in Indian history, up to the present, focusing on women's rights and opportunities, with bibliography and readings suggested for classroom use.

Sakala, Carol. *Women of South Asia: A Guide to Resources*. Millwood, NY: Kraus International Publications, 1980 (faculty background/student reference). An excellent annotated bibliography.

Towards Equality: Report of the Committee on the Status of Women in India. India, Ministry of Education and Social Welfare. December, 1974 (faculty background/student reading). A detailed examination of disadvantages suffered by Indian women in many realms of life. Also available in a condensed version. An irreplaceable reference source.

Wadley, Susan S. "Women and the Hindu Tradition." *Signs, Journal of Women in Culture and Society*. Vol. 3, No. 1, 1977: 113–125 (student reading). Discusses Hindu concepts relating to feminine powers and ideal roles.*

*The above two articles, by Jacobson and Wadley, are also available in a single volume: Jacobson, Doranne, and Susan S. Wadley, *Women in India: Two Perspectives*. Columbia, MO: South Asia Books, 1992.

AUDIOVISUAL AIDS

Jacobson, Doranne, *Women and Work in South Asia*. St. Louis Park, MN: The Upper Midwest Women's History Center Collection, 1989. Sound filmstrip or sound filmstrip in videocassette, 100 color images of women at a variety of work activities in urban and rural areas, through seasonal cycles. Available with instructor's manual for $50 from The Upper Midwest Women's History Center Collection, 6300 Walker Street, St. Louis Park, MN 55416. Intended for students. Other materials on South Asian women available from this publisher.

Anthropology: India

Stratification, Inequality, Caste System: India

Owen M. Lynch

I. INTRODUCTION: CENTRAL POINTS

India, inheritor of one of the world's most complex and rigid systems of stratification, the caste system, is also the world's largest functioning democracy. It therefore provides an excellent case study of:

• The organization of society based on inequality believed to be inherent in one's caste and inherited from parents. Such inequality is considered the natural order of the universe, and the organization of a division of labor on the basis of groups ranked and rewarded according to such inequality.

• The problems arising from a system of protective discrimination for India's lowest castes, the Untouchables.

• The conflicting but legitimate demands that arise when a society attempts to change from organization on the basis of caste to organization on the basis of class.

• The relationship of ideology to a system of social stratification.

II. MAJOR TOPICS

SPECIFICATION OF THE PROBLEM BY CORRECT QUESTION

Before considering the caste system itself, three confusing and confused questions when discussing the caste system must be distinguished and the one asked in this essay noted.

1. What is **a** caste? This question focuses on defining characteristics or traits— such as endogamy, distinct rituals, and the like— of a unit, or particular group, within the caste system rather than about those characteristics defining the caste system itself. A system, such as the solar system, is not understood in the same terms as a unit in the system, such as the planet Earth.

2. What is **the** caste system? This question examines the Indian caste system as a prototypical model of other caste-like systems. The present discussion is restricted to this question and to defining as well as describing the caste system of India, which is culturally unique.

3. What is **a** caste system? This question suggests a generalized, theoretical, and cross-culturally applicable model of a caste system. Such a model could be used to compare the system relating between blacks and whites in the United States with that relating the races in South Africa or that relating the Burakumin and the general population in Japan.

When students of stratification ask one of these questions but answer it in terms of another, confusion results.

THE CASTE SYSTEM OF INDIA

Definitions. Caste System: An ordering of society into categories (varna) containing groups of people (*jāti*) that are a) **hierarchically** ranked according to inherent inequality expressed in a language of purity and pollution, and b) **interdependently** organized such that each group theoretically specializes in an occupation necessary for the survival of the whole society.

Varnas: A set of hierarchical social categories (Brahman or priests, Kshatriya or rulers and warriors, Vaishya or merchants and businessmen, and Shudra or menials and workers) found throughout India, believed to be religiously ordained, and into which the various castes or *jāti* can be placed in rank order.

Jāti: An organized, usually endogamous, named, self-conscious group often associated with a distinctive occupation, having its own way of life and customs, and generally restricted to certain local areas in India. *Jāti* are the operative units of the caste system and number in the thousands.

Rules of the System. It was perhaps no accident that chess originated in India. Chess is a game of almost infinite combinations of moves and strategies. No one player can know and foresee every possible move. The game is played with several types of chessmen organized in a hierarchy of importance. A few simple rules, largely unchanged over the course of millennia, organize the chessmen into an exceedingly complex system. As in chess, India's caste system is defined by, and has functioned for centuries on, the basis of two simple rules. Those rules are: interdependence and hierarchy.

a) **Interdependence**. In Indian terms, **interdependence** finds clearest expression in the hegemonic, Hindu ideology of the varnas or classes. There are four ranked varnas: the Brahman or priests, the Kshatriya or warriors and rulers, the Vaishya or merchants and businessmen, and the Shudra or laborers and workmen. Varnas are national social categories not actual groups, just as the middle class in the United States is a social category but not an actual group, such as Troop 122 of the Boy Scouts. Within each of the four varnas are organized groups or castes (*jāti*). A particular village generally has several, sometimes many *jāti*s, and taking India as a whole, their number is in the thousands. Different *jāti*s are most often found only in particular regions of India.

According to orthodox Hindu religious teaching, the varnas originated in the sacrifice of the macrocosmic, primeval man, as recounted in the sacred text, *Rig Veda*. In the sacrifice, the Brahman came from the head, the Kshatriya from the shoulders, the Vaishya from the thighs, and the Shudra from the feet. Just as in the macrocosmic body from which they came, each varna has a definite function in maintaining the life of the social whole or society. Brahmans are supposed to think, provide for the intellectual needs of society, act as priests, and make sacrifices to the gods. Kshatriyas are needed to rule, protect others, and maintain order. Vaishyas are required for commerce and agriculture, while Shudras are needed to perform the more menial tasks necessary for society. Added to these four, but not included in the theory, is the chandala category, that of the Untouchables, whose function is to remove and shield the upper castes from sources of pollution by working with polluting substances such as leather (tanner), excrement (sweeper), and blood- or sweat-stained clothes (launderer).

What does the varna theory mean? First of all, it is descriptive providing an ideal **model of reality** and of how society should be organized through a division of labor. Each of the varnas, and often each separate caste (*jāti*) within it, contributes some distinctive function or occupational specialization, **as its duty**, for the benefit of the whole society. Since it is rooted in religious cosmology, the model legitimates the caste system and provides a taken for granted ontology for it. To go against the duties of one's caste disturbs not only the social order, but also the natural order of the universe. Thus, the *Bhagavad Gitā* says that it is better to carry out one's own caste duty poorly than to do that of another well. For those Indians who accept this doctrine, it is as fundamental as the Ten Commandments are for Jews and Christians.

Second, the varna theory is prescriptive, providing a **model for reality**. Following the rule of interdependence the many castes in an Indian village have been organized into a cooperative system, often called the jajmani system which when it also follows the rule of hierarchy is really the caste system as carried out in the everyday reality and behavior of India's villagers. In Indian villages members of various **castes** work as clients for landowners or patrons called jajman. For example, a member of a carpenter caste provides tools and plows; a member of the launderer caste washes the soiled clothes of the jajman household; the leatherworker tans hides, makes country shoes, and works in his jajman fields; the tailor stitches garments; and the priest officiates at the rituals of his jajman's family. The right as well as the duty to work for a particular jajman is inherited within a family and not by an individual.

In return for these goods and services, the jajman oversees the farming of his land and gives harvest grain and other gifts to his clients. Often, these payments were made at traditionally assigned rates which varied according to caste, not according to amount of work done. The jajman also gives nonreciprocal gifts called *dān* which rid his family and the village of inauspiciousness. Each of the client castes also provides political support as well as ritual services at various ceremonies for their jajman. The system is, then, simultaneously, economic, ritual, and political and the role of the jajman, not necessarily the high ranking Brahman, is central to it in all these ways. In theory, although not necessarily in reality where conflicts between jajman and between jajmani and their clients often exist, the caste system is kept together by organic solidarity without conflicts of interest among the varnas and the castes within them.

b) **Hierarchy**. The second rule of the caste system is **hierarchy**, which follows from the theory of the varnas in that Brahmans originating in the superior part of the primeval man's body, the head, rank highest and the Shudras originating from the feet rank lowest. Each of the castes (*jāti*) of the different varnas in an Indian village is ranked in terms of purity and pollution, a language for talking about inherent inequality between groups of people and other things, just as color is a language for talking about differences between so-called races in the United States and South Africa.

Because purity and pollution are a language, the meaning of the words is partially dependent on their use in social situations, as is the meaning of black and white in the American language of color. Thus, in one part of India fish may be considered polluting and Brahmans forbidden to eat it but for Brahmans in another part of India it may be considered pure and essential to their diet. The important point is that some things be identified as pure and others impure, so that they can index or symbolize inherent inequalities, including moral inequalities, between different *jātis*. Just as "All men are created equal" may seem natural and indubitable to an American, so too "All castes of human beings are created unequal" may seem natural and indubitable to an orthodox Hindu. Both views are social constructions of reality, not parts of the natural world.

Because purity and pollution is a language for talking about inequality, different castes often use it as a language of argumentation about small differences of relative rank in the case of hierarchy. This is particularly true of the middle ranked castes, although the high rank of Brahmans and low rank of Untouchables remain stable. Thus, between villages and even between neighboring regions the rank of a particular caste may vary slightly within its varna, just as its rank may vary somewhat up or down over time. Such movement, however, does not challenge, but rather confirms, the rule of hierarchy by accentuating the taken-for-granted cultural fact that rank is important.

Units of the System. Because each caste (*jāti*) is understood to be different and unequal in inherent quality (*jāqtidharma*), the moral character and behavior of each is expected to be different. Expected behavior is in part a function of inherent quality. A member of the Rajput *jāti* is supposed to possess the qualities of a ruler, and a predisposition to aggressive behavior, eating meat, and consuming alcohol. Such stereotypical beliefs are both the source and the result of actual behavior.

Each caste (jāti) differs from other castes in the customs it follows, in the rituals it observes, in its origin myths, and in its sense of identity. For example, among Brahman jātis of Maharashtra state, elderly ladies and widows of all ages are not supposed to eat onions and garlic. Most castes circumambulate the sacred fire seven times at the time of marriage; but the Chaube jāti of the Brahman varna in Mathura city circumambulate it three times on one day, four on another. Such customs are often well-known and used as markers of caste identity.

Many castes have traditional councils (panchayat) to enforce their customs and rules, as well as to settle conflicts among their members. Excommunication from the caste is the ultimate sanction; it leaves the person and his family isolated from potential marriage mates and from neighbors with whom he can socialize and seek assistance.

As already mentioned, each caste tends to be associated with a traditional occupation which passes as a family right from father to son. Agriculture, however, is an occupation open to members of every caste, as are modern occupations in factories and offices.

Just as the varna theory explains and legitimizes the inherent inequality of the varnas and the jātis in them, so too do the religious notions of karma and rebirth explain and legitimize the individual's membership in his or her jāti as well as lend support to the hegemonic varna theory. According to the notion of karma every action in this life has a good or bad consequence that results in rebirth in another life. Thus, an individual's caste rank in this life is due to his own actions in a past life. All one can do, therefore, is accept one's jāti membership in this life and work to reduce bad karma so as to be reborn in a better life or jāti.

CONSEQUENCES OF THE CASTE SYSTEM

The caste system has had profound consequences for Indian society. First, because castes differ from one another according to their inherent moral qualities, the different customs and inequalities between them are considered as natural as the difference between dogs, cats, and insects. Socially, individuals are judged and treated according to unequal caste rank; one's jāti is more important than one's individual abilities. Interaction between members of different castes is thus restricted. Individuals are expected to marry within their own caste and to avoid eating food prepared by a member of a lower caste. More important, one's opportunities within the society at large are extremely restricted, particularly for castes of the Shudra varna and the Untouchable category.

Second, viewed from the nonorthodox Hindu viewpoint, the caste system with its hegemonic, religious ideology of the origin of the varnas has worked to the benefit of those castes at the top and to the disadvantage of those at the bottom.

Third, the system has allowed for caste mobility, except for the Untouchable caste, through what is called Sanskritization. Sanskritization is the process whereby a low caste or tribal group in India attempts to change its socially recognized varna rank by emulating over a number of generations the customs, rituals, ideology, and way of life of an elite or dominant caste of a higher varna. If a *jāti* in a lower varna should improve its economic circumstances, then it may develop an origin myth claiming membership in a higher, usually the Kshatriya, varna; its members emulate the behavior of that higher varna, and after a few generations the upwardly mobile *jāti* may be recognized as belonging to that higher varna. There is no intermarriage among *jāti*s in this process, nor is there individual mobility; the *jāti* as a whole is mobile. Because each *jāti* is unique in its customs and way of life and because an individual's identity is determined by the *jāti* to which he belongs, it is virtually impossible for an individual to pass as a member of a different *jāti*. An individual who tries to do so may be successful for a time, but sooner or later, when he or his children wish to marry, he will be unable to bring forward relatives linking him to other known members of the *jāti*. Thus, the caste system itself remains stable and mobility within it does not disturb the order of society.

Fourth, the system has survived for centuries, despite repeated invasions, colonial rule, and recurrent famines, droughts, and natural disasters. Under it the land was tilled and goods and services provided for the survival of all, the enrichment of some, and, at least in the nonorthodox Hindu view, the exploitation of others. The myth of the origin of the varnas also provided a hegemonic ideology to legitimate the system as grounded in religious belief about the origins of society.

CHANGE IN THE SYSTEM— FROM CHESS TO MONOPOLY

Although India's caste system continues to operate according to the two rules of interdependence and hierarchy, especially in the villages, which account for 80 percent of the population, the rules of the game are rapidly changing. Having achieved independence in 1947, India chose in 1950 to become a federal, secular, and democratic republic under a parliamentary system of government. The Indian Constitution guarantees basic rights to all its citizens including the right to equality and equal protection before the law, the right to individual ownership of property, and the right to constitutional remedies. The practice of untouchability, as well as discrimination on the basis of caste, race, sex, or religion, have been legally abolished. As equal citizens before the law, Indians, literate and illiterate alike, possess the right to vote. As a result, Indian voters from all castes, classes, and stripes of political opinion have mobilized into interest groups and changed their society into a democratic arena of competitive politics. Parliamentary democracy, without eliminating the caste system, has thus brought with it a new mode of integrating Indian society. Two consequences have been the creation of the protective discrimination policy to uplift India's Untouchables and the development of a mixed caste/class system.

Protective Discrimination. In 1981 India's Untouchables were estimated to number 107 million or about 15.7 percent of the total population. Traditionally they were not included in the varna system because they were considered to be unclean and polluting to upper castes. In villages they were forced to live in separate hamlets, apart from other castes; they were the poorest of the poor, powerless and despised. Untouchables worked as laborers for upper-caste landowners and were subject to many discriminatory practices including forced labor, restrictions on dress, denial of entry into Hindu temples, and enforced deference to members of the upper castes. They were denied the possibility of education, particularly the opportunity to learn Sanskrit, the language of the sacred texts defining their polluted condition, and Brahman priests would not officiate at their rituals.

Early in this century the British colonial administrators attempted to change the condition of Untouchables by granting to them certain privileges in education and employment. Those Untouchable *jāti* eligible for these privileges were put on a list or schedule; even today Untouchables continue to be known as scheduled castes. Mahatma Gandhi called them Harijans, Children of God, but educated scheduled caste members today reject that term because it connotes upper-caste paternalism and the idea that Untouchables are childlike and unable to take proper care of themselves.

Independent India has built upon British policy, and committed itself to eliminating the problem of Untouchability. The goal, however, remains elusive. Just because the Indian Constitution outlaws the practice of Untouchability does not mean the caste system and caste privilege have been abolished. In fact, castes have rights in Indian law and may even exist as legal corporations.

In addition to legal provisions, the government of India has implemented a policy of **protective discrimination** for Untouchable castes, in an effort to redress the profound injustices Untouchables have suffered and to achieve a measure of **social** equality. The policy of protective discrimination departs from the nineteenth century liberal notion that advancement must be on the basis of **individual merit** which assumes equal opportunity is open to all individuals. It moves toward a notion of **social equality** which assumes that, before individual merit can be equally open to all, groups in society must achieve equality through representation and positions of power in all institutions of society whereby they can control, if not eliminate, prejudice and discrimination on the basis of group membership. The policy implies that equality will not be achieved merely by legally declaring equal rights, and abolition of discrimination as well as of the practice of untouchability. Rather government, because of the weight of historical and religious tradition against Untouchable castes, must intervene and create conditions for them to become equal participants in all aspects of Indian society.

The policy of protective discrimination has three arms:

reservation of elective political offices, reservation of jobs in the central and state governments, and provision of educational benefits and preferences. The Constitution mandates that one in seven seats in the national and state legislatures be reserved for members of the scheduled castes. These seats represent a reserved constituency where only Untouchable candidates may stand for election, although electors in such a constituency are from both scheduled and nonscheduled castes. One problem with reserved constituencies is that the majority of scheduled caste people live outside of them. Thus, nonscheduled caste legislators represent the majority of scheduled caste people, while a small minority of nonscheduled caste people find that they must turn to scheduled caste legislators for assistance.

A second and more significant problem is that scheduled castes constitute less than half of the voting population in national constituencies and more than half in very few of the state-level constituencies. This means that nonscheduled castes can, although do not necessarily, determine which scheduled caste candidate is elected. It must be noted that in the nonreserved constituencies open to the general population, few if any scheduled caste candidates have ever been elected. Thus, if the reserved constituencies are abandoned, then no members of the scheduled castes are likely to be elected to legislative positions in the government.

Reservation of seats in the legislatures is, then, the most important part of the protective discrimination policy, because without it Untouchables would have little or no voice in government; other policies to remedy their condition would probably disappear. The Constitution originally mandated the reservation of elected seats for a period of ten years in the hope that it would be sufficient for attitudes toward Untouchables to change. That initial mandate has been renewed four times since its inception, indicating the government's commitment to eliminating the problem of Untouchability despite the strong and ever-growing opposition of many of its upper caste citizens.

In terms of education, the protective discrimination policy provides tuition, books and sometimes meals at the state level, and college scholarships at the national level. Scheduled caste literacy increased from 10.3 percent in 1961 to 14.7 percent in 1971, although the increase among the rest of the population was even greater. The program has resulted in the creation of a cadre of educated Untouchables able to represent and fight for Untouchable rights. Many have also been helped to get and keep better jobs.

Finally, in terms of employment, the policy reserves positions in the national and state civil services for Untouchables in proportion to their population in the nation and in the states. This arm of the policy has been somewhat effective, but mostly at the lower clerical end service levels. Untouchables are still underrepresented in the higher-level administrative posts and are virtually unrepresented in the private sector. Even when qualified Untouchable candidates for higher-level positions are available, reserved jobs often go unfairly to other candidates. For many reserved positions the basic qualifying conditions have been lowered for the scheduled castes. Thus, beneficiaries are resented by members of higher castes who insist that jobs should be awarded on the basis of individual merit and that they are being discriminated against. Thus, the Indian government has found it difficult to achieve social equality for all its citizens while at the same time recognizing the rights of individual merit.

Protective discrimination, therefore, is pursued in the face of great resistance, hostility, and resentment of members of non-scheduled castes. In recent years reported atrocities against representatives of scheduled castes have greatly increased, despite new laws for their protection. The government insists that it is moving as fast as possible without tearing the nation apart; Untouchables, who yearn for full integration as well as for full and uncontested recognition of their rights and equality with other citizens, feel that it is moving much too slowly. Nevertheless, 90 percent of India's Untouchables live in rural areas where discrimination is greatest and governmental protection weakest. Of rural Untouchables, in 1964, 34 percent were landless agricultural laborers, while in 1971 this figure had risen to 52 percent because even when Untouchables own land it is most often minuscule in amount and of marginal productivity.

Just as Untouchable castes have become more politicized, so too have other castes. Castes in India, like ethnic groups in the United States, have become interest groups, forced to compete with one another in the new game of parliamentary politics. This game has weakened the interdependence, but not necessarily the hierarchy, among castes, particularly in rural areas. Indeed, in India's cities today, castes continue to exist, but the caste system does not. Although the traditionally dominant upper castes still tend to monopolize positions of power and influence, they are increasingly coming under attack by lower-ranked castes. Many lower-ranked castes, referred to as the "backward classes," are themselves trying to obtain privileges similar to those given to Untouchables. The issue of social equality of castes (*jāti*) has become more important than either individual merit or caste hierarchy.

Development: Transition from a Caste to a Class System. The government of India has also made great efforts to improve the conditions of all its citizens. After independence each state passed laws to limit the amount of land any one person could own and also to abolish holdings by wealthy absentee landlords. To date the new laws have been unsuccessful, and distribution of land to poorer laborers and tenants has been minimal. Significantly, the laws still uphold the right to private ownership of property including land. Some landlords have avoided legal limits on land ownership by registering land in the name of relatives; others have evicted tenants who had been holders of traditional tenancy rights.

Members of castes who had hereditary rights to a share in the harvest from the lands of the jajman have in many cases been slowly reduced to laborers paid in cash for work done only at specific times. Some landowners have replaced human labor with tractors and other machines. Moreover, many landowners today prefer to go to town where they can buy mass-produced factory goods rather than use the products of the local service castes, such as the potter, the tailor and the like. The condition of both laboring and service castes is in many cases worse than it was under the traditional caste system.

India has also made great efforts to increase agricultural production by extending irrigation facilities, expanding fertilizer production, and making credit more easily available. High-yield varieties of seed have created what is known as the "green revolution." An important result of these programs concentrating on production is that distribution of wealth has become even more unequal. Laws favoring private ownership of property and competition in the market economy are said to promote efficiency and production, yet their unfortunate consequence has been to enshrine profit as the overriding motive. These changes have exacerbated rural under- and unemployment. In the cities industrial growth has been phenomenal, yet insufficient to absorb the growing army of unemployed, many of whom come from the scheduled castes. Thus, progress has created a small new class of the very wealthy, and has increased the multitude of the poor.

Although the rule of hierarchy, under which the castes are ranked, remains, the rule of interdependence among castes has begun to wither and be replaced by the rule of individual competition in the market economy. The game of chess has given way to the game of Monopoly, where success is measured by the accumulation of money and the ownership of private property. The hierarchy of caste is now cross-cut and complicated by a hierarchy of class. In the caste system economic status, political power, and caste status tended to coincide. In the new system these measures of status have to some extent diverged. As a democracy, India has found it difficult to balance respect for **individual rights** such as the ownership of private property and allocation of jobs on the basis of individual merit, against the demands of **social and distributive justice**, such as the guarantee of a living wage, an adequate diet, and the creation of genuine equal opportunities for all, regardless of caste rank (status level). [*Readers are referred to the essay on "Religion in a State Society: India," by Lawrence A. Babb, for additional discussion of the definition of caste.*]

III. ISSUES FOR DISCUSSION

1. Consider the argument that hierarchy is necessary to ensure that the web of interdependence, through the division of labor, is maintained for the benefit of all castes in the caste system. Consider as well the argument that class stratification is necessary to motivate, by unequal economic rewards, individuals to train for and perform the more difficult jobs required by society. If all jobs are necessary for a society to function well, as, for example, Untouchables to remove sources of pollution, then who is it that decides which jobs are more necessary, more difficult, and more rewarded than others and on what bases are those decisions made?

2. Compare India's policy of protective discrimination with the policies of affirmative action in the United States. Consider them in light of the underlying need and the rationale given for them, and results for both individuals and society. Compare progress made in the United States in the more than a century since the Emancipation Proclamation and in India since the promulgation of its Constitution in 1950.

3. According to the orthodox Hindu viewpoint, the caste system is not exploitative; attempts to change the system, therefore, are an unwarranted interference with religious freedom. Compare this to the argument that the American class system is open with equal opportunity for all, and that individual initiative and competition redound to the benefit of all. In your comparisons take into account the viewpoints of representatives of both Untouchables and the upper castes, as well as those of the different classes and races in U.S. society.

IV. SELECTED READINGS

Dumont, Louis. *Homo Hierarchicus: The Caste System and Its Implications,* revised English edition. Chicago: University of Chicago Press, 1980 (faculty background). A classic, controversial, and influential theory of the caste system.

Klass, Morton. *Caste: The Emergence of the South Asian Social System.* Philadelphia: Institute for the Study of Human Issues, 1980 (faculty background). A review of theories, as well as a new "eclectic" theory, of the origins of the Indian caste system.

Kolenda, Pauline. *Caste in Contemporary India: Beyond Organic Solidarity.* Prospect Heights, IL: Waveland Press, 1985 (student reading). A brief but comprehensive introduction to the caste system, includes a discussion of underlying theories and changes taking place.

Lynch, Owen M. *The Politics of Untouchability: Social Mobility and Social Change in a City in India.* New York: Columbia University Press, 1969 (student reading). An ethnographic and historical study of an Untouchable caste in the midst of change.

Reheja, Gloria Goodwin. *The Poison in the Gift: Ritual Prestation and the Dominant Caste in a North Indian Village.* Chicago: University of Chicago Press, 1988 (student and faculty reading). A revisionary theory of "centrality" concerning the caste system as well as an ethnographic description of how it works in village India.

Anthropology: Indonesia

Family and Kinship in Indonesia

John R. Bowen

I. INTRODUCTION: CENTRAL POINTS

The rich diversity of societies in Indonesia make it an excellent case study for illustrating important variations in family and kinship organization. Indonesian materials provide a clear counterpoint to the European and American social forms with which students are familiar. Among points to be highlighted with Indonesian examples are:

• In many societies, systems of kinship and marriage are the **major, generalized institutions** for the regulation and interpretation of social life. Three distinct kinds of kinship emphasis are very well illustrated through Indonesian materials: the bilateral web of kinship, the corporate kin or descent group, and systems of marriage exchange.

• Kinship systems **shape local responses** to economic, political, and religious change. Of special importance in Indonesia has been the challenge posed by Islamic social ideas to preexisting social forms, including marriage exchange and the transmission of property. Scholarship on Indonesia provides a set of case studies in the dynamic interactions of society, economic change, and religious ideologies.

• Kinship systems shape and are shaped by **dominant cultural** conceptions. Indonesian cases are useful for showing how ideas of person, gender, time, and emotions are made concrete and public through determinate social forms such as kin terms, names, and genealogies.

• Rituals, especially life-cycle or life-crisis rituals, provide meaning and order at the points of critical transition in the family or kinship network. Indonesia is a rich source of material on ritual importance, in particular, mortuary rituals that mediate between the living and the dead.

II. MAJOR TOPICS

THE DIVERSITY OF INDONESIAN FAMILY AND KINSHIP

Throughout most of human history, and in most societies today, kinship and marriage play a more salient role in everyday life than is the case for many Americans. Nearly every possible kinship form can be found in Indonesia, and the country provides an excellent set of cases for showing the different ways of structuring society. Good material is available on the role of rituals, the diverse cultural categories that inform social life, and the adaptive responses of local societies to challenges posed by supralocal social forms and ideologies. Of particular importance in the Indonesian case have been the social frameworks prescribed by Islam and the new opportunities afforded by trade and cash-cropping.

Common Features. Indonesia contains over three hundred distinct ethnolinguistic groups (or "cultures"). Most Indonesians speak languages of the Malayo-Polynesian family (the major exceptions are the Papuan language speakers of West Irian and several eastern islands). In their forms of family and kinship they share certain broad features, some of which, as Reid has shown, are shared with other Southeast Asians.[1] These features set them off from many societies of Melanesia, Africa, and the Americas.

The major common element of Indonesian kinship are **cross-sex pairs**: husband-wife and brother-sister. In most societies the nuclear or extended family is the basic unit of production and consumption, even when several such families coreside. Ties to sons and daughters are preserved and valued. In mythology and cosmology as well, a brother-sister or husband-wife pair appear as the initial social unit. Kinship, accordingly, is **reckoned bilaterally**. Sons and daughters, and their descendants in turn, retain ties to a family regardless of descent ideology. In most cases objects of value are transmitted to sons and daughters. Even when one gender-defined line is favored over the other the preference is not absolute. If sons are favored to remain in a house or village and inherit the family land, the possibility is usually kept open for daughters to play this role instead (and vice-versa). A bilateral kinship grid thus underlies the diverse kinship-and-marriage constructions in Indonesian societies.

This basic bilateralism supports relatively **egalitarian ideas of gender**. Husbands and wives tend to cooperate on many tasks, including those of agriculture, trade, and child care. The radical separation of men and women that one encounters in much of Melanesia and Africa is rare here.[2]

On top, as it were, of this bilateral kinship network are **diverse and changing social structural emphases**, including social rank (in Java and South Sulawesi), kin-based corporate groups (in much of Sumatra), and marriage exchange and alliance (in eastern Indonesia). These arrangements have specific political and economic implications, and have accommodated the supralocal pressures of cash-cropping, national integration, and religious conformity. I have chosen to highlight several case studies for which teaching materials are available. Each case study provides opportunities for drawing particular connections between kinship and other social domains.[3]

Case Studies.
   a) **The Javanese Web of Kinship.** The Javanese provide a good example of a society in which ties of bilateral kinship provide a broad base for social interaction. As documented by Hildred and Clifford Geertz, the Javanese case offers special features for in-depth study: a **status hierarchy** that had its apex in the traditional court and that is reflected in the many levels of politeness in the language; a strong **sense of shame**, inculcated in the **socialization** process; the coexistence of very different **socioreligious orientations** that make Java an excellent case for the study of modern, plural societies.[4]

Javanese patterns of social interaction center on the family, and on loosely-bounded networks of kin and neighbors. Kinship is reckoned bilaterally, and, for those following older patterns rather than Islamic law (discussed below), inheritance is divided equally among all children. The Javanese kinship system does not delineate bounded groups; rather, it sets out a pattern for the showing of respect or familiarity to all others with whom a person interacts. Speech and other behavior are highly determined by the relations of differential status between individuals. The Javanese language contains several levels of style; Javanese is more strongly inflected for status than, for example, European languages, which indicate status in the choice of pronouns and voice tone.[5]

The Javanese child is taught that he/she lives in a hierarchical social world and that he/she is to adopt attitudes of fear, shame, and respect toward others. H. Geertz (1961) describes this process very clearly; it could usefully be contrasted with Western socialization patterns and with the Japanese. Whereas Japanese dependence on the mother tends to produce a person who seeks to give absolute loyalty to a leader and a group, the Javanese style of socialization, in the context of an open-ended, bilateral kinship network, produces a generally deferential but not group-oriented individual.

The key family and neighborhood ritual is the *selamatan*, a ritual meal held for many occasions that brings blessings and, through the pattern of invitation, demarcates the salient social network.[6] **Because of the absence of corporate kin groups, other political, economic, and religious differences loom saliently for Javanese.**[7]

b) **Sumatran Corporate Groups**. In contrast to the bilateral Javanese kinship system, many Sumatran societies are structured by kin groups in which descent reckoning plays a dominant role. In these societies, property and other rights are transmitted within the group. Differences in kin group structure affect responses to outside economic, political, or socioreligious pressures. The study of these societies illustrates both the important contemporary role played by kin groups and the adaptive responses by people in such societies to social change.

The *Minangkabau* people of West Sumatra are one such group. The Minangkabau case shows the relations among social structure, economic activities, and a particular social openness toward change. In Minangkabau society, **corporate kin groups** have rights over the transmission of land and status titles. Membership in these kin groups is **figured matrilineally**, and men marry out of their group and into another. Many men thus live on the social margins of their village. This feature of Minangkabau society and the scarcity of agricultural land have led many men to leave the homeland for a period of years to earn money elsewhere in Indonesia, or to study in Indonesia or abroad, and then return home to purchase rice land and acquire status titles. The general pattern of migration extends to families as well. Minangkabau men and women are heavily represented in the urban areas of Indonesia, both in trades and in cultural circles.

Minangkabau men returning from work and study bring with them new ideas and resources. In the early decades of the twentieth century, for example, some of these men studied the new current of Islamic reformism in the Middle East, and new ideas of Indonesian nationalism on Java. West Sumatra became a center for religious renewal, educational reform, and cultural innovation. Minangkabau men and women played disproportionately large roles in the creation of the Indonesian nation and an Indonesian literature. Kato documents this historical process in his study, *Matriliny and Migration.*

Matriliny perdures despite strong pressures for change among the Minangkabau and among the related people of Negeri Sembilan, Malaysia. Islamic teachers have urged that the corporate claims of the matrilineage be abandoned in favor of a bilateral kinship system like that of the Javanese. The increased availability of new cash crops, such as rubber and coffee, has given to fathers resources that they can pass on to their own children (thus cross-cutting the matrilineal system). But these matrilineal societies have preserved their material and ideological core by retaining control over rice land.

Other Sumatran societies with corporate kin groups have responded to these same change pressures in different ways. In the Angkola Batak society, people have begun to emphasize the nuclear family over their corporate groups. The Angkola have promoted the refiguring of their society through the new media of cassette recordings and newspaper columns.[8]

c) **Marriage Exchange in Eastern Indonesia**. In many of Indonesia's societies the regular **exchange of women or men between kin groups** is an important basis for social communication, cooperation, and ideology. The social importance of marriage exchange is especially well-documented among the societies of **eastern Indonesia**.[9] These Indonesian cases provide excellent illustrations of the importance of exchange in social life, and can usefully be compared to exchange in Western societies of gifts, cards, and money. These cases also show how marriage can become the overall structuring principle of a society. The eastern Indonesian exchange systems are excellent illustrations of the exchange theories of Marcel Mauss and Claude Levi-Strauss. These theories assert that the exchange of persons and goods between social groups form the basis for social organization in many societies, especially in small-scale, non-industrialized societies.

Eastern Indonesian societies frame their views of society and of the cosmos in terms of the societal unit of the house. Houses, which may contain one or several families, often form the basic social and political units in the society, regardless of how descent is reckoned. They often are ranked as elder vis-à-vis younger houses.

Exchange between houses is conceived of as the "flow of life" within the society, and in some cases is conceived of as the regular movement of daughters from "wife-giving" houses to "wife-taking" houses. Ritual speech styles accentuate the social importance of these events of marriage exchange.[10] Ritual speaking in eastern Indonesia is structured around pairs of terms. Speakers bring order to the world (at a marriage or after a calamity) by speaking of events in terms of paired categories. The emphasis on pairs in speech is part of a broader emphasis on dual classification that binds together kinship and marriage, cosmology, and speech forms. For example, ritual speakers seeking to protect the community from harm may emphasize the distinction between forest spirits that live outside the community and spirits that live in the community, and associate that distinction with the distinctions of left and right, night and day, female and male, and so forth. This series of oppositions thus describes a total cosmology. The speaker then, through his speaking, strengthens the boundary between the community and the harmful spirits that lay outside, thereby protecting the community and also reinforcing in listeners' minds the structure of the cosmos.

THE DYNAMICS OF FAMILY AND KINSHIP: SPECIFIC TOPICS

Ritual and Kinship. The organized, regular sets of activities that we call "ritual" provide a dynamic form for the family and kinship. In particular, life-cycle or **life-crisis rituals** provide meaning and order at the points of critical transition in the family or kinship network. These points include (but are certainly not limited to) birth, the transitions to adolescence and adulthood, marriage, and death.

The management of death, through **mortuary ritual**, is especially important in most Indonesian societies. Mortuary rituals repair a torn social fabric, prepare the spirit of the deceased for the afterlife, and provide ways for the living to make meaning out of the loss and deal with their pain, anger, and suffering. These rituals establish the society's relation to the cosmos and so carry with them special powers and dangers. Attitudes toward life and death are strongly shaped by these rituals in many societies, in Europe as well as Asia; the example of **secondary burial** is especially effective in teaching this point.[11]

In many Malaysian and Indonesian societies, the gradual decomposition of the corpse has led people to posit a corresponding gradual departure of the soul from the community. This departure must be aided by rituals of appeasement, aid, or exorcism. The rituals often involve disinterment and a secondary burial ritual through which the soul of the deceased is sent into a distant land of the dead. Disinterment is practiced in the West as well (e.g., the Christian practice involving ossuaries) and provide instructive examples for cross-cultural comparisons.[12]

Of particular interest in the Indonesian cases is what Metcalf has called the "inherent bilocality of the dead," that is, the desire of the living to keep the dead distant but at the same time near for purposes of aid and comfort. These ambivalent attitudes toward death, and indeed the same ideas about transition from the world of the living to the world of the dead, appear among the *Islamic Gayo* as well[13], where they are linked to Islamic doctrines of the soul and Islamic mortuary chants.[14]

A second Indonesian case is that of the *Toraja* of South Sulawesi.[15] Toraja society is stratified into genealogically-determined social ranks. Mortuary ritual once was the occasion where those other members of the community with high rank demonstrated their inherent— and inherited— powers by their large gifts of meat. Sacrifices made at the funeral by the deceased's children also determined the relative size of their shares of the estate. Mortuary ritual thus was the occasion for social dramas in which social rank and family continuity were determined. More recently, however, some Toraja of low rank have obtained sufficient wealth to best the nobility at these ritual occasions. Further complicating these changes is that many of the newly rich are also Christian converts, and find that the older ritual forms conflict with their new beliefs. Mortuary ritual thus has been at the center of debates about the nature of family, the society, and religion.

Transmission of Wealth. In both the Toraja and Minangkabau societies described above, the **intergenerational transmission of family wealth** has been a central issue. Similar debates over inheritance have occurred in many other Indonesian societies as well, and particularly in Islamic societies where **Islamic inheritance laws** can be seen to require that older inheritance forms be changed or annulled.

Islamic rules of inheritance, as interpreted in most Indonesian societies, specify the awarding of estate shares to all children, in the ratio of two shares for males to one share for females.[16] Other categories of heirs receive shares as well. These rules conflict with practices that either (a) award equal shares of an estate to all children regardless of gender (as in much of Java) or (b) award shares only to those children, sons or daughters, who remain in the kin group after marriage (as in much of Sumatra). Local inheritance systems in much of Indonesia also typically favor the youngest child in cases where he or she cares for the parents in their old age.

Local accommodations to Islamic law have varied. Because Islamic rules allow for the giving of up to one-third of the estate as a pre-mortem gift, some of the variance can be accommodated within Islam itself. Some Minangkabau Islamic authorities have allowed matrilineage land to be classed as a corporate estate that remains outside the rules of inheritance (on analogy to a pious foundation, *waqaf*). Some Muslims regard the application of Islamic rules as optional rather than required, and thus allow local practices as long as no party contests the division in a court. Islamic courts, whose jurisdictions vary throughout the country, often encourage this tolerance of local practices, sometimes acting as unofficial arbiters.

Categories of Kinship, Gender, and Person. Indonesian kinship systems often contribute to the overall cultural shape of the society, that is, **the relation among its symbols and meanings**. Indonesian cases are useful for showing how ideas of person, gender, time, and emotions are made concrete and public through determinate social forms such as kin terms, names, and genealogies. C. Geertz's (1966) analysis of notions of person, time, and conduct in Bali shows how traditional calendars, which feature several interlocking cycles, orient the Balinese toward time as cyclical or punctuated. Balinese systems of kinship and naming suppress personal identity in favor of one's formal status present and future rather than toward the past. These features of time-reckoning and kinship forms also supported the overall "ceremonialization" of Balinese life: the attempt to keep social interactions at a formalized level.[17]

Urbanization and Government Policies. As more Indonesians have moved into the major cities, new forms of association have emerged that extend the circle of kin out to others of the same or similar origins. Thus, rotating social circles (*arisan*) have become important forms of association in Jakarta, binding together people either through kin reckoning or through a sense of shared culture.

III. ISSUES FOR DISCUSSION

1. What roles does kinship play in your life? How do relations of kinship and marriage function differently in Indonesia?

2. Why do people practice secondary burial? What are the possible psychological and social advantages of this practice? Is there anything comparable in the United States?

3. [a project rather than a question] How do parents in the United States divide wealth among their children? What do state laws dictate concerning the division of an estate? Compare Islamic law: what are the important differences?

NOTES

1. See Reid 1988: chapter 4.

2. See Atkinson and Errington, 1991.

3. All complete references are given at the end of the paper. I have chosen, when possible, references that are (as of late 1989) in print in paperback format.

4. H. Geertz (1961) analyzes the Javanese family, its functions and rituals, and the processes of socialization.

5. C. Geertz (1960:248-260) provides a clear overview of the Javanese system.

6. C. Geertz (1960: Part One) describes the *selamatan* in detail.

7. Jay (1969) is an excellent source for a lecture overview of how the patterns of social interaction are structured within a Javanese village. Both C. Geertz (1960) and Jay (1969) describe the overlay of religious and political divisions in Java.

8. See Rodgers (1986). Bowen (1988) shows the responses of the Gayo people in the northern part of Sumatra, and contrasts their response to that of the Minangkabau and the Karo Batak.

9. Fox, ed. (1980) contains descriptions of these marriage exchange systems for particular societies, and Fox (1980) provides an overview of these systems.

10. As is shown in the essays in Fox, ed. (1988). (See especially the introduction by Fox and the essay by Forth.)

11. Huntington and Metcalf (1979) discuss the effectiveness of Indonesian mortuary rituals as rites of transition. They discuss at length the case of The Berawan of Borneo.

12. Metcalf has summarized the argument in a brief article (Metcalf 1978).

13. Bowen, 1984.

14. Huntington and Metcalf (1979) also compare Indonesian with other societies, including contemporary American society.

15. Volkman, 1985.

16. See discussion in Bowen, 1988.

17. This article on Bali and H. Geertz's (1961) description of Javanese person-categories and emotions form a nice cross-cultural contrast for teaching purposes.

IV. SELECTED READINGS

Atkinson, Jane, and Errington, Shelly, eds. *Power and Difference: Gender in Island Southeast Asia*. Stanford: Stanford University Press, 1991 (faculty background).

Bowen, John. "Death and the History of Islam in Highland Aceh." *Indonesia* 38 (1984):21–38 (faculty background).

Bowen, John. "The Transformation of an Indonesian Property System: Adat, Islam, and Social Change in the Gayo Highlands." *American Ethnologist* 15 (1988):274–93 (faculty background).

Fox, James, J. Introduction to *The Flow of Life*, edited by James J. Fox, pp. 1–20. Cambridge: Harvard University Press, 1980 (faculty background).

Fox, James, J., ed. *To Speak in Pairs*. Cambridge: Cambridge University Press, 1988 (faculty background).

Geertz, Clifford. *The Religion of Java*. New York: Free Press, 1960. [Paperback, Chicago: University of Chicago Press, 1970 (faculty background/student reading).]

Geertz, Clifford. "Person, Time, and Conduct in Bali." Reprinted in *The Interpretation of Cultures*, pp. 360–411. New York: Basic Books, 1973 (faculty background/student reading).

Geertz, Hildred. *The Javanese Family*. 1961. Reprint. Prospect Heights, IL: Waveland Press, 1989 (faculty background/student reading).

Huntington, Richard, and Metcalf, Peter. *Celebrations of Death*. Cambridge: Cambridge University Press, 1979 (faculty background/student reading).

Jay, Robert. *Javanese Villagers*. Cambridge, MA: M.I.T. Press, 1969 (faculty background).

Kato, Tsuyoshi. *Matriliny and Migration*. Ithaca: Cornell University Press, 1982 (faculty background).

Metcalf, Peter. "Death Be Not Strange." *Natural History* 87 (6, 1978):6–12 (student reading).

Peletz, Michael. *A Share of the Harvest*. Berkeley: University of California Press, 1988 (faculty background).

Reid, Anthony. *Southeast Asia in the Land of Commerce*. Vol. 1. New Haven: Yale University Press, 1988 [Forthcoming in paperback] (faculty background/student reading).

Rodgers, Susan. "Batak Tape Cassette Kinship: Constructing Kinship Through the Indonesian National Mass Media." *American Ethnologist* 13 (1986):23–42 (faculty background/student reading).

Volkman, Toby. *Feasts of Honor*. Urbana: University of Illinois Press, 1985 (faculty background/student reading).

FILMS

A series of films produced by the Canadian government and available through the Canadian embassy in Washington, D.C., depict family life in contemporary Indonesia, particularly in urban areas. Of particular interest is the film entitled "Marvel," which shows family life in Jakarta through the eyes of a small boy from the Minangkabau region.

Anthropology: Indonesia

Islam in Indonesia: A Case Study of Religion in Society

John R. Bowen

I. INTRODUCTION: CENTRAL POINTS

Case materials on Islam in Indonesia are ideally suited for exploring the relation of a world religion to a variety of social and cultural contexts. They also provide a useful counterpoint to Middle Eastern cultures, which most students associate with Islam.

• Indonesia has the largest Muslim population of any nation. About 85 percent of Indonesia's 190,000,000 people are Muslims.[1] Indeed, Indonesia, Pakistan, India, and Bangladesh are the four largest Muslim societies and account for over one-half of the world's Muslim population. Islam in Indonesia is of particular interest in view of the fact that **most Muslims live in South and Southeast Asia,** and that Arab peoples make up only a small minority (perhaps 15 percent) of the world's Muslims.

• The diversity among Indonesia's Muslims (who live in as many as three hundred distinct cultures) shows how **Muslims**

have adapted Islamic ideas and traditions to a wide variety of cultural settings.

• Muslims in many societies hold a great variety of opinions on key religious, social, and political issues. It is important to point out this diversity in light of the uninformed notions of "Islamic politics" and "Muslim fundamentalism" that are conveyed in the U.S. media. Indonesia provides excellent materials for the study of **the internal diversity of this religious tradition**.

• Muslims in Indonesia live in a **multiconfessional nation-state**, in which Christians and Muslims work together in trade, education, government, and other domains. There has been little communal conflict; the Indonesian case suggests ways in which religious communities can live in relative harmony in a complex, modern nation-state.

II. MAJOR TOPICS

THE ISLAMIC CONTEXT

The word *islam* means submission to God. The prophet Muhammad saw his mission as bringing all people back to the religion of Abraham. Thus it gives special status to the "people of the book," a category that includes Christians and Jews. Muhammad is, for Muslims, the last in a succession of prophets.[2]

Muhammad began to receive revelations about 610 A.D. in Mecca, in what is now Saudi Arabia, fled to Medina in 622 (the event that marks the beginning of the Islamic calendar), and died after making the first pilgrimage (*hajj*) to Mecca in 632. Disputes over succession to the position of Muhammad's deputy, or caliph, led to the division between the Shi'i and the Sunni sects of Muslims, a division that continues to be deeply felt today. Muslim armies spread out over other Arabic-speaking lands during the following century. The late sixteenth century saw the formation of two major Muslim empires in South and Southeast Asia: the Mughal dynasty, which ruled most of South Asia until the accession of the British Raj in the nineteenth century, and the Mataram kingdom in Java, which lost control to the Dutch in the eighteenth century.

Today there are about 880 million Muslims in the world, about one-sixth of the world's population. Just over one-half of them live in South and Southeast Asia, with Indonesian Muslims by far the most populous. Between 80 and 85 percent of all Muslims live outside the Arab world, thus the importance of studying Muslim ways of life in non-Arab, as well as in the more frequently studied Middle Eastern settings. The following list of the ten most populous Muslim societies, with the number of Muslims listed for each, may be useful (figures, in millions, are calculated from the 1990 *World Almanac*):

1. Indonesia, 160
2. Pakistan, 110
3. Bangladesh, 94
4. India, 92
5. Nigeria, 57
6. Turkey, 55
7. Egypt, 52
8. Iran, 50
9. USSR 32 (conservatively estimated)
10. Morocco, 25 / Algeria, 25

A HISTORICAL OVERVIEW OF ISLAM IN INDONESIA

Early History. The earliest Muslim kingdoms grew up in Indonesia against a background of Hindu-Buddhist kingdoms, particularly the large kingdom of Majapahit on Java. They were small trading principalities established on the coasts of Sumatra, Java, and Sulawesi (Celebes) between the fourteenth and sixteenth centuries. By the early seventeenth century several important kingdoms had acquired control of large territories and of segments of the international trade in foodstuffs, spices, and cloth. Most important were Aceh on the strategic Straits of Malacca; Mataram, based in Central Java with port outlets on the northern coast; and Gowa in south Sulawesi.

Islamic ideas of power, probably derived from the northern Indian sultanates, were important to the new Muslim states. Rulers represented themselves as Muhammad's deputies (caliphs) and as the "shadows of God on earth." In Java, earlier Hindu-Javanese ideas of the ruler as possessing special powers were joined to new Islamic ideas. For a ruler to convert to Islam was to gain a new source of moral authority and to enter more easily into links with other Muslim states and with Indian Muslim traders.[3]

Modern Reformist Movements. One must distinguish among different kinds of reform movements within Islam. The label "fundamentalism" is particularly unfortunate in describing these movements, for at least three reasons. First, most Muslims would think of themselves as relying on scriptures for guidance, and thus could be seen as "fundamentalists"; but then the term loses any descriptive power. Second, the term implies an absence of debate or critical thought. But Muslim reformists have been engaged in the critical reevaluation of their traditions for centuries, and have produced highly scholarly, complex discussions of scripture and its role in social life. Third, different reform movements have emphasized very different goals: some, political change; others, the purifying of social and ritual life; still others, the modernizing of Muslim society.

Movements for ritual or social reform probably have been part of Indonesian Muslim life and Muslim reformist movements since the coming of Islam. Generally these movements have called for Muslims to rid their societies of non-Islamic elements and to bring religious practice in line with the dictates of scripture. One of the best-known drives to purify society was the Padri movement in West Sumatra in the early nineteenth century. This movement was directly inspired by the Arabian Wahhabi movement, and sought to replace the local matrilineal social system with Islamic law.

But twentieth century Indonesian reformists also have been influenced in one way or another by Islamic modernism. The modernists, or "young group" as they were called in Indonesia, were inspired by the writings of the Middle Eastern scholars Jamal al-Din al-Afghani (1839–1897) and Muhammad 'Abduh (1849–1905). Reacting to what they saw as a stagnation in Muslim societies brought about by undue reliance on accumulated authority, al-Afghani and 'Abduh called for a return to Muslim scriptures as the sound foundation for Muslim life. They called on Muslims to throw off the non-Islamic accretions that had corrupted their societies and to apply their own powers of reason to the interpretation of scripture rather than rely on the accumulated weight of tradition. They and their Indonesian followers argued that the resulting purification and renewal of Islam would enable Muslims to participate fully in the modern world.

Inherent in the anti-traditionalism of Indonesian modernism is a tension between two divergent schools of thought. One holds that Muslims should build a new society on Islamic principles, and thus seeks to enforce Muslim law and norms whenever possible. This school contributed to the rebellion by Muslims in different regions against the central, pluralistic government in the 1950s and early 1960s. The second school within modernism seeks to delimit the sphere of religious determination, and urges Muslims to study secular subjects openly, without constraints of

Muslim tradition. Thus many modernists quote the statement of the prophet Muhammad to the effect that "you know your own affairs better than I do," but add that one also must follow Muhammad's example in religious matters.

In seeking to refashion Indonesian social institutions, modernist leaders of both types in the 1920s and 1930s built new schools in which modern languages and sciences were taught alongside religious matters. The Muhammadiyah modernist organization, for example, has emphasized education and supports such social welfare institutions as orphanages and hospitals.[4]

Islam in Political Life. Muslims and Muslim organizations played a major role in the anticolonial movements of the early twentieth century, and many Muslim leaders urged that Indonesia become an Islamic state. But when independence was declared in August 1945, Sukarno (the first president) and other influential leaders (nearly all of them Muslim) decided instead on a pluralistic state based on a general belief in one God. They were wary of alienating the new nation's important Christian minorities, who also had played important roles in Indonesia's struggle for independence. Muslim parties have played a major role in Indonesian political life since that time.

In the legal system of Indonesia today, Muslim courts exist alongside civil courts and traditional forms of dispute resolution. In some provinces the Muslim courts implement family law (marriage, divorce, inheritance) for all Muslims; in others, their jurisprudential scope is narrower. Because of the direct effects on property rights, the implementation of Muslim inheritance law has been a particularly salient issue. Many of the three hundred or more Indonesian cultures in which Muslims live have their own norms for distributing property. Often these norms leave land in the hands of a corporate group, sometimes a lineage. [*See the essay on "Family and Kinship in Indonesia."*] Two trends have increased the pressure to change these norms. Modernists have emphasized the rights of sons and daughters to fixed shares of an estate. The rise in cash-cropping has intensified the demands for this partition and distribution. In general one could say that Islamic inheritance law has been applied in a greater percentage of cases in recent years than has civil law.[5]

PRACTICAL RELIGION

Indonesians show a great deal of diversity in the ways they practice Islam in their daily lives. Yet several complexes of ritual and other social activity provide a recognizable unity to Muslim life throughout the archipelago (as well as points of similarity to much of South Asia). These complexes also are foci of debate between Muslims who adhere to long-standing practices and those reformists who seek to transform Muslim practice. The most interesting and important dynamics of Indonesian Muslim life lie in these debates.

The Five Pillars. Most Muslims agree on the central place occupied by the "five pillars of Islam" in religious life; they are acts required of all Muslims.

a) **The Confession of Faith.** "I attest that there is no other deity but God, and I attest that Muhammad is his Messenger (or: Apostle)."

Pronouncement of the confession is the first pillar. It is repeated frequently in worship, as the first part of a marriage ritual, and in the call to worship, which is cried out before each of the five worship times during the day.

b) **Worship (Salat).** Normally performed five times daily and involves prostrations in the direction of Mecca. These worship rituals are an important way of defining time for Indonesian Muslims. The congregational worship at midday on Friday is a socially important way of bringing together people, men and women, in a community or an urban neighborhood, and often is the occasion for announcements and for additional prayer recitations. For many Indonesians, the congregational worship service has become a model of how society ought to be constructed.

c) **Fasting During the Month of Ramadan.** Observance of the fast varies widely: in Aceh most restaurants are closed; in Java many people observe only several days out of the month.

d) **The Giving of Obligatory Alms in the Forms of an Annual Tithe on Wealth and a Head Tax.** These sums are collected locally, usually within a village, and then redistributed for assistance to the poor, for the upkeep of the mosque, and for support of several other categories of people. But in Indonesia and Malaysia, government arrogation of collection rights has led to discontent and varying degrees of non-payment.

e) **The Pilgrimage (Hajj) to Mecca for Those Capable of Undertaking It.** The pilgrimage provides a very important communications link between Indonesia and the Middle East; the rapid growth of the pilgrimage in the mid-nineteenth century led to a rapid influx of new, reformist ideas and to subsequent political and ritual changes throughout Indonesia. In Most larger Muslim villages in Sumatra, Java, and Sulawesi there will be one or more persons who have been on the pilgrimage. The title of returnee, *hajj*, can carry substantial prestige.[6]

Scripture. The basic scriptures of the Islamic religion are the Qur'an (Koran), verses revealed to the prophet Muhammad by the archangel Jibra'il [Gabriel], and the *hadith*, reports of Muhammad's statements or deeds. Also important guides for Muslims are the opinions of Muslim scholars as recorded in books of law and theology.

For Muslims, the Qur'an is God's major gift to humans. Its significance for Muslims thus has been compared to that of Jesus for Catholics, as the most direct link between humans and God. The very sound of the words and shape of the letters contained in the Qur'an are of great religious importance to Muslims. (In this the Qur'an more closely resembles the Hebrew Bible than it does the Christian Gospels.) Indeed, many Muslims argue that there cannot be a "translation" of the Qur'an, with the implications of cross-linguistic transparency that the term implies, only "interpretation" from the original Arabic into another language.

Thus Indonesian Muslims, as well as those living elsewhere, attach great importance to the recitation of the Qur'an. Boys and girls begin to memorize sections of the Qur'an, in the original Arabic, at a young age; some will have recited all its verses by the time they reach adolescence. The biennial national Qur'an Recitation Contest includes competitions at the village, subdistrict, district, and provincial levels, and attracts large audiences. But recitations of Qur'anic verses also are offered to God on behalf of the deceased (see below), and verses, written on scraps of paper, serve as talismans to ward off attack or protect one during a journey. Although many Indonesian Muslims draw on the meaning of Qur'anic verses in deciding social issues, for many the primary significance of these verses lies in the immediate power conveyed by the sound or shape of their letters.

The hadith, reports of what the prophet Muhammad did and said, constitute a second basic guide for the Muslim. Many of these reports were written down only many generations after Muhammad's death, and thus arguments over religious issues often turn on disputes about the reliability of individual transmitters. (In some respects the hadith are analogous to the four synoptic Gospels in Christianity.) More generally, the way of life followed by Muhammad, called his sunna, serves as a guide for many Muslims. Even minor elements in his life, such as the colors he wore (white and green) and the kind of dates he would have eaten, have taken on religious significance for many.

Religious scholars, called ulama among others, apply scripture to current issues. Because there is no formal hierarchy or set of leadership offices among Indonesian Muslims, anyone may, on the basis of learning or other accomplishments, urge that his/her interpretations be followed. Scholars also act as sermon-givers for the Friday congregational worship service. The Indonesian government often attempts to persuade (or coerce) important scholars to promote official policy but has no direct control over their statements of opinion. Thus in the late 1970s considerable debate took place among sermon-givers concerning the advisability of the national family planning program. Both sides quoted a hadith in which Muhammad exhorted Muslims to "have many pious children." Some scholars emphasized the **many** and opposed all forms of birth control. Others, siding with the government, emphasized the word **pious**; they observed that parents have only so much energy, and urged couples to have only two children so as to ensure that they would grow up to be pious Muslims. (By and large, the program was accepted by Indonesian Muslims and has been rather successful.)

Also available are many Indonesian-language books, volume collections of hadith, manuals on marriage, divorce, and inheritance, and books of spiritual exercises. Many of the classical, Arabic-language books also are available to Indonesians in translation.

Ritual Meals. Throughout Southeast (and South) Asia, Muslim communities hold frequent ritual meals, called *slametan* on Java and *kenduri* in most of the rest of the Indonesian archipelago. These meals are held for a wide variety of purposes. They mark the major calendrical occasions, including Muslim holidays and stages in the agricultural cycle. They celebrate and sanctify occasions in the life cycle, including birth, a seventh-day naming and initiation ceremony, circumcision, completion of stages in Qur'an study, marriage, and death.

Ritual meals generally include the serving of ritually meaningful foodstuffs, especially rice cakes, that stand for natural elements or human attributes, the burning of incense, the saying of prayers to God, and the pronouncement of statements of intent that define the intended effect of the meal. Qur'anic verses also may be recited. Feast-goers send the essence of the food (as locally defined) and the benefit of the verses to spirits of the deceased, spirits of the place, or to God. They expect in return assistance in healing the sick or ensuring a good crop.

Meals are held to celebrate Muslim holidays. Holidays are scheduled according to the Islamic lunar calendar, which recedes eleven days in each solar year. Three holidays are celebrated throughout the archipelago. Muhammad's birth is celebrated in the third lunar month of the year with feasts at which scholars recount stories about the prophet's life. The day after the end of the month of fasting (the ninth month) is a major feast day, on which Muslims visit each other and ask forgiveness for their sins of the past year. Finally, in the twelfth month is celebrated the holiday of sacrifice. By sacrificing an animal in the name of God, Muslims commemorate the willingness of the prophet Ibrahim to sacrifice his own son. The sacrificed animal also is thought to serve as a vehicle for the long journey to the place of judgement after the resurrection of the soul.[7]

Chants for the Dead. Rituals held to commemorate the death of a community member are especially important to many Indonesian Muslims, but also have been sharply criticized by reformists. In many societies, men and women gather at the house of the bereaved on the first, third, seventh, and fortieth or forty-fourth evenings after a death. There they chant together in order to create merit for the deceased. The chants are entirely in Arabic and include repetitions of Qur'anic verses, of the phrase "there is no deity but God" (part of the confession of faith) and long prayers directed to God. The verse repetitions are chanted by all those present; the invocations are sung by a specialist, someone who has memorized a long series of phrases in which he praises God, praises the prophet Muhammad and his companions, and asks God to send his blessings on the deceased and on other Muslims throughout the world.

Modernists object to these practices. They deny that one can affect the fortunes of the deceased. They ask rhetorically: How can one person make up for the sins of another? In their objections they insist on a strict separation between the value of reciting sacred verses for oneself and the possibility of transferring merit through such recitations.[8]

Education. Indonesian Muslims place great weight on education for both boys and girls. Prior to this century religious education consisted mainly of memorizing portions of the Qur'an and reading elementary books of religious instruction. There were no graded classes; one studied under a teacher along with other students of different levels of accomplishment. Schools of new types have flourished in this century, and have become the center of Muslim social, political, and economic activity as well as religious instruction. Religious schools today vary in their curricula from a highly traditional focus on religious topics to a broad instruction in spoken languages (Arabic and English) and modern sciences.

Of particular importance on Java is a group of schools headed by an intermarrying network of religious scholars. This network has been the basis for the sociopolitical organization Nahdatul Ulama or NU. NU was a major political party in the 1950s and continues to be a major force in Indonesian politics; it is based on allegiance to this small group of highly prestigious scholars. It permits the holding of ritual meals and other elements in Javanese tradition. NU schools stress the reading of past and present Muslim scholarship, and hold consistently to one of four Muslim legal traditions, the Shafi'i.

A very different kind of school emphasis emerged in Sumatra in the 1920s and 1930s. Called the "schools movement," this modernist-inspired drive for school reform was decidedly anti-traditionist. Schools were organized into classes, and instructional materials were ordered from Cairo and Mecca, with the help of Arab scholars living in Indonesia and Indonesians studying (and in some cases teaching) in the Middle East. The Muhammadiyah modernist organization quickly became allied with the schools movement, which spread throughout Indonesia. The modernist schools emphasize facility in Arabic, and in their religious teachings draw on the opinions of several of the law schools.[9]

CASE STUDY: CULTURE AND RELIGION IN JAVA

One issue dividing students of Indonesian Islam is the degree to which some (the more traditional) religious forms are mixtures of Islamic and pre-Islamic ideas. This issue has arisen in particular with regard to Javanese religious life.

One position, developed by Clifford Geertz, is that Javanese society is (or was, in the early 1950s, when he conducted the study,) divided into three streams: the high culture of the Javanese nobles with its stress on mysticism and etiquette, the low culture of Javanese peasants with its many spirits and ritual meals, and the self-consciously Islamic culture of the merchants, students, and scholars, which saw itself as opposed to many features of the Javanese past. In this view, the basic elements of Javanese culture, including ritual meals, the art of shadow puppetry, and the ideas of power and rank suffusing the Javanese kingdoms evolved from indigenous and Hindu ideas, prior to the introduction of Islamic ideas. Islam was adopted as an additional religious layer rather late in Javanese history.

A second position holds that Javanese culture is suffused with Islamic ideas and in fact is the outcome of a process of religious adaptation. Advocates of this position argue that Islamic mystics, known as Sufis, propagated a form of Islam that was in keeping with Javanese interest in spirits and the power of unseen forces. They reinterpreted pre-Islamic ideas in Islamic terms. Thus, these scholars argue, the ritual meal in traditional Javanese culture was modified to conform to the custom as practiced throughout the Islamic world. Even the power of Javanese kings came to be viewed through an Islamic lens: the king was no longer an incarnation of a Hindu deity, but the "shadow of God on earth," an idea taken from Persian Muslim political thought.

What is clear is that Javanese religious life shows the adaptation of Islamic traditions to a particular set of Javanese emphases. Islam entered a Java where large kingdoms had already developed an elaborate court culture based on a mixture of animistic and Hindu ideas. Most Javanese Muslims acknowledge this cultural heritage, in which an emphasis on refinement and self-control is combined with Islamic ideas. For Javanese, authority involves the absorption of power within the self, the capacity to smoothly control others without being flustered or showing emotion. Refinement is epitomized by the lithe heros of shadow puppet theater, who effortlessly defeat giants; it is reflected in one's mastery of the elaborate system of speech levels in the Javanese language, and in the control of desires attained through meditation.

Sufism provided a Muslim framework that validated this idea of inward control. Meditation and abstinence refocus thought away from the outer world and toward one's inner self, and finally toward God. Some Sufi scholars taught that God was present in oneself. Whether or not one sees the present-day Javanese emphasis on self-control as pre-Islamic or as part of Sufism, it seems clear that a fit between indigenous and Sufi ideas was crucial to the propagation of Islam on Java.

Muslim rituals also have been shaped to fit indigenous concerns. On Java, the ritual meal, although present throughout the archipelago and indeed in other Muslim societies, takes on a Javanese character. The meal maintains social and emotional equilibrium, a persistent Javanese concern, by involving everyone in a neighborhood or village on an equal basis (despite their otherwise marked social inequalities). "When you give a ritual meal," said one Javanese quoted by Geertz, "nobody feels different from anyone else."

Funerals, though conducted according to Islamic rules, also reveal the Javanese concern for controlling emotion and reaching a state of detachment. The relatives of the deceased pass under his/her body several times when it is on the litter, give away money as a sign of their willingness to let the deceased go, and feature at the funeral meal a large, flattened-out rice cake that symbolizes the flat character of their emotions.[10]

ISLAM AND ECONOMICS

Because the early coastal Islamic states and societies were focused on trade, a number of writers have ventured a link between entrepreneurship and Islam, or at least the reformist varieties of Islam. The link passes by way of an emphasis on the individual and his/her rational application to a particular task. The affinities with Max Weber's Protestant ethic thesis are suggested.

Indeed, Islam as a set of duties and creeds does, like the ascetic Protestant faiths studied by Weber, highlight the responsibility of the individual for his/her actions. Modernist Muslim thought, in particular, emphasizes the role of work and the value of reason in disciplining the individual to overcome the dangerous seduction of the passions. This struggle is an individual one, and dictates that trade should be pursued in an individualistic way. Thus, in Javanese towns, indigenous commercial activity has focused on the short-term sale transacted by the individual trader, not the accumulation of capital or the growth of a firm. (Here is a significant difference from the Protestant case, where the accumulation of capital was a sign of one's own elect status.) Furthermore, a man who wishes his son to start in trade will not take him on as his apprentice, but will set him up with some capital and send him off to peddle as best he can. The person who mixes friendship or kinship with business has not yet really understood the religious value of commerce as a path to self-control.

These religious values may have initially spurred commercial activity, but have hindered the growth of firms, particularly given the competing presence of overseas Chinese entrepreneurs, who can draw on extensive kin networks to raise and move capital.[11]

The study of Islam in Indonesia thus shows how a world religious tradition is interpreted in diverse ways. Within Indonesia, Muslims hold diverse positions on the proper Islamic ways of conducting rituals or dividing an estate. But Indonesians also share certain cultural features that differentiate them from Muslims elsewhere in the world. All Muslims, whether they live in Indonesia, Morocco, or England, share a belief in God and His revelations, and perform the same central Islamic rituals. But they differ in their ways of life. Many Arab peoples, for example, place high value on the outward expression of grief and rage, and seek to protect honor at all costs. Relations between men and women are relatively segregated. These cultural values have become, for many Americans, characteristics of "Muslims." By contrast, most Indonesians emphasize self-control and emotional stability. Men and women in Indonesia, and in most of Southeast Asia, interact relatively freely. Any religious tradition contains the possibility of diverse views and cultural emphases; to realize this is to accord the same respect for others that we hold for ourselves.

III. ISSUES FOR DISCUSSION

1. In what ways do local versions of Islam vary? What is wrong with making general statements about "Islamic social life?" or "Islamic ritual?"

2. How do we distinguish between features of a religion and features of a culture? How would you isolate the features of Judaism or Christianity?

3. What does it mean to say that the Qur'an is to Islam as Jesus is to Christianity? Do you accept the parallel?

NOTES

1. Muslim is an adjectival form of Islam. I suggest using Muslim when discussing the variety of ideas and practices held by the world's Muslims and reserving Islamic for aspects of the core doctrines of the religion.

2. Denny (1985) provides a clear introduction to Islam. Consult his index and glossary as a guide for overview sections of lectures.

3. See the short articles by Milner and Ricklefs in Ibrahim (1985).

4. See the articles by Kartodirdjo, Noer, and Roff in Ibrahim (1985).

5. The articles by Boland and Samson in Ibrahim (1985) provide an overview of Islam and politics; Bowen (1988) is a case study in legal and economic change.

6. Denny (1985) provides an overall review of the pillars. Bowen (1989) explores the public importance of worship in three Indonesian cases. Scott (1987) draws an interesting comparison between resistance to alms collection in Malaysia and resistance to the tithe in France.

7. Woodward (1988) emphasizes the Islamic roots of the Javanese meal and contrasts in this regard with the analysis in Geertz (1960, Part I).

8. Bowen (1984) is an analysis of controversy over funeral ritual in a Sumatran community.

9. In Ibrahim (1985) see the articles by Rahardjo, Noer, and Abdullah.

10. The sources for this discussion are Geertz (1960) and, arguing for the second position, Woodward (1988).

11. Geertz (1963) examines the problem this presents for Java. These economic issues return us to the general problem of "modernity," on which see the articles by Swift and Hassan in Ibrahim (1985).

IV. SELECTED READINGS

Bibliographic Note: The reader edited by Ibrahim et al. is a very useful source for short articles, suitable for classroom use. The articles are also very useful for lecture preparation. The articles by Bowen, Scott, and Woodward provide succinct case studies of the points mentioned above. Clifford Geertz' *Religion of Java* is an excellent book for students; full of detail but clearly written. His *Peddlers and Princes* is a bit dryer, but a good source for lecture preparation.

Bowen, John R. "Death and the History of Islam in Highland Aceh." *Indonesia* 38 (October, 1984): 21–38.

Bowen, John R. "The Transformation of an Indonesian Property System: Adat, Islam, and Social Change in the Gayo Highlands." *American Ethnologist* 15 (1988):274–93.

Bowen, John R. "Salat in Indonesia: The Social Meanings of An Islamic Ritual." *Man* (N.S.) 24 (1989):299–318.

Denny, Frederick Mathewson. *An Introduction to Islam.* New York: Macmillan, 1985.

Geertz, Clifford. *The Religion of Java.* Chicago: University of Chicago Press, 1960.

Geertz, Clifford. *Peddlers and Princes.* Chicago: University of Chicago Press, 1963.

Ibrahim, Ahmad; Siddique Sharon; and Hussain Yasmin, eds. *Readings on Islam in Southeast Asia.* Singapore: Institute of Southeast Asian Studies, 1985.

Scott, James C. "Resistance without Protest and without Organization: Peasant Opposition to the Islamic *Zakat* and the Christian Tithe." *Comparative Studies in Society and History 29 (1987): 417–452.*

Woodward, Mark R. "The *Slametan*: Textual Knowledge and Ritual Performance Central Javanese Islam." *History of Religions* 28 (1988):54–89.

Anthropology:
Indonesia

Hierarchy and Stratification: The Case of Java

Robert W. Hefner

I. INTRODUCTION: CENTRAL POINTS

The people of Java, an island of the Southeast Asian nation of Indonesia, are renowned for their concern for status in interaction, which is expressed in a richly elaborate system of linguistic and social etiquette. In all exchanges, the relative status of the speakers is explicitly indicated through linguistic and behavioral markers. Over the last two centuries the form and meaning of this status system have changed dramatically, as the role of Java's aristocracy diminished and a more complex, but less rigid system of stratification took shape. The system of etiquette that originally underscored the clear barrier between aristocrats and commoners has been "popularized," and is today used by commoners to establish relative status among themselves. Of relevance to anthropologists, linguists, and sociologists, the Javanese example illustrates that status can be conceptualized in ways quite different from the common understanding of status in the West, and demonstrates the complex relationship between status in interaction and status ranking in society as a whole. In particular, the example raises three points:

- the role of status in behavior and language;
- the influence of politics on identity and stratification;

* the changing nature of social hierarchy in the context of a developing nation-state.

II. MAJOR TOPICS

The Javanese are an ethnic population of some seventy million people living in eastern and central Java and (as a result of recent migrations) southeastern Sumatra. Comprising almost one-half of its total population, the Javanese are the largest of Indonesia's more than three hundred ethnic populations. Their influence on modern Indonesian national culture is great.

EARLY HISTORY

The roots of Javanese civilization reach back sixteen hundred years to a time when India's Hindu-Buddhist religious tradition was introduced to the island, as it was to early centers of state power elsewhere in Southeast Asia. Recast in a distinctively Southeast Asian form, Hindu-Buddhist ideas influenced everything from state organization and ceremony to language and the arts. In the sixteenth century, however, Java's last major Hindu--Buddhist (i.e.,non-Islamic) kingdom fell to an alliance of Muslim-Javanese principalities. This fall set in motion a process of Islamization that ultimately resulted in the conversion of most Javanese to Islam, which had first diffused from India to Sumatra in the thirteenth century and to Java in the fourteenth and fifteenth. Despite this change, Java's courts preserved much of the cultural pomp and ceremony of the earlier period. Indeed, they appear to have developed extant traditions of hierarchy and stratification to an even higher degree of cultural elaboration.

TRADITIONAL SOCIAL STRATIFICATION: ARISTOCRATS, TRADERS, AND PEASANTS

The social order that took shape during the "classical" period of modern Javanese history (from the 17th to the 19th centuries) was organized around a simple, tripartite division of society into aristocrats (*priyayi*), traders, and peasants. The aristocrats were the members of both preeminent and lesser principalities, or courts. Javanese kingdoms from Hindu-Buddhist times up through the coming of colonialism were much more federationist alliances of assorted principalities than they were centralized bureaucracies of the Chinese or Japanese kind. The alliance was apical, however, and there was a preeminent court—or courts, one, two, or three, depending on the period and on how one counts. From the late sixteenth to mid-eighteenth century, there was essentially one preeminent court, or sultanate, and a host of lesser courts. In the middle of the eighteenth century, this dominant court split in two and then one of the two split in two creating three "preeminent" rulers vying for power; in general during this period, however, only two of these rulers had real power and we usually refer to premodern Java as having two preeminent courts. Within this general framework, it must be realized that the lesser courts often achieved a good measure of autonomy relative to the preeminent courts.

Although historically there was some mobility from the lower strata into aristocratic ranks, most aristocrats were of noble birth, and were acutely aware of their superiority in rank to the mass of commoners (traders and peasants alike) whom they referred to as "little people" (*wong cilik*). From the perspective of the aristocrats, political power and social rank were but visible expressions of spiritual preeminence; thus it was only natural that the gentry stood at the pinnacle of both the social and spiritual hierarchy. Unlike their counterparts in feudal Europe, however, the aristocrats were not a landholding class. Their privileges and wealth depended instead on their control of peasant followers. In principle only Java's kings had title to land. Rather than giving the gentry right over land, the royal courts rewarded them by giving them rights over specific numbers of peasant households, many of which were located in dispersed territories. The territorial dispersion of these designated peasant followers made it extremely difficult for the aristocrats to mount serious challenges to royal authority. Rights over manpower were also subject to renegotiation as relations between the central courts and lesser aristocrats changed.

Strict limits were also placed on traders and trading wealth. Linked more strongly to the inter-island trade throughout the Indies than to the internal courts (referring to the two preeminent courts of the premodern period) Java's merchants identified less closely with the status-conscious ways of the courts than did the gentry. In the sixteenth century, as today, the loyalty of the merchant class was more likely to be directed toward orthodox Islam (as opposed to the syncretistic Islam professed by the gentry). At times, too, they were vocal opponents of aristocratic privilege. In part to limit the power of the Muslim merchant class, the courts licensed large-scale trade, often according monopoly rights to Chinese and other ethnic minorities less likely to mount challenges to court authority. In the face of several serious rebellions, the courts also appealed to Dutch forces for help. Having established a small trading port in West Java in 1619, the Dutch took advantage of these political crises to wrest control over ever-larger areas of Java, a process that culminated in 1830 with the establishment of colonial rule over the entire island. Throughout most of the subsequent period, which lasted until 1949, the Dutch authorities used the Javanese aristocracy to give an air of legitimacy to their rule. The aristocracy thus continued to exercise some influence on the rural population, but its role was increasingly subject to political challenge by Muslims and "Javanist" religious leaders, as discussed below.

While aristocrats generally regarded Java's peasantry as an undifferentiated, common mass, there was in fact significant stratification within the peasant community. In the largest portion of the island where the two preeminent courts had (until the nineteenth century) exercised direct power, village officials invariably took advantage of their ties to central government to strengthen their economic position. Since offices in village government were usually transmitted from father to son, this linkage of village to state created a peasant elite, defined more by access to political office than simply wealth or economic class. The imposition of Dutch colonialism at first disrupted this peasant hierarchy by reorganizing agriculture for the production of export crops. But the continuing influence of the colonial state in the rural economy ensured that functionaries' ties to government remained as important a determinant of status and wealth as economic class. This remains the case in modern Java.

THE CULTURE AND LANGUAGE OF HIERARCHY

It was in this context of a village-based gentry dominating the peasant and trading segments of society that Java's modern culture of hierarchy took shape. With a keen sense of its own spiritual and social preeminence, the court aristocracy developed one of Asia's most elaborate systems of ritual and social refinement. Unlike the modern West's conceptualization of power in materialist, "blood-and-muscle" terms (but not unlike concepts of power among the European aristocracy during and after the Renaissance), the animating assumption of the Javanese hierarchy was that authority was above all the product of and demonstrated in spiritual refinement. Spiritual excellence was expressed in both an inner (*batin*) life of orderly control, achieved through mystical practice, and an external (*lahir*) life of smoothly polished etiquette.

This etiquette system required that every actor have a keen awareness of his or her place in the social hierarchy. With this peculiar vision of its role, the Javanese aristocracy supported a ritual and aesthetic tradition that, in its members' eyes, clearly distinguished them from the mass of ordinary commoners, whom they considered barely superior to animals.

Nowhere was this emphasis on self-control, social harmony, and spiritual superiority more vividly expressed than in the development of Javanese "language levels." Building on a system of honorific language that may have developed in Java during the period of Indian influence more than a thousand years earlier, these language variants probably took on their modern form at the central Javanese courts between the seventeenth and nineteenth centuries. In the nineteenth and twentieth centuries, they diffused from the aristocracy to broader segments of Javanese society. Among some subcommunities— orthodox Muslim traders, for example— or areas of eastern Java where the influence of the central courts was never strong, language levels are not as important an aspect of social interaction as they are in inland central Java, the island's cultural heartland, where they are a defining feature of speech, transforming every verbal interaction into a complex commentary on the relative status of the actors.

The language levels actually involve a range of speech features, including vocabulary, morphology, intonation, and speed and rhythm of delivery. The appropriate level is determined by an evaluation of the relative status and intimacy of those communicating. In every linguistic exchange, speakers must choose from among several distinct linguistic varieties which signal and assert their notions of their relative standing. This selection of an appropriately intimate or distant form, similar to the familiar-formal distinction expressed in many European languages (*tu-vous* in French), is an intrinsic element of Javanese speech, of which actors are always and sometimes agonizingly aware. The distinctions in Javanese, however, are considerably more complex than the binary *tu-vous* distinction in European languages; they involve a richer variety of vocabulary and morphology, and often require a speaker to select from three, four, or even five variants of the same word. The consequences of this linguistic system for speakers are quite clear: in every exchange speakers must comment in explicit detail on their relative status. In speaking Javanese, one cannot but acknowledge one's position in the social hierarchy.

There are three basic speech levels: low Javanese or *Ngoko*; high Javanese or *Kromo*; and a middle level called *Madyo*. Ngoko is the language children learn first, and it is the level adults use in more intimate contexts or with social subordinates. With the largest number of lexical items, it is the core around which the other levels are built. Kromo, or high Javanese, is the language used in speaking with people of higher status, or with people with whom one is not intimate. In addition to its distinctive features of morphology and intonation, Kromo is characterized by a more formal etiquette and indirection in expression. The relative status of speakers is also marked in choice of vocabulary: there are approximately one thousand Ngoko words for which there are also Kromo variants. Sometimes there is more than one Kromo term, each of which indicates a slightly different measure of status gradation. There are only a small number of specifically Madyo items; basically, this middle level comprises a continuum of respect between Ngoko and Kromo, in which high and low forms are mixed, depending on the status of the person the speaker is addressing or talking about. Madyo is thus a kind of compromise language level, used with superiors for whom Kromo would be too high, or with intimates with whom Ngoko would be disrespectful. Familiarity alone does not relieve speakers of the obligation to signal their relative status in the most precise way.

LINGUISTIC HIERARCHY AND SOCIAL DIFFERENTIATION

The system of language levels is complex, but the preoccupation with relative status is its most basic feature. Before the nineteenth century, when the boundary between aristocracy and peasantry was more rigid, full mastery of the levels was achieved only by aristocrats and members of the subordinate population who had occasion to interact regularly with them. Java's popular arts— especially *wayang* shadow puppetry and *wayang wong* theater— also served to disseminate an elementary understanding of the system among a broader population. In areas of the island where these art forms were uncommon (such as far eastern Java), however, even modest familiarity with the complexity of the levels was rare.

In the course of the nineteenth and twentieth centuries, use of the levels spread into larger areas of the countryside. Migration from the densely populated terrains of inland Central Java played an important role in this process, as did Javanese newspapers, literature, and mass education especially after the first decade of the twentieth century, when they became more widely available.

With the consolidation of the colonial state in the nineteenth century, Java experienced spectacular population growth which resulted in mass migration to the far corners of the island. Government penetration into the once-remote areas linked the local social hierarchy all the more firmly to the machinery of state, creating what was, in effect, the first effective island-wide administration since the sixteenth century. This development also helped to standardize the cultural expressions of status hierarchy, of which the status-sensitive language levels were a key component.

While unifying the island politically and administratively, the colonial regime also engendered deep antagonisms among the native population by drawing Javanese aristocrats into the system of forced labor and land expropriation established for the government's massive programs of commercial cultivation. In using the native aristocracy in this way, the colonial government ultimately alienated much of the peasantry from their traditional rulers, resulting in a crisis of political legitimacy. The resulting vacuum of leadership was eventually filled by rural religious leaders— orthodox and unorthodox Muslims alike—who led, unsuccessfully, agrarian protests against the colonial administration. (In the twentieth century these rural movements would give way to more sophisticated Muslim and nationalist— "Javanist"— organizations.) Rising rural tensions exacerbated the estrangement of the peasantry from the aristocracy, driving a wedge between the two social groupings that would widen in the twentieth century. The diffusion of the language levels (and related aspects of social hierarchy) into rural society was thus not a matter of a homogeneous peasantry imitating the styles of an esteemed aristocracy. These and other cultural changes were instead promoted by peasant elites who benefited from the changes brought about by colonialism, and adopted the language levels to mark their own power and refinement. Status markers once reserved for *priyayi* elites were now being appropriated by influential peasants with aspirations to high status.

Resentment of Europeans, colonialism, and the Javanese gentry prompted many people to search for political means with which to challenge colonialism and the hierarchical system it now supported. Many Javanese looked to Islam as the best solution to the crisis of Javanese identity. Muslim leaders had long held themselves aloof from Java's courtly traditions and, in the nineteenth century, the expansion of Islamic boarding schools (*pesantren*) throughout the countryside provided the peasantry with greater exposure to Muslim religiosity. Many in rural Java continued to reject Muslim orthodoxy, however, and in the middle decades of the twentieth century these Javanese turned to the nationalist and communist parties to provide a non-Islamic vehicle for their political aspirations. Though use of the language levels spread throughout Java during this period, the cultural and stratification system of which they had once been part had decisively changed.

SOCIAL HIERARCHY IN CONTEMPORARY JAVA

Since Indonesia gained its independence (in 1949) the organization and meaning of Javanese social hierarchy have continued to evolve. The courts and their aristocrats have been almost totally eclipsed by a new class of bureaucrats. Traditional Javanese notions of status, such as those associated with indirection in speech and status-sensitivity in interaction, do influence this new elite's behavior. With its emphasis on bureaucratic structures, economic development, and modern consumer goods, however, the new elite is promoting new social values and engendering new patterns of social hierarchy. Continuity between the traditional and contemporary social hierarchy is thus highly selective, drawing on some traditional notions of hierarchy, but doing so in an organizational context having greater similarities with other developing Asian states than with premodern sultanates.

Popular society is changing as well. From 1949 to 1965 rural Java was beset with political conflict and severe economic decline, thus undercutting developments that might have heightened rural inequality. In the period since 1966, however, a more Western- and capitalist-oriented government has succeeded in placing severe limits on all forms of political activity and in launching a number of programs for economic development. While many urban and rural people have enjoyed increased prosperity, for the moment the gap between rich and poor appears to have widened. Meanwhile, such modern consumer goods as radios, televisions, and motorbikes have diffused into the countryside, bringing with them new notions of wealth and status and unleashing aspirations for new ways of life. Though it would be premature to talk of the demise of Javanese traditions, there can be little question that traditional Javanese notions of status and consumption are now giving way to more market-oriented and "Indonesian" lifestyles.

Use of the Javanese language levels remains widespread, and indeed if anything has spread with mass education. Their meaning and the contexts in which they are used, however, have changed significantly since the early nineteenth century. The process of popularization begun at the end of that century has been completed. Though effective mastery of the speech levels still varies with social class and region, today this has less to do with aristocrat vs. commoner distinctions than it does with status differences within popular society as a whole. As segments of the rural population have acquired new wealth and, to a limited degree, expanded education, they have also sought to take on linguistic airs once restricted to the aristocrats.

Today, as in the late nineteenth century, there are contrary developments working to undercut the spread of hierarchical social styles. Schools, radio, and television have disseminated the national language, Indonesian, to most of the Javanese population. Promoted at independence to provide a common language for Indonesia's three hundred language groups, Indonesian is a more democratic language than Javanese in that it lacks the latter's language levels, allowing speakers to address each other without the ever-present attention to relative status characteristic of Javanese. In urban areas where Javanese regularly interact with non-Javanese, the population now relies heavily on Indonesian. In rural areas, use of Indonesian is less widespread but even here Indonesian provides an occasional respite from the status concerns of Javanese speech. Popular society is changing in other ways as well. The political and economic changes that have swept the countryside have in many areas severely eroded the strength of village-based "Javanese" traditions. Education, advertising, and the media have convinced many rural youths of the backwardness of traditional ways and have turned their eyes toward new consumer goods and lifestyles. The demise of village-based traditions has also abetted the advance of orthodox Islam into areas of the countryside which had been only nominally Islamic. Though varying widely, Islam's progress is in fact a continuation of a process of social reorientation that began with the crisis of authority in the nineteenth century that resulted from the collaboration of the gentry with the Dutch. Not so much a democratizing force as a new form of social hierarchy, Islam will likely play an important and perhaps increasing role in Java's future.

THE FORM AND MEANING OF SOCIAL HIERARCHY

In all societies, social hierarchy involves more than the simple ranking of social groups. Status and stratification have an inherent cultural dimension as well. Not merely a frill added on to the reality of social rank, the culture of hierarchy— the myriad ways in which relative social positions are understood and expressed— is a crucial aspect of personal identity and a society's organization. Here in Java language and etiquette have long played a key role in the expression of hierarchy but their form and social organization have changed in a way which reflects transformations in Javanese society as a whole. A system of linguistic and social elaboration that originally served to distinguish aristocrats from commoners slowly changed and became an index of high social standing among all Javanese. The generalization of this cultural style was in part related to the demise of the aristocracy, brought about by their integration into the colonial state. These same developments, however, also set in motion broader changes that have challenged rural traditions and unleashed aspirations for new ways of life. Pressures for change have only increased in recent years. While modern development has thus helped to disseminate the etiquette and language of Javanese hierarchy, it has also set other developments in motion, developments that promise to change the form and meanings of stratification in this Southeast Asian society. A system of linguistic and social elaboration that originally served to mark aristocratic preeminence, slowly changed, becoming an index of high social standing in society as a whole. Popularization of the culture of hierarchy brought with it fundamental change in its social organization and meaning, and was a consequence, in part, of the integration of rural society into the colonial state. The spread of language levels, though sometimes referred to as "levels of politeness" or "vocabularies of respect," had less to do with politeness than with changes in the political culture. "Polite" forms previously reserved for the aristocracy were extended to rural-based elites. The events that ensured the spread of this culture of hierarchy, however, also set in motion other processes that promise to bring further changes to hierarchy and stratification in Java.

III. ISSUES FOR DISCUSSION

1. How do we as Americans think about status? Do we use speech to signal relative status? Compare American with that of the Javanese speech. What does this variation indicate as to how we think about language and status?

2. Discuss the impact of Dutch colonialism on Javanese society. How did colonialism affect the role of the aristocracy? How did colonialism influence the advance of Javanese Islam? What impact did it have, finally, on the system of status ranking in Java as a whole?

3. "Modernization" is sometimes assumed to undermine the values of traditional societies. The process in Java is more complex and selective: some aspects of social hierarchy have been preserved, but others have changed. Discuss the ways in which "traditional" notions of hierarchy have changed in recent years.

IV. SELECTED READINGS

Errington, J. Joseph. *Language and Social Change in Java: Linguistic Reflexes of Modernization in a Traditional Royal Polity.* Ohio University Monographs in International Studies, 1985 (suitable for graduate students and faculty). A sociolinguistic study of the language levels and language change among gentry elites in Central Java.

Geertz, Hildred. *The Javanese Family: A Study of Kinship and Socialization.* New York: The Free Press, 1961 (suitable for all levels). A readable classic study of Javanese socialization with great insight into the teaching of politeness and status.

Kartodirdjo, Sartono. *Protest Movements in Rural Java.* Oxford University Press, 1973 (suitable for all levels). The best historical source for the impact of colonialism on nineteenth-century rural Java, and the subsequent estrangement of peasants from the gentry.

Keeler, Ward. *Javanese Shadow Plays, Javanese Selves.* Princeton: Princeton University Press, 1987 (suitable for graduate students and faculty). Not simply a discussion of Java's most esteemed art form, but a densely argued introduction to Javanese notions of self and society, with special insight into the role of language.

Smith-Hefner, Nancy J. "Women and Politeness: The Javanese Example." In *Language in Society* 17:535–554 (1985) (suitable for all levels). An overview of the problem of linguistic politeness in Java and the West, particularly as it relates to the gender.

Wolff, John U., and Soepomo Poedjosoedarma. *Communicative Codes in Central Java.* Cornell University Southeast Asia Program, 1982 (suitable for graduate students and faculty). The best single linguistic overview of Javanese language levels.

Anthropology: Japan

Urban Life in Japan

Theodore C. Bestor

I. INTRODUCTION: CENTRAL POINTS

It goes almost without saying that Japan is among the most highly urbanized societies in the world; by some measures, over 80 percent of its population lives in urban areas.[1] Contemporary Tokyo is often regarded—with hope or with despair—as a harbinger of the world's postindustrial urban future. But at the same time, the roots of Japanese urban life extend far into the past, and the heritage of preindustrial urban life—ways that developed out of the creative tension between warriors and commoners in the cities of the Tokugawa period (seventeenth through mid-nineteenth centuries) continues to exert strong influences on contemporary Japanese.

The field of urban studies has ill-defined boundaries, and at least in the study of Japanese history and contemporary society, no single issue or theme has emerged to unify the diverse interests of historians, anthropologists, sociologists, political scientists, architectural historians, and urban planners, all of whom lay claim to the study of Japanese urbanism in its various dimensions. Nevertheless, several general topics of interest to sociologists, anthropologists, social historians, and behavior-oriented political scientists focus attention on the social structure of Japanese cities, on the nature of Japanese urbanism as a cultural system, and on the processes of urban development that have created contemporary forms of urban life.

The study of Japanese cities, their development, and the patterns of urbanism they embody is significant for several reasons.

Japanese cities include world famous urban centers such as Tokyo and Kyoto which, of course, are intrinsically significant and interesting in their own right.

These urban centers and dozens of other less well-known cities also represent historically rich and currently vital patterns of urban growth and development that can illuminate many of the processes and outcomes of social change that have shaped contemporary Japanese society, its economy, and its politics. That is, the study of Japanese cities can shed considerable light on Japanese society itself.

A final dimension is more explicitly comparative; Japanese cities provide a test case against which to compare the processes of urbanization and the textures of urban life in other societies, and to evaluate the applicability (and limitations) of general theories about urban society— the urban condition— that generally are drawn from the Western experience since the industrial revolution.

There are several major avenues along which such comparative questions may be pursued. In the sections that follow I briefly summarize three approaches: the evolution of urban society; urbanization and modernization; and contemporary urban social integration. Although the first two of these approaches involve substantial historical components, it is important to note that they focus more or less directly on questions about the development and character of contemporary Japanese society as well.

II. MAJOR TOPICS

THE EVOLUTION OF URBAN LIFE IN JAPAN

In examining the origins of urban society and the development of preindustrial cities in Japan, the history of Japanese cities and the various forms that urban life have taken over the past millennium and a half can be viewed in terms of comparisons with urban centers of other societies and in light of general theories and typologies of urban development.

Japanese cities offer the potential for comparative study along avenues suggested by a wide variety of general theories or concepts of urban life, including: V. Gordon Childe's "urban revolution," Gideon Sjoberg's "preindustrial city," Robert Redfield's and Milton Singer's "cultural role of cities," and Max Weber's and Karl Marx's divergent views of the role of the bourgeoisie and urban political institutions in stimulating the demise of feudal regimes and the development of modern industrial capitalism.[2] The challenge—and indeed the merit—of using Japanese cities to illustrate or discuss the applicability of these general theoretical frameworks is that although Japanese cities may amply illustrate particular phases implied by these models, the internal patterns of historical development and transformation do not necessarily correspond to the evolutionary processes (stimulated by developments in technology, demography, economic stratification, or state power) that these models variously propose as major causal factors.

Several important phases of Japanese urban development suggest comparisons with the rise and development of cities in other parts of the world, along such lines as the role of state formation in stimulating urban growth, the diffusion and adaptation of urban models (the "demonstration effect"), the social and political structure of preindustrial urbanism, or the effects of colonial encounters on urban growth. Examples from the Japanese case that might be used to illustrate such comparisons include:

• the rise of indigenous protourban centers in the Kinki region (surrounding present-day Kyoto, Nara, and Osaka) which accompanied the emergence of state organization before the sixth century;

• the development of imperial capital cities along Chinese models, following the importation of Chinese institutions of government, economic organization, and social structure after the sixth century;

• the emergence of feudal castle towns (from the fifteenth or sixteenth through the nineteenth century) which were dominated by the warrior classes but in which distinctive forms of bourgeois urban culture developed for the first time in Japanese history;

• the influences of port towns and quasi-colonial settlements in stimulating diffusion of Western economic, political, and social institutions, particularly in the nineteenth century;

• the twentieth century development of massive industrial cities at the core of a mass society.

The final two of these topics will be dealt with in more detail in the following section on *Urbanization and Modernization*. Here I will discuss briefly Japanese cities during the feudal period as an example of how they may illustrate comparative questions about the nature of preindustrial cities.

Gideon Sjoberg's famous characterizations of the preindustrial city were framed as a response and corrective to then prevailing views that Western industrial cities were the sine qua non of urbanism. Drawing on data from many premodern societies (although Japan was not one of the cases he examined in any detail), he argued that the nature of technological, economic, political, and social processes in premodern (or "feudal") societies was sufficiently similar to have given rise to a characteristic form of urban life. Premodern Japanese cities, especially during the Tokugawa period, do indeed conform to many (although by no means all) of the major features he identified: a technological and economic order based on preindustrial sources of energy; poorly developed economic institutions; sharply defined class structure based on traditional patterns of ascription with only inconsequential social mobility; spatial segregation within cities that reflect hereditary class, occupational, and ethnic divisions; family or clan as major units of social organization and integration; highly centralized and autocratic political institutions that rely heavily on personalistic patron-client bonds rather than legal or bureaucratic procedures; literacy and education limited to members of the ruling elites; and religion as a major proscriptive force ordering the daily lives of urban residents.[3]

Sjoberg's attempts to define the preindustrial city as representing a distinguishable and widespread stage along a more or less universal sequence of urban development has been widely criticized along a number of lines: for giving precedence to technological factors at the expense of political, economic, demographic, or social ones; for using a "negative" definition that depends on somewhat circular logic (defining preindustrial cities as those that are not industrial, and from that extrapolating a developmental sequence); or for ignoring differences among cities within a given society or among cities in different societies that might arise as a result of their different places in regional, national, or transnational networks of trade, political dominance, and so forth.

Nevertheless, for discussions of urbanism in premodern societies, Sjoberg's typology is a valuable starting place and material on premodern Japanese cities can be highly illustrative.[4] In addition, Sjoberg's typology can be useful in discussions of the transition from premodern to modern cities and of the preconditions for modern urbanization, which are the topics of the next section.

URBANIZATION AND MODERNIZATION

A second major approach to Japanese cities focuses on urbanization and modernization (or industrialization) since the later half of the nineteenth century (that is, since the start of industrialization and associated urban growth). This approach can be further divided into two somewhat different, although closely interrelated, perspectives. The first looks at "urbanization without breakdown," the second at urbanization in terms of "preconditions for development." The "urbanization without breakdown" approach examines the ways in which Japan speedily developed into an industrialized society and underwent massive urban growth while avoiding many of the dislocations, social upheavals, and breakdowns of established economic, political, and social institutions that have accompanied this transformation—or stalled it entirely—in other developing societies. This is not to deny or minimize the profound and wrenching social changes and problems that industrial urbanization caused for many Japanese,[5] but in comparative terms, Japanese urban growth followed a relatively smooth path as cities managed to absorb massive population increases, sustain the continuity of social and cultural institutions, and serve as centers for the entire society's further economic and social development. Put another way, Japanese cities by and large did not become mired in intractable problems of over-population, poverty, and social alienation that might otherwise have impeded Japanese development by diverting social, political, and economic resources in attempts to solve urban problems.

An excellent case study which can be used to illustrate the social dynamics behind urbanization without breakdown is Ezra Vogel's article, "Kinship Structure, Migration to the City and Modernization."[6] Vogel argued that the role of traditional family institutions in managing the flow of migrants to cities—the degree of control families exercised over who could migrate, what resources would be available to them, what jobs they would take in the city—was crucial to the smooth urbanization process, as was the development of urban institutions—such as employment practices and patterns of urban nuclear family life—that were conditioned in response to the role played by traditional rural family units.

Closely related to and intertwined with the general urbanization without breakdown perspective is one that looks at urbanization in terms of "preconditions for development." In essence, this asks the question of "why and how" in the light of "urbanization without breakdown." That is, it examines what constellations of political, economic, social, demographic, and cultural factors existing before the Meiji Restoration (1868), which marked the beginning of Japan's modernization effort, help account for Japan's ability to industrialize and urbanize with such relative ease. Many of the features of preindustrial society identified as contributing to this transformation are factors common in other, Western, cases of successful industrial urbanization: levels of commercial development, rates of literacy, demographic transitions. Other traits (most notably political stability and continuities in government authoritarianism, or the relative dearth of bourgeois political consciousness and ideologies of individualism) stand in distinction to the Western experience of industrial urbanization.

A useful, if now slightly dated, summary of some of the social, economic, and political continuities between premodern and modern Japanese cities that can contribute to a discussion of preconditions for development is John W. Hall's essay, "The Castle Town and Japan's Modern Urbanization."[7] Hall argued that the patterns of centralized, bureaucratic control, of economic growth, and of literate, sophisticated urban culture contributed substantially to the ease with which the urban infrastructure of Japan sustained and adapted to the social change wrought by industrialization and the growth of a modern state.

Both approaches, whether concerned with breakdowns or with preconditions, naturally lead to questions about contemporary urban social life and its character.

CONTEMPORARY URBAN SOCIAL INTEGRATION

Finally, a third approach considers contemporary patterns of Japanese urban social life as a comparative lens through which to analyze the nature of urban life—its necessary conditions, problems, and potentials—simply as a contemporary phenomenon. That is, Tokyo or Osaka or Sapporo or Sendai is as valid a case study of a contemporary city in an advanced industrial society as is Toronto or Oslo or Seville or Seattle. Thus, appropriate avenues for comparative consideration include an examination of such phenomena as social class structure, employment patterns, and the effects of education on mobility; of the ways in which family organization and kinship change to conform to the demands of urban life; of the nature of urban ethnicity; of the role of neighborhood communities in sustaining the livability of cities; and of the process of suburbanization. Each might be used to demonstrate in fundamental ways the similarities of urbanism and ur-

banity in Japan to the patterns of urban life found in other industrial societies but also to reveal in the overall patterns of urban
integration a society that remains distinctly different from most
Western societies.

In this section, I will briefly outline several closely interrelated
domains of urban life that seem to contribute to the social stability and integration of contemporary Japanese urban life: family
patterns, patterns of corporate life, and community organization.

Family Patterns. In the previous section, I mentioned Vogel's
study of the role of traditional patterns of kinship in facilitating
migration to cities in a relatively smooth fashion. Vogel's larger
study (*Japan's New Middle Class*) examined the structure of middle-class, white-collar families in a Tokyo suburb; his analysis
argued that a number of features of middle-class life are functionally related to one another. In particular, he looked at the emergence of the nuclear family and the dynamics of relationships
between husband and wife, and between mother and children, as
conditioned both by typical patterns of the husband's employment
in a large, all-embracing (i.e., quasi-paternalistic) bureaucratic
organization or firm and by the educational ambitions that become a family's sole means of ensuring the social advancement of
its own children in the next generation. He argued persuasively
that for members of this important group in urban society, family,
education, and corporate employment are inextricably linked by social and psychological processes that ensure the relative stability (if
not conservatism) of this class and that contribute substantially to
the social integration of family, residential community, educational
institution, and workplace throughout the urban system.[8]

Although the particulars of family life and its relationship to
work and career vary greatly from class to class, other studies
that address the relationship between family organization and the
structure of economic enterprises generally support Vogel's overall
model of integration between family structure and economic activity, albeit in widely diverse ways. Bestor's "Tokyo Mom-and-Pop"
and Dorinne Kondo's *Crafting Selves* discuss patterns of family
organization and familial ideologies in the small-scale sector of the
economy, while Matthews Hamabata's *Crested Kimono* examines
family ties among the quasi-aristocratic families that control
many of Japan's largest industrial and financial empires.[9]

Patterns of Corporate Control. The social organization of business,
particularly of corporate workplaces, similarly illustrates the ways

in which the institutional arrangements of the urban economy promote an all-encompassing sense of social belongingness and connectedness, and a social integration which permeates much of urban life. Several of the studies mentioned above address these issues, but more particularly Thomas Rohlen's *For Harmony and Strength*— an ethnographic analysis of a Japanese bank— demonstrates ways in which the corporate context becomes the overriding social environment for its employees, not only shaping their daily work lives and their individual patterns of career advancement, but significantly structuring their relationships with the wider society outside the bank.

Community Organization. A final aspect of urban social integration that I want to discuss briefly is that of urban community organization. While cities in many societies contain discrete, well-bounded urban communities (often organized along ethnic, religious, or sharply defined class cleavages), Japanese cities generally lack communities so defined. Nonetheless, Tokyo and other major cities are divided into well-organized and clearly defined neighborhoods that play major roles in organizing residents for a wide variety of administrative, public sanitation, social welfare, recreational, economic, political, and ritual purposes. Although by no means do all residents participate in local organizations, the groups and institutions active at the local level play a major role both in the delivery of services to urban areas and in sustaining or creating a sense of local belonging and identification that mitigates against alienation and anonymity.[10]

Comparative study and discussion of any or all of these dimensions of contemporary Japanese urban life can proceed in at least two directions. One would be to identify those particular patterns of Japanese social life that contribute to the integration and stability of contemporary cities. But a perhaps more fruitful and fundamental comparative urban question turns on whether the patterns of urban life that we are accustomed to considering (generally under the heading "urban problems") are the necessary products of urban life or whether our views of the urban condition are unduly narrowed by the problems many Western cities face.

III. ISSUES FOR DISCUSSION

1) What kinds of cities are there in different societies (or at different historical points)? What kinds of change— technological, economic, demographic, social, political, cultural— contribute to

the transformation of cities from one type to another? How does the historical development of Japanese cities fit into any or all of these processes?

2) Industrialization in most societies is accompanied by massive urban growth. Why should this be so, and what are some of the social, demographic, economic, political, or cultural consequences of this process in various urban societies? Does the Japanese case reflect the same kinds of processes as other societies?

3) What factors contribute to urban social disorder or alienation in many cities around the world (including cities in advanced industrial societies as well as in developing societies)? Are similar factors present or absent in Japanese urban life? What are the social forces in Japanese urban life that seem to contribute to overcoming or preventing urban social disorder or alienation?

NOTES

1. Internationally standardized definitions of urban areas or urbanized populations are notoriously slippery. But the often quoted comparison that Japan has roughly half the population of the United States living in the area of California (or half the population of the EC in the area of France) gives a good indication of the density.

2. Gideon Sjoberg, *The Pre-Industrial City* (New York: Free Press, 1960); V. Gordon Childe, "The Urban Revolution," in *Town Planning Review* 21 (1950):3–17; Robert Redfield and Milton Singer, "The Cultural Role of Cities," *Economic Development and Cultural Change* 3 (1954):53–73; Max Weber, *The City* (New York: Free Press, 1958).

Ulf Hannerz, *Exploring the City* (New York: Columbia University Press, 1980) and Richard Fox, *Urban Anthropology: Cities in Their Cultural Settings* (Englewood Cliffs, NJ: Prentice-Hall, 1977) provide overviews of urban theory relevant to this discussion. Richard Sennett, ed., *Classic Essays on the Culture of Cities* (New York: Appleton Century Crofts, 1969); Irwin Press and M. Estellie Smith, eds., *Urban Place and Process* (New York: Macmillan, 1980); and George Gmelch and Walter Zenner, eds., *Urban Life: Readings in Urban Anthropology*, 2nd ed. (Prospect Heights, IL: Waveland Press, 1988) are collections of social science writings on urban theory.

3. From this list alone, several key points at which Japanese cities diverge from Sjoberg's idealized model include: relatively widespread literacy; relatively minor role played by religion in ordering the daily lives of urbanites; and relatively common (though officially proscribed) social mobility between classes.

4. James L. McClain's *Kanazawa: A Seventeenth-Century Japanese Castle Town* (New Haven: Yale University Press, 1982) is the single most comprehensive account of the structure and life of a Japanese city during this period.

5. Much of the recent historical scholarship on development and industrialization in the late nineteenth and early twentieth centuries has

made precisely this point, that Japan's development was based on great social inequalities, exploitation, and emiseration, and that the process was hardly as smooth or as inevitable as is sometimes suggested.

6. E. F. Vogel, "Kinship Structure, Migration to the City and Modernization," in *Aspects of Social Change in Modern Japan*, ed. R. P. Dore (Princeton: Princeton University Press, 1967), pp. 91–111.

7. J. W. Hall, "The Castle Town and Japan's Modern Urbanization," *Far Eastern Quarterly* 15 (1955): 35–56.

8. E. F. Vogel, *Japan's New Middle Class*, 3rd ed. (Berkeley: University of California Press, 1991). Merry I. White, *The Japanese Educational Challenge* (New York: Free Press, 1987) addresses many of the same issues from the perspective of the educational system. See also Anne E. Imamura, *Urban Japanese Housewives* (Honolulu: University of Hawaii Press, 1987) for more recent research on suburban life in Tokyo.

9. Theodore C. Bestor, "Tokyo Mom-and-Pop," *Wilson Quarterly* (Autumn 1990):27–33; Dorinne K. Kondo, *Crafting Selves* (Chicago: University of Chicago Press, 1990); Matthews M. Hamabata, *Crested Kimono* (Ithaca: Cornell University Press, 1990).

10. Theodore C. Bestor, *Neighborhood Tokyo* (Stanford: Stanford University Press, 1989) is an ethnography of social life and local institutions in one urban community. Also, David H. Bayley, *Forces of Order* (Berkeley: University of California Press, 1976) examines the relationship between communities and the police in Japan and the United States to understand how social control is maintained in both societies.

IV. SELECTED READINGS

Bestor, Theodore C. *Neighborhood Tokyo*. Stanford: Stanford University Press, 1989 (faculty and student reading). An ethnography of daily life in an ordinary Tokyo community, focusing on local social ties and institutions and on the ways in which seemingly traditional patterns of community life and ideology are created and maintained as a response to social changes.

Dore, Ronald P. *City Life in Japan*. Berkeley: University of California Press, 1958 (faculty background). The classic study of Japanese urban life, an overview of community life in an older section of Tokyo.

Imamura, Anne E. *Urban Japanese Housewives*. Honolulu: University of Hawaii Press, 1987 (faculty and student reading). A study of suburban housewives and their family and community roles.

Kondo, Dorinne K. *Crafting Selves*. Chicago: University of Chicago Press, 1990 (faculty and student reading). A reflexive ethnography of gender, class, and identity in an artisanal Tokyo neighborhood.

McClain, James. *Kanazawa: A Seventeenth-Century Japanese Castle Town*. New Haven: Yale University Press, 1982 (faculty background). A detailed social history of a major castle town.

Seidensticker, Edward. *Low City, High City*. New York: Alfred A. Knopf, 1983 (faculty and student reading). A historical account of twentieth century Tokyo, focusing on the passing of the old merchant quarters of the Low City; a sequel, *Tokyo Rising*, (New York: Alfred A. Knopf, 1990) traces Tokyo's history up to the 1990s.

Vogel, Ezra F. *Japan's New Middle Class*. 3rd ed. Berkeley: University of

California Press, 1991 (faculty background). A study of white-collar middle-class families in suburban Tokyo and the interaction of family patterns with corporate employment and the education system. Recently updated by Suzanne Vogel in a third edition.

In addition to the above titles, there are several bibliographic essays that cover Japanese urban life. They include:

Bestor, Theodore C. "Urban lifestyles and popular culture." In *Handbook of Japanese Popular Culture*, edited by Richard G. Powers and Hidetoshi Kato, pp. 1–37. Greenwich, CT: Greenwood Press, 1989.

Narita, Ryuichi; Ogura, Kinichi; and Yoshie, Akio. "Japan." In *Modern Urban History in Europe, USA and Japan: A Handbook*, edited by Christian Engeli & Horst Matzerath, pp. 129–148, 427–435. Oxford, New York, and Munich: Berg, 1989.

Smith, Henry. "Tokyo as an Idea." *Journal of Japanese Studies* 4 (1978): 45–80.

Anthropology: Japan

Rural Society in Japan: Past and Present

William W. Kelly

I. INTRODUCTION: CENTRAL POINTS

Japan has long fascinated social scientists and historians for both its stability and its dynamism. It has had some form of central state authority for almost fifteen hundred years and was the first and by far the most successful non-Western society to industrialize. The nature of Japan's rural society and economy has been crucial to its historical experience as a pre-modern agrarian state and as an industrializing nation-state. Rural Japan thus presents an important case for **any** study of the nature of preindustrial states and of socioeconomic change. The following themes will be discussed:

• **Agrarian Ecology, Technology, and Productivity**. Wet-rice cultivation is an ecological system radically different from that of European temperate-zone grain farming. The requirements of growing irrigated rice have affected settlement patterns, social relations, and long-term technological progress.

• **State-Peasant Links**. The Japanese experience belies a linear political trajectory for preindustrial states. Japanese history has not been characterized by the progressive growth of an ever-stronger central authority, but rather by oscillations between periods of centralized authority and periods of regional autonomy.

Control of cultivators and production has always been crucial to this dynamic.

• **Population Dynamics**. Documentation for studying the early modern demography of Japan is among the best in the world, and permits us to understand the population characteristics of modernization. Rapid population increases in the seventeenth and early eighteenth centuries were slowed considerably by conscious practices to limit family size in the late eighteenth and nineteenth centuries. A generally expanding rural economy meant that per capita aggregate output was rising.

• **Rural Social Organization**. Households and villages have been the elemental units of rural society for two thousand years. However, the Japanese countryside has also been structured by administrative districts, irrigation networks, voluntary associations like pilgrimage groups, and commercial links. The scale and boundaries of these many units have not often overlapped. Rural Japan is thus organized not by a simple nesting of groups but as a complex set of organizational overlays.

• **Agriculture's Role in Industrialization**. The Japanese rural experience of the last two centuries illuminates the material, social, and ideological preconditions necessary for successful modernization as well as the vital contributions that agriculture can make to industrialization itself.

• **Farmers and the Advanced Industrial State**. Agriculture's declining place in the national economy has stirred much debate in Japan, as in other industrial states, about the future of the countryside in such societies. Contemporary Japan presents a striking contradiction between farm crisis and rural prosperity.

II. MAJOR TOPICS

AGRARIAN ECOLOGY, TECHNOLOGY, AND PRODUCTIVITY

Asian wet-rice was originally a tropical swamp crop, and its becoming the staple of Japanese agriculture required considerable technological ingenuity, social effort, and political pressure over the past two thousand years. Japan is a temperate zone archipelago of four major islands and thousands of small islands, with an area about the size of Italy and about one and one-half times that of the British Isles. Its natural vegetation is luxuriant and its coastal waters abundant, but its landform is largely forested mountains, bisected by numerous short and steeply graded rivers. This "corrugated" topography has limited agriculture and settlement to the coastal plains and interior basins that constitute only about one-fifth of its already small land mass.

Productivity in European grain farming is rooted in and limited by soil fertility, and depends on increasing the scale of operations and greater inputs of complex machinery. Wet-rice, with nutrients supplied and fixed by an aqueous medium, can yield high per-unit outputs through improvements in seed varieties, better water supply and drainage, manuring and fertilizing, and more intensive labor inputs. This has given a particular shape to Japanese agricultural development: extensive breeding of cold-resistant and region-specific rice varieties; sophisticated river control, ponding, and field drainage techniques; proliferation and refinements of hand tools; elaborate green manuring and composting schedules; and transplanting, multiple weedings, and other intensive labor practices. These have had important ecological and social consequences.

Ecologically, wet-rice cultivation requires a support system of water, leaf and tree materials for fertilizer and feed, and fields for complementary dry crops. Japan, in effect, is a country of some two hundred small river basins, each composed of a plain and its surrounding mountains, and constituting a relatively contained and integrated ecological unit. The forests, scrublands, rivers, and dry crop fields have had to be exploited and managed as a resource system within these small basin units.

Socially, because cultivation is intensive, farming operations have seldom been large, and small holders (as owners or tenants) have predominated. Moreover, because of the small-basin resource system, agriculture in Japan has created multiple and cross-cutting lines of cooperation and competition among foresters, farmers, and fishing folk, and among farmers themselves, who both share and compete for access and use of necessary resources.

STATE-PEASANT LINKS

While there is frequently a tendency to think of preindustrial states as emerging and growing progressively larger and stronger, the case of Japan cautions against such a linear model. Rather, Japanese history may be seen as oscillating periods of centralized authority and regional autonomy. These oscillations can be followed through the roughly five periods of Japanese history:

300 BCE to 700 BCE	Increasing stratification within local groups fueled conflicts among large clans in western Japan. The Yamato clan emerged as preeminent, and developed central state institutions around an emperorship that combined indigenous Shinto and imported Confucian and Buddhist notions of authority.
700 to 1100	This new aristocratic state was centered at the flourishing court capital of Heian (Kyoto), in west central Japan.
1100 to 1600	With the decline of the aristocratic elite, central authority fragmented during centuries of struggle among military houses and among Buddhist monastic establishments, which often had regional bases of power.
1600 to 1868	In the early seventeenth century, the entire country was consolidated under the bureaucratic-feudal rule of the Tokugawa shoguns. Tokugawa power began devolving to regional lords by the early nineteenth century.
1868 to 1945	This first part of Japan's "modern century," which was characterized by nation-state building, capitalist industrialization, and imperial expansion, ended in the country's defeat in World War II.
1945 to present	In the latter part of its "modern century," Japan recovered from the wartime devastation and since then has grown rapidly into the world's second-largest economy.

Control of rural cultivators and the product of their labors has always been crucial to this dynamic of centralization and decentralization, and Japan offers a fascinating study of state policies toward rural society and their unintended consequences. There have been four great land reforms in Japanese history: the seventh-century Taika reforms, late sixteenth-century cadastres undertaken by Hideyoshi and subsequent Tokugawa reform policies, the land tax revision of the 1870s, and the post-World War II land reforms. Each was essentially an effort to reestablish a viable countryside of small-holding, self-cultivating, taxpaying cultivator households. And each embodied certain contradictions that ultimately precipitated serious political and economic problems for the state and cultivators alike.

In the seventh century, the state claimed public ownership of all paddies, forests, and meadowlands; it mandated a periodic household census and apportionment of paddy lands to cultivators, who were to make tribute payments directly to state administrators. However, to promote new land development, in subsequent centuries it granted extensive exceptions to noble families and religious establishments. This eroded the fiscal base of state land revenues, and enriched and emboldened the provincial military elite who eventually usurped court authority.

In the late sixteenth century, the general Hideyoshi undertook a national land cadastre as part of his efforts to unify the country. Registration, measurement, and uniform taxation schedules were enforced by the first Tokugawa shoguns to regain direct appropriation of rice tax. Again, however, the state's inducements to develop paddy land resulted in much new land that escaped full taxation, while fluctuations of climate and market left many peasants vulnerable to pressures to pawn, sell, or abandon their land. By the early nineteenth century, large absentee holdings and undertaxation were causing great fiscal difficulties for the Tokugawa shogunate.

The new Meiji elite moved quickly to conduct a new cadastre, restore property rights to cultivators, and institute a national cash land tax. These measures, however, soon contributed once again to concentrations of landholdings and widespread tenancy in the early twentieth century. It was this tenancy that the post-World War II land reform addressed. This reform was highly effective in recreating a rural population of independent small holders, but its legal limits on ownership have prevented farmers from achieving significant economies of scale now possible with mechanization, and contributed to the virtual disappearance of full-time rice farmers.

POPULATION DYNAMICS

Population estimates of pre-seventeenth century Japan are very tentative; they generally infer gradual growth from about five million people in 300 CE to a range of ten-fifteen million in the early 1600s. For the Tokugawa period, however, Japan has the best demographic data of any early-modern society. The temple household registries, which survive for a number of areas in series over long periods of time, together with national surveys and other records, are a unique historical archive for understanding family demography and population dynamics prior to modernization.

Research on these materials has documented for the seventeenth century a rapid rise in population, an expansion of cultivation acreage and output, and the growth of large urban concentrations, including the explosive growth of the capital, Edo (Tokyo), which became the largest city in the world by 1720. At the same time, extended family groups gave way to smaller households which maintained independent farming enterprises. There was much regional variation in the particular customs of succession and inheritance, but the general preference among the rural population was for a "stem family," in which a single son or daughter takes a spouse and remains, while other siblings marry out. Thus, in a stem family, succeeding generations of husband-wife pairs reside together and sustain a family line.

In the eighteenth and nineteenth centuries, population growth slowed considerably, and there is strong evidence of infanticide and other measures to limit rural family size. Formerly, this was attributed to profound poverty and famine which, according to the theories of Malthus, checked population growth. Recent research has shown that the overall rural economy, both agricultural and non-agricultural production and trade, continued to expand. This suggests that efforts to limit family size were more deliberate. The prevalence of adopting heirs or sending out excess children and evidence of sex-selective infanticide are now interpreted as strategies to maintain a gender balance and family labor force appropriate to family resources.

RURAL SOCIAL ORGANIZATION

Households and villages have been the elemental units of rural society for two thousand years. Despite variations according to time and place, their character and form have always been shaped by both state intervention and local circumstance. Wet-rice ecology predisposed nucleated settlements of cultivator households, which were internally connected by a variety of village groupings, including male and female youth groups for unmarried adolescents, rotating credit circles, pilgrimage associations, and shrine parish guilds.

The village as focal point was further strengthened over the centuries by state efforts to assign social control and tax collection responsibilities to small residential collectivities which were ordered in hierarchical chains of administration. In the seventeenth through nineteenth centuries, for example, self-regulating villages were constituent units of larger "village groups," several of which formed the jurisdiction of local districts within the domain.

However, in addition to administrative hierarchies, the Japanese countryside was also structured by multi-village irrigation networks, linkages among area shrines and temples, and commercial activities like trading circuits, markets, and labor recruitment chains. The boundaries of these units often did not coincide. In this sense, the organizational pattern of rural Japan has not been simply a nesting of small households within discrete village settlements, but a complex set of organizational overlays.

Much of the regional variety in household form and succession preferences was homogenized as a result of by the state's promulgation in 1896 of the national Civil Code, which attempted to enforce a patriarchal and patrilineal version of the stem family. Revisions of the Civil Code in the late 1940s were intended to democratize and nuclearize family form, although in the countryside a significant number of three-generation households remain. More influential than legal change has been the appeal of a metropolitan lifestyle; the spread of "middle-class consciousness" throughout rural Japan has further standardized family form and lifestyle and largely eliminated urban and rural differences.

AGRICULTURE'S ROLE IN INDUSTRIALIZATION

As noted in the introduction, the Japanese experience of the last two centuries illuminates the material, social, and ideological preconditions necessary for successful modernization as well as the vital contributions that agriculture can make to industrialization itself.

The question of European industrialization, as Simon Kuznets argued forty years ago, is not how poor countries industrialized and got rich, but rather how they got rich enough to industrialize. What were the crucial antecedents to their takeoff to industrial prosperity? This has become a key question in research on the early-modern period. Developments in Japan in the eighteenth and nineteenth centuries demonstrate that while the European take-off was exceptional, it was not unique. Japan, too, shared these preconditions, many of which were features of rural society and economy:

- a growing rural economy, with stable population levels, provided a basis for general prosperity (although it was not equally distributed);
- an infrastructure of schools, state administration, and trans-

portation networks extending into the countryside; growth of significant rural industries ("protoindustrialization") in many regions (e.g., cotton spinning, silk reeling, papermaking);
 • state and local regulation of resource extraction which curbed overexploitation of forests and soils and stabilized local ecologies; and
 • popular advocacy of the value of thrift, pragmatism, literacy, agricultural experimentation, and self-governance.

In short, Japan in 1868, poised on the verge of modern nationhood, had a number of material, social, and cultural features that in retrospect were vital to its rapid industrial and urban transformations.

In the late nineteenth and early twentieth centuries, the rural sector continued to make several essential contributions to Japanese industrialization. The agricultural land tax was the major source of government revenues, land rents provided important funds for private investment, and the export of silk and cotton goods earned crucial foreign currency. Rising agricultural production was essential to feed the growing urban markets. And rural family patterns both promoted and regulated migration to cities. That is, the stem family ideology stipulated that one member of the next generation would remain to succeed to the family farm; in being sloughed off, his siblings were free to join the urban work force. After World War II, the complete mechanization of rice agriculture further freed surplus farm labor for the expanding industrial recovery and growth of the 1950s and 1960s.

FARMERS AND THE ADVANCED INDUSTRIAL STATE

Rural Japan is no longer agricultural Japan. Like the United States and northern European countries, the population engaged in farming has declined precipitously in the past three decades, yet the future of agriculture and the role of rural society in industrial Japan continues to be hotly debated by policy planners and scholars. Japan is the essential non-Western case for understanding state and agriculture—and the state of agriculture—in advanced capitalist societies. It presents the stark paradox of a relatively prosperous countryside and a gravely imperiled agricultural sector.

Crop subsidies, equipment loans, a vigorous agricultural cooperative movement, and non-farm employment opportunities have made part-time small-scale rice farming the predominant form of agriculture today. Mechanization has created one of the most technologically advanced and economically inefficient farming systems in the world; farming units are underscaled and overcapitalized. This crisis is exacerbated by conflicting pressures on the national government; it has made tremendous investments in and commitments to agriculture, yet it faces intense foreign demand to liberalize food imports.

Ironically, the same government programs that have produced the agricultural crisis have also brought enormous infrastructural improvements to rural society. Many of the road networks, telephone and sewer lines, community centers, and other public service facilities that have significantly improved and "metropolitanized" rural life have been constructed with subsidies from the basic agricultural assistance programs or ancillary programs. By such measures as household income, car ownership, and house size, rural life compares favorably to urban life, even as educational and economic opportunities continue to lag appreciably.

III. ISSUES FOR DISCUSSION

1. What have been the ecological and social consequences of wet-rice cultivation in Japan?
2. What have been the implications of Japan's political history for state-peasant relations?
3. The peasant village is often seen as the elemental unit of the countryside. How true has that been for rural social organization in Japan?
4. What has been agriculture's contribution to industrialization in Japan, and what is now its fate in the industrial society?

IV. SELECTED READINGS

Dore, Ronald P. *Shinohata: Portrait of a Japanese Village*. New York: Pantheon, 1978 (student reading). A splendid ethnographic account of a village in the post-World War II decades, with an opening chapter on early twentieth-century developments.

Ogura, Takekazu. *Can Japanese Agriculture Survive? A Historical and Comparative Approach*. Second edition. Tokyo: Agricultural Policy Research Center, 1980 (faculty background). An exhaustive survey of agricultural history, policy, technology, and prospects.

Smith, Thomas C. *The Agrarian Origins of Modern Japan*. Stanford: Stanford University Press, 1955 (faculty background). Still a comprehensive and reliable overview of agricultural development and rural society in the Tokugawa centuries.

Totman, Conrad. *Japan Before Perry*. Berkeley: University of California

Press, 1981 (student reading). A highly readable history of Japan to 1868, with useful emphasis on rural development and ecological themes.

See also the many entries in the *Kodansha Encyclopedia of Japan* (1983) and the relevant articles in the *Cambridge History of Japan* (1988-).

Anthropology: Japan

Gender Roles: The Case of Japan

Nancy Rosenberger

I. INTRODUCTION: CENTRAL POINTS

II. MAJOR TOPICS
    WOMEN'S SUBORDINATION: CHANGES THROUGH TIME
    GENDER RELATIONS REPRESENTING DIFFERENT DOMAINS OF LIFE

I. INTRODUCTION: CENTRAL POINTS

In the area of gender roles, Japan presents students with a challenging contrast to American values and current ideals. Although Japan is highly modernized in terms of industrial lifestyle and material consumption, most women and men retain separate and stereotyped roles. The Japanese case thus provides an interesting perspective on the values and pace of change in gender relations in the United States.

Japan presents a case where gender roles and gender relations vary historically and socially among different socio-economic groups. This is particularly interesting in the light of the purported "homogeneity" of Japan.

Japan is an example of a society in which gender relations are closely linked with important cultural values that underlie social process.

Japan is an excellent example of an industrialized society in which quality education and a large role in the work force have not benefitted women's status to the extent social science theory would predict.

The Japanese case illustrates a situation where adult men and women exist in very different worlds, and raises questions as to the kind of power Japanese women have in society.

II. MAJOR TOPICS

WOMEN'S SUBORDINATION: CHANGES THROUGH TIME

In studying Japanese history and society, it is important to remember that gender roles are not fixed, but vary through time and according to context.

Although Japanese women never have had autonomous economic or political strength, they have had more power as wives in some eras and classes of society than in others. In the Heian period (794–1192) several women who were consorts of the emperor wrote diaries and novels describing life at the court. In Murasaki Shikibu's *The Tale of the Genji*, the world's first novel, we see a world in which upper class women live either in houses set up for them at court, or in their natal homes, raising children whose fathers are men of the court. The women wait for those men, or other lovers, to visit them. Emperors kept consorts at court because the women's presence and childrearing for the Emperor created alliances between the Emperor and the women's various clans.

During the Muromachi period (1392–1573), many of the elite began to take up the practice of making political alliances by marrying a woman from an allied clan. Wives would enter into the residence and lineage of the husband. This contributed to an increased subordination for women as wives among the elite. The arrangement guaranteed military strength in this period of wars among strong clans.

This pattern in which the wife was firmly entrenched within the household of her husband was rigidified among the samurai class during the feudal Tokugawa period (1630–1868), when the country was united under the Shogun in Edo (Tokyo). The wives of the highest-ranking feudal lords were pawns in the political system, forced to live in the capital, away from their domains, as "hostages" to guarantee the loyalty of their husbands to the shogunate. Samurai wives were strictly trained to sacrifice personal desires for the prosperity of the household, both in everyday management of the household and in times of crisis. For instance, defeat of a husband in war was often followed by the suicide of his wife and children.

GENDER RELATIONS REPRESENTING DIFFERENT DOMAINS OF LIFE

In feudal times, particularly from the seventeenth through mid-nineteenth centuries (Tokugawa), relations between men and women varied according to context. During this period men could frequent the urban "pleasure quarters," which constituted a wide variety of entertainments, including sexual services. At the more elite end of the spectrum were *geisha*, women trained in cultural amusements (dance, musical instruments, singing, witty conversation) who might also provide sexual services for selected patrons. Other women in the pleasure quarters were simple prostitutes, engaged for sex but lacking the skills and refinements of other entertainments. Within the home, the relationship was one of obligation; both wife and husband had responsibilities to the household and the wife had a strict obligation to respect her husband. These hierarchical relations were supported ideologically by Confucian ethics and practices. Outside the household, gender relations for men were characterized by emotion, specifically, the emotional bonds between the man and a paramour. The puppet plays of seventeenth century playwright Chikamatsu describe these relations of marriage and adultery that were particularly prevalent among the wealthy and powerful merchant class. His heroines usually are either devoted wives or passionate prostitutes. A man may have them both as long as he keeps them in separate realms of his life; if he is overwhelmed by passion, suicide is the only recourse for him and his lover.

In the Meiji period (1868–1912), the samurai ideal of the husband-wife relationship was encouraged among peasants through legislation and education. This ideal flourished particularly among the growing urban middle class. An especially poignant example of this can be found in the novel *The Waiting Years* by Enchi Fumiko. After bearing several children, the heroine spends most of her married life finding several young mistresses for her husband and then caring for them as part of the household. In this case, it is clear that the wife's identity is as a member of her husband's household rather than as an emotional or sexual partner to her husband. Thus, the relationship between husband and wife involved reproduction and official household status; passions were tolerated but kept unofficial in the husband's relationship with mistresses.

Although in modern times the number of geisha has greatly decreased, "hostesses" and "companions" are still important in facilitating men's entrance into this world where hierarchy is muted and relaxed social links can be forged among men. They help men participate in a context of relaxation and harmony that women are considered adept at creating simply because of their biological sex and social gender. It is now framed, however, within the higher economic power of males.

GENDER ROLES AMONG PEASANTS

The samurai ideals of primogeniture, patrilineality and patrilocal residence were encoded in law in the Household Code of 1898. Yet the samurai ideal that positioned the wife in the household and the man in public life did not penetrate all levels of Japanese society by the twentieth century. Japanese peasant women and men worked together in the rice fields. Love marriages, supported by young men's and young women's groups in the village, were commonplace. Inheritance of the household by a woman was the rule in some places even in the early twentieth century, and inheritance of the household by a woman along with her married-in husband was quite common when she had no brothers. In Ella Wiswell's 1930 study of rural Kyushu, as described in *The Women of Suye Mura*, we find women marrying several times, having pre-marital pregnancies or pregnancies of questionable paternity, dancing and joking obscenely, and drinking heavily. Women were an integral part of all aspects of village life. On the other hand, they worked harder than the men and felt jealous of their husbands who went off to town to take up with prostitutes. The extent of women's subordination varied regionally. In the rural northeast husbands and fathers-in-law had more authority over wives than in the southwest because households themselves were embedded in a strict hierarchical system. In contemporary Japan, differences occur according to class more than region. The "proper" relationship, in which the husband is the master, punctiliously cared for by his wife, is not observed to the same extent in working class households as in professional households.

GENDER AS COMPLEMENTARY

Japanese like to portray the relationship between man and woman as one of complementarity, each doing his or her part so that society functions smoothly. Often the feminine and masculine are portrayed in terms of the negative and positive principles of *yin* and *yang* complementary powers, with each containing a bit of the other. The man (yang) is likened to a powerful horse running a short, swift race. He is positive and outward-oriented, thus well-suited to public life. The woman (yin) is his opposite, associated with darkness and inner spaces and thus suited to the private sphere. With the development of industrial capitalism in Japan, these "natural" characteristics have made women seem well suited to domestic responsibilities whereas men are "naturally" more capable in corporate occupations. Such ideas of complementarity give a sense of meaning to women in subordinate roles. However, they also reproduce unequal relations between women and men because masculine characteristics are in practice valued above feminine characteristics in most spheres of Japanese life.

GENDER ROLES WITHIN THE HOUSEHOLD

A woman's status in the patriarchal household must be viewed throughout the life cycle. Hierarchies in multi-generation agricultural and business households (now rapidly decreasing) subordinate women, but also allow movement toward dominance. If a woman marries a firstborn son who was to inherit responsibility for the household, she would be under the authority of her husband, father-in-law, and, most directly, mother-in-law in the household hierarchy. Even today there are many women in their fifties who harbor bitter memories of having had to endure a domineering mother-in-law. Women who marry younger sons or who bring a bridegroom into their natal homes (in the absence of a male heir) do not experience the lower end of the hierarchy so vividly. A wife living in the mother-in-law's household gains status and authority by producing children, particularly sons. She will become matriarch upon the retirement or death of the mother-in-law. Multigenerational households can still be found in modern Japan, but most young women avoid marrying into agricultural households because of the hard work and the fear of a domineering mother-in-law. That inheriting sons on farms sometimes bring in wives from the Philippines indicates the extent of this problem.

The man's relations with his children in such a household, particularly the elder son, are more distant and sterner than his wife's. Also, he generally feels more emotionally tied to his mother than to his wife. While the male househead tends to dominate the female househead in major household decisions, gender is not the only determining factor of hierarchical power. His mother typically has strong influence; and, alternately, if he married into his wife's family, he is a weak figure in the eyes of his wife's family and village society.

THE CHANGING HOUSEHOLD HIERARCHY

In modern Japan, the domestic power of Japanese women has two main sources. Politically and economically, it stems from her position as female househead and, frequently, her control over the purse strings, a control that is more complete among urban than rural women. Wives of many company workers receive the husband's salary out of which she pays household expenses and gives an allowance to the husband. Emotionally, a woman's power is a result of her intimate relationship with her children, especially her eldest son. Having sacrificed for them and coddled them, she earns feelings of debt and gratitude from her children. In some modern Japanese psychological therapies, the feeling of deep gratitude and debt to mothers is rekindled through meditation, becoming the basis for renewed meaning in life. According to modern law, a widow inherits half of her husband's estate, but in fact she often chooses to depend on her close relationship with a son, entrusting him with her share of the inheritance.

In contemporary Japan the traditional household hierarchy is weakening. In 1987, 60 percent of households in Japan were nuclear. Inheriting sons and their wives often live apart from their parents until the elders retire or need the assistance of the younger generation. Often they do not live together until the mother-in-law is widowed and/or not able to live alone. However, women in their forties and fifties are often expected to care for elderly in-laws. The example of a working woman in Tokyo who drove several hours every Sunday to take home-cooked food for the week to her husband's parents is not particularly remarkable. It is not uncommon for women in Tokyo and other cities to quit work in order to care for their own or their husbands' parents who live with them or nearby.

In cases where an aging mother lives with her son, the tendency is for the daughter-in-law to be in charge and for the older woman to provide household services, especially if the younger one works. In this situation, the older woman often feels that the hierarchy has been turned upside down: in her youth she had to endure a mother-in-law and now, in her old age, she has to submit to her daughter-in-law. Consequently, many older women now prefer to live with their married daughters because they have a closer emotional relationship.

As the vast majority of men now work outside of the home, gender relations are much less a function of the home environment than when farming and business were household concerns. Gender differences create a seemingly natural difference between a public company sphere and a private domestic sphere. As a middle-aged executive in a medium-size firm said to me, "Society works well if women stay at home and men go to work. If my wife worked, I'd have to eat cold dinners and wear unironed shirts to work."

This characterization is particularly applicable to couples where the woman is at home caring for younger children. At this time, the intimacy of early marriage, whether a "love marriage," or an arranged marriage based on mutual approval, tends to dissipate. It is assumed that mothers should establish close emotional bonds with their children and continue to have primary responsibility for their physical, emotional, and educational needs. If children are socially maladjusted or unsuccessful in school, mothers are often blamed either for working full-time and paying too little attention to the children or at the other extreme, for showering their children with too much attention. Fathers spend much time away from home, because of cramped living space and the demands of their jobs and after hours socializing with their colleagues. The traditional image of the father as disciplinarian is changing; often absent, he relates increasingly to the children through the presents he brings home.

On the other hand, it is not uncommon on weekends to see families shopping together or young fathers in parks caring for their small children. Especially among the younger generation, the ideal of the nuclear family, enjoying leisure time together is quite strong. This is reflected by changes in the style of house plans and furnishings. Examples show designs with a common room for parents and children with separate space for grandparents to be by themselves. Whereas before sleeping rooms and futons (sleeping mats) made sleeping arrangements flexible with the assumption that children would sleep with their parents or grandparents, the current ideal is to have separate bedrooms for grandparents, parents and children, with separate beds for each.

Thus, even while the ideology of mother's devotion to children remains strong, practices that favor generational and individual independence are also popular.

MIDDLE-AGED WOMEN

The world of middle-aged women is quite separate from that of their husbands. With men absent and aging parents less dominant, women have almost complete authority over the domestic sphere. They may feel much more in charge of their lives (especially after children are in school) than do their husbands who are placed in a competitive hierarchy at work. Middle-aged women may experience strain from isolation or feelings of uselessness, but usually derive satisfaction from friendships, hobbies, volunteer activities, and work.

Important regional differences exist among middle-aged women that are in part sustained by varying attitudes towards menopause. In a northeast provincial city in the early eighties most women still held the ideal that middle-class housewives should not work, yet they had few tasks during the day. Women interviewed complained of many symptoms, classifying most aches and pains as menopausal from their late thirties to mid-fifties. Many women used these physical manifestations as proof that they needed to stay home and care for their household, despite their shrinking responsibilities therein. In contrast, in a small village in northeast Japan, where multigenerational households involved in agriculture and fishing were flourishing, women downplayed menopausal symptoms but admitted to a few with some pride. They were described as evidence of the important sacrifices of childbearing and hard work that these women had made to build up their households. In some cases, the menopausal symptoms were the impetus for the mother-in-law to receive more care from family members, especially her daughter-in-law. Another contrast was found in Tokyo where many women denied having problems with any menopausal symptoms. They were moving away from the household as the center of their worlds and the image carried by menopause symptoms would have pulled them back. They wanted to get jobs or establish independent activities with friends during the hours their children were at school and husbands at work. In sum, we can see a general movement among women toward an ideology of leisure time and work for pay outside the household, a movement that increases with urbanization, western influence, and the reduced economic functions of the household.

WOMEN IN THE WORK FORCE

Young rural women were the first work force in Japanese silk and cotton weaving factories in the late 1800s and early 1900s, making up 60 percent of all factory workers in 1876. They were recruited off farms in poor rural areas where advance payments for daughters as workers could build a new house or buy several rice paddies. The daughters became indentured servants with a contract to work a certain number of years and penalties if they did not. They often worked 12-hour days or longer in factories with little light and were confined in dorms when off work. Until the Factory Act of 1911, even girls of eight or nine did such work. Promises to give the workers lessons in flower arranging or other domestic skills were not fulfilled, but the girls were still considered dependents of their families rather than independent workers.

Although women workers were valued for their docility and obedience, some did strike beginning in 1886, and many more participated in strikes throughout the early twentieth century. Neither the companies nor the government responded to workers' demands with decisive improvements in pay, working hours, or working conditions. The much-touted life employment system was developed during this time to retain skilled male workers, but its benefits did not extend to women who mainly did manual factory work. Thus, women's cheap and flexible labor has been and continues to be one pillar supporting Japanese industrial growth.

At present, more than half of Japanese women work outside the home. This may appear to challenge the traditional pattern of husbands at work, and wives at home. Yet responsibilities to the household and its members continue to be the focus of concern and source of identification for most women. As in other industrialized societies, there is an M-curve to women's employment patterns. In 1987, 73 percent of women between the ages of 20 and 24 worked. Most work full-time, earning as much money as men their age and often enjoying it in international travel and stylish clothes before marriage. Women's magazines have burgeoned in number for this age group. They encourage free spending to consume items that will give a "personal style." However, such magazines are also full of articles on marriage, sometimes debating whether to marry but ultimately concentrating on how to find a marriage that will insure a sound economic future with consumer status. Following this advice, most women do marry in their mid to late twenties. The employment rate for women then dips to around 50 percent for 10 years during early marriage, and then rises back to 60 percent from 35 to 39 years of age, and to 65 percent from 40 to 54 years of age.

An important point, however, is that slightly over half of all women workers are employed on a part-time or "temporary" basis, working six to eight hours a day. They earn low hourly wages without benefits or job security. They are the "reserve army of labor" which gives flexibility to the Japanese economy. Significantly, part-time women workers say that they prefer this situation because it gives them time to do their household chores, and they can readily quit if household necessities demand it. Thus, for the most part women define themselves first as mothers and wives, work being a way to help pay for children's education or a means to get out of the house.

GENDER RELATIONS AT THE WORK PLACE

The organization of the work place supports this identification of men with work and women with home. In large companies, young unmarried women are valued for their sexual attractiveness; they are referred to as "flowers" of the work place and sometimes addressed as "sister." Besides clerical support, they provide a domestic grace to the office as they serve tea to the men and their guests. In company dorms, young women are encouraged to learn domestic skills by cleaning, doing laundry, and taking courses for "bridal preparation" such as tea ceremony or flower arranging. An older single working woman told me that men in her company shun her because she no longer spoils them as the younger women do. On the other hand, middle-aged part-time workers sometimes provide motherly support for the men. In almost all cases, even younger men have higher status than women. Men make the decisions and interface with important people both within and outside the company.

In 1987, the average pay for men was twice that for women. Even those women who do continue working full-time are rarely eligible for the same line of promotions as men, and tend to stay in clerical positions. Most women experience social pressure from company superiors to quit at marriage or when they have children, despite the fact that the law now prohibits forced retirement and requires maternity leave. In a few areas such as publishing, banking, and insurance, women are generally not pressured to resign and some receive promotions. Such opportunities are slowly increasing, but the general attitude among employers is that hiring women on the same promotion tracks as men is too risky. They will probably quit because of children, if not because of pressures from husbands. Even women who are hired on promotion tracks find that they rarely get the kinds of training, transfers, and promotions that their male counterparts receive. The importance of after hours socializing in bars and restaurants to develop personal ties with superiors also remains a barrier to women's upward movement.

When women reenter the job market after raising children, their possibilities are usually limited to low-level positions with small enterprises that pay low wages. Even teachers and nurses cannot return to work full-time at the same institutions where they worked in the past. They must work part-time at smaller, less prestigious institutions. Although women can retrain in areas such as medical and legal clerical work or nutrition, their options for jobs are limited over age 35. Universities are just beginning to develop classes for older students, but most aim at general education rather than professional training. Large and medium Japanese companies have mostly depended on young men with general university educations for their new hires, with companies providing training in corporate culture and the specifics of the job. This system works against the possibility of women entering such companies after raising children.

Nevertheless, examples of women executives can be found, mostly in small or medium-size companies. They often gain these positions through family connections. Women executives are able to function effectively in relations with both male subordinates and male counterparts, suggesting that gender is not the overriding determinant of status: the status ascribed to a position of authority takes precedence over that ascribed to gender.

GOVERNMENT POLICIES AND WOMEN

Japanese government policies encourage women to take on a number of different, sometimes contradictory, roles. As a whole, however, all of these roles ensure that women will aid Japan in sustaining high economic growth. On one hand, they are urged to work. In the national pension system, women will get the highest benefits if they work long years at increasing salaries, just like men. Their pension benefits decrease when they quit jobs to get married or have children or if they later work for another company with a different pension system. On the other hand, some receive support for staying home. Women who are married to salaried employees in medium or large companies are encouraged to be full-time housewives because their husbands are now required to pay into an individual pension account for their wives. Women who are married to men self-employed in agriculture or small business, however, must pay into their own pension accounts, and thus have a greater incentive to work. Thus, the pension system holds in place the ideology that wives of richer households should not work while these of poorer households should contribute economically.

Government policies encourage women to work part-time. Men can continue to claim their wives as tax deductions if the wives make no more than about $7,000 per year. In short, women get a variety of messages from government policies precisely because the government needs women to fulfill a number of disparate roles to support the high growth economy. They need women at home to care for children, especially those children who are future government and company leaders. They also expect women to care for elders at home when necessary. By not supporting enough institutions to care for children and the elderly, the government implicitly appeals to women's "inherent" sensitivity to human relations and concern for the family. At the same time, the economy is short of labor. Women are needed in the work force, but if many of them can be employed at low wages and without job guarantees, high economic growth will be protected even in times of hardship.

EDUCATION

The statistics on women in the labor force do not reflect the high level of education attained by the average Japanese women. In 1987, 94 percent of all Japanese matriculated through senior high school, in virtually equal numbers for men and women. Thirty-one percent went for higher education, although three times as many men as women went to four-year universities. Ten times as many women as men went to junior colleges where the most popular courses are home economics, the humanities, and pre-school education. Companies prefer to hire women graduates from high school or junior college rather than four-year colleges because they can be expected to work longer before marriage. Even female graduates from the highest-ranking universities are at a disadvantage, since the better jobs, that is, those that lead to career advancement, are generally obtained through old-boy networks built on university ties, which are all but closed to women.

WOMEN'S RIGHTS AND PARTICIPATION
IN POLITICS

During the late 1800s and early 1900s, privileged urban women were beginning to fight for women's rights. They failed in their attempt to have prostitution banned, but did get prostitutes' contracts and debts cancelled in 1872. Concubines got equal rights in the family from 1870. In journals of the day, educated women encouraged debate on monogamy, the power of mothers-in-law, and divorce of women who fail to bear children.

Those fighting for women's rights argued for equal education for women in practical subjects. They discouraged the practices in elite families of confining their daughters' education to artistic skills and the belief in peasant families that girls need no education. Elite young woman were called "daughters in boxes," but feminists of the time said, "putting daughters in boxes is like growing flowers in salt." This quest for limited freedoms within the boundaries of the household must be measured against the then progressive idea that women should train their children in morals and religion, rather than being simply a borrowed womb. The ideology of "good wife, wise mother" held great appeal to women against a background of work in households where they received little credit for their contributions.

Kishida Toshiko and other women campaigned for the vote for women taxpayers and property owners in the 1870s, but their hopes were dashed by ensuing political repression. The 1890 Constitution went so far as to prohibit women from gathering for political meetings, observing the legislature or ascending the throne.

Suffragists such as Hiratsuka Raicho and Ichikaua Fusae led the fight for the 1922 revision of these prohibitions on women. Arguments for birth control made little headway, and struggles for civil rights for women in the 1930s succumbed to the war efforts. It was not until 1945, during the American Occupation, that Japanese women gained the rights to vote and run for political office. They also were given broader rights to file for divorce, and the postwar divorce rate soared. The new law diminished the power of the male househead.

Thus women gained much legal independence after World War II, but in practice things changed slowly. Although now legally equal to men at home and work, social pressures continue to force women to make decisions that do not necessarily reflect their true aspirations. I have mentioned pressures to quit work and marry between about 25 and 28. A single woman at 30 is viewed as having slim chances of finding the ideal mate with a high education and employment with a top flight company.

Women have the right to practice birth control, which was encouraged at the end of World War II. However, the pill has never been legalized and abortion is still one of the main ways of preventing birth. The Japanese government is beginning to worry about the falling birth rate, for in the early 2000s each working person will be supporting four dependents if the current rates of population growth and levels of life expectancy continue unchanged. Government agencies even have considered making special payments to women who have more than one child.

Women have right to file for divorce, but because of employment opportunities that are vastly inferior to men, women often feel economically constrained to remain married. In 1982, couples divorced at the rate of 1.4 per 1000, low in comparison with other industrialized countries. A significant change is that couples are divorcing later in life: in 1982, 37 percent of divorcing couples had been married for ten years. A bulge becomes noticeable in the statistics among women in their late forties. Women tend not to file for divorce until then so as not to jeopardize the educational, marriage and employment opportunities of their children. Teachers, employers, and future in-laws, view children of divorced families as risks because they are thought to be less stable.

In the postwar period, women have been active in citizen movements concerned with such issues as pollution, consumer rights, and nuclear dangers. Now voting in greater numbers than men, women's representation in local assemblies is notable, although there are few women in the national legislature. In the world of politics, as in that of employment, old-boy networks, which are crucial for monetary support, do not include women. An exception to this is Doi Takako, former head of the Socialist Party. Her party has not been able to successfully challenge the strong Liberal Democratic Party that has ruled almost continually since World War II.

CHANGES AND CONTRADICTIONS IN
THE CONSCIOUSNESS OF JAPANESE WOMEN

Although the terms "women's lib" and "feminist" are known in Japan, the principles and debates of the feminist movement as observed in the United States are not part of the consciousness of most Japanese women. In fact, such words in Japanese have a negative image that connotes women's power over men, an image most women cannot afford to be associated with. Demands for equal job opportunities and an equal division of labor at home have been noticeable only among a few highly educated urban women. Magazines that appeal to more independent women tend to feature articles on such issues as living alone, the significance of turning 35, sex as a spiritual act and reactions of husband, children and mother-in-law when a housewife returns to work. Debate about women's roles and gender relations goes on. For the most part, however, Japanese women continue to make small changes within the framework of hierarchies at school, home and work in which men are superior. Women writers urge other women to gain economic independence, to rebel against husbands and to even consider the single life as acceptable. Women in government agencies work toward gaining better benefits and job stability for part-time women workers.

Japanese women have great diversity among them in terms of regions, occupations, socio-economic levels, as well as individual life histories. Yet they are all affected by wide-ranging ideologies that emerge from powerful institutions such as government, schools, and mass media. All Japanese women are familiar with the injunctions to be gentle, patient, nurturing, modest, and deferential "like a woman." They know that women are expected to serve others, especially men older than they in a hierarchy. At the same time, all except the oldest Japanese women are exposed to a mass media highly influenced by western ideas. Here Japanese women meet images of themselves in which they develop individuality, have sexual appeal, and enjoy spontaneous pleasure through the consumption of goods and entertainment. These two sets of ideas are contradictory, yet they co-exist in women's lives. Japanese women who take ideas of individual choice beyond the department stores and into their lives feel frustration as to how to express their independence, yet still be considered mature Japanese women. They exist at an intersection that is confusing, yet offers the potential of creating a new way of being a woman that is neither Japanese nor western.

III. ISSUES FOR DISCUSSION

1. How would you judge Japanese women's "power," in the broad sense of that word. Is she always subordinate? Does she have some kinds of power that men do not have?

2. How are gender relations reflected in broader social relations

and social organization in Japan? Would the social order be upset if the position of women were to change significantly?

3. Hierarchy is very important as a way of organizing people and getting things done in Japan. How are gender relations involved in hierarchical organization? Are women ever free of hierarchical constraints?

IV. SELECTED READINGS

Bernstein, Gail Lee. *Recreating Japanese Women, 1600-1945.* Berkeley: University of California Press, 1991 (faculty and student reading). This is a collection of short articles that analyzes the multiplicities of women's histories in Japan. Each article breaks down stereotypes of a homogeneously submissive Japanese woman or accounts for the historicity of those stereotypes.

Edwards, Walter. *Modern Japan Through Its Weddings: Gender, Person and Society in Ritual Portrayal.* Stanford: Stanford University Press, 1989 (faculty and student reading). Edwards' ethnography describes the lavish weddings popular in Japan. Marriage rituals present bridge and groom, each as an incomplete individual, in need of marriage to become finished. The book includes case studies of courtship procedures leading up to marriage, breaking down boundaries between arranged and love marriages.

Hane, Mikiso. *Peasants, Rebels and Outcastes: The Underside of Modern Japan.* New York: Pantheon Books, 1982 (student reading). Hane chronicles the lives of the lower classes during the build up of Japanese industrial and military strength in the late nineteenth and early twentieth centuries. Of particular interest are chapters on the problems experienced by rural women, women textile factory workers and prostitutes.

Kondo, Dorinne. *Crafting Selves: Power, Gender and Discourses of Identity in a Japanese Workplace.* Chicago: University of Chicago Press, 1990 (faculty and student reading). Kondo's ethnography of a small confectionary factory in downtown Tokyo highlights the relations of power among the older male company head, the male artisans, and the female part-time women workers. She shows that women's gendered actions have contradictory results of power and powerlessness.

Lebra, Joyce; Paulson, Joy; and Powers, Elizabeth, eds. *Women in Changing Japan.* Stanford: Stanford University Press, 1976 (student reading). This book contains short articles on women working in many different spheres of life, such as factories, bars and farms. It includes statistics and ethnographic examples.

Lebra, Takie. *Japanese Women: Constraint and Fulfillment.* Honolulu: University of Hawaii, 1984 (student reading). This very readable book describes the positions of women in a small Japanese city throughout the life cycle. It is based on data that the author collected through extended interviews in Japan, and offers many illustrations of customs, their rationales, and their variations.

Lo, Jeannie. *Office Ladies, Factory Women.* Armonk, NY: M.E. Sharpe, 1990 (student reading). This is an ethnography of the practices and concerns of secretaries and factory workers in a Japanese manufacturing firm. Lo describes the differential treatment of women based on educational and socio-economic levels as well as the restrictive practices in dorms and company that direct women out of the company and into marriage.

Pharr, Susan. *Political Women in Japan.* Berkeley: University of California, 1981 (faculty and student reading). This book describes three types of political involvement among women. Political socialization, political activism and the strains of pursuing a politically active role are discussed.

Saso, Mary. *Women in the Japanese Workplace.* London: Hilary Shipman, 1990 (faculty and student reading). Saso studies working conditions of women in Japanese factories not only in Japan, but Ireland and Britain as well.

Seivers, Sharon. *Flowers in Salt.* Stanford: Stanford University Press, 1983 (faculty and student reading). This book describes the struggles of women who spearheaded Japanese women's movements in the late nineteenth and early twentieth centuries.

Smith, Robert, and Wiswell, Ella Lury. *The Women of Suye Mura.* Chicago: University of Chicago Press, 1982 (student reading). In this book the notes of Ella Wiswell recorded in the agricultural village of Suye Mura in the 1930s provide picture of rural women quite at odds with the staid morals of the upper classes. This book also presents a fascinating contrast to the structured village life described in Wiswell's late husband John Embree's ethnography *Suye Mura* and is an important contribution to women's history in Japan.

Anthropology: Japan

The Family in Japan

Stephen R. Smith

I. INTRODUCTION: CENTRAL POINTS

The Japanese family is a fascinating case for comparative study in both history and the social sciences. Traditional Japanese domestic organization presents a striking counterpoint to Western expectations of family structure and content. The family is also an adaptive institution, not fixed forever, but evolving in response to the changing demands of life in Japan. Yet, at the same time as the traditional family is being transformed, elements of that institution can be found pervading the rest of contemporary Japanese society.

• The traditional Japanese family (*ie*) was a corporate body which was modeled on kinship but functioned on principle intended to insure the survival of the institution.

• The Japanese family has, over the last century, undergone a remarkable change, reflecting the economic, political, and social transformation of the nation.

• Elements of traditional domestic organization persist, however, not only in the modern family, but also in other institutions.

II. MAJOR TOPICS

THE TRADITIONAL JAPANESE FAMILY: THE IE

The Japanese term for the "traditional family" is *ie* (pronounced "ee-eh"). The term is similar to the English word "house" in that it can mean the building in which people live or it can have the more figurative sense of a family as ongoing institution, as in the case of the royal houses of Europe. The *ie* as domestic grouping, then, is considerably different from the "nuclear" or "conjugal" group that is ordinarily evoked by the English word "family;" for this reason, and other reasons to follow, the Japanese term will continue to be used here.

The *ie* is, first and foremost, a corporate body. While each nuclear family necessarily is transformed into others, or ended, by the marriage and death of its members, the *ie* ideally should continue through the generations. The pivotal role in the institution of the *ie* is that of household head. The head, the retired head, the successor apparent, their spouses and children, and other members of the *ie* each fill roles that are arranged in a clear hierarchy of deference and responsibility. Occupants of roles come and go, but the roles and the *ie* persist.

In premodern Japan, the *ie*, not the individual, was the minimum unit of society. One's social identity was derived from the status of one's *ie* and one's role within that *ie*. The achievements, and sins, of one member could alter the status of the entire *ie*, hence the fate of an individual member was directly linked to the behavior of others. Likewise, one's role in the *ie* significantly affected life inside and outside the family. For example, whatever a young man's individual character or talents might be, his position as firstborn son and, hence, successor designate, ordinarily assured him of preferential treatment.

The *ie* should also be seen as an economic institution, a unit of production. It is made up of not only the personnel but also the resources and economy of the *ie*. The resources might include a house, land, tools, and livestock, or perhaps a restaurant or warehouse of goods. The economy of the *ie* might be farming or entertainment service or retail trade, plus secondary forms of economic production. Resources and participation are allocated so as to insure the survival and prosperity of the *ie*, the corporate family, not according to the needs, wants, or "rights" of its individual members.

FAMILY STRUCTURE

In the jargon of the social sciences the multigenerational, coresident *ie* is a "stem family." While the *ie* is a type of extended family, it is quite distinct from the pattern we might anticipate. Our expectations of an extended family are more likely met in the "joint family" pattern such as is found in China [*See the essay on "Family Organization in China"*]. In this latter case there can be more than one married couple in each generation, e.g., three adult brothers, as well as their wives and children (married and unmarried), might all live together with their parents. In the case of the *ie*, or Japanese "stem family," however, there can be—by definition—no more than one married couple in any given generation. Hence, an *ie* might be made up of a grandparent couple (or widowed individual), one married child with spouse, and one married grandchild, plus any number of unmarried individuals in each generation.

If only one child per generation stays in the *ie* after marriage, who stays and who goes? Ideally, it is the firstborn son who will stay. Not only will he and his wife and children continue to live in the house, but he is groomed from childhood to succeed to the household headship (male primogeniture). Upon the death or retirement of his father, the eldest son enters the role of ultimate authority in *ie* matters. As head, he will stand as public representative of the *ie*, make final decisions on the allocation of *ie* resources, and have power over *ie* members. It is his responsibility to insure that, in turn, he has a successor who takes over headship and continues the *ie*.

And what becomes of nonsuccessor children? Although certain circumstances may permit the younger sons to remain in an affiliated status (see *dōzoku* below), they are normally expected to find an independent source of livelihood and upon marriage they would leave their natal *ie* to join a different *ie* or, more likely, to establish a new *ie* of their own.

Likewise, it is expected in the *ie* system that daughters will marry and, with some exceptions, leave their natal *ie*. If a woman marries a designated successor she will move into his natal household (patrilocality). There is a cliché in East Asia about new brides (*yome*) suffering under the tyranny of their mothers-in-law. The cliché is not without some truth in the case of traditional domestic organizations, and is particularly apt in China, where all women might expect to live, at least temporarily, in the homes of their in-laws. But in Japan, where only one married son remains in any stem family, many brides wed nonsuccessors and the young couple establish a new *ie* in an independent residence (neolocality). One should not, therefore, accept this stereotype of a bride's lot as being applicable to all Japanese women, much less to all women in East Asia.

Relations between *ie* members are based on a very clear hierarchy. Those above may expect to be obeyed and are in turn expected to show benevolence and concern for those below. Those below are expected to be compliant and loyal, while they may expect guidance and aid from those above. Generally speaking, status is a product of age and gender. Elders have authority over juniors; men are of higher status than women. There are two notable exceptions to this generalization. The head of the *ie*, no matter what his age, is the highest authority. And, when a woman marries into her husband's family she is on the lowest rung of the hierarchy, no matter what her relative age (this will change with time, the birth of children, and, most importantly, the succession of her husband to headship).

MEMBERSHIP AND RECRUITMENT IN THE IE

The *ie* includes not only living members, but also the ancestors and yet unborn descendants. Continuity (survival) of the *ie* is the first obligation of the living, out of gratitude to those who went before and benevolent responsibility to those who will follow. Even more unexpected, from an American perspective, is that fact that, while roles in the *ie* are modeled on the roles within the biological nuclear family, distant kin and even non-kin can be members. Shared blood is not a prerequisite for membership in the Japanese stem family, e.g., a biologically unrelated foreman in a farm household or a maid in a merchant house can be a full member of the *ie*.

Ideally, to every *ie* there is born at least one son who grows into a competent adult so that he can take over headship, as well as sire a new generation. But when nature is not kind enough to provide an appropriate successor, other arrangements can be made.

If no children are born at all, a successor may be adopted. What is notable about adoption into an *ie* is that it is an adult of recognized competence, not a child, that is adopted, for the purpose of the adoption is to secure an heir apparent of the *ie*, not to find emotional satisfaction in parenthood. If the *ie* has daughters, but no sons, a man will be brought in as a husband to a daughter, then adopted. An adopted male successor is called a *yōshi*. It is also possible for there to be a son (or sons) who is (are) believed to be inadequate to the task of headship; a more distant kinsman, or even a highly respected non-kin member of the *ie*, may be adopted into the position of successor, thus superseding the biologically closer candidate for headship.

Like a bride, the adopted successor (*yōshi*) abandons the name of his *ie* of birth, takes the name of his new family, and becomes a full member of the adoptive *ie*. Because the *yōshi* enters the *ie* much like a bride—a stranger in the family, without a power base, dependent—being an adopted successor is widely held to be undesirable. On the other hand, becoming an adopted successor may also be seen as providing a viable future for sons who are not destined to become head of their natal *ie*.

MARRIAGE AND DIVORCE

Marriage and procreation are essential to the continuation of an *ie*. Furthermore, through the creation of useful links with other families, the union may improve the social or political or economic circumstances of an *ie*. The decision as to whom one marries, therefore, is not left to the transient passions of the young couple. Instead, marriages are arranged and the couple might not see each other, much less be in love, before the wedding. Mutual affection, even love, may reasonably be expected to grow between a husband and wife through years of shared experience, but love is not necessary to the union. Of course, parents try to take into consideration the feelings of their children in finding them a mate, but the union is ultimately between *ie*, not individuals.

When we accept that marriage is intended, above all else, to insure the continuity of an *ie*—and not to satisfy the romantic desires of individuals—it is easier to understand the expectations and behavior of *ie* members. Marriages are monogamous, but extramarital sexual activity is tolerated (even expected) for men (although never for women). In premodern times a marriage might not be legally registered until the new wife (*yome*) got pregnant, and the groom's *ie* might send the new wife back to her natal *ie* if she did not bear children. Either a *yome* or a *yōshi* might be returned, even after a number of years, if they did not satisfactorily adapt to the ways of their in-laws' house or if they proved incapable of fulfilling their expected tasks. Divorce, however, is rare; after all, assuming that men fulfill their role as *ie* manager and provider, while women prove to be "good wives and wise mothers," personal satisfaction in the husband-wife relationship is not the central issue. Men, however, can get a divorce more easily than women can, on the ground, for example, of adultery.

EXTENDED IE NETWORKS: DŌZOKU

In the discussion of the "traditional Japanese family system," there also arises the issue of extended, formalized relationships between *ie*. This pattern is generally referred to as *dōzoku*, although the word is a scholarly invention used to cover numerous local practices.

A *dōzoku* would ordinarily come into being when it is time for a nonsuccessor child to marry and establish an independent *ie*. If his parent's *ie* is wealthy enough, rather than send their son out to find his own source of livelihood, they may set him up with the resources to start an economically viable *ie*. For example, a prosperous farm *ie* might give a son land and tools, or a successful *ie*-run pharmaceutical business might expand by setting up a retail shop run by a daughter and an adopted son-in-law. The original *ie* is known as the *honke*, "main" or "stem house," while the new *ie* is called the *bunke*, or "branch house." With luck, each *ie* in the *dōzoku* continues through the generations. The *honke* may generate further *bunke*, and each *bunke* can potentially bud off *bunke* in relation to which it would stand as *honke*. Like non-kin members of the *ie*, unrelated *ie* may request, and be accepted in, a *bunke* relationship vis-à-vis another *ie*.

As with the *ie*, it can be seen that the *dōzoku* is less a set of purely kinship-based relations than an economic organization expressed in a kinship mode. A *dōzoku* is initiated under the unusual circumstances where an *ie* has enough economic surplus that it can part with sufficient resources to establish the livelihood of a dependent *ie*. In compensation for the initial endowment or for regular economic support, *bunke* take a subordinate role to the *honke*. All member *ie* of the *dōzoku* are hierarchically ordered based on their relative closeness to the *honke* line. Subordinate *ie* show deference to their superior *ie*, for example by playing supporting parts on ceremonial occasions. More importantly, *bunke* must supply labor and/or materials to the *honke* and defer to the economic strategies of their superiors; on the optimum day for harvesting, for example, *bunke* members first labor in the fields of the *honke*. Interestingly enough, if the fortunes of houses should happen to change over time, the *dōzoku* hierarchy may be reorganized to reflect economic predominance, rather than biological relatedness or historical development.

VARIATION AND CHANGE IN THE TRADITIONAL FAMILY

In the discussion thus far, the predominant features of what is recognized as the "traditional Japanese family system," the *ie/dōzoku* system, have been presented. Before proceeding, a consideration of the meaning of "traditional" will be helpful. The word is all too often applied naively to some vague past for which the issue in question is assumed to have always been true, for all the people, throughout the society. But when, for example, do we find the "traditional American family"? In the 1950s? Before World War II? Before the turn of the century? Would the family configuration be the same for the rural poor family as for the suburban middle class family or urban upper class family? Would expectations of the family be the same in Connecticut, Kansas, and California? When dealing with familiar topics, it is obvious that there is variation in social institutions over time, class, and region. To speak with any validity about "the traditional family" in Japan, one must recognize the possibility of the same degree of variability.

The multigenerational, coresidential stem family pattern never was, and never could be, the universal form of Japanese domestic organization. The *ie* system was, instead, a frequently achieved cultural ideal reflecting class and political ideology. It is also a scholarly model, a useful aid in academic analysis. The *ie* system should not be reified, however, into a static description of all Japanese domestic organization.

To the extent that the *ie* system ever had any universality, it was during a relatively brief historical period (1898–1947) when it was the legal norm. To better understand variability and change in family structure, we will simplify Japanese history into three periods: Premodern (1603–1868), Prewar (1868–1947), and Postwar (1947 to the present).

Premodern. Premodern Japan, for our purposes, is coincidental with the Tokugawa Period (1603–1868). At that time Japan was a feudal society. Most of the population were farmers (about 80 percent) living in rural hamlets, governed by samurai bureaucrats (6 percent) who lived in castle towns along with merchants and artisans (10 percent). The *ie* ideal was essentially a samurai model for domestic organization. Yet because stem family practices so successfully protect *ie* resources from dispersal, the most prosperous families in any class aspired to a samurai-like pattern. The poor managed as best they could.

In matters of marriage there was considerable class difference.

Samurai families adhered most closely to the arranged marriage model, with the betrothal being negotiated by parents, and acquiesced to by the young couple, for the good of the *ie*. Peasant marriages, on the other hand, were based on love. When romance developed between a young couple of the same hamlet (interhamlet marriages were strongly opposed), representatives of the young men's group would recommend a union to the respective families. If a family objected, the youth group would refuse to lend its labor in such absolutely vital tasks as rethatching the family roof until the parents capitulated.

There were also significant regional variations in *ie* practices. For example, male primogeniture predominated as a pattern of succession, but in certain areas of northeastern Honshu the first child, be it male or female, stayed in the family and brought in a mate, while all others moved out. On the southern coast of Japan there were also areas of (predominantly male) ultimogeniture, where the last child born would succeed.

Of equal importance to acknowledging the temporal, class, and regional variation in the *ie* system is recognizing that, by the very developmental nature of family life, not everyone could be living in the idealized multigenerational *ie* of head, retired head, and successor, each with a wife and unmarried children. Nonsuccessor sons regularly established new households without any possibility of being joined by the senior generation. The living die; babies do not get conceived. The best laid family plans are thwarted or delayed. Thus, while many people may have spent part of their lives in a multigenerational *ie*, at any given time, many did not.

Likewise, the *dōzoku*, the model of hierarchically organized and reciprocally dependent *ie*, was, in fact, exceptional.

Prewar. Prewar, or early modern, Japan would ordinarily date from the Meiji Restoration (1868) to the end of World War II (1945). Certainly the rush to modernization following the Meiji Restoration initiated many of the economic, social, and political forces that would produce the postwar family pattern. Yet for our purposes, a more significant period within this larger historical context opens in 1898 and closes in 1947. The former date marks the promulgation and enforcement of the Meiji Civil Code books on relatives and inheritance, while the postwar Constitution of 1947 brought the legal demise of the *ie* system. Meiji oligarchs turned to the West for much of their legal system, then they looked inward for family law. Under the Meiji Civil Code, customary samurai *ie* patterns became the law of the land. For the first

time male primogeniture was required. Heads of peasant households, who once had functioned simply as the formal spokesmen
in collective family decisions, now found themselves legally invested with power over the lives of *ie* members.

Just because laws existed in the Civil Codes does not mean
that people behaved according to the law. But for the first time, at
the turn of the century, for a period just short of fifty years,
samurai practices— which today are naively assumed to have been
universally "traditional"— became through legal fiat, the requisite
pattern of family organization.

Postwar. The postwar period has seen the removal of all the legal
supports of the *ie* system and the recision of authority of the
household. The new Constitution of 1947, in essence, declared
the individual and not the *ie* to be the minimum unit of society.
Marriages are to be made through the free will of both partners.
Marriage is explicitly based on the equality of the sexes, as are the
grounds for divorce. Consent of the household head is not necessary for the marriage of legal adults (at age 20). Unitary inheritance by the first son has been replaced. Under article 900 of the
contemporary Civil Code, if a person dies without leaving a will,
the surviving spouse (wife or husband) is entitled to one half of
the inheritance, and children inherit equal proportions of the remainder. Similar distribution is granted as forced shares in the
case of a contested will.

It should not be assumed, however, that in the postwar period,
any more than in the prewar period, legal statute is reflected in
universal behavior. Unitary inheritance is much less common,
because there is seldom a family economy to preserve; where
there is an enterprise that would be destroyed by divided inheritance, it is not uncommon for "nonsuccessor" children to sign
away their claim to inheritance. In exchange, the heir (whoever it
may be) provides his siblings with an education, perhaps a financial start, and takes care of the parents in their old age. While the
law guarantees that the grounds for divorce are equal for both
partners, financial settlement practices (small lump sum, no ali-
mony) and custody rules (no joint custody, presumption that the
initiator of divorce will not get custody) discourage women from
ending an unhappy marriage.

But it is not only the legal supports of the *ie* system that have
changed. So too have the social, economic, and political bases for
much of the *ie* system. Approximately 80 percent of *ie* were rural,
farming households in the Tokugawa Period while today barely 6

percent of families farm. As one might expect, the Japanese family has been transformed by the processes of urbanization, industrialization, and Westernization so that the demographic structure of the family looks much like that in the West. The modern Japanese term for "family" (*kazoku*) defines a social reality much closer to American preconceptions than does the term *ie*.

POSTWAR CHANGES IN THE FAMILY

What, then, has Japanese domestic organization come to look like? With the *ie* system officially gone, what has changed? And what has remained the same?

For one thing, the size of the family has declined. Although the number of members in the **average** *ie* was never as high as the ideal, the size has declined steadily in the postwar period, for a number of reasons. To begin with, Japanese women are having fewer babies, down from average of over four in the 1940s to fewer than two in the 1980s. A decline in fertility correlates, worldwide, with the growth of industrialization. Peasants need children to take care of them in their old age and they need to have many children to insure that some survive to maturity. Children on a farm can also add valuable labor to the household economy (for example, by tending flocks) from an early age. Modern, industrialized nations have social security programs, old age insurance, company pensions, and other alternatives to reliance on one's children. Infant mortality is reduced to a negligible level, hence those children that are born usually reached adulthood. Furthermore, children are usually a financial burden on a family in an industrial economy because their labor is of little value until they are into early adulthood if they pursue higher education.

The number of multigenerational households in postwar Japan is also in decline, further diminishing the size of the average family. In the last thirty years the number of families with three generations living together has dropped from almost half to approximately 15 percent. Concomitantly, there has been a steady growth in households of singles and of couples without children. The net result has been a drop in average household size from five persons in the 1950s to just over three, and a steady nuclearization of the Japanese family.

Just as the size and configuration of households have changed, so too have roles and relationships within the family. Since the *ie* has diminished in importance, marriage has become less an issue of conjoining households than of individual preferences. During

World War II approximately 70 percent of marriages were arranged (*omiai*) while 30 percent were "love" (*renai*) marriages; today those proportions are reversed. The issue of succession does not arise in the families of wage earners, there being few *ie* resources to govern. Most couples begin married life in a new residence of their own, so few women spend their adult life in servitude to a tyrannical mother-in-law. The separation of gender roles has been exacerbated in the modern family, at least as compared with circumstances where men and women work side by side in a family economy. Men, as wage earners who are absent from home much of the time, try to create an aura of family authority, although they have no legal claim to power. Women, as mothers at home raising children, take proprietary control of domestic arrangements. The husband/wife bond is still not as strong as the American ideal and, whereas the essential relationship of the *ie* was that between head and successor, in the contemporary Japanese family the emotional bonds between mother and children have become extremely (some would say pathologically) powerful.

PERSISTENCE OF THE IE IDEAL

Yet, despite the apparent "modernization" of the Japanese family, the *ie* ideal continues to shape practices inside the family and out. Where economics justify keeping a business "in the family," junior and senior generations tend to live together or in very close proximity. Also, while most Japanese families are, at any given time, nuclear, many Japanese still spend part of their lives in a modified stem family. It remains the common practice for aged parents to live with one of their children. Therefore, a child might live in a nuclear family only to about the age of ten, when grandparents move in, creating a three-generation household. That child might marry in his/her mid-twenties and begin a new nuclear family, but fifteen or twenty years later, his/her parents move in, once again forming a three-generation household. And, for a while, after the death of the parents and the departure of the children, the family comprises simply the middle-generation who, in turn, might eventually move in with their children and grandchildren, to live out the final years in a three generational family.

IE-LIKE ELEMENTS IN OTHER INSTITUTIONS

The persistence, or recrudescence, of *ie*-like elements in nonfamily contexts is an important aspect of contemporary Japanese society. It is common to establish one's relative social position for interaction by addressing strangers by kin terms. For example, one may get the attention of a waitress by calling her "older sister" or offer to help an elderly woman and address her as "granny." More fundamental than the use of kin terminology is the formation of hierarchical relations that are well recognized as recapitulating familial relations. The *senpai/kohai* relationship, as between students of different grades or coworkers with different degrees of seniority, is modeled on that of older and younger brothers; the junior shows deference while the senior aids the junior in learning the ways of the institution. Even more explicitly familial is the *oya/ko*, or "parent/child," relationship. In this case, there is significant status difference between the senior and the junior; the junior is expected to show great loyalty and commitment to the senior who, in turn, should always be looking out for the "child's" best interests. The *oya/ko* quality is the essence of relationships between master and disciple or boss and worker, but the most striking example of such relationships is in the world of organized criminals (*yakuza*), where low-level gangsters commit themselves to the service of a higher level boss, and the parties refer to each other as "child" and "parent."

It is also widely recognized that Japanese business organizations have both spontaneously, and self-consciously, taken on qualities of the *ie*. Members of large firms, like members of *ie*, derive their social identity as much (if not more) from the status of the institution than from their specific professional skills. In Japan, the success or failure of a company can directly influence the perceived social status of its employees to an extent incomprehensible to most Americans.

Japanese firms, especially those that have life-time employment policies, do everything possible to encourage loyalty; hard work of their employees, including fostering a familial ideology, and the concept of the enterprise as "one *ie*" (*ikka*) is taken quite seriously. Such enterprises resonate with expectations of familiar intracompany relations because, like the *ie*, the company consists of not just personnel, but also resources and shared economic endeavor. The company is paternalistic; work relations go beyond mere contractual labor for pay. Expulsion from a firm, as from a family, is not done except for truly egregious misconduct. A clear hierarchy of status governs relations, with status and remuneration based not so much on productivity as on seniority. Slightly senior members, like older brothers, are expected to form *senpai/kohai* relations of assistance with their junior colleagues.

Managers take parental (*oya*) interest in the lives of their employees, for example, by taking responsibility for finding them marriage partners.

III. ISSUES FOR DISCUSSION

1. It is a misleading cliché that all Asians live in "extended families." What is the nature of the extended family in Japan? How does it compare with the Chinese case? To what extent do Japanese live in multigenerational families?

2. In terms of the organization of the *ie*, what were the functions the family served in premodern Japan? How does that compare with the contemporary family in Japan? In the United States?

3. Convergence theory predicts that modernization will produce the same family patterns everywhere. How well do the Japanese data fit this theory?

4. We tend to see kinship as coterminous with biological relatedness and family, and as having little significance outside those spheres. To what degree is the *ie* a kin unit? To what degree are other Japanese institutions familial?

IV. SELECTED READINGS

Befu, Harumi. *Japan: An Anthropological Introduction.* New York: Harper and Row, 1971 (faculty background). Although the contemporary material is now dated, this book has an excellent chapter on kinship and the *ie* system.

Bernstein, Gail Lee. *Haruko's World: A Japanese Farm Woman and Her Community.* Stanford: Stanford University Press, 1983 (student reading). This delightful ethnograph of life in a contemporary farm family is always popular with undergraduates. There is relatively little presentation of generalizations about family, and the focus really concerns farm life in the context of modern Japan, but with explanatory lectures, this can be a very useful text.

Bestor, Theodore C., ed. *Teaching Guide on the Japanese Family.* New York: The Japan Society, 1988 (faculty background). Intended as a teachers' guide to accompany a film series on the Japanese family, this pamphlet provides an overview of domestic organization, as well as analyses of three films (*Early Summer, Mother, Family Game*) that are available for classroom use.

Hendry, Joy. *Marriage in Changing Japan.* Rutland, VT, and Tokyo: Charles E. Tuttle Company, Inc., 1981 (student and faculty reading). This ethnograph presents the empirical data on marriage in village in Kyushu as well as abstractions concerning the history of marriage and family. Pertinent generalizations are dispersed throughout the book and it is too long for a single assignment. However, it might work well in the context of a larger unit on rural life.

Hendry, Joy. *Understanding Japanese Society*. London: Croom Helm Ltd., 1987 (faculty and student reading). This anthropological introduction to Japan has a short chapter on the family system that would be an appropriate assignment for undergraduates.

Long, Susan Orpett. *Family Change and the Life Course in Japan*. Ithaca: Cornell University, China-Japan Program, East Asia Papers #44, 1987 (faculty background). An excellent review of the issues and models of Japanese domestic organization used in sociological and historical study.

Nakane, Chie. *Kinship and Economic Organization in Rural Japan*. London: Athlone Press, London School of Economics Monographs on Social Anthropology #12, 1967 (faculty and student reading). This book is a classic, an extensive and detailed analysis of kinship and the *ie* system in a farm setting.

Vogel, Suzanne H. "Professional Housewife: The Career of Urban Middle Class Japanese Women," *The Japan Interpreter* 12 (1978): 16–43 (student reading). An excellent summary of the ideal family home life of the white collar worker (*sarariman*) and his stay-at-home wife. This material is particularly useful and important in compensating for the unfortunate preponderance on rural families.

Anthropology: Korea

Changing Gender Relations: The Korean Case

Laurel Kendall

I. INTRODUCTION: CENTRAL POINTS

In common with other East Asians, Koreans cite their Confucian tradition, either in blame or rationalization, as the source of women's subordination, both past and present. But both in the past and in the present, the lives of Korean women often confound the stereotypical expectations of a Confucian society. The Korean case bids us, once again, to look beyond an articulate ideology of female subordination to the varied and contradictory substance of women's lives. Significant dimensions of Korean women's experience have always fallen outside the Confucian gaze. In contemporary Korea, a selective reading of the past justifies women's subordination in transformed social circumstances, but this reading is actively contended by a lively women's movement.

Some common aphorisms defining woman's place are cited throughout the Confucian world and echoed in nearly every depiction of Korean women: "Man is respected and woman abased." "A man is as high as the heavens and woman, like the earth, is to be trod upon." "A woman follows her father before marriage, her husband after marriage, and her son in widowhood." Confucian ideology is mustered to "explain" the hardships endured by women in traditional peasant families, and to account for discrimination in education and employment today. The assumed docility of dutiful daughters has been touted internationally to encourage foreign investment in industries capitalizing upon the cheap labor of young unmarried Korean women. Son preference persists in the face of stringent family planning, facilitated by new reproductive technologies.

But the Korean roots of this tradition are no deeper than a few centuries, introduced by the founders of the Choson dynasty (1392–1910) as a blueprint for social reform. While the social institutions that evolved as a consequence of the "Confucian transformation" bear much in common with those of China, subtle but significant variations in the structure of social relationships gave Korean women a more positive image as actors in family and ritual life. A tenacious female-centered ritual complex, with female shamans as its professional specialists, has long enjoyed an uneasy coexistence with male-centered Confucian rites.

In the modern period, while education and employment opportunities have opened worlds of experience to women, the older assumption that male and female inhabit separate spheres imposes constraints upon the employment and career opportunities of married women. With respect to marriage, young women favorably compare courtship and consent to the more restrictive circumstances under which their mothers and grandmothers married. A few voices of alarm have been raised, however, as women follow their Western counterparts in accepting market standards of commoditized beauty as a measure of self-worth in a competitive marriage market.

Korea thus provides an excellent example of how assumptions of a uniform and static "tradition" obscure gender relationships through time and across social classes. Because Korea shares with China both Confucian ideology and many related institutions, the Korean case also forces a comparative consideration of the degree to which this common heritage defined (and did not define) women's lived experiences, both in the past and in the present. Finally, because Korea has shifted from a predominantly rural to majority urban, underdeveloped to industrial society in the space of one generation, it provides a bold and immediate example of the impact of this transformation upon a gendered division of labor, marriage, and family life.

II. MAJOR TOPICS

THE CONFUCIAN TRANSFORMATION

The evolution of a "Confucian" family system during the Choson period (or Yi Dynasty, 1392–1910) transformed the status and social experience of Korean women. Both advocates and iconoclasts cite Korea's Confucian heritage to explain the present circumstances of Korean women. In the Confucian scheme, fathers transmit family honor and ancestral virtue to their sons through an unbroken line of male-linked kin. Sons repay their debt of gratitude through filial piety. Sons accept the father's authority for the sake of family welfare and reputation. Sons support aging parents. Sons sustain the living family's link with the past through periodic offerings of wine and rice to the family's ancestors, and sons sustain the family's link with the future by providing male heirs. From a male perspective, membership in the Confucian family is lifelong, indeed more than lifelong, for the boy who grows up to become a patriarch will, in season, be commemorated as an ancestor. There is thus an unambiguous preference for boy babies over girls, an unambiguous acknowledgment of the social and ritual worth of brothers over sisters, of men over women.

Women experienced traditional family life as discontinuity, a daughter lost the known world of her natal home and community, and was exiled to a potentially hostile new environment. Daughters were called *chulga woein*, "once married out, a stranger." Although to varying degrees, they maintained ties with their own kin and, with their knowledge of two distinct communities, women were instrumental in matchmaking.

Before the modern period, even fifty years ago, a woman was married young, often in her mid-teens, the better to learn the customs of strangers. The marriages of brides and grooms who were little more than children were appropriately considered a family matter. Matches were made by the elders of the house, with an eye toward prestigious alliances among the upper classes and a concern for strength, endurance, and resourcefulness among the lower. The very poor might sell a daughter in childhood, to be raised by her future mother-in-law.

By Confucian precept, separation and complementarity characterize the ideal relationship between husband and wife. In an earlier Korea, this distinction relegated the upper-class wife to the innermost courtyard of the house from which she ventured forth under a face-concealing veil or in a closed palanquin. A woman's relative invisibility was a measure of personal honor and family reputation. At the other end of the social spectrum, bond servants or slaves (who made possible the sequestered life style of the highborn lady), peddlers' wives, and peasant women hard at work appear in genre paintings and early photographs with bare heads, shorter skirts, and brief jackets. Occasionally, the painter portrays such women beside a steam, bared to the waist as they bathe or wash clothes. Also visible were dancing girls (*sadang*), courtesans (*kisaeng*), and shamans (*mudang, mansin*), practitioners of despised (*ch'ŏn*) professions who sang and danced in public.

Neither the construction of kinship as an exclusive linkage of fathers and sons, nor the subordination of wives to their husbands' kin, nor the rigid sequestering of upper-class women was a Korean practice until the seventeenth century. In the preceding Koryŏ (918–1392) and early Choson periods, daughters were both valued and valuable; they inherited family property in their own right, along with their brothers, and participated in family rituals for their ancestors. Although she married young, a woman's early married life was spent among her own kin; she joined her husband's family as a full adult who had already proven her worth by producing children. Sons-in-law could be regarded as members of the wife's family with none of the onus that would accrue to adopted-in sons-in-law in later centuries. Divorced and widowed women remarried without social stigma and veiling was not a common practice.

The Confucian transformation is known, almost exclusively, through documentary evidence of the lives of upper-class women. Even so, it provides a powerful example of a relatively recent reformist agenda, in many respects antithetical to what had gone before, that came to wield the authority of "ancient custom."

WOMEN IN HOUSEHOLDS

In an earlier Korea, the bride and groom were strangers who met for the first time on their wedding day, a not unusual circumstance in rural Korea even thirty years ago. A person of more immediate consequence for the bride than the groom, whose face she might not recognize in daylight until months after the wedding, was the mother-in-law whose favor she had to win by diligence and obedience. As with any novice, the bride's actions were carefully scrutinized and critically appraised. The birth of her first male child was impatiently anticipated, and sometimes encouraged through rituals, prayers, tonics, and moxibustion.

The relationship of a brother's wife and a husband's sister was also potentially difficult. Initially, the unmarried sister was in a position of strength vis-à-vis the new bride, potentially jealous, and capable of telling tales to subvert the new bride's good intentions. But from the sister's perspective, the bride's arrival was a harbinger of her own fate, and if her mother was already dead, the sister's subsequent marriage rested precariously in the hands of the brother's wife who would arrange the match. Over time, the brother's wife would become the gatekeeper who governed the married sister's access to her natal home and her recourse to the resources and support of her own kin.

The word *sijipsari*, "life in the in-laws' house," is sometimes used in common speech to connote any difficult and trying new situation. The difficulty of traditional *sijipsari* was compounded by the bride's isolation from her own kin and community. But *sijipsari* was a training period, and there was an end to it. All but the first son and his family were expected to leave the parents' home in sequence, when they and their wives had attained maturity, maintaining ties of "family" through labor exchange and ritual veneration of their common ancestors. In good times, the new household would be endowed with a house site and lands in the same community. Unlike the Chinese, Koreans never idealized the family as a collectivity of grown sons living harmoniously together under one roof. As a consequence, Koreans never shared in the Chinese view of women as dark, destructive forces who pulled the family apart with their quarrels. In Korea, inequalities of inheritance were a function of the acknowledged inequality of brothers, the senior brother being favored as the primary heir, the eventual head of the "big house."

The certainty that *sijipsari* would end, and the existence of clear hierarchical relationships among women, probably also diminished the real level of tension among coresident brothers' wives. Ethnographers usually describe this relationship as close and cooperative, not marked by the ferocious quarrels described in Chinese ethnography.

The wife of a second or third son could anticipate becoming the mistress of her own home, eventually managing her own household and honoring her own household gods. The wife of the eldest son and primary heir endured a longer tenure under her mother-in-law's roof, but she became the mistress of the main house upon the older woman's death or retirement. Then, as the respected "senior mother" or "senior grandmother" of the family, she would be a source of advice and council among the subordinate kin. The wives of eldest sons, and especially the wife of the first son of the senior line of a local lineage, the eventual lineage head, were selected with particular care. Because the head household led the lineage in its social, moral, and ritual life, heris' wives were formidable women who managed large and complex households where the hospitality given guests and the quality of ancestral offerings were measures of family reputation.

Whatever the hierarchical status of her household, a Korean wife's abilities as a hard worker and frugal manager were recognized as a measure of the prosperity, harmony, and reputation of her household. While women in the West have been idealized as the bearers of civilizing impulses in a world governed by pragmatic, often loutish, men, Confucian Koreans saw males as the more cultivated gender whose flights of idealism might be counterpoised to the earthy common sense of their wives.

The wife's traditional role as pragmatic manager, however, can be a double-edged sword in present-day Korea. While it may be advantageous for a wife to receive her husband's paycheck and thereby save him from excesses of hospitality, and while it is also assumed, at least tacitly, that women will attempt to maximize the family's capital through investment, the financial activities of women are viewed with deep suspicion. Whether it be the usually innocuous activities of traditional rotating credit associations (kye), more serious speculation in real estate and investment, or conspicuous consumption in the preparation of a daughter's dowry, the financial dealings of women often appear in the media under the banner of "social problem."

RITUAL LIFE

Korean women have maintained a body of largely unwritten ritual practices that affirm the mistress of the household as a positive presence who acts on behalf of the entire domestic group. Women's religious traditions include honoring a collectivity of household gods for the health, harmony, and prosperity of the domestic group, making offerings at shaman shrines, Buddhist temples, and on sacred mountains, and sponsoring major shaman rituals. Birth and menstruation, pollutions associated with women's bodies, impose only temporary limitations upon these sacred activities and on the work of female shamans. Although excluded from the core Confucian ritual of ancestor veneration, women, through their rituals, deal with the dead as suffering and potentially harmful presences who must be distanced from the living and released from hell. The link between the living and the articulate, aggrieved dead, is maintained by female professional shamans who also invoke and placate the gods of home and community.

Official (male) attitudes toward female ritual have varied with time and circumstance. Dynastic officialdom disapproved of dancing shamans and their potentially fraudulent rituals, but folklore recounts how some of these same officials recanted in a moment of personal crisis or when confronted with a particularly compelling performance. Twentieth century progressives, both male and female, saw these activities as "superstition," an obstacle to progress and a measure of the degradation of Korean womanhood. More recently, Korean scholars have lauded these same practices as embodying the ancient spirit of the Korean people; for some, ancient shamans were thus necessarily male. Korean feminists cognizant of Western writing on "goddess religion," on the other hand, have very recently begun to regard shaman practices and women's rituals as a repository of Korean female strength and inspiration.

Women have also played an important role in the phenomenal spread of Korean Christianity—roughly 25 percent of today's South Korean population is Christian—both as proselytizing "Bible women" and as visible and active members of congregations, although only recently have they been accepted into the higher levels of the church hierarchy. Some Korean theologians fault "women's Christianity" as being larded with "superstitious" elements derived from women's older religious tradition. Syncretistic elements may be discerned in Pentecostal groups where inspired women give healings and lead prayer groups. Because of the Korean missions' early commitment to education, including education for women, a Christian background often figures in the biography of a distinguished female educator or social reformer.

CONTEMPORARY MARRIAGE

In south Korea today, the men and women who marry are young adults, not children; they have been educated, have some experience of the world, and many have an earning capacity independent of the family enterprise. These changes insure that the modern bride's experience of the Korean family will be very different from the traditional expectations described above and, indeed, from the experiences of many Korean women barely a generation ago. Contemporary courtship practices, even for matchmade couples, encourage affection and romantic anticipation; the new wife now has a claim on her husband's affections that may best that of her mother-in-law.

Conversations about matrimony in Korea turn on the distinction made between "love marriage" (*yŏnae*) and "matchmade" (*chungmae*). Like practices that have emerged in twentieth century Japan, China, and Taiwan, modern Korean matchmaking implies a formal first meeting of the intended couple, representatives of their families, and the matchmaker, followed by an opportunity for the couple to converse in private and then decide whether to pursue a courtship. Matchmaking seems to flourish among the upper-middle-class, where men with good prospects are wed to daughters of wealthy families.

Most matchmakers are amateurs, a mother's friend or a relative. Professional marriage bureaus (*kyorhon sangdamso*) claim that the services they provide are suited to the needs of modern people who live apart from family and community. The most notorious of all professional matchmakers are those known as Madame Ttu (Madame Procuress), women who claim huge fees for matching the sons and daughters of the wealthy and powerful. The stereotype of the female matchmaker, at once positive and negative, is in many respects similar to that of the female shaman; both are noted for their keen perception and way with words, but are also suspect as potential deceivers and avaricious manipulators.

Student culture favors romance, but graduation may bring an end to all but the most sincere courtships. Men face compulsory military service and, often, additional professional training. Middle-class women, however, are encouraged to marry by the age of twenty-four and when they declare their intention of waiting for a college sweetheart, they incur increasing pressure to be matchmade.

Women workers who manage to save toward their dowries view marriage as a gateway to middle-class respectability. Among women with limited prospects, however, particularly those whose earnings have been absorbed by the needs of poor families, consensual unions are common. Although their marriages may be legally registered with the birth of the first child, poverty forces many couples to postpone the wedding ceremony that confers social adulthood. Some social welfare organizations provide free weddings to aid these couples as "good works."

The costs of weddings are not ceremonial alone. Weddings assume at least a token exchange of clothing and jewelry; proper weddings assume extensive exchanges between two families. The bride's family bears the greater burden, providing extensive gifts to the groom and his family as well as the couple's household goods and furnishings. Wedding costs and the variety of ceremonial exchanges have been elaborated over the last two decades. Brides and their families are now seen as investing in the career of a promising groom. The groom's side holds the initiative in courtship, a situation underscored by a new media-engendered emphasis on glamour and charm as criteria of feminine self-worth.

Policymakers and social reformers consider contemporary marriage practices excessive and unwholesome. Popular opinion blames brides and their mothers for fanning the fires of status-enhancing conspicuous consumption. A more sympathetic view holds that insofar as daughters join husbands' families, mothers are pressured to send them in style, lest they incur scorn and humiliation from their in-laws. Cases of physical abuse by husbands who anticipated larger dowries are well-known.

WOMEN AND THE FAMILY IN SOUTH KOREA TODAY

The new bride is far less likely to reside under her mother-in-law's roof, extremely unlikely to do so amid a larger community of husband's siblings and brothers' wives. An average household size of 4.6 suggests that at a given moment in time, most Korean families are nuclear, composed of parents and unmarried children.

With the older age at marriage, life in the in-laws' house ceased to be an extended training period for raw youth. Where some families still seek to instruct a bride through coresidence, the period is brief, usually less than a year. In the years that span Korea's industrial transformation, 1966 to 1980, households including parents and married children declined from 23.31 percent to 16.46 percent of all households. Most noticeable was a decline in the number of households where a married couple resided with both of the husband's parents, from 6.66 to 1.85 percent of all households, suggesting that widows or widowers were joining the households of married children, a later development in the family cycle. That aging, infirm, retired, or widowed parents now join the households of vigorous middle-aged children implies a very different dynamic in the relationship between a young and vulnerable daughter-in-law and a mother-in-law in her prime. Now it is the older woman who expresses anxiety over the potential tyranny of a daughter-in-law.

The implications of kinship for an urban population contrast with those of an agricultural household. In a traditional farming community, the most desirable marriages were with an eldest son, both for the economic advantage of his larger inheritance and for the prestige of his status within the family and local kin group. In modern Korea, these unions are considered the most onerous and a challenge to the matchmaker. In a competitive and inflationary urban setting the old advantage of a larger inheritance and local status pale against the burden of responsibility for aging parents and unmarried siblings.

CHILDREN AND FAMILY PLANNING

Korean feminists complain that women have entered the consciousness of development planners only with respect to family planning. Nevertheless, south Korean family planning is one of the world's success stories. The rate of population increase has dropped from 2.88 per hundred between 1955 and 1960 to 1.56 per hundred between 1980 and 1985. Son preference remains a commonplace of Korean life, and a potential obstacle to family planning; family planning posters celebrate happy one-daughter families. Feminists argue that insofar as population limitation is a national priority, equality of the sexes is also in the national interest. But there are other, grimmer possibilities. A few physicians now acknowledge the use of amniocentesis to monitor female foetuses for selective abortion. (Officially illegal but widely practiced, abortion has, until recently, been a major means of birth control.)

The emergence of urban families with fewer children will likely lead to a different style of parenting, of more attention focused on few children by fewer adults, and almost exclusively by a non-working mother. The bond is enhanced as mothers find it necessary to monitor their children's schoolwork in the face of competitive examinations. The consequences of a pro-natalist society suddenly transformed into a nation of one- or two-child families bears comparison with Japan, which went through a similar change after the Second World War, and with urban China, where similar demographic processes apply but where a larger proportion of mothers are consistently employed outside the home.

WOMEN AND WORK

Insofar as much of the work that women do is invisible, occasional, and either not or only partially remunerated, it often eludes consideration and is underreported in labor force participation statistics. In an earlier Korea, the degree to which a woman's work was public, performed outside the house walls, was a measure of abasement. The sequestered or veiled lady required a servant or slave to draw water from the well, beat laundry in the stream, and visit the market. In peasant households, it was a mark of both affluence and distinction that one's own wife visited the fields only to deliver a copious lunch, but many women of less advantaged households worked at transplanting rice, weeding, and harvesting. Some were even hitched to plows in the absence of oxen.

Early travellers to Korea have remarked upon the range and variety of women's work. Foodstuffs grown in kitchen gardens were processed through a seemingly endless round of drying, salting, or pickling. Cloth was loomed both for domestic consumption and as a medium of exchange and taxation. Clothing was unstitched and then reassembled with each rigorous laundering at the stream bank. Both laundry and needlework were the resources of women who covertly maintained the economic "face" of destitute households. All of these activities could be performed in the respectable confines of a woman's realm. The following woman-identified professions were performed in the public sphere at the cost of disapprobation.

The *kisaeng* (artist-courtesan) and the *mudang* (shaman) were considered outcast professions requiring women to perform in public for pay, but *kisaeng* were valued for their artistic and literary accomplishments, and *mudang* were the sacred vehicles of the gods and ancestors. Women peddlers have a long history in Korea, both as members of the peddling associations that monopolized long-distance trade in the last century, and as casual workers hawking produce, the products of cottage industry, food, or water. Some form of peddling has carried many Korean women and their families through the hardships of war, abandonment, widowhood, or economic failure.

On Cheju Island, where men are long absent at sea or on the mainland, diving women participate in a distinctively female profession that vests them with economic independence and a strong sense of collective female self-worth. In contrast to the mainland agriculturalist's standard of patrilineal kinship, Cheju families have been described as "matrifocal." Mainlanders consider the strength and independence of island women to be further testimony to the lack of propriety found in seaside villages.

WOMEN WORKERS TODAY

South Korean women are found in virtually all occupational fields and, in most instances, in steadily increasing numbers. Their numbers are small in engineering, security work, driving, welding, and tool and machine production, all perceived to be "masculine" occupations. They constitute the vast majority of workers in textile and garment production, telephone operation, accounting, nursing, stenography and typing, domestic service, and unpaid farm labor. Many women are in the less-favored "informal sector," working as petty traders, domestics, or casual labor.

Korean women earn far less than Korean men. This is due, in part, to the lesser value accorded female-dominated jobs, in part, to the fact that women are often expected to terminate regular employment upon marriage, with little seniority. In 1985, the average male wage was 386,346 won, while that of female workers was 180,319 won, well below half, a pattern that has been consistent throughout the period of industrialization.

FACTORY WORK

Although small numbers of young, unmarried women have worked in Korean factories and in the service sector since the colonial period, an unprecedented number of young women came to the cities seeking wage work beginning in the late 1960s. Without this pool of cheap, educated, and initially docile female labor the south Korean economic miracle could not have taken place.

As elsewhere in Asia, a daughter's wage work must be understood in the context of family economic strategies as her potential contribution to maintenance, the education of younger siblings, and her own dowry. On the other hand, a work life outside family supervision and with even residual pocket money introduces the working daughter to a new youth culture where the definitions and expectations of womanhood are renegotiated.

As in other developing economies, one of the attractions of young women workers to their prospective employers is the likelihood that they will marry in their mid-twenties and terminate regular employment. Salary increments based on seniority will reach an early ceiling, and workers without any long-term interest in their occupation will be less inclined to agitate for better conditions and pay. Korean working women have not, however, been docile.

Unions have been most effective in organizing women in the

textile and garment industries. The late 1970s saw numerous strikes and protests by women workers. In 1979, the death, under suspicious circumstances, of a woman protester from the Y. H. Trade Company ignited a firestorm of discontent, contributing to the collapse of the Park Chung-hee regime. In the face of severe suppression of labor activities in the early 1980s, union membership by women workers suffered a gradual decline, picking up again in the climate of labor unrest that marked the end of the Chun regime in 1987. Organizers now face the added burden of criticism that agitation for higher wages is driving multinational investors from Korea.

MARRIED WOMEN AND WORK

The assumption that middle-class respectability implies a non-working wife is not unique to Korea, although traditionalists will ascribe it to the logic of the old Confucian dichotomization of female and male spheres as "inside" and "outside" space. Married women who work out of necessity are nearly always restricted to the less-favored "informal sector," working as petty traders, domestics, or casual labor. A married woman may find herself doing piecework for a subsidiary firm under contract to the factory that paid her a better wage before her marriage. The bias against continued regular employment after marriage and the contradictory possibility that some married women will need to work insures the existence of a trained, fluid, and immanently exploitable female labor pool on the margins of industrial employment.

RURAL WORKING WOMEN

In rural south Korea in 1985, there were 160 men between the ages of 20–24 for every 100 women in the same age group. Rural daughters who have gone to the cities seeking work are increasingly reluctant to marry back into the countryside. The inability of rural bachelors to lure a wife back to the farm has attracted national media attention.

While rural women of even middle age will readily cite the numerous improvements in domestic work wrought by electric appliances, easy-care fabrics, and ready-made clothing, the amount and variety of agricultural work done by women who remain in or return to the countryside has risen steadily over the last two decades as a consequence of the rural labor shortage. Sixty percent of all unpaid female workers are in agriculture, although the figure has declined more than 10 percent in the last six years as a consequence of the scarcity of women in the countryside. Most rural women work as unpaid family labor on farms managed by husbands, fathers, or sons. Like other working women, they bear the dual burden of household responsibilities and their extra-domestic tasks.

Rural women remain nearly invisible to the gaze of development planners. Power tools are developed to facilitate the traditionally male tasks of plowing and harvesting. Men are given both training in the new technologies and access to loans to purchase the new equipment. Women's work, both in the home and in the field, is not a development priority.

WOMEN'S MOVEMENT

South Korean feminism betrays many of the cleavages of opinion that have appeared in the American movement. An older reformist tradition, identified with legal and social welfare issues, claimed it's most significant victory in the 1989 reform of the Korean Family Law. Another Culture, a collective of scholars, writers, and artists begun in the 1980s, has challenged the gendered premises of Korean life from the writing of poetry to linguistic usage within the family. The separatist stand of Another Culture is criticized by members of the Marxist-oriented Women Students' Movement, whose spokeswomen argue that women must work within the larger struggle to transform the fundamental social and economic inequalities of Korean life. Another Culture counters (with the familiar argument) that women's issues will necessarily be slighted when women accept uncritically the hegemony of a movement led by men. These two intellectual polarities exist in an uneasy alliance with grass roots women's organizations emerging from the labor movement, farmers' movement, and consumer's movement under the banner of Korean Women United. Attempts by this broad, synthetic organization to define a direction have provoked an ongoing debate that testifies to the vitality and complexity of women's issues in Korea beneath the simplicity of Confucian clichés.

III. ISSUES FOR DISCUSSION

1. "Confucian" ideology is usually described as the source of Korean gender relations both in the past and in the present. Is this an adequate and complete explanation?

2. In what ways are changes in how Koreans marry linked to other changes in the way Koreans live (e.g., education, work, migration, residence after marriage).

3. In what ways have Korean women's life experiences been defined and circumscribed by their social class, both in the past and in the present.

IV. SELECTED READINGS

NOTE: Much of the material on Korean Women is published in Korea. Your best source for ordering it is the Royal Asiatic Society, Korea Branch. C. P. O. Box 255, Seoul, Korea. Allow at least two months for shipping.

Cho, Uhn, and Hagen, Koo. 1983. *Capital Accumulation, Women's Work, and Informal Economies in Korea.* Working Papers. East Lansing: Michigan State University, April, 1983. For the instructor and interested students.

Chung, Sei-wha. *Challenges for Women: Women's Studies in Korea.* Translated by Shin Chang-hyun et al. Korean Women's Institute Series. Seoul: Ewha Woman's University Press, 1986. Historical articles on the women's movement, and good information on contemporary women and work. For the instructor and interested students.

Committee for the Compilation of the History of Korean Women. *Women of Korea: A History from Ancient Times to 1945.* Edited and translated by Yung-Chung Kim. Seoul: Ewha Woman's University Press, 1977. Summary translation of a longer work in Korean. Positivist history with a slight Christian bias. Useful as a general resource.

Harvey, Youngsook Kim. *Six Korean Women: Biographies of Shamans.* St. Paul: West Pub. Co., 1979. For the instructor and interested students.

Janelli, Roger L., and Janelli, Dawnhee Yim. *Ancestor Worship and Korean Society.* Stanford: Stanford University Press, 1982. Chapter 2 provides a good description of traditional households, for students. Chapters 6 and 7 include a gendered reading of religion, for the instructor.

Kendall, Laurel. *Shamans, Housewives, and Other Restless Spirits: Women in Korean Ritual Life.* Honolulu: University of Hawaii Press, 1985. For the instructor and students with specialized interest.

Kendall, Laurel. "Ritual Silks and Kowtow Money: The Bride as Daughter-in-law in Korean Wedding Rituals." *Ethnology* 24/ 4: 253–268. For the instructor.

Kendall, Laurel. *The Life and Hard Times of a Korean Shaman: Of Tales and the Telling of Tales.* Honolulu: University of Hawaii Press, 1988. Light reading as a prompt to classroom discussion.

Kendall, Laurel, and Peterson, Mark, eds. *Korean Women: A View from the Inner Room.* New Haven: East Rock Press, 1983. Variety of articles on women in families. Of particular interest are the Wagner and Peterson

son articles on the Confucian transformation, Cho's article on diving women, and Harvey's account of adopted daughters-in-law.

Kim, Choong Soon. *Faithful Endurance: An Ethnography of Korean Family Dispersal.* Tucson: University of Arizona Press, 1988. Personal narratives of divided families that can be given a gendered reading, for the instructor and interested students.

Mattielli, Sandra, ed. *Virtues in Conflict: Tradition and the Korean Woman Today.* Seoul: Royal Asiatic Society, Korea Branch, 1977. Articles on a range of topics. Martina Deuchler's description of the Confucian transformation is particularly useful for students.

Research Center for Asian Women. *Women of the Yi Dynasty. Studies on Korean Women Series 1.* Research Center for Asian Women. Seoul: Sookmyung Women's University, 1986. Articles on a range of topics, for the instructor.

Rutt, Richard, and Kim Chong-un. *Virtuous Women: Three Classic Korean Novels.* Seoul: Royal Asiatic Society, Korea Branch, 1974. "The Song of a Faithful Wife" is a rare example of a popular work with a female hero, good for prompting discussion.

Sorensen, Clark W. *Over the Mountains are Mountains.* Seattle: University of Washington Press, 1988. Chapter 5 includes a good description of women's work in peasant households with some indication of change. For the instructor.

Sorensen, Clark W. "The Myth of Princess Pari and the Self-Image of Korean Women" *Anthropos* 83: 403–419. Interpretation of a shaman song featuring a female hero, for the instructor and interested students.

Yu, Eui-Young, and Phillips, Earl H. *Korean Women in Transition: At Home and Abroad.* Los Angeles: Center for Korean-American and Korean Studies, California State University, 1987. All-too-brief accounts of women in the professions, low income women, factory women. Background information for instructor and students with special interests.

II
Economics

Economics:
China and Japan

Japan and China as Case Studies in Introductory Courses in Economics

Thomas G. Rawski

*To accommodate the structure of a wide variety of economics courses, the ECONOMICS section of the Guide has been organized somewhat differently from other sections. Professor Thomas Rawski has identified ten topics that are commonly the subjects of introductory economics courses and suggested how the economic practices of **Japan** and **China** can be used to illustrate basic concepts. Suggested readings are indicated immediately following each subsection. Issues for discussion, covering all ten subject areas, are listed at the end of the entire entry.*

I. COMPARATIVE ECONOMIC SYSTEMS

JAPAN

The case of Japan is excellent for a course in economic systems. It is similar to the United States in industrial structure (small farm sector, huge service sector, urbanized, high educational level, etc.), income level, technology, and many other indicators, but quite different in a number of areas such as labor relations, corporate strategy, and savings behavior.

Labor Relations. We can discuss contrasting models of employer-employee relations. In the "American model," workers are hired as needed on a contract basis. Both employers and workers are free to terminate these relations on short notice. Both sides gain in flexibility. Workers are not strongly loyal to their employer and feel free to quit even if this will harm their employer. Job switch and mid-career lateral transfer are not uncommon and are seen as enhancing upward mobility (of workers) and injecting new ideas into sluggish organizations (benefiting managers). Companies are not loyal to employees, who can be laid off or fired in case of business slowdown, corporate merger, or other exigent circumstance.

In the "Japanese model," employees may be hired for the duration of their careers under the system known as "permanent" or "lifetime employment" when they graduate from junior high, high school, or college. For such workers and their employers, there is a sacrifice of independence and mobility for the sake of assured mutual commitment and stability. Benefits are clear. This system creates unity of long-term interest between workers and management, with both sides knowing that their economic fortunes are inextricably intertwined. This system discourages protracted labor disputes— it is no surprise to find strikes relatively rare under this style of labor contracting. If business is bad or if the nature of business changes, management will transfer workers to different jobs or locations. Workers tend not to insist on restrictive work rules, because they see internal reshuffling as part of an effort to improve the company fortunes which, if successful, will benefit them in the form of higher incomes (semiannual bonuses are linked with company profitability) and the prestige of being associated with a prosperous company.

Important qualification to these contrasting models comes when we recognize that the system of "lifetime employment" covers at most one-fourth of the Japanese work force. Large numbers of Japanese are employed in conditions that include substantial possibility of unexpected dismissal, that do not come under the "seniority wage" system observed in large firms with substantial cadres of permanent employees, etc. Comparisons of U.S. and Japanese blue-collar workers show that the gap between quit rates, for instance, is not as large as might be expected. Also, many American workers and employers develop strong ties of mutual loyalty and maintain long associations. Finally, the Japanese system is under pressure to change. As the pace of structural change accelerates, the costs of long-term employment for worker and company seem to increase, leading to widely publicized instances of dismissals and mass resignations from companies that had previously not experienced such phenomena.

References

Clark, Rodney. *The Japanese Company*. New Haven: Yale University Press, 1979 (student reading).

Cole, Robert E. *Japanese Blue Collar: The Changing Tradition*. Berkeley: University of California Press, 1971 (student reading).

Cole, Robert E. *Work, Mobility and Participation: A Comparative Study of American and Japanese Industry*. Berkeley: University of California Press, 1979 (student reading).

Pascale, Richard, and Rohlen, Thomas P. "The Mazda Turnaround." *Journal of Japanese Studies* 9.2 (1983):219–63 (student reading).

Corporate Strategy. Here again, contrasting U.S. and Japanese models can be used to advantage. On the U.S. side, we think of corporations—financed primarily by self-owned funds (stockholder contributions and retained earnings)—pursuing strategies that place considerable emphasis on short-term financial gain. Executives are acutely conscious of current market performance of their companies' shares, especially because their compensation package frequently includes stock options whose value is directly related to current stock performance. Outside corporate directors add to the pressure to increase current returns, as does the threat of takeover by minority shareholders or corporate raiders motivated by perceived disparity between a corporation's actual worth and the value of its outstanding shares.

The Japanese model is considerably different. Customary levels of corporate indebtedness have long exceeded comparable U.S. norms by substantial amounts. With relatively underdeveloped stock, corporate bond, and venture capital markets, expansion-minded Japanese firms have depended largely on bank loans to raise needed funds. High levels of indebtedness focus corporate attention on rapid expansion of output as a means to lower fixed costs by "spreading overhead" over a larger volume of production. The tendency of Japanese executives to pay less attention to short-term financial results than their U.S. counterparts is reinforced by patterns of shareholding and also by differences in corporate behavior.

Japanese firms typically hold large blocks of shares in other firms with which they conduct regular business. Banks (which, in the United States, are not permitted to hold shares of nonfinancial corporations) hold blocks of stock in their main client firms. Business groupings (called *keiretsu*– like Mitsubishi, Sumitomo, or Hitachi) may hold shares of their fellow group members. The purpose of these holdings is not to achieve short-term gain, but to affirm corporate solidarity and fraternal ties among enterprises linked by business interdependence. With large blocks of stock held in friendly hands and, in general, not for sale under normal market conditions, Japanese executives are far less concerned about hostile takeover or sudden emergence of hostile minority shareholders than are their U.S. counterparts. Shareholder meetings offer no opportunity for "corporate gadflies" to challenge management actions; such behavior is prevented by the presence of *sokaiya*, shady toughs who eject unruly participants from the hall. Furthermore, most corporate directors are insiders– members of management or executives from associated firms. Thus the corporate environment of large Japanese firms is much different from what we observe in the United States, with results that translate into considerable differences in behavior, as illustrated, for example, in the following discussions of topics 4, 5, and 6.

References:

Aoki, Masahiko, ed. *The Economic Analysis of the Japanese Firm.* Amsterdam: North Holland, 1984 (faculty reading).
Clark, Rodney. *The Japanese Company.* New Haven: Yale University Press, 1979 (student reading).

Savings Behavior. The ratio of savings to national income is considerably higher in Japan than in the United States. This is partly because Japanese governments save more than their U.S. counterparts (especially in recent years, when Japan implemented Ronald Reagan's advice by cutting government deficits, while the United States did the opposite under Reagan's presidential leadership). Differences in household savings patterns account for much of the difference between the two national savings rates. Japanese households save far more (as a percentage of household income) than their U.S. counterparts. Furthermore, substantial saving rates are regularly observed even among Japanese households with low incomes, whereas in the United States, only high-income households are substantial net savers (i.e., they save more than they borrow, both in terms of annual flows and of maintaining positive net stocks of financial assets). Although there is no widely accepted explanation for these significant behavioral differences, discussion of possible explanations provides an opportunity for students to exercise their understanding of a variety of theoretical and empirical aspects of the analysis of consumer behavior. The following is a brief list of possible explanatory factors.

a) **Bonus System**. Japanese wage earners receive monthly wage or salary payments. In addition, they are paid large semiannual bonuses (in midsummer and at year's end), each equivalent to several months' regular salary, which resemble the "transitory income" aspect of Milton Friedman's analysis of consumer behavior. If wage earners use monthly income flows to finance regular consumption, they might regard the bonus payments as "transitory" rather than "permanent" income (the payments do fluctuate with company fortunes) and save extremely high fractions of their bonus receipts. This could raise the ratio of savings to income.

b) **Retirement System**. In the past, it was often argued that high savings rates were needed to enable households to compensate for the low level of social security payments to retired persons. Although it is no longer true that Japan's social security system offers far smaller payments than are found in other advanced nations, the retirement system remains different from what is found in the United States and Europe. Most "permanent employees" retire relatively early, often at age 55. On retirement, they receive large lump-sum payments, but no regular pension flows. It is therefore possible that Japanese save unusually large amounts because they cannot expect to receive regular income flows from pension contributions made during their working lives.

c) **Lack of Consumer Credit**. Until very recently, Japanese consumers had little access to bank loans for such purposes as purchase of homes, cars, or other consumer durables. With real estate prices far higher (as a multiple of typical household incomes) than in other industrial nations, high savings rates are essential prerequisites to real estate purchases.

d) **Taxation**. Until recently, the Japanese tax system encouraged saving by exempting substantial amounts of interest income from personal income tax. The U.S. tax system discourages saving by applying full income tax rates to nearly all financial assets. The U.S. system also encourages borrowing, particularly to finance home-buying, by allowing a large (though decreasing) range of personal interest payments to be deducted from personal income before tax is computed, effectively obliging the government to repay a portion of loans that qualify for this special treatment.

References:

Hayashi, Fumio. "Why is Japan's Saving Rate So Apparently High?" with comment by A. Ando and P. Roemer. In *NBER Macroeconomics Annual 1986*, edited by Stanley Fischer, Cambridge: The M.I.T. Press, 1987 (faculty reading).

Sato, Kazuo. "Saving and Investment." In *The Political Economy of Japan, 1: Domestic Transformation*, edited by Kozo Yamamura and Y. Yasuba, Stanford: Stanford University Press, 1987 (faculty reading).

CHINA

The case of China works well in a comparative systems course because a) it is very different from the United States in terms of income level, economic structure, system of resource allocation, attitude toward private enterprise, and many other dimensions, and b), because recent Chinese experience presents enormous contrasts, e.g., between the extreme collectivism of agricultural organization during the Great Leap Forward (1958–60) and the essentially private household farm system of the 1980s. Perhaps the most interesting aspect of the Chinese case comes under the rubric of "plan vs. market," where Chinese experience shows the strengths and limitations of both approaches to economic organization, and also presents fascinating problems of transition from a planned to a more market-oriented system.

Strengths and Weaknesses of Planning. Discussion of this topic can follow familiar lines traced in Soviet history. Indeed, large chunks of standard works such as that by Peter Wiles can be applied to China by simply changing "Moscow" and "Stalin" to "Peking" and "Mao." The history of the People's Republic of China (PRC) displays the advantages of administrative resource allocation in achieving rapid structural transformation of a rather undeveloped economy. Even though recent research shows that China's prewar economy, in which the role of government was quite small, achieved substantial growth in a market environment, there can be no doubt that the market economy could not have matched the rapid expansion of "heavy industry" during the 1950s and early 1960s. After all, when the survival of the United States was last challenged (in World War II), we immediately switched from market allocation to a system of administrative allocation of war-related materials despite the drag on efficiency by the resulting Byzantine bureaucracy. The reason for this is that the quickest way to transfer production from washing machines to mortars is **not** to raise the price of mortars, but to order Maytag, Whirlpool, etc., to produce mortars and deny them access to steel, machine tools, bank loans, or skilled workers for any purpose other than manufacturing weapons. Thus even U.S. experience confirms the superiority of a plan system when rapid structural change is crucial and all other considerations are secondary.

Although the benefits of the plan system are very real, as China's new industrial strength and rising life expectancy can attest, the costs of administrative resource allocation are often high. Socialist planning generates strong pressures to increase physical output at the expense of quality, variety, timeliness, customer service, and financial performance. With prices functioning primarily as accounting devices rather than as signals to guide allocation of resources, the relationship between price or cost and scarcity or economic value becomes increasingly distant. If prices are known not to reflect scarcity costs, there is no clear-cut criterion for deciding which projects or products are valuable and which are not. Thus economic policy decisions are based increasingly on subjective criteria even if economic analysis is not politically dangerous (as it was in China for long periods between the late 1950s and the late 1970s). With enterprise managers striving to increase the flow of output almost regardless of costs or consequences and political factors at the forefront of economic decision making at all levels of government, massive inefficiency and waste cannot be avoided. There are numerous examples of the results: coal shipments filled with rocks; pipelines built in locations devoid of natural gas deposits; suppliers unaware of the existence of new plants; official orders to transfer land and labor out of grain production at the very moment of collapsing harvests; "frozen" technology which allows no improvement in product quality despite advances in engineering knowledge and changing economic circumstances (such as the world energy shortage which brought no changes in the relative or absolute prices in China of coal, oil, and related products, even though both coal and oil can be exported and China is chronically short of foreign exchange).

References

Komiya, Ryutaro. "Japanese Firms, Chinese Firms: Problems for Economic Reform in China." *Journal of the Japanese and International Economies* 1.1 and 1.2 (1987):31–61, 229–247 (faculty reading).

Perry, Elizabeth J., and Wong, Christine, eds. *The Political Economy of Reform in Post-Mao China.* Cambridge: Harvard E.A.R.C., 1985 (faculty reading).

Rawski, Thomas. "China's Industrial System." In United States Congress, Joint Economic Committee, *China: A Reassessment of the Economy,* 1975 pp. 175–198; also in *Comparative Economic Systems: Models and Cases,* edited by Morris Bornstein. Washington: U.S. Government Printing Office, 1978 (faculty reading).

Wiles, Peter. *The Political Economy of Communism.* Oxford: Blackwell, 1962 (faculty reading).

Wang, George C. *Economic Reform in the PRC.* Boulder, CO: Westview, 1982 (faculty reading).

Transition from Plan to Market. During the past decade, China's government embarked upon an episodic and unsystematic, but nonetheless bold and wide-ranging program of economic reform designed to inject elements of a market economy into a system formerly dominated by administrative investment decisions and resource allocation. The rationale underlying reform efforts is similar to arguments heard in the USSR, Eastern Europe, and socialist oriented Third World nations in which economic innovation is often stifled by state bureaucracies. The deregulation initiatives of the Carter and Reagan administrations also arise from ideas not dissimilar to those articulated by reform-minded Chinese economists.

If economic actors devoted their full energies to producing and delivering commodities and services desired by business and consumers rather than spending a large share of their effort in complying with and manipulating official regulations, and if officially sponsored monopolies found their comfortable bailiwicks invaded by profit-hungry rivals immune to the protestations of the sponsoring agencies of entrenched enterprise, productivity could increase, perhaps spectacularly. In the Chinese case, arguments for reform have been fueled by growing awareness of impressive economic gains elsewhere in East Asia. If the Chinese entrepreneurs of Hong Kong and Shanghai can dazzle international markets with a variety of merchandise of ever-higher quality, complexity, and sophistication, why should China be content with producing simple and cheap items, and why should Chinese residing in the People's Republic be denied access to the swiftly rising living standards of neighboring Chinese communities?

In some areas, Chinese reform efforts have amply fulfilled the expectations of domestic and overseas critics of the former plan system. In agriculture, farm management has shifted to a system of household control from the collective arrangements that prevailed for two decades after the creation of communes in the late 1950s. Although acreage controls and compulsory state grain procurement (at artificially low prices) still constrain farmers' freedom of choice, the typical Chinese farmer now enjoys substantial opportunity to determine crop selection, land use, allocation of labor among various farm activities and between farming, handicrafts, transport, peddling, off-farm employment, etc. These changes have brought a decade of impressive increases in grain output (even as land and labor move out of this segment of farming), with even faster expansion of cotton, oilseeds, livestock, and other subsidiary crops and truly spectacular output increases in rural construction, commerce, manufacturing, and other non-farm economic activities. Following these successes, Chinese reform advocates see agriculture as an inspiration for their efforts to implement more problematic changes in the urban economy. Looking at the swift progress in the countryside, it is easy to conclude that urban reform experimentation is valuable despite the absence of clear-cut success; once the right policy approach is determined, the experience in the farming sector suggests that the payoff to successful reform may be very high indeed.

Services is another area in which reform efforts can claim considerable success. Following the commodity orientation of socialist planners everywhere, Chinese officials actively squeezed resources from the service sector, to the detriment of consumer welfare and business convenience. The results were especially evident in the cities, where the numbers of restaurants, barbershops, bathhouses, repair stations, and other service facilities actually declined during the 1960s and 1970s despite continuing population growth. Expansion of the service sector, together with intense competition between state and collective or private service establishments have brought palpable benefits to both urban and rural residents, who now find a growing array of service establishments actively competing for their custom. City streets are now filled with vendors of vegetables, newspapers, maps, refreshments, and books; repair stalls for shoes, bicycles, and motor vehicles are common; expanded taxi companies face competition from private operators; private construction companies work on projects formerly reserved for state building corporations; employees of state agencies, factories or research institutes are now allowed to act as private consultants, often referred to as "Sunday engineers." These are a few of the many options now open to Chinese in their dual roles as income-earners and consumers.

The impact of reform on the industrial sector, the largest component of China's economy in terms of contribution to national product, is more problematic. A number of studies, including influential World Bank reports, have concluded that the reform program has brought no sign of increase in multi-factor productivity within state-owned industrial establishments. Although subsequent studies report that productivity has turned upward during the reform period, it remains clear that industrial reform cannot be termed an unmitigated success.

The experience of industry highlights intriguing aspects of the reform effort. An economy traversing the path between plan and market is not easy to analyze. At times, even attempts to describe the current state of affairs are quite difficult to contemplate. It is clear that, as might be expected from the "theory of the second best" (which teaches that removal of particular restrictions to competition may fail to improve economic circumstances if other restrictions cannot be eliminated), partial steps toward a market system do not necessarily lead to improved productivity or efficiency. Decentralization of investment decisions offers a striking example.

In the past, central determination of investment allocations gave rise to massive inefficiency because of the inability and/or unwillingness of central officials to evaluate proposed capital progress on the basis of the economist's cost-benefit criteria. Reformers claimed, with obvious reason, that decentralization of investment decisions would place control over capital spending in the hands of local personnel familiar with local conditions.

But familiarity with local conditions has not always enhanced the quality of investment decisions. Areas that formerly exported locally grown raw materials (tobacco, cotton, etc.) for processing by large urban factories have rushed to erect local processing plants and diverted raw materials to these new facilities. The reason for this is that China's price system undervalues raw materials relative to processed goods. This means that a tobacco-growing locality can increase its own industrial employment and tax revenue by constructing small-scale, high-cost, inefficient manufacturing facilities that produce inferior products. The outcome benefits local workers and local government, but the nation suffers a decline in product quality, increased production cost, and excess capacity as regional embargoes starve large-scale processors of essential raw materials. These practices are so extensive that Chinese observers have called for wholesale closure of new plants on the grounds that they are less efficient than older facilities.

The proliferation of inefficient small-scale processing industries continues because government officials have failed to implement appropriate tax/price reforms. If the farmgate price of tobacco were allowed to rise and/or if large taxes on raw tobacco squeezed the (currently huge) profit margins available to processing industries, efficient processors could regain access to raw materials by outbidding rivals burdened with higher production costs. In the event, a combination of internal trade restrictions and price distortions has created a situation in which well-intentioned economic reforms appear to have brought a deterioration of performance by encouraging large numbers of investment projects which, while profitable to their sponsors and participants, may actually reduce China's national product.

This sad history raises intriguing questions about the sequencing of reform which is now the subject of intense discussion among Chinese economists. Price reform is clearly desirable, but also politically difficult and indeed dangerous. The benefit of price reform is apparent. As the economy becomes more oriented to the market, an increasing share of economic decisions are based on profitability, which in turn is determined by the prevailing price configuration. If producers, workers, sellers, and consumers seek pecuniary advantage in an environment in which prices fail to reflect social costs, income-seeking decisions may systematically move the economy away from, rather than in the direction of, an optimum of productivity and efficiency. The case of small tobacco processors graphically illustrates the negative consequences that may ensue from pursuit of profit in an inappropriate price environment.

But prices perform important distributive functions in China's economy. Without a strong tradition of accepting changes in relative advantage brought about by market-driven price changes, every significant price adjustment becomes an intensely political decision. An increase in the price of energy, for example, while clearly appropriate on analytic grounds, pits the political and economic interests of provinces and ministries that produce and sell energy against the wishes of ministries, regions, and groups that represent large energy consumers. In this environment, efforts to implement substantial price reforms often become bogged down in a hopeless quagmire of competing interest groups. The problem is further exacerbated by the downward rigidity of certain prices (most notably urban wages), which means that significant price reform inevitably adds to inflationary pressures, which have already aroused fierce political opposition from China's articulate and privileged urban populace. In this situation, Chinese economists who formerly advocated immediate price reform as a prerequisite to meaningful adjustment in other sectors have changed their views, arguing that price reform can follow decentralization, expansion of markets, and other policy initiatives. Sweeping price reform continues to appear on lists of reform objectives, but implementation has been repeatedly postponed, evidently because of the strong political resistance to major changes in relative prices.

This experience raises the question of how to evaluate the costs and benefits of various types of price reform. Which prices cause the most damage (in the form of waste and inefficiency) if left unchanged? Interest rates, which are currently well below the rate of consumer price increase? The international exchange rate of the Chinese currency, which clearly overvalues the Chinese yuan (no one can doubt that demand for foreign exchange would far exceed current reserves if the public were allowed to freely convert yuan to foreign currency at present official rates)? The artificially low prices of energy, minerals and agricultural products? While general price reform is clearly infeasible over the next several years, it is entirely possible that the Beijing government has enough determination and political clout to ram through major changes in one or two key price groups. Which groups should be the focus of attention for Chinese economists?

References

Chen, K.; Jefferson, G.; Rawski, T.; Wang, H.; and Zheng, Y.; "Productivity Change in Chinese Industry, 1953–1985." *Journal of Comparative Economics* 12 (1988):570–591 (faculty reading).

Naughton, Barry. "The Decline of Central Control Over Investment in Post-Mao China." In *Policy Implementation in Post-Mao China,* edited by David M. Lampton. Berkeley: University of California Press, 1987 (student reading).

Reynolds, Bruce L., ed. *Reform in China: Challenges and Choices.*
Armonk, NY: M.E. Sharpe, 1987 (student reading).
Tidrick, Gene, and Chen, Jiyuan. *China's Industrial Reform.* New York:
Oxford, 1987 (student reading).
World Bank. *China: Socialist Economic Development* (3 vols.). Washing-
ton: World Bank, 1983 (student reading).
World Bank. *China: Long-term Development Issues and Options.* Balti-
more: Johns Hopkins, 1985 (student reading).
Wong, Christine. "Material Allocation and Decentralization: Impact of the
Local Sector on Industrial Reform." In *The Political Economy of Reform
in Post-Mao China,* edited by Elizabeth J. Perry and Christine Wang.
Cambridge: Harvard E.A.R.C., 1985 (student reading).

II. INTERNATIONAL ECONOMICS:
TRADE AND FINANCE

JAPAN

Japan presents excellent opportunities for case studies in the
area of international economics. Japan has enjoyed remarkable
success in penetrating international markets with a succession of
new (to Japan) and, more recently, genuinely innovative products.
The so-called New Industrial Countries (NICs) are now following a
similar path, with Korea, especially, consciously emulating Japan
not only in its choice of new products but in many aspects of
industrial organization and managerial structure. Several aspects
of Japan's participation in the international economy can contribute to discussions of international economics:

Specialization and Division of Labor. Japan illustrates the enormous benefits available through development of special skills in
certain types of economic activity. Standing in isolation, Japan,
with its meager endowment of natural resources (approximately
70 percent of all energy products and 99 percent of petroleum
must be imported, along with large proportions of mineral ores,
food, and fiber), could hardly aspire to the increased living standards attained during the 1920s and 1930s, not to mention the
large postwar increases that have brought Japanese consumption
standards near the level enjoyed by citizens of the wealthiest
nations of Europe and North America. Japan's success at raising
productivity and living standards by exporting the products of
skill and industry while importing the bulk of its energy and
material supplies demonstrates the potential benefits of international trade. The experience of Japan and the NICs constitutes a
powerful argument against those who decry the international

economy as a vehicle of exploitation that benefits the rich at the expense of the poor. Japan's history shows that both rich and poor nations can benefit from trade—Japan has done so first as a poor nation and now as a wealthy and powerful participant in the international economic community.

Product Cycle. Japan offers a useful vehicle for studying the product cycle. Take cotton textiles and steel as examples. Following Japan's opening to foreign trade in the mid-nineteenth century, cotton textiles emerged as a leading import. Attempts to manufacture cotton goods, initially conceived as a protectionist reaction to import surplus, eventually created a powerful industry that first took over the domestic market and, following World War I, emerged as a major international exporter. Export of textiles continued to expand rapidly during the 1950s, so much so that serious trade friction developed between Japanese exporters and governments in the United States and Europe, which complained that Japanese exports were unfairly disrupting their own textile markets and hurting domestic producers. The "textile problem" still exists, and Japan is still involved, but now as a wealthy importing nation that acts to restrict imports into its own domestic market and exports only high-quality luxury goods. Rising wages have caused Japan's textile industry, once a leading employer, to decline in the face of competitive pressure from the NICs, which deploy similar equipment and technology and benefit from wage levels far lower than Japan's. Japan has maintained its record of rapid export growth by redeploying workers in industries that require levels of technology and skill that the NICs cannot yet attain.

Steel offers a similar history. Japan's steel industry, begun during the late nineteenth century, achieved substantial scale under the arms-oriented policy of the 1930s but was largely destroyed by U.S. bombing during World War II. During the 1950s, steel emerged as a leading target of official development promotion efforts. By the 1960s, Japan had developed a large and highly competitive steel industry that bought high quality resources from all over the world, processed these materials in Japan, and then delivered finished products overseas for less than the price of local products in the importing nations. The effect on foreign steel industries, especially in the United States, where local mills were slow to adopt continuous casting and other new technologies, was severe. Ironically, Japan's own steel industries now face decline, and for exactly the same reason that U.S. steel producers wilted under Japanese pressure ten and twenty years ago. Japan has a large steel industry with considerable excess capacity. Relatively slow growth of the domestic economy (dating from 1973) means that the growth of domestic demand for steel is much slower than in the past. For this reason, domestic producers are slow to replace existing production facilities with new plants and equipment. Aging equipment and rising wages make Japan's steel markets, both overseas and, increasingly, at home, a target for competition from Brazil, the NICs, and other rising steel producers whose domestic markets are growing rapidly and thus can support speedy adoption of the latest production technology, often with the cooperation of Japanese engineering firms.

References

Inoguchi, T., and Okimoto, D., eds. *The Political Economy of Japan: The Changing International Context.* Stanford: Stanford University Press, 1989 (student reading).
Patrick, Hugh, and Tachi, Ryuichiro, eds. *Japan and the United States Today: Exchange Rates. Macroeconomic Policies and Financial Market Innovators.* New York: Columbia University Center on Japanese Economy and Business, 1986 (student reading).

III. FOREIGN ECONOMIC POLICY

CHINA

China presents an interesting topic from the perspective of foreign economic policy because of its history of sudden policy reversals. During the decades prior to World War II, China's economy remained, with the exception of very limited tariff restrictions, almost completely open to international trade and investment. Although Chinese patriots decried the inability of their government to restrict foreign business activities on Chinese soil, the activities of foreign enterprise, and the opportunities they created for Chinese enterprise, clearly contributed to the growth of per capita output and income that seems to have occurred during the prewar decades.

After the Chinese Communist party established the PRC in 1949, China quickly moved to rigorous control over foreign trade and virtual elimination of foreign investment. The 1950s witnessed an enormous transfer of industrial technology from the Soviet Union and Eastern Europe, concentrated in approximately 160 giant enterprises in the steel, engineering, power, and other "heavy" industries, which perhaps constitutes the greatest transfer of technology in world history. At the same time, China reoriented its trade toward the USSR and its East European allies. Following the emergence of a Sino-Soviet rift in the late 1950s, China began a long retreat toward autarchy that brought the volume of foreign trade down to very low levels. During this period, China trumpeted the virtues of self-reliance as a strategy for rapid economic development. The wartime experience of many nations illustrates that enforced isolation can reveal surprising reservoirs of innovation, a lesson that emerges also from China's swift recovery from the disastrous Great Leap Forward campaigns of 1958–60. At the same time, the costs of self-reliance, in the form of missed opportunities for export expansion (textiles, other labor intensive manufactures, energy products) and expensive efforts to duplicate products that could be imported at a fraction of the domestic production cost (the new Baoshan Steel Plant at Shanghai may be an excellent example), were increasingly obvious.

Beginning in the late 1970s, China's leaders embarked on a stunning reversal of its former policy of isolation. Commodity trade has expanded swiftly. Vigorous efforts have been made to attract foreign investment, including creation of export processing zones (based on experience of NICs elsewhere in Asia) and opening of a number of coastal cities to foreign investment. Chinese banks, insurance firms, and trust companies now participate in international financial markets, and Chinese representatives have begun active participation in various international economic bodies including the World Bank, International Monetary Fund, and Asian Development Bank. Perhaps most important for the future, large numbers of Chinese students have been sent abroad, primarily to U.S. institutions, for postgraduate study, initially in the physical sciences, but now in economics and other social sciences as well. Here again, East Asian experience argues against those who deny the benefits flowing from extensive participation in the international economy by low-income nations.

References

Ho, Samuel P.S., and Huenemann, Ralph W. *China's Open Door Policy: The quest for Foreign Technology & Capital.* Vancouver: University of British Columbia Press, 1984 (student reading).
Lardy, Nicholas R. *China's Entry into the World Economy: Implications for Northeast Asia and the United States.* New York: Asia Society, 1987 (student reading).

JAPAN

Here an important topic concerns the extent of Japanese protectionism. All nations are protectionist. The United States maintains a wide range of protectionist policies, including tariffs; import quotas on textiles, sugar, automobiles, and many other goods; "buy American" laws and regulations; and a host of special restrictions on individual industries and products (e.g., scholars supported by U.S. government funds must use U.S.-flag airlines; Alaskan oil cannot be exported and must be shipped southward on U.S.-flag carriers; books printed outside the United States cannot receive protection from its copyright laws).

Japan also maintains a variety of policies designed to protect domestic firms against overseas competitors. But is it more protectionist than the United States? Can the success of Japanese firms in U.S. and other international markets be ascribed to "unfair" trading practices on the part of Japanese business and government? Do Japanese officials and businesses maintain such close and mutually supportive ties that the business-industry grouping can be fairly described by the sobriquet "Japan Inc.," with its implication of sinister conspiracy against foreign, especially U.S., firms? Or, as Japanese and even U.S. officials complain, is the bilateral trade imbalance partly the result of inadequate sales effort by U.S. businesses that lack the language skills, market intelligence, and determination that have supported Japanese firms in their effort to penetrate North American markets?

Although it is easy to document cases of Japanese resistance to foreign market penetration—e.g., quotas on import of rice, citrus products, and beef; endless foot dragging over allowing U.S. security firms to become full members of the Tokyo Stock Exchange; idiotic comments by high officials about supposedly unique characteristics of Japanese snow and Japanese intestines as justification for import restrictions on skiing equipment and beef (if foreign skis were useless on Japanese snow or if foreign beef upset Japanese digestion, a policy of free trade would eliminate all imports as soon as Japanese skiers and gourmets discovered these problems!)—it is difficult to demonstrate that Japanese efforts to handicap foreign firms are more pervasive or more successful than parallel efforts elsewhere. A number of foreign firms—including Coca Cola, Nestle, and IBM—have operated successfully in Japan for decades. The recent success of U.S. fast-food chains in Japanese cities indicates reasonably open markets. And the emergence of large U.S. balance-of-trade deficits with other trading partners, as well as with Japan, suggests that economic factors, rather than unusually effective protectionist policies in Japan, stand behind the reversal of long-standing trade patterns in recent decades.

References

Bergsten, Fred C., and Cline, William R. *The United States-Japan Economic Problem.* Washington: Institute for International Economics, 1987 (student reading).
Murakami, Yasusuke, and Kosai, Yutaka, eds. *Japan in the Global Community: Its Role and Contribution on the Eve of the 21st Century.* Tokyo: University of Tokyo Press, 1986 (student reading).
Sato, Ryuzo, and Rizzo, John A., eds. *Unkept Promises, Unclear Consequences: U.S. Economic Policy and Japanese Response.* New York: Cambridge University Press, 1988 (student reading).
U.S., Congress, Joint Economic Committee. *Japan's Economy and Trade with the United States.* Washington: U.S. Government Printing Office, 1985 (student reading).

IV. INTERNATIONAL BUSINESS AND MARKETING

JAPAN

Instruction in these subjects can benefit from both general and specific information about Japan. At the general level, simple microeconomic analysis can show how differences in employment practices and capital structure can lead to variations in pricing strategies that can easily give rise to cries of "foul play."

Suppose two firms, one U.S., one Japanese, are identical in every respect except that (a) the Japanese firm has more bank loans and less owned funds than the U.S. firm and (b) the Japanese firm practices "lifetime employment" and cannot dismiss employees under any foreseeable circumstance. Thus, while total and average production costs of the two firms are identical, the Japanese firm has higher unit fixed costs and lower unit variable costs than its U.S. rival.

Now let these two firms compete. Prices begin to fall, and both firms experience losses. Textbook microeconomics teaches that profit-maximizing firms may continue operating at a loss in the short-run, but only if they can cover all of their variable costs and some of their fixed costs. If price falls so low that sales revenues fail to cover variable costs, a profit-seeking firm is expected to produce nothing.

As prices fall, the U.S. firm may reach the so-called "shutdown point." But when this happens, the Japanese rival, although experiencing identical losses, still manages to cover all of its (considerably lower) variable costs, and thus has no need to cease production. From the viewpoint of the U.S. firm's managers, it seems obvious that the Japanese rival is engaged in "dumping." How could anyone continue to produce and sell at such ruinously low prices? But in fact, a switch of executives might not change results at all. After looking at the Japanese firm's accounts, an American businessman might choose exactly the same strategy as his Japanese predecessor, and vice versa. Clearly, institutional differences can create significant variations in business practice.

Turning to more specific issues, the financial press is filled with fascinating case studies of Japanese business activities in the United States and other foreign nations that illustrate both the strength and the weaknesses of Japanese business practice. The success of Wacoal (a producer of lingerie) and of Aprica (baby carriages) are remarkable because they illustrate the success of Japanese business in gathering information about foreign customs relating even to intimate personal and family matters. Consider the difficulty of researching child-rearing practices in a foreign culture in sufficient detail to inform manufacture of a product that fond parents, concerned only about the safety, comfort and intellectual development of their infant boy or girl, will choose in preference to items turned out by domestic manufacturers with decades of relevant experience.

Equally relevant is the growing experience of Japanese management in the U.S. setting. Japanese firms have acquired or established a wide range of businesses in the United States, ranging from machine shops to auto factories and securities houses. Their efforts to find a workable compromise between methods developed for the well-disciplined Japanese work force and traditional U.S. management practices geared to less docile U.S. workers provide insight into the interaction between cultural background and economic behavior on both sides of the Pacific.

References

Aoki, Masahiko, ed. *The Economic Analysis of the Japanese Firm.* Amsterdam: North Holland, 1984 (faculty reading).

Yamamura, Kozo. "A Technical Note on Japanese Firm Behavior and Economic Policy." In *Policy and Trade Issues of the Japanese Economy,* edited by K. Yamamura. Seattle: University of Washington Press, 1982 (student reading).

V. GOVERNMENT AND BUSINESS: INDUSTRIAL ORGANIZATION AND PUBLIC POLICY

JAPAN

Here, we come to topics for which the study of Japan and East Asian NICs raises fundamental issues about the nature of capitalism. Scholars of Japan engage in fierce debate about whether Japan is truly a market economy or whether, as eloquently argued by Chalmers Johnson, Japan has pioneered a new variety of capitalism in which government officials occupy central roles in determining economic strategy and resource allocation between investment and consumption and, within investment, among various industries and even between various enterprises in particular industries. Is it true, as argued by Johnson, that Japanese government agencies, especially the Ministry of International Trade and Industry (MITI) and the Bank of Japan (BOJ) have played crucial roles in shaping the course of private economic activity, exercising a degree and quality of influence that extends far beyond normal practice in the capitalist states of North America and Western Europe?

Johnson's claim that, by articulating and implementing "market-conforming" policies, MITI and associated agencies have contributed crucially to the acceleration of Japan's economic growth and thus hold the key to Japan's superior record of development in the postwar era, has not gone unchallenged by economists who downplay the role of government and emphasize the role of private market forces in explaining Japanese economic success. These authors point to MITI's numerous failures, including initial denial of foreign exchange to Sony, then a fledgling firm seeking to import transistor technology, and to the use of government funds to support Japan's merchant marine and other weak sectors rather than to "promote winners."

Although the resulting debate shows no sign of dying away, it appears that Johnson's view best fits the "high growth period" of the 1950s and 1960s, when the government's control over foreign exchange allocations and bank loans created impressive leverage for imposing its will on all but the most independent and recalcitrant business leaders. In the 1970s and 1980s, when Japanese firms were increasingly able to escape domestic regulation by borrowing and investing overseas, Johnson's view of MITI and BOJ as central determinants of Japan's economic course seemed less compelling.

Another important issue revolves around the need for Japan to revise its mix of economic policies in the wake of its emergence as a leading economic power that can easily afford high living standards for its citizens. In a rapidly changing world, mental attitudes often lag far behind economic realities. Thus we find Japanese officials and business leaders thinking anachronistically of Japan as a tiny, weak, and isolated nation, while American leaders sometimes behave as if a stern lecture (as if to a stubborn child) will cause Japan to abandon its own self-interest in favor of Washington's current whims. Kozo Yamamura has described a whole complex of Japanese policies designed thirty-forty years ago to promote savings, investment, and growth which are now thoroughly outdated, but still very much in force. He calls these policies Japan's "shackles of success," and urges Japan to contribute to its own economic health and to the world's by relaxing constraints on personal consumption, imports, etc., that make no sense in today's circumstances.

Finally, studies of government treatment of individual industries (e.g., biotechnology), or of specific types of policy (e.g., antitrust), can be used to compare official interaction with business in Japan and elsewhere.

References

Johnson, Chalmers. *MITI and the Japanese Miracle.* Stanford: Stanford University Press, 1982 (student reading).

Tresize, P. "Politics, Government and Economic Growth in Japan." In *Asia's New Giant: How Japan's Economy Works,* edited by Hugh Patrick and Henry Rosovsky. Washington: Brookings Institution, 1976 (student reading).

Saxonhouse, Gary R. "Industrial Policy and Factor Markets: Biotechnology in Japan and the United States." In *Japan's High Technology Industries,* edited by Hugh Patrick. Seattle: University of Washington Press, 1986 (student reading).

Yamamura, Kozo. "Shedding the Shackles of Success: Saving Less for Japan's Future." In *The Trade Crisis: How Will Japan Respond,* edited by Kenneth B. Pyle. Seattle: Society for Japanese Studies, 1987 (student reading).

Yamamura, Kozo. "Japanese Research and Antitrust: Japanese vs. American Strategies." In *Japan's High Technology Industries,* edited by Hugh Patrick. Seattle: University of Washington Press, 1986 (student reading).

CHINA

Discussion of government and business in China can usefully focus on two types of approach that officials can take, and indeed have taken in the past, toward the economy. The first is a policy of direct control, under which important decisions, and even day-to-day choices, are made by administrators who are relatively unconstrained by and frequently unaware of market forces. The second is a policy of indirect control through manipulation of what the Chinese call "economic levers"— commodity prices, interest rates, tax rates, money supply etc.— which allows producers and consumers to seek financial advantage in an environment whose broad parameters are shaped by public policy. If the government desires that farmers grow more grain and less cotton, direct control means ordering them to change their cropping pattern; indirect control involves raising the price of grain, taxing land sown with cotton, or offering fertilizers at specially low prices to farmers who deliver increased grain crops to state warehouses.

There is ample evidence of the potential for successful indirect controls in China's economy. Chinese farmers, workers, and consumers respond readily to price incentives. Ever since the 1950s, farmers have repeatedly responded to higher prices for specific crops by increasing output of those crops. Individual Chinese make determined efforts to secure urban residence permits, which ensure access to a wide range of special benefits created by the long-standing urban bias inherent in Beijing's economic policies. The current rush of young Chinese to migrate to Shenzhen and Hainan illustrates their responsiveness to opportunities for high incomes, as does the new aversion of rural youth to military service, formerly viewed as an avenue of upward mobility, but now seen as distinctly inferior to business opportunities in local farm economies.

Despite the potential of indirect control, China is now burdened with the legacy of several decades of direct controls. Millions of officials at every level, both inside and outside the government, have built careers essentially on their power to **prevent** fellow citizens from acting in their own financial self-interest. In addition to socialist ideology, which teaches that pursuit of personal financial gain may damage the public good, a shift to indirect control naturally arouses opposition from the former practitioners of direct control, who stand to lose power, authority, respect, and perquisites, even if their titles and salaries are not at stake. To appreciate the depth of resistance, one must recall the extent of controls, which have extended to such matters as fuel consumption quotas for individual machines, restrictions on commodity movement across administrative boundaries, administrative assignment of apartments, travel permits, and even permits for bearing children.

Furthermore, the institutional prerequisites to effective indirect controls are often absent. Tax policy cannot be used to manipulate relative costs unless there are effective means of enforcing laws and regulations. Managing the money supply presupposes that bank managers observe the central bank's guidelines for limiting credit. Difficulties in these and other areas stand in the way of extensive replacement of direct with indirect controls.

In the present environment characterized by a confusing mixture of direct and indirect control, two avenues stand available for Chinese reform advocates. Reform from above, in which government directives are used to push economic structure and behavior in desired directions, has achieved beneficial results—for example, by introducing profit-retention schemes to focus enterprise attention on financial performance—and have certainly not exhausted their potential. Devaluation of the Chinese currency and commercialization of urban housing, both under serious consideration in Beijing today, represent possible initiatives that promise considerable improvement in economic efficiency.

Another approach, which can be undertaken together with "top-down" reforms, is to create institutions designed to encourage trends that will themselves intensify the pressure for desirable modifications in economic behavior. The best example of this is the spectacular growth of collective and private industry, which, during the 1980s, grew at (possibly exaggerated) rates approaching 25 percent annually, and now accounts for more than one-third of China's industrial output. Lacking access to the massive subsidies and extensive bureaucratic protection enjoyed by sheltered enterprises in the state sector, collective and private establishments can prosper only by turning out products that appeal to buyers on the basis of quality, style, cost, and delivery—the same areas in which state industry is notoriously lax. Just as opening the door to firms like Federal Express and UPS has shaken up slothful giants in the American air transport and delivery sectors, official encouragement of private and collective industries may prove more effective than "top-down" policy announcements in forcing China's state industries toward a more commercial, flexible, demand-oriented posture than they have adopted in the past. From this perspective, reforms intended to provide firms outside the state sector with expanded opportunities to obtain funds, raw materials, skilled workers and college graduates may have their largest impact on the state sector.

References

Lardy, Nicholas R. *Agriculture in Modern China's Economic Development.*
   New York: Cambridge University Press, 1983 (student reading).
Solinger, Dorothy J. *Chinese Business Under Socialism: The Politics of
   Domestic Commerce in Contemporary China.* Berkeley: University of
   California Press, 1984 (student reading).

VI. ECONOMICS OF THIRD WORLD HUNGER

Poor countries tend to squeeze agriculture as a means of obtaining resources to finance the development of other economic sectors. Rich nations subsidize the small numbers of households remaining on the farm. Both China and Japan fit this pattern. China has consistently used low farm prices and high markups on textiles and other consumer manufactures purchased by farmers to extract resources for national development programs directed almost exclusively to urban, especially industrial projects. Strict controls over internal travel and residence were required to prevent large numbers of farmers from abandoning the land to pursue lucrative urban opportunities, as is common in other Third World nations. In recent years, relaxation of travel restrictions has brought a flood of temporary migrants to China's cities even though rural reform has done much to reduce the formerly large gap between urban and rural incomes. In Japan, agricultural policy mimics the transition from national poverty to wealth. Following the 1918 rice riots, Japan's government shipped in large quantities of colonial rice to keep domestic food prices and urban political passions in check. During the 1950s, Japan adopted a policy of raising rice prices to allow farm incomes to keep pace with the earnings of urban "salarymen." The result is a system of massive subsidy financed by the public, which pays large multiples of world market prices for such staples as rice and beef. Artificially high crop prices plus capital gains engendered by Japan's land boom have made Japan's cosseted farmers into one of the richest socioeconomic groups.

JAPAN

Analysis of Japan's present farm economy offers a window for viewing the entire complex of official policies that stands behind the postwar success of the Japanese economy. Japan's farmers, like their counterparts in Western Europe and North America, produce huge crop surpluses that are purchased by government agencies at inflated prices and stored, at further expense to the public, in official warehouses. Just as the European Common Market accumulates lakes of wine and mountains of butter, Japan's storehouses bulge with "new rice," "old rice" and "old old rice." In Japan, television advertisements vainly exhort the public to eat more rice, just as American dairymen urge their fellow citizens to "drink [vastly overpriced] milk for health."

The effects of farm policies, however, go far beyond enriching several million farmers. High rice prices keep land under cultivation and restrict the supply of land available for building houses and other amenities. This is true even in the outskirts of Tokyo, where passengers arriving at the Narita airport drive through rice paddies en route to the center city. The limited supply of land fuels the skyrocketing of real-estate prices. In Tokyo, land accounts for 80–90 percent of residential property values; as much as 98 percent of highway construction budgets may be expended on land acquisition. Sky-high land prices contribute to high rates of household savings and reduce the average and marginal propensity to consume out of household income.

This whole complex of forces forms part of Yamamura's "shackles of success" that, in his view, unnecessarily restrict the growth of consumption levels and of Japan's total output. Opening Japanese markets to imports of rice, beef, citrus fruits, and other heavily protected farm products, coupled with gradual reduction of farm subsidies (both recently begun, albeit very slowly) can be expected to reduce domestic food prices and to curb, if not reverse, the upward spiral of land costs. Both trends could permit the real level of consumption to rise, and also divert funds from unnecessary subsidies to rich farmers (most of whom pursue non-farm occupations as well as securing harvests of rice and subsidies) to support increased domestic production in various non-farm sectors. This in turn would relieve pressure on the state budget, and possibly provide room for additional public investment without enlarging the national debt.

References

Sanderson, Fred. "Managing Our Agricultural Interdependence." In *U.S.-Japanese Agricultural Trade Relations*, edited by Emery N. Castle and Kenzo Hemmi. Baltimore: Johns Hopkins University Press, 1982 (student reading).

Yamamura, Kozo. "Shedding the Shackles of Success: Saving Less for Japan's Future." In *The Trade Crisis: How Will Japan Respond*, edited Kenneth B. Pyle. Seattle: University of Washington Press, 1987 (student reading).

CHINA

The recent history of Chinese agriculture can be used to illustrate a number of significant issues normally raised in the study of development economics.

Incentives. China's agricultural experience, like that of the USSR and Eastern Europe, supports the view that private farming is normally more productive and efficient than collective or communal farming. It was widely understood that the huge communes into which Chinese farmers were herded during 1958 and 1959 were dreadfully inefficient. Together with foolish policy and bad weather, large communes eroded incentives to such a degree that harvests fell precipitously, producing in 1959–61 near-famine conditions whose dimensions are only now becoming clear. Once control over production and distribution was returned to smaller "production teams" consisting of several dozen households, foreign observers anticipated that the grossest inefficiencies of the collective system had been eliminated.

This turned out not to be the case, with the result that many outside observers (including the author of these pages) were stunned at the surge of farm production that followed the return to household farming in the late 1970s. Whether this growth, which has slowed somewhat in recent years with the flight from the land and especially labor from low-paying farm work, represents a temporary forward thrust toward a relatively static production frontier or a permanent increase in the growth rate of food supply above population growth, remains to be seen.

Comparative Advantage. China's agricultural experience reinforces the basic lesson of economic theories of international and interregional trade concerning the substantial benefits available when individuals, communities, and nations specialize in producing commodities to which their resources and talents are well-suited and sell them to outsiders in return for supplies of import goods rather than producing everything for local consumption. During the 1960s and 1970s, underdevelopment of commerce and transport systems and Beijing's enforcement of "self-reliance" edicts at all levels obliged North China's wheat-growing regions to produce sugar beets and required the rich canefields of Fujian and Guangdong to be shifted into grain-growing. The result was an all-around reduction in incomes and living standards whose magnitude is visible in the huge improvements reported for commercial farming areas (e.g., Shandong peanut growers) following the resumption of market-oriented production beginning in the late 1970s.

Agriculture's Impact on the National Economy. With the share of farm output in national product declining steadily, it is easy for economists to belittle the importance of maintaining healthy growth in agriculture. The impact of agricultural reforms on China's balance of payments illustrates the mistake of dismissing farming too quickly. During the 1950s, China's trade surplus depended heavily on exports of raw and processed (e.g., cotton textiles) farm products. During the 1960s and 1970s, agriculture was weak, and so, in consequence, was China's trade balance, not only because slow farm growth meant stagnant exports, but because food and cotton emerged as significant components of China's import bill. In the 1980s, China has succeeded in supporting a vastly expanded scale of imports, in large part because growing farm output has restored China's international trade in farm products to a strong surplus position.

A strong farm sector seems essential to maintaining reform momentum throughout the economy. As long as agriculture appears dynamic, urban food supplies are assured and reform advocates can cite farming as a success story in their campaign to achieve the "four modernizations." If farm output lags, reform opponents will be able to argue not only that market orientation is "not socialist," but, more tellingly, that it "does not work."

Dietary Change. A final issue concerns the impact of changes in the national economy on the domestic demand for farm products. Study of international data reveals regular patterns of dietary change during the process of industrialization. In particular, we expect income growth to be accompanied by rapid increases in the demand for sugar and meat. Consumption of meat is of particular significance in countries like China (and also Japan), where available farmland per person is extremely small (and, in China, declining steadily in terms of both quantity and quality as flat, well-drained lands are occupied by housing, roads, railways, and factories). Since 1000 calories of beef or pork require the harvest from a much larger plot of land than 1000 calories of wheat or rice, a shift toward a high-protein diet seems likely to generate intense pressure on China's dwindling stock of farmland. Signs of such pressure are already visible in articles complaining that Chinese consumers are spending "too much" of their incomes on meat, and suggesting that the public should be "persuaded" to stick to the poor man's diet of grains and vegetables.

References

Lardy, Nicholas R. *Agriculture in Modern China's Economic Development.* New York: Cambridge University Press, 1983 (student reading).
Perkins, Dwight, and Yusuf, Shahid. *Rural Development in China.* Baltimore: Johns Hopkins University Press, 1984 (student reading).
Parish, William L., ed. *Chinese Rural Development: The Great Transformation.* Armonk, NY: M.E. Sharpe, 1985 (student reading).

VII. ECONOMIC DEVELOPMENT OF UNDERDEVELOPED AREAS

The subject of development economics was created during the 1950s and 1960s, largely based on information and case studies about South Asia, Latin America, and Africa. Although the success of East Asian nations in raising living standards, increasing exports, and mastering new technologies has naturally attracted increasing attention from economists in the field, it remains true that the attention devoted to East Asia in courses and texts in development economics falls far short of the region's significance as measured, for example, by its share in the total population of developing nations. Both China and Japan provide ample illustrative material for discussing numerous topics that form important segments of the standard curriculum in development economics.

CHINA

China offers valuable case-study material for courses in development economics because a) it is the largest developing nation, b) its lack of dependence on, and indeed ignorance of, economic trends in the international community has led China to adopt policies quite different from those pursued elsewhere and c) dramatic policy shifts make China itself a fascinating laboratory for important issues in the development field.

One major area that displays all these features is that of choice of industrial emphasis and industrial technology. China began in the 1950s with strong emphasis on building large-scale plants in steel, engineering, and other basic industries, with minimal attention to short-term comparative advantage and to the development of consumer products other than what was deemed absolutely essential to maintain the population at spartan levels of consumption. Unlike most nations, which promise to spread industrial investment over disparate regions without fulfilling such commitments, China did invest heavily in manufacturing bases outside of early-developing coastal centers of industry. Beginning in the late 1950s, and for two decades thereafter, China, again unlike most latecomers to industrialization, committed substantial resources to the development of small-scale industrial facilities operating "alternative" industrial technologies that required less capital, both quantitatively and qualitatively, per unit of labor than the large-scale units built with Soviet assistance during the 1950s. More recently, emphasis has shifted toward expansion of consumer industries, across-the-board technology importation from advanced industrial nations, and renewed attention to industrial expansion in long-established manufacturing bases.

This experience sheds light on several controversies that form regular components of the curriculum in development economics. China's industrialization suggests that, despite significant temporary contributions in such sectors as building materials and chemical fertilizers, creation of large numbers of small-scale industrial plants based on alternative technologies that are already obsolete in the advanced nations does not offer a viable development path that can significantly economize on the foreign exchange costs, capital needs, and time required to pursue a long-term industrialization process. Small-scale plants did economize on imported equipment and transport facilities, but their products were often of high cost and low quality, and their need for fuel, materials, electricity, and transport capacity sometimes conflicted with the requirements of more sophisticated plants capable of producing superior products at lower cost.

China's experience accords with the current view shared by many development economists that emphasizes the limits of "import-substituting industrialization," in which nations systematically develop domestic manufacturing capacity, especially in the intermediate and capital goods sectors, to supply commodities formerly imported from abroad. China's policy of import-substitution was successful in that a wide range of industrial products, some quite sophisticated (rockets, computers, pharmaceuticals, petrochemicals), are now available, often in large volume, from domestic producers. At the same time, however, the high cost and low quality of many of these products, and of the production facilities where they are manufactured, means that these successes have come only at great expense. The cost of import substitution includes China's failure to progress rapidly in developing labor-intensive manufactures more appropriate to China's resource endowment and more suited to expanding national export potential than the industries that have received highest national priority and, in consequence, the lion's share of investment funds over the past four decades. Comparison of China with the smaller industrial nations of East Asia produces clear indications that China's de-emphasis of labor intensive consumer manufactures has unnecessarily slowed the pace of development, retarded the growth of nonagricultural employment, and also raised the resource cost of increments to total output in the People's Republic.

China's innovations in regional policy also appear to have produced mixed results. On the one hand, nearly all of China's provinces have by now built large industrial bases. But at the same time, production costs in most industries located in China's interior regions remain far higher and productivity is far lower than in long-established manufacturing centers in coastal areas and in the northeast. The importance of "learning curves" in manufacturing make it natural to expect high costs in new industrial regions during the initial production experience. But many of China's interior regions now have decades of experience with large-scale industry dating back to the 1950s (and in some cases, even earlier). The failure of costs and productivity to converge toward levels achieved in regions (especially Shanghai) that have received far less investment since 1949 suggests that the costs of artificially accelerating the industrial development of interior regions (compared to what might have occurred under a market regime) have been extremely high. Development of industrial strength by investing primarily in coastal regions whose prior industrial experience in the prewar market economy demonstrated their suitability as manufacturing bases might have produced a similar amount of industrial growth at a far smaller sacrifice of consumption. For a poor country, substantial consumption loss may be a high price to pay for improved geographic dispersion of industrial facilities that offer little long-term prospect of achieving high levels of efficiency despite policies (such as industrial product prices that fail to reflect transport costs) geared to favor interior regions over the coast.

Distribution is another important subject in development economics for which China's experience offers a valuable case study. During the early days of development economics, little attention was paid to income distribution, as practitioners assumed that a rise in national income would automatically benefit the vast majority of citizens in low income countries. Beginning in the 1960s, this assumption, derisively termed the "trickle-down theory" was questioned by authors who insisted that, without careful attention to distributive issues from the start of development, even substantial increases in national income could leave large groups of citizens no better-off, or even worse-off, than before. These concerns, whose validity was verified by the experience of many developing nations, led to the development of a "basic needs strategy" that called for emphasis on directly providing for food, potable water, shelter, and basic medical care for low income strata in developing nations rather than waiting for a general rise in per capita incomes to bring gradual improvements in opportunities available to the poorest households and individuals.

From this perspective, China, which undertook land reform in the early 1950s, introduced rationing of basic consumer staples soon thereafter, and created corps of paramedics to provide low-cost medical services to its rural populace, appeared to be well in advance of most national and international planning agencies. More than anything else, it was the perceived egalitarianism of Chinese economic policies that led economists to begin discussing a "Chinese model" of development with possible relevance to other low-income nations.

China's record in this area appears mixed. The impact of the "basic needs" approach is visible in many parts of China; visitors rarely report seeing large numbers of people in obvious need of food or medical care (although one does see occasional beggars on the streets of large cities, and Chinese reports speak of impoverished rural regions in which tens of millions still lack adequate supplies of basic foodstuffs). Rapid, indeed unprecedented, increases in average life expectancy (from about forty years in the early 1950s to over seventy years in the 1980s) confirm the impression that the vast majority of Chinese have received adequate supplies of commodities and services required for survival.

At the same time, the widespread impression of China as a nation of unusually equal income distribution seems mistaken. The land reform and anti-business campaigns of the 1950s, and also the transition to collective farming in the late 1950s, attacked primarily local inequalities, raising the incomes of the local poor at the expense of rich people in the same locality. But large inter-regional income differentials that marked China's rural economy were hardly affected by official policies toward farming. Furthermore, the pronounced urban bias of Beijing's economic policies enlarged the inherited gap between the living standard and life chances of urban and rural residents. This is visible from many perspectives, but most notably in the extreme determination with which urban youth fought to reverse edicts under which they were "sent **down**" to the countryside. As a result, some empirical studies indicate that China's income distribution in the 1970s was not markedly different in important respects from India's, or even from China's income distribution during the 1930s.

We can speculate that the reforms of the past decade have had mixed effects on equality in China. On the one hand, the widely remarked increase in farm incomes has undoubtedly contributed to a narrowing of the gap between average incomes of rural and urban residents. At the same time, however, since rural reforms have offered the greatest benefits to rural communities that can tap into the marketing system of nearby urban centers, it is entirely possible that the degree of inequality within the rural economy has increased under the reforms. Increased opportunities for migration from farm to town and between rural areas has presumably acted to mitigate this tendency by allowing inhabitants of the poorest regions (who also tend to dominate the roster of poorest households and individuals) to escape from the inhospitable environment that mired them in long-term poverty under the former regime of strict migration controls.

JAPAN

Japan represents an interesting case study of income distribution because of its surprising combination of strong pro-business policy orientation and unusually even distribution of income. This appears to represent a validation of the widely discredited "trickle-down" approach under which the general public, including low-income groups, can be expected to benefit from a substantial rise in the national average of per capita output and income.

There can be little doubt that, when compared to the welfare-state establishments maintained by governments in Western Europe, Canada and even the United States, Japan's government appears relatively little concerned with the distribution (as opposed to the size of) the economic pie. The ratio of government spending to national product is low in international terms. Government policy is widely regarded as being attuned to the interests of business rather than of consumers. A wide variety of official business consultative groups ensure that the government is constantly kept aware of the economic interests of the business community, especially of large enterprise. Close relations between the civil service and the higher ranks of the corporate world add to the climate of intense mutual communication between business and government. The small business community expresses its interests through national business associations and through close ties with legislators representing individual communities. Tight restrictions on expansion of large retail outlets and massive farm subsidies illustrate the continuing ability of small business groups (retailers and farmers) to influence official policy in ways favorable to the economic interests of their members.

In contrast to this picture of effective lobbying by representatives of large and small business, Japan's citizenry appears woefully underrepresented in its role as consumers of products and services. There is no equivalent to the vociferous public interest lobbying associated in the United States with the name of Ralph Nader. Consumer groups often acquiesce in public policies — such as stringent limitation of food imports— that run counter to the economic interest of the households they purport to represent.

Under these circumstances, it is perhaps surprising to discover that no serious case can be made for the proposition that Japan should be included in the list of nations in which large segments of the population have failed to share in the benefits of economic growth. Not only do the statistics show a distribution of income that is quite egalitarian compared to results in other nations, but we also find that "middle-class behavior"— substantial household savings, successful completion of high school education, etc.— extends to low- as well as middle- and high-income groups. As a result, in Japan, unlike the United States, we find no substantial "underclass" of persons whose training and experience differ so widely from the norm that they are essentially unable to participate in the economy on the same basis as their fellow citizens.

One qualification to the picture of Japan as a society which systematically neglects (or attaches low priority to) distributive problems but nonetheless achieves an unusually equal income distribution comes from the legacy of the American postwar occupation period (1945–52). It might be argued that various reforms instituted during these years, including rural land redistribution, dissolution of the largest business combines (*zaibatsu* holding companies), strengthening of trade unions, and reform of the compulsory education system, constitute fundamental changes that exercise an important influence on income distribution even four decades later. In this sense, it might be argued that Japan fits the category of "reshape distribution first, expand the economy later" rather than the laissez-faire pattern of "trickle-down."

References

Bronfenbrenner, Martin. "Economic Welfare." *The Political Economy of Japan, 1: Domestic Transformation,* edited by Kozo Yamamura and Yasukichi Yasuba. Stanford: Stanford University Press, 1987 (student reading).

Eberstadt, Nick. "Material Poverty in the People's Republic of China in International Perspective." In U.S., Congress, Joint Economic Committee, *China's Economy Looks Toward the Year 2000,* 1 (1986):263–290 (student reading).

Inoguchi, Kuniko. "Prosperity Without the Amenities." In *The Trade Crisis: How Will Japan Respond?,* edited by Kenneth B. Pyle. Stanford: Stanford University Press, 1987 (student reading).

Perkins, Dwight H., et al. *Rural Small-scale Industry in the People's Republic of China.* Berkeley: University of California Press, 1977 (student reading).

Rawski, Thomas G. "The Simple Arithmetic of Income Distribution in China." *Keizai Kenkyu* [Economic Research] 33.1 (1982):12–26 (student reading).

Riskin, Carl. *China's Political Economy: The Quest for Development Since 1949.* New York: Oxford University Press, 1987 (student reading).

World Bank. *China: Socialist Economic Development* (3 vols). Washington: World Bank, 1983 (student reading).

World Bank. *China: Long-term Development Issues and Options.* Baltimore: Johns Hopkins University Press, 1985 (student reading).

VIII. LABOR ECONOMICS: WORKER MANAGEMENT

To be effective, systems of labor-management relations must satisfy partially conflicting requirements for security (to foster worker morale), flexibility (to promote productive efficiency), and uncertainty (to goad both workers and managers to greater effort in pursuit of higher productivity and lower costs).

JAPAN

Japan, as noted above, distributes its work force according to two patterns: the "permanent" or "lifetime" employment system, encompassing roughly one-fourth of the work force, which combines high employee security, high employer flexibility (in how to deploy the work force), and a minimum of uncertainty; and a much more market-oriented arrangement affecting the majority of the work force, in which workers gain little security, face much uncertainty, and offer little of the loyalty that characterizes relations between employer and worker in the lifetime employment sector.

The merits of the Japanese labor system, with its record of rapid productivity growth, flexible adjustment to new technologies, and minimal labor strife, are widely recognized. Weaknesses of this system also deserve close attention.

There is growing evidence that the accelerating rate of technical progress and structural change creates increasing difficulty for the permanent employment system. Rapid evolution of product varieties and international shifts in the locus of comparative advantage make it increasingly difficult for employers and (especially highly skilled) employees to anticipate that current business relationships, however mutually beneficial in the short run, can be expected to endure for several decades. Japanese managers chafe at the restrictions imposed by the lifetime employment custom, and yearn for the relative flexibility of the American system in which "pink slips" can be issued to employees whose talents no longer match the firm's requirements. We may anticipate a gradual increase in both voluntary and involuntary job mobility within the large-scale corporate sector of Japan's economy that has formerly been the bastion of lifetime employment (at least for regular male employees).

Another important weakness in the Japanese labor system concerns the inability to make good use of a substantial fraction of the current and potential labor force. This includes women, who, with few exceptions, are excluded from the permanent employment system and from "professional" and managerial positions. Senior citizens, for whom early retirement from the "lifetime employment" system is a virtual necessity because, under the *nenko* or seniority-linked wage system associated with "lifetime employment," the most experienced personnel receive the highest base wages, represent another group whose skills are not fully utilized under present labor-market arrangements. With growing labor shortages and substantial elements of the work force systematically under-utilized under current institutional arrangements, it is important to note that Japan is presently not capable of using large numbers of immigrant or "guest" workers, a vehicle that adds flexibility to labor market conditions in Western Europe and particularly in the United States. There are sociocultural obstacles to every avenue for overcoming the labor shortage.

CHINA

China is presently pursuing reforms intended to create a more fruitful mix of security, flexibility, and uncertainty for employees of large organizations. The vibrant economies of Hong Kong, Singapore, Taiwan, and of overseas Chinese communities around the entire Pacific Rim, and also the recent explosion of small business activity in the People's Republic itself, demonstrate conclusively that Chinese culture, with or without a socialist polity, offers no obstacle to dynamic economic change. Workers in large Chinese enterprises, however, have shown little inclination to exert the degree of effort visible in the small-business sector. Inappropriate institutional arrangements appear at the root of this problem.

Workers in state-controlled Chinese enterprises are cocooned in security and experience almost no risk. Enterprises maintain themselves as small communities, within which essential services, quite literally from cradle to grave, are provided at little or no cost. Pay and perquisites have little connection with individual or even enterprise performance. As the Chinese put it, "all eat from one big pot" with little regard for the economic success or failure of enterprise units. As a result, the pace of work is generally slow, and shirking, loafing, and absenteeism are commonplace.

Recent reforms have begun to change these conditions by allowing successful enterprises to retain a portion of their profits to be used, among other things, to construct employee housing and welfare facilities and to enlarge employee paychecks. In principle, this means that outstanding individual workers and employees of enterprises that record superior performance stand to gain materially relative to other workers, thus increasing incentives to do a better job. While these reforms have undoubtedly provided some incentives, their effect is limited. Within enterprises, bonuses are typically distributed with little regard for individual merit. Failure to implement price reform makes it easy for unprofitable enterprises to demand official subsidies on the grounds that profitability has little connection with social benefit or economic efficiency. Under these circumstances, adroit gamesmanship on the part of enterprise officials may outweigh customer service, cost reduction, or productivity gains as a determinant of overall employee compensation (including housing and other non-cash benefits) within the large-enterprise sector of China's economy.

Another salient issue concerns the extent of worker control within Chinese enterprise. During the Cultural Revolution years (1966–76), it was commonplace for Chinese officials to insist that the workers were "masters of the enterprise" and to claim that worker congresses and other labor exercised considerable control over the direction of enterprise development. The falsity of these assertions is now clear. Professional managers and Communist party leaders within large enterprises wield enormous power over every aspect of their subordinates' lives. The reality of comprehensive, arbitrary authority makes it extremely difficult for workers to exercise independent control or authority over enterprise operations. These circumstances encourage patron-client relationships between leaders and subordinates.

General absence of labor mobility reinforces the arbitrary authority of managers and limits the independence of workers. Once Chinese are taken on as regular employees of large enterprises (including government agencies), transfers between units, or even across organizational boundaries within a single unit, are unusual. Employees typically cannot change jobs without the permission of their current employer, who has no reason to accept a reduction in his own work force, especially if the departure of a skilled or experienced person is involved. Employers threaten recalcitrant employees with loss of housing, of party membership, or a variety of other privileges available through the work unit but not in the marketplace. Given the severe housing shortage in most urban areas, employer control over housing is a particularly potent threat to would-be job-changers.

For this reason, housing reforms now under discussion in Beijing offer substantial opportunities to reinforce reforms in employment systems. If housing were commercially available, dissatisfied employees could consider moving to new positions, and employers could seek needed skills through market searches rather than cumbersome labor allocation procedures. If incoming workers were forced to leave housing provided by their former employers, they or their new employers could purchase housing on the open market. This sort of reform, together with the slow but unmistakable expansion of labor mobility now evident in China's cities, could quickly change the attitude of employers toward their workers. If employees could respond freely to offers from outside units, management would be forced to regard the work force as a valuable asset rather than, as is now common, as enterprise property to be disposed of with little regard for personal dignity and satisfaction.

References

Dore, Ronald. *British Factory, Japanese Factory*. Berkeley: University of California Press, 1973 (student reading).

Kamata, Satoshi. *Japan in the Passing Lane*. New York: Pantheon, 1982 (student reading).

Walder, Andrew G. *Communist Neo-traditionalism: Work and Authority in Chinese Industry*. Berkeley: University of California Press, 1986 (student reading).

IX. FINANCIAL MANAGEMENT: MONEY AND BANKING

In the United States, monetary policy represents an indirect mechanism through which government attempts to influence the level of economic activity by regulating interest rates and controlling the growth of credit. The influence of monetary policy is general rather than aimed at specific industries. Conditions in Japan and China are quite different. In Japan, extreme dependence of corporate business on bank loans and of the small number of large commercial banks on loans from the Bank of Japan has, in the past, allowed government to use the banking system as a tool for obtaining a high degree of general and even specific leverage over economic activity. In the 1980s, internationalization of Japan's financial system and gradual strengthening of the financial position of large business has significantly weakened these controls. In China, where monetary policy formerly acted as a minor adjunct of economic planning, authorities are just beginning to grope toward a new role for interest rates and credit controls as indirect "economic levers" for regulating activity under new semi-market conditions.

JAPAN

Compared to the United States, Japan's banking system is marked by a high degree of concentration in many directions. Deposits and loans are concentrated in the hands of a small number of large banks, known as "city banks," that operate branches throughout Japan. The financial resources of large corporations are drawn to a substantial extent from bank loans proffered by the same city banks. Major corporations obtain most of their loans from a single financial institution. The banks themselves tend to grant the maximum possible amount of loans relative to their capital and deposit base, and the resulting state of chronic "overload" makes them most anxious to obtain loans and to discount commercial paper through the Bank of Japan, Japan's central bank.

These arrangements, which reflected conditions in Japan's financial markets during the 1950s, 1960s, and early 1970s, created opportunities for close government regulation over the activities of the banking system and of individual banks. Control over banks created an avenue for close control over allocation of funds among industries and even, within industries, among individual firms. Government regulation of the banking system was a key factor in the Japanese government's policy of regulating investment activity and controlling corporate behavior on a case-by-case basis to a degree almost unknown in the United States.

The foundation of this system was quite simple. The economy was expanding rapidly, and in every industry major rivals were engaged in fierce struggles for corporate dominance that focused on market share. High fixed interest costs, partially fixed labor costs (due to the "lifetime employment system") and widespread scale economies (not least because the strong seniority component in the wage system gave a cost advantage to firms that expanded fastest and drew in the most low-paid young workers), placed a premium on rapid growth. Given Japan's weak financial markets, rapid growth required massive bank loans. With banks dependent upon the Bank of Japan for funds to fuel their own drive for expansion, it was relatively easy for officials of the Bank of Japan to direct bank lending toward industries that government agencies identified as high priority areas, to discourage investment in sectors viewed as relatively unimportant (especially in conjunction with official exchange controls of the 1950s and 1960s), and to use access to bank loans as a carrot/stick to secure corporate compliance with a wide range of administrative "suggestions" or "informal guidance" offered by government officials. The result was a system of detailed official intervention in private business decisions extending far beyond anything known in American business practice.

The same dependence of corporations and banks on the Bank of Japan provided a powerful vehicle for macroeconomic control. During the 1950s and 1960s, rapid expansion of Japan's domestic economy sent imports shooting ahead of exports, leading to periodic balance-of-payments difficulties. When such difficulties arose, the Bank of Japan restricted credit, leading to short, sharp recessions that curtailed investment, curbed imports, and quickly rectified the nation's external trade imbalance. The momentum of economic growth and investment demand was so strong that, once credit curbs were lifted, expansion resumed with renewed vigor. A similar strategy of abrupt credit restriction was successfully implemented to halt the inflation that followed the sudden oil price increases of the mid-1970s. Even though Japan imports most of its energy needs and virtually 100 percent of its oil requirements, this policy of tough monetary restriction spared Japan the lingering inflationary pressures that discomfited the economies of the United States and Canada into the early 1980s, even though these nations, as major oil producers, experienced far less economic dislocation from the "oil shocks" of the 1970s than Japan.

Rapid development of domestic financial markets, internationalization of Japan's financial system, and strengthening of corporate balance sheets have all contributed to a steady weakening of official control over corporate behavior in the 1980s. Steady growth of retained earnings has left major corporations far less dependent on bank loans now than in the past. If funds are required, domestic and even foreign capital markets can be tapped. This means that "informal guidance" is much more difficult to enforce than in the past, because the implicit threat of denying recalcitrant firms their accustomed access to loans from domestic "city banks" carries little weight in the boardrooms of international corporate giants like Toyota, Sony, or Matsushita, each of which commands preferred access to banks and nonbank creditors in the financial markets of London, New York, and Hong Kong as well as Tokyo and Osaka.

References

Royama, Shoichi. "The Japanese Financial System: Past, Present and Future." *Japanese Economic Studies* 12.2 (winter 1983/4):3–32; also in *The Management Challenge: Japanese Views*, edited by Lester Thurow, pp. 82–102. Cambridge: The MIT Press, 1985 (faculty reading).
Feldman, Robert. *Japanese Financial Markets*. Cambridge: The M.I.T. Press 1986 (faculty reading).
Hayden, Eric. "Internationalizing Japan's Financial System." In *Japan's Economy — Coping with Change in the International Environment*, edited by Daniel Okimoto, pp. 89–122. Boulder, CO: Westview, 1982 (faculty reading).

CHINA

During the period of central planning (roughly 1952–1978), monetary policy had little independent existence in China. Planners assigned output targets, investment projects, and allocations of labor and materials to individual enterprises, along with lines of credit deemed sufficient to execute production and investment assignments. Banks were expected to issue loans geared to firms' production and investment tasks, and to monitor performance to ensure compliance with official directives. At the macroeconomic level, planners expanded the amount of currency in circulation in accordance with their expectations about the growth of household purchasing power, which was closely associated with wage payments and agricultural procurement outlays, both part of the annual economic plan. Thus monetary matters were almost entirely subordinate to quantity planning, and monetary decisions followed almost automatically from decisions about allocation of commodities and personnel. At the microeconomic level, financial agencies remained subordinate to production units, which used the primacy of physical output targets in the national economic system to justify their demands for credit to meet "the needs of production." Financial criteria were clearly subordinate, and insistence on their fulfillment could even lay financial officials open to charges of "pursuing the capitalist road" by placing profit ahead of production.

In the recent reform environment, the passive role formerly assigned to financial agencies has begun to change. Reformers advocate a reduction in official control over detailed microeconomic decision-making, and seek to create an environment in which production and commercial units can increasingly pursue their own economic self-interest within a framework of overall, indirect controls managed by the state. The banking system, with its potential for controlling credit flows and setting interest rates, plays an important function in the indirect control mechanisms desired by reform advocates.

During the past decade, institutional changes have changed the face of China's financial system. There is now a separate central bank and several important commercial banks, each with a substantial network of local branches. Competition is now visible among major commercial banks, and small numbers of private banks even exist in some localities. Enterprises now must pay interest charges for funds received from banks, and their access to bank loans is conditional upon their commercial prospects. As profit-seeking enterprises in their own right, banks are expected to refrain from lending to would-be borrowers who are unlikely to be able to repay.

Implementation of these reforms has encountered significant difficulty. At the microeconomic level, the traditional dominance of producer interests has proved difficult to eradicate. Officials in Beijing experience difficulty in restraining local bankers from making excessive loans, including loans that are unlikely to be repaid, especially when attempts to restrict credit run counter to the interests of local political bosses. The financial discipline embodied in requirements that loans be repaid is regularly breached by provision of government subsidies to firms that would otherwise be insolvent. Thus financial criteria crumble in the face of the socialist taboo against dismissing workers associated with insolvent enterprises. At the macroeconomic level, China's central bankers lack the experience required to confidently manipulate interest rates and credit control in order to influence the level of economic activity. When credit is restricted, enterprises, instead of restricting investment activities as expected by the center, often choose to curtail production, correctly anticipating that stagnant or falling output will cause political leaders to order a halt to credit restrictions. A further problem of the late 1980s was the tendency for depositors to withdraw funds from the banking system as consumer price inflation outstrips official interest rates, leading to a situation in which converting funds into physical commodities promises greater returns than maintaining financial assets.

References

Byrd, William. *China's Financial System: The Changing Role of Banks.* Boulder, CO: Westview, 1983 (faculty reading).
Dernberger, Robert F., and Ekhaus, Richard. *Financing Asian Development: China and India.* New York: Asia Society, 1988 (faculty reading).
Hsiao, Katherine H. *Money and Banking in the Chinese Mainland.* Taipei: Chung-Hua Institution for Academic Research, 1984 (faculty reading).

X. FINANCIAL MANAGEMENT: TAXATION AND FISCAL POLICY

CHINA

Revenue sharing between center and provinces is a feature of China's fiscal system that exercises significant influence over the policy options available to China's leaders. As noted above, China is unusual among Third World nations in that it devoted not only promises but also funds and resources to the development of backward regions. Revenue sharing, under which Shanghai, Jiangsu and other province-level units with large fiscal resources regularly remit substantial shares of their tax revenues to the center for transfer to regions with small revenues and/or fiscal deficits, is an important aspect of this redistributive policy.

Although we think of prereform China as a "command economy" in which resources were tightly controlled by national officials, one of the significant developments of the 1960s and 1970s was the gradual decline of central control over fiscal revenue, which came increasingly under the jurisdiction of the provinces. The reasons for this retreat from central control are not well understood, but its consequences were of great significance for

Chinese economic policy during the 1980s.

In recent years, the central government's shortage of funds and resultant lack of control over economic activity have become increasingly apparent. Each year, Beijing announces its determination to reduce the scale of domestic investment. Each year, the volume of investment financed through the central government's budget declines. But each year, the overall investment total rises because of uncontrolled activity by provinces, localities, and, more recently, by collective and private investors whose operations largely escape Beijing's purview.

The center's fiscal weakness is also reflected in the composition of investment. China's economy suffers from a chronic shortage of transport and other infrastructure investment. Central officials frequently articulate their intent to divert massive funds to improve transport facilities, but have proved incapable of implementing these programs. With most funds firmly under provincial control, and given the extreme difficulty of horizontal cooperation among bureaucratic rivals, development of railway lines and other infrastructure facilities that cut across bureaucratic lines is severely restricted by the center's fiscal weakness. Even major projects involving China's international standing have been obstructed by uncontrollable bureaucratic rivalries. At times, the center has been forced to issue public appeals for provincial donations to finance so-called key national projects. The contrast between the fiscal weakness of the national government and China's status as a "command economy" cries out for careful investigation.

References

Lardy, Nicholas R. *Economic Growth and Distribution in China*. New York: Cambridge University Press, 1978 (faculty reading).

Naughton, Barry. "The Decline of Central Control Over Investment in Post-Mao China." In *Policy Implementation in Post-Mao China*, edited by David M. Lampton, pp. 51–80. Berkeley: University of California Press, 1987 (faculty reading).

Lyons, Thomas P. *Economic Integration and Planning in Maoist China*. New York: Columbia University Press, 1987 (faculty reading).

ISSUES FOR DISCUSSION

1. To what extent can Japan be considered a market economy? On the one hand, the share of government spending in national product is no greater than in the United States. On the other hand, the government's influence is pervasive.

2. Chalmers Johnson insists that

> Japanese institutions such as labor unions, joint stock compa-
> nies, and the banking system (and also governmental economic
> policy) function in different ways and with very different results
> than in the U.S . . . . Japan has invented and put together the
> institution of capitalism in new ways.

Hugh Patrick and others find nothing remarkable about private institutions or public policy in Japan. They see

> the basic source of Japan's economic growth as . . . a vigorous
> private sector which, taking advantage of the private market
> mechanism, has energetically, imaginatively, and diligently en-
> gaged in productive business investment, commercially oriented
> research and development of a supportive system of labor-man-
> agement relations. Business entrepreneurs were and are the
> engine of growth.

What do you see as the fundamental factors underlying Japan's long-term economic expansion? How have these factors contrib-uted to determining the structure and behavior of Japan's econ-omy?

3. China recorded significant economic gains during the pre-reform period 1949–1976. Why then the pressure for reform? What are the main objectives of the economic reform effort? If you were a consultant to the Chinese government, how would you suggest they evaluate their progress in achieving the goals of economic reform?

4. Suppose that, as a consultant to the Chinese government, you were told that no more than two or three reforms can go forward at once. Which reforms would you urge them to move forward immediately? Which would you recommend be delayed? Why?

5. What are the advantages and disadvantages of Japan's sys-tem of employer-employee relations compared with America's? If the American system is superior or if the two have offsetting strengths and weaknesses, how have the Japanese managed to wrest large shares of many important markets for manufactured goods (steel, automobiles, VCR equipment, microchips, etc.) from American producers? If Japanese systems are clearly superior to our own, why has the United States, with its historic legacy of practical "Yankee ingenuity," failed to adopt this superior ap-proach to labor relations?

6. Is Japan protectionist? Is the United States protectionist? If both nations are protectionist, what is the meaning of numerous

complaints of "unfair trade practices" on the part of the Japanese? What is the difference between Japanese restrictions and U.S. restrictions? Are American complaints largely a case of "sour grapes" arising from our growing inability to compete in the marketplace for manufactured goods?

7. The United States is loudly urging Japan to open its doors to more agricultural imports (including U.S. beef, oranges, rice, etc.) to liberalize its financial system, and to modernize retailing by allowing more big supermarkets and shopping malls. If the Japanese take our advice, Japanese consumers will benefit from lower prices, and Japanese firms will have access to more funds at lower interest rates. Won't this just strengthen the competitive power of Japanese firms?

8. Most Americans think that "socialism" doesn't work and that it makes little sense for people to work hard unless they expect higher incomes as a reward for greater effort. But when the existence of our nation was seriously threatened after Japan's attack on Pearl Harbor in 1941, we immediately installed a "socialist" system of economic planning under which government officials determined the distribution of major industrial goods and consumer purchases were restricted under a system of rationing for gasoline, meat, sugar, and many other goods. To this day, our Defense Department obtains its military hardware under a system that looks more like Chinese socialism than market capitalism. Furthermore, we expect our military personnel to risk their lives not for money, but for honor; outstanding performance is rewarded not with cash, but with badges and medals. Doesn't this mean that we put a lot of faith in "socialism"?

9. The share of U.S. products in world exports of manufactures has dropped sharply in the past several decades. Many people attribute this relative decline to management problems. American managers are accused of myopic concentration on current profits. Japanese managers, by contrast, are said to excel at long-term planning. If we look at the share of world manufactured exports produced by U.S.-owned corporations, however, there has been no decline. But if American managers can't compete, their weakness should be reflected in the performance of American-run plants overseas as well as at home. So it seems that the problem of lagging exports is confined to manufacturing operations **located in the United States** rather than those **run by American managers**. To what should we attribute the poor competitive performance of manufacturing operations located in the United States? Labor? Unions? Our education system? Government regulation?

10. Consider the relationship between economic change and political change in China. China's leaders want to build a strong and prosperous economy, but they fear that any relaxation of strict political control will lead to their quick departure from political leadership (look what happened to the Communist leadership in Poland, East Germany, etc.). Chinese intellectuals and student leaders who talk about "democracy" oppose the dictatorship of the Communist Party, but they also would oppose any system that might place effective political power in the hands of China's vast farm population. All these people are concerned (for different reasons) about the degree to which economic reform and political liberalization must go together. What do you think?

III
Political Science

Political Science:
China

Totalitarianism, Authoritarianism, Democracy: The Case of China

Andrew J. Nathan

I. INTRODUCTION: CENTRAL POINTS

China since 1949 has had three regimes: Mao Zedong's, Deng Xiaoping's, and the post-Deng regime which China seems to be entering as this is written, even though Deng is still alive. Mao's regime was a kind of totalitarianism, yet it differed in important ways both from other regimes like Stalinism and fascism and from the abstract concept of totalitarianism developed by social scientists. Deng's regime was a kind of "postmobilizational authoritarianism," but it too deviated in certain ways from the general authoritarian type. The question about the post-Deng regime is whether it will become a version of democracy. It is too early to say, but one can analyze the forces pushing China in that direction and current Chinese understandings of what a democratic regime would be.

Analysis of post-1949 China's three regimes will help students understand the concepts of totalitarianism, authoritarianism, and

235

democracy more clearly. At the same time, the exercise will help them understand how the Chinese political experience and political values resemble or differ from those of peoples elsewhere in the world.

THE CONCEPT OF REGIME

By a regime is meant the key elements of a country's political organization (including formal and informal aspects) that are relatively persistent over time and that are fundamental enough so that they help to explain how the political system works. The concept may also include major patterns of social relations and major economic policies and structures that are set up or maintained by the political authorities.

Except in the case of a revolution, there is no easy way to identify when one regime ends and another begins. Often we identify a regime with a certain ruler, both for convenience and because new rulers often make fundamental changes in political arrangements. But when referring to a regime by the name of its leader or ideology, we should not prejudge the extent to which the regime is actually the creation of that one leader or is dominated by the dictates of the ideology that gives it its name. Likewise, we need not assume that the structure of the regime is invariant during the time span of its existence. Constant change is a feature of politics; in speaking of a regime one is speaking of features that exist and are important during a large part of a regime's existence. Such features may take shape in the early part of a regime, work out their logic during the middle of a regime, and enter a decline in the later period of a regime. At a finer level of analysis one could speak without error of a series of regimes rather than of a single regime.

THE CONCEPTS OF TOTALITARIANISM, AUTHORITARIANISM, AND DEMOCRACY

The concepts of totalitarianism, authoritarianism, and democracy will be defined in the appropriate sections below. In general, they present two difficulties to those who would apply them. First, they are highly aggregative concepts; each attempts to cover with one label the essential features of many different and complex political systems. If the concepts are defined too narrowly, they will not fit China or any other case beyond the original ones they were defined to describe, since each new case is bound to have some special characteristics that are different from the original examples. But if the terms are defined too broadly, they will include regimes that are different in important ways. With proper definition, however, the concepts can help us locate a regime in a category with others that are fundamentally similar. They can also help us analyze how the given regime resembles and differs from the others in its class.

A second problem with these concepts is that they are simultaneously analytical and evaluative. They are used not only to classify regimes into empirical types but also to label them in a way that involves making a value judgment. The dangers here are that we might misclassify a regime as democratic because we like it, or as totalitarian because we disapprove of it, without paying adequate attention to how it really functions. On the other hand, we might merely label a regime without carrying out a detailed evaluation of its successes and failures. So long as such pitfalls are avoided, however, the concepts can help to clarify a regime's key features while also guiding us toward an evaluation of its historical record.

II. MAJOR TOPICS

MAO'S REGIME

Mao's Regime as Totalitarianism. The concept of totalitarianism had its origins in the 1930s as an ideal of fascist ideologues who were seeking a political order that had the capability to provide total organization for society. After World War II, it was refurbished as a social science concept. Commentators have criticized the concept as still bearing the birthmarks of its ideological origins, because it attributes to its subjects a mystical, overwhelming power and invulnerability to change that no regime in history has ever had. One of the most influential definitions defines totalitarian systems by six characteristics: a totalist ideology, a single ruling party led by a dictator, a secret police that carries out political terror, a monopoly of mass communications, a monopoly of political organizations, and monopolistic state control of the economy. The classic totalitarian systems are usually said to be Hitler's Germany, Stalin's Soviet Union, and Mao's China.

There are several ways in which the Maoist regime departed from the classic concept of totalitarianism. The police played a less important role in creating political terror than in Stalin's Soviet Union or Hitler's Germany, since the terror was created mainly through the work unit. The military was a more important factor in inner-party politics, serving as a trump card in the hands of Mao Zedong, while both Hitler and Stalin relied more on the loyalty of their secret police organizations to buttress their rule and kept the military effectively out of politics. Although Mao was the dominant Chinese Communist leader and the subject of a cult of personality, his power was intermittently checked by the authority of his colleagues among the top leaders. His power was based less on personal charisma than Hitler's and Stalin's and more on a combination of personal loyalty to him among the other leaders (especially the military) and his authority as an ideologist.

Moreover, some theories of totalitarianism claim that these societies are classless, because they reduce everyone to a mass. This may not have been true of any such system, but it is certainly wrong in case of Maoism, which was highly stratified in several ways, including by the class status system, by the system of bureaucratic ranks, and by the social cleavages between rural and urban residents and between state and nonstate employees.

Finally, most versions of the theory of totalitarianism pessimistically saw these systems as unchangeable. In fact, they have proven rather fragile. In China, the breakdown had already gone quite far in the late Mao years, due to the ideological exhaustion of the population and the rise of corruption resulting from unchecked power. It seems that the exaggeration of the permanence of this kind of regime grows out of the ideological origins of the concept, which glorified these systems as something completely new and able to remake human nature.

If there was ever a regime in world history that came close to totalitarianism, however, Mao's China was it. The concept highlights well several aspects of Mao's regime:

• The broad scope of the regime's political control—the repression of all civil society and of nearly all individual autonomy. The system of control mechanisms (units, class labels, political campaigns, the party network) added up to a unique achievement in the social technology of control. While no control system is absolutely perfect, research has turned up very little in the way of gaps in the Maoist system until its late years, when it began to decline in effectiveness.

• The monolithic nature of the political system. Political authority was highly centralized in the hands of a small number of people. No political system is ever totally centralized, and in Mao's China too the central authorities had to fight continuously against bureaucratic obstacles to its programs presented by the needs and procedures of various bureaucratic hierarchies and local political units. But the center had ample power to override local bureaucratic priorities when it wanted to.

• The centrality within this control system of both ideological belief and terror, with the two operating in a kind of symbiosis.

- The aspiration to remake totally not only society but nature and human nature.
- The aim not only to control, but to mobilize people.

Among totalitarian systems, Maoism most closely resembled Stalinism, which should not be surprising considering Maoism's origins. The common points between the two regimes included exploiting the countryside to industrialize and creating a sharp urban-rural gap; establishing a command economy with huge, inefficient industrial enterprises; enforcing a rigid ideological orthodoxy; and creating a cult of personality. But Maoism differed from Stalinism in having a much less highly developed planning system with more economic decentralization and more small and local enterprises; in developing an ideology that was more voluntarist and more utopian; in the lesser role of police and the different sociology of terror; in the creation of the unit and class status systems, both lacking in Stalin's Soviet Union; in Mao's relation to his colleagues and subordinates, which was never as absolute or as bloodthirsty as Stalin's except for 1966–68; in the relatively greater vigor of the party; and in the greater influence of the military in politics.

After Mao's death, Chinese writers often referred to Maoism as a form of fascism. So far as this involves the idea that Maoism was a totalitarian system that was oppressive and unjust, it is true enough. But within the broad totalitarian type, Maoism and fascism are distinguished from one another by some important differences. Maoism's ideology was Marxist, while all forms of fascism have been based on self-styled fascist ideologies that usually included a myth of racial superiority. Fascist systems relied far more than Maoism did on the police, police terror, and paramilitary organizations, and far less on social and party organization. The class base of fascist regimes was the petty bourgeoisie, while Maoism was an avowedly proletarian movement that came to power with peasant support and, as a regime in power, created a broad base of support among a wide range of classes it labeled "progressive." Finally, although both Maoism and fascism were developmental, industrializing regimes, fascism was based on an alliance between big capitalists and the state, rather than on a state-owned economy that did away with capitalism.

Origins of Mao's Regime. When the Chinese Communist Party under Mao Zedong came to power in 1949, the new leaders faced the need to promote rapid industrialization in a continentally huge, backward agrarian economy by relying mostly on capital drawn from within that economy. The Maoist regime can be understood as a unique ensemble of economic, social, and political institutions that resulted from a failed effort to impose a Stalinist development model on a Chinese economic and cultural reality.

To understand why the Chinese Communist leaders first tried to adopt, and then modified, the Stalinist model, one needs to analyze the circumstances the new regime faced when it came to power.

First, the new regime faced a threatening international environment. As the two superpower blocs emerged after World War II, China found itself located on the boundary of their spheres of influence, so that any expansion of its influence would bring it into conflict with one or both. China was surrounded by countries that feared its potential, shared more land and sea borders with other countries and political entities than any other nation, and was highly vulnerable to invasion both by land and by sea, especially given its economic backwardness. The stronger of the two blocs, led by the United States, viewed Chinese communism with firm hostility, especially after American and Chinese troops fought in the Korean War. China turned to the other bloc, led by the Soviet Union, for protection against the American threat, but the overwhelming Soviet interest was to reach some sort of accommodation with the United States rather than to protect China. These conditions dictated that the Chinese leaders' top priority was to build up the industrial base for a strong, militarily self-reliant and secure national defense. They sought not just economic growth, and not entry into the Western-dominated world market as an exporter, but industrial and military self-sufficiency.

Second, the new leaders faced a threatening security situation at home. The Chinese Communist Party (CCP) had come to power by winning a civil war, yet this victory did not give the regime a strong mandate for building socialism. Rather, its civil war victory reflected the disgust of broad sectors of the population with the corrupt Nationalist Party (Kuomintang, or KMT) rule. Many sectors of the population gave only weak loyalty to the new regime or opposed it. There were local insurgencies, subversion, bandits, KMT forces in the Southwest as well as in Burma and Taiwan. Tibet was still not under Chinese control. Landlords and businessmen formed a potential opposition force. And the regime had only cool support from the intellectuals, many of whom were hoping for intellectual freedom rather than for the discipline that the CCP hoped to impose.

The third condition facing the regime was that China was a

continental country with a huge and poor population, having no real alternative to self-reliant development. The Soviet Union gave substantial economic assistance, but it faced a development crisis of its own and its means were limited, so this aid was limited; and it all came in the form of loans. Western aid was out of the question, and even had this not been the case, American priorities lay in the development of Europe and to some extent Japan. China in 1949 had only a small industrial sector. The rural agrarian economy was the only conceivable source of the massive capital needed for self-reliant, rapid industrialization.

Fourth, in the late 1940s in many parts of the world, capitalism commanded little respect as a development model while Stalinist socialism was considered to have scored remarkable achievements, bringing the Soviet Union from backwardness to the status of a world-class industrial power in three decades under wartime conditions. Not only the CCP leaders, but virtually the entire Chinese intellectual class, believed that capitalism was a wasteful and unfair economic system while state planning was both an equitable and a rational way to direct capital to serve national needs rather than the consumption needs of a small class.

For these four reasons, the Mao regime aligned itself with the Soviet Union in international affairs and began to impose a Soviet model on its economy and society. This model involved establishing state control over the agricultural surplus and agricultural investment by organizing the peasants into collective farms and using the capital accumulated from agriculture to invest in a relatively small number of large, vertically integrated heavy-industrial firms and infrastructure projects.

After only a few years, however, the Chinese Communists began to turn away from Soviet model and experiment with their own variant of Stalinism. This shift can be explained in terms of the same four sets of circumstances that explained the adoption of the Stalinist model. First, in the international scene, the Soviet search for accommodation with the United States, beginning with Stalin and becoming more pronounced under Khrushchev, left China feeling isolated in the face of its most potent and threatening enemy, the United States. Second, in the domestic political arena, the Chinese leaders saw the Soviet Union as trying to subvert their autonomy by building up a pro-Soviet bloc within the Chinese regime. In response, they conducted a series of purges and political campaigns to wipe out pro-Soviet forces in the party and economic structure. Third, economically, the Soviet model did not work as well as the Chinese leaders expected.

Although Soviet aid was substantial, it was limited. The early years of rapid construction created their own bottlenecks in transport, energy, construction materials, and other areas. The agricultural surplus did not increase as rapidly as the leaders expected it to. Expecting more rapid growth, the CCP leaders were disappointed and resolved to try new experiments to produce the extremely rapid economic growth that they believed was possible. These experiments led into the disastrous Great Leap Forward (1958–1960). Finally, intellectually, the Chinese leaders began to reassess the appropriateness of the Soviet model for China. Mao took the lead in this effort, developing a critique of the Soviet model as "revisionist" and articulating a separate model he deemed more suited to China, which depended more on human willpower, on what he called "unbalanced development," and on political mobilization. These theories undergirded both the Great Leap and the subsequent and also disastrous Great Proletarian Cultural Revolution (1966–69). Mao's anti-Sovietism, adopted in the search for autonomy, went hand in hand with the search for China's own model. China found itself in international isolation, on terms of enmity with both superpowers, and driven even further into the need for self-reliant economic development.

The institutions of Maoist China thus become a hybrid between the original half-realized Stalinist pattern and various other patterns, some drawn from the party's Yanan experience, some from the KMT and Japanese traditions, some developed as experimental, on-the-spot adjustments to immediate economic or political problems. This history explains why Maoism as a regime partially resembles and partially differs from Stalinism.

Characteristics of Maoism. The economic structure of Maoism consisted essentially of repressing consumption so as to raise state-controlled investment to very high levels. Its social structure fixed individuals in dependency on party secretaries in their work units in order to enforce social conformity despite these low levels of consumption. Its political structure penetrated society to provide a high degree of social control, and centralized power in the hands of a few decisionmakers at the top.

In the long run, the system generated strong social cleavages that became axes of socio-psychological tension that broke out in the violence of the Cultural Revolution. It also permitted abuses of power at both the unit and the national levels that ultimately led to a "crisis of faith" more complete than that suffered in the Soviet Union and provided the impetus for Deng's reforms.

Ten features characterized Mao's regime:

1. Capital for development was drawn predominantly from the domestic economy, with little coming from foreign aid or trade. A very high rate of accumulation (forced savings) of about 30 percent of GNP was achieved by repressing consumption, with investment flowing from the countryside to the cities, from agriculture to industry. Many of the regime's key political and social institutions were adopted in order to make these high accumulation rates possible. In the early years, the accumulation came almost exclusively from the agrarian economy, through a mechanism called the "price scissors" by which the state purchased agricultural commodities at low prices and sold agricultural inputs and consumer goods at relatively high prices. The exploitation of countryside by city gave rise to the major and still existing social gap in China, that between rural and urban dwellers.

The accumulation strategy consisted essentially of pressing peasants to minimum living standards, at or below the average standards of the 1930s. Urban living standards were also kept low, although not as low as rural. The repression of living standards became the regime's largest political liability and the key reason why Deng's reforms were urgently necessary after Mao's death.

The commune system—Maoism's most characteristic, classic institution—was put into place, after several years of disappointment in the rural harvest, partly in an attempt to realize quickly what the leaders believed was the potential for increases in productivity, but even more importantly to assure state control over the surplus that existed, which the leaders thought was being squirreled away by the peasants.

2. Forced rapid industrialization focused on a small number of huge, vertically integrated state-owned factories. Efficiency was not a criterion. Major inputs were set at low prices to encourage enterprise growth. This left the legacy of today's need for price reform, the rock on which the reform process foundered in 1988–89.

3. A "command" or administered economy that relied neither on a well-developed plan nor on market mechanisms for coordination but responded to orders from above. This system enabled the leaders to make successive efforts at "breakthrough development." The lack of plan or market forms of coordination encouraged village and enterprise "cellularization," excessive local autarky, self-sufficiency, and vertical integration of enterprises, and left no real alternative to breakthrough development or what Mao called "creative imbalances."

4. Rural-urban segregation, expressed in a household registration system that forbade rural residents from changing their place of residence. Peasants were tied to the land in order to enforce the low rural standard of living and to prevent excess rural population from flooding the cities.

5. The "unit" system, which tied both rural and urban residents to a work or residential unit that controlled virtually all functions of their lives, including jobs, education, marriage, housing, medical care, recreation, and political education.

In the countryside, the key kind of unit was the commune, with its subsidiary levels of the production brigade and production team. The functions of the commune system were to achieve state control of the surplus, to mobilize excess labor for investment, to achieve social control, and to spread technological innovation. In the cities, the major kinds of units were factories, schools, offices, and neighborhood committees. The functions of these urban units were to help with political and social control and to allocate jobs, housing, medical care, and other benefits, and thus help keep down the level of consumption so that funds could be directed to investment.

Because assignment to a unit was normally for life, the system provided the political authorities virtually complete control over individuals' geographic and social mobility. Dominant and unchecked power within the unit was normally exercised by the party secretary.

Political terror was implemented in China not through the police but predominantly through the unit. The unit system rendered each person vulnerable to the whims of the unit party secretary. The class status (chengfen) system created a permanent class of targets, to whom others could be added by the process of giving them negative political "labels." As in other socialist systems, the use of terror grew out of the siege mentality of the regime vis-à-vis real and imagined class enemies.

6. The class status system, under which each individual was assigned a pair of labels— one describing his or her class origin (father's class), and one describing his or her own class (normally inherited from the father). The system originally grew out of the temporary administrative needs of land reform teams who had to take land away from landlords and rich peasants and give it to poor, and some middle, peasants. It was extended to cities gradually during the 1950s. Originally intended to be temporary, it became fixed in place as heightened political tensions especially after the Great Leap Forward led to a search for class scapegoats.

Among competitive urban young people, the "good class" vs. "bad class" cleavage became a crucial dynamic in the factional struggles of the Cultural Revolution.

7. A high level of ideological mobilization, carried out through political campaigns, study groups, and a massive institutional system of propaganda media and political-ideological education. The regime used ideology to legitimate itself, to provide a sense of identity and solidarity to citizens, to mobilize the population, and as a language for communicating policy priorities. Some CCP leaders believed in the possibility of using ideological indoctrination to remake human nature and create a new kind of citizen who was selflessly dedicated to socialism and the national interest.

Chinese Communism was characterized by a distinctive mentality, involving the personality cult of Mao, asceticism and self-denial, definition of human value in terms of political virtue, and dehumanization of the class enemy. The fervor was such that for many years most acts of political repression were not carried out by police or party cadres but by civilians acting against one another. The Maoist ideological system began to crumble in the late 1960s and early 1970s, as a result of the ending of the Cultural Revolution, the sending down of urban youth to the countryside, and the alleged coup attempt and death of Mao's chosen successor, Lin Biao.

8. A Leninist-style system of single-party dictatorship, closely modeled on the Soviet system. The elite party, comprising about 5 percent of the population, regarded itself as the vanguard of the proletariat and of the progressive forces generally. It was motivated by a strong sense of mission and of infallibility because of its command of an ostensibly scientific ideology. The party exercised strong internal discipline over its members: the careers of both party members and nonmembers were controlled by the party organization department and its subsidiary organs via a Soviet-style *nomenklatura* (the list of jobs to be filled by party appointment).

The Chinese Communist Party penetrated society even more deeply than the Soviet Communist Party. It had members in all but the lowest levels of all kinds of units, and wherever they were located, party members were the dominant people in their units. The party thus had a low level of differentiation from other power structures in civilian sector. Since the party was located in virtually every unit, it was able to take over the administrative functions that might otherwise have been performed through other hierarchies. The party not only reigned but ruled, not only led society but actually ran most units in society.

9. The supreme leader. Power was not only concentrated in the party, but within the party was highly concentrated in the party center. At its apex, the party center consisted of at most thirty to forty individuals who had the authority to make all major decisions. Among them power was highly personalized, uninstitutionalized, and fluid.

Mao was the dominant leader. He did not have absolute power and often had to struggle for his way, but he had predominant power, thanks to his compelling ideological vision, his record of leadership successes, his political skills, and his direct and exclusive control of the military.

Mao was a man who understood little about practical economics and was suspicious of intellectuals and experts. He had enormous self-confidence and nervous energy and enjoyed conflict and crisis. Over the course of time he was able to violate with impunity party norms that called for deliberate, collective decision-making among the top leaders, and to push his own vision in a series of economic and political experiments that were designed to prevent China from becoming revisionist and to lead the country rapidly into communism, which Mao identified with a high level of industrial development and public-spirited devotion to the collective welfare regardless of personal interest.

10. An autonomous army, loyal only to Mao. The role of the army in Mao's China was distinctive among socialist states. Although, as in other socialist states, the Chinese army had a commissar system and a system of party organizations intended to assure party control, in fact the military reported only to the Military Affairs Commission, which in turn reported only to Mao. In political crises within the leadership, this was a crucial source of Mao's power.

DENG'S REGIME

Deng's Regime as a Postmobilizational Authoritarian Regime. Mao died in 1976, and after an interlude of political maneuvering Deng Xiaoping acquired the leading role in Chinese politics in 1978. Chinese communism under Deng could no longer be called totalitarian, because it substantially relaxed political mobilization and terror, allowed the emergence of some independent groups and institutions in the economy and among intellectuals, gave citizens more individual freedom, and to some extent limited the exercise of power and made it more predictable. But it was still not a democratic regime because of the monopoly of power in the hands of a single political party, indeed, in the hands of a few top leaders.

The processes of reform in China resembled those in other socialist states. In each case reform aimed chiefly at improving economic performance and standards of living. It brought about reduced political mobilization, relegitimation of the regime on a technocratic rather than revolutionary-utopian basis, and a change in the makeup of the elite to bring in younger, better educated, more technically competent leaders at every level.

This evolution was well explained by the theory of postmobilizational regimes developed by Richard Lowenthal, Chalmers Johnson, and others. According to this theory, communist systems in their early phases are modernizing regimes that rely on mass political mobilization and state control of the economy to achieve industrialization. But such regimes cannot maintain a high state of revolutionary tension indefinitely. People become exhausted and disappointed in the failure to realize the utopian vision. At the same time, the regime's success in creating modern, large-scale industry requires it to adopt more sophisticated economic structures, to rely more on technocrats, to adopt regular procedures and rational regulations, and to create a less politicized, more meritocratic and liberal society. Modernization thus imposes its own dynamic on the mobilization regime, ushering it into the "postmobilization phase" or phase of "mature communism."

What this theory failed to predict was that the mature communist systems would prove as unstable as they have. In Eastern Europe in 1989, most of the postmobilizational Communist regimes collapsed. In China, Deng's regime confronted a severe crisis. Economically, although Deng's reforms succeeded in improving both living standards and economic performance, they failed to solve the key problem of the inefficiency of state enterprises. Meanwhile they generated both inflation and corruption, which aroused popular opposition. Politically, people— especially urban residents, and among them particularly students and intellectuals— proved unwilling to settle for the limited political freedoms and rights they were granted under reform communism. After the repression of the Mao years, a desire for intellectual and political freedom became a political force of its own. Thus in the spring of 1989, political demonstrations to commemorate the popular leader Hu Yaobang snowballed into a massive and prolonged nationwide urban movement that threatened the existence of the regime. This movement was crushed in June with military force.

These events reflected a crisis both in the regime and in theory about such regimes. For the regime, the crisis of 1989 signaled that the legitimacy crisis inherited from Mao's regime could not be solved without fundamental political change. Deng and his senior colleagues had been unwilling to break with the most fundamental political characteristics of the old regime, partly because they were themselves of Mao's generation. Under the slogan of "socialism with Chinese characteristics," they looked for new solutions that would preserve the monopolistic authority of the party. As it turned out, the regime could stabilize itself only temporarily by improving economic performance, but a legitimacy based solely on economic performance evaporated when performance faltered.

As for the crisis in theory, most analysts had assumed that postmobilizational authoritarian regimes would be able to stabilize themselves short of making a transition to democracy. In retrospect it appeared that analysts had underestimated the fragility of these regimes, overlooked internal forces that threatened their existence, and failed to investigate their possible paths of development after the phase of reform communism.

Deng's Reforms. The legacy Deng inherited from Mao's regime was an economic, social, and political crisis. Economically, the Maoist development program had produced substantial development. Industry had grown at an average rate of 11 percent a year, China was industrially self-sufficient, and 60–70 percent of GNP was produced by industry and commerce. However, the new industrial system was technologically twenty to thirty years behind the West, was extremely inefficient, and faced energy and transport bottlenecks. Because the Maoist economy grew by suppressing consumption, living standards had not increased since the 1950s, and there was a widespread popular impression that the Maoist program was an economic failure.

Socially, the political campaigns of the Mao years had created a huge number of "unjust, false, and wrong cases"— instances of political persecution, criminal convictions, demotion or loss of jobs, internal exile, erroneous application of class labels, denial of access to schooling, and so on— which led to a wave of demands for redress after Mao's death. These cases probably numbered in the tens of millions, enough to create vast social pressure for reform.

Politically, the regime was no longer able to legitimize its rule by appealing to a vision of Communist utopia. People had become skeptical of the party's programs and of its right to rule. The party leaders themselves, many of them victims during the Cultural Revolution, felt the need to make changes in the system to ensure that abuses of the party's normal collective decision-making processes could not occur again.

The international environment was far less threatening to Deng's regime than it had been to Mao's. Thanks to Mao's opening to the United States from 1971 onward and the changes in American foreign policy resulting from the U.S. defeat in Vietnam, China no longer regarded the United States as a serious security threat except in the special arena of Taiwan, where China continued to suspect the United States of encouraging Taiwan's de facto independence. The Chinese also evaluated the Soviet threat as receding under Mikhail Gorbachev from the mid-1980s on. Deng announced that China should take advantage of what he thought would be a prolonged period of international peace to solve its internal problems.

To resolve these problems, the regime undertook far-reaching reforms in Chinese communism. Deng's regime tried to reform economic institutions so as to increase living standards and efficiency; to redress the grievances of individuals who had been harmed under Mao; to create a new legitimacy based on economic performance rather than a vision of a future utopia; and to institutionalize the party's own decision-making processes to improve the quality of its leadership. Deng, however, made it clear that these reforms aimed to save, not dissolve, Chinese communism. He articulated "four basic principles" that reform should never challenge: socialism, dictatorship of the proletariat, Marxism-Leninism-Mao Zedong Thought, and Communist Party leadership.

In the first ten years of reform (late 1978 to early 1989), the Deng regime changed some of the elements of the Mao system more than others.

1. While maintaining high rates of state accumulation and investment, the authorities relaxed the price scissors. Peasants were allowed to sell much of their crop on free markets, and the state substantially raised the prices it paid for crops it purchased from the peasants. As a result, rural living standards increased and became roughly equivalent to urban levels. The regime dissolved the communes, leasing land to peasant households for fifty-year terms, in effect restoring traditional household agriculture. Peasants who could not find enough work to do in agriculture were

allowed to set up small factories or migrate to cities and towns looking for work.

2. More autonomy was given to large, state-owned factories to manage themselves in an effort to increase their efficiency. Initial steps were taken to raise the prices of industrial inputs like energy and steel to more realistic levels and to free the prices that industrial enterprises could charge their customers. Permission was given for the development of small and medium-sized private enterprises (some of them labeled "collective").

3. The regime took advantage of the more relaxed international environment to pursue an "open door" policy that drew in billions of dollars of foreign trade and investment. It endeavored to move away from the "command economy" to a version of "market socialism" in which major enterprises would remain state-owned but would operate in a market environment. The market environment in turn would be guided by the state through its control of banking, taxation, and other "economic levers." During the decade of reform the transition to market socialism was not completed, and there were periodic efforts to reassert and improve planning, as well as debate over the possibility of moving beyond market socialism to a true market economy based on privatized ownership of enterprises.

4. Rural-urban segregation was substantially eased. Although peasants were still forbidden to move permanently into cities, they were encouraged to move to small rural towns to work in factory jobs and were allowed to look for work (usually in construction) even in big cities.

5. The "unit" system was virtually dissolved in the rural areas with the demise of the communes. In the cities, it remained substantially in place except for self-employed entrepreneurs and workers in private enterprises. But the hold of urban units on their members was somewhat weakened by the decline of ideology and the rise of an embryonic labor market that gave people at least a possibility of switching to different jobs.

With the decline of both the unit and ideology, political terror greatly decreased. People were still punished for political deviance, and some leading dissidents, such as Wei Jingsheng, were jailed for long terms. But campaigns of political persecution within units fizzled out because neither party secretaries nor unit members were willing to disrupt normal routines for values that were no longer widely believed.

6. The class status system was abandoned.

7. The regime continued its efforts at political education

through political campaigns, study groups, and the propaganda media. It no longer demanded a high level of participation from ordinary people, however. The regime tolerated people's opting out of politics to pursue private concerns, and it increasingly allowed intellectuals inside and outside the party to debate sensitive issues publicly within limits. The goal of reforming human nature was pushed off into the distant future, and various philosophical and policy issues that had been regarded as closed were reopened for discussion.

8. The Leninist-style system of party dictatorship, constituting perhaps the most essential of Deng's four basic principles, was carefully maintained. Reforms were made, however, to institutionalize the party's internal procedures and to limit its interference in the work of government organs and economic enterprises.

9. Deng Xiaoping tried to avoid becoming another Mao by restricting himself to relatively modest official posts (vice-premier, chairman of the party's Central Advisory Commission, chairman of the Military Affairs Commission) and promoting others to the key posts of party general secretary and prime minister. Yet Deng never managed to shake the essentially personal nature of power in the CCP top command. He remained the supreme leader whose assent was needed for all crucial decisions, although he shared power somewhat more than Mao did with other senior leaders.

Deng was not much more of an economist than Mao, but his instincts were pragmatic. In guiding the reform, he encouraged subordinates like Zhao Ziyang to present policy proposals formulated by experts from specialized institutes. But the advice of the experts often conflicted, and Deng often made compromise decisions in order to maintain a consensus among senior party figures, including both those in office and those formally retired. Because of these factors, the reform unfolded in an experimental, inconsistent way. It went furthest in the countryside, remained a mixed success in the urban economy, and made relatively few inroads into the structure of the party.

10. Under Deng, the army remained largely independent, reporting directly to Deng as chairman of the Military Affairs Commission. The military accepted cuts in its budget and manpower in return for substantial modernization of arms and training. It proved its loyalty to the party elders in the operations of May and June 1989, putting down the democracy movement that almost toppled Deng's regime.

The Post-Deng Regime: Possible Transition to Democracy? Both Mao's and Deng's regimes claimed to be democratic. Mao spoke of a "people's democratic dictatorship" and Deng of "socialist democracy." The idea behind both terms was that the Chinese Communist Party represented the highest interests of the Chinese people, and that such rule in the people's interest was democratic, with or without their participation and consent. In retrospect, it is doubtful that Mao's or Deng's China were democratic even on their own terms, since they did much to harm as well as to serve the people's interests. But this question may be inherently unanswerable.

The dominant conception of democracy in the West, and one that has enjoyed growing influence in China since Mao's death, is that it is a system of open competition for political power through elections, in conditions in which the freedoms to compete politically, to articulate diverse political ideas, and to vote are effectively protected.

As this is written, Deng Xiaoping is still alive and exercises much influence, although he has resigned from his last official post as chairman of the Central Military Commission. In a certain sense, the post-Deng era can be said to have started, because the crisis of 1989 has caused a retrenchment in Deng's reform policies and has brought about an intensification of the power struggle to succeed him. Three generic possibilities for China after Deng are that the Communist regime will collapse as in Eastern Europe; that it will stabilize itself as an authoritarian communist system, providing an exception to the Eastern European example; or that it will enter a period of transition toward democracy. This is not the place to speculate on which of these scenarios will occur. In rounding out the discussion of regime types, however, it is suitable to consider three sets of factors that affect the possibility of a democratic transition and that would probably shape a Chinese democratic regime if it came into existence.

First, there is the question of whether China's level of development is high enough to provide the social, economic, and cultural preconditions for democracy. Social scientists have identified no absolute threshold of development required to qualify a people for democracy, but China is now clearly above the minimum level in simple economic terms and far above it in social development and communication facilities. GNP per capita in 1980 was already above the level found in the three poorest stable democracies of the 1970s. By the end of this century, GNP per capita will probably match or exceed the level enjoyed by the eight poorest democracies in the early 1970s (India, Sri Lanka, the Philippines, Turkey, Costa Rica, Jamaica, Chile, and Uruguay in ascending order of wealth). China is more industrialized than other poor and lower-middle income countries, is relatively highly urbanized, and has a population that is relatively well educated. Despite increasing polarization of wealth in recent years, China still has a relatively equitable distribution, which is generally considered a helpful condition for democracy. It has strong police and military institutions, which are as necessary in a democracy as in a dictatorship to keep the peace.

In terms of political culture, democracy is generally thought to require widespread acceptance of such values as dignity, autonomy, and respect for persons; belief in individual rights; trust, tolerance, and willingness to compromise; commitment to democratic procedures and values; public spirit; and nationalism, among others. Evidence on Chinese political culture is scattered and unscientific but suggests that the Chinese people increasingly have these attributes. The Beijing demonstrations of 1989, with their public spiritedness, spontaneous public order, and spirit of tolerance, seemed to support this impression.

Second, there is the question of what a Chinese version of democracy might be like. The Chinese yearning for democracy goes back at least to the late years of the nineteenth century. But the Chinese understanding of democracy has always differed in certain ways from mainstream Western conceptions, reflecting the influence of traditional political thought and Chinese cultural values. Chinese democratic theorists have tended to see democracy less as a way of regulating inevitable social conflicts and adjudicating clashing individual and group interests than as a way of mobilizing popular energies to strengthen the state and serve a higher common interest. They have viewed individual rights less as limits on the state than as privileges granted and defined by the state in order to encourage people to give their best for the social order as a whole. Most Chinese democratic theorists have hoped that democracy would not merely regulate ongoing social conflicts but bring them to resolutions acceptable to all; would not merely enable diverse opinions to be expressed but would lead to a consensus on correct solutions for policy questions facing the nation.

The institutions of a democratic China, if it came into existence, would probably evolve from the present structure. The system would probably have a single supreme legislature like the National People's Congress, unicameral and not subject to judicial review. It might have a single dominant party like those in Taiwan and Japan that stays in office permanently. This would most likely be the Communist party, because they would enter the democratizing transition with enormous advantages— size, organizational sophistication, control over resources— and would use them to fight and win elections. Protecting the vested interests of party members and party-chosen bureaucrats would be high on the agenda of the politicians who engineer the transition.

A factionalized opposition would probably develop out of the existing satellite parties as well as some exile democratic organizations acceptable to the communists. Elections would be short and hard-fought, with manifestoes and personal attacks, and would draw high participation rates, but many of the voters would be mobilized on the basis of personal ties to the candidates or payoffs from political machines rather than issues. Some broad version of socialism would continue to be the official ideology and few politicians would question it. The press, freed from government control, would be intensely partisan, with every journal serving the interests of some party, party faction, or social group. Readers would still have to read between the lines, and much of what they read would not be true. The military would continue to serve as a silent arbiter, its interventions kept as much as possible from the public eye, and would continue for a long time to owe its primary loyalty to the ruling party.

Third, there is the question of how a transition to democracy might take place. Theories of democratic transition generally emphasize the point that if such a transition occurs peacefully and from above, it takes place because it serves the interests of some members of the political elite to take the risks associated with embarking on such an unpredictable process. Such a transition might be initiated as a result of a factional dispute within the regime or during a leadership succession crisis, when one faction seeks to reach out to the public for support to defeat another faction. Or it could be initiated as a result of a renewed outbreak of social disorder arising from the regime's still unresolved legitimacy crisis. Generally the transition to democracy is long-drawn-out, turbulent, and in some sense inconclusive, since once it begins there will always be forces in the political system claiming that the process has not gone far enough.

Whether the post-Deng regime will move in this direction cannot be predicted with certainty at this time. But one can no longer argue, as used to be argued in the past, either that China is too backward for democracy or that communist authoritarian systems are too stable to evolve in that direction.

III. ISSUES FOR DISCUSSION

1. What are the essential attributes of democracy? To what extent must a country meet certain developmental or cultural standards before it can realistically hope to have a democracy?

2. Are there any other types of regime besides totalitarian, authoritarian, and democratic?

3. Are all democratic regimes normatively superior to all authoritarian and totalitarian regimes in every way, or are authoritarian or totalitarian regimes preferable to democratic regimes in some ways or in some situations?

4. Why do people obey a totalitarian or authoritarian regime?

IV. SELECTED READINGS

Chan, Anita. *Children of Mao: Personality Development and Political Activism in the Red Guard Generation.* Seattle: University of Washington Press, 1985 (student reading). An insightful account of how young Chinese tried to adapt to the demands the Mao system placed on them, in light of the theory of authoritarian personality.

Harding, Harry. *China's Second Revolution: Reform After Mao.* Washington, DC: The Brookings Institution, 1987 (student reading). A comprehensive account of Deng's "consultative authoritarianism."

Johnson, Chalmers, ed. *Change in Communist Systems.* Stanford: Stanford University Press, 1970 (faculty reading). Discussion of the theory of Communist societies' "mobilization phase" and "postmobilization phase."

Linz, Juan J. "Totalitarian and Authoritarian Regimes." In *Handbook of Political Science*, vol. 3, edited by Fred I. Greenstein and Nelson W. Polsby, pp. 175–411. Reading, MA: Addison-Wesley, 1975 (faculty reading). A summary and comparative application of the concepts of totalitarianism and authoritarianism.

Meisner, Maurice. *Mao's China and After: A History of the People's Republic.* New York: Free Press, 1986 (student reading). A history and analysis of both Mao's China and Deng's, paying special attention to the clash between democratic and authoritarian values.

Nathan, Andrew J. *Chinese Democracy.* Berkeley: University of California Press, 1986 (student reading). An analysis of how Chinese have understood the concept of democracy from the late nineteenth century through the early 1980s.

Nathan, Andrew J. *China's Crisis*. New York: Columbia University Press, 1990 (student reading). Discusses the origins of the crisis in Deng's regime and the prospects for a post-Deng transition to democracy.

White III, Lynn T. *Policies of Chaos: The Organizational Causes of Violence in China's Cultural Revolution*. Princeton: Princeton University Press, 1989 (faculty reading). Analysis of how the unit system, class status system, and system of political campaigns created the social tensions that exploded in violence during the Cultural Revolution.

**Political Science:
China**

Mobilization and Participation: The Case of China

Jean C. Oi

I. INTRODUCTION: CENTRAL POINTS

The case of participation in China illustrates the importance of studying institutions and the political context in which that must operate. All citizens in China "participate" in the political system, but depending on the political context, the channels of participation vary in form and effectiveness. Voting in elections, writing letters to the editor, speaking out at public meetings, or putting up "big-character posters" may constitute effective forms of interest articulation, or they may be examples of mobilization— acts of forced participation required of all loyal citizens.

Yet, in spite of the unpredictability of formal channels of interest articulation and their limited effectiveness, citizens in China have pursued their interests through informal modes that often rely on covert, sometimes illegal means. Like citizens of many third world countries who have limited input into the policy formulation process, Chinese have learned to pursue their interests on an individual level by means of personal relations.

A study of participation in China forces those who are familiar only with developed pluralist systems to rethink their basic assumptions about what constitutes participation and what are the necessary economic and political contexts for effective interest articulation. It also suggests adopting a broader definition of participation that would include "all those activities through which an individual consciously becomes involved in attempts to give a particular direction to the conduct of public affairs."[1]

II. MAJOR TOPICS

FORMAL CHANNELS OF POLITICAL PARTICIPATION.

China has many formal channels of participation, and citizens are provided with a variety of ways to articulate their interests.

Pluralistic Modes. Many forms of political participation common to pluralist systems exist in China, including:
- elections
- letters to newspapers
- demonstrations
- meetings
- mass organizations and advocacy groups (Women's Federation, All China Trade Unions, Communist Youth League, etc.)

The Mass Line. In addition to forms familiar to pluralist systems, the Chinese Communists have provided alternative forms of participation under the "mass line style of leadership." The following were extensively used during the Maoist period:
- "Big-character posters" displayed in public places. These posters were written by citizens to call attention to the mistakes and crimes of officials, or to express various demands and opinions. Such posters are no longer legal.
- "Work teams" to investigate complaints of misconduct or wrongdoing at the local level, including political problems. These teams are composed of personnel drawn from various walks of life, usually from urban areas, and often from schools and bureaucratic offices.
- Small group meetings where local citizens, usually from the same work unit along with their immediate supervisor, discuss their recent activities, study documents, and hear each other's opinions on various matters. These meetings include criticism-self

criticism sessions where members criticize each other's mistakes or problems and where an individual engages in "self-criticism" and admits to his or her mistakes.

Developed during the Chinese Communist Party's struggle for power, this highly participatory style of leadership calls for leaders to be one with the people, for policies to be "from the masses to the masses." The above mechanisms are suppose to help leaders go to the people, investigate concrete situations, gather materials to formulate their policies, and then return to the people to explain and implement the policies, and to make any necessary modifications.

LIMITS ON THE FORMAL CHANNELS OF POLITICAL PARTICIPATION

Shifting Political Winds. The effectiveness of formal channels of participation depends on the political and economic contexts in which they must operate. Depending on the ideological position of the leadership, power struggles at the top, economic constraints, and the psychological makeup of the top leaders, the leadership may one day solicit criticisms but the next day ignore that information and punish those who offered the criticism. Consequently, in China, the effectiveness of these channels is turned on and off like a faucet. A prime example is the Hundred Flowers Campaign (1956–57), which quickly turned into the Anti-Rightist Campaign (1957). The political context quickly changed from one that solicited criticism and honest airing of views to one that punished those who loyally offered their true opinions during the previous period. Like the democracy embodied in the concept of "democratic centralism," debate is allowed to take place and criticism may be offered, but only as long as the leaders want such input. Once a policy decision is made, all must unquestioningly and enthusiastically carry it out.

Like shifts in wind, during certain times formal channels have been effective means of interest articulation. An example is the late 1970s, right after Mao's death and the arrest of the "Gang of Four," when the new leadership was trying to discredit the radicals. At that time people were encouraged to write letters to the editor and to come forth with their problems. Similarly, when Deng Xiaoping was fighting to return to power after being purged during the Cultural Revolution, he supported the mass outpouring of complaints known as "Democracy Wall." But at other times, it is impermissible and even dangerous to express criticisms using these same channels. For example, after Deng Xiaoping defeated Hua Guofeng and firmly established power, he quickly and effectively quelled the Democracy Wall movement, banned further use of big-character posters, and arrested the most outspoken of the demonstrators.

In practice some of the formal channels for participation, such as work teams, have always had a dual character, serving as instruments of control as much as channels for interest articulation. Again, the degree to which they serve one function or the other depends on the political context. During the early period of the regime, in the land reform campaigns, peasants generally welcomed work teams as problem solvers and redistributors of land. By the mid-1960s, however, when the political context was highly charged and the ideological radicals were in control, work teams were often feared rather than welcomed at the local levels. They were perceived as instruments of state control, sent to regulate policy implementation and punish those at the local levels for not correctly following policy.

In the decade and a half since Mao's death, amid increasing economic liberalization, there have been signs of movement toward political reform and a renewed emphasis on the rule of law. For example, local elections have become more democratic. Choice is provided on the ballot, and villagers can freely elect their officials. Although the winner is still approved by the upper levels, evidence suggests that there is less direct interference from above, and more attention paid by the candidates to the interests of the village electorate. In addition, people theoretically have more input into the decision-making process because of the new provision allowing for the direct election of representatives to the people's congresses up to the county level, rather than the appointment of these representatives by the higher-level authorities. Likewise, workers seem to be enjoying some success in making their voices heard. In factories, there are indications that since the reforms in industry—the institution of the tax-for-profit system that makes managers responsible for profits and losses—workers have been more able to influence their work unit leaders. Factory managers, anxious to meet quotas, make profits, and earn bonuses, seem to be making concerted efforts to please workers.

Unfortunately, the progress of the 1980s was limited and has proven to be transitory. There was no institutional reform at the very center of power, subjecting China's top power holders to rules and regulations. The brutal suppression of the student demonstrators in the spring of 1989 serves as a cruel reminder that economic reforms do not necessarily lead to similarly far-reaching reforms in the political sphere. It is unclear whether changes, such as reform of the election laws, will officially be rolled back in the aftermath of the crackdown, but it does seem almost certain that in practice the party will once again play an active censor's role in screening appropriate candidates, who now almost certainly will have to tow the correct ideological line. In short, China has once again entered a period when the faucet for legitimate participation through open public channels has been turned off.

Organized Dependency. The effectiveness of channels of political participation is also dependent on the economic context in which they operate. In China, participation carries with it economic costs. During the Maoist period, citizens were highly dependent on their leaders, not just for promotions, but for their overall economic, social, and political well-being, and thus they were hesitant to alienate these leaders. Getting ahead, getting a better apartment, more food, and better clothes were not just a matter of money. Common necessities of life, including housing, job assignment, food rations, and travel, and "luxury" items such as televisions and bicycles were rationed before 1978. Rationing and the closing of free markets devalued money as a means of exchange. Ration tickets were needed to gain the right to buy goods with money. Housing and jobs were allocated; travel out of one's home area was by permission only. The key to success was good relations with those officials in charge of allocation. In such an economic context, what Walder has termed "organized dependency," people thought more than twice about alienating their local cadres. Even if work teams came to investigate, locals were hesitant to speak out for fear of retribution—there was no guarantee that the work team would make changes in the leadership, or that the changes would be permanent.

The Necessity of Participation. Given the unpredictability and limited effectiveness of formal channels of participation, one might suppose that citizens would simply avoid participating. The opposite was the case in China, however, especially before the 1978 period. A unique feature of political participation in China is that citizens do not have the luxury of nonparticipation. Particularly in the Maoist context, in spite of the limited and unpredictable effectiveness of the formal channels, everyone had to attend meetings, speak out, write big-character posters, vote, and criticize those labeled as "enemies of the people." To do otherwise would be to leave oneself open to criticism and punishment. In a campaign, when the entire population is mobilized for a specific task defined by the leadership, whether it be for killing sparrows and rats, overtaking the West in steel production, or criticizing those "taking the capitalist road," the mass line was tightly integrated with a mobilizational style of leadership, where participation was mandatory.

The strategy chosen by many was to participate as required by the political context, but to do so in a passive manner. Over time, politically astute citizens learned to sleepwalk through the various campaigns, to do whatever was required of them, but little more. During the Maoist period political participation was mobilized and in large measure **ritual**. Because one never knew which interests would be considered politically suspect and the consequences of articulating such interests, citizens generally learned to control their public expressions of interest. To survive, people followed their leaders or recited or paraphrased the "political line" expounded in the most recent editorial in such government newspapers as *People's Daily*. People learned to adopt the appropriate outward attitudes and express them when necessary. They did not speak out unless they were forced to. They made self-criticisms, but only enough to conform and show evidence of remorse. They criticized their friends and family in public meetings, but usually only to the extent that they themselves would not be accused of protecting or supporting the person under attack.

There have been, however, major exceptions to political participation as ritual. The massive demonstrations in Beijing and other cities in the spring of 1989 clearly were free expressions of interest and stand as the largest and most significant act of participation by citizens in post-1949 China. The analytical question for those who study participation is why citizens risked the costs of participation at this time. The answer is certainly complex, but one would suspect that the size and scale of public participation during the Tiananmen demonstration in 1989 were in part related to the loosening of controls—both economic and political—over the course of the economic reforms instituted since 1978. The brutal suppression of those demonstrators stands as a cruel reminder of the costs of overt participation and the limits of political reform in China.

INFORMAL CHANNELS OF INTEREST ARTICULATION

In spite of the limitations on the effectiveness of formal channels of political participation, citizens in China did and will continue to participate in the political system, affect policy, and pursue their interests.

In contrast to pluralist systems, citizens in China most commonly use informal, often covert means to pursue their interests, outside of the formal policy-making process and the public arena of formal meetings. The reliance on informal channels in China highlights a point often made about participation in many less developed countries, namely, that formal channels of participation are not the only or even the most common means by which citizens pursue their interests. Chinese citizens often pursue their interests by the **nonarticulation** of interests. In other words, they use informal, often covert means to resist policies after they have been decided. This includes strategies designed specifically to evade state policies and to cultivate relations with officials to maximize one's position under state policies.

Participation During Policy Implementation. Like citizens in developing countries, those in China are forced to pursue their interests during policy **implementation**. Because citizens have so little input in policy making, they resort to taking action when that policy is implemented at the local level. Instead of lobbying for higher grain rations or higher grain procurement prices, peasants deny the state its legally prescribed share by submitting false reports or hiding production. Rather than being able to legislate effectively for higher wages, workers can demonstrate their displeasure and serve their own interests by participating in work slowdowns. Local officials responsible for the regulation of state policy can register their dissatisfaction by minimal implementation of official policies.

While participation during policy implementation cannot make direct and immediate changes to policy, it does have an affect. Though the system usually does not come to a halt, it still functions, but only to a minimal degree. Over time, the costs can be great enough to force a change in policy. The reforms in agriculture, specifically those concerning the production and procurement of grain, are major examples of this.

Personalistic Relationships and the Pursuit of Interests. Like citizens in many Third World countries, Chinese citizens pursue their interests not as groups, but on an individual basis, through the use of personalistic relationships. Rather than actively working to change the system, individuals pursue their own narrow self-interests. Instead of working in the formal arena to lobby for reform, many rely on personal connections and particularistic relationships to make the most of the economic and political context, to get ahead and take advantage of scarcity and rationing.

Contrary to images derived from the totalitarian model, local officials charged with implementing policies are not a dedicated, impersonal core of ideologically driven bureaucrats, but political actors subject to local interests and pressures. Individuals do not always act in groups, nor do they necessarily even articulate their interests in public forums. In China, citizens commonly purse their interests through the cultivation and manipulation of personalistic relationships, including kinship and clientelist ties. The pursuit of interests during the policy implementation process is possible precisely because of the prevalence of clientelism.

Again, the form that this participation takes is shaped by the economic and political institutions of the Chinese state—the organized dependency described above. The use of clientelism as an elite-mass linkage and the strength of clientelist politics are strengthened by the communist system that exists in China—central planning, the closing of markets, rationing, and the scarcity that has resulted. The same organized dependency that undermined the effectiveness of the formal channels of political participation has provided political actors at all levels, particularly those at the grass-roots level who have the most intimate contact with the people, with a personalization of authority over state and collectively owned goods and services. This, in turn, has caused people actively to cultivate the favor of cadres who control those resources on which their economic well being depends, in the hopes of gaining privileged access in a situation of scarcity.

Students might ask why it is so significant that people rely on connections. In most societies some people rely on some personalistic ties to get ahead. In China, however, the practice is rampant and extends to almost all aspects of life, from buying extra food to securing housing. Reliance on personal connections, the "old-boy network," kin or clan ties, or what the Chinese often refer to as "going through the back door" is recognized as a necessary and effective operational code for everyone from peasants to high officials. These actions that one might otherwise simply call corruption or evasion are in the Chinese context strategies of survival. The Chinese case thus superbly illustrates the structural causes of such illegal behavior.

A key question is how much this situation of dependency and clientelism has changed in the wake of the economic reforms. Economic liberalization has lessened people's dependence on the work unit for common necessities. The reopening of free markets has meant that people have the option of going outside of the official system if they do not want to tow the line. At the same time, the need to cultivate particularistic relationships has not diminished. What has changed are the basis of exchange and, perhaps, the officials who control the sought-after resources. In the countryside, for example, local cadres no longer directly determine peasant incomes, but they still have a big influence on the profits that individual farmers can make through their control of access to key agricultural inputs, such as fertilizer and diesel fuel.

Regardless of the extent of economic changes, in the wake of Tiananmen crackdown, the political context requires that citizens again rely on informal rather than formal channels to pursue their interests, at least for the near future.

III. ISSUES FOR DISCUSSION

1. How economic and political structures affect modes of participation.

2. The reliance on informal modes of participation, i.e, patronage systems during the earlier part of this century in the United States and why this has decreased over time. Also the prevalence of such practices and the prospects of their demise in China.

3. Should one view "corruption" as a form of participation?

4. Causes for mass participation in demonstrations in Tiananmen Square, spring 1989.

NOTE

1. Townsend, James, *Political Participation in Communist China.* (Berkeley: University of California Press, 1969) p.4.

IV. SELECTED READINGS

Burns, John P. *Political Participation in Rural China,* Berkeley: University of California Press, 1988 (student and faculty reading). A comprehensive discussion of different modes of political participation for rural residents in China that builds on Townsend. Discusses both formal and informal modes through which peasants pursue their interests.

Falkenheim, Victor. "Political Participation in China," *Problems of Communism* (May–June 1978):18–32 (student reading). Good introduction to what political participation means in practice, and why citizens rely on informal methods to pursue their interests.

Nathan, Andrew. *Chinese Democracy,* Berkeley: University of California Press, 1986 (student reading). One of the best analytical discussions of democracy in China. It not only deals with various democratic

movements, such as Democracy Wall and reforms in the electoral
system in the post-Mao period, but addresses the issue of the existence of a democratic tradition in Chinese history.

Oi, Jean C. *State and Peasant in Contemporary China: The Political Economy of Village Government,* Berkeley: University of California Press,
1989 (student reading, particularly chapters 6 and 7). Detailed study
of how the institutional structure of the rural economy has shaped
peasant political behavior. Focus is on informal modes of participation.

Townsend, James. *Political Participation in Communist China,* new ed.
Berkeley: University of California Press, 1969 (faculty reading). One of
the best overall discussions of political participation from both an
ideological and institutional perspective. (Students may be assigned
sections on participation by Townsend and Womack in James
Townsend and Brantly Womack, *Politics in China,* 3rd ed. [Little,
Brown, 1983] pp. 258–392.)

Walder, Andrew. *Communist Neo-Traditionalism: Work and Authority in
Chinese Industry,* Berkeley: University of California Press, 1986 (faculty reading). Looks at how the organization of urban work and life
have created a condition of organized dependence that shapes political
behavior and expression of interests by China's workers.

**Political Science:
Taiwan**

Political
Transition
on Taiwan

Edwin A. Winckler

In this paper, **China** *refers to all the territory that is now administered by the People's Republic of China (PRC) and the Nationalist authorities on Taiwan.* **Taiwanese** *refers to people who migrated to Taiwan from southeast China before 1895, and their descendants.* **Mainlander** *refers to people who first migrated to Taiwan from the rest of China only after 1945, and their descendants.* **Taiwan** *refers simply to the physical island and its inhabitants, without reference to administrative status, which is in dispute between Taiwanese, mainlanders, and the PRC.*

I. INTRODUCTION: CENTRAL POINTS

SUMMARY

For most of its postwar political history, Taiwan was an authoritarian regime. In the early postwar period (1945–1960), the largely mainlander Nationalist state consolidated its rule over a largely Taiwanese society, at first using much coercion. In the middle postwar period (1960–1975), political control remained strict and opposition organizations remained banned, but export-driven economic prosperity and machine-style local patronage alleviated political tensions. In the late postwar period (1975–1990), the

267

Nationalists hesitantly completed a shift from "hard" to "soft" authoritarianism, gradually allowing some political opposition but still maintaining Nationalist dominance. As of 1990 Taiwan was halfway through a transition from authoritarianism to democracy, having liberalized authoritarianism but not yet institutionalized democracy. The question for the 1990s was whether Taiwan would consolidate a liberalized authoritarianism, as some conservatives still hoped, or negotiate a democratic system, as most others wished.

So far, Taiwan's democratization has been a particularly successful case of "transition through transaction"— the gradual, peaceful negotiation between a still robust Establishment and an increasingly strong Opposition of mutually acceptable rules for political competition (as earlier in Spain and Brazil). This contrasts with democratization resulting from the breakdown of an authoritarian regime (as in the Philippines and most recent East European cases), or the violent overthrow of an authoritarian regime by armed rebellion (as in some Latin American cases and Romania). Taiwan's combination of diverse supranational influences, a strong national party-state, and a vigorous subnational economy and society provides rich materials from which to debate alternative explanations of how it became the first quasi-Leninist regime, and first Chinese political society, to initiate democratization.

Politically, the bare facts of the Taiwan case are as follows. Originally part of the Chinese empire, Taiwan was ruled by Japan from 1895 until 1945 as a model of colonial modernization, then returned to Nationalist China. When the communists conquered the mainland in 1949, the Nationalists retreated to Taiwan, bringing their military, party and parliamentary institutions with them. Mainlanders dominated central government power and policy, while allowing Taiwanese limited political scope in local elections. From 1975, however, U.S. patronage declined, and young Taiwanese began replacing old mainlanders within the Nationalist party-state. Socioeconomic modernization renewed public demands for democratization and facilitated emergence of an informal political opposition. Around 1980 the Nationalists repressed what they regarded as a too radical opposition. However in 1986 mainlander President Chiang Ching-kuo (CCK) initiated a dialogue with the remaining moderate opposition, which soon declared itself a formal party, with grudging Nationalist acquiescence. By 1990, direct local elections had consolidated about 30 percent of the popular vote behind this new Democratic Progressive Party (DPP), and indirect elections had confirmed Taiwanese Lee Teng-hui as CCK's successor as chairman of the Nationalist Party or Kuomintang (KMT) and government president. Phased reelection of national representative bodies promised to make legislative institutions responsible to the Taiwan public by the early 1990s. Demands for direct election of the president raised the possibility of asserting popular sovereignty over the executive in 1996 or 2002.

Taiwan illustrates the strengths and limits of some alternative approaches to analyzing political development, differing in the levels they emphasize and the ideologies they reflect. Supranational, national and subnational processes have all contributed to the outcome. Liberal, radical, and conservative orientations all contribute to our understanding. In the lesson plan below, the introduction summarizes these issues, which the teacher might present at the beginning of the unit, and the students might debate at the end. Pedagogically, however, these themes are best developed historically: the interactions between levels emerge only when all three are narrated together. Consequently the body of the lesson plan begins with an overview of processes that have extended across the imperial, colonial, and Nationalist periods on Taiwan (1500–1895, 1895–1945, 1945–2000?). Then we review the main political characteristics of the early, middle, and late postwar periods on Taiwan (1945–1960, 1960–1975, 1975–1990). Only then do we examine some key aspects of Taiwan's late postwar democratization (the formation of the main opposition party, the growing role of elections, and the continuing issue of political independence for Taiwan). Fortunately there are now enough background books and analytical articles about the Taiwan case to implement this plan.

ANALYTICAL THEMES

Liberal, radical, and conservative orientations in western scholarship each have their own interpretations of the role of the supranational, national, and subnational levels in political development in general, and on Taiwan in particular.

Globalism. Taiwan is a useful example of how global processes shape national political development. Historically an extension of imperial China, Taiwan began its socioeconomic modernization under Japanese colonialism, and continued postwar under Chinese Nationalist rule, with American and Japanese participation. Both its authoritarianism and its democratization were largely externally derived. Taiwan's authoritarianism began under imperial China, intensified under the Japanese, and was reinforced by the Nationalists. Taiwan's democratization originated in Japanese, Nationalist, and American ideals. Externally-oriented economic development strengthened society's demand for political democratization. Finally, the long-delayed reorientation of the United States from the Republic of China (ROC) to the PRC, and a global tide of democratization, left the Nationalist state with little alternative but to democratize.

Different interpretations highlight different supranational processes in this globalist narrative. Conservatives emphasize regional geopolitical interactions, which produced first U.S. intervention to protect the Nationalist state from communism (permitting much authoritarianism but requiring some democracy) and later U.S. disengagement (forcing the Nationalist state finally to come to terms with Taiwan's society). Liberals celebrate the global diffusion both of democratic ideals and of the economic preconditions for realizing them. Radicals interpret all of these—early postwar Cold War, middle postwar trade expansion, and late postwar democratization—as aspects of the global development of capitalism. Even in the radical account, however, global processes contain conflicting tendencies that affect different countries differently, in each country both promoting and retarding democratization.

Statism. Recently some political sociologists have gained much attention for rediscovering the potency of states. Statism, both as political practice and as academic analysis, emphasizes the autonomy of states from social forces and the initiative of states in launching social policies, in all political systems—totalitarian, authoritarian and democratic. East Asian specialists have always known the region was highly statist. Historians and anthropologists provide "conservative" analyses of the persistence of institutions and culture, regarding modern East Asian authoritarianism as a legacy from the past. Radical political economists consider it a concomitant of dependent development. Liberal political scientists analyze the domestic mix of leadership, military, party, and government institutions. These national institutions manage both conflicts among themselves and demands from their supranational and subnational environments. Some institutional analysts view Taiwan as a party system in transition from one party to several (e.g., Tien). Others give equal attention to all institutions, particularly warning against neglect of the military (e.g., Winckler).

Statism too provides a persuasive narrative of Taiwan's politics. Imperial, Japanese, and Nationalist authoritarianism reinforced each other, giving the postwar Nationalist state on Taiwan exceptional autonomy, which it used to reform society, steer the economy and dominate culture. Early postwar statism suppressed opposition and middle postwar statism coopted it, leaving late postwar statism strong enough to outcompete the opposition that it then allowed to emerge. The state itself decided both the timing and the terms of transition from authoritarianism towards democracy. Eventually, the Nationalists can claim to have implemented their founder Sun Yat-sen's program of gradual transition from warlord militarism through tutelary democracy to full democracy. Even a future Taiwanese democracy is likely to remain quite statist— society will delegate much authority to the state to maintain stability, and government will intervene much in society to solve problems. Incidentally, a statist account need not assume complete state unity and rationality. Rather, the story could include much rivalry between institutions, and a decisive role for the Leader in forcing political reform on them.

Socioculturalism. Subnational processes are often less visible than supranational and national ones, particularly in authoritarian regimes. Nevertheless it is worth constructing a society-centered narrative of Taiwan's political development. Liberal political science assumes that politics is an expression of society, and that economic development will eventually lead, through social modernization, to the democratization of authoritarian regimes. Radical critiques of authoritarianism too assume both some class basis for, and some mass opposition to, most authoritarian regimes. Historians have always emphasized the conservative social ideals of the traditional Chinese state. Historical sociologists have recently argued that traditional Chinese society outgrew the traditional Chinese state, requiring society itself to organize much of local political-economic as well as sociocultural life.

Clearly this was the case for pre-1895 Taiwan, which was an undergoverned maritime frontier. Japanese administration penetrated society more deeply, but still left Taiwanese local elites some role. After 1945, the Nationalists at first suppressed these elites, but later accommodated many, allowing them to pursue local political and economic objectives so long as they did not challenge Nationalist rule. Meanwhile some postwar processes gradually increased mass influence— the pluralizing effect of modernization and the growing leverage of Taiwanese soldiers, administrators, entrepreneurs, and workers. Through the early and middle postwar periods the Nationalists succeeded in preventing any opposition from organizing to give political expression to these social forces. However, by the late postwar period, such repression became too costly. Political opposition gradually formalized, emboldening organizers of social movements (consumers, environmentalists, workers, farmers). This sociocentric narrative allows, but does not require, much coordination between political opposition and social movements, or between moderate and radical wings of the political opposition.

II. MAJOR TOPICS

HISTORICAL BACKGROUND

History not only provides a backdrop and leaves a legacy, it also reveals long-run processes still at work in Taiwan's postwar political development.

Imperial China. Some postwar processes began in the imperial period. At the supranational level, European expansion brought westerners to Taiwan even before extensive Chinese settlement, provoking China to strengthen its claim to Taiwan. Eventually, however, the western powers awarded Taiwan to Japan. At the national level, unlike most of the non-western world, China successfully resisted western conquest, and therefore later modernized independently. Finally, at the subnational level, migration from China's southeast coast gradually laid the foundations for modern Taiwan— a society that is culturally Chinese, but socially oriented to local communities on Taiwan.

Japanese Colonialism. Japanese occupation inaugurated many processes that continue into the postwar period. At the supranational level, Japan's upward drive in the Pacific brought Japan into competition with the United States, causing Japan to accelerate economic and political development on Taiwan. (Postwar, both America and Japan used Taiwan as an export platform for competition with the other, again accelerating Taiwan's development.) At the national level, Japan imposed order on both lowland Chinese and upland aborigines. It built a modern state that penetrated to the bottom of Taiwanese society, facilitating postwar Nationalist political control and economic mobilization. At the subnational level, Taiwanese elites gradually mastered the game of demanding self-rule within the Japanese empire, lessons they later applied in lobbying the Nationalist state for political liberalization. Meanwhile socioeconomic modernization and military mobilization laid the basis for postwar mass political participation.

POSTWAR DEVELOPMENT

Taiwan's postwar political development falls into three periods—early, middle, and late.

1945–1960. In the early postwar period the main supranational process affecting Taiwan's political development was the Cold War, which forced U.S. support of the Nationalist state. The main national process was the Nationalist's securing control of Taiwan through hard-authoritarian political repression and state-led economic development. State control left little latitude for subnational initiatives.

The late 1940s saw the end of World War Two, the outbreak of the Cold War, and Nationalist defeat on the mainland and retreat to Taiwan. The Nationalist preoccupation was first regaining control of Chinese territory from Japan, then combating communism, then ensuring survival. Taiwanese at first celebrated their liberation from Japanese colonialism, then protested a carpet-bagging Nationalist provincial administration, then resigned themselves to subjugation to the exiled Nationalist central government.

In the early 1950s, the outbreak of the Korean war required the United States to protect the KMT, and enabled the Americans to force the Nationalists to implement social reforms and launch economic development. Inauguration of local elections began the process of co-opting old Taiwanese local elites and creating new, Nationalist-dependent ones.

By the late 1950s two Taiwan Straits crises (in 1954 and 1958) had confirmed the separation of Taiwan from the mainland—the communists could not take Taiwan, but neither could the Nationalists retake the mainland. Consequently the Nationalists gradually redirected their attention to developing Taiwan as a model for future mainland development. Mainlander intellectuals and Taiwanese politicians moved toward formation of an opposition political party.

1960–1975. In the middle postwar period the main supranational process affecting Taiwan was the American shift from organizing regional military alliances to promoting global economic development, a strategy for which Taiwan was the earliest exemplar. The main national process was gradual succession from Chiang Kai-shek to his son Chiang Ching-kuo, and further consolidation of the dominance of the Nationalist state over Taiwanese society, particularly through the success of economic development. The main subnational process was individual pursuit of the opportunities for upward mobility created by rapid economic growth.

In the early 1960s, the Kennedy administration considered opening dialogue with China, and pushed global trade liberalization. Economically, Taiwan progressed from aid to trade; politically, it regressed with the suppression of efforts to form an opposition party. Taiwanese shifted rapidly from agriculture to industry and from countryside to city.

In the late 1960s, intensification of the Vietnam War and outbreak of the Cultural Revolution postponed Sino-American detente, gave the U.S. defense relationship with Taiwan a new lease on life, and spurred Taiwan's exports. The beginning of a smooth succession from Chiang Kai-shek to Chiang Ching-kuo precluded significant regime change. The Nationalists marginally increased Taiwanese political representation, but further developed Nationalist party organization and further reduced opposition activity.

The early 1970s finally saw the beginning of U.S. diplomatic disengagement from Taiwan and detente with the PRC. Nationally, leadership succession continued. Chiang Kai-shek remained as a decreasingly active president. Chiang Ching-kuo assumed an increasingly active premiership, courting reformist intellectuals and the Taiwanese public. The combination of prosperity, repression and reforms temporarily reduced opposition political activity to practically nothing, allowing the KMT to attempt a transition from local machine to good government politics.

1975–1990. In the late postwar period, the main supranational process affecting Taiwan's political development was the decline in tension between the capitalist and socialist blocs (depriving Taiwan of U.S. protection but reducing the likelihood of communist attack) and the rise in economic conflict between capitalist countries (producing trade frictions between Taiwan and the United States but generating still more business for Taiwan). The main national political process was the incipient normalization of the Nationalist state, including the end of dynastic strongmen, the revival of legislative institutions, and the conversion of the KMT into an electorally competitive party. At the subnational level, education and incomes approached developed-country levels, a maturing middle class began asserting some leadership over society, and a formal political opposition emerged.

In the late 1970s the United States finally shifted its formal diplomatic relations from the ROC to PRC, though continuing informal relations with Taiwan. Chiang Kai-shek died and Chiang Ching-kuo completed his succession to the party chairmanship and government presidency. Incipient political liberalization permitted a surge of opposition activity, which led in turn to temporarily renewed repression. The Nationalists jailed most of the more assertive opposition leaders for long terms.

In the early 1980s, Taiwan demonstrated that it could survive American political derecognition and global economic stagnation, despite initial international enthusiasm for Tengist reformism in China. CCK resumed cautious liberalization—relaxing tensions with the PRC, promoting Taiwanese within the Nationalist elite and tolerating political opposition. A series of local and national elections allowed the informal opposition to demonstrate its staying power and gain experience.

In the late 1980s, PRC political and economic regression again raised Taiwan's international reputation vis-à-vis the PRC, but global democratization increased the pressure on the Nationalists for political reform. Chiang Ching-kuo died and Lee Teng-hui succeeded him, continuing reform. Both the liberalization of civil society (lifting of martial law, emergence of social movements, explosion of cultural cosmopolitanism) and the democratization of political institutions (legalization of opposition parties, reelection of national representatives, broadening of political debate) accelerated.

RECENT DEMOCRATIZATION

This section provides more detail on some key aspects of democratization on Taiwan in the late postwar period—the gradual emergence of political opposition, the increasing role of elections, and the continuing issue of independence for Taiwan.

The Emergence of Opposition. Throughout the postwar period the Nationalist party-state left some political space for Non-Nationalist politicians, contenting itself with about 70 percent of votes and positions. In the early postwar period, the non-Nationalists still included many ardent opponents of KMT rule. By the middle period most non-Nationalists were non-partisan independents running as individuals. The story of the late period is the gradual occupation of non-Nationalist political space by committed oppositionists, mostly at the expense of independents, not Nationalists.

This story begins with the "breakthrough" elections of 1977 when non-Nationalists captured four of twenty-one local executive posts and 21 of 77 provincial assembly seats. Some of these were long-standing local oppositionists, some were recent defectors from the KMT, some were resolutely non-partisan, and some later joined the KMT. Preparations for 1978 elections to the National Assembly and National Legislature helped clarify who wished to remain independent and who wished to join the incipient opposition. When the 1978 campaign became too radical and the United States transferred diplomatic recognition to the PRC, the Nationalists postponed the election. Reactions to these events created radical versus moderate tendencies within the opposition. The moderates remained within the law, calling on the Nationalists simply to implement their own constitution. The radicals pushed organization of a formal opposition political party and held mass political rallies, both illegal. The Nationalists arrested the radicals but, as a safety-valve, allowed some moderate oppositionists to continue their parliamentary and publishing activities.

When elections resumed, 70 percent of the public continued to support the KMT, with the remainder split between non-partisan independents, moderate oppositionists and radical oppositionists (the wives and lawyers of the jailed radicals). CCK again maneuvered the system toward political liberalization, trying to get reactionaries and progressives within the KMT to agree on political reforms, and encouraging moderation and discouraging radicalism within the incipient opposition. However the Nationalist establishment dithered while the opposition radicals grew daily more daring. The opposition again moved toward more formal political organization, this time more cautiously, first "recommending" candidates, then "supporting" them. Finally, knowing that both the Nationalist party and he personally were running out of time, CCK ordered direct communications between Nationalist progressives and opposition moderates. In spring 1986 he announced that martial law (in force on Taiwan since 1947) would be suspended, and the organization of opposition parties legalized. As the fall 1986 elections for national representatives approached, a few radical oppositionists in the United States announced plans to form a party there. Oppositionists on Taiwan, meeting to consider their fall campaign strategy, unexpectedly decided to declare themselves a formal political party, even though the Nationalists had not yet completed the necessary legislation. After some internal debate, the KMT acquiesced, choosing to treat the opposition's announcement as a declaration of intent rather than as an illegal act. Thus was the Democratic Progressive Party formed, with many other would-be opposition parties soon to follow.

One interpretive issue surrounding these events concerns the balance between external influences, Establishment initiative, and Opposition pressure. This author sees all three as essential. Democratization in other countries and modernization of Taiwan's society increasingly made democratization the only rational option for the KMT. However it was only CCK's sophistication and decisiveness that finally forced the KMT to choose that option. (Tunjen Cheng has emphasized opposition pressure, while Andrew Nathan has emphasized CCK's leadership.) Another interpretive issue concerns the nature of the political system from which, through which, and toward which the various participants thought they were moving. This author assumes that what the Nationalists thought they were embarking on was a transition from "hard" authoritarianism (the KMT retaining power by suppressing opposition through whatever force might be necessary) to "soft" authoritarianism (the KMT retaining power by using their institutional advantages to maintain a majority against a permanently minority opposition). Their objective was to stabilize the system in "soft authoritarianism," thereby postponing as long as possible a perhaps inevitable transition to democracy. As of 1990, that is basically what has happened, though the system has slipped toward democracy faster than even progressive Nationalists originally envisaged, as reactionary Nationalists had warned. Such peaceful slippage is what opposition moderates hoped, and opposition radicals doubted, would occur.

The Role of Elections. As the above shows, in the late postwar period, elections played an increasing role in Taiwan's political development. Elections, particularly of the president, had always been occasions for Nationalist party congresses and policy pronouncements, the state creating what it regarded as an appropriate atmosphere for itself. However, as the KMT switched its reliance from police power to popular poll, anticipation of elections increasingly shaped both public policy and personnel choice. Moreover, the KMT faced significant electoral dilemmas— how to increase intraparty democracy without destroying campaign discipline, how to decrease reliance on local factions without losing contests. The DPP, too, faced major electoral dilemmas. Taiwan's single-vote multi-member electoral system makes it easy for a minority party to obtain representation, but difficult for a minority party to achieve a majority. Under the system on Taiwan, in elections for parliamentary bodies, each voter casts only one vote, but each constituency contains from one to ten seats, three to five in most constituencies. One candidate can win with a third to a fifth of the vote, which the opposition commands in most localities, guaranteeing it at least some representation. However, members of the same party run against each other for these multiple seats, requiring strong party organization to limit candidacies and allocate votes. The Nationalists became very good at this, the opposition much less so. Moreover, the DPP was caught in a vicious circle: because it had not won many positions, it had little demonstrated administrative competence, which worried voters, who continued to award it few positions. Meanwhile, other new parties entered the field, including potentially strong labor representatives.

In the "triple" 1989 elections (for national legislators, provincial assemblymen and local executives), the KMT attempted to use intra-party primaries to increase democracy and weaken factions. For its part, the DPP resolved on a bold strategy for overcoming its dilemma. It ran some of its strongest candidates for local executive, which are one-on-one races that tend to mobilize most voters behind the two leading candidates, as in most Anglo-American elections. The DPP hoped that the excitement surrounding the local executive races would then spill over into the parliamentary contests, boosting its proportion of parliamentary votes and seats. Capturing local executive posts would give the DPP administrative experience, while increasing its parliamentary vote would show that the DPP could, in the long run, win a national majority. In the event, the DPP's gambits succeeded better than the KMT's. Instead of taming factions, the KMT's primaries exacerbated them, and caused some factions to place their own survival above Nationalist victory. The KMT still captured 70 percent of the positions, but only 60 percent of the vote. The public preferred young reformers to old hacks. On the non-Nationalist side, the public ignored other new parties, giving strong support to the DPP, though still some support to some independents. The DPP won an unprecedented six local executive posts. In parliamentary races, an alliance of radical DPP candidates favoring Taiwan independence did better than expected.

The interpretative issues surrounding these events concern both the nature of the outcome and the processes that produced it. Was the KMT performance a victory or a defeat? The KMT itself called it "defeat within victory", showing that even its progressives still hoped to maintain a "soft authoritarian" 70 percent of the popular vote. Was the decline to 60 percent a prelude to further slippage, or an adjustment to a more realistic and stable level? Probably the latter. How much of the increase in DPP vote (from

22 to 30 percent) resulted from a shift in voter sentiment toward them, and how much from the fielding of more candidates in previously uncontested constituencies? Probably about half and half.

The Issue of Independence. A key aspect of Taiwan's late postwar democratization has been the handling of an issue that is potentially explosive, both externally and internally: whether Taiwan should formally declare itself a new country. Supranationally, independence is explosive because the PRC might use force to prevent Taiwan's secession from the concept of "one China," and the United States would not protect Taiwan. Nationally, independence is explosive because the Nationalists base both their reason for existing and their claim to Taiwan on fervent adherence to the concept of "one China." Subnationally, independence is explosive because many Taiwanese have long yearned for an independent state to represent them internationally, and the opposition has long tried to use this issue to mobilize support. If there is any issue that could derail Taiwan's democratization, independence is it.

Given the Nationalists' pursuit of de facto independence, their position has been that the less said about de jure independence the better. Nevertheless, before he died, CCK himself announced that he considered himself Taiwanese, and some regarded this as an informal declaration of Taiwan's de facto independence. Moreover, largely to preempt opposition appeals, the Nationalists have vigorously reasserted Taiwan's de facto independence, buying diplomatic relations with more countries and demanding admission to more international organizations. For its part, the opposition has long had three levels of aspiration—the right to discuss the question, the right of the people on Taiwan to decide the issue, and independence itself. Most polls show the general public less concerned about this issue than opposition politicians, but it is not clear to what extent this just reflects long suppression of its discussion. In principle, advocacy of independence remains forbidden but, in practice, by the 1989 elections it was widespread. Pro-independence candidates won twenty of 32 races they entered, garnering about ten percent of the vote.

The interpretive issues surrounding independence again highlight the interplay of supranational, national and subnational processes. Is the PRC now too enmeshed in the "complex interdependence" of external political and economic relations, including those with Taiwan, to use force against Taiwan? Is Taiwan's anomalous international status a failure to achieve classical international ideals, or a harbinger of further future decline in the significance of political sovereignty for all states? Would the Taiwanese in North America who advocate independence return to Taiwan to live with its consequences? Can the Nationalists transfer their legitimacy from representing "China" to representing "Taiwan"? For the opposition, is the independence issue a way out or a dead end? Only the post-postwar era, beginning in the 1990s, will tell.

III. ISSUES FOR DISCUSSION

1. The Nationalist state has always claimed to be a democracy. What definition of democracy is appropriate to Taiwan and, under that definition, when would Taiwan start to be a democracy?

2. What are the advantages and disadvantages, for an eventually strong democracy, of a gradual, negotiated transition from authoritarianism to democracy like that on Taiwan? Discuss the roles in that process, both past and future, of conservatives and progressives within the Nationalist establishment, and moderates and radicals within the Taiwanese opposition.

3. In Taiwan's political development, what have been the roles of supranational processes (external geopolitics and political-economy), national processes (personal leadership and authoritarian institutions) and subnational processes (resilient opposition and robustly modernizing society)? Are they equally important or not?

4. In Taiwan's political development, what have been the roles of conservative processes (institutional and cultural legacies from the past), liberal processes (liberalization of markets and modernization of society), and radical processes (political oppression and class conflicts accompanying capitalist development)? Are they equally relevant or not?

IV. SELECTED READINGS

Cheng, Tun-jen. "Democratizing the Quasi-Leninist Regime in Taiwan." World Politics 41, 4 (1989): 471–499 (student reading). The best single article on subsequent democratization.

Cheng, Tun-jen, and Haggard, Stephan, eds. Political Change in Taiwan. Boulder, CO: Lynne Rienner, 1991 (faculty background). Provides useful recent discussion of Taiwan's political transition.

Clough, Ralph. Island China. Cambridge: Harvard University Press, 1978 (faculty background). Still the best introduction to Taiwan's postwar situation, particularly as an object of American policy.

Gold, Thomas. State and Society in the Taiwan Miracle. Armonk, NY: M.E. Sharpe, 1986 (faculty background). The best introduction to Taiwan's postwar political economy.

Tien, Hung-mao. *The Great Transition: Political and Social Change in the Republic of China.* Stanford: Hoover, 1989 (faculty background). The only, and magisterial, book-length introduction to Taiwan's postwar politics.

Winckler, Edwin A., and Greenhalgh, Susan, eds. *Contending Approaches to the political economy of Taiwan.* Armonk, NY: M.E. Sharpe, 1988 (faculty background). Relates the Taiwan case to comparative theory, with two papers by Winckler on political development.

Winckler, Edwin A. "Institutionalization and Participation on Taiwan: From Hard to Soft Authoritarianism?" *The China Quarterly* 99 (1984): 481–499 (student reading). A short article sketching Taiwan's late postwar political system.

Winckler, Edwin A. "Taiwan Transition?" In *Democratization in Taiwan*, edited by Tun-jen Cheng and Stephan Haggard. Boulder, CO: Lynne Rienner, 1991 (student reading).

Political Science:
India

Democracy
and Political
Participation
in India

Paul R. Brass

I. INTRODUCTION: CENTRAL POINTS

India is often called the world's largest democracy. Its postindependence history of elections, political parties, and interest group representation provides an excellent basis for contrasts and comparisons with similar institutions and processes in the industrialized countries of the West and Japan. Its history also contrasts with that of other postcolonial countries, raising the question of why India's parliamentary system has persisted where others have not.

Four major aspects of India's post-Independence political development deserve special notice:

• The nearly unbroken history of competitive elections at the national and state levels in this subcontinental federal parliamentary state demonstrates the value of elections in a developing country as a means of inducting previously unmobilized groups into the political process.

• The Indian party system provides the leading example of the "predominant" or "one-party dominant" system, which has been associated also with other Western and non-Western countries, including Japan, Turkey, and Italy.[1]

• Post-Independence Indian experience with processes of social mobilization and political institutionalization contradicts the prevalent argument that rapid increases in the former "tend to produce political decay" unless offset by special measures to restrict their impact upon political organizations and political participation."[2]

• The great number of interest associations in Indian politics confirms the importance of a vigorous group life for the peaceful articulation of demands and discontent in representative systems. The distinctive character of many of these interest associations and intermediary groups between the people and the state also demonstrates one of the great strengths of the Indian representative system, namely, its ability to adapt alien, that is, British, parliamentary institutions to the institutions, practices, and values of its traditional society.

II. MAJOR TOPICS

ELECTIONS AND POLITICAL MOBILIZATION

Pre-Independence Elections and Party Formation. Parties, elections, and representative government came gradually to India during British rule. The Indian National Congress, the party which led the nationalist movement and took power after Independence, was founded in 1885. In the intervening years, the Congress went through several transformations. It began as a pressure group petitioning the government for political and administrative reforms. After the 1920s, the Congress became a mass membership party alternating between the use of strategies of mass mobilization under the leadership of Mahatma Gandhi and contesting elections to provincial and national legislatures. From 1935, with the introduction of provincial self-government, the Congress began the third change towards a governing party in the majority of provinces of British-ruled India, culminating in its emergence as the ruling party of the country at Independence in 1947.

The first elections to the central legislature occurred under a highly restricted franchise after the Morley-Minto Reforms of 1909. Further political reforms in 1919 and 1935 brought increases in the numbers of Indians elected to the central legislature, extension of the electoral principle to the provinces, and expansion of the franchise. However, universal adult franchise was not introduced until after Independence.

Opposition to the Congress during British rule came principally from the Muslim League, a party founded in 1906, whose leaders ultimately chose the goal of separation of the Muslim-majority areas to form the independent sovereign state of Pakistan. Several post-Independence Indian political parties also trace their origins to the period of British colonial rule. The Communist Party of India (CPI) was founded in 1925. The Socialist parties originated as a group within the Indian national Congress founded in 1936 as the Congress Socialist Party. Post-Independence parties identified with militant Hindu nationalism developed out of the Rashtriya Swayamsevak Sangh (RSS), a Hindu revivalist organization founded in 1925.

Several regional (state) parties also have their sources in earlier movements. The Dravida Munnetra Kazagham (DMK) and its splinter, the All-India Anna DMK (AIADMK) in the contemporary state of Tamil Nadu are descendants of earlier Tamil nationalist movements which developed in the late nineteenth and early twentieth centuries. The Akali Dal, the principal party of the Sikh religious community in the Punjab, originated in a gurdwara (Sikh temple) reform movement in the 1920s.

On the eve of Independence, however, the two principal parties contesting for power at the Center and in most of the states were the Indian National Congress and the Muslim League. The creation of Pakistan left the Indian National Congress as the overwhelmingly dominant party in India, well placed to establish its supremacy over all other rivals in the first two decades of post-Independence electoral and party competition.

Post-Independence Elections. There have been ten general elections in India since Independence; the latest was held in May-June 1991. In addition to elections for the national parliament, there have been numerous elections to the legislative assemblies of each of the twenty-four states of the Indian Union. Also, since many of the states have undergone periods of instability, under India's parliamentary system mid-term elections have often been called in such states. The cumulative impact of these and other elections has been to produce a situation comparable to that in the United States in the sense that, in both these huge democracies it often appears that elections, far from being periodic affairs, are a continuing, constant part and focus of the political scene.

Voter Turnout. Turnout rates in India compare favorably with those in presidential elections in the United States. In 1984, the

Election Data, Indian Parliamentary Elections, 1952–84[1]

Year	Electorate (in millions)	Polling stations	Votes Polled (in millions)	Turnout (percent)
1952	173.2	132,560	80.7	46.6
1957	193.7	220,478	91.3	47.1
1962	217.7	238,355	119.9	55.1
1967	250.1	267,555	152.7	61.1
1971	274.1	342,944	151.5	55.3
1977	321.2	373,908	194.3	60.5
1980	355.6	434,442	202.3	56.9
1984	375.8	479,214	238.4	63.4
1989	498.6	589,449	298.9	59.6

Source: Robert L. Hardgrave, Jr. and Stanley A. Kochanek, *India: Government and Politics in a Developing Nation*, 4th, ed. (San Diego: Harcourt Brace Jovanovich, 1986), p. 302; for 1989, Election Commission of India, Press Information Bureau.

1. Excluding Assam, where elections could not be held.

Indian turnout (63.4 percent) was nearly ten percentage points above the American turnout (53.9 percent) in the presidential election of that year.

There has been a gradual increase in voter turnout in Indian elections, in both national (parliamentary) and state (legislative assembly) elections since the first general elections, held in 1952 (see table). The average turnout rate in the first four parliamentary elections was 52.5 percent, and in the next five it was 59 percent.

Although there has been a general increase, there have also been marked fluctuations in the parliamentary vote, with three notable peaks above the 60 percent level in 1967, 1977, and 1984. The first peak in 1967 was associated with widespread popular discontent over a number of issues, of which rising prices and food shortages were the most significant. The 1977 election followed the relaxation of the "emergency" authoritarian regime imposed on the country by Prime Minister Indira Gandhi from 1975 to 1977. The defeat of the Congress party in that election constituted a rejection of several notorious features of her emergency regime, particularly forced sterilization for family planning purposes. The 1984 election followed the assassination of Mrs. Gandhi, which in turn was a consequence of the turmoil and violence in the state of Punjab.

Intensity of interparty competition, which is commonly considered to produce increased rates of voter turnout, was a minor factor in the election of 1967, a major factor in 1977, and of no consequence in 1984. That is, there was a limited anti-Congress electoral alliance among opposition parties in 1967, a complete merger of the largest opposition parties in the 1977 elections, and a disintegration of the non-Congress opposition in 1984. Moreover, in 1989, when a largely united opposition faced the Congress, voter turnout declined.

As in the United States, voter participation varies considerably among the states of the Indian Union. In contrast to the United States, however, where the national presidential elections consistently produce higher rates of turnout, the pattern in India is less consistent. State elections, closer to the interests and sentiments of the people and frequently more intensely competitive, often generate more enthusiasm and participation than do parliamentary elections.

The average turnout by state (the fifteen largest states) in legislative assembly elections in India ranges from a high of 74 percent in Kerala to a low of 40 percent in Orissa, a difference of more than thirty percentage points. Intensity of interparty competition is strongly associated with high turnout rates in state elections. Turnout in states where there is intense competition among parties tends to be between ten to fifteen percentage points higher on the average than in states where the Congress is the dominant party.

Why should intensity of interparty competition be so clearly related to voting at the state level and not at the national level? The main reason is that there is no coherent national opposition with an alternative leadership in most elections. The first election in which such an opposition did appear, in 1977, did precipitate a high turnout.

Voters and Nonvoters. Studies of turnout rates in India by various social, personal, and ethnic categories suggest the following general features. Voting rates by sex, initially much higher among men than among women in a society where female modesty and subordination to men's wishes on political matters have been traditionally valued, has evened out with successive elections, though male voting generally remains somewhat higher than female. Similarly, rural-urban differences in voting behavior also have tended to even out in successive elections within each region of the country. The only consistent social attribute which cuts across regional differences is education which, virtually among all social groups in India as elsewhere, tends to lead to higher voting rates.

One of the most important determinants of both turnout and voting for particular parties in India is caste. At the local level, in particular constituencies, prominent persons often influence members of the same *jāti* both to come out and vote heavily and to vote for a particular candidate or party. In larger areas, numerous *jātis* are often viewed as belonging to a broad caste category with a common designation. Thus, any caste category, including Brahmans, Rajputs, Yadavs, for examples, may include dozens or even hundreds of *jātis* (sometimes called "sub-castes"). The caste category in this sense is neither a corporate group nor the same as varna, but a potentially mobilizable group of similar or related *jātis*. Some caste categories have been mobilized effectively across large areas both to turn out and to vote predominantly for particular political parties.

The caste categories of India are often divided into three groupings according to ritual status and wealth. At the top, the elite castes include those who fall into the two highest varnas, particularly Brahmans and Rajputs (Kshatriyas), among others. All such castes comprise at most a quarter of the Hindu population of the country. In the middle are so-called backward castes whose members have lacked social or religious prestige, have had less favorable access than the elite castes to educational opportunities and government jobs, and who work primarily on the land as cultivators or laborers. They are estimated to comprise approximately half the Hindu population of the country. At the bottom are the so-called untouchables, designated officially as Scheduled Castes— comprising approximately a fifth of the Hindu population—whose condition has traditionally been so wretched that they have been placed on a schedule (hence the official designation), entitling their members to special privileges in the form of political, educational, and employment reservations.

In rural areas, persons from the highest castes, and especially from the predominant landowning castes, have been presumed to vote at higher rates than those from lower castes; they have even been suspected of controlling the votes of the latter or, where this is not possible, of physically preventing them from voting. However, beginning in 1971, the Congress party, under Mrs. Gandhi's leadership, deliberately set out to mobilize the poorest voters, who come primarily from the low castes. As a result, estimated turnout rates for low caste voters have been as high as and often higher than the rates for the general population as a whole.

Turnout rates among the aboriginal tribal populations (nearly 8 percent of India's total population), who are often as poor and disadvantaged as the low castes, have generally been somewhat lower than the national rate. Estimated turnout rates for the large Muslim minority population (more than 11 percent of the total population) have been quite varied from region to region, sometimes higher, sometimes lower than the general population in particular states.

A plurality of the Indian rural population, however, are neither high caste nor low caste nor minorities, but come from a broad range of the above described backward castes of intermediate ritual status, some of whose members are relatively well-off peasant farmers, others of whom are on average barely above the lower castes in economic well-being. Studies of particular constituencies have revealed a pattern of gradual incorporation of particular castes from within this broad category in election after election. A typical pattern has been a challenge to the Congress from an opposition party that has mobilized a particular backward caste in a region. If the Congress suffers a loss of electoral support, it will move to draw into voting in the next election another previously unmobilized caste by selecting a candidate from amongst its ranks to contest against the opposition.

As competition for the vote of this broad range of intermediate castes has intensified, prominent political leaders from both the Congress and the opposition have vied with each other by promising benefits, notably the allocation of jobs in government and the public sector and places in educational institutions for their members. Resentment among the elite castes who feel threatened by a potential loss of advantage in education and employment, and sometimes from the lower castes as well who feel their own rights to benefits will be eroded if those benefits are likewise extended to other castes, has in several states in India precipitated considerable intercaste violence. Intercaste conflict on the matter of reservations for backward castes has reached a new level of intensity since August, 1990 when the central government announced its intention to introduce a policy of reserving twenty-seven percent of jobs under its control for backward castes. The issues raised by India's policies of "protective discrimination" for the low and backward castes are similar to those which have come up in relation to affirmative action policies in the United States.

Overall, the most important conclusion is that voting rates have increased throughout large segments of the electorate in successive elections in such a manner as to even out differences between sexes, the literate and illiterate, urban and rural populations, minorities and nonminorities, high castes and low castes, and the like. Competitive political mobilization has been the principal factor in this process. The primary differentiating factor in turnout rates is region, that is, state or a territorially compact, culturally distinctive segment of a state rather than social class or other individual and group differentia.

POLITICAL PARTIES AND PARTY SYSTEM

One-party Dominant System. The most common label placed upon the Indian national party system by scholars of India and comparative party politics has been "one-party dominant system" or "predominant party system." Several features distinguish this type of party system from one-party and hegemonic party systems, on the one hand, and two-party and multi-party systems, on the other hand. These features include the existence of other parties which are free to contest elections against the dominant party; however, the dominant party invariably wins a majority of seats in parliament, though not necessarily a majority of votes.[3]

How well does this label apply to the Indian case? Until 1967, the Indian National Congress, the dominant party and the party of Independence, held a virtual monopoly on governing power at the federal government level and in most of the Indian states. In 1967, however, the representation of the Congress in parliament was reduced to a bare majority and, after the elections, the party lost power in half the Indian states. The predominance of the Congress in the system was restored, however, as Mrs. Gandhi consolidated her power between 1967 and 1977. In the 1977 general elections which followed the relaxation of Mrs. Gandhi's emergency regime, a new opposition party, called the Janata party, was formed through a merger of the leading non-Congress parties in the northern party of the country. Janata at last, thirty years after Independence, succeeded in displacing the Congress from power at the national level and in most of the states in the state legislative assembly elections which followed.

In mid-1979, however, the Janata coalition disintegrated and fell from power; after the return of the Congress to power under Mrs. Gandhi's leadership in 1980, the opposition was unable for another decade to achieve sufficient unity to effectively challenge the Congress in parliamentary elections. In 1984, the Congress, under the leadership of Mrs. Gandhi's son, Rajiv, won an unprecedented popular vote, nearly 50 percent, and an equally unprecedented seat share of 77 percent in the Lok Sabha (the lower house of the Indian parliament).[4] Then, in 1989, a new Janata coalition (the Janata Dal), centered in north India, combined with several regional parties in other parts of the country to defeat the Congress and form the second non-Congress central government in India's post-independence history. The National Front, however, failed to win a majority of seats in parliament and could form a government under Vishwanath Pratap Singh only with the support of other parties in the House, namely, the Bharatiya Janata Party (BJP) and the Communist Party of India (Marxist [CPM]). However, the BJP withdrew its support to the V. P. Singh government in October, 1990 on issues relating to reservations for backward castes and the temple/mosque controversy in the city of Ayodhya in north India. The National Front government was then replaced by another minority government headed by a faction from the Janata Dal led by Mr. Chandrashekhar, supported in Parliament by the Congress. In the general elections held in May–June, 1991, in the midst of which the Congress leader, Rajiv Gandhi, was assasinated, the Congress was nevertheless returned to power with a minority government under its new leader, Mr. P. V. Narasimha Rao.

Despite the success of the opposition in 1977 and 1989, there seems no other appropriate designation for India's national party system during the first forty years than "predominant" or "one-party dominant" system. There are, however, two important differences from the ideal model. The first is the fact that the Congress never polls a majority of votes in the country as a whole, which means that a united opposition can defeat the Congress; though this happens rarely, the Congress-dominated system is truly competitive and alternation in power is a genuine possibility. Second, in a sense, it might be more accurate to say that India simply does not have a "national" party system; its party configuration varies within each state and, for the country as a whole, from election to election. Within each state, there will be a different set of parties contesting against the Congress in the state legislative assembly elections. In every national election, new political parties enter the fray. The principal opposition party in Parliament also has changed in every general election.

State Party Systems. In the United States, the two-party system now prevails in nearly all the fifty states and the two parties are the same everywhere, at least in name. The Canadian federal parliamentary system is more diverse than that of the United States in the sense that the dominance of the two main parties varies significantly from province to province, and there are strong third parties in several provinces. In India, however, aside from the universal presence of the Congress, variation from state to state in the configuration of the leading parties and in the structure of interparty competition is very great.

In the 1980s, state party systems could be divided roughly into three broad types: one-party dominant systems, comparable to the prevailing pattern of Congress dominance in the country as a whole; one-party dominant systems in which there existed one institutionalized non-Congress party, but not one strong enough in most elections to bring the Congress down except in alliance with other non-Congress parties; and competitive party systems. In general, over the past two decades, in contrast to the situation at the national level, the pervasiveness of one-party dominance has declined and the number of states with truly competitive party systems has increased.

The Leading Political Parties. The Indian National Congress, founded in 1885 and the leading party in Indian politics since independence, is ideologically a party of the Center. It has pursued economic development through centralized planning, based on a mixed economy, in which socialist ideals are proclaimed but not practiced. Agrarian reforms have been modest. Programs for the poor have been adopted, but no radical restructuring of economic and class relations in town or country has been undertaken. Congress policies also have been secular. In the Indian context, secular means that no privileged status is granted by the state to any religious group, but that all are tolerated, several actually receive some benefits directly from the state, and religious minorities are protected, once again in principle though not always in practice.

The Left of the Indian political spectrum was occupied until 1974 by both Communist and non-Communist parties. The non-Communist Left, comprising several socialist parties, emerged after Independence, largely through defections from the Congress itself, as the major opposition force in several states and with a combined total of 21 seats out of 489 in the Lok Sabha. Of the 21 seats, 12 were won by the Socialist party and 9 by the Kisan Mazdoor Praja Party (KMPP). The non-Communist Left reached its peak of representation with 36 seats in the Lok Sabha in 1967 (of which 23 were won by the Samyukta [United] Socialist Party and 13 by the Praja Socialist Party), after which it disintegrated while its leaders and rank and file joined either the Congress or, in 1977, the new Janata coalition.

The Communist Left, unlike its socialist counterparts, has persisted, despite a major split in the original Communist party of India (CPI) in 1964 into a rump CPI and the Communist party of India (Marxist) or CPM. The CPI adopted a policy of supporting India's first Prime Minister, Jawaharlal Nehru, and later Mrs. Gandhi and of allying at times with the Congress against so-called parties of the Right, while the CPM has maintained a consistent policy of militant opposition to the Congress. Both have adhered faithfully to a non-violent, reformist, parliamentary path. Their economic and social policies are not much different from those of the Congress, except that when they have been in power, the Communist parties have implemented more serious and more effective, but still quite moderate policies of agrarian reform.

Two features have distinguished the Communist parties from their counterparts in other parts of the world. The first is that, earlier than elsewhere—from 1951 in fact—the Communist movement opted for and has adhered to a parliamentary path. Second, more than anywhere else, the Communist parties have been accepted by most other parties as legitimate participants in the political process. They have been the principal governing party in two of India's major states, West Bengal and Kerala, for long periods of time.

In the post-Independence period, there has been only one party on what might be called the traditional Right, that is, a party representing the interests of the urban and rural rich. The Swatantra party, founded in 1959, achieved representation in the Lok Sabha and some strength in the legislative assemblies of several states for the decade from 1962 through 1971, after which it, too, disintegrated and its remnants joined the Congress or, later, the Janata coalition.

One distinctive political party which has persisted since independence, originally called the Jan Sangh, but now the Bharatiya Janata Party (BJP), advocates militant Hindu nationalism. It may be considered a party of the Right because it is more inclined than the Congress toward a free enterprise system, opposes centralized economic development planning, and has been even less interested than the Congress in agrarian reform. Its cultural policies include the adoption of Hindu values, symbols, history, and ideals as national symbols and as vehicles of education for the youth of the country, irrespective of their religion. It is accused of being anti-Muslim and unsympathetic to minorities in general. While its leaders deny this accusation, they also say that too much attention has been paid to the problems of minorities, particularly Muslims, who should be "Indianized."

Another distinctive party was the Lok Dal, which sought to represent the interests of the middle-sized cultivating peasant groups with viable economic holdings in the range of between 2.5 and 25 or so acres. Its policies favored reorientation of economic development planning to favor agriculture rather than industry, labor-intensive rather than capital-intensive enterprises in industry and agriculture, provision of off-farm employment to rural unemployed and under-employed masses, and higher prices for agricultural produce. In the 1980 elections, it won forty-one seats in the Lok Sabha, more than any other party, but it then suffered a stunning reduction to only three seats in the 1984 elections, which produced a landslide victory for the Congress. The Lok Dal merged into the Janata Dal coalition before the 1989 elections.

There are also a number of regional political parties in India confined to particular states. In the deep southern state of Tamil Nadu, the ruling party is the DMK, representing the regional nationalism of the Tamil-speaking people. It opposes any attempts to use or teach the Hindi language (the official language of the country) in the state, and calls for a reorientation of national-state relations in favor of greater regional autonomy. In the neighboring state of Andhra, the Telugu Desam takes a similar stance in relation to the dominant Telugu-speaking people of the state. To the north, in the strife-torn province of Punjab, the Akali Dal is the leading party of a religious group, the Sikhs, who form a majority in the state but are a minority elsewhere. In the northeastern state of Assam, the Asom Gana Parishad rose to power in 1985 in the aftermath of massive and often violent demonstrations demanding the expulsion of hundreds of thousands of allegedly illegal migrants who have entered the country across the international border from Bengali-speaking Bangladesh.

Mobilization and Institutionalization. Huntington, one of the most influential theorists of political development in developing countries, has argued that most such countries have not been undergoing political development at all, but rather "political decay" produced by excessively rapid economic, social, and political mobilizations without stable party organizations to channel them. The evidence from India, however, contradicts for the most part the hypothesized relationships between mobilization and decay.

Comparisons among the fifteen major Indian states in levels of political institutionalization, rates of economic growth, and rapid and sustained increases in voter turnout reveal two types of relatively stable political contexts. The first involves a replication at the state level of the predominant or one-party dominant system. The two best examples of this situation in the past have been Maharasthra and Gujarat, two states in western India that enjoy relatively high rates of voter participation and economic growth. Although the latter state has experienced extreme forms of urban ethnic violence associated with the rapid mobilization of low- and "backward"-caste voters, the overall political context has remained relatively stable, with the Congress being a more effectively institutionalized dominant party than in most other Indian states.

Political stability and institutionalization of party organization have been even stronger in states which have undergone quite rapid rates of economic, social and political change in a context of intense interparty competition. These states—Kerala, West Bengal, Karnataka, Tamil Nadu, and Andhra Pradesh—have mean turnout rates of between 58 and 74 percent and are at the very top among the fifteen largest states in this respect.

In contrast, instability and lack of political institutionalization have been most pronounced over the past two decades, particularly in the north Indian Hindi-speaking states of Rajasthan, Uttar Pradesh, Madhya Pradesh, and Bihar, and the eastern state of Orissa, where rates of economic growth and turnout have been low and social heterogeneity has been extreme, that is, where social groups are fragmented rather than organized into large, coherent, highly mobilized formations. These states have had party systems which were one-party dominant, but weakly so; their institutionalized opposition parties were until recently not strong enough to pose a continuing effective challenge to the dominant congress.

Political stability and party institutionalization, therefore, are most positively associated in India with high and rapid rates of economic growth, social mobilization, and political participation in a context of intense interparty—but not necessarily two-party—competition. Political instability and political decay, in contrast, have been concentrated in states with the lowest rates of economic development and social and political mobilization. The balance of the argument, therefore, between traditional democratic views which place a high value on adversarial politics and contrary views which call for reducing the intensity of party competition and engaging in "selective mobilization" of the population while strengthening political organizations to minimize instability is in favor of the former insofar as India is concerned.

REPRESENTATION: INTEREST GROUPS AND INTERMEDIARIES

Interest Groups. Indian group life is extraordinarily diverse and comprises not only a multiplicity of interest associations but a range of different types of associations and intermediaries, some of which play uncommonly, if not uniquely, important roles in Indian politics in comparison to Western democratic states.

There are in India a full range of organized interest associations that are familiar in the West: trade unions, chambers of commerce and industry, professional associations of doctors, lawyers, and journalists, trade associations of cloth dealers, wholesale commodity dealers, and the like. However, they are important primarily in the organized sector of the economy dominated by large-scale bureaucratic organizations, which comprise only about 10 percent of the working population of the country. Moreover, these groups have less policy influence on the whole than their counterparts in the West. They tend also to be highly fragmented, again in contrast to the situation in most industrialized societies where a single large organization often dominates over other interest groups in particular sectors of the economy or professional life.

A second type of interest association in Indian politics is the large, amorphous, unorganized type of movement or "demand group" which arises from time to time among broad sectors of society, such as peasants, students, language, or regional groups. In the 1980s, among the most prominent of such movements were those associated with the mid-sized peasant cultivating communities of northern and western India. Under their chosen leaders they rigidly eschewed involvement in party politics and were closed to party politicians; they articulated their demands, particularly for fair agricultural prices, directly to the state authorities. Such movements in India among peasants and other sectors have often been far more important and effective than the activities of organized interest groups.

There are two other types of interest associations which have been quite important in modern Indian history and politics. These are revivalist movements and caste associations, which may take the shape of either organized interest groups or demand groups, making traditional values and institutions in Indian society the source of their strength. In their efforts to reform current practices by returning to supposedly original sources of faith or cultural practice, they have in fact transformed indigenous religious or cultural values and institutions they sought to protect. The political significance of the religious movements lies in their demands for state patronage and protection and in the effects they have in sharpening the boundaries between different communities, which often precipitate religious communal conflicts.

Caste associations typically do not base themselves in the localized village corporate caste entities, but claim to represent widespread caste categories. Their leaders seek to promote the interests and welfare of members, but the caste associations may also be used by their leaders as springboards for their entry into politics or by political parties as sources of political mobilization.

In these and other respects, the Indian caste associations epitomize the process of adapting traditional values and institutions to modern political forms which is the essence of party and interest-group politics, of mobilization and representation in India today.

Intermediaries. Organized interest associations can represent only a small segment of Indian society. Demand groups and mass movements are sporadic and often focus on a single issue. The day-to-day interests of ordinary people in India, especially in the rural areas, are more effectively represented by a range of informal intermediary groups and individuals who move between the villagers and the state and local administration. Two prominent examples of this type of intermediary grouping are factions and "brokers" or "touts."

Factions are leader-follower groups, based on a merging of instrumental and transactional with affective ties; they operate as informal associations in villages, in local and state representative assemblies, and in political party organizations. They are intermediary associations in the sense that they operate as informal groupings "representing" particular interests within formally organized groups.

"Brokers" and "touts" are persons, usually of middle caste status sometimes with unsavory reputations, who make a living out of acting to gain for villagers the services and benefits to which they are legally entitled, but which in practice the bureaucrats jealously guard and provide often only upon persuasion accompanied by payment. Brokers gain for the villagers the loans and subsidies to which they are entitled, timely supplies of agricultural inputs, access to hospitals in times of medical emergency, and the like.

These intermediary groups and individuals, like revivalist movements and caste associations, are characteristic forms by which traditional and modern, local and regional, individual and group interests are linked in Indian society. They demonstrate a few of the multiplicity of ways in which the British parliamentary system has been adopted through both traditional and modern forms of mobilization and representation in a still mostly agrarian, fragmented, culturally diverse society.

III. ISSUES FOR DISCUSSION

1. Evaluate the arguments for and against the desirability of adversarial systems of party competition in culturally diverse developing countries.

2. Compare India's "predominant" or "one-party dominant" system with, for example, the Japanese party system.

3. Compare the roles of interest associations and intermediaries in India and the United States.

NOTES

1. Giovanni Sartori, *Parties and Party Systems: A Framework for Analysis*, vol. I (Cambridge: Cambridge University Press, 1976), pp. 192–201.

2. Samuel P. Huntington, *Political Order in Changing Societies* (New Haven: Yale University Press, 1968), p. 86.

3. In electoral systems such as India's, where constituencies are won by the candidate who polls the largest number of votes, i.e., a plurality, and where there are a multiplicity of candidates, the largest party usually wins many seats with less than a majority of the votes.

4. The Rajya Sabha, the Upper House, is elected under a different franchise separately from general elections to the Lok Sabha.

IV. SELECTED READINGS

Brass, Paul R. *Caste, Faction, and Party in Indian Politics*, Vol. I: *Faction and Party* and Vol. II: *Election Studies*. Delhi: Chanakya, 1984 & 1985 (faculty background). Essays on party systems, political participation, factionalism, and the influences of caste, class, and community in elections.

Rudolph, Lloyd I., and Rudolph, Susanne H. *In Pursuit of Lakshmi: The Political Economy of the Indian State*. Chicago: University of Chicago Press, 1987 (student reading). More than half the book is devoted to parties, politics, and interest associations, with an original discussion of the latter in comparison with interest groups in Western countries.

Weiner, Myron. *India at the Polls*. Washington, DC: American Enterprise Institute, 1980 (student reading). A vivid account of the national election campaign, with the results presented also in an appendix containing numerous valuable tables.

Weiner, Myron, and Field, John O. eds. *Studies in Electoral Politics in the Indian States*. 4 vols. Delhi: Manohar Book Service, 1974, 1975, 1977 (faculty background). Detailed background studies including analyses of party systems in particular states and voting behavior among specific sections of the population.

Political Science:
India and Pakistan

The Military in India and Pakistan: Contrasting Cases

Stephen Philip Cohen

I. INTRODUCTION: CENTRAL POINTS

Armies everywhere face outward, toward their neighbors (friend and enemy alike), and also look inward, toward their own societies. The modern armies of India and Pakistan provide a remarkable case study of inward and outward divergence even though they had a common origin in the old British-Indian army. It is also worth including the Bangladesh army in our comparison— it was split off from the Pakistani army when Bangladesh was created in 1971 and retains features of both of its parents.

The most significant points of comparison among these three armies are:

• their very different domestic political roles— the armies of Pakistan and Bangladesh are active politically, while the Indian military establishment is under tight civilian control;

• the different ways in which they accommodated themselves to culturally and ethnically diverse societies— within a secular context in India and the avowedly Islamic identity of Pakistan;

• the different ways in which these armies prepare against external and internal enemies of varying degrees of military strength and sophistication— ranging from nuclear to guerrilla warfare.

These points of comparison also suggest that the study of armies—and armed forces in general—transcends any single disciplinary perspective. Besides the obvious importance of the historical evolution of armies as institutions, the study of the military draws upon the skills of the anthropologist and sociologist (for the relationship of an army to the society and culture that support it), the political scientist (for the comparative domestic political role of the military), and the student of international relations (since the size, quality, and performance of a military establishment will affect a state's foreign and security policies).

II. MAJOR TOPICS

A COMPLEX TRADITION

Elements of the colonial British-Indian army system are visible in Pakistan and Bangladesh as well as in India. All retain something of its professionalism and unique social and organizational structure, but they differ in terms of the relationship between civilian and military authority— and none looks exactly like the colonial parent.

A series of reforms, extending over thirty years after the Mutiny of 1857, turned the British-Indian army into a professional force. Deployed extensively in the nineteenth and twentieth centuries as imperial "enforcers," Indian army units saw action in China, Europe, the Middle East, and Africa.

While the British army played an important role in the conquest and governance of India, it was not the dominant political institution. Ultimate authority rested with the government in London; local responsibility was vested in the viceroy, who governed through a skilled civilian bureaucracy. The commander-in-chief of the army in India was the second highest official of the colonial regime, and while there were occasions when the viceroy was challenged by the military, control by British civilian bureaucrats and political appointees remained strong in both principle and practice.

Recruitment. The army's organizational makeup was important to its military success in British India. The officer corps was entirely British through the late 1920s, and even at the time of independence only a quarter of the officers in combat units were Indian. These officers, British and Indian, were chosen and promoted through rigorous competition. The best were as good as any officer in a modern Western army, and the Indian army produced a number of distinguished generals during World War II (e.g., Auchinleck and Slim). British-Indian army officers—whether British or Indian—were particularly knowledgeable about India's complex social structure, and had to acquire a high level of proficiency in one or more Indian language. This was necessary since the social structure of the British-Indian army was deeply rooted in Indian society. With the exception of some technical units (artillery, engineers) and the navy and air force, Indian army recruitment was intimately linked to India's complex ethnolinguistic structure, and closely tied to particular castes, regions, and religions.

The army's recruitment was often misleadingly described as being based on the "martial races" of India. The British developed a theory of "martial races" in the late nineteenth century, at the same time racial theories swept through Europe. The idea that some castes or ethnic groups possessed certain attributes (such as valor, bravery, and fighting qualities) to a greater degree than other groups was also embedded in India's Hindu tradition and the traditions of the Islamic conquerors of South Asia. In fact, the British had recruited heavily from "non-martial" regions of India (Bengal, Bihar, and most of South India) in the eighteenth and early nineteenth centuries, and they used troops from these regions to conquer what had become (by the 1890s) the "martial races" of Punjab, Rajasthan, the Himalayan kingdoms, the Northwest Frontier Province, and Baluchistan.

The British also favored some religious groups over others. Sikhs were brought into the army in large numbers after the Mutiny, and proved loyal to the British who had just defeated them; Muslims from the Urdu-speaking areas which had revolted during the Mutiny were de-recruited, not to be taken back in until World War I, fifty years later, and even then not trusted with their own independent units.

Defense Production. The British also built a state-owned arms production establishment in India, which, however, rendered the Indian army self-sufficient only in basic weapons. Because of pressure from British industry to restrict the spread of advanced military technology, and because of the fear that a well-equipped Indian army might someday pose a challenge to British rule itself, the Indian army received equipment inferior to that operated by the British army (whose units were also based in India). Thus, the Indian army (as opposed to the British-Indian army) was slow in acquiring artillery and rapid-fire weapons, and the Indian air force and navy were equally ill-equipped; this was to have important economic and military consequences for both successor states. The Indians were inadequately equipped when they confronted the Chinese in a dispute in 1962, and the newly independent Pakistan had to search abroad for even the most basic weapons.

Partition and Inheritance. This complex political, social, and economic background influenced the post-independence policies of the successor states of India and Pakistan in different ways.

Partition left Pakistan weak militarily. In the old British-Indian army there had been fewer Muslim officers, proportionately, than Hindu and Sikh officers, and they were relatively junior in rank. Pakistan thus had to retain five hundred British officers on a contract basis to help organize its armed forces. Moreover, it received very few of the armaments factories (most were located in regions that went to India). Finally, the Muslim soldiers that opted for Pakistan were predominantly from the Punjab and the North-west Frontier Province (Punjabis and Pathans).

While fine fighters, these regions did not produce in large numbers the skilled technicians needed to keep a modern army operating. Furthermore, Muslims from East Bengal—which was to become East Pakistan, and later Bangladesh—had not seen service in the British-Indian army during World War II and few Muslim Bengalis had become officers.

There were important differences in the political inheritance of the two states. Pakistan's founding father, Mohammed Ali Jinnah, was dying when his country came into existence, and his chosen successor, Liaquat Ali Khan, was assassinated in 1951. Moreover, Jinnah's political party, the Muslim League, had few roots in the provinces and districts that formed the new state of Pakistan. While India lost Mahatma Gandhi to an assassin's bullet in 1948, it did have the benefit of Jawaharlal Nehru's leadership until his death in 1964, and he was assisted throughout his tenure by an array of competent bureaucrats, politicians, and an effective political party, the Indian National Congress.

Several strategic developments affected the political role of the two armies. Ironically, each country became the other's chief enemy— thus ending the British strategy of defending the subcontinent with an integrated military force under a single political command. Pakistan also soon became embroiled in a border dispute with neighboring Afghanistan; it was not until the late 1950s that India began to feel pressure along its northeastern borders from the newly revived People's Republic of China. Both India and Pakistan turned to other countries for military assistance: in the late 1950s India obtained American, British, and Soviet help and earlier, in 1954, Pakistan received substantial American assistance because of its perceived role in containing both Chinese and Soviet influence (a role expressed in its membership in two Western-sponsored alliances, SEATO and CENTO).

DIVERGENT POLITICAL ROLES: CIVIL-MILITARY RELATIONS

Different Political Paths. By the mid-1950s the domestic political orders of India and Pakistan had begun to evolve in different directions. Pakistan has been under military rule, or military-dominated civilian governments, for about twenty-five of its forty-four years; India has had a stable democracy for most of the post-independence period (except for the years of Indira Gandhi's dictatorial "Emergency," 1975–77).

Pakistan's Political Weakness. The reason for political instability in Pakistan was the weak and fragmented party system it inherited. Although young and inexperienced, its army was reasonably professional— and originally had no political ambitions. While the country was divided into West and East Pakistan (the latter becoming independent as Bangladesh in 1971), and with a thousand miles of hostile Indian territory in between, other states (notably, Indonesia) have coped with equally difficult geographic circumstances and an even more divergent ethnolinguistic structure.

The root cause of Pakistan's political problems lay in the lack of cohesion among its political parties. They failed, on the one hand, to put down roots in the countryside and cities and obtain support beyond a thin crust of landed and moneyed elites and, on the other, to demonstrate that they could effectively govern. Party politics became corrupt and parochial by the early 1950s, and national affairs began to revolve around fratricidal issues of provincial and ethnic competition. In becoming an independent state, where South Asian Muslims could live free from domination by the subcontinent's dominant Hindu population, Pakistan was confronted with the problems of nation-building and extreme economic and social disparities both within the two wings of Pakistan and between them (the east was much poorer than the west).

As in many other new nations at the time, the army seemed to be the only institution that had maintained its integrity after independence. As did the armies of Indonesia, Burma, Turkey, South Korea and many in Latin America and Africa, Pakistan's army eventually seized power in 1958. Led by General Ayub Khan, the coup was greeted with considerable popular support. Ayub and his fellow generals were committed to the reform and transformation of Pakistani politics, not merely the restoration of order.

This task proved to be beyond the army's capabilities, and Ayub was eventually deposed by his own commander-in-chief, Yahya Khan, in 1969. Yahya soon held national elections, but the bitterness and antagonism between East and West Pakistan had reached huge proportions; the 1970 election was won by East Pakistan's leading political figure, Sheikh Mujibur Rahman, but the army and the dominant West Pakistani political figure, Zulfiqar Ali Bhutto, jointly kept Mujibur from assuming power, and a tragic and bloody civil war broke out in the towns and villages of "sonar Bangla"—beautiful Bengal. The civil war was terminated by Indian military intervention and the defeat of the Pakistan army. The new state of Bangladesh was proclaimed in December 1971, the first country created by force of arms in the postwar period.

Pakistan's agonies were not yet over. After Zulfiqar Ali Bhutto came to power in 1972, he instituted a series of political and economic changes which, while popular, frightened many; he also enmeshed the army in the repression of dissent in the province of Baluchistan. By 1977 Bhutto had polarized what remained of Pakistan; although he was still the country's most popular politician, the army—led by the man he had appointed its head, Zia ul-Haq—seized power in a coup that year, and subsequently tried and executed Bhutto.

There then followed a long period of "controlled" political activity, in which the military carefully regulated the areas of civilian political participation and the issues that were "fit" to be publicly discussed. Gradually, however, the pressure was relaxed and political activity increased. Zia became president (while retaining command of the army) and was moving toward a democratic election when he and several close aides died in a plane crash in

August, 1988. This obviated the demand of Bhutto's daughter and popular political leader, Benazir, for revenge against Zia, and thus, paradoxically, made it easier for the army to step back and allow elections to be held in November 1988. A little over a year later, Benazir's own popularity was on the wane, and with encouragement from the military she was successfully challenged by more conservative forces in a national election held in late 1990. Nevertheless, Pakistan has held two relatively free national elections in a row, and while the armed forces have not been passive onlookers, they have not directly intervened in the political process.

The military remains Pakistan's central political institution, although its officer corps prefers to see itself as an apolitical defender of national sovereignty. Whoever comes to power in Pakistan will have to accommodate the wishes, beliefs, and institutional demands of the military, especially the army. And because **armies are complex, deeply rooted institutions that are slow to change, the officer corps will not soon come to see itself as the mere servant of any government that happens to rule Pakistan**. On the other hand, history demonstrates that military officers have repeatedly failed in the past to govern effectively, and, further, that at times their excursions into politics, in contravention of their staff college doctrine, have hurt the army's purely military role. Pakistan's soldiers (like India's) have general contempt for politics and politicians, and are susceptible to the argument that civilian government is desirable if only to keep the army free from contamination by politics.

Bangladesh. Dhaka's politics have been, since 1972, something of a variant of Islamabad's. The flamboyant Sheikh Mujibur Rahman early lost his charisma, and was eventually assassinated ushering in a period of army rule which shows no sign of abating. As in Pakistan, in Bangladesh the army regards itself as a professional service, above politics, and contemptuous of "corrupt politicians" and their scheming ways. And, as in Pakistan, opposition groups have grown up demanding that the army withdraw from politics (in this case, the two leading opposition parties are headed by the daughter of Mujibur Rahman and the widow of a popular general, Zia ur-Rahman, who was himself assassinated by disgruntled fellow officers). But Bangladesh, beset by a high population growth rate and a very low economic growth rate, and with virtually no industrial base, has problems that will not be solved in the foreseeable future by any government, civilian or military. The armed forces are likely to hang on to power; the military cannot dismount the tiger, and probably does not want to. **Without a serious external threat the Bangladeshi army can afford to decline as a professional fighting force as it concentrates on political matters, and would prefer to do so rather than give up the perquisites and advantages of power.**

The Indian Case. New Delhi is unusual in the non-Western world in that the hand of civilian control over the armed forces is even firmer than in most Western and Communist states. Upon independence the new Indian government took a number of steps to ensure that the military would be even further subordinated to civilian control than it had been during the British colonial period. The status of the military as a whole was reduced, and the position of commander-in-chief abolished; officers were recruited from a wide geographical and social base, and encouraged to focus on professional military matters; the three service chiefs (army, navy, air force) were put on an equal basis, even though the army was by far the largest and most powerful service, and a complicated system of bureaucratic and fiscal control was expanded and strengthened.

On external issues the Indian army is usually required to take the advice of a proficient foreign service; on domestic matters it is subordinated both to civilian bureaucrats and a political system which reaches deep into Indian society, and which remains legitimate and effective. While Indian generals have the usual soldiers' contempt for "politics"—which are becoming increasingly venal—they know that the task of governing a country the size of a continent is beyond them; Pakistan and Bangladesh provide chastening examples of failed military rule. Finally, they are usually well-rewarded for professional—and obedient—careers, and a number of retired senior officers routinely find employment in India's vast network of government-controlled public sector enterprises.

NEW SOCIAL AND IDEOLOGICAL PATTERNS

There are two salient features of the relationship of society to army in India and Pakistan. The first is the link between the army's social base and its political influence, the second is their relationship to modern, advanced technology, some of it useful for military as well as civilian purposes.

Region and Power. The distribution of ethnic, caste, and linguistic groups in Pakistan and India has influenced the broader social and political role of the armed forces in South Asia. The provinces that became West Pakistan were once a major recruiting ground for the British-Indian army; the Northwest Frontier Province and Punjab together provided almost 40 percent of the army, including the officer corps. After 1947 these regions provided the overwhelming number of soldiers and officers to the Pakistani army (about 80 percent), although they constituted less than half of the total population of the country. This meant that when the army came to power in Pakistan in 1958 the nation was in effect governed by one province, the Punjab. This was resented by the East's majority Bengali community, whose lack of representation in the armed forces constituted a major grievance. Even after East Pakistan split off from West Pakistan, this imbalance has continued to affect Pakistani politics: **that the Punjab, now 60 percent of the population, is the center of military and political power is deeply resented by other provinces, especially Sind and Baluchistan**.

India never had to face this problem. Its political heartland, comprising the Hindi-speaking states of Uttar Pradesh, Bihar, and Madhya Pradesh, has no significant representation in the armed forces. India's Punjab provided a disproportionate number of soldiers and officers, but is politically insignificant on a national scale. **Thus, political power and military power are divided in India, and its diverse and pluralistic army is far more representative than that of Pakistan**. Practically, this means that when the army is called in to maintain law and order in a troubled region, it can draw upon soldiers from another province or region; in Pakistan, trouble in the major cities of Punjab, especially Lahore, would mean trouble for the army, which would have to ask its own Punjabi officers and soldiers to fire upon relatives and friends.

Modernity and Ideology. India and Pakistan are undergoing rapid, unprecedented social and economic change. This has affected their armed forces, whose organizations are rooted in a nineteenth century tradition yet are compelled to face adversaries, primarily each other, who possess the most modern weapons. The two countries have pursued two different strategies for bridging the gap between available weapons and technology and their own capabilities to produce them.

Pakistan has clung more tightly to the British theory of

"martial races" than India, while aggressively searching for outside sources of advanced weapons. The Pakistani army cultivated the notion that one Pakistani was worth ten or fifteen Indians on the battlefield (especially if the latter were not Sikhs or Gurkhas, who were accorded considerable respect). Pakistani officers emphasized the unifying and strengthening force of Islam, and taught their soldiers that war against India was war against the infidel—a jihad. Pakistan was, of course, the first state founded on the principle of Islam, and that it focused on Islam's martial and militant traditions was understandable.

However, the disaster of 1971—the civil war and division of Pakistan into two separate states—led to a reexamination of these doctrines and a more realistic assessment of religion as a decisive factor in war. It was clear that while West Pakistani soldiers fought valiantly, they had been badly outnumbered by forces in the East, which had the benefit of superior equipment from India. **Thus, since 1972, Pakistan has greatly expanded its own defense production sector, improved the quality of training and discipline within the army, and clandestinely pursued the nuclear option.**

The Indians early abandoned the "martial races" theory, since it was divisive in the context of a democratic political system. With a special role preserved for castes and religious groups that had traditionally found a place in the armed forces, a number of new regiments drawn from the south and east were raised. The resulting reduction in quotas for Sikh soldiers (who had been vastly overrepresented) led to a serious problem in the mid-80s: growing Sikh disaffection and the demand for a separate nation, Khalistan.

The Indians early sought to build a defense industry. With Western and Soviet help, India can now produce most components of a range of modern aircraft, ships, tanks, and missiles, although its drive toward self-reliance is years behind schedule and billions of dollars over estimated cost. **India also has a large nuclear infrastructure and is equally capable of exercising its nuclear "option" at short notice.**

THE MILITARY AND EXTERNAL POLICY

Strategic Defense. Both India and Pakistan inherited responsibility for the defense of the South Asian subcontinent. In the northeast, India and China fought a significant war in 1962, and their border is still disputed; in the northwest, Pakistan, with its military and intelligence services, was instrumental in checking and reversing Soviet military aggression in Afghanistan and helped the Afghan mujahedin fight the superpower to a standstill. The Bangladeshi army plays no significant external role; almost completely surrounded by India, its energies are directed entirely inward; while reasonably competent, its officers and soldiers do not have access to modern equipment, nor are they in close contact with any foreign military establishment.

Extraregional Contacts. Both the Indian and Pakistani armies have also been active in nearby regions—as was the British-Indian army. **Pakistan** has trained a number of Gulf and Arab armies and air forces and, until recently, maintained a significant military presence in Saudi Arabia. The **Indian** military has also trained a number of Asian and African services, and has recently been used as a "peacekeeping" force in the island states of Sri Lanka and the Maldives.

India-Pakistan Conflict. Of course, the great historical irony of post-partition South Asia is that **the two successor states spend most of their energies in preparation for war against each other**. They fought in 1949, 1965, and 1971; in the latter conflict India inflicted a decisive defeat on Pakistani forces in East Bengal. Pakistan regrouped, and today maintains a credible army and air force, although it would lose to India in an extended war. Its covert nuclear program is designed to serve as a deterrent to both Delhi's assumed nuclear capability and its conventional military superiority. **The two states have thus reached something of a stalemate, although at increasing levels of armament and economic cost**.

India as an Expanding Power. The most significant recent military development has been the acquisition by India's armed forces of a regional, and perhaps interregional, capability. With its greater population and industrial base, and its higher levels of education and technology, India has been able to maintain a million-man army, a large and modern air force, and the largest navy in the Indian Ocean. Further, India has learned how to use its arms in combined operations, and to operate simultaneously in different sectors. This was vividly illustrated in early 1967 when, in the midst of military maneuvers against Pakistan, India's generals dramatically increased their force levels against China and began planning for an operation in Sri Lanka. India's modern navy (with two carriers) and significant airlift capability will give it an interregional military capability within the next decade.

Two Professional Militaries. Thus, both the Indian and Pakistani armed forces have to be counted among the most advanced in the non-Western world. Despite their very different domestic roles, each is regarded highly for its professionalism and high standard of training. The Indian military has the additional advantages of posessing large quantities of advanced equipment and its own defense production facilities, and of being relatively undistracted by domestic political responsibilities. Either or both could be significant in extraregional security and foreign policy developments in the decades to come.

III. ISSUES FOR DISCUSSION

1. Since both the Indian and Pakistani armies were created from the same organization, what factors best explain their very different political involvements since 1958, when the Pakistani army seized power?

2. What are some of the advantages and disadvantages of attempting to recruit a military organization from highly complex, multiethnic societies such as India or Pakistan?

3. Which factors best explain the continuation of military professionalism in India and Pakistan, when it seems to be in decline in Bangladesh?

4. How does the existence—or absence—of competent political leadership affect the professionalism and political role of the military in a new nation?

IV. SELECTED READINGS

Three recent books provide a survey of the political and social roles of the Pakistani army:

Cheema, Pervaiz Iqbal. *Pakistan's Defense Policy, 1947–58.* New York: St. Martin's Press, 1990 (faculty and student background).

Cohen, Stephen P. *The Pakistan Army.* Berkeley: University of California Press, 1984 (faculty and student background).

Rizvi, Hasan Askari. *The Military and Politics in Pakistan.* 4th ed.; Lahore: Progressive, 1987 (faculty and student background).

For a narrative history of the social, cultural, and political origins of both armies see:

Cohen, Stephen P. *The Indian Army: It's Contribution to the Development of a Nation.* Berkeley: University of California Press, 1971; revised edition; New Delhi: Oxford University Press, 1990.

Recent events are summarized in:

Cohen, Stephen P., "The Military and Indian Democracy." In *Democracy in India*, edited by Atul Kohli. Princeton: Princeton University Press, 1988.

A good survey of Indian security policy is:

Thomas, Raju G.C., *Indian Security Policy*. Princeton: Princeton University Press, 1986.

All titles good for faculty and student reading.

Political Science:
Indonesia

Authoritarianism: Indonesia

Benedict R. O'G. Anderson

I. INTRODUCTION: CENTRAL POINTS

President Suharto of Indonesia is today the longest-surviving military head of state in the world. This fact, and Indonesia's huge (almost 185 million) population, strategic location between the Indian and Pacific Oceans, and history of bitter class, religious, and ethnic conflict, make the study of his authoritarian New Order regime of exceptional comparative interest.

Indonesia's New Order regime, established in the wake of economic catastrophe, extreme political polarization, and massive domestic bloodshed, offers useful comparisons with other such long-lived, military-dominated regimes (e.g., Franco's Spain, Pinochet's Chile, and Martinez's El Salvador), and contrasts to more usual, short-lived military dictatorships.

The mechanisms created by New Order authoritarianism for controlling and containing political participation are comparable to those of other regimes in the Third World.

As a regime profoundly dependent on external economic, tech-

311

nological, and military support, yet ruling over a strongly nationalist country, the New Order's efforts to establish ideological legitimacy invite comparison with other Third World regimes facing similar dilemma (Chile, Egypt, Pakistan, and so forth).

President Suharto's long tenure in comparison with other military heads of state raises questions about the importance of the personal political skills to regime survival. It is often argued that successful authoritarian regimes, by their very nature, create the social forces that finally destroy them. Is Indonesia good evidence for this argument? (Compare, for example, South Korea and Taiwan.)

II. MAJOR TOPICS

The independent state of Indonesia was born in August 1945, in the vacuum that developed in the period between the surrender of imperial Japan (which had occupied the country during the Pacific War), and the return of the Dutch colonial regime. A bitter four-year armed struggle against the Dutch ensued, resolved finally by American-sponsored negotiations at the end of 1949. This "revolution" was, however, never under the control of single political party or military group; participating in it were Muslims, secular nationalists, socialists, Communists, Japanese-trained military officers, and independent, armed youth-organizations of different kinds. Most of the fighting took place in the more advanced, populous western islands of Java and Sumatra, which therefore, after independence, tended to dominate political life.

At the end of 1949, a constitutional democratic order was established, and free and open legislative elections were held in 1955. The results showed how deeply divided the country was once the colonial enemy was removed. About 80 percent of the vote was divided among four large, antagonistic political parties: Masyumi, a party of reformist and fundamentalist Islam, with a strong base in the islands outside Java; Nahdlatul Ulama, a party of conservative, rural Islam, based mainly on Java; the Nationalist party, speaking for a statist secular nationalism, with strength among civil servants, *abangan* (a term applied to that section of the population that is nominally Muslim, but in practice Hindu-Buddhist/animist) village and small town elites on Java, and various declining aristocracies in the Outer Islands; and the Communist party, with strong support in the small working class and the *abangan*-oriented sectors of the huge Javanese peasantry. Alongside these giants were the important, if much smaller,

Socialist, Catholic, and Protestant parties. Cabinets were formed on the basis of unstable coalitions among antagonistic parties, greatly undermining the prestige of constitutional democracy and encouraging regional, ethnic, and religious-based rebellions, the most serious of which were Islamic-fundamentalist in character.

The military, shaped by its Japanese training and the experience of fighting the dispersed, locally-based anti-Dutch guerrilla war of 1945–1949, was also deeply divided; many of the regional rebellions that broke out after 1950 were led by dissatisfied military men, veterans of the revolutionary struggle. The Army High Command's gradual success in suppressing these rebellions— thanks to American (for the army) and Soviet (for the young navy and air force) support— solidified the top officer corps, and made it more and more Javanese in personnel and outlook.

Constitutional democracy was overthrown in 1957–58 by an uneasy partnership of left-leaning charismatic President Sukarno and the right-leaning Army High Command. In its place came so-called Guided Democracy, an authoritarian regime with a radical-populist rhetoric and an anti-Western foreign policy, but with conservative military control of the outer regions and of the advanced sectors of the economy, following the nationalization of Dutch corporate enterprises in 1957. Between 1958 and 1965 Indonesian society became increasingly polarized politically and impoverished economically. To balance the power of the military Sukarno encouraged the three Java-based giant parties to expand (Masyumi had been banned for its involvement in the regional rebellions). But since elections were prohibited under the prevailing martial law, this expansion took place mainly among mass organizations (of youth, students, women, peasants, workers, intellectuals, and so on), which increasingly competed with one another on an around-the-clock basis—day in and day out, through rallies, mass meetings, parades, recruitment drives, village intrigues, and campaigns for control of campus institutions— thereby creating ever-greater political tensions. In this atmosphere, the Communist party, in particular, made rapid strides, to the point that it would probably have won a plurality if elections had been permitted. At the same time, the economy went into a tailspin, the result of recklessly inflationary fiscal policies, hostility to foreign enterprise, and military corruption and mismanagement of the nationalized sector. By the summer of 1965, inflation had become hyperinflation, with prices rising daily and fixed salaries becoming virtually worthless. The result was society-wide insecurity and fear, accentuated by rumors of the president's poor health and impending death.

On the morning of October 1, 1965, Lieutenant-Colonel Untung, an obscure battalion commander in the Presidential Guard, went on the radio to announce that he had taken decisive action to protect the president from a plot organized by what he referred to as a Council of Generals, and masterminded by the C.I.A. That evening, his "coup" was countercouped by General Suharto, commander of the army's elite Strategic Reserve. It then transpired that Untung's group had murdered six of the army's top generals. Seizing this opportunity, Suharto proclaimed that Untung was a Communist pawn. Between October 1965 and the spring of 1966, the military, aided by youthful Christian and Muslim vigilantes, launched a massive pogrom against the Communist party and its political allies. Hundreds of thousands were murdered, imprisoned, tortured, and orphaned. In March 1966, Suharto compelled Sukarno to sign over all executive power, and within two years arranged for himself to become the country's second president.

IDEOLOGICAL LEGITIMATION

The initial justification for the authoritarian "New Order" which Suharto began to build after 1966 was the need for drastic solutions to the problems and conflicts of the postrevolutionary era: Communism had to be wiped out root and branch; purposive, pragmatic, and coherent policymaking had to replace futile ideological conflict among political parties; a demoralized, fragmented bureaucracy had to be centralized and reanimated; inflation had to be controlled and modernization of the economy seriously undertaken; and a dangerously self-isolating, anti-Western foreign policy had to be abandoned.

In positive terms, the New Order regime's ideological program, designed to meet these needs, consisted of six elements. (1) A permanent legal ban on any form of Marxism. (2) Compulsory adhesion of all legal political and social organization to the Pancasila, the state philosophy (stressing belief in one God, nationalism, humanitarianism, popular sovereignty, and social justice). This philosophy, formulated by Sukarno in the last days of the Japanese Occupation, had originally been designed to create the broadest possible consensus among Indonesia's immense variety of ethnic, ideological, and religious groups. But during the contentious 1950s it had increasingly been exploited by Christian and *abangan* Muslims as a political weapon against militant Islam. The New Order, dominated by *abangan* military officers, continued to use it, even more comprehensively, for the same purpose. (3) Elevation to constitutional principle of the Doctrine of (the military's) Dual Function (Dwifungsi), whereby the armed forces have permanent responsibilities both in matters of security/defense and in political, social, and economic affairs. (4) Promulgation of "monoloyalty" for all civil servants, including teachers and faculty members at state universities. Officials were forbidden to have any "external" party affiliation, and were required to give absolute loyalty to the government and their bureaucratic superiors. (5) Institution of the doctrine of the "floating mass," whereby, except during elections, the masses of the population were to be insulated from organized political activity, so as to concentrate on the tasks of development. (6) Inauguration of a campaign for "accelerated modernization," aimed at achieving agricultural self-sufficiency and rapid industrialization in cooperation with international lending institutions, friendly foreign governments, and private foreign capital.

THE POLITICAL CONTEXT OF INSTITUTIONALIZATION

Domestic. The scale of the massacres in 1965–66 did not merely destroy the Indonesian Left for a generation; it created a pervasive atmosphere of fear among its old working class and peasant constituencies, even among those elements involved in non-Communist organizations. The new regime had little difficulty in dismantling all worker and peasant organizations not under its direct control. The anti-Communist (and, a little later, the anti-Sukarnoist) campaign resulted in massive purges of the civil service and even the military itself, giving Suharto and his associates extraordinary patronage opportunities in filling the tens of thousands of resulting vacancies.

Suharto's position was initially strong, and he took careful, intelligent steps to strengthen it. As a veteran of the army of the Revolution of 1945–49 he had impeccable nationalist credentials, and as the "savior" of the country from Communism he gained the personal gratitude of a wide array of anti-Communist groups. He was careful also to create a quasi-legal aura around his assumption of office, to discourage any subsequent coups against his rule. The People's Consultative Assembly, the body constitutionally designated to select presidents— with its large military component, and with its left-wingers purged— first made him acting president in 1967, and then full president in 1968. Sukarno was quietly put under house arrest, where he remained till his death in 1970.

At the same time, many highly mobilized anti-Communist groups— especially Muslims, and middle-class elements— who felt they had shared in the battle, expected to be rewarded with a share in power, and hoped for a genuine civil-military partnership in a reasonably open, newly democratic political system.

External. Suharto's quick destruction of the world's third largest Communist party, at a time when the Vietnam War was going badly for the United States, earned him strong and lasting support in Washington. Indonesia's strategic location astride the sea lanes between the Pacific and Indian Oceans (through which submarines as well as surface fleets have to pass), and the importance of her natural resources (especially oil) made it even more imperative to help the forty-five-year old general consolidate his rule. American leadership drew Japan, the major Western European countries, and international lending agencies, into a so-called Inter-Governmental Group on Indonesia (IGGI), which ever since has annually provided Indonesia with very substantial amounts of aid. In return, on the advice of his American-trained team of economists and technocrats, Suharto reopened the country to foreign capital on very generous terms, dismantled many bankrupt nationalized enterprises, liberalized trade and currency regulations, and put an end to strikes and other forms of labor protest. As a result, the Sukarno-era hyperinflation was quickly stabilized, and a long economic boom began, which was accelerated, at the end of 1973, by the huge increase in world oil prices engineered by OPEC (of which Indonesia is minor member).

INSTITUTIONALIZATION

Suharto recognized early on that long-term stability required that the authoritarian New Order have at least a veneer of legality, including some form of legislative and electoral politics. At the same time, he was also aware that institutions would have to be created to contain the dissatisfaction of groups unlikely to have much trust in parliamentarism— particular factions in the military, students, militant Muslims, and the urban poor.

Parties, Elections, Legislatures. At the time of the banning of the Communist party and its allies, ten legal parties still existed in Indonesia. But by 1973, the regime had collapsed these into two—

one containing all former Muslim parties and their adherents; the other, a ragtag fusion of the right-wing elements of the National-ist, Catholic, and Protestant parties, and various other non-Muslim groups. Coercive manipulations by Suharto's extralegal "Special Operations" intelligence group (see below), and, after 1973, government funding of these pro forma "opposition" parties gave the regime control of their leaderships. At the same time, the government created its own quasi-party, called Golkar (an acro-nym for Golongan Karya-Functional Groups), to control the elec-toral process and the legislative bodies that emerged from it. The origins of Golkar lay in the revolutionary period, when President Sukarno and others, believing that the political parties did not give sufficient representation to regional, professional, and minor-ity interests, created a special category of parliamentarians to speak for these "functional groups." This form of representation disappeared during the period of constitutional democracy, but was reintroduced under Guided Democracy primarily to give legis-lative voice to the powerful military and its allies. The earlier anti-party animus was, under the New Order, turned into a major instrument of state. Advertising itself as being "above parties," enjoying more than ample funding by the government, and mak-ing maximal use of the coercive hierarchies of the territorial mili-tary and the military-controlled Ministry of the Interior, Golkar has handily won every election since 1971. With the huge patron-age at its disposal in a time of economic boom, Golkar has delib-erately tried to incorporate compliant elements of as many organized interests as possible: military factions, civil servants, Muslims and Christians, as well as businessmen, professionals, and intellectuals, to say nothing of ethnic minorities. The result is that though it lacks all policy cohesion, it serves loyally to ensure the government complete control over Parliament and the People's Consultative Assembly. (As a further safeguard, both these bodies contain large non-elected military factions appointed personally by the president).

The electoral process is tightly controlled to ensure permanent regime success. Under the doctrine of the "floating mass," the political parties (but not Golkar) have been prohibited from organ-izing branches at the village level. All party candidates must be screened by the state's security apparatus, which has the right to disbar anyone without explanation. Furthermore, the president has the legal right to remove any obstreperous parliamentarian, though the party he or she represents keeps its overall numerical representation. Political parties are prohibited from criticizing the government. The Muslim party may not use Islamic symbols in electioneering. Most importantly, the military and Interior Ministry hierarchies have strict orders to use their powers to coerce the rural population into producing majorities for Golkar. The result has been a series of "elected parliaments" which are both pliant and unrepresentative. In addition, arguing that the "majority rule" voting system of Western constitutionalism is unsuited to Indonesian culture and traditions, Parliament is required to reach its decisions by "consensus," a system that forces potential opposition groups to lobby quietly with the Golkar majority rather than present a visible and forceful minority opposition to the public. Finally, since Golkar is basically controlled by the minister of the interior, the minister of defense, and the commander-in-chief of the armed forces, all appointed by the president, and since he also has the right to remove any of its parliamentary representatives, Suharto is always assured of "reelection"— something that has occurred now five times since 1967.

Interest Groups. For controlling private interest groups, the New Order has generally adopted a corporatist institutional structure. Workers, fishermen, and peasants, insofar as they are organized at all, have been forcibly enlisted in monolithic state-controlled apparatuses, designed nominally to represent their interests within the national consensus, but actually to enforce labor discipline. A parallel attempt to incorporate all youth and student organizations within a national student federation has been much less successful, but the campaign of "campus normalization," a series of draconian decrees enacted after nationwide student protests in 1978, has largely controlled youthful opposition by prohibiting all political activity and organizing in the nation's universities. The legal profession's once generally independent organization has been undercut by being forced to accept the mass membership of military lawyers. Only the business sector has been able to exercise some autonomous influence on the government because of its importance to the program of "accelerated modernization."

The Revival of Traditional Aristocracies. The New Order regime has shrewdly pursued a policy of reviving regional aristocracies which seemed near collapse in the 1945–65 period. The public justifications for the policy have been: (1) a return to authentic Indonesian traditions; (2) recognition of regional identities; and (3) the development of tourism, which benefits from glittering displays of aristocratic pomp. Unstated reasons include the effort to gain solid support from a naturally conservative stratum, and, more importantly, to fragment the regions vis-à-vis the center by offering them leaderships which inevitably, in a huge multiethnic archipelago, have merely local appeal. The Ministries of the Interior and of Tourism have cooperated closely to implement the overall policy.

The Security Apparatus and the Military. As in other authoritarian regimes, intelligence agencies have proliferated and greatly increased their power under the New Order. In the early years of the regime, Suharto, unsure of his full control of the military, relied heavily on an unofficial "Special Operations" apparatus organized directly out of the presidential palace. Though headed by a powerful general, it recruited heavily among educated civilians (particularly from the Catholic minority), and made frequent use, especially in elections, of petty hoodlums. Disliked by all the real military intelligence services, its power declined in the late 1970s, and collapsed in 1983 when several thousand of its hoodlums were liquidated by military death-squads operating in mufti. Over time, the military intelligence services—whose tasks include surveillance of the military itself—have been unified, centralized, and put under the control of long-time presidential confidants. In turn, the intelligence apparatuses are tightly integrated with the executive instruments of repressive control, especially the territorial military command hierarchy. Until 1988, territorial commanders doubled as agents of Kopkamtib, an immensely powerful, extraconstitutional agency empowered to take almost any measure to ensure "national security."

Central to New Order authoritarianism have been the steady institutionalization of the Doctrine of the (military's) Dual Function and, concurrently, the fairly strict implementation of the professional principles of rotation and tour of duty. As noted above, in the New Order's early days, the Dual Function principle was used to pack the national and provincial legislatures with powerful military blocs, and to appoint military officers to strategic positions in all "civilian" ministries, government agencies, and state enterprises. It served also as a useful way of comfortably retiring surplus officers, and easing serious promotion blockages. In the 1980s, the system has been regularized, in that all officers are now required to serve terms in these nonmilitary capacities before rotating back to the main military hierarchy. Performance in civilian functions is for the first time becoming a criterion for promotion. In addition, two-year terms of duty have increasingly become the norm. The effect has been to "normalize" military penetration of the state at all levels, but also to break up emerging officer cliques which might be tempted to challenge the president's power.

SAFETY VALVES

The New Order regime has been rich enough and shrewd enough to offer some carefully monitored channels for "letting off steam." While the regime has full control of television and radio, private capital dominates the press. The most popular newspapers and magazines are often very cautiously critical. Religious schools must be licensed, and are monitored, but are otherwise generally let alone. Non-governmental organizations, especially those concerned with environmental issues, are permitted to be active except where the financial and political interests of the military are directly affected. And in spite of the regime's constant exhortations to citizens to return to the virtues of their ancestors, it has done very little in practice to interfere with the spread of a new teenage culture, feminist and gay-liberation groups, and, more generally, American-style consumerism among the middle classes.

Religious and ethnic conflicts have, with some brutal exceptions, been handled adroitly. While "political" Islam has been largely suppressed, the state has subsidized the construction of mosques and certain types of religious schools, senior government officials ostentatiously go on the pilgrimage to Mecca, and civil marriages are now no longer recognized. In public, Christian groups have been quietly protected, while behind the scenes they have heavily penetrated the intelligence services and the officer corps. Concessions to ethnicity have come typically in the appointment of "local sons" to provincial governorships and mayorships, while behind-the-scenes central control is ensured by the fact that the recruitment pool is predominantly military. For reasons outlined above, the government has also promoted the revival of "colorful" local (ethnic) aristocracies. Where these policies have failed, however— most notably in West New Guinea and formerly Portuguese East Timor— bloody military occupation has been resorted to. Yet these regions are so remote from the center, and so thinly populated, that the state's stability is not seriously threatened by continuing local armed resistance.

THE FUTURE OF NEW ORDER AUTHORITARIANISM

For all its successes over the past quarter of a century, the New Order's long-term stability can not be taken for granted. At seventy, Suharto is an old man by Indonesian standards, and talk of the succession is becoming increasingly public. But over the years he has taken such good care to eliminate all credible alternatives to himself that no generally acceptable successor has emerged; in the event of his death, severe intramilitary conflict is likely, into which civilian groups will probably be drawn. While IGGI financial support is likely to continue indefinitely, the Indonesian economy remains heavily dependent on exports of oil and natural gas, and hence is vulnerable to severe price fluctuations beyond its control. Serious economic troubles could easily break up the regime's existing political support. On the other hand, if the current industrialization proceeds satisfactorily, it is plausible to expect the same political consequences for military rule that can be observed in economically buoyant South Korea, Taiwan, and Thailand: the rise of increasingly wealthy, self-confident, and politically ambitious entrepreneurial and professional groups, and, more generally, a politically influential middle class. Historically, such middle classes have always (in the long run) opposed military rule, except where there is real fear of a radical Left. In Indonesia, while such a Left is not yet in sight, a huge constituency of exploited workers, dispossessed peasants, and urban poor provides fertile ground for its reemergence.

III. ISSUES FOR DISCUSSION

1. Does the Indonesian case plausibly support the argument that nothing guarantees a modern authoritarian regime longer life as much as its having been established in the wake of civil war or extensive massacres? Compare with other long-stable authoritarian regimes.

2. Most military regimes fall because of internal divisions among the military itself and because it is difficult to convince the vast civilian majority that military rule is acceptable once an emergency situation has ended. Why has Indonesia's military been so united since the late 1960s? How successful has the Dual Function Doctrine been in legitimizing the New Order? Will this success last?

3. Economic success is essential for the survival of most authoritarian regimes in the Third World, but this success depends

on powerful external support. Compare the position of the United States vis-à-vis Indonesia with its positions vis-à-vis comparable regimes in Pakistan, South Korea, Taiwan, and Egypt, for example.

4. All strong authoritarian military regimes rely heavily on military intelligence for control of the political process. Why is this so, and what are the short- and long-term political consequences? Compare the Indonesian case with other military regimes in the Third World.

IV. SELECTED READINGS

Anderson, Benedict R. "Old State, New Society: Indonesia's New Order in Comparative Historical Perspective," chapter 3 in his *Language and Power: Exploring Political Cultures in Indonesia*. Ithaca: Cornell University Press, 1990 (student reading). Structural comparison of New Order Indonesia with mature Dutch colonial governance of the Netherlands Indies.

Dunn, James. *Timor, a People Betrayed*. Milton, Queensland: Jacaranda Press, 1983 (student reading). The best introduction to the East Timor problem, by a former Australian consul in Portuguese East Timor.

Emmerson, Donald K. "The Bureaucracy in Political Context." In *Political Power and Communications in Indonesia, edited by Karl Jackson and Lucian Pye*. Berkeley: University of California Press, 1978 (student reading). Fine analysis of how Suharto built the ramshackle civil service of the 1950s and 1960s into a powerful, authoritarian machine.

Liddle, R. William. "Soeharto's Indonesia: Personal Rule and Political Institutions." *Pacific Affairs* 58 (1985): 68–90 (student reading). Good discussion of the difficult question of how far Suharto has managed to institutionalize his regime, so that it can continue largely unchanged after his death.

MacDougall, John A. "Patterns of Military Control in the Indonesian Higher Central Bureaucracy." *Indonesia* 33 (1982): 89–121 (student reading). The best detailed study of how the military controls the state apparatus.

Osborne, Robin. *Indonesia's Secret War. The Guerrilla Struggle in Irian Jaya*. Boston: Allen and Unwin, 1985 (student reading). Solid study of the brutal repression of West Irianese nationalism by the Suharto regime.

Suryadinata, Leo. *Military Ascendancy and Political Culture, A Study of Indonesia's Golkar*. Athens, Ohio: Ohio University, Monographs in International Studies, Southeast Asia Series, No. 85: 1989 (student reading). Important, up-to-date analysis of the state party Golkar—how it operates, and is operated.

Political Science:
Indonesia

Political Culture in Indonesia

Benedict R. O'G. Anderson

I. INTRODUCTION: CENTRAL POINTS

With at least two hundred significant ethnolinguistic groups; with the largest at least nominally Muslim population among contemporary nation-states, but also with powerful Catholic, Protestant, and Hindu-Buddhist minorities; with a history of colonization by Dutch bureaucrats and planters and occupation by Japanese militarists; and with experience of revolutionary-nationalist, constitutional-democratic, charismatic populist-authoritarian, and military-dominated regimes, Indonesia offers abundant comparative material for the study of political culture. Issues of particular importance to political scientists, historians, and anthropologists include:

• The nature of precolonial political cultures, their social base, and their adaptation to conditions of modern life.

• The impact of colonial education and colonial political styles.

• Problems of political integration after the attainment of independent statehood.

• The relationship between religious belief and political orientation.

• The conflict between Western ideologies of different stripes and older, indigenous value-systems.

II. MAJOR TOPICS

PRECOLONIAL POLITICAL CULTURES

Indonesia's present boundaries are the outcome of three hundred years (c. 1610–1910) of gradual Dutch colonial expansion in the vast archipelago. Throughout its precolonial history, none of its major islands was ever under the control of a single indigenous dynasty, in sharp contrast to China and Japan. The most highly-evolved political system developed in Java, but this was also the island on which Dutch power was earliest and most deeply implanted. At the other end of the spectrum were the remote, fragmented, profoundly underdeveloped "stone age" populations of (West) New Guinea, while in between were an array of petty monarchies, tribal chieftainships, and autonomous village "democracies."

The early political culture of western Indonesia (4th–13th centuries A.D.) developed under the influence of Mahayana and Tantric Buddhism, as well as Sivaitic Hinduism. Beginning in the late thirteenth century Islam began to penetrate the archipelago from the west, brought mainly by Persian, Indian, Arab, and Chinese traders and missionaries. Overwhelmingly Sunni in orientation, it was profoundly affected by Sufi mysticism, especially as developed in Persia and Gujerat. By the end of the sixteenth century the institutional bases of Hindu-Buddhism (priesthoods, monasteries, caste systems, temple-complexes) had been obliterated, except in the island of Bali and its immediate periphery. But under an institutional Islamic veneer, Hindu-Buddhist mystical and animist residues continued (even up to the present) to be powerful and politically influential. Right through the early colonial period, kingship in particular retained an essentially pre-Muslim character.

Given mountainous (volcanic) topography, deep tropical forests, poorly developed communications (except by water), sparse populations, and largely unmonetized economies, the central problem for ancient rulers was how to create a durable state. Dynasties rarely lasted more than three generations, and royal capitals were moved, abandoned, or destroyed with great rapidity. Hence the focus of "political thought" was the nature of power, and how it could be accumulated, in contrast to the modern Western way of thinking which, born in a powerful, stable institutional framework, has worried much more about power's use. Ancient political thought in Java conceived of power as something concrete, not abstract—a manifestation of the divine, and thus existing in natural phenomena, in sacred objects, in human beings, and in the invisible world. It was thought to exist in a stable cosmological "sum," such that its accumulation in one site (a king, a shrine, a mountain) necessarily meant its diminution somewhere else. This accumulation could be achieved by ascetic practices, by the acquisition of magically powerful persons (albinos, dwarves, diviners) and things (daggers, precious stones, relics), and by sexual prowess and alliance. Since all power was of the same "stuff," it was generally believed that close connections existed between political and natural life: eruptions, floods, epidemics, and famines were thus read as signs that the real power of the ruler was leaking away.

The difficulties of state-building in the context of the belief system described above deeply affected political practice. Enormous energies were devoted to the construction of spectacular monuments, which, aside from their usually religious function, served also as advertisements—the official TV, so to speak—for the ruler, and helped attract the sedentary, productive agricultural populations needed to supply his granaries and armed forces. In societies where kinship was the strongest social bond, rulers naturally practiced polygamy, not only to demonstrate their divine fertility, but also to build political coalitions with kinship networks other than their own. Personal prowess was essential in a context where no Chinese-style mandarin bureaucracies yet existed, and in languages where there was no word for "institution."

Since Islam made its way more by trade and mission than by the sword, its influence on political culture developed slowly. Its most long-lasting impact came from its dismantling of the institutional structure of Hindu-Buddhism. What resulted was the phenomenon of the *abangan* or "statistical Muslim," the man who was circumcised, married, and buried by Muslim rites, because there was no institutionalized alternative, but who ate pork, fasted not during Ramadan but on moonless nights, placed trust in magical daggers, took wives and concubines as often as he pleased, and worshipped the spirits of his ancestors and a plurality of gods as much as Allah. To this day, "statistical" Muslims probably outnumber "real" Muslims in populous Java, so that the country's official 90 percent Muslim affiliation conceals the fact that in political-cultural terms "real Muslims" are an angry, frustrated minority.

DUTCH COLONIAL INFLUENCE.

The most important impacts of Dutch colonial rule derived from the fact that it began early in the seventeenth century, and for two hundred years was exercised, not by a state, but by the largest multinational corporation of the time, the United East India Company. The company was interested solely in making money: it had no substantial interest in educating natives, or converting them. Moreover, it had its base in newly Protestant Holland, which scarcely had enough Protestant clergy to minister to its own needs. Unlike the contemporary Spanish in the Philippines, or the Portuguese in Brazil, the Dutch made no serious attempt at Christianization till the middle of the nineteenth century, and permitted Muslimization to continue. (Meantime, the Philippines had become 90 percent Catholic). And because Holland was a republic, and the Company stingy, no effort was made for almost three hundred to introduce the Dutch language to the local elites. Uniquely among all colonial rulers, the Company adopted the policy of ruling through a pidgin version of the simple Malay that was the trading lingua franca of the archipelago. Hence, even before the advent of nationalism around 1900, the company had inadvertently created a **local** language of administrative unification, which, once people forgot its origins, became an uncontroversial national language. The contrast with India, which was ruled by the British through English and still has no accepted single national language, is instructive.

When an independent Holland became a monarchy for the first time, in 1815, and turned Indonesia into a regular colony, it was a desperately poor, weak, small, and backward European country, which held its colonies only on British sufferance. Eager to make maximal profits, and lacking the self-confidence to undertake a "civilizing mission" in the French, British or American imperial style, the Dutch, for most of the nineteenth century, relied heavily on propping up the traditional ruling classes and the political culture they represented in order to maintain control. Modern education began, very cautiously, only in the twentieth century.

Religious Change. In nineteenth-century Holland, a powerful religious revival encouraged a quite new missionary effort in the Indies, targeted especially at remote, pagan, mountain-dwelling peoples. Thanks to mission schools, initially mostly Protestant, later also Catholic, these hitherto remote, illiterate populations moved rapidly ahead, i.e., were educated, joined the civil service and army, and immigrated to the cities. Many were fearful of Islam in part because of missionary prejudices, in part because they had often been oppressed, in their pagan days, by Islamicized coastal populations. Meantime, Islam in the archipelago was also changing as the result of more rapid communications with the Middle East, where reformists and fundamentalists, resisting Western penetration and Ottoman autocracy, were challenging old accommodations and developing a self-consciously political Islam. Especially in urban areas in the Indies, adherents of this type of Islam actively opposed not only the conservative rural ulama (Islamic wise men), but Christian missions and those local elites whom they regarded as collaborators with a colonial regime hostile to the Faith. Muslim activists did much to pioneer the independent schools, charitable organizations, scouting movements, and women's groups which later laid the base for the nationalist movement. The modernist Islamic ideas of the equality of Muslims before Allah and the importance of applying rationality to social life contributed— together with certain strands in Christianity— to undermine the traditional magical conceptions of power, and the authoritarianism of both colonial bureaucracy and indigenous monarchy.

The Impact of Marxism. Marxism was brought to the Indies, well before the Bolshevik revolution, by a small group of dedicated Dutch radicals. Before the colonial regime decided to expel them, they had managed to recruit some very able young Indonesians, who then spread the word among the receptive laborers on the huge plantations, in the railway system, and in the ports. In 1920, the first Communist Party in Asia was founded. Although it became affiliated with the Comintern of Lenin and Stalin, it was very much a homegrown product, working easily with Islamic radicalism and older strains of peasant millenarianism. When (against Comintern instructions), it opened an armed rebellion against the colonial regime in 1926–27, the insurrection blazed most fiercely in two of the most strongly Islamic regions of the archipelago.

But the Marxist critique of imperialism and colonialism also captured the imagination of the burgeoning non-Communist intelligentsia that was being created (finally) by the colonial school system in the 1920s and 1930s. After the crushing of the Communist insurrection, these groups—social democrats, radical nationalists, reformist Muslims, progressive Christians, and so forth—known collectively as the Pergerakan (the Movement) generally adopted the anticapitalist, antifeudalist, and anti-imperialist vocabulary that Marx had originated. "Socialism," albeit interpreted in often conflicting ways, became a powerful element in the emerging "Indonesian" political culture.

INDONESIAN NATIONALISM

A self-conscious "Indonesian" nationalism appeared only after the rise of radical Islam and radical Marxism, but it quickly incorporated them. The central factor was the rapid spread, and acceptance, of what came to be called Bahasa Indonesia as the language of the nation now beginning to be imagined. Although, for the strange reasons suggested earlier, pidgin Malay had long been the on-the-ground language of colonial administration, it originated in the ancient trading lingua franca of the islands, and was the property of no single, important ethnolinguistic group. Its adoption as a national language threatened no one, and its simple grammar, democratic (unhierarchical) vocabulary and now Romanized spelling made it easy to learn. From 1890s on, it was increasingly adopted by the native press and was officially proclaimed "our" language at a big multiethnic Youth Congress in 1928.

Another important factor was the highly centralized nature of the colonial bureaucracy and the colonial school system, which brought children from all over the archipelago into standardized classrooms, with standardized curricula and textbooks, within an educational hierarchy whose center was the colonial capital Batavia (Jakarta) itself. Finally, there was the marginality of the Dutch language itself, which had none of the international prestige of English or French, and therefore proved far less culturally seductive. Altogether, these conditions created a sturdy nationalism by the 1930s. As articulated by the charismatic young politician Sukarno, it was radical and populist, Marxist-influenced, and at the same time conscious of the need to make political room for religious and ethnic diversity.

JAPANESE OCCUPATION AND THE REVOLUTION

The Japanese invasion in 1942, and occupation during the next three years profoundly affected the growth of Indonesian political culture. Dutch planters and officials were interned and their language prohibited; for the first time Bahasa Indonesia became the official language of state as well as nation. But it was Japanese militarism and pan-Asianism that wrought real change. The prestige of Japan had been rising in Indonesian eyes since its spectacular victories in the Russo-Japanese War. The Japanese conquest of all Southeast Asia, and the ease with which Japanese armies contemptuously routed the Dutch, made the "Japanese model" now especially attractive. Late colonial Dutch rule had been civilian, routine, commercial, and "Western." Japanese rule was militarist, wartime-violent, ceremonial-fascist, and "Asian." Ruler and ruled were now "elder brother and younger brother," united in racial solidarity against the white West. "Traditional" values of a generally authoritarian kind were revived and given official support as being "genuinely Asian." Perhaps most important of all, the Japanese, for their own wartime reasons, gave military training to substantial numbers of young Indonesians, emphasizing Bushido values and national identity. These youngsters were fully aware that mighty Japan was a military dictatorship, unlike any of the Western colonial powers.

The suffering imposed on the Indonesian people by Japan's wartime exactions, the sudden collapse of the Japanese in August 1945, and the inability of Holland (only just liberated from the Nazis) quickly to reimpose colonialism, created a revolutionary situation in the fall of 1945. Japanese arms quickly fell into the hands of many different groups. The two most prestigious nationalist politicians, Sukarno and Hatta, proclaimed Indonesia's independence, and the stage was set for a bitter four-year conflict till The Hague was forced finally to concede a transfer of legal sovereignty in 1949. The Revolution, as it quickly came to be called, drastically transformed Indonesian political culture. Millions of Indonesians of all social classes and most ethnic groups were drawn into the struggle, giving radical nationalism a far broader social base than ever before. But the struggle was controlled by no one party, religion, organization, or ideology. The relative weakness of the revolutionary government itself meant that long-suppressed forces of social radicalism were unleashed. In many areas colonial collaborators—local royalties, aristocracies, and officials—were overthrown, imprisoned, and even killed. A profound, unplanned and uncoordinated democratization of society took place, and for the first time in Indonesia's history parties of the Left (Socialist and Communist) played leading public roles in political life. At the same time, the absence of an all-powerful colonial ruler permitted the increasingly violent expression of ideological antagonisms. For the first time, armed conflict between leftists and rightists, Muslims and Christians, peasants and landowners took place. And the legitimacy of militarized politics, which had been undermined by the sudden collapse of Japan, acquired new currency in the struggle to get rid of the Dutch once and for all.

INDONESIAN POLITICAL CULTURE AFTER THE TRANSFER OF SOVEREIGNTY

In 1949, the new, internationally recognized, Indonesian state emerged weak, divided, and desperately impoverished from the multiple traumas of successive colonial regimes and four years of revolution. A constitutional democracy was formally instituted primarily because no organized political group— civil or military, on the Right or the Left— was sufficiently powerful or united to impose an alternative. But the system had few genuinely committed supporters. Dutch colonial capitalism had largely stifled the growth of an indigenous business class, leaving space only for a dependent, politically vulnerable, Chinese commercial minority. The college-educated intelligentsia was pitifully small— a few thousand people in a population by then approaching one hundred million.

Through the 1950s the political culture appeared increasingly to fragment. Free elections held in 1955 produced no clear majority but rather four dominant, often antagonistic major parties: Masyumi, representing reformist and fundamentalist Islam, strong in urban areas and the islands outside Java; Nahdatul Ulama, representing traditional, syncretic Islam, strong mainly in heavily-populated rural Java; the Communist Party, with powerful support in Sumatra's plantation belt and among the *abangan* peasantry and urban workers of Java; and the Nationalist Party, based mainly among *abangan* civil servants, professionals, and village elites on Java, and threatened local aristocracies in the Outer Islands. The freely elected Constitutional Assembly, created to draft a new constitution, was unable to resolve the ideological impasse between those who favored some form of Islamic state and those (Christians and *abangan* Muslims) who opposed it. Furthermore, dissatisfaction with the outcome of the Revolution and with government economic policies favoring poor populous Java over resource-rich Sumatra and Sulawesi produced a whole series of local rebellions. Yet the depth of Indonesian nationalism meant that only one of these— the long-Christian South Moluccas where the colonialists had traditionally recruited their native soldiery—had secession in mind; all the rest were intended to increase the rebels' say in national politics.

THE RISE OF AUTHORITARIANISM

The crisis of parliamentary democracy in the late 1950s encouraged the reemergence of authoritarian elements in Indonesia's cultural traditions. The two most important strands were articulated by the charismatic Javanese-Balinese President Sukarno, and by the military's high command.

Denouncing Western-style democracy as divisive and alien to Indonesian society and as a betrayal of the radical-nationalist impulse of the Revolution of 1945–49, Sukarno managed, between 1956 and 1959, to impose a system he called Guided Democracy. At the ideological level, the president drew eclectically on Marxism and a mythologized version of *abangan* tradition to mobilize the population behind him on the basis of hostility to Western capitalism and imperialism, as well as "decadent" Western culture: Indonesia should have its own form of socialism, its own cultural personality, and a consensual style of political decision-making originating in traditional village life. At the practical level, the system elevated the president to the position of supreme arbiter of political life; it rejected reformist-fundamentalist Islam as beholden to the alien Middle East, and social democracy as aping the West; it imposed censorship and undermined the political parties while encouraging the formation and mobilization of popular organizations. However, while Sukarno's rhetoric was radical and his support (to balance the growing power of the military) for the Communist party was public, he also identified himself with precolonial monarchs, enjoyed "palace politics," and exploited popular belief in mystical and millenarian beliefs to bolster his own position.

The military, with support from both the United States and the USSR, emerged from the civil wars of the 1950s as the most powerful institution in the country after the presidency. Its authoritarianism derived from its origins under the Japanese military occupation, its embrace of the ethos of modern military professionalism, and the worldview of the *abangan*-oriented Javanese rural elites of which, by the late 1950s, its officer corps was mainly composed. What it shared with the president was hostility to political Islam, a dislike of political parties, and the belief that state power shall be concentrated at the center. On the other hand, it was violently anti-Communist (especially after

1957, when Sukarno, angered by the continuing Dutch refusal to turn over West New Guinea despite the terms of the 1949 settlement, ordered the nationalization of all Dutch enterprises in the archipelago— and the army took control in the name of the state); it was covertly sympathetic to the United States, which had been training its officers since the mid-1950s; and it believed in bureaucratic order rather than popular mobilization. An unstable alliance between the two strains of authoritarianism finally broke down in the aftermath of the mysterious "coup" attempt of October 1, 1965, when six senior generals were killed by units of the Presidential Guard. Blaming the murders on the Communist Party, the army leadership, in the person of then General Suharto, organized, with the assistance of Muslim and Christian civilian vigilantes, a vast massacre of party members and sympathizers. By 1966, President Sukarno had lost all effective power; he was succeeded by Suharto, and placed under house arrest until his death in 1970.

THE POLITICAL CULTURE OF SUHARTO'S NEW ORDER

The New Order regime, in place since 1966, has been completely dominated by a military which, as a result of the previous civil wars, is disproportionately *abangan* Javanese. The outlook of the officer corps, of which President Suharto is quite representative, is profoundly authoritarian, but at two different levels. Publicly, emphasis is laid on the modern military values of discipline, patriotism, and corporate loyalty. Much is made of the army's heroic role in what is now called the War of National Liberation, and, after 1950, in preserving national unity against Communist, Muslim, and ethnic insurrections. Not far below the surface, however, are residues of Japanese influence, and traditional superstition. Off stage, Suharto consults mystics and astrologers, collects objects said to be invested with magical powers, and visits ancient shrines. Especially in recent years, he has established marriage ties with one of the old royal families, and often behaves like a Javanese monarch.

Alongside the authoritarianism of the military, are three other authoritarian tendencies which the New Order regime has turned to its own advantage.

Modernization and Industrialization. Lacking Sukarno's charisma, and coming to power when Indonesia's economy was near collapse, Suharto has sought to build up long-term legitimacy by casting himself as Indonesia's modernizer. For this purpose, he allied himself from the start with a small group of American-trained economists and technocrats, who provided much needed expertise, won the confidence of the World Bank and the International Monetary Fund, and attracted a huge and continuing out-pouring of aid from the United States, Western Europe, and Japan. For the technocrats, who lacked any political base, Suharto's rule provided the political stability, the insulation of the state from popular pressures, and the crushing of labor unions and peasant associations necessary to attract major foreign investment. The economic success of New Order modernization has created a substantial, if fragile, new Indonesian middle class, which, if not authoritarian in itself, has been willing to support authoritarian rule in exchange for economic advantage. For all these groups, "modernization" has justified not merely the suppression of the traditional Indonesian Left, but a pervasive denial of political rights of the great bulk of the population.

Christian Minorities. The prominent role played by devout Muslims in the crushing of the Communist party aroused their own hope of gaining power, alarming not only the *abangan* officer corps and most civil servants, but also the Catholic and Protestant minorities. The New Order regime has recruited heavily from these minorities in staffing its varied intelligence agencies, whose prime function since the early 1970s has been to spy on and repress Muslim activism. The triumph of Khomeini's Islamic revolution in Iran has simply reinforced Christian fears and willingness to back the regime's anti-Muslim policies.

Aristocracies. Because most of the local aristocracies collaborated with the Dutch colonial regime, and represented "feudal" backwardness in the minds of committed nationalists, they were severely weakened in the 1945–65 period. Since 1965, they have made a strong comeback, for three related reasons. First, as traditional authorities, they are overwhelmingly conservative in outlook. Second, since they have only local bases, they are no threat to the New Order, which can indeed use them to show that it respects Indonesia's local ethnical loyalties. Third, reviving local aristocratic pomp has contributed greatly to the rapid expansion of Indonesia's tourist industry.

OPPOSITION

The stability of the New Order regime over the past quarter of a century has been based on an authoritarian coalition of military officers, civil servants, religious minorities, and ethnic aristocracies. But the coalition's ascendancy does not mean that other strands in Indonesia's political culture have disappeared, even if they are at the present time heavily repressed. If "Indonesian socialism" is anathema to the New Order, it remains attractive to a variety of groups who consider themselves, privately, on the Left: surviving members of the once twenty million-strong Communist Party's "family" of organizations, left-wing nationalists, and groups of young Muslim, Christian, and secular intellectuals influenced by neo-Marxist and *dependencia* thinking. The popularity of Islam has been increasing, to judge by mosque attendance and new conversions, not least because of its hostility to the regime's often "feudal" style, support for aristocracies and privileged Christians, and close alliance with the West. Nor can it be denied that as a result of twenty-five years of political repression, the powerful impact of the Western mass media, the rise of a visible urban youth culture, and the fading memories of the traumas of 1965–66, there is renewed interest in liberal democracy and constitutionalism, though these terms are rarely used in public.

III. ISSUES FOR DISCUSSION

1. Compare the impact of Dutch colonialism on Indonesian political culture with that of British, French, or American colonialism in regions under their domination.

2. How would you explain the fact that although Indonesia is listed as the most populous Muslim nation in the world, Islam has never been "in power" there?

3. Given Indonesia's extreme cultural and religious diversity, what factors have helped give it a national identity?

4. The authoritarian political culture of today's Indonesia has strong traditional roots, but it also represents a self-conscious reaction against the populist, revolutionary-socialist, and democratic strains so prominent in the country's first twenty years of independence. Compare this kind of "reactive" authoritarianism with that in other "postrevolutionary" Third World countries.

IV. SELECTED READINGS

Anderson, Benedict R. O'G. "The Idea of Power in Javanese Culture,"
    Chapter 1 in his *Language and Power: Exploring Political Cultures in
    Indonesia.* Ithaca: Cornell University Press, 1990 (student reading). A
    reconstruction of precolonial "political thought" in Java, and assessment of its influence on modern Indonesian politics.

Boland, B.J. *The Struggle of Islam in Modern Indonesia.* The Hague: Nijhoff, 1971 (student reading). The best full-length study of the subject.

Feith, Herbert, and Castles, Lance, eds. *Indonesian Political Thinking, 1945–1965.* Ithaca: Cornell University Press, 1970 (student reading). Broad-gauged, well-selected anthology of speeches and essays by representatives of most of Indonesia's political-cultural traditions, with a fine interpretative introduction by Feith.

Liddle, R. William. *Politics and Culture in Indonesia.* Ann Arbor: University of Michigan, Center for Political Studies, 1988 (student reading). Excellent, brief, up-to-date synthesis of existing research on Indonesian political cultures, with special emphasis on the New Order.

McVey, Ruth T. "Nationalism, Islam and Marxism: The Management of Ideological Conflict in Indonesia." Introduction to Sukarno *Nationalism, Islam and Marxism* (trans.). Ithaca: Cornell Modern Indonesia Project, 1969 (student reading). The best brief discussion of Sukarno's thought and its relationship to problems of Indonesian unity.

Political Science:
Indonesia

The Political
Role of the
Military:
Indonesia

Benedict R. O'G. Anderson

I. INTRODUCTION: CENTRAL POINTS

Indonesia, a sprawling archipelagic territory strategically positioned between the Pacific and Indian Oceans, and the world's
fifth most populous nation, offers an excellent case for studying
the role of the military in the Third World.

Although in significant respects military dominance of Indonesian political life is comparable to the pattern of civil-military
relations in many Third World countries, it is also deviant in that
the Indonesian officer corps claims this dominance to be permanent, and the claim is enshrined in the present constitutional
order. Indonesia thus falls into the very small minority (fewer than
10 percent) of military-dominated states where the officers belong
to a group that Eric Nordlinger terms "ruler-type praetorians."[1]

Indonesia is also useful for comparative purposes because its
military was originally formed, not by European colonial powers, but
by Imperial Japan, during World War II. It thus shares certain
special authoritarian features with the militaries of Burma and
South Korea.

The transformation of the Indonesian military from a revolutionary guerrilla force fighting against Dutch colonialism (1945–

49) into a right-wing, semiprofessional organization closely linked to the Western powers and Japan shows with great clarity the pattern of dependency of would-be professional militaries in non-industrialized societies on weapons, military-related high technology, and training provided by advanced industrial societies, especially the United States.

The policies pursued by the Indonesian military with regard to the huge variety of religious and ethnolinguistic groups among Indonesia's almost 185 million citizens offer important comparative data for the study of problems of national integration in Asia and Africa.

II. MAJOR TOPICS

DUTCH COLONIALISM

Beginning with trading posts established on Java and in the fabled Spice Islands (Moluccas) in the early seventeenth century, the Dutch gradually expanded their East Indies empire to include, by 1910, all of maritime Southeast Asia except for British northern Borneo, the Spanish and American Philippines, and tiny Portuguese East Timor. While the vast majority of the populations had accepted Islam to various degrees, Catholic and Protestant missions gained substantial numbers of converts, especially among previously animist ethnic minorities. As in many British and French colonies, these Christianized minorities were disproportionately recruited into the colonial military because they were believed to be both trustworthy and peculiarly dependent on the protection of the empire. The Dutch exploited the colony's natural resources by promoting plantation agriculture (rubber, sugar, coffee, and tea) and mining (oil and tin)— especially on the western islands of Java and Sumatra— in the process creating the largest proletarianized agricultural work force in pre-World War II Southeast Asia. But colonial education policy was exceptionally conservative. In 1940, when the population of the colony was close to eighty million, there were fewer than 650 youngsters enrolled in tertiary-level Western-style educational institutions. The educated civilian elite was thus very small, and heavily concentrated on Java. Finally, in comparison with the British in Burma (which in the late 1930s already had a native Burmese prime minister) or the Americans in the Philippines (which in the same era had a Filipino president of sorts), the Dutch gave Indonesians very little practice in constitutional self-government. The colonial legislature was chosen through a highly restricted franchise and had very little real power; nationalist politicians and journalists were under constant surveillance and harassment by the colonial bureaucracy's political police.

THE JAPANESE OCCUPATION

In March 1942 the armies of imperial Japan crushed feeble Dutch resistance and began an occupation of the archipelago which lasted for a little more than three years. The Japanese disbanded the small Dutch colonial army (which numbered just over forty thousand) and interned most of its senior personnel. They also abolished the legislature, shut down all political parties, and imposed full wartime press censorship. Furthermore, they broke up the colony into three completely separate zones: Java, Sumatra (each controlled by the army), and the Eastern Archipelago (administered by the navy). For the first time Indonesians experienced military rule.

In late 1943, however, with the Pacific War now going against them, the Japanese army leaders decided that in the event of an American invasion they would need the assistance of armed Indonesians. In Java, the so-called Peta army was created which eventually numbered sixty-six battalions. Sumatra followed suit on a slower, smaller scale. The Japanese naval administrators in the east, however, blocked any such development in their zone. The Peta was trained as a guerrilla force, with each battalion being locally recruited and deployed. It had no central staff, and no officers above the level of battalion commander. On the other hand, it was heavily indoctrinated in the Japanese military ethic, especially its radical-nationalist variant. Of special importance was the example of the political role of the military in Japan itself, which during the 1930s completely overshadowed that of the civilians in government.

THE REVOLUTION (1945–49)

The unexpectedly sudden Japanese surrender on August 15, 1945, following the American atomic attacks on Hiroshima and Nagasaki, and the Russian invasion of Manchuria, created a vacuum of power in the Indonesian archipelago. Holland, under Nazi occupation till the spring of 1945, was in no condition to reestablish colonial rule by force of arms. The British, assigned the task by the Potsdam agreement accepting the Japanese surrender in Indonesia, were seriously undermanned, and gave top priority to their own colonies of Burma, Malaya, and the Straits Settlements. The British commander, Lord Louis Mountbatten, radioed the Japanese administrators to disband any armed groups they had trained and to prevent any changes in the political status quo. The local Japanese commanders did disband the Peta and its Sumatran equivalents, but did little to prevent the proclamation of Indonesian Independence on August 17, 1945, by Sukarno and Hatta, the two preeminent nationalist politicians. In the weeks that followed, a civilian republican government was set up which won substantial popular support. The suffering of the war years— famines, harsh taxation, forced labor on a huge scale, and hyper-inflation— had created a revolutionary situation, in which radicalized Indonesian youths played the central role. By the time the Dutch and British appeared, large quantities of Japanese weapons had fallen into Indonesian hands, and a four-year armed struggle for Indonesian independence was under way.

Unlike almost all other modern militaries, that of Indonesia grew from the bottom up. Ex-Peta officers tried to reassemble their subordinates, but had to do so on the basis of popularity, not command, and were successful only where they were lucky enough to seize local Japanese arsenals. But they were in competition with many other youth groups, which had no intention of becoming military professionals yet wished to defend the country's independence on the basis of an Islamic, Socialist, Communist, or other ideology. Field commanders got together to elect their superiors, and so on up to the very top. In 1945, the thirty-year-old revolutionary, General Sudirman, who had not completed high school, was **elected** commander-in-chief, a position he held till his death in 1950; the civilian leadership of the country felt compelled to acquiesce.

Other peculiarities of the revolutionary Indonesian military which were to have decisive consequences for its later historical role were: (1) A peculiarly flat age-pyramid, in which almost all military personnel, from generals down to privates, were between sixteen and thirty years of age. Seniority in terms of years served, so important to the authority structure of "normal" militaries, was largely absent; and the fact that, in view of their youth, it would be years before any officers would retire, was a source of grave discontent among the lower ranks in the postrevolutionary years. (2) A critical shortage of educated staff officers, mainly the result of the Peta's odd structure and training. It proved necessary to recruit veterans of the Dutch-era military, some of whom had been given emergency staff training on the eve of the Pacific War.

Needed, but tainted as Dutch collaborators, these men were often in severe conflict with the Peta veterans. (3) Absence of the normal military monopoly of access to the instruments of war, as powerful armed "struggle organizations" sprang up alongside the military and competed with it for guns, supplies, money, recruits, and popular support. Inevitably, fighting broke out at various junctures between the military and such groups, especially those identified with Muslim or Marxist ideologies. Yet many military men also had friends and relatives in these struggle organizations, so that the official state army was also much more porous to outside influences than the usual professional military. (4) The lopsided geographical distribution of military training by various Japanese authorities (and the temporary 1945–46 occupation of eastern Indonesia by the Australians). This meant that the revolutionary army was overwhelmingly an army of Java and Sumatra. Most of the fighting against the returning Dutch was carried out on these islands, so when Holland finally granted legal independence at the end of 1949, the military was "national" only in name and aspiration, not on the basis of recruitment. (5) Dutch superiority in training and firepower forced the Indonesian military to revert to the guerrilla style of fighting it had learned from the Japanese. Guerrilla warfare, however, required intimate military involvement in local politics, administration, and economic life. When the Dutch paratroopers, dropped into the Republican capital in December 1948, succeeded in capturing President Sukarno, Vice-President Hatta, and many senior civilian government leaders in December 1948, the guerrilla army essentially took charge of the continuing nationalist resistance. By the end of 1949 many army officers were convinced that it was they, and they alone, who had finally secured their country's freedom.

In all this, the contrast to Vietnam, the other major Southeast Asian country that had to fight militarily for its independence, is striking. In Vietnam, nationalist leadership was from the start firmly held by Ho Chi Minh and his Communist comrades, and the Vietnamese army was formed by, and under the control of, the Communist Party. In Indonesia, no single party or personality dominated, and every revolutionary cabinet was a complex, often conflictual, coalition. Each party had armed youth affiliates, but none was decisively stronger than any other. Civilians never effectively controlled the military, but the military itself was so loosely structured, so locally oriented, and so internally rivalrous that it could not dominate the population or the government in any permanent way.

CONSTITUTIONAL DEMOCRACY (1950-57)

The circumstances under which Holland finally yielded sovereignty to Indonesia had decisive consequences for the Indonesian military. The critical factor was not any Indonesian military victory (compare General Giap's stunning victory over the French at Dien Bien Phu), but rather American intervention. In the early phase of the Revolution, Washington had supported The Hague, which it regarded as a wartime ally, and as essential for building a solidly anti-Soviet Western Europe. By the end of 1948, however, after Sukarno, Hatta, and more conservative elements in the military had crushed an abortive rebellion by the Indonesian Left on Java, it shifted its position. Since the Dutch financed their war effort largely out of Marshall Plan funds, they could not sustain it for long in the face of American opposition. The settlement imposed by Washington turned out to have two especially damaging consequences. First, an infant Indonesia that had been economically devastated by years of Japanese rule and revolutionary warfare was forced to assume the huge public debt of the Dutch colonial state, including the bills run up during the period 1945–49. Independent it might now be, but it was nearly bankrupt. Second, the western half of the island of New Guinea was withheld from the transfer of sovereignty pending further negotiations. (The Dutch wished to maintain some presence in East Asia, and moreover thought the remote, undeveloped region might be a suitable home for members of loyal Eurasian and Christian minorities who were not welcome in Holland). Unresolved for the next thirteen years, the issue enormously envenomed Dutch-Indonesian relations, gave the military a new "liberation" mission, and helped undermine the credibility of parliamentary government.

Indonesia started out as a parliamentary democracy primarily because there was no plausible alternative. In the vast island country an authoritarian regime was still impossible. There was no navy or air force to permit the forcible imposition of a central will. No military group or political party had a genuinely national stretch or organization. The charismatic president, Sukarno, was hugely popular, but had no political party of his own, and presided over a ramshackle bureaucracy which combined revolutionary republican elements with collaborator holdovers from the antirevolutionary Dutch regime. But Western-style constitutional democracy has its own doctrine of civil-military relations, one which firmly subordinates the military to civilian authority. Nothing in the Indonesian military's experience or training made this doctrine seem justifiable or sensible; all its various factions, however much they might dislike each other, resented the "back to the barracks" logic of the 1950s constitutional system. After all, they were national heroes, unlike the collaborator militaries of neighboring Malaya and the Philippines.

Without solid economic, cultural, or political foundations, parliamentary government quickly collapsed, despite the successful holding, in 1955, of the only free and fair elections Indonesia has ever known. For these elections showed the country evenly divided between four mutually suspicious giant parties (two Muslim, one Communist, and one "secular nationalist"), as well as substantial Catholic, Protestant, Socialist, and other smaller parties. Provincial rebellions erupted almost at once: first in the Protestant Moluccas, led by local veterans of the Dutch colonial army, who feared reprisals for their antinationalist role in 1945–49; then in Muslim Aceh, a revolutionary stronghold which the Dutch never reconquered, led by Muslim religious leaders angered by the government's attempts at centralization and secularization. Everywhere, local militaries were crucial. Accustomed to running their own affairs, they disliked being subordinated to either civilian or military leaders in Jakarta, the national capital located on Java. Especially in Sumatra, with its agricultural and mineral wealth, its close economic ties to Singapore, and its revolutionary experience, hostility to Jakarta grew. As early as 1951, the army on Java felt compelled to begin the difficult transition from a huge, badly armed, popular guerrilla force into a much smaller, well-armed, centralized counterinsurgency force, capable of putting down rebellions in most parts of the country (even on Java).

Two processes greatly aided this fundamental transformation: one was the logic of postindependence demobilization and failed provincial rebellion; the other was intervention by the United States, and later, the USSR. With the end of the armed struggle against the Dutch, most "struggle organizations" either disbanded or sought integration into the official military. Few were accepted, because a desperately poor government was trying to reduce, not expand, the army. When regional rebellions were suppressed, often with great difficulty, the military men from those regions were removed from the national army, which thereby gradually assumed a more and more Javanese character. On the other hand, the military high command, humiliated by the need for endless negotiations with ex-revolutionary comrades defying the central government, began to look for the external help needed to give it decisive control. As early as 1954, it began sending officers for training to the United States, in order to organize elite para-troop units, obtain better weapons, and develop an effective air and naval capacity. The civilian cabinets, for their own reasons, cooperated in this effort. President Sukarno, however, concerned to maintain room for maneuver in foreign policy and in dealing with the army, pushed for the Socialist bloc to become the main suppliers of the navy and the air force, expecting to exploit inter-service rivalries.

Up until 1957, no rebellion had had serious international impli-cations. But late in that year Washington, alarmed by the rapid growth of the Indonesian Communist Party, lent substantial CIA support to a coalition of Muslim, Christian, and military rebels in Sumatra and Sulawesi, which in February 1958 proclaimed a rival government to that in Jakarta. At almost the same time, negotiations with Holland over West New Guinea completely col-lapsed. Sukarno declared nationwide martial law and confiscated the vast Dutch corporate assets in the country. His intent was to ensure the loyalty of the military on Java by giving it control of this corporate wealth in the military on Java, thereby guarantee-ing its loyalty, and to create a new political system in which the military would have an important legal and political role.

GUIDED DEMOCRACY (1959–1965)

The central government's decisive success in the civil war of 1958 effectively destroyed the local militaries in Sumatra and Northern Sulawesi which had been active since the revolution. In their place entered victorious occupation forces from Java. The Java-nese ethnic group, already very strong in the officer corps, became overwhelmingly dominant; the army was now much more nar-rowly based than hitherto, but it was also much more united and disciplined. The Army High Command and Sukarno now joined forces to replace the liberal Constitution of 1950 with a strongly authoritarian one originally drawn up in the last months of the Japanese Occupation. The elected parliament was abruptly re-placed by one appointed by the president, in which military offi-cers had strong representation for the first time. From then on, presidential cabinets always included a large number of generals and colonels. But the military was still too internally fragile to challenge the charismatic, left-leaning president for supreme power. Indonesia was thus spared the coups which were inaugu-rating full military dictatorships in neighboring Burma and Thai-land.

Military control of the country's major productive assets, after the nationalizations, strengthened the hand of the Army High Command, which found it could begin to address the "promotions problem" that derived from the officers' youth, by pensioning people off very comfortably in jobs with the new state corporations. But at the same time, the military's new economic power made it much more corrupt and conservative than hitherto. Under Guided Democracy, with military personnel now managing businesses in which the labor force had long been successfully organized by the Communist Party, the hostility between the party and the senior officer corps increased sharply. The antagonism was heightened by Sukarno, who gave the party public support as a counterweight to the growing power of the military.

By 1964, the Guided Democracy regime was in severe difficulty, despite its 1962 success, with the help of the Kennedy Administration, in getting Holland to relinquish West New Guinea. Sukarno's increasingly anti-Western foreign policy (which frightened off foreign investment), military mismanagement and plundering of the nationalized sector, and years of heavy budget deficits, caused a hyperinflation of catastrophic proportions. With their legal salaries rendered almost worthless, civilian and military officials felt compelled to practice corruption on a massive scale. At the same time, popular unrest and social conflict, especially over land reform, greatly increased.

THE "COUP" OF OCTOBER 1, 1965

Early on that morning, Lt.-Col. Untung, an obscure battalion commander in the presidential guard announced on the national radio that he had had to take drastic measures to protect Sukarno from an imminent coup plotted by a Council of Generals with the complicity of the C.I.A. Among these measures were the formation of a mixed military-civilian revolutionary council to run the country, and the abolition of all army ranks above his own, that of lieutenant colonel. He also denounced the Army High Command for corruption, sexual scandals, and abuse of those in lower ranks. That same day, however, Untung was "countercouped" by General Suharto, commander of the army's elite paratroop strike-force. It then transpired that six top generals had been killed by the Untung forces.

To this day, much remains obscure about the Untung "coup." Though many observers believe it originated in internal antagonisms, deriving from the military's unusual origins in the Japanese Occupation and the Revolution, Suharto and his associates denounced it as a Communist plot. Media manipulation of the deaths of the six generals contributed to an already explosive atmosphere caused by the hyperinflation. A vast, bloody pogrom, directed by the military but involving mass participation by youthful Muslim and Christian vigilantes, ensued. Upwards of five hundred thousand "leftists" were massacred, and hundreds of thousands of others imprisoned and tortured. By the spring of 1966, the Communist Party was obliterated. Fatally weakened by these events (and his attempts to halt the massacres), Sukarno was forced to sign over his powers to Suharto in a second, bloodless coup on March 11, 1966. By March 1967 Suharto had become acting president, and a year later president. So he has remained to the present.

THE NEW ORDER (1966–   )

Under the New Order regime established by Suharto, the Indonesian military has been in full control of the country's political life for almost a quarter of a century. The purging of thousands of civilian officials on suspicion of pro-Sukarno or Communist sympathies gave the new president an extraordinary opportunity to solve the military's "promotion problem" by replacing the purged civilians with military personnel. The United States, Japan, and Western Europe, elated by the fall of Sukarno, and the obliteration of the largest non-ruling Communist Party in the world (at a time when the Vietnam War was already going badly), rushed to give Indonesia enormous amounts of aid, which helped to control inflation. Foreign investment, encouraged especially by the effective elimination of trade unions, poured in. And in 1973, as a result of Indonesia's participation in OPEC, its government suddenly became extremely wealthy. For the first time in its independent history, the country's economy began to develop rapidly.

Taking credit for this sustained development, for having saved the country from Communism in 1965 and from the regional rebellions before that, as well as for its central role in the armed struggle for independence between 1945 and 1949, the officer corps has insisted on the right to a **permanently** dominant place in the country's political life. This stance, codified in the Doctrine of the Dual Function (strictly military, and politico-economic), and enshrined in the Constitution, legitimizes military control over national and regional legislatures, strict military censorship of the media, military manipulation of elections, and draconian internal security measures.

GENERATIONAL CHANGE

By the early 1980s most of the officers who as youngsters had joined the Peta and the army of the Revolution had finally reached retirement age. While they continued to dominate political life, they could no longer run the army directly. In their place have come the so-called Cadets. So bloated with aspiring officers was the post-revolutionary military in the 1950s, that it was not until 1958 that a military academy was set up—along American lines. Members of the first graduating classes (1960, 1961, 1962) now hold almost all top military positions, though they have had to wait an average of ten years longer than the generation of 1945 to reach them. In terms of education, these men are much more professional than their seniors, but they have much less combat and political experience. Their prestige, too, is substantially less than that of their predecessors, since they were too young to participate in the events of 1965–66, let alone 1945–49. Moreover, their numbers are considerably fewer. These factors have led some observers to believe that after Suharto's death the officer corps will have to be more accommodating to increasingly impatient civilian groups, and perhaps will even be obliged tacitly to revoke the Dual Function Doctrine.

Other observers are more pessimistic, focusing their attention on changes in military life that emerged in the 1970s and 1980s. The first of these has been the rise in power of military intelligence vis à vis other branches of the army. Most top-ranking officers have spent a good part of their careers in intelligence work, directed not externally to foreign threats, but to real or imagined domestic threats to the New Order regime. The second is that under the Dual Function Doctrine many of these men have spent as much time in civilian as in military jobs, and have grown accustomed to the amenities that come with these jobs. Both factors have led to a significant decline in the army's strictly military competence.

This decline is best evidenced by the protracted warfare in the former Portuguese colony of East Timor. When the Salazarist dictatorship in Lisbon collapsed in April 1974, the population of the eastern half of Timor (north of Australia) began to assert claims to freedom and self-determination as did the peoples of Angola, Mozambique, and Guinea Bissau, Portugal's colonies in Africa. Claiming that an independent East Timor (especially one run by the popular, left-nationalist Fretilin organization) would become a base for Communist penetration of Indonesia (which includes West Timor), Suharto ordered the invasion of the territory in December 1975. A quick and easy victory was expected, not least because the invading force was heavily armed with American weapons. (Furthermore, President Ford and Secretary Kissinger, visiting Jakarta the day before the invasion, raised no objections, although such use of American munitions violated an Indonesian-American agreement dating back to 1958). But as of this writing in late 1989, the fighting continues in the hills of the territory. Meantime, an estimated third of the 1975 population has died in the fighting itself, or as a result of forced resettlement, crop defoliation, and famine. Most of the Indonesian field commanders are of the Cadet generation, and they have distinguished themselves not by their battle skills but by the physical brutality and political insensitivity of their performance. A similar pattern, if on a lesser scale, has been evidenced in the army's efforts to suppress the Free Papua Movement, a loosely-organized insurgency in West New Guinea, which since the late 1960s has fed on the deepening discontent of that vast, remote, and disadvantaged region.

III. ISSUES FOR DISCUSSION

1. Compare the political roles of the Indonesian military with the roles of other Third World militaries: a) those originally formed by Japanese militarists (e.g., South Korea and Burma); b) those participating in armed struggles for national independence (e.g., Algeria and the PRC).

2. Suharto is today the longest-ruling military head of state in the world. In what ways has the peculiarity of the Indonesian military's history contributed to the longevity of his regime?

3. Compare the relationship of the United States to the Indonesian military with similar ties in other parts of the Third World (e.g., U.S.-Chile, U.S.-Egypt).

4. Discuss the role of ethnicity and of Indonesia's ethnic diversity in influencing the military's political behavior.

NOTE

1. *Soldiers and Politics: Military Coups and Governments.* Englewood Cliffs, NJ: Prentice Hall, 1977. pp. 26–27.

IV. SELECTED READINGS

Anderson, Benedict. *Java in a Time of Revolution.* Ithaca: Cornell University Press, 1972 (student reading). Chapters 2, 7, 11, 16. Fullest account of the military's birth during the Japanese Occupation and early Revolution.

Sundhaussen, Ulf. *The Road to Power, Indonesian Military Politics 1945–1967.* Kuala Lumpur: Oxford University Press, 1982 (student reading). Detailed study focusing particularly on the periods of constitutional democracy and Guided Democracy. Generally sympathetic to the military.

Crouch, Harold. *The Army and Politics in Indonesia.* Ithaca: Cornell University Press, 1978 (student reading). Deals mainly with Suharto's rise to power in the late 1960s.

Jenkins, David. *Suharto and His Generals: Indonesian Military Politics 1975-1983.* Ithaca: Cornell Modern Indonesia Project, Monograph Series, 1984 (student reading). Experienced journalist's analyses of extensive interviews with both loyalist and disaffected generals. Vivid personality portraits.

Budiardjo, Carmel, and Liong, Liem Soei. *The War Against East Timor.* London: Zed Books, 1984 (student reading). Well-informed, critical account of the counterinsurgency war in East Timor, and the politics behind it.

Political Science: Japan

Bureaucracy in Japan

T. J. Pempel

I. INTRODUCTION: CENTRAL POINTS

Japan, the first Asian country to join the ranks of the industrialized democracies, is an excellent example of a non-Western, but thoroughly modern, national bureaucracy. As such, it provides a useful and informative case for study in comparison with the United States specifically or with other industrialized democracies in general.

• The Japanese case is a good example of bureaucracy as planner and agent of change.

• Because it has been closely linked to political leadership, the Japanese bureaucracy provides an important contrast to countries where bureaucrats and politicians tend to have separate and even antagonistic roles.

• Because Japan has consciously limited and systematically downscaled the size of its bureaucracy, the Japanese case invalidates the presumption that bureaucratic expansion is inevitable.

• In view of its history of having been reformulated several times, once, for example, in explicit imitation of the Prussian model, and once by American bureaucrats, the Japanese bureaucracy is an excellent case for examining the interaction of competing bureaucratic traditions.

II. MAJOR TOPICS

PREMODERN HISTORY

Heavily influenced by Chinese models in so many areas, Japan also adopted a Chinese style bureaucracy as early as the Nara period (710–794). Bureaucratic organizations subsequently emerged at various times throughout the country. It was not until the establishment of centralized feudalism under the Tokugawa shogun in the early 1600s, however, that the first seeds of a modern **national** bureaucracy were sown. Even then, the Tokugawa government exercised direct control over only about one-quarter of Japan, with the remainder largely under local control. In these local regions too, however, bureaucratic forms of governance flourished as, over time, samurai warriors became de facto civilian administrators. Nonetheless, in both shogunal and local bureaucracies, vassalage, birth, and chance were far more often the keys to administrative rank, official duties, and promotion than were proven technical competence or systematic regulations. Yet throughout the roughly 250 years of the Tokugawa regime (1600–1868), civilian administration increased in areas such as tax collection, justice, finance, construction, and religious supervision. Gradually, in both national and local governments, proven competence, not heredity, came to determine both assignments and promotions.

The military and commercial threats to national sovereignty posed by the Western powers in late nineteenth century were the principal catalysts toward the creation of the service as we know it today.

BUREAUCRACY UNDER THE MEIJI SYSTEM

A series of steps taken during the early years of the Meiji government provided the groundwork for a truly modern national bureaucracy. The model for much of Japan's government organization, and especially its national bureaucracy, was Bismarck's Prussia. By implication this made it a relatively close approximation of Max Weber's ideal bureaucracy. The national bureaucracy, under a small core of oligarchies, was designed to lead the nation's modernization and industrial development efforts. Bureaucratic activity had strong legalistic underpinnings, Tokyo Imperial University was created for the explicit purpose of training servants of the state. Civilian and military bureaucracies were separated and put on a par; both were given explicit mandates to serve the emperor and the nation, rather than a specific region or class. Careers in the civil service were secure. Written rules assigned separate responsibilities to different offices. Demonstrated competence in such areas as military science, finance, foreign language, engineering, and technology soon became keys to an individual's success. In all of these ways, the Japanese bureaucracy took on modern trappings quite quickly.

Training. From 1869 on, a rigorous examination system determined entry into most levels of the civil service. Exams were targeted to identify the generalist rather than the specialist, much as in Britain. Legal training was the primary factor in determining entrance to and mobility in the national service. Senior civil servants through the prewar (and well into the postwar) period came disproportionately from Tokyo University, especially from its Faculty of Law. In 1937, for example, 74 percent of the senior civil servants had graduated from Tokyo Imperial University, 47 percent from its Faculty of Law; an additional 9 percent came from Kyoto Imperial. (Moreover, 85 percent of the prefectural governors came from these two universities.)

Open testing for admission to the universities and for entry into the civil service meant that the bureaucracy was far more meritocratic, and less class-based, than most European bureaucracies at the time. This undoubtedly contributed heavily to the widespread public support and prestige which the civil service enjoyed. At the same time, arrogance and disdain for public input was not uncommon among those who had been so recruited.

Political Ties. Under the Meiji system, the bureaucracy was free from patronage control by political parties but was closely tied to the political system as a whole. Senior civil servants were appointed by, and directly responsible to, the emperor, just as were cabinet members. As "servants of the emperor," they were sharply proscribed from any involvement in electoral and party politics. Only the most senior ministers were expected to have any political ties and these were rarely to the parties. Nor were civil servants or ministers legally responsible to the cabinet, the prime minister or the parliament. The "National Rescript to Soldiers and Sailors" served as an imperially sanctioned ban on all partisan activities by members of the military. In addition, "right of supreme command" required additionally that the armed forces report directly to the emperor, leaving them even more explicitly outside of electoral or political responsibility. As a consequence, during this period Japan had two very separate bureaucracies, one civilian and one military, with neither particularly subject to control by elected officials.

The military was able during the late 1920s and early 1930s to manipulate its direct ties to the emperor so as to gain control over large areas of government policy formation. In this it was often joined by a number of "new bureaucrats" in the civilian agencies, individuals committed to high levels of national planning and resource mobilization directly under their own lines of authority.

Both civilian and military bureaucracies were integral components of the government of prewar Japan, exerting extensive controls over most facets of national policy. Bureaucratic agencies drafted most of the laws submitted to the National Diet, and they frequently relied on extra-legislative ordinances to exert direct bureaucratic control. Local governments were typically subject to close legal, financial, and personnel controls by the powerful Home Ministry. Many former bureaucrats were eventually appointed to the House of Peers, from which they gained no small measure of prestige. Others entered politics, most typically by appointment to cabinet positions or prefectural governorships, rather than by running for office. Thirty-six percent of the prewar cabinet ministers, for example, were former bureaucrats. Unlike their counterparts in the United States, Britain, or even France, Japan's civil and military bureaucracies were relatively free from major checks by electoral or parliamentary organs of government. Far more frequent than political penetration of the bureaucratic world was bureaucratic penetration of politics. For example, only eight of the forty-four cabinets formed between 1890 and the end of World War II were formed by the heads of political parties.

Despite the anti-democratic dimensions of this system, there is widespread agreement that much of the industrial and social transformation that Japan underwent in the late nineteenth and early twentieth centuries was due to strong bureaucratic leadership in many spheres of Japanese life. What the bureaucrats lacked in political responsibility they made up for in their clarity of vision and technical efficiency.

BUREAUCRACY UNDER THE U.S. OCCUPATION

Following Japan's defeat in World War II, the American forces that occupied the country introduced a series of sweeping political, economic, and social changes. Many affected the bureaucracy: the military bureaucracy was eliminated; the Home Ministry was reorganized; many functions of the national government were transferred to local authorities. The National Personnel Law altered various features of the civil service, and a retrenchment program cut back the size of the civil service. Most importantly, the powers of elected officials, political parties, and the National Diet were greatly enhanced, thereby reducing bureaucratic influence. Yet, the bureaucracy was not restructured as an integral component of politics; far more attention was given, particularly after the first wave of Occupation reforms, to increasing bureaucratic efficiency and to the internal rationalization of tasks. Thus, when looking at the total picture one cannot but conclude that the structure and character of the Japanese national bureaucracy itself was only minimally affected. Bureaucrats continued to be drawn from the same social and educational background as previously; administrative discretion remained broad; direct control by elected officials over administrators remained minimal; and the powers of bureaucratic agencies vis-à-vis the political organs of government remained considerable.

THE CONTEMPORARY BUREAUCRACY

Overview. Today Japan's bureaucracy is structurally similar to, though generally smaller than, those of many of its counterparts in Western Europe. It is highly meritocratic and staffed with some of the nation's most talented individuals (see *Recruitment*, below). It is deeply imbued both with a sense of mission, as well as a willingness to aggrandize its own authority in order to achieve that mission. It has close ties to the governing political party (and to many of the opposition parties as well) but its individual members are rarely involved directly in partisan or electoral politics while they hold office. Unlike the national bureaucracy in the United States, where many high-level positions change hands when a new administration takes office, in Japan it is far more often the politicians who change and the bureaucrats who remain. The national bureaucracy is also an exceptionally small organ of government that is continually reexamined.

Organization and Structure. The National Civil Service Law (October 21, 1947) and the National Government Organization Law (July 10, 1948) provide the main legal outlines of Japan's national bureaucratic service. In addition, there are an extensive local civil service and about 100 public corporations. Together these three bureaucratic entities employ over five million full-time public employees (komuin). Although this represents a nearly tenfold increase in the size of Japan's bureaucracy since the 1940s, this figure is significantly lower than that for most other major industrialized countries. While differences in administrative structure, institutional variation, and methods of calculation make precise comparisons difficult, government employees represent approximately 6–9 percent of the total populations of the United States, France, West Germany, and Britain; in Japan the figure is only 4.5 percent. In terms of proportion of the total employed population, Japan's government employees represent about 9 percent of the total compared to between 14 and 20 percent for the other four countries. Nevertheless, Japan is often thought of as a bureaucratized country.

Approximately 1.2 million individuals work as full-time personnel for the national government. Of these some 300,000 are employed by the Defense Agency; over 350,000 more work in one of the five government services (posts, national forestry, government printing, the mint, and the alcohol monopoly); slightly more than 125,000 work for the Ministry of Education. This leaves approximately 420,000 who make up the general administrative staff of the national government.

There are twelve main ministries (*sho*) which, along with the Office of the Prime Minister (*Sorifu*), form the principal administrative organs of the national government. In addition, there are a number of agencies and commissions, such as the National Archives, the Science Council of Japan, the Department of the Imperial Household, the Tax Administration Agency, the Immigration Service Agency, and the like, which are collectively referred to as "external organs" (*gaikyoku*). Technically outside the direct lines of ministerial organization and charged with overseeing special areas of administration substantially different from, or overlapping, those of the main ministries, these external organs hold slightly less prestige. For most practical purposes, however, they may be considered similar to the ministries.

The twelve main ministries and most important agencies are headed by a minister with one, or occasionally two, vice ministers. These officials are almost invariably elected Diet members and the only politically appointed officials in a ministry or agency; below them are members of the career civil service.

The most senior civil servant in each ministry and agency is the administrative vice-minister, who oversees all administrative matters within that ministry. From him extend a number of relatively clear lines of hierarchy. Each ministry is typically divided into from six to twelve functionally arranged bureaus (*kyoku*), and these in turn are either sub-divided into departments (*bu*) or divided directly into sections (*ka*). It is these sections, employing anywhere from twenty to thirty people, which form the working units of each ministry.

Most ministries and agencies also include a number of auxiliary organs such as research institutes, museums, and libraries, as well as up to several dozen advisory committees (*shingikai*), which provide policy input from outside interest associations, professionals, journalists, and policy experts. Each national ministry and agency also maintains local offices to gather information and provide other services associated with the agency's mission. These offices are staffed by members of the national civil service and are separate from the offices of local government.

Civil Service System. Responsibility for overseeing the national civil services in regard to recruitment, promotion, compensation and adjudication of disputes lies with the National Personnel Authority, a semi-autonomous body somewhat analogous to the U.S. Civil Service Commission. The Management and Coordination Agency (formerly the Administrative Management Agency), under the Office of the Prime Minister, is charged with overseeing the organizational needs and efficiency of individual agencies.

On paper, civil service positions are well-classified. There are eight main classes: administrative, taxation, security, marine, education, research, medical, and a final catch-all. Most of these classes are further subdivided.

Recruitment. As with the prewar service, there is little horizontal entry into the top or middle ranks of the civil service. Rather, most personnel are recruited in their early twenties, after completing their university education, and promotion involves a long and fairly predictable series of steps up the career ladder, leading eventually to retirement in their mid-fifties. Entrance and promotion are based on examinations. Most recruits are male, although in the last three or four years an increasing number of females have been recruited and are being promoted along with their male counterparts.

The most important exam is the Principal Senior A-Class Entrance Examination (*Kokka komuin shiken jokyu ko*). This is a rigid exam for the top tier of the civil service. Those who pass the exam can expect an appointment at grade six and to advance rapidly to a top position, usually to one of the top three grades, before retirement. Those who fail must seek employment elsewhere.

Although there has been some reduction in the dominance of Tokyo University in the civil service, roughly 35 percent of the successful applicants continue to be Tokyo graduates; an additional 15 percent or so come from Kyoto University. Usually only fifteen or so of Japan's 460-odd universities see ten or more of their graduates succeed in the exams.

Career Patterns. Most members of the national bureaucracy remain with a single government agency throughout their careers, although many will be seconded temporarily, one or more times, to other agencies. Advancement tends to be principally a function of seniority, and groups of individuals hired together tend to be promoted together, with some adjustments made according to ability. Individuals rarely remain in a single position for more than two or three years, and transfers are designed, among other things, to ensure that all senior officials will have a broad familiarity with most of an agency's or ministry's functions.

During the course of a civil servant career, there are many opportunities to acquire additional skills. Courses in such areas as foreign language, computers, and economics, are often offered by an agency. The National Personnel Agency maintains a program for those having special potential to be sent abroad for two years of advanced education, including language training.

In principle, all promotions in the civil service are governed by civil service regulations and are not subject to interference by political parties or other partisan considerations. In point of fact, appointments at the level of bureau chief and above are subject to additional scrutiny by the cabinet and the ruling party. As a result, promotion to top positions in the bureaucracy is by no means immune from political influence.

Most successful civil servants can expect to head a section after approximately fifteen years of service, to be an assistant bureau chief after twenty-two to twenty-five years and bureau chief three years thereafter. The top post of administrative vice-minister, available only to a limited few, is achieved after twenty-eight to thirty years. It is usually held for two or three years, after which the vice-minister and most of those who entered the agency with him are expected to resign their posts. Their age at this point is usually in the low- to mid-fifties.

Competition and Coordination. Individual agencies and ministries within the national bureaucracy enjoy a considerable degree of autonomy, which often results in intense interagency to agency competition (as well as intra-agency competition among different sections or bureaus). Certain ministerial competitions have reached epic proportions such as that between the Ministry of Finance and that of International Trade and Industry; between the Ministry of Posts and Telecommunications and that of Education; or, more generally, between the "economic" ministries and the "service" ministries. Coordination among such autonomous power bases is never easy, and in Japan as elsewhere, tunnel vision and compartmentalization are a part of bureaucratic life. At the same time, a variety of structures exist to mitigate this tendency, ranging from alumni clubs and informal study groups on particular issues to more formally structured bodies such as the weekly conference of administrative vice-ministers, or issue-specific interministry teams. That most of the senior officials have been trained as generalists, rather than technical specialists, also undoubtedly helps in brokering complicated issues of jurisdiction and agency power.

Post-bureaucratic Careers. Bureaucratic rejuvenation is spurred by relatively early retirement. On the other hand, most retiring officials have an economic and psychological need to remain active in the work force, and society is eager to take advantage of their expertise. Thus a common phenomenon is the "descent from heaven" (*amakudari*) whereby retired bureaucrats gain employment with a public corporation, a think tank, an affiliated agency, or a private corporation previously overseen by the agent and his agency. The implicit assumption frequently made is that the rehired official will serve as a useful bridge between his new and his former employer.

Bureaucrats as Elected Officials. Japan's civil servants do not participate overtly in the political world while in office. Unlike French bureaucrats, they do not serve as formal advisors to the cabinet. Nor is there a *grands corps* concept allowing Japanese civil servants to move freely between administrative and political posts, or to run for office while retaining bureaucratic status.

Unlike their West German counterparts, Japan's bureaucrats cannot sit in the Diet. In contrast to the system in the United States, they do not serve with politicians on "presidential teams." The lines separating politics and bureaucracy in Japan remain relatively clean; when a bureaucrat does enter the world of electoral politics it is usually after retirement.

Only a small number of bureaucrats who retire each year enter electoral politics. Conversely, former bureaucrats have traditionally constituted a substantial proportion of the Diet members from the Liberal Democratic party (LDP), and an even greater proportion of their party's leaders. As early as the 1953 elections, some 25 percent of the elected officials were former bureaucrats. These included a core of supporters of Prime Minister Yoshida Shigeru, who plucked a number of talented younger bureaucrats from the civil service to stand for elective office under the Liberal party. This 25 percent figure has remained relatively constant over the postwar period, although it has declined somewhat of late. Moreover, about half of the prefectural governors during the mid-1970s had previously been in national or local government service. What is perhaps most remarkable, in the twenty-five years following the formation of the LDP in 1955, the office of prime minister was held by former bureaucrats for twenty years and by men who could be described as professional politicians for only five years.

Evidence in the last decade suggests that the influence of former bureaucrats within the LDP is on the wane. Essentially, politics has become a lifetime career path, with entry at the top or middle levels becoming increasingly difficult. Most politicians today have not served for many years in the bureaucracy; rather, they have come up through local parliamentary election. Most bureaucrats who enter politics now do so by resigning in their early to mid-thirties, after perhaps only ten years with an agency, rather than waiting until after retirement. Moreover, unlike the earlier corps of bureaucrats-turned-politicians who had served principally in economic or diplomatic ministries, such as Finance or Foreign Affairs, most of the officials now leaving the bureaucracy for the political world come from ministries such as Construction, Home Affairs, or Agriculture, Forestry, and Fisheries, agencies with direct pork barrel and partisan connections that make the transition to electoral politics quite logical.

The Bureaucracy and Policy Formation. Certainly, there is no modern bureaucracy today that is divorced from politics. While bureaucrats and the agencies they represent cannot enter the world of electoral politics, this is not to say that they do not influence political decisions. They do so most importantly in the area of policy formation. One survey of members of the national bureaucracy showed a full 80 percent believed that it was they, and not the elected politicians, who were addressing Japan's general policy problems. This figure compared to only 21 percent of the British and 16 percent of the West German officials surveyed. Japan's senior bureaucrats see themselves as pro-active, rather than re-active on policy questions. This perception is matched by actual performances.

Bureaucratic expertise is a key component of their influence. Agencies have a great deal of influence in the conceptualization of issues. They are most often charged by parliament with investigating politically sensitive problems. Reports submitted to the agencies by their various attached advisory commissions often form the core of new legal proposals. Ultimately, about ninety percent of all legislation passed in the parliament is first drafted by bureaucratic agencies. Top-level bureaucrats are typically the equivalent of floor managers for such bills once they are introduced in the Diet. Moreover, most bills are broad in nature and include provisos deferring the specifics of implementation to subsequent bureaucratic ordinances. In fact, much of the actual legislation in Japan consists not simply of laws enacted by the Diet, but of precisely such extra-parliamentary ordinances issued by agencies solely on their own authority. Agencies also utilize the so-called power of administrative guidance vis-à-vis the organizations under their purview. This involves little more than the sometimes subtle, oftentimes blunt, cajoling of such organizations to adjust their behavior to accord with agency priorities. Post-retirement careers also serve as a tool of bureaucratic influence in many spheres. Most national bureaucratic agencies thus have a wide range of tools with which to shape and influence public and private policy-related activities within the country.

Much of a bureaucratic agency's influence is a function of the rapid turnover of cabinet ministers and vice-ministers. With some important exceptions, few ministers hold their positions for more than a year, making it difficult for most of them to maintain close day-to-day supervision over staffs whose members have fifteen to thirty years of accumulated expertise.

At the same time, such power is subject to checks by political parties, interest groups, the media, single-issue movements, the

Diet, and a host of other political actors which provide important counterweights. Moreover, since senior-level promotions within a bureaucracy are closely scrutinized by the LDP, it follows that the thinking of senior officials is generally attuned to the broad goals of the country's elected officials.

Bureaucrats vs. Politicians. One of the ongoing disputes among scholars of Japanese politics concerns the relative degree of influence over policy making exerted by bureaucrats versus elected officials. Without recapping this debate, suffice is to say that there is general agreement on the trend showing that members of the Liberal Democratic party are taking an increased interest in, and exerting greater influence over, an ever larger range of policy issues. At the same time, in view of the close links— personal, organizational, and ideological— between these politicians and national bureaucrats, these battles for influence are far closer to intrafamily quarrels than they are to full-fledged turf battles. The two groups may demonstrate different skills and immediate concerns but their ultimate values and objectives are usually quite similar.

Public Unionization. Close cooperation between senior bureaucrats and leaders of the LDP is not always matched at the lower levels of either the national or local civil service. Employees of agencies at both bureaucracies have been highly unionized since the postwar years. Explicit strikes by most officials are banned in most agencies, although strikes for the "right to strike" have actually occurred. Collective bargaining is allowed in some spheres, such as the postal service, the railways, and the telegraph and telephone services.

Administrative Reform. As noted above, Japan's bureaucracy remains comparatively small. This is largely a result of a series of administrative reform measures undertaken over the past forty years, to reduce systematically the size and complexity of government agencies and governmental paperwork. An important series of measures undertaken in the late 1960s and early 1970s involved reductions in the authorized size of most agencies, often by 5 percent, implemented over several years. The cumulative effect was a de facto freeze in the size of the national bureaucracy, and a cut in the number of government agencies and public corporations.

The most recent series of administrative reform, referred to by its Japanese acronym, *rincho*, was begun in the early 1980s. In addition to further simplifying administrative paperwork and reducing agency size and complexity, it resulted in the privatization of many of Japan's public corporations, including the telephone system and the national railways. Among the two more widely recognized consequences of this reform were, first, the not incidental diminished political strength of Japan's public sector unions; and second, a strong reaffirmation of the long-standing commitment to minimalist government and to a lean, if highly efficient, national bureaucracy.

III. ISSUES FOR DISCUSSION

1. Compare the role of the bureaucracy in Japan to that of the United States or any other country with which you are familiar.
2. Examine the strength and weaknesses of the prewar Japanese bureaucracy in terms of the tradeoff between economic development and political democratization.
3. What factors would suggest that Japan's bureaucracy is "political" and what would suggest it is not?
4. If you were a member of the LDP charged with scrutinizing promotions in the civil service, what traits would you most look for? What would be the probable consequences if your standards were adhered to?

IV. SELECTED READINGS

Inoki, Masamichi. "The Civil Bureaucracy: Japan." In *Political Modernization in Japan and Turkey*, edited by Robert Ward and Dankwart Rustow, pp. 283-300. Princeton: Princeton University Press, 1964 (student reading). A fine overview of the prewar Japanese bureaucracy in a developmental context.

Johnson, Chalmers. "Japan: Who Governs?: An Essay on Official Bureaucracy." *Journal of Japanese Studies* 2 (1975): 1-28 (faculty background). An examination of the influence wielded by bureaucrats in policy making and other areas relative to that of other political actors.

Johnson, Chalmers. *MITI and the Japanese Miracle*. Stanford: Stanford University Press, 1982 (faculty background). An exceptionally detailed study of a single agency and its role in national economic development.

Kumon, Shimpei. "Japan Faces Its Future." *Journal of Japanese Studies* 10 (1984): 143-166 (student reading). An examination of the administrative reform efforts of the early 1980s.

Pempel, T.J. "Organizing for Efficiency: The Higher Civil Service in Japan." In *Parliaments and Parliamentarians in Democratic Politics*, edited by Ezra Suleiman, pp. 72-106. London: Holmes and Meier, 1984 (student reading).

**Political Science:
Japan**

Japanese
Democracy
and Political
Culture: A
Comparative
Perspective

T. J. Pempel

I. INTRODUCTION: CENTRAL POINTS

Japan is an excellent case for the comparative study of the connections between democracy and culture.

• It is a country with a well-established system of constitutional democracy having roots in the nineteenth century; it has
been constitutionally and electorally democratic since the end of
World War II.

• Democracy in Japan also has strong social and cultural underpinnings. Despite a hierarchical Confucian tradition, the country is largely egalitarian in its educational, economic, and
informational systems.

• Because Japanese democracy, like that of any country, is far from perfect, it is a good case study for examining ideal conceptions of democracy in contrast to practical democratic realities.

• Japan resembles other advanced industrial countries in terms of its political and social institutions and customs, but as a non-Western culture it presents an ideal case for a comparative study of democracy as a system capable of transcending cultural differences and incorporating practices particular to a given culture.

Democracy is a term that has very positive connotations. Most countries in the world, representing widely differing political, social, and economic systems, describe themselves as democratic; the multiplicity of forms, people's democracy, revolutionary democracy, capitalist democracy, democratic republic, liberal democracy, representative democracy, and federal democracy, demonstrates the popularity of the concept and the disparate political systems to which the name is applied.

Bypassing a broad theoretical debate on the relative merits of these many different versions of democracy, three points should be made. First, as commonly used by Western social scientists, the term democracy usually implies the right of citizens to determine their form of government and to choose those who will constitute that government; the requirement that government be responsive to a greater or less extent to the preferences of citizens; and the requirement that citizen preferences be weighted relatively equally.

By these standards, contemporary Japan stands comfortably with the so-called advanced industrialized democracies of Western Europe, North America and Australasia. This was not the case prior to the end of World War II, but since 1945 Japan's political system has taken on most of the features usually associated with the Western democracies, among which Japan is usually considered.

At the same time, in Japan as in these other countries, democracy is far from absolute and there is room for increased democratization.

II. MAJOR TOPICS

HISTORICAL LEGACIES

The Tokugawa Period, which lasted from 1600 until the Meiji Restoration of 1868, provided several important contributions to Japan's subsequent development. First of all, decentralized feudalism prevailed. Under this system, the country was divided into some 250 fiefs, each headed by a hereditary lord (daimyo) administered by his loyal samurai vassals. But from the capital city of Edo (now Tokyo) a single military authority, the *shogun*, exercised strict overall national control. Meanwhile, in the capital city of Kyoto, overall symbolic unity was represented by an emperor and a hereditary imperial family which traced its lineage to a mythological descent from the Sun Goddess. Thus, from early history, Japan enjoyed at least the trappings of national unity and the experience of centralized government making its subsequent transition to a modern nation-state substantially easier than in countries lacking such traditions. For many, the experience of rule by a military caste also left a legacy that legitimated military predominance during the early years of Japan's industrialization and that is drawn upon even today by the numerically small but influential right wing.

In addition, the prevalence of wet rice agriculture and the overall crowdedness of the country necessitated extensive collaboration among members of the same family and families within the same villages, making the group, rather than the individual, the primary social unit. Even today, Japanese shun excessive individualism as detestable "egoism" and gravitate toward collective behavior. The give-and-take of such group activity, however, also provided fertile soil for the subsequent respect given to the rights of others and for overall democratization at the popular level.

The Tokugawa period was also one in which Japan's leaders deliberately isolated the country from Western influences, heightening both the governmental and popular sense of national uniqueness and separateness. Ethnic homogeneity, geographical demarcation of the island country, the distinctive Japanese language, and the commonly accepted nativist religious practices, called Shinto, all added to this perception. Shinto, under the formal leadership of the emperor as high priest, was subsequently institutionalized as an official state religion following the Meiji Restoration and again provided a dimension of national and cultural unification as well as separation from others. Although Japanese today enjoy freedom of religion and the position of the emperor has been legally circumscribed, Shinto practices, both popular and emperor-led, remain widespread.

Tokugawa Japan provided many strengths on which the modern Japanese nation-state could draw as modernization and industrialization began. But it should be clear that democracy was neither a goal nor an outcome of the Tokugawa system. The same can be said of the Meiji system which followed. Under the Meiji Constitution, in effect from 1889 until 1947, democracy was neither the principal goal nor an underlying axiom of the Japanese political system. Rather, the constitution was designed to facilitate national cohesion and consolidate centralized authority. Rapid changes in society were deemed necessary by Japan's modernizing elite to enable the country to industrialize and modernize quickly and thus protect its sovereignty from Western imperialism. Because a strong central authority was seen as indispensable to this effort, the constitution's drafters designed political institutions that would ensure a strong central government capable of acting purposefully and with minimal opposition; democratic checks against the powers of the nation's rulers were not a concern.

The constitution, modelled on that of Bismarck's Prussia, was the emperor's "gift" to his people; it was neither a popularly derived nor a representatively ratified document. Under it, the emperor's authority, as articulated through his advisors, was supreme. The two-house parliament included one, the House of Peers, that was purely appointive and based largely on heredity and service to the state; powers of the elected House of Representatives were severely circumscribed. Most importantly, elected officials had no guaranteed right to determine the composition of the executive branch of government. Instead, the cabinet and prime minister were chosen by the emperor and his advisors.

Although the electoral backing of the lower house ultimately became an important factor in the formation of governments during the 1920s, it was always but one of many relevant factors. This point was particularly salient during the 1930s when the army, constitutionally exempt from civilian and cabinet control, became the major force in cabinet selection.

The vote was limited to males of high economic status until universal male suffrage was introduced in 1925; women did not win the right to vote until 1947. Local government leaders, including prefectural governors, were appointed, not elected. State Shinto circumscribed religious freedoms. A tight web of laws restricted the rights of citizens to organize labor unions, political parties, and interest groups; the media were subject to strict censorship; the police, the military, and right-wing terrorist groups subverted the civil liberties of citizens in numerous ways. Citizens' duties to the state far outweighed the constitutional and legal guarantees of citizens' rights.

Comparative Perspective. Despite all of the valid criticisms that could be levelled at the authoritarian character of prewar Japan, two points are important from a comparative perspective. First, the prewar Japanese political system contained the potential to become more democratic, and indeed it did so with time. Popular votes, political parties, the parliament, and citizen rights had by the 1920s gained vastly greater authority than they had enjoyed in the late nineteenth century. Counter governmental organizations such as labor unions had also gained greater autonomy and influence. Anti-governmental, including Marxist, parties were able to organize and achieve a measure of popular support during the 1920s and 1930s in spite of government and police efforts to suppress them. Some newspapers, and many intellectuals, struggled to achieve a commendable degree of autonomy, even during the war.

Second, during the late nineteenth and early twentieth centuries, the Japanese political system was by no means unique in its circumscription of democratic rights and privileges. Other countries may have been more democratic in many ways, but in the United States, for example, slavery was legal until 1862, and in many regions of the country blacks faced severe and explicit legal barriers to citizen equality at least until the passage of the Civil Rights Act of 1965. In Great Britain, Catholics, Jews, and agnostics could not even become members of the parliament until well into the nineteenth century, and the House of Lords, with its undemocratic privileges for the British nobility, was a powerful impediment to democratic government until the reforms of 1911. Universal male suffrage was severely restricted in Britain until 1884 and in much of the rest of Europe until after World War I; women did not get the right to vote in the United States until 1920, in Britain until 1929, in France until 1945, and in Switzerland until the 1970s. Union organizers had to confront hostile police, courts, and private security forces in the United States and most of Europe until the 1920s and later in many instances.

Such comparisons are not meant to belittle the very real institutional barriers to democracy that existed in the prewar Japanese political system. Nor do they imply that democracy was meaningless in these other countries until well into the twentieth century. Rather, they make the point that while Japanese institutions were far less than fully democratic, they did allow for increased democratization of the political system over time. Moreover, to the extent that democratization is an evolutionary process, Japan can be said to have trailed many other countries but by not more than a few decades.

It may be concluded then, that the postwar democratic system in Japan has roots in the late nineteenth and early twentieth centuries, and the introduction in 1947 of more democratic processes and institutions did not involve a total break with the past.

CONTEMPORARY JAPANESE DEMOCRACY

Political Restructuring under the U.S. Occupation. During the six and one-half years of the Occupation following Japan's surrender in 1945, numerous changes were introduced in an effort to create the political, social, and economic conditions the American forces believed would transform Japan into a peace loving democracy.

The most important change was the deliberate restructuring of the political system to ensure democracy. A totally new constitution written by the Americans replaced the Meiji constitution. Under it, popular sovereignty replaced imperial fiat. A wide array of personal and political rights were guaranteed to all citizens. The National Diet, or parliament, became "the highest organ of state power," and membership in both houses was determined solely through popular elections. Cabinets were to be formed by the Diet, and the prime minister and at least half of the cabinet had to be elected parliamentarians. Local governments, down to the town and village levels, were also made elective. The civil and criminal codes were drastically overhauled to make laws compatible with the democratic principles of the constitution. In the same spirit, numerous social and economic changes were also introduced.

Rights of Citizens. Japan's postwar constitution provides one of the most extensive catalogs of rights guaranteed to citizens anywhere. These in turn form the basis of the freedoms commonly associated with of democracy. Among the most prominent are the right to equality under law and the freedom from discrimination based on race, creed, sex, social status, or family status (Art. 14); freedom of conscience (Art. 19); religious freedom (Art. 20); freedom of residence and occupation (Art. 22); academic freedom (Art. 23); the right to a minimum standard of wholesome and cultured living (Art. 25); the equal right to education (Art. 26); the right of workers to organize and bargain collectively (Art. 28); and freedom from search and seizure without specific warrants (Art. 35).

Beyond these general rights are a number of specifically political guarantees. Among the most noteworthy are the right to choose public officials through universal suffrage and the secret ballot (Art. 15); the right to petition for political change (Art. 16); the freedom of speech, the press, and expression (Art. 21); the right of access to the courts (Art. 32); the right to hear charges upon arrest and to have legal counsel (Art. 34); the right to a speedy trial; and the right to refuse to testify against oneself (Art. 38).

These are meaningful guarantees, not simply paper promises. At the same time, even a superficial familiarity with Japanese society and life will reveal many instances in which reality falls short of the constitutional ideal. Those instances having political implications may be categorized as follows: economic and social discrimination; education; and the intrusion of the state.

Economic and Social Discrimination. Economic and social discrimination is probably neither less nor more significant in Japan than in the other industrialized democracies. There are areas where it is somewhat different, and many where it is interesting for comparative purposes. Class counts in Japan, as in all capitalist countries, but in Japan family background is surely far less significant than in Britain, for example, or France. Moreover, statistical comparisons of economic equality invariably show Japan to be more economically egalitarian than most other industrialized countries, including the United States, France, England, and Germany. A widely cited statistic notes that 90 percent of its citizens identify themselves as "middle class." Unemployment tends to be much lower in Japan than in most other democracies. Broad access to health care, low and declining crime rates, long life expectancy, and a wide distribution of consumer durables all suggest that the differences between the "haves" and the "have nots," while by no means absent, are far less pervasive in Japan than in many other industrialized democracies.

Yet in areas such as jobs, housing, education, marriage opportunities, and general social interaction, there is widespread and accepted discrimination against several minority groups, including members of Japan's traditional untouchable caste, the *burakumin*, descendants of Korean or Chinese immigrants, many (particularly non-white) foreigners, the remnants of the Ainu tribes in the northern island of Hokkaido, and the physically handicapped. While most such discrimination is not legal, it is nonetheless pervasive and seldom subject to redress before the court.

Discrimination against women is endemic, particularly in jobs and education. Despite a constitutional provision guaranteeing sexual equality and the Employment Opportunity Law, passed in

May 1985, Japanese women still earn less than one-half the salaries of their male counterparts; many attend only junior colleges while their male peers attend four year universities and the availability of child care is inadequate. Various other forms of gender discrimination are common as well.

Education. For the formal rights of citizenship to be meaningful, a nation's citizens must have the educational and informational bases on which to make informed political decisions. Japan has one of the most extensive educational systems in the industrialized world, with 40 percent of those between 18 and 22 attending institutions of higher education, compared to about 48 percent in the United States, 26 percent in both France and Germany and about 21 percent in Britain. Moreover, the quality of Japanese education is high: there are few dropouts; its students invariably outperform their foreign counterparts in international test competitions and literacy is virtually 100 percent.

At the same time, many valid criticisms could be levelled at the Japanese school system. First, conformity is emphasized over individuality. This is manifested in rigid dress codes and behavioral standards, an emphasis on rote memorization of facts, and the importance placed on standardized tests. Second, ever since the 1950s, the government has frequently attempted to reintroduce moral education into the curriculum, in an effort to instill greater patriotism and respect for Japanese (predemocratic) traditions. Third, the government has been similarly engaged in what many have seen as the rewriting of Japanese history, censoring in particular the negative interpretations of Japan's foreign policy and actions during the prewar period. For many, both within Japan and throughout Asia, these latter two efforts revive the specter of prewar nationalist indoctrination, or even a return to right-wing extremism. While there are a number of right-wing groups politically active in Japan, most have limited memberships and even less governmental or mass influence.

These problems are at the heart of any comparative study of the relationship between education and democracy, and raise the question of when "education" ends and "indoctrination" begins. One would be hard pressed to find democracy that did not attempt to instill in its younger citizens a sense of patriotism and loyalty, and to teach a less than candid version of the national history. While these are important concerns, Japan is today by all measures a vastly different country from its prewar days.

State Intrusion and the Non-Political Sphere. An important, but often overlooked component of democracy is the citizen's freedom from the state. And, indeed, the Japanese citizen enjoys the right to lead a private life free from the harassment of mobilization campaigns, the requirement to participate in state-run religious services, police surveillance, forced service to state projects, and the like. Most Japanese are free to lead their daily lives without political or state interference, and to have families, pursue hobbies, engage in sports, buy from a variety of available food and clothing, work and socialize without government oversight. At the same time, the government does collect taxes; all citizens must be registered; several radio and television stations are under government auspices; virtually all government and semi-governmental agencies engage in public relations activities designed to convince the citizen of the meritorious nature of their work; strict laws govern various aspects of social behavior, from drunken driving to safety standards for drugs and toys, to inheritance rights. Customs clearance regulations, intrusive officials, and seemingly omnipresent police officers make it clear that the Japanese state is a factor in citizens' daily lives. In short, there is a relatively clear demarcation between "public" and "private" that allows the citizen a wide sphere of nonpolitical activity. While the committed democrat could argue for changes at the margins of many of the intrusions by the Japanese state, most of these do not appear to be vastly different from those in other countries. On balance, the privacy of the citizen in Japan accords well with the maintenance of a democratic political culture.

BETWEEN CITIZEN AND STATE

If the first requisite of democracy involves the rights of the citizen, the second is surely the need for mechanisms that permit the articulation of citizen preferences and their translation into the formation of government. Three such mechanisms are: the media, interest groups, the voting system, and political parties.

The Media. Politically independent, competitive, and widely accessible mass media are critical in providing information to enable citizens to form reasoned opinions of political matters. Contemporary Japan has one of the world's highest rates of newspaper readership, with three national dailies blanketing the country with morning and evening editions, plus countless numbers of local and specialized papers. Books and magazines appealing to a wide range of interests also sell widely. Total publications greatly outnumber those in most European countries on an absolute basis; on a per capita basis, Japan is roughly on a par with most of these countries. Virtually every household has radio and television receivers. Foreign literary works, journals, and other forms of information and criticism are also widely available. In short, the Japanese citizen suffers from, if anything, information overload.

Many have observed a disturbingly conformist quality to Japan's major newspapers; others have noted that a great deal of deference is shown to those in power. Yet editorials are generally critical of government or official actions; numerous diverse sources of information find their way into the press; scathing criticism is common outside the mainstream press; and the papers have doggedly pursued government corruption, such as came to light in the Lockheed and the Recruit scandals.

Interest Groups. A second important link between citizens and government in a democracy are interest groups. In Japan, virtually any social interest one might imagine seems to be organized, suggesting that it is a vigorously democratic society. Some groups, of course, are vastly more influential than others. But typically most pursue their political or nonpolitical ends by organizing widely, lobbying lustily, endorsing or withholding endorsement of political candidates. Petition drives, fund raising, informational meetings, boycotts, leafletting, marches, sitdowns and direct confrontations with officials are among the wide range of strategies these interest groups adopt. Although frequently criticized for the alleged as self-serving, these groups are testimony to the relative freedom of association in Japan and to the vigor with which that freedom is exercised.

Elections and Political Parties. All Japanese citizens aged twenty and over are eligible to vote. There is no literacy requirement or poll tax; registration is relatively easy; voter turnout, even in local elections, is typically high between 65 and 75 percent, which is high by international standards.

In addition, citizens have a relatively wide range of choices among candidates, except in elections at the municipal level where candidates are often uncontested. Throughout the postwar period, there have been at least three and at times seven major political parties contesting for national office. These range from the relatively conservative Liberal Democratic Party (LDP), which is pro-business, pro-agriculture and pro-United States, to moderate and more radical socialist parties, such as the Japan Socialist Party (JSP) and the Democratic Socialist Party (DSP), to the Japan

Communist Party (JCP), which is legal, and to the Clean Government Party (CGP) which is affiliated with a large Buddhist religious group. Some, however, run as independent or as unaffiliated candidates. Moreover, by virtue of its multi-member distinct system, the voter can often choose among a number of candidates from the same party. Declaring one's candidacy is a relatively simple matter entailing few legal barriers, actually getting elected is another matter.

Two points deserve elaboration. First, Japanese voters have available to them a wide range of choices among candidates, parties, and political philosophies. In addition to candidates who represent strongly nationalistic and right of center positions, Japan has a strong Marxian tradition as well. In this sense, the party spectrum in Japan is analogous to that in much of continental Europe. Certainly, Japan's election and party systems provide a greater range of choice than is available in single-member district systems and/or two- or three-party systems such as those in Britain, Australia, Canada, Germany or the United States.

All election systems have their peculiar biases, however, and the Japanese case generally favors both the larger and the smaller parties to the disadvantage of the middle-size parties, which tend to gain fewer seats in proportion to their total votes; the discrepancy is relatively small, however. In addition, election fraud occurs in Japan, but not more often than in most other industrialized democracies.

Second, the Japanese case is noteworthy for the extensive gerrymandering of its districts, which results in an overrepresentation of rural areas at the expense of urban areas. In addition, the peculiarities of the Japanese election system make it very difficult to vote **against** a party, since although several parliamentarians are returned from each district, a voter can vote for only one candidate. Thus, in contrast to Britain or the United States where a successful candidate typically receives about 50 percent of the total vote cast or more, in Japan most winners need only 15–20 percent of the vote. Thus, small groups of well-organized supporters for any candidate can insure his/her election, often with only 15 percent of the total vote in a constituency. This phenomenon also makes it difficult to determine whether national issues have any direct effect on local voting. Thus, while several distinctly anti-democratic biases can be detected in Japan's party and election systems, suggesting important areas of criticism, they by no means invalidate the broader claims to a democratic system of translating citizen preferences into the formation of governments.

INSTITUTIONS OF GOVERNANCE

In the broadest sense, Japanese government institutions are parallel to those of many other parliamentary democracies. The cabinet is chosen by the National Diet, which is constituted through regular and free elections. So long as a cabinet enjoys the confidence of a majority of the Diet members, it can remain in power. On the other hand, unlike presidential systems in which the chief executive is chosen for a prescribed term through a popular election, in parliamentary systems, the cabinet can be forced to resign immediately through a vote of no-confidence. Japanese prefectural and city governments lack the specific powers often found in federal political systems such as those of West Germany, Canada, Australia or, the United States, but they have most or more of the powers found in centralized systems such as Sweden, France, or England.

In these respects, Japanese political institutions are not dramatically different from those in most other political democracies. At the same time, a discussion of formal institutions leaves unanswered at least two further questions. First, just how much actual power do elected officials have? If those subject to popular control are not in fact the political system's real decision makers, then surely democracy is circumvented. And second, once in power, just how responsive are policy makers to public control?

Power of Elected Officials. Despite its constitutional guarantee as the "highest organ of state power," the Japanese Diet is not widely accepted as such by many academics and critics. Certainly, it is not the actual lawmaking body that the United States Congress is, although Congress is much more the exception than rule among democracies. Still, the Diet is principally a ratifier of decisions made elsewhere. At least three major candidates for the "elsewhere" can be cited: big business, the bureaucracy, and the Liberal Democratic Party.

Big Business. Those who argue that big business wields the real power in Japan point to a variety of factors, most of them linked in some way to Marxian economic analysis. Certainly in the standard juxtaposition of business and organized labor, the latter holds very little real power in Japan, and is much weaker politically and economically than labor in virtually any other industrialized democracy. Japan is home to some of the largest corporations and banks in the world, with higher levels of concentration than in most other major countries. And there is no question but that public policy has been good to big business over the past three decades, while Japanese consumers and owners of small shops have often borne the costs of Japan's macroeconomic successes.

At the same time, the government has taken action in such areas as involving environmental cleanup, tax revision, liberalization of imports, change in the retirement age, financial and stock market liberalization, and so forth, despite strong opposition from big business. But more importantly, perhaps, the influence of big business in Japan has rarely been shown to be significantly greater than in other industrialized democracies. Much of the criticism leveled against the allegedly undemocratic powers of Japanese big business is in fact a broad scale criticism, applicable to varying degrees to virtually all capitalist countries.

Bureaucracy. The relative power of the elected Japanese Diet and the non-elected bureaucracy has been debated for several decades; similar questions of power are likewise debated in other democracies. There is very little question but that most laws are drawn up by senior civil servants, not legislators. Most of the preliminary investigations and fact-finding are also done by the national bureaucracy, and great discretion is left to bureaucrats to implement laws which are typically crafted very broadly. Many former bureaucrats retire to take up political careers often in the LDP, and one in four LDP members has a bureaucratic background. Elected officials hold only the top two posts in a government agency and usually for only brief terms, leaving the bulk of the day-to-day activities in the hands of the more permanent civil service. While most of these or similar criticisms may be made of bureaucracies in other industrialized democracies, comparative evidence strongly indicates that the Japanese bureaucracy is particularly influential.

At the same time, it is important to note that the bureaucracy is virtually under the political control of the Diet and the ruling Liberal Democratic Party. Even if many bureaucratic agencies appear to be acting autonomously, it is rarely suggested that they are acting **against** the political wishes of the parliamentary majority. Thus, if the bureaucracy in Japan is powerful, as indeed most evidence suggests, its power remains subject to the parliamentary majority.

Liberal Democratic Party. Finally, there is strong evidence to suggest that real decision making in Japan takes place within the long ruling Liberal Democratic Party, and that only after the party has reached some form of agreement does the Diet as a body become meaningfully involved in legislation. Indeed, very rarely does a bill that has been approved by the LDP get turned down in Diet, largely because to the near ironclad discipline the party enjoys. Yet in interpreting this phenomenon as it relates to Japanese democracy, two points, at least, should be mentioned. First, the LDP has been returned as the majority party since 1955, usually receiving more than twice as many votes as its nearest competitor. As such, it has a certain legitimate claim to rule. Hammering out a consensus among its members before approaching the Diet does not in itself thwart the democratic process.

Second, there are strong cultural and procedural norms in Japan that operate against what the Japanese usually refer to as "tyranny of the majority." Although there have been a number of occasions when the LDP has used its majority to ram through controversial legislation, the norm is that of cross-party consensus building. Usually the LDP tries to ensure support for its proposals by one or more opposition parties; few government bills pass with only LDP support. Indeed, many sessions of the Diet have been effectively shut down when opposition party members refused to attend until compromises had been worked out with the ruling party.

Finally, the power of the opposition parties is also a function of their electoral strength and public opinion. Compromises are most frequent when the parliamentary majorities of the LDP are slimmest and when issues gain wide attention in the press and among the citizenry. In short, again there are many democratic checks on what might otherwise appear to be a grossly undemocratic system of governance.

Government Responsiveness beyond Elections. In the above consideration of just how responsive Japan's institutions are to changing public preferences, it was noted that government must be sensitive to media concerns, to opposition demands, and to interest group pressures. The Japanese government's responsiveness to citizen pressures outside of regular elections, however, can perhaps best be measured by the effectiveness of the various citizens' movements that developed around such issues as pollution, consumerism, and taxation. For the most part these movements spring up when existing institutions such as bureaucratic agencies, local governments, political parties, or interest groups fail to deal adequately with pressing issues of concern to large numbers of citizens. Resorting to a variety of public protest tactics and appealing to the court system, the powers of non-established authorities, the media and other mechanisms, these movements seek to force an otherwise non-receptive government to act on their demands. Such protests do not always work; but the success of several of the more famous is testimony to the capacity of public opinion to effect change.

CONCLUSION

The above analysis suggests that in most important respects, Japanese democracy is roughly comparable to most other industrialized democracies in Western Europe, North America, and Australasia. Japan certainly has as much right as any of them to describe itself as a democracy, even though there, as elsewhere, practices fall short of democratic ideals.

III. ISSUES FOR DISCUSSION

1. Compare Japanese democratic institutions with those of any other country with which you are familiar. What are the relative advantages and disadvantages of each? Where does each fall short of democratic ideals?

2. Compare the lives of Japanese citizens in their "non-political" lives with the lives of citizens in a country whose government makes greater demands on their time and services. How important is the tradeoff between the freedom to participate in political actions and the freedom **not** to participate?

3. Compare democracy as practiced in a presidential system such as the United States and in a parliamentary system such as Japan. Which system gives citizens greater potential influence and control? In what ways and with what tradeoffs?

IV. SELECTED READINGS

Krauss, Ellis, and Takashi Ishida. *Japanese Democracy.* Pittsburgh: University of Pittsburgh Press, 1989 (student reading). A collection of analytic essays that attempt to evaluate different aspects of Japanese democracy, including the media, local government, opposition parties, and education.

McCormack, Gavan, and Sugimoto Yoshio. *Democracy in Contemporary Japan.* Armonk, NY: M.E. Sharpe, 1986 (faculty background). A selection of critical essays that point out a number of areas in which Japanese democracy falls short of the ideals.

Pempel, T.J. *Policy and Politics in Japan: Creative Conservatism.* Philadelphia: Temple University Press, 1982 (student reading). A textual overview of Japanese politics that examines six cases of public policy formation, all with a comparative democratic perspective.

Pempel, T.J. *Japan: Dilemmas of Success.* New York: Foreign Policy Association, 1986 (student reading). A broad overview of contemporary Japanese culture, politics, and economics written for the generalists.

Verba, Sidney, et al. *Elites and the Idea of Equality.* Cambridge: Harvard University Press, 1987 (faculty background). A cross-national study of various aspects of elitism and equality that demonstrates among other things a number of ways in which Japan is more democratic in practice than several other important democratic regimes.

Political Science: Japan

Political Parties and Representation: The Case of Japan

T. J. Pempel

I. INTRODUCTION: CENTRAL POINTS

One of the most stable democracies in the industrialized world today, Japan provides an excellent case for the study of political parties and representation.

• Japan was the first non-Western country to adopt a parliamentary system of government (1890) and universal male suffrage (1925).

• Political parties and popular elections played an important part on governance even before World War II, and have determined the formation Japan's governments since then, making Japan one of the few non-Western examples of electoral representation.

• Despite the existence of a competitive multi-party system, Japan's governments have been formed exclusively by the conservative Liberal Democratic party since that party's formation in 1955, making Japan an unusual example of uninterrupted conservative rule among advanced industrialized democracies.

- The similarities and differences in Japan's electoral and party systems as compared to those of Western industrialized democracies make it a fascinating case for those generally interested in the comparative study of those systems.

II. MAJOR TOPICS

ELECTIONS, PARTIES, AND PARLIAMENT UNDER THE MEIJI CONSTITUTION

Soon after the Meiji Restoration (1868) which marks the beginning of Japan's modernization effort, the young Emperor Meiji issued the Charter Oath, which provided that "an assembly widely convoked shall be established, and thus great stress shall be laid upon public opinion." In April 1869, Japan's first deliberative assembly was convened, and over the next two decades successive local and national assemblies were established. During this period, proto-parties developed in various parts of the country. For the most part, however, their membership was limited and based on highly personalistic ties, making the political bases they could claim to represent conspicuously narrow. Moreover, the assemblies were typically appointed, not elected, and their powers were severely circumscribed.

It was not until 1890 that Japan had a representative body that could meaningfully be compared to the parliaments of Western Europe and the United States. In that year, the Imperial Diet (Teikoku Gikai) was convened, in accordance with the Meiji Constitution, promulgated one year earlier. As was true of many of its Western counterparts, however, Japan's Diet was sharply restricted in its powers. As in Prussia and France, a strong state and an able bureaucracy were viewed as the keys to political rule. Sovereignty thus remained vested in the emperor. It was he, and not the parliament, who appointed the cabinet, and it was to him that the individual ministers and the cabinet as a whole were responsible. A national bureaucracy was created to deal with matters of day-to-day administration and governance, and it was given a wide array of powers; the powers of the Diet were correspondingly circumscribed.

Structure and Powers. Japan's prewar bicameral Diet was structurally similar to that of Britain. The upper chamber, the House of Peers, was appointive and hereditary and essentially insulated from electoral control. The lower chamber, the House of Representatives, was elective, but in the beginning, suffrage was limited to perhaps one percent of Japan's population, rendering invalid any claim to national representation. Although he never exercised it, the emperor retained the right of absolute veto over all legislative acts. Diet sessions of parliament were limited to three months a year, leaving most of the real governance of the country to the national bureaucracy and to the imperially appointed cabinet. The powers of the Diet were restricted even when it was in session: cabinet ministers could attend and speak in either house, they had free access to all parliamentary committees and could introduce, amend, or withdraw bills on any subject; government bills took precedence over parliamentary bills. Only the emperor could propose constitutional amendments (although he never did so), and laws passed by the Diet required the countersignature of a cabinet minister. The Diet generally conducted its debates publicly, but could be forced into secret session when so requested by the cabinet. The financial and budgetary powers of the Diet were sharply circumscribed to ensure virtual cabinet autonomy in money matters. Finally, the cabinet could dissolve the parliament at will; no provision was made, however, for a parliamentary vote of no-confidence that would force the resignation of a cabinet.

Dissent and Integration. Despite all of these formal boundaries around parliamentary powers, over the succeeding forty years Japan's parliament became an integral part of the governing system, while elections and political parties became expanded sources of influence over national politics.

In the first election, held in 1890, suffrage was restricted to the nation's major taxpayers, about one percent of the population. Political parties were opposed by many of Japan's cabinet officials and behind-the-scenes power brokers as being contrary to the national interest. As a consequence, Japan's elections throughout the decade were marked by sharp confrontations and pitched battles between party politicians and the police; in sessions of the Diet, elected officials frequently opposed the government on such matters as the budget and taxation, with neither side willing to compromise. Nevertheless, by the turn of the century, the political parties had gained sufficient influence over electoral and parliamentary processes to force government leaders into a series of accommodations that expanded party and parliamentary powers considerably, making them integral parts to the governing process.

The most critical aspect of this accommodation involved a reduction in the government's reliance on the land tax for revenues, thus easing economic burdens on Japan's wealthier landlords. In exchange, the parties, through which these landlords generally exercised power, increasingly supported various government initiatives. Interested in the reelection of their members, the party sought to maintain control over local pork-barrel and patronage projects such as roads, schools, railways, and other efforts that created local jobs. The parties also began to draw membership and financial support from the emerging urban industrial and commercial classes. As a further indication of the closer association between government and parties, several government leaders, including Ito Hirobumi, one of Japan's foremost senior statesmen, joined political parties in which they assumed leadership positions. By the turn of the century, some 20 percent of Japan's elected parliamentarians were former government bureaucrats.

In 1918, Hara Kei, leader of the largest political party, the Seiyūkai, was the first commoner to become prime minister, demonstrating the extent to which the parties, the Diet, and the electorate support had increased their powers and become integral to the governance of the country. From 1922–32, a period during which there was generally peace abroad and prosperity at home, every cabinet was formed by the leader of either the Seiyūkai or the Minseitō, depending on which political party had the largest number of seats in the Diet. With the introduction of universal male suffrage in 1925, many anticipated that Japan was on a historical trajectory toward electoral and parliamentary control comparable to that attained in much of Western Europe and North America.

Ideological Polarity and the Demise of Electoral Control. While the two major parties were exchanging power during the 1920s, a number of parties on the left—variously described as socialist, social democratic, and communist—emerged and began to attract support. Most of them were linked to the fledgling labor union movement which was developing a degree of strength, mostly in urban areas and in the more industrialized sectors of the economy. Both the parties and the union movement were beset by internal divisions and overt police repression. Even at their high point in the late 1930s, the unions enrolled only about 7 percent of the national work force, and all the left-wing parties combined drew only about 10 percent of the total vote. Even so, they were seen by both the politically and economically powerful as posing a challenge to the established parties and the ongoing political system.

At the same time, in response both to the rise of the left and to changes in Japan's domestic and international situation, opponents on the right also began to gain strength. Associated primarily with the military and civilian right-wing organizations, these groups took advantage of domestic dissent over Japan's international politics and its aggression in northern China as well as over ideology per se to launch continuous attacks on the hard left and the more moderate center. Eventually, they gained control of Japanese politics and held it for most of the 1930s. Throughout the years of the Second World War, elections continued to be held and the mainstream parties were active in the Diet. But party and parliamentary influence was severely circumscribed by the policies of both military and civilian right-wing groups, some of which included high government officials, which effectively ensured, not "government by election," but "government by assassination."

Summary: Limits on Parliamentary and Electoral Controls. Despite progress toward increased party and parliamentary influence, the principle of parliamentary control was by no means widely accepted in prewar Japan. Thus when the Minseitō platform called for "parliamentary-centered government" on the eve of universal male suffrage, the party was sternly rebuked by the Home Ministry, which insisted that the overarching principle of Japanese politics was the sovereignty of the emperor.

Japan adopted and then abandoned a series of electoral systems during the prewar period, which made it exceedingly difficult for a single political party to gain an absolute majority in the lower house of the Diet. In only four of the twenty-two elections held between 1890 and 1946 did a single party garner such a majority. This made it difficult for any single party, or for parties in general, to lay even a weak claim to a popular mandate, and thereby to gain a predominant role in the selection of governments and the formation of public policies.

At most, seventeen of the forty-four cabinets formed between 1890 and the end of World War II can be said to have been party cabinets. And of these seventeen, eight were headed by retired bureaucrats who took up positions as party leaders, and another by a retired general who did the same. What is even more revealing, during the entire prewar period not a single election resulted in the defeat of an incumbent political party. Cabinets changed, of course, as did party in parliament, but the dominant pattern was for the cabinet to change **before** the party majority, contrary to what one would expect in a parliamentary form of government.

At the same time, the roles played by the parties, elections, and the Diet should not be completely dismissed. Throughout most of the prewar period a basis was laid for the expansion of representative democracy that put Japan far ahead of most of its Asian neighbors. This democratic development process was brought to a decisive halt during Japan's military expansion in the 1930s and the Second World War, but its prewar experiences with democratic institutions provided a valuable basis on which to build a representative government after the war.

POSTWAR PARTIES AND REPRESENTATION

The Occupation of Japan. Following its defeat in World War II, Japan was occupied by the U.S. military for almost seven years. The American Occupation authorities oversaw a number of radical changes in the Japanese political system, including the introduction of a completely new constitution. Most of the changes were designed to enhance the power of the individual voter and to expand the role of elections, the parliament, and political parties. The constitution was based on popular sovereignty; the legislature was declared to be "the highest organ of state power, and the sole lawmaking organ of the state"; the bicameral Diet was retained, but the appointed House of Peers was replaced by an elected House of Councilors; the cabinet was made responsible to the Diet; the suffrage was expanded to include women; and the voting age was reduced to twenty.

The Occupation also released most political prisoners from jails; many Japanese who had gone overseas into voluntary exile were repudiated. Meanwhile, large numbers of officials who had supported the wartime government were purged from political office. These acts led to a democratic revitalization of the political left and to an overall reshuffling of party fortunes. Several prewar parties recombined in the late 1940s, but the Occupation-led changes induced an entirely new group of individuals to enter electoral politics. In the first postwar election, some 246 proto-political parties contested for office; over 80 percent of the lower house election of April 1946 had never served before.

The Japan Socialist party (JSP) and the Japan Communist party (JCP), both with labor union support, did rather well electorally under the new system, and in 1947–48 Japan was headed by coalition governments that included the JSP. This was to be the only time, however, that the country experienced a left-of-center government.

Election System. The history of party development and the character of both intra- and inter-party competition in Japan can be traced in large part to Japan's unusual electoral system. In fact, there are two electoral systems, one for the House of Councilors, or Upper House, and a different one for the House of Representatives or Lower House.

Elections for the **House of Councilors** take place at three-year intervals and are two-tiered: only half of the members, who serve for a term of six years, stand for election at a time. Thus, as in the U.S. Senate, the terms of office overlap. Of the 252 members of the Upper House, 100 are elected in a national constituency and 152 are elected in local level constituencies. Until recently, the election for the national constituency involved open competition among all candidates. Each voter could cast one ballot in the national constituency; the fifty seats that were up for election went to the top fifty vote-getters. As can be imagined, this meant that personal popularity and name recognition counted for a lot; quite often popular television and media personalities were the top vote-getters. Also, candidates who represented narrowly based interest groups such as veterans, doctors, and atomic bomb victims could easily be elected as long as he/she could gain all the votes of the members of the group.

Recently, the national constituency system was changed and elections are now on the basis of slates presented by the major political parties. Voters now cast their ballots for the party slate of their choice and the top names on the slate are returned in proportion to the total number of votes received by the slate as a whole. While this change gives the parties greater control over the composition of their slates, the absolute fortunes of the parties have not been greatly affected.

The local constituencies for the House of Councilors return from three to eight representatives, depending on the population of the district. As with the national constituency, each elector gets only one vote, which means that smaller parties can do well if they are able to consolidate the votes of their supporters. The system also generates a good deal of intra-party competition among candidates from the larger parties since the bloc of their potential supporters is relatively fixed and each individual can vote for only one of the party's several candidates.

The system for electing the 511 members of the **House of Representatives** involves what is known as a single ballot multimember district system. In the U.S. House of Representatives, or the British House of Commons, each electoral district elects one representative, and each voter gets one vote. If there is more than one candidate, the candidate with the largest number of votes wins. In most instances, a winner will receive close to, or more than 50 percent of the total number of votes cast. In Japan, by way of contrast, each district returns typically from three to five representatives, depending on the population of the district. (Lately, a few exceptions have broadened this range to two to six representatives.) Thus, there are several "winners" per district, as many as five or six in many populous districts. Yet each voter still gets only one vote. This means that a "winner" might be seated with only 10–15 percent of the district's total vote.

This system has many consequences. For one thing, it makes it possible for small political parties enjoying support from no more than 5–10 percent of the national population to gain representation in the Lower House. In addition, the system also poses problems for individual candidates and for political parties. Should a party run only one candidate? That would ensure that all their supporters within the district could deliver their votes to that candidate, heightening his or her chance for election. But it also means that a party following such a strategy could never achieve a majority of seats in the parliament since there are only 123 districts and parliament has 511 seats. Alternatively, if a party's supporters in the district are many, the party could run several candidates and hope to elect two or three candidates per district, but in doing so they always run the risk that their supporters' votes will be divided in such a way that none of their candidates are elected in a specific district. This heightens intra-party tensions among those parties that choose to run more than one candidate per district. It also often pits candidates from some of the smaller parties against one another more than against the larger parties. This system as a whole also serves in this way as an important contributor to the factions which pervade the larger Japanese parties, namely the LDP and the JSP. Candidates who wish to run in a given district under the name of either of the large parties, compete to gain the backing of that party—a backing linked to the candidate's standing in a particular faction and that faction's relative power within the party. Finally, the system makes it possible for voters to vote against a specific representative whom they might oppose, either for corruption, ineptitude, age or the like, while continuing to support that representative's political party; they simply transfer their vote from the member of the party whom they wish to punish to another candidate from the same party. This feature has been an important feature in the ability of the ruling LDP to rejuvenate itself while retaining parliamentary majorities.

In addition to this unusual feature, the districts are extremely imbalanced, with rural areas grossly overrepresented, despite periodic efforts to correct the worst inequities by adding limited numbers of seats to urban districts. The most recent effort to rectify some of the extreme imbalances led to an expansion in the range of representatives returned from each district. Despite these changes, rural representatives still need far fewer votes to be elected than their urban counterparts.

Unlike the Upper House elections which occur at fixed times, those for the Lower House take place only when the house is dissolved by the cabinet. This must occur at least once every four years, but usually occurs more frequently.

Election Campaigns. Under the Public Offices Election Law, voter qualifications are kept to a minimum. Any Japanese who has attained the age of twenty and who has three months' residence in a particular city, town, or village is eligible to vote in all elections. There are no literacy or poll tax requirements; voting is by secret ballot; elections are relatively peaceful and generally recognized as honest; voter turnout is moderately high, usually running about 70–75 percent for national elections.

Under the Election Law, entering one's candidacy for office is a simple matter. All that needed are several hundred dollars bond and notification of the local election board; the bond is returned if a candidate secures a sufficiently high number of votes. Actually winning office, however, is extremely difficult without the support of one of the major parties.

There are tight formal limits on campaign expenditures, speechmaking, and publicity. The official campaign season lasts only three weeks. Door-to-door campaigning is prohibited; no food, drink, or campaign buttons may be distributed; the number of posters, mailings, speeches, and media appearances are limited. Each candidate may make three television appearances at public expense for four-and-one-half minutes each. Because nothing may be done to "raise the ardor" of the citizenry, bands, sirens, parades and the like are also illegal.

But in fact, campaigning is a year-round process that costs millions of dollars per seat. Most restrictions are circumvented through *kōenkai* (clubs), study meetings, gifts to interest groups by "friends of the candidate," and so forth. Soundtrucks blaring the candidates' names criss-cross each district constantly throughout the campaign. Meanwhile, the candidate typically can be found wearing white gloves and a white sash with his or her name emblazoned across the front, bowing politely to constituents in front of the district's largest train station. Enough bows, plus enough money, ensure victory. Incumbency is invariably the greatest asset, however, and in most elections it is rare for more than 15–18 percent of the successful candidates to be "new faces," a figure comparable to the United States, Britain and Canada, countries with the lowest turnover rates in the industrialized world.

At the heart of the election campaign is the individual support group (*kōenkai*), a body of supporters whose loyalty is to a specific candidate, rather than to a political party. Virtually every successful candidate from the larger parties has such personal support groups, designed to ensure their continued reelection. Such support groups are developed and maintained through personal connections, patronage, frequent mailings, festive activities, and the like, all of which are presumed to increase the loyalty of *kōenkai* members to the specific candidate. This should materialize during the actual campaign period in the form of votes and other electoral assistance. These *kōenkai* have become so institutionalized that they are often transferrable from one politician to another, quite often from father to son, a fact which accounts in large measure for the number of second or third generation politicians being elected from the same district over several decades.

Party Factions. Japan is frequently alleged to have factions, not parties. It is true that Japan's larger parties have well-organized, identifiable, and institutionalized factions that persist over long periods of time. Even the smaller parties have internal divisions based on ideology, personality, or both. The complicated electoral system for the House of Representatives is one major contributor to the factionalization of parties; so is the intra-party process of becoming a party leader. Since the selection of a party leader rests heavily on the support of the elected parliamentarians from each party, it is advantageous for anyone desirous of achieving the post to develop personal ties to as many of these parliamentarians as possible. Within the LDP, those anxious to achieve cabinet or top party posts have a similar incentive. An exchange relationship is thus created; in exchange for financial support, campaign assistance, and help in gaining key parliamentary or party posts from the actual or potential faction leader, the faction member is expected to lend support to the faction leader's effort to become party leader. Careers thus become linked. With time, the individual parliamentarian can work his or her way up to higher ranks within the faction as well as within the party and the government just as the faction leader improves his position within the party hierarchy. Along the way, faction members will also often be called upon for support on other matters usually related to intra-party personnel matters, but occasionally including intra-party policy disputes.

In the past, most LDP faction leaders either became prime minister or else came close, died, and passed on their organization to a loyal lieutenant. Thus, Prime Ministers Hatoyama, Kishi, Ikeda, Sato, Tanaka, Miki, Fukuda, Nakasone, and Takahashi, among others, all headed their own factions. But of late, many prime ministers, including Suzuki, Uno, and Kaifu, lacked their own factions. They were typically backed by strong faction leaders who were thus capable of exercising a good deal of behind-the-scenes power over prime ministerial decisions.

Party Dominance. During the forty odd years since the end of the war, the Japanese party system has undergone a series of transformations as parties combined and broke apart, new parties arose, and the fortunes of parties ebbed and flowed. Prior to 1955, it made sense to think of Japan's as a true multi-party system. Under the Occupation, at least five major parties competed vigorously with one another across a wide ideological spectrum. Toward the end of the Occupation in 1952, and over the next few years, the two major conservative parties, the Liberals and the Democrats, began to establish preeminence, and Prime Minister Yoshida Shigeru (a Liberal) was the central political figure of the time.

In 1955, the left and right two main wings of the Japan Socialist party combined to form a unified party. A month later the Liberals and the Democrats united to form the Liberal Democratic party. Over the next several years, these two parties dominated elections, receiving around 95 percent of the total votes between them. Since the LDP usually received from 55–60 percent of the total, with the JSP receiving about 35 percent, however, many cynics referred to the system, not as a two-party, but as a one-and-a-half-party, system.

The LDP continued to control all of the cabinet posts and to hold clear majorities in both houses of the Diet throughout the 1960s and 1970s but its predominance, along with that of the JSP, weakened somewhat as several smaller parties began to carve out national niches for themselves. This process started with the Democratic Socialist party which split from the JSP in 1960, drawing its electoral and financial support largely from Domei, one of Japan's two largest labor federations. Then in 1964, a quasi-religious Komeito, or Clean Government party, began to win seats nationally. In the early 1970s, the Japan Communist party (JCP), which had been dormant following the anti-left wing purges of the American Occupation in the late 1940s and early 1950s, also began to reestablish its electoral base, largely in urban areas. Finally, in 1976, a LDP splinter group, the New Liberal Club (NLC), was established. (It subsequently merged back with the LDP in 1986.) Most of these smaller parties gained only between 6–11 percent of the vote in each election, but they provided viable electoral and ideological alternatives to the two major parties and their combined strength posed a threat to long-term LDP hegemony. During the 1970s the LDP's margins of victory grew increasingly narrow, and for a brief period at the end of the decade it held roughly an equal number of seats as the combined opposition parties. Continued LDP dominance suddenly looked far less probable than some form of coalition government.

A major comeback by the LDP occurred when it posted a major victory in the double election of 1980, in which both the lower and upper house seats were contested at the same time. Subsequent elections in 1983 and 1986 reinforced the LDP's rebound, leaving the JSP and the minor parties largely on the margins of political power. In fact, in a move more important for its symbolic than for its numerical impact, the NLC dissolved and its members rejoined the LDP.

The cumulative picture suggests that the LDP has remained the unquestioned dominant party throughout the post-1955 period. It has typically held more than twice as many parliamentary seats as the next largest party in the Lower House, has formed every cabinet and has been the primary force behind all major public policy initiatives. The only serious challenge to LDP dominance followed the 1989 Upper House election where the LDP lost its majority and has been forced on many pieces of legislation to seek compromise with one or more of the smaller opposition parties. It is valid, therefore, to view the entire postwar period as one of single-party predominance, despite the changing configurations and fortunes of the opposition parties. In this regard, Japan is unusual among the advanced industrial societies, although the conservative Christian Democrats in Italy have enjoyed a continuous, if a somewhat less solid, majority throughout the postwar period, and the Swedish Social Democrats enjoyed forty-four years of uninterrupted left-of-center control from 1932–76.

Parliament and the Bureaucracy. Under the LDP rule, the Diet retained its formal role of designating the prime minister, and all laws had to pass through the parliamentary process. Yet at the same time, the LDP itself and the national bureaucracy became far more central to political initiative. Particularly when the LDP enjoys a comfortable majority, legislation generally emerges from negotiations between a bureaucratic agency and LDP headquarters. Only after party, and later, cabinet approval, is the bill introduced into the Diet.

Bureaucratic influence is also noteworthy in the proportion of former bureaucrats who become parliamentarians. During most of the 1950s and 1960s about 30 percent of LDP Diet members were former bureaucrats. Ex-bureaucrats were even more prevalent in the cabinets and in top party posts. This situation was moderated during the mid- to late–1970s, when the government and the opposition held almost equal numbers of seats, and where opposition members often controlled committees in the Diet. Then, cross-party compromise was much more common, and many government proposals were defeated or revised, demonstrating that the powers of the LDP were by no means unchecked. Bureaucratic influence also fell off as fewer members of the LDP came from the ranks of officialdom, and as more and more "pure politicians" held high office. And increasingly, many of the former bureaucrats in the LDP come, not from the "administrative ministries" such as Finance, International Trade and Industry, or Foreign Affairs, as had been true before, but from the more "political ministries" such as Construction, Home Affairs, and Agriculture.

As the profile of Japan's elected officials has changed and as the LDP has reestablished its predominance, policy expertise among party officials has also increased. Today, many Diet members belonging to the LDP have extensive backgrounds in such fields as education, health, taxation, defense, and the postal system. Frequently castigated in the popular press as members of zoku (tribes), these experts do indeed challenge bureaucratic dominance over policy matters; they have also enhanced the policy-making influence of the Diet and have raised the status of elected officials. In this sense, since Japan's parties and the Diet have traditionally been viewed as relatively weak, this shift would suggest an increase in the powers of the very bodies which are critical to representative democracy.

III. ISSUES FOR DISCUSSION

1. Compare the evolution of parties, parliament, and elections in Japan with those in the United States or any other country

with which you are familiar. What important similarities and differences emerge? What consequences flow from these?

2. Imagine yourself a young Japanese anxious for a career in politics. Lay out your game plan to become a key member of the National Diet.

3. Compare the consequences of the Japanese electoral district system and campaigning to practices in the United States or any other country. What kinds of changes in the Japanese system would you be tempted to make and why?

IV. SELECTED READINGS

Curtis, Gerald L. *Election Campaigning Japanese Style.* New York: Columbia University Press, 1971 (student reading). A participant observer's description and analysis of the election campaign of a single candidate for the House of Representatives.

Curtis, Gerald L. *The Japanese Way of Politics.* New York: Columbia University Press, 1988 (student reading). A recent survey of party and electoral politics that focuses on the Liberal Democrats, but deals with all parties.

Krauss, Ellis J. "Conflict in the Diet: Toward Conflict Management in Parliamentary Politics." In *Conflict in Japan,* edited by Ellis S. Krauss, Thomas P. Rohlen, Patricia G. Steinhoff, pp. 243–293. Honolulu: University of Hawaii Press, 1984 (faculty background). An examination of intra-parliamentary politics during the period in which LDP control was least secure and compromise between government and opposition most frequent.

Pempel, T.J. "Uneasy Towards Autonomy: Parliament and Parliamentarians in Japan." In *Parliaments and Parliamentarians in Democratic Politics,* edited by Ezra Suleiman, pp. 106–153. New York: Holmes and Meier, 1986 (faculty background). A comparative overview of the changing role of Japan's parliamentarians and parliament that contains numerous quantitative indicators on parliamentarians and their actions and attitudes.

Scalapino, Robert A. "Elections and Political Modernization in Prewar Japan." In *Political Development in Modern Japan,* edited by Robert E. Ward, pp. 249–291. Princeton: Princeton University Press, 1968 (student reading). A good overview of the prewar system including electoral data.

Political Science:
Korea

Political Development in South Korea

Han-Kyo Kim

I. INTRODUCTION: CENTRAL POINTS

Any discussion of the political development of South Korea should focus on the following key issues: its relations with North Korea, its economy, and its halting democratization process. These issues have preoccupied the Koreans for more than four decades; the United States, a longtime ally and trading partner of South Korea, has an abiding interest in each of them.

In August 1945, during the last days of World War II, the division, at the thirty-eighth parallel, of the Korean peninsula was hastily arranged, with the southern zone occupied by the U.S. military, and the northern zone by the Soviets. The division was perpetuated in 1948 with the creation of two rival regimes: in the South, the Republic of Korea (ROK), with its capital in Seoul and in the North, the Democratic People's Republic of Korea (DPRK), with Pyongyang as its capital. An inconclusive war (1950–53) has left a bitter legacy of distrust and hostility between the two sides which even today are separated by a 150-mile demilitarized zone (DMZ).

As the decade of the nineties begins, with its promise of an end to the Cold War, the tension between the two heavily armed Korean protagonists persists. How has this tragic division affected the pattern of political development in South Korea? Does an external threat impede the development of democratic politics? Does the yearning for reunification impose an unbearable burden on the young political system of ROK?

II. MAJOR TOPICS

IMPLICATIONS OF A DIVIDED KOREA

The postwar division of Korea is perceived by Koreans on both sides as a callous act of injustice inflicted upon them by the victorious Allies in World War II. Korea had been a politically unified and culturally homogeneous nation since the days of Koryo dynasty (918–1392). Under the Choson dynasty (1392–1910), Korea had attained a high level of cultural sophistication as well as stable and highly developed sociopolitical institutions.

Although thirty-five years of Japanese colonial rule (1910–1945) sacrificed Korean pride and independence, it preserved the unity of the nation. The promise of an end to the harsh rule by Japan was included in the wartime proclamations issued at Cairo (1943) and Potsdam (1945). But at the time of Japan's surrender in 1945, the Allied nations had no political blueprint for an independent Korea. As the Soviet forces poured into Korea from the north, the United States proposed—and the Soviet Union readily accepted—a plan to divide Korea into two zones of military occupation.

Divided Korea quickly became an arena of contest between the two superpowers, under whose aegis contending political forces were organized among the Koreans. The United States sponsored the creation of the ROK under the staunch anti-communist leadership of Syngman Rhee, while the USSR handpicked Il-sung Kim to head the communist regime in the North. The civil war that erupted in 1950, when the North invaded the South, reflected the prevailing Cold War polarity with the United States and its allies involved on the ROK side and the USSR and China (PRC) on the DPRK side.

The war took heavy tolls in lives and property on both sides and ended inconclusively in 1953 with an armistice agreement that left Korea as divided as before but also more heavily armed and vengeful. Frosty military confrontation across the fortified DMZ has required militarization of the two Korean societies. In the South, a large share of national resources is devoted to national defense; the presence of more than 40,000 U.S. troops demonstrates the continuing significance of the bilateral mutual security pact signed in 1953.

DEMOCRACY IN SOUTH KOREA

The turbulent political history of South Korea is characterized by numerous changes in regime, several revisions of the Constitution, two military coups (1961 and 1979), and frequent waves of popular demonstrations. Despite the constitutional affirmation of popular sovereignty, and elections in 1963, 1967, and 1971, voters were denied their right to elect the president between 1972 and 1987. The election and the rules of the National Assembly, the unicameral legislative body, are often subject to such manipulation that its roles and functions are compromised. The independence of the judiciary has been called into question. Although the most recent and relatively democratic redaction of the Constitution asserts the autonomy of provincial and local government units, this has not been achieved. The list of democratic principles that are espoused but not honored in fact is long.

Nevertheless, democracy has been the rallying cry of the political opposition and of the republic's five successive regimes, referred to as "republics" by South Koreans, since 1948. The first, led by Syngman Rhee, lasted twelve years, until it was topped as a result of student protests in 1960. The second regime lasted barely a year before it was overthrown by a military junta led by General Chung Hee Park. Park eventually took off his uniform and remained in the presidency, heading the "Third" (1963–72) and "Fourth" (1972–79) Republics, until his assassination in 1979, which ushered in a brief "spring in Seoul." Another military group, however, led by Doo Hwan Chun, quickly emerged triumphant and turned back the political clock. President Chun did step down in 1988 when his single seven-year term expired and opened the way for his protégé, Tae Woo Roh, to succeed him.[1] Roh was designated by Chun to be the ruling party's candidate; he ran in and won the popular election in 1987. Roh's term, which under the revised Constitution is limited to five years, began amidst expectations of democratic change. There indeed have been some liberalizing changes but not enough to satisfy opposition groups. Is democracy possible in South Korea in light of its nondemocratic traditional culture? Do the frequency and manner in which regime changes have been effected signify a lack of political legitimacy? What form should political participation take? Indeed, what is **political development** in the Korean context? Does the Korean case represent a variant on the general themes found in the scholarship on political development? Or is *sui generis?*

These complex questions demand careful analysis of the situation inside Korea as well as of Korea in a regional and global context. It is hoped that the general discussion that follows will stimulate further investigation for answers to these questions.

ECONOMIC DEVELOPMENT

The spectacular economic performance of ROK in the three decades beginning in the early 1960s has earned it the title "Little Japan," and recognition as one of the "Four Tiger Cubs," or "Four Dragons," alongside Taiwan, Hong Kong, and Singapore.

South Korea's record looks particularly impressive because of its earlier image as a hopelessly impoverished country which subsisted on foreign handouts after 1945 and particularly after the Korean War. Between 1962 and 1985 its real GNP per capita is estimated to have tripled to over $2,000. (The 1990 estimate is about $5,000 in current dollars.) Its trade statistics are even more impressive. Whereas in 1965 its exports amounted to just $175 million, the 1987 figure showed $47.28 billion, or a better than 270-fold increase in twenty-two years. In 1986, ROK for the first time ever had a surplus in its balance of trade amounting to more than $4 billion.

These remarkable statistics reflect two general policy thrusts that have been consistently observed through a series of multiyear economic plans: (1) export-led economic growth; and (2) an industrialization scheme based initially on labor-intensive import-substitution industries (such as textiles) and then, more recently, on capital- and technology-intensive industries.

What is obvious to students of political economy is that the implementation of these economic policies in the initial stage of Korea's economic recovery were made possible by the interventionist orientation of the ROK government, beginning with the Park regime. The state's intervention in economics, which is consistent with the traditional Confucian notion that the ruler had the moral responsibility to provide for the economic well-being of the people, was clearly a major factor in ROK's economic growth during the past three decades.

ROLE OF GOVERNMENT IN
INDUSTRIAL DEVELOPMENT

Touted as one of the fastest growing NIEs (newly industrialized economies), ROK has received much attention from students of political economy, including those concerned with dependency theory: Does the Korean "miracle" disprove the gloomy forecast of impoverishment of the "periphery"? To those concerned with economic development strategies, what does the Korean case say about the role of state in economic growth? Has the political system— more specifically, the bureaucracy— been able to formulate and implement effective economic policies? Is there a "Korea Inc."? More broadly, the seeming "disparity" between **political** and **economic** development raises questions about the relationship between these two facets of modern change. Is there a causal relationship between them, or are they basically independent of each other?

The remarkable Korean record, and indeed similar stories from other NIEs in East Asia, may challenge the validity of the dependency theory that explains— and forcasts— lasting economic and political domination of the third world nations by the industrialized nations of the world. That South Korea was on the "periphery" prior to President Park's assumption of power in 1963 is beyond doubt. But how could a peripheral Korea undergo basic economic transformation and development while remaining closely tied to the capitalist world order? A possible answer to this question may be that East Asian "bureaucratic/authoritarian" systems, which encourage collaboration between technocrats and a relatively small group of modern entrepreneurs, have a peculiar mix of sociocultural factors which permits an accelerated pace of industrialization and export expansion, thereby breaking out of the vicious cycle of economic dependency on the "core" nations. The traditional Confucian emphasis on the value of education, a strong work ethic, and cultural homogeneity are some of the sociocultural factors that may be relevant.

JAPAN AS A MODEL

Japan has had a far-reaching impact on the South Korean economy. It was not until 1965 that the ROK government normalized its relations with Japan, the long delay having been largely due to their history of bitter relations earlier in the century. Quickly thereafter, however, Japan began to replace the United States as the primary source of capital, machinery, and technical know-how for South Korea. But more importantly, ROK economic policies seemed to emulate the policies Japan had followed at earlier stages, moving from the import-substitution phase into the multi-phased export expansion programs. Many Korean business leaders feel more at home in the Japanese business environment and have closer personal ties with their Japanese than with their American counterparts. Even the Korean term *chaebol*, denoting the largest family-controlled business empires is an import from Japan, where the same Chinese characters are pronounced *zaibatsu*.

To the extent that Japan's political economy merits the term "Japan Inc.," is a similar characterization of Korean economy justified? A short answer would be "yes"; a close partnership between the state (or bureaucracy) and business in pursuit of national economic goals does exist in Korea as in Japan. Of course, this partnership is subject to continual ·change as the economy grows in size and complexity; "Korea Inc." today may show features which no longer exist in its Japanese counterpart.

SOCIOECONOMIC CHANGE

The scope and the speed of Korea's economic development have had steady and irreversible impacts on its social structure and way of life. The tempo of urbanization has engulfed more than a half of South Korea's 42 million residents, nearly one quarter of whom live in the capital city of Seoul alone. Traditional family and community structures have been transformed. Manufacturing and service sector employment has eclipsed farming, and the urban middle class and organized labor have grown significantly. There is a high degree of social mobility.

These and other socioeconomic changes have led to the rise of new interest groups and to the decline of communal ties as a factor affecting voter preference, as in other modernizing societies. These changes were not, however, necessarily in the direction of democratic development. The initial, almost dizzying, economic success of the 1960s was used to justify the creation of the re-pressive Yushin regime in 1972 which succeeded in keeping up the momentum of economic growth even during the difficulties resulting from the "oil shock." The brief economic setback in 1980 is widely attributed to political instability resulting from the "spring in Seoul" following the collapse of the Yushin regime in 1979.

From this overview of the development of the South Korean

economy it is clear that state intervention was primarily responsible for initiating the industrialization process and that political stability has impacted directly on economic performance. The Korean case also suggests that economic development and democratic politics do not necessarily correlate, and that they may at times move in opposite directions. Economic development and the attendant social changes (such as the growth of the middle class) are no guarantee that political democracy will prevail.

THE QUEST FOR DEMOCRACY

Political and Economic Ramifications of South-North Tensions. Anticommunism has overridden virtually all other political considerations in ROK. In the wake of certain liberal reforms undertaken by the Roh administration (1988-), academic study of Marxism-Leninism and North Korea is beginning to enjoy greater tolerance. But strict anti-communist laws are still in place, and any radical left-wing group is liable to persecution and suppression. In the name of national security, certain civil rights and political freedoms have been curtailed. During the Yushin Reform ("Revitalizing Reform") in 1972 delicate relations with the DPRK were cited as an excuse to proclaim the life-term dictatorship of President Park.

While it is debatable that ROK is a "garrison state" predicated on a total war strategy, it appears undeniable that the constant threat, real or presumed, posed by North Korea to its security has hampered the development of an open political system in South Korea. National security and anti-communism have been invoked time and again to justify repressive laws and policies limiting individual rights and political freedoms.

At the same time, one may speculate that such a threat may have stimulated efforts for national development. In military and economic spheres, such efforts are obvious, but even in politics, such challenges may have spurred efforts to create and develop a strong leadership institution and bureaucracy.

An important corollary to the division of Korea and military tensions is the political ramifications of the question of reunification of Korea. Popular pressure for a unification has always existed in both Koreas, but it has acquired new impetus with the end of the Cold War, the reunification of Germany, and the introduction within ROK itself of certain liberal reforms.

For nearly twenty years after the 1953 armistice, the two Koreas had not talked to each other. In 1972, they began a dialogue which, despite frequent and long interruptions, has continued. Both regimes have exploited the issue for propaganda gains and internal political ends, but neither side has been willing to risk a permanent rupture in the peaceful exchange.

There are obvious parallels between the Korean and the German situations, but there also are significant differences. The power differentials between ROK and DPRK are not as decisive as those that existed between West and East Germany; the enmity and distrust run deeper in Korea than was the case in Germany, partly due to the bitter memories of the war; and the first generation of revolutionary leaders is still firmly in power, at least in North Korea, a situation which tends to inhibit compromise and minimize the impact of worldwide detente on the Korean peninsula.

The recent surge in the popular demand for national reunification in South Korea poses a major challenge to the political system. The on-again off-again pattern of the South-North dialogue and the attendant media hype have created a continually rising tide of expectations. The ROK government has at times tried to dampen these expectations, but has not always been successful. (It has also taken a number of steps to enhance its capability in policy-making and implementation in this area, again with only partial success. Consequences of mismanagement may be dangerous and the ROK's political stability is in balance.)

Tradition of Student Protest. South Korea may today have the dubious distinction of being the only East Asian country where street demonstrations are almost routine year-round. Radical students usually constitute the core activists and may be joined at times by opposition politicians, civil rights advocates, reform-minded members of the clergy, unionists, and infrequently, general citizenry. Demands— of varying revolutionary intensity— for democratic reforms make up their slogans. More often than not, these demonstrations result in violent clashes with the police, although the casualty lists are usually surprisingly short.

The role of students in these demonstrations requires a brief explanation. First, the tradition of protest goes back to the pre-modern period. During the Choson dynasty, the Confucian literati class, especially those who were not bureaucratic office-holders, had the presumptive right and duty to act as self-appointed critics of the government. In the early modern period this tradition was inherited by students in secondary or higher educational institutions. Moreover, during the Japanese colonial period, anti-Japanese nationalist sentiment added fervor and a sense of patriotic mission to various student demonstrations, of which the March First Movement (1919) is the most celebrated.

Since liberation in 1945, student groups espousing a range of ideologies have been active in the political maneuvers that precede the establishment of a new ROK regime. In 1960 students were instrumental in toppling the twelve-year regime of the octogenarian autocrat, Syngman Rhee. Twenty years later, another massive uprising spearheaded by students erupted in the southwestern city of Kwangju. Each of these and other similar instances has created its own martyrs and myths, and constitutes a monument to student activism.

A second explanation for student activism concerns the political structure that has traditionally left little or no room for loyal opposition. The Japanese colonialists had proscribed any form of political activity; schools and religious establishments were the only Korean organizations allowed to exist. In the 1919 Movement, it was the students who led mass demonstrations and religious leaders who signed the 1919 proclamation of Korean independence. In the late 1950s, opposition parties were largely suppressed until students took to the streets. In short, the students have often been the only mobilizable opposition to an authority that sought to emasculate political parties and other organizations.

FUTURE PROSPECTS

The South Korean record in the development of democratic institutions and procedures has thus been shown to be wanting. The office of the chief executive has grown too powerful and immune to constitutional restraint. Electoral contests, even when tolerated, have often been subject to illegal constraints and tampering by the ruling group. Political parties as institutions have remained underdeveloped. Negotiation and compromise, the cornerstones of nonviolent political behavior, have tended to be equated with betrayal or surrender.

On the other hand, even the most willful office-holders have paid homage to democratic principles. The people of Korea genuinely believe in democracy, and have become aware of their collective strength. In 1960, 1979, and 1987, the people brought down autocratic regimes against seemingly hopeless odds. The level of political sophistication among the people continues to rise.

The record of the present regime appears to point to a slow, if unsteady, movement toward a more open political system. Such optimism seems warranted despite violent street demonstrations and other signs of political unrest. Democracy in South Korea may not share all the features of its Western counterparts; nor is it likely to develop at the pace and in the manner of other democracies in the world. Nevertheless, the evolution of a democratic political system peculiar to Korea and suited to conditions there is possible, or even probable in the long run.

The question of political development *per se* requires a definitional clarification. If political development is understood to include three key sets of variables: i.e., a) institutional development that Samuel Huntington argues is a key factor for political stability, b) political culture, and c) system capability; South Korean democracy is weak in some areas and promising in others. The state-building process since 1945 has been beset by external as well as internal difficulties. In certain areas, such as bureaucracy, economic technocracy, or the defense and other security-related establishments, ROK has developed complex and capable institutions. On the other hand, those institutions that citizens look to for the protection of democratic freedoms and an open political process have remained weak.

In terms of political culture, while South Korea's past record has not been very reassuring, future prospects appear hopeful. Confucian legacies have nurtured what Jacobs (Norman Jacobs, 1985) has called a patrimonial social order that has been accepted for centuries. The bureaucratic/authoritarian system is the political expression of this patrimonial order. At the same time, however, the opposite concept of popular sovereignty has gained wide acceptance. Whatever emerges out of the intermeshing of these two sets of beliefs and attitudes, the outcome is likely to be more "modern" than traditional.

Assessment of system capabilities is an easier task. South Korea has proved that its political system is capable of survival and of rendering a credible performance in the face of enormous challenges. Successive ROK regimes have had to confront the tensions in relations with North Korea, economic hardship, and demands for democratic reforms. Throughout successive regimes, the ROK as a state has retained its legitimacy by virtue of its economic performance. More basically, ethnic and cultural homogeneity have enabled Korea to proceed directly to state-building and state-maintaining operations without expending its resources on nation-building endeavors.

On the basis of the preceding analysis, one may conclude that South Korea has experienced considerable progress in political development, especially in terms of its system capabilities; as a result, the society is likely to move in the direction of democratic change in the years to come. But because of certain variables that are unique to Korea, and may be expected to endure, it would be imprudent to draw lessons from the Korea for application to other cases. The Korean record is a variation on general themes, but not an example of novel theorems.

III. ISSUES FOR DISCUSSION

1. Although Korea, China, and Japan share certain common cultural legacies that can be conveniently referred to as Confucianism, the modern history of political and economic changes in these countries show much divergence. In addition to the obvious geopolitical factors, what other factors are there to help explain the different paths and patterns of modern changes in these East Asian countries?

2. Often we assume that economic development and political development are closely interrelated. There may even be a form of causal relationship. What does the story of South Korea tell us in this respect? Affirm, refute, or modify the preceding statement.

3. Does the presence of serious military threat impede the development of democratic politics? Is the checkered record of democracy in South Korea due—at least partially—to the perceived danger of another armed conflict on the peninsula? Does military tension provide a convenient excuse for authoritarian behavior of the government?

NOTE

1. The 1980 constitution provided for a single seven-year term (indirect election). The 1987 constitution provided for a single five-year term (popular direct election).

IV. SELECTED READINGS

Jacobs, Norman. *The Korean Road to Modernization and Development.* Urbana and Chicago, IL: University of Illinois Press, 1985 (faculty background). A work in political sociology that defines Korea as a patrimonial society that may have undergone some modernization, but hardly any development.

Jones, Leroy P., and Sakong, Il. *Government, Business, and Entrepreneurship in Economic Development: The Korean Case.* Cambridge: Harvard University Press, 1980 (faculty background). A largely descriptive study of Korean economic history that includes profiles of Korean business leaders. Part of the useful Harvard series on the modernization of ROK.

Kihl, Young Whan. *Politics and Policies in Divided Korea: Regimes in Contest.* Boulder, CO: Westview Press, 1984 (student reading). A general descriptive introduction to politics in North and South Korea.

Kim, Chong Lim. *Political Participation in Korea: Democracy, Mobilization and Stability.* Santa Barbara, CA: Clio Books, 1980 (advanced student and faculty reading). An anthology of analytical studies by several authors; Chapter Ten by the editor is particularly useful.

MacDonald, Donald Stone. *The Koreans: Contemporary Politics and Society.* Boulder, CO: Westview Press, 1988 (student reading). Another descriptive study that is suitable for classroom use.

Political Science: The Philippines

Political Parties and Political Representation: The Philippines

Carl H. Lande

I. INTRODUCTION: CENTRAL POINTS

Until the early 1970s, Western observers generally regarded the Philippines as a showpiece of American-style democracy. Its 1935 Constitution, establishing a presidential-congressional system of government based on the American model, was set aside in 1972, however, when President Ferdinand Marcos declared martial law and ruled the country as a dictatorship. In 1981, he introduced an almost equally authoritarian presidential-parliamentary government, similar to the French system. The Marcos dictatorship was brought to an end in 1986 through a combination of forces, including the presidential campaign mounted by Corazon Aquino, the revolt of the military, and the mass demonstrations of "people power." A slightly altered version of the 1935 Constitution was put into place and optimism was restored. In 1990, however, at the time of this writing, with successive military coup attempts against the government of President Aquino, the future of Philippine democracy is once again in question.

The weakness of Philippine democracy, for many Filipinos, lies not in the structure of government but rather in the nature of Philippine politics, particularly its political party system. It is a system not without virtues: the political parties traditionally have been excellent instruments for national integration, reaching across all social classes, binding together all regions of the archipelago, and winning equal support in cities and in the countryside. But the parties have not been effective instruments for choice or change, a failure that can be explained in part by the lack of any fundamental policy differences between opposing parties, which in turn can be explained by the hierarchies of patron-client relationships on which all mainstream parties are based. As a result, party loyalty traditionally has been weak. Ineffective defenders of democracy, the two major parties were unable to prevent the declaration of martial law in 1972 or to regain a significant role after democracy was restored in 1986. The parties that have emerged since then are little different from the earlier ones, and appear no better able to present choices to the voters or to formulate and implement programs for socioeconomic reform.

In a course on political party systems the Philippine case would be useful in demonstrating:

• the importance of mass support;

• the effects of clientelism and how clientelist politics may prevent political parties from establishing ties with specific social groups and thus from becoming institutionalized;

• the importance of a party's ability to establish an identity and maintain stability by taking positions on controversial issues and pursuing programmatic policies.

II. MAJOR TOPICS

THE SETTING

Philippine society in most provinces is marked by a sharp division between absentee landowners, both large and small, and the landless peasant sharecroppers and agricultural laborers who must depend on them for access to land and for various forms of assistance. This pattern of rural dependency, together with customary patron-client relationships that pervade Philippine society, helps to account for the vertical, cross-class structure of Philippine political organization, including the organization of political parties.

Philippine society also is marked by narrow loyalties to village, town, province, and regional language groups. The largest of the latter are the Ilocanos of Northern Luzon, the Tagalogs of Central and Southern Luzon, the Bicolanos of the Bicol Peninsula, the Waray, Cebuanos and Hiligaynon of the Visayan Islands and Northern Mindanao, and several Muslim groups with separate languages who are the original inhabitants of Western Mindanao. Most important for national party politics are provincial and language group loyalties. Provincial party leaders depend on the provincial loyalties of voters in dealing with national party leaders. Linguistic-regional loyalties foster interregional contests for national political leadership. As a result, election analyses show, regional language is a more powerful predictor of voting in national elections than are socioeconomic factors.

THE STRUCTURE OF PHILIPPINE POLITICAL COMPETITION

The present Philippine political party system is the outgrowth of an almost unbroken history of competitive electoral politics reaching back from the present Philippine Republic, through the American colonial period, to Spanish colonial times.

During the Spanish period, from the mid-sixteenth century until 1898, national and provincial government positions were restricted to appointed Spaniards. At the local level, however, mayorships were held by members of the Filipino elite, who were elected by the principal citizens— those with education or substantial property— of the municipality. Municipal histories, often compiled by amateur local historians, show that these elections, held annually or biennially, resulted in a frequent turnover in municipal offices which were rotated among members of certain leading families. Thus began, at the local level, what was later to become an enduring pattern of intense rivalry among prominent families for the power, privilege and prestige of higher levels of elective office.

Early in the American colonial period that began in 1898 after the Spanish-American War, Filipino political participation was extended both upward and downward from the municipality. Beginning in 1902 provincial governors were elected, first by municipal councilors within the province, and later directly by the voters. In 1907 the first elections were held for the new Philippine Assembly, the lower house of a bicameral national legislature; membership in the upper house was appointive until 1916, when it too became elective. Finally, in 1935, with the establishment of the semi-autonomous Philippine Commonwealth, the first presidential election was held.

Together with this upward extension of the sphere of electoral politics, participation also moved downward within the municipalities. While in Spanish times the right to vote for municipal officials had been restricted to members of the local elite, American rule brought a progressive extension of suffrage, culminating in 1937 with the enfranchisement of women.

The gradual elimination of property and educational limitations on the franchise meant that the vote, which previously had been restricted to local elites who generally resided in cities where a municipal government was located, was extended to poor and less educated voters in the surrounding villages. To win the votes of this expanding electorate, candidates built pyramids of political leadership and support. Candidates for provincial offices used their wealth, which was usually considerable, to gain the support of prominent political figures in the municipalities. These municipal leaders, in turn, developed their own base of support among influential villagers, including their tenants, who built their following among kin and neighbors. Through such multi-tiered patron-client systems, inherent in each political party, votes were delivered upward in return for the downward flow of material rewards: public works projects for localities and public works jobs for individuals, in addition to cash bribes and a variety of other collective or individual rewards. Patron-client pyramids of this type continue to constitute to a large extent the structure of each of the parties.

PARTIES BEFORE MARTIAL LAW

The two major political parties that developed after the war traced their origins to 1907, when a number of parties were formed to contest the first elections to the National Assembly under American colonial rule. The strongest were the Partido Nacionalista and the Federal Party. The former controlled the legislature until the Japanese invasion of 1942, and the latter, later renamed Partido Nacional Progresista and then Partido Democrata, remained in opposition until it dissolved in the early 1930s, weakened by their repeated defeats at the hands of the Nacionalistas. The main objective of both parties was the early attainment of Philippine independence from American colonial rule. But the issue best served the Nacionalistas who, as the leaders of the Philippine representation in the colonial government, could claim credit for winning independence through peaceful negotiations with a willing American government.

In 1934, independence was promised after what was planned to be a ten-year period of semi-autonomy under a Philippine Commonwealth government headed by an elected president. That independence came, almost on schedule in 1946, immediately after the end of the Japanese occupation. With its nationalist goal achieved, soon after the wartime death of its pre-eminent leader Commonwealth President Manuel Quezon, the now wholly ascendant Partido Nacionalista split in two. One half of the party, led by Quezon's successor in the presidency, Sergio Osmena, kept the old party's name. The other half called itself the Liberal Party; its leader, Manuel Roxas, another Quezon lieutenant, became the first president of the new Republic of the Philippines.

From 1946 until 1972, the Nacionalistas and Liberals maintained a near monopoly of Philippine politics, alternating the presidency and the control of Congress between them. The high frequency and extent of the cyclical swings of voter support from one party to the other was due in part to the readiness of political leaders to change their party attachments when that was to their advantage. This two-party dominance came to a sudden end in 1972 when the twice-elected President Ferdinand Marcos, a former Liberal turned Nacionalista, invoked martial law and closed down the Philippine Congress.

PARTIES DURING THE MARCOS DICTATORSHIP

The two political parties offered little resistance to the imposition of martial law. Some party leaders joined Marcos; others issued periodic statements of criticism. But neither party was able to organize public opposition to the new regime. By 1978, when Marcos called elections for a new Interim National Assembly, little remained of the old parties. Marcos had created a new political organization of his own, the Kilunsang Bagong Lipunan (KBL) or New Society movement. In opposition were various small new parties, most of them with narrow local or regional bases of support. Only thirteen of their members were elected to the new legislature, in part because of the falsification of the vote count by or with the complicity of new Commission on Elections, whose members were hand-picked by Marcos.

Six years later, in 1984, when new elections for the Assembly were held, the opposition parties had combined into several "umbrella groups," some of which chose to boycott the elections. One, the United Democratic Opposition (UNIDO), decided to contest the elections. Its candidates won a third of the Assembly seats, presenting the president with a significant legislative opposition for the first time since the imposition of martial law.

By the end of 1985, when Marcos called a "snap" presidential election to reaffirm his claim to national leadership, all of the new opposition parties and umbrella groups, except the Communist-led National Democratic Front, decided to contest the election with a single opposition slate. Their presidential candidate was Corazon Aquino, widow of the slain Marcos opponent Benigno Aquino and nominal heiress to the leadership of the Partido Demomcratico Pilipino-Laban (PDP-Laban), a party formed by her late husband and other Marcos opponents in 1978. Her vice-presidential running mate was UNIDO's leader Salvador Laurel. This team was victorious in the February 7, 1986, election, and, with the assistance of a popularly-supported military revolt, assumed office shortly thereafter.

THE POST-MARCOS PARTY SYSTEM: MORE OF THE SAME?

The coalition that had been formed to oust the autocratic Marcos began to fragment once it attained power. The first important defector was Secretary of Defense Juan Ponce Enrile, a holdover from the Marcos government who had turned against his chief in the military revolt that followed the snap presidential election. In 1987 he was to become the leader of the opposition Grand Alliance for Democracy (GAD) and then its only member in the restored Senate. Next to draw away from Aquino was Vice President Salvador Laurel. For accepting second place on the presidential ticket, Laurel had been promised the prime ministership. But when the Marcos-era presidential parliamentary system was replaced by a presidential-congressional form of government, that post ceased to exist. Laurel was left with the vice presidency, the secretaryship of foreign affairs and the prospect of playing but a minor role in domestic policymaking. In increasing disagreement with Aquino over policy he became a semi-oppositionist, though for a time his UNIDO party remained a part of the majority coalition.

By May 11, 1987, when elections for a new congress were held, the candidates represented four coalitions: (1) President Aquino's newly-formed Lakas ng Bayan (Strength of the Country) which included PDP-Laban, most of the remnants of the Liberal Party, and UNIDO; (2) Enrile's Grand Alliance for Democracy; (3) a group of Marcos loyalists, Union for Peace and Progress-Kilusan Bagong Lipunan (UPP-KBL); and (4) Partido ng Bayan-Alliance for a New Politics (PNB-ANP), a coalition led by members of the Communist Party. The pro-administration Lakas ng Bayan swept the field, winning 22 out of 24 Senate seats and 135 out of 193 elective seats in the House of Representatives. (Seven additional members were appointed to represent peasants, labor, women, veterans, the elderly, and the disabled.)

When Aquino became president as the candidate of the anti-Marcos coalition, she was urged by her advisors to form a new administration party of her own, distinct from the multi-party coalition, and even from her late husband's PDP-Laban. This she declined to do, preferring to remain simply the coalition leader. But in September 1988, the president's brother and brother-in-law took the initiative to create such an administration party, the Laban ng Demokratikong Pilipino (LDP) or Philippine Democratic Party. Then ensued a tide of party-switching to the LDP by members of the coalition in the House of Representatives. That included most members of PDP-Laban and numerous members of the Liberal Party. In the lower house, most members of Laurel's UNIDO also switched, leaving the vice president with but a few of his earlier followers. Later, he joined with Enrile in an attempt to revive the old Nacionalista party. Even some former Marcos men joined the tide of party switching. By mid-1989, 159 of the 200 members of the lower house were members of the LDP. Only 17 remained in other coalition parties. The rest made up the opposition. In the much smaller 24-member Senate, old party ties proved more durable. While the coalition had won 22 of that chamber's 24 seats, only six senators had joined the new LDP as of mid-1990. The rest were aligned as follows: Liberals 7, PDP-Laban 3, UNIDO 2, Independents 4, Grand Alliance for Democracy 1. (One senator had resigned to become Foreign Secretary.) This allowed Senate Liberal party leader Jovito Salonga to win the Senate Presidency. While still nominally a member of the dominant coalition, he has maintained some distance between himself and the Aquino administration.

As in earlier years, party-switching by elected officials is fostered by the lack of clear differences between the policies of different parties. Even when a party leader has attempted to formulate his own policies, he has not been able to impose them on fellow party members, who feel entitled to vote as they please.

The only party with a clearly distinctive program is the Communist Party of the Philippines (CPP). Formed in 1930, the party won its earliest successes during World War II when it built an effective anti-Japanese guerilla movement, the Hukbalahap, in Central

Luzon. But the "Huks" were suppressed militarily in the early 1950s while most of the party's leaders were arrested. In the late 1960s a younger Beijing-oriented leadership breathed new life into the party by organizing urban labor, students, and peasants. The party's most powerful weapon, however, has been its New Peoples Army, a guerrilla force which by the end of Ferdinand Marcos' rule had organized armed units in the outlying parts of most Philippine provinces. While itself illegal, the CPP has numerous fronts, the oldest of which is the National Democratic Front. A newer front, the previously mentioned Partido ng Bayan-Alliance for a New Politics (PNB-ANP) was formed to run candidates at the 1987 elections but fared poorly in that contest, winning two seats in the House of Representatives and none in the Senate. Still, the PNB-ANP coalition won eight percent of the national senatorial vote, giving it a small but probably enduring electoral base for future growth.

PROSPECTS: THE ENDURING FEATURES OF PHILIPPINE PARTY POLITICS

The post-Marcos political parties have brought together old and young politicians in fresh combinations and under new party names. But much remains unchanged. As before 1972, linguistic regionalism continues to be a powerful divisive force in Philippine politics. To win the presidency and control the Congress, a party must attract influential leaders and, through them, gain voter support in all regions.

But as before, all parties except the Communist Party and its associated fronts remain loose coalitions of self-made and self-financed provincial leaders. The power of these leaders, most of whom are members of prosperous land-owning families, depends to a great extent on the loyalty of their personal political followings and their ability to mobilize broader electoral support among voters in their towns and provinces. The clientelist nature of political life reinforces regional loyalties, but to ensure access to governmental resources, governors and members of Congress must campaign together in national political parties. But party unity remains weak and on substantive public policy questions parties show little party cohesion in Congress.

As in the past, party-switching remains endemic. As this is written, in late 1990, an overwhelming majority of the members of the lower house have joined the new LDP party of the administration. But the unity of that party is not assured; it could easily split apart. In the long run, a competitive two-party system, much like that of the pre-martial-law years, is likely to reappear. As in 1946, the new majority party could split if two popular leaders of the 1986 anti-Marcos coalition were both determined to seek the presidency, and neither was willing to yield to the other. That would create new party alignments, influenced in part by the regional origins of the rival presidential contenders and their running-mates.

As before, the new political parties— the Communists excepted— remain "catch-all" parties that differ little from each other in their vegetative policies. None— again with the exception of the Communists— has built strong ties to a particular sector of Philippine society. None but the communists have championed the interests of the peasant majority. All other parties in the Congress are united in blocking serious agrarian reform. Whether real programmatic differences will develop between the major parties remains to be seen. As long as all major parties maintain their multi-tiered cliental-patron structure and are successful in mobilizing the votes of the poor behind the candidates representing an enduring, relatively homogeneous provincial elite, sharp programmatic differences between opposing parties are not likely to appear.

If the Communist Party and its New Peoples Army were to abandon armed struggle in favor of purely peaceful electoral competition, as some of their leaders have proposed, it could in time become a serious competitor for the votes of the poor and disaffected. Aside from the communists, however, parties of the democratic left remain in an embryonic state. The new Social Democratic Party, formed in 1989, remains untested at the polls. Unless, like the CPP and its PNB-ANP front, it can organize or win the allegiance of major peasant and labor organizations, the new Social Democrats are not likely to become a significant force in national politics.

POLITICAL THEORY AND THE PHILIPPINE PARTY SYSTEM

Samuel Huntington has said that "the stability of a modernizing political system depends on the strength of its political parties. A party, in turn, is strong to the extent that it has institutionalized mass support." The institutional strength of parties, he suggests, is measured by their ability to survive their founders; by their organizational complexity and depth, that is, their links to and support from mass social and economic organizations; and by the degree to

which political activists and power-seekers identify with their parties rather than merely seeing them as the means to other ends.
"In a highly developed political system," Huntington concludes, "it
is rare for political leaders to shift from one party to another, and
the movement of social groups and classes from one party to
another is usually a complex and lengthy historical process."

By all but the first of these tests, most Philippine political
parties have proved weak. While the two post-independence parties outlasted many of their national leaders, neither party had
built special or enduring ties with specific social groups, and
neither engendered strong and enduring loyalties among the rank
and file of provincial political leaders. Instead, politicians, voters,
and social groups have moved easily from one party to another as
their interests dictated. As Huntington might have predicted, the
pre-1972 Philippine political system as a whole proved to be weak
and unstable. The post-Marcos parties have been even less able to
meet his criteria for strong parties. That may help to explain why,
despite the broad popular support for the restoration of democracy
shown in 1986, that democracy remains dangerously unstable.

In a seminal article, "Cleavage Structures, Party Systems and
Voter Alignments," Seymour Martin Lipset and Stein Rokkan have
argued that during the periods of emancipation and mobilization
that preceded the appearance of fully mobilized nation-states in
Western Europe, different types of social cleavages commonly influenced political party alignments. Over time, the salient lines of
cleavage have been, successively, those between the central nation-building culture and ethnically, linguistically, or religiously
distinct subject populations; between the nation-state and the
historically established privileges of the church; between landed
interests and the growing interests of industry; and finally between owners and employers on the one side and agricultural
tenants, laborers and industrial workers on the other. As rival
political parties take opposing sides along these lines of cleavage,
interparty contests become debates about the major social and
economic issue of the age. Elections then decide a controversial
issue for a time, until it is reopened at a later election. Successive
elections make possible purposive, albeit cyclical, change: two
steps to the left, one step to the right, and two steps to the left
once again. Over time, all groups develop a stake in a system that
makes such change possible.

But when political parties are indistinguishable, as they are in
the Philippines, elections do not decide fundamental issues of
public policy. And when all parties are equally dominated by con-

servative interests, as are the parties of the Philippines, which are based on patron-client relations, elections cannot serve as mandates for socio-economic reform. That significant sectors of the Filipino intelligentsia have become advocates of violent, revolutionary change, and have succeeded in winning substantial support among the nation's poor is understandable in the light of the above.

III. ISSUES FOR DISCUSSION

1. Is the Philippine political party system unique? Where else are similar party systems to be found? Have they had similar consequences?

2. How did the American policy of moving quickly toward the development of democratic institutions affect the Philippines? Compare the Philippines with other countries of the region where different colonial policies were pursued.

3. What, in your opinion, are the prospects for the survival of democratic institutions in the Philippines? By what means could these prospects be improved?

IV. SELECTED READINGS

Friend, Theodore. *Between Two Empires: The Ordeal of the Philippines, 1929–1946.* New Haven: Yale University Press, 1965 (faculty background). An excellent account, including the roles and rivalries of Nacionalista party leaders Manuel Quezon and Sergio Osmena.

Hayden, Joseph Ralston. *The Philippines. A Study in National Development.* New York: Macmillan, 1950 (faculty background). The standard work on pre-World War II Philippine government and politics.

Huntington, Samuel P. *Political Order in Changing Societies.* New Haven: Yale University Press, 1968 (student reading). See Chapter 7 for an excellent discussion of the importance of strong political parties in the developing countries.

Lande, Carl. H. *Leaders, Factions and Parties: The Structure of Philippine Politics.* New Haven: Yale Southeast Asia Studies, Monograph Series No. 6, 1965 (student reading). An analysis of the Philippine party system before martial law.

Liang, Dapen. *The Development of Philippine Political Parties.* Hong Kong: South China Morning Post, 1939 (faculty background).

Lipset, Seymour Martin, and Rokkan, Stein. "Cleavage Structures, Party Systems and Voter Alignments: An Introduction." In *Party Systems and Voter Alignments: Cross National Perspectives,* edited by Seymour M. Lipset and Stein Rokkan, pp. 1–63. New York: Free Press, 1967 (faculty background). Useful for understanding the relationship between social conflict and politics in the Philippines.

Wurfel, David. *Filipino Politics: Development and Decay.* Ithaca, NY: Cornell University Press, 1988 (student reading). The best recent study of Philippine politics by an acknowledged expert.

Political Science: Thailand

Political Development and Political Participation in Thailand

Clark D. Neher

I. INTRODUCTION: CENTRAL POINTS

The history of Thailand over the past two decades illustrates how a Third World country, emerging from an autocratic past, can develop both politically and economically, through astute adaptation of Western political institutions and economic policies which were appropriate to traditional Thai ways.

As the only nation of Southeast Asia never to have been colonized, the Thais never had a foreign culture thrust upon their soil. As a result, they were able to choose and mold a political system which fit their indigenous culture.

Thailand's success in developing politically, however, is striking given the fact that for centuries the government was autocratic in form and spirit. Power was the privilege of a small elite, the coterie of officials surrounding the monarch, who were not accountable to the people and whose authority was enhanced by an aura of divinity attached to the highest levels of office. Those who ruled

415

were believed to possess superior ability and moral excellence. Common citizens exhibited little interest in affairs beyond their own village.

Even after the 1932 revolt, in which the absolute monarchy was overthrown and a constitutional monarchy established, politics remained in the hands of a small elite group, now mostly civilian bureaucrats and military generals. The coup d'etat became the primary means by which governments changed leadership. The military emerged as the dominant institution and has controlled political power in Thailand for about five of the past six decades. Politics in Thailand has been monopolized by military leaders and a small number of ranking government officials with no external competition or balance from forces outside the bureaucratic arena. That monopoly was confirmed in February 1991 when the military carried out a successful coup d'etat against the legitimate civilian government. The basis of political power was highly personalized and subject to informal political manipulations and loyalties.

Historically, the patron-client relationship has been the basis of Thai society. Patron-client ties are hierarchical, face-to-face relationships of reciprocity: but the relationship is not one of equality since the superior, with greater resources at his command, has power over the subordinate. Patrons use their resources and influence to provide benefits for their clients. The client reciprocates by offering his patron such benefits as labor, deference, or other services.

These patron-client ties have been at the heart of Thai politics, as political and military leaders form cliques and factions based on their personal relationships. Factional infighting has been the "stuff" of Thai politics, with coups determining how and when governments change.

Although both personalism and patron-client relationships remain important, they are no longer at the center of Thai politics. In the past two to three decades, Thai politics has evolved in the direction of increasing development and participation.

The success of the Thai people in fashioning a political system that has a high capacity to cope with the changing needs and demands of the people makes the Kingdom of Thailand an excellent case study for understanding political development themes. Namely,

• the evolution and professionalization of political institutions and the rise of pressure groups designed to represent the interests of an increasingly pluralistic society;

• increased democratization, expanding the involvement of citizens in the political sphere;

• reduced importance of personalism as well as increased importance of laws and governmental institutions in determining public policy;

• rapid economic development and its impact on political development.

II. MAJOR TOPICS

PRINCIPAL POLITICAL INSTITUTIONS OF THAI SOCIETY

Constitutions. The Thai propensity for redrafting the national constitution has been referred to as "faction constitutionalism," whereby each successive draft reflects, makes legitimate, and strengthens major shifts in factional dominance. Thai constitutions have not been considered the fundamental laws of the land; rather, they have functioned to facilitate the rule of the regime in power. Since 1932, Thailand has been governed under thirteen constitutions.

The most recent semi-democratic constitution, promulgated in 1978, struck a balance between democracy and military dominance. It called for a bicameral parliament with an appointed upper body, the senate, and an elected lower body known as the assembly. This constitution was in force until February 1991 and remained intact longer than any of the previous documents and was the underpinning for the semi-democratic system that emerged, a system in which Western-style democracy is balanced with military involvement in governmental affairs.

Military. Since the overthrow of the absolute monarchy, the Thai military has played the dominant role in Thai politics. Of the forty-nine cabinets during the period 1932 to 1991, twenty four were classified as military, eight as military-dominated and seventeen as civilian governments. The civilian governments, which were the most unstable, were often replaced by military regimes following army coups.

The reasons for military dominance include the weakness of civilian governments and the fact that the military is the most highly organized institution in the kingdom. In the face of perceived external and internal threats to Thai security, the military has proclaimed itself the only institution capable of protecting Thai sovereignty. Moreover, the hierarchical nature of the military is congruent with the nation's highly centralized political culture. Until 1991, the military had acquiesced to the administration of civilian Prime Minister Chatichai Choonhawan, partly because of his immense popularity and partly because he gave the military a free hand in determining its personnel matters. Former Army Commander-in-Chief Chavalit Yongchaiyut, himself a potential candidate for the position of prime minister, viewed Chatichai's administration as supportive of military interests. Moreover, following the Indonesian model, where the army plays a national development as well as a security role, the army has launched civil development projects, manned by army units, in all four regions of the country.

The fact that there was no successful coup d'etat between 1977 and 1991 is testimony to the professionalization which the army underwent in the four decades since 1932. The fact that communist insurgency has been wiped out and that there is no credible external threat to Thai security also undermined the major rationale for military intervention in governmental affairs. Nevertheless, two unsuccessful coups, in 1981 and 1985, and one successful coup in 1991 are reminders that the military is still a part of Thai politics.

Bureaucracy. For most of the modern era, Thailand has been a bureaucratic polity with the arena of politics located within the bureaucracy itself. The bureaucracy has been the bedrock of stability in a political system where top leadership positions change unpredictably. While coups may bring new factions into power, the bureaucracy continues its policy role with little overt change in direction. The military allows the civilian bureaucrats to run their ministries with a minimum of interference.

The formerly exclusive nature of the bureaucracy has been widened in recent years by the inclusion of technocrats who have assumed important positions within the government and have introduced a more rational element to the policymaking process. These highly educated officials have public service values rather than the traditional values of hierarchy, personalism, and security.

Moreover, the bureaucracy is no longer the only arena of politics. Extrabureaucratic institutions such as parliament, political parties, and pressure groups now play a significant role in determining public policy. Still, the bureaucracy is a powerful body in determining the direction and implementation of policies.

Parliament. From 1932 until the 1970s, elections in Thailand were held when the ruling groups became convinced that they could control the process and enhance their power. Today, elections provide more meaningful choices among candidates who represent alternative ideas. The parliament, no longer just a rubber stamp of the prime minister, engages in public debate about important issues.

In the present semi-democracy, although the senate is still dominated by the military, it has lost much of its influence. In 1989, for example, a constitutional amendment was passed making the speaker of the elected lower house, rather than the speaker of the appointed senate, the president of parliament. Another sign of parliament's higher standing has been the growing reluctance of military leaders to criticize members of parliament.

In the 1988 parliamentary election, eleven parties won seats. Prime Minister Chatichai eventually brought five of these parties into his coalition; the others formed the opposition. The parliament includes an unprecedented number of Sino-Thai business executives. In the past, Thailand's Chinese minority had generally confined their activities to the economic sphere. Their increased involvement in political affairs has raised concerns among some that an emerging "bourgeois polity" will be dominated by Chinese Thai.

Political Parties. In the past, political parties centered around individual political personalities. They had rudimentary organization only and were almost devoid of programs or issues. Elections often included over twenty parties, most of which were established for a particular candidate in a specific election.

Since the short-lived democratic period of 1973 to 1976, when a student-led revolt led to a temporary period of civilian rule, there has been a movement toward party institutionalization. The organizational apparatus for the major parties now remains intact after an election and plays an important role in the strategies of both the ruling coalition and the opposition. The parties are increasingly building long-term links with the citizenry and maintaining party discipline so that they can exert greater influence on policymaking and gain important posts in coalition governments.

Thai political parties can be placed on a spectrum from liberal to conservative; only a minority of the voters make choices based on issues. There are clear party strongholds in Bangkok and in other areas of the nation. In the last several elections, parties have been fewer in number, more coherent in structure, and better able to represent citizens' demands. Prime Minister Chatichai is leader of the conservative and pro-business Chat Thai party. Because his party won the largest plurality of votes in the 1988 election, Chatichai became a clear candidate for the position of prime minister.

Monarchy. Theoretically and legally above politics, the Thai monarch is the national symbol, the supreme patron who reigns over all, and the leader of the Buddhist religion. The prestige and veneration of the monarchy have grown since the 1950 coronation of King Phumiphol Adunyadej, who recently became the kingdom's longest reigning monarch.

In the 1980s, the king has become more involved in Thai politics. He supported the government of Prime Minister Prem Tinsulanond in both 1981 and 1985, when the military attempted to overthrow his administration. The king's strong stance against the attempted coups helped to defuse the crises and heightened his prestige and influence. In February 1991, the King acquiesced to the military coup leaders, but called for them to act responsibly and in the interests of the Thai people.

The universal veneration of the Thai people for their monarch has raised concerns about a potential succession crisis. The king promoted his daughter, Princess Sirindhorn, to the rank of *maha chakri* (crown princess), thereby placing her in the line of succession along with her brother, Crown Prince Vachiralongkorn. While there has never been a reigning queen, the crown prince has been widely criticized for his lack of serious commitment and discipline, while the princess is universally admired for her intelligence and dedication. At present, however, the crown prince has become more involved in ceremonial duties and it appears that he is being trained to succeed his father.

Peasantry. About 70 percent of the Thai people live in rural areas as farmers. As modernization has arrived, Thai farmers have become increasingly sophisticated in economic matters, moving from subsistence to surplus agriculture. More and more rural Thais engage in political activity, interact with officials, join interest groups, participate in village projects, and are knowledgeable about governmental processes.

Changes in the countryside in the past several decades have significantly affected the lives of the vast majority of Thais. Roads now penetrate into formerly isolated areas. Electricity is almost universally available. Transistor radios, motorcycles, television, and daily newspapers are an integral part of village life. Agricultural diversification has introduced cash crops into the Thai economy. Whereas twenty years ago rice constituted more than 90 percent of agricultural output, today the percentage is under fifty.

Sino-Thai Business Community. Traditionally, the Chinese minority (about ten percent of the population) dominated the Thai economy while the Thai majority prevailed in politics. In the past decade, however, a fundamental change has occurred in Thai politics with the Sino-Thai becoming more involved. Because of the high degree of Sino-Thai assimilation (compared to all other Southeast Asian nations), the expansion of the middle class, the new importance of technocrats in the bureaucracy, and the realization that government policies do affect the state of the economy, business interests have become increasingly involved in political matters.

The rising importance of the Sino-Thai dominated middle class (in a nation which had no such class until recently) has prompted some analysts to suggest that Thailand has developed from a bureaucratic to a bourgeois polity. This new class of entrepreneurs, technocrats, and government officials tends to view military rule as an anachronism, unsuited to the nation's well-being. As this class expands, the traditional personalistic form of politics is giving way to a more stable, pluralistic and institutionalized political system.

DEMOCRATIZATION

Prime Minister Chatichai Choonhawan. The most auspicious sign of Thai democratization was the rise to power of Chatichai Choonhawan, the first elected member of parliament to become prime minister since 1976. Chatichai assumed his position following the 1988 elections, when the political party he led received a plurality of votes. The way for civilian leadership under Chatichai was opened when his predecessor, General Prem Tinsulanond, decided not to accept another term as prime minister. Prem, who had led Thailand during a period of stability and economic growth since 1980, had been deemed acceptable to both civilian and military forces and had been expected to continue in office. The smooth transition from Prem to Chatichai was an encouraging sign of Thailand's evolution toward democracy. Chatichai assumed power without relying on the support of the army; the constitutional provisions for elections worked well in the transfer of political power.

Chatichai had served as minister of foreign affairs, minister of industry, and deputy minister under previous administrations. Because of his close ties to business interests and flamboyant lifestyle, most analysts believed his tenure as prime minister would be short. However, Chatichai initiated a number of highly popular policies, thereby enhancing his *baramee* (charisma) in the minds of the populace.

Chatichai raised the salaries of government officials and the minimum wage for laborers, introduced controls on the environmentally unsound practices of the logging industry, and stood up to the United States on trade and other economic issues. His idea to develop war-ravaged Indochina as a trading market was especially popular with the business community who sought to open economic ties with the Vietnamese.

Chatichai's policies were supported by his coalition majority. Oppositionists spoke out against many of his initiatives, and the press was free to present all sides of the controversies. Military leaders publicly expressed support for Chatichai's administration and did not intervene until 1991.

Despite Chatichai's widespread support, questions were raised about the government's stability and effectiveness. The traditions of personalism and factionalism did not entirely disappear with the development of democracy. Even among the coalition partners, factional infighting remained the norm as party leaders vied for the most influential cabinet positions.

A related problem, that of corruption, continued to affect the political process. The phenomenal economic growth rates of the 1980s brought large amounts of capital into the system. While this provided the financial resources for economic development efforts, there were charges that officials were using public funds for private gain. When the military overthrew Chatichai's administration, the coup leaders cited pervasive corruption as the chief reason for the action.

The stability of Thailand's semi-democracy was partially a function of the government's capacity to meet the needs of the citizenry. The economic boom thus contributed to the government's stability. A second potential difficulty related to the monarchical succession issue, as discussed earlier. The important symbolic role of the monarchy could change fundamentally with the succession of the crown prince.

ECONOMIC DEVELOPMENT

Economic Growth. For several decades, Thailand has sustained a seven percent annual growth rate, a rate equalled by only a few other developing nations. More remarkably, the kingdom's economic growth in 1987 to 1990 was about 10 to 11 percent, the highest of any country. During these boom years, the inflation rate was under 4 percent.

Coincident with these high growth rates was the expanding export sector, which in the late 1980s grew about 24 percent each year. Manufacturing now accounts for a larger share of the gross domestic product than does agriculture. Foreign investment has grown at a similarly rapid rate, with Japan, Taiwan, the United States, Hong Kong, and South Korea as the leading investors.

While 70 percent of the Thai people are in the agricultural sphere of the economy, the number engaged in rice farming is decreasing. Thai farmers have diversified to crops such as vegetables, fruits, maize, tapioca, coffee, flowers, sugar, rubber, and livestock. Although the farming areas have not developed economically as rapidly as urban areas, the standard of living in the countryside has improved noticeably in the past decades. Nevertheless, the urban bias of Thai economic development is clear both from the government emphasis on manufacturing and the higher percentage of budget allocations centered on Bangkok.

The factors responsible for the kingdom's economic successes include a commitment to free-market, export-driven policies, carried out by highly trained, and generally conservative, technocrats. Those in charge of economic policy carefully screen development projects to ensure that they will contribute to overall economic growth. These new officials, who are Western educated, are not as steeped in personalistic, clientelist politics as their predecessors or their peers in neighboring countries.

An important component of sustained economic development is bureaucratic stability. Although coups have been the standard mechanism for changing governments, they have rarely undermined the continuity of policy. The Thai government has adhered to a consistent set of policies, with incremental (rather than fundamental) changes introduced.

The involvement of Thailand's Chinese minority cannot be overestimated as a factor explaining the vibrancy of the economy. This dynamic minority has provided leadership in banking, export-import manufacturing, industrialization, monetary policy, foreign investment, and diversification. As a result of the autonomy granted the Chinese, this entrepreneurial minority has reinvested its profits within Thailand, and comparatively little capital has left the country.

Another element in Thailand's economic development has been its ability, in just one generation, to lower its population growth from 3.0 percent to 1.5 percent. The decrease is credited to a massive government-sponsored education program that has changed attitudes about optimum family size and made birth control devices readily available. The result is a higher standard of living for families, higher educational attainment and literacy, and lower poverty rates.

Obstacles to Economic Growth. The greatest obstacle to continued economic growth is the poor state of the infrastructure. Bangkok's thoroughfares are clogged with automobiles and port facilities cannot handle the growing ship traffic. Electricity and telecommunications are unreliable.

A second problem is the depletion of Thailand's natural resources, especially its forests. Floods, soil erosion, and droughts have resulted from the government's almost total lack, until recently, of control over the logging industry.

The number of college graduates in the "hard" sciences and technology is not sufficient to meet the country's developmental needs. Thai universities produce only a third of the engineers required, and higher salaries in the private sector attract qualified graduates away from the public sphere.

One further source of difficulty for the Thai economy stems, ironically, from its very success. Foreign investment and trade have made the Thai economy vulnerable to the vagaries of the world's capitalist system. Economic policymakers have thus far diversified imports and exports sufficiently to ensure that a downturn in one sector will not cripple the overall economy.

SUMMARY

Thailand has evolved into a semi-democracy with new institutions available for more effective political participation. These new institutions have been assimilated into existing cultural patterns. Thai leadership has been able to cope with the tensions which have arisen from the process of democratization. The Thai political system meshes with the personalism and status hierarchy that have been an important part of Thai culture.

At a formal level, there is open participation, a free press, and free elections. At an informal level, Thai society is still dominated by a small proportion of the society that controls the military, economic, and political spheres. Today, the Thai people tend to regard their government as legitimate, because of both the progress made toward democratization and steady economic growth.

The prospects for parliamentary democracy depend on the capacity of the government to meet the economic and security needs of the people, the continued vibrancy of the economy, the restraint of military leaders, and a smooth monarchical succession. The continued strengthening of such democratic institutions as the parliament and political parties, and the concomitant decrease in personalism and self-interested and corrupt policymaking are likewise crucial.

Thailand today is fundamentally different from the country it was just a decade or two ago, when the military-dominated bureaucracy controlled society. With democratization and economic development flourishing simultaneously, and new groups emerging to challenge the traditional power elites, Thai society has evolved into a more confident, stable, and vibrant nation. The military coup in 1991 has detoured but not destroyed the evolution toward democracy. The appointment of an interim civilian prime minister following the coup is indicative of the military's concern for legitimizing the government.

Because semi-democracy involves the participation of most groups within the society, the political system is accepted as legitimate by the rulers and the ruled. Thais do not feel oppressed by their government leaders and (with rare exceptions) civil liberties are protected. Thailand's time-tested capacity to cope with changing demands and to assert its own destiny remains intact.

III. ISSUES FOR DISCUSSION

1. What unique characteristics of Thai society make political development and participation more likely to succeed than in other Third World nations?

2. What relationship is there between Thailand's political and economic development? Can one kind of development occur without the other?

3. Is it possible for a Third World country to adapt all aspects of Westernization? Would Thailand's government be more effective with a more Western-style democracy?

IV. SELECTED READINGS

(All these books are available in paperback and are appropriate for faculty and students.)

Neher, Clark. *Politics in Southeast Asia.* Cambridge, MA: Schenkman Publishing Co., 1987. An overview of the politics in each of the nations of Southeast Asia, with an emphasis on Thailand.

Ramsay, Ansil, and Mungkandi, Wiwat. *Thailand-U.S. Relations*, University of California-Berkeley, Institute of East Asian Studies Research Papers, 1988. A collection of essays on domestic Thai politics as well as on Thai relations with the United States. Chapters by Ansil Ramsay, Suchit Bunbongkarn, and William Overholt are particularly readable for students without a background in the area.

Girling, John L.S. *Thailand: Society and Politics*. Ithaca: Cornell University Press, 1981. The most detailed, but now somewhat out-of-date analysis of Thai politics. Excellent background chapters for students focusing on political history and political culture.

Morell, David, and Samudavanija, Chai-Anan. *Political Conflict in Thailand: Reform, Reaction, Revolution*. Cambridge, MA: Oelgesclager, Gunn and Hain, 1981. Insightful discussion of factional struggles for power among Thai politicians. Focus on the student-led revolt of October 1973 and the reasons for the return of the military in 1976.

IV
Sociology

Sociology:
China

Comparative Revolution: The Case of China

Andrew G. Walder

I. INTRODUCTION: CENTRAL POINTS

It would be difficult to justify the exclusion of China from a course on comparative revolution. While relevant to a very wide array of questions, the Chinese case is especially useful in teaching about several of important themes that have dominated the study of revolution in recent years. They are:

• The role of mass poverty and hardship in generating the discontent that can fuel revolutionary movements;

• The role of foreign invasion and devastating warfare in generating both opportunities for revolutionaries and mass support for their appeals;

• The role of organization and strategy in enabling revolutionary challengers to mobilize sufficient resources to defeat incumbent states having superior military power;

• The role of a prior condition of state breakdown, or its opposite, state cohesion, in determining whether a mass-supported revolutionary challenge will succeed or be defeated.

Having spawned a revolution which, together with that of Russia, was the most momentous of the twentieth century, and the-prototype for the guerrilla warfare so prevalent since the end of the Second World War, China has never been far from the thoughts of comparative theorists. Its long process of dynastic decline and revolution has informed a number of distinguished comparative studies. Barrington Moore's *Social Origins of Dictatorship and Democracy* (1966) placed landlord-peasant relations at the center of attention, and highlighted China's inability to resolve the "peasant question" as the primary explanation for its communist revolution. Eric Wolf's *Peasant Wars in the Twentieth Century* (1969) examined the rural roots of communist success. Later, Theda Skocpol's *States and Social Revolutions* (1979) would highlight the historical conjuncture of peasant rebellion, international pressure on the prerevolutionary state, and a lack of cohesion between ruling class and state apparatus as the necessary combination of circumstances for a major social revolution.

China's process of revolution was long and complex, beginning with dynastic decline, internal peasant rebellion, and imperialist aggression in the last half of the nineteenth century, and continuing through successive waves of abortive republican revolution, social disintegration and warlordism, large-scale foreign military invasion, and guerrilla warfare in the first half of the twentieth. This long historical process throws into vivid relief virtually every explanatory factor that students of revolution have considered: the abrupt impact of a Europe-centered world economy and state system; mass poverty and endemic peasant unrest; the growth of organized workers' movements and ensuing urban insurrections; the emergence of modern nationalism; guerrilla strategy, organization and warfare; and repeated and egregious instances of state breakdown. Chinese case materials would therefore greatly enhance any course on revolution, whether taught thematically or case-by-case.

II. MAJOR TOPICS

POVERTY, DISCONTENT, AND PEASANT REBELLION

The argument that there is a direct link between economic hardship and collective violence has been challenged repeatedly in recent decades by analysts of revolution. Increasingly, analysts have moved away from models that posit a direct relationship between the level of hardship and the level of collective violence, and have focused on other factors: for example, community organization, class formation fostered by changes in the organization of production, the availability of competent leadership, and local circumstances that provide opportunities to act. This shift in

scholarly attention was stimulated in part by the failure of historical studies of western Europe and North America to uncover clear
temporal or statistical links between levels of economic hardship
and collective disorders.

Like other traditional agrarian societies, China had a long history of mass poverty, periodic famine, and peasant rebellion. Several dynasties were in fact toppled by large peasant rebellions;
others were so weakened by them that they soon passed from the
historical scene. One of the long-standing verities of conventional
Chinese historiography is that the end of a "dynastic cycle" was
typically marked by an increase in such rebellions, which in turn
were caused by a deteriorating dynastic structure that contributed to an increase in mass hardship by failing, for example, to
maintain water works or provide traditional famine relief.

Whether there was in fact a neat relationship between dynastic
decline, mass poverty, and rural rebellion as traditional
historiography sometimes assumes is unclear; it is generally,
however, agreed that qualitatively different forces were set in motion in the late nineteenth century to bring about the end of
Imperial China and usher in the modern era of revolution. Since
throughout its history China had periodically suffered large-scale
famine without major political repercussions, it is clear that even
if economic hardship was a necessary condition of rebellion, other
factors must have been at work to mobilize the people to take
effective political action.

The search for a connection between hardship, peasant rebellion, and China's modern revolution has focused on the following
questions:

1) What was the origin of traditional patterns of rural banditry
and local rebellion, and what was the relationship between these
traditional rebels and the Communist movement in the 1930s and
1940s?

2) Were there changes in the nature of Chinese village organization that made economic hardship more intolerable and politically explosive in the modern period?

Researchers have found that rural banditry and traditional secret societies were often a response to material deprivation, and
were especially prevalent in poorer regions and among deprived
social classes. However, research has uncovered two distinct traditional rebel types, and neither contributed to the rural revolutionary movement of the Communist party. One type of rebel
organization was "predatory" in nature: peopled by poor or dispossessed peasants, it survived in hilly or marshy hinterlands, and

preyed periodically on settlements. Sometimes these predatory groups would grow or coalesce into a sufficiently large organization to challenge local government control for brief periods, or even incite serious regional rebellion.

The second type of traditional rebel organization was "defensive" in nature: established by village notables or leading clansmen and enrolling poorer members of the community or lineage as soldiers, these local indigenous militias defended the village against predatory attack and promoted community interests in disputes with other villages. Sometimes they developed common customs and rituals and coalesced into regional forces that led rebellions against state authority.

Neither type of traditional rebel organization made a ready ally for the Communist movement: instead, they either provided competing outlets for disaffected peasants or were political rivals of the Communists. Predatory rebels, while certainly alienated from the mainstream of society, were motivated by self-enrichment through plunder. It was an orientation that clashed sharply with the discipline of Communist troops and rural cadres, whose strategy it was to provide effective government and rent relief in rural areas. In liberating areas that had long been strongholds of predatory rebels, Communist cadres took on the tasks of defending the villages they had organized against predatory attack, and of pacifying or eradicating these traditional bandits.

Defensive rebel organizations, on the other hand, were political rivals of the Communists. Dominated by the same village elites whom Communist cadres sought to replace, they stressed community and clan rather than class and national allegiance. Communist cadres had to undermine these local militias before they could establish an effective government of their own and recruit local peasants into the greater Red Army.

In sum, not only was there no simple relationship between economic hardship and traditional peasant rebellion—poor peasants were recruited into both defensive and predatory organizations—but there was a largely antagonistic relationship between traditional peasant rebellion and the Communist revolution.

Other scholars have argued that changes in the traditional Chinese village altered the equation between economic hardship and peasant rebellion in the modern period. Drawing insights from Barrington Moore's discussion of the role of local granaries and famine relief in Imperial China, and from Eric Wolf's discussion of the impact of the spread of "North Atlantic capitalism," some students of revolution have pinpointed the decline of the traditional corporate village as the precursor of modern peasant rebellion.

This argument was developed by students of Southeast Asia, and has generated considerable controversy within that field in recent years [*See the essay on "Comparative Revolution: The Case of Vietnam"*]. It has found some proponents among students of the Chinese revolution who argue that corporate village institutions, such as kinship organizations, traditionally provided famine relief and guaranteed, to the best of their ability, a substance level of existence. According to these analysts, however, once world markets penetrated rural areas they stimulated a number of changes that undercut traditional village subsistence guarantees: land became a commodity, resulting in a decline in common grazing, foraging, and hunting areas and restrictions on traditional water rights; wealthy villagers turned to nonagricultural enterprise in towns, neglecting their traditional village and kin obligations and even turning their village properties over to paid agents; and specialization in single-crop commodity production was encouraged, leaving the peasantry newly vulnerable to fluctuations in world demand and prices.

Proponents of this view claim that such non-violent changes in village economy and institutions prepare rural areas for revolution. They argue that there exists a traditional "moral economy" of the peasant, in which the subsistence guarantee is an inalienable right— a right violated increasingly as the corporate village economy changes and agriculture shifts to commodity production. Recurring natural disasters pose a threat to traditional subsistence rights, resulting in peasant outrage that can develop into political rebellion; peasants turn to revolutionary parties to reclaim these traditional rights. Communist parties, therefore, find support among the peasantry because their egalitarian, anti-capitalist and anti-imperialist stance appears to champion traditional values against alien institutions and cultural practices. Such scholars as Edward Friedman (*Backward toward Revolution*) and Ralph Thaxton (*The World Turned Rightside Up*) have applied this novel argument to the case of China, but their approach and supporting evidence have been the subject of considerable controversy as have similar approaches to the study of Vietnam. **Key areas of contention are whether traditional village institutions in fact provided subsistence guarantees, and whether world markets had penetrated the vast Chinese countryside to such an extent as to significantly transform peasant agriculture in the rebellious districts in the hinterland.**

WAR, NATIONALISM, AND REVOLUTION

One important, though recently neglected, general argument about modern peasant revolutions based on the study of China is that contained in Chalmers Johnson's *Peasant Nationalism and Communist Power* (1962). Johnson argues that an upsurge of peasant nationalism was responsible for the mass support that underlay several postwar communist revolutions. He bases his thesis primarily on a study of the Communist movement from 1937–1945, arguing that Mao's peasant-based strategy of revolution did not meet with great success until the Japanese invasion and occupation. During that time the Communist party turned from its earlier radical policies of rural land redistribution toward moderate programs of tax reform, while at the same time appealing to the people's anti-Japanese sentiments. Frequent atrocities by undisciplined Japanese troops, as well as the brutal expropriation and pacification policies of the occupation, generated for the first time a sense of nationalism among peasants in vast areas of the country where Communist guerrillas were the only Chinese forces operating. Johnson argues that these conditions and growing sentiments pushed peasants into the Red Army and allowed the Communist party to ride to power on nationalist sentiments. Johnson suggests his thesis is of general relevance to the case of Yugoslavia as well; it could also applied to Vietnam, Korea, and other cases in Asia. This view holds that it is nationalist ideology, not rural hardship or class struggle, that impels Communists to power via a rural strategy. **In ignoring the relevance of rural social and economic conditions, however, this argument has not found many adherents among political sociologists.**

ORGANIZATION, STRATEGY, AND MASS MOBILIZATION

Over the past two decades a broad group of scholars has conceived a "resource mobilization perspective," which stresses the importance of organizational capacity, solidarity, discipline, and strategy to effective collective action and successful political challenge. Such theorists of social movements as Charles Tilly, William Gamson, and Mayer Zald, among many others, conceptualize revolution as essentially a contest between competing political organizations. As a result of their works, the process of political mobilization became dominant concern of scholars in the field during the 1970s.

Having pioneered a successful guerrilla organization and strategy that would inspire many subsequent imitators, and having united the Chinese mainland, against overwhelming odds where a succession of governments, warlords, and parties had failed, the Communist party of China is perhaps the prototypical case of an effective organization that determined the outcome of a revolution.

Scholars have identified several facets of Communist organization and strategy in rural areas, although placing varying degrees of emphasis on them:

1) Intensive and continuing ideological training and strict political supervision that served to maintain discipline among troops and cadres.

2) Stable, effective village government, free from corruption, in "liberated areas."

3) "Selective incentives" offered to family members of Red Army recruits in the form of preferential treatment in the administration of tax and land policy, and, conversely, the penalization of opponents through discriminatory treatment in these areas.

4) Policies that benefitted the peasantry as a class: rent reform, tax reduction, redistribution of land from collaborationist landlords or Nationalist officials to the landless.

5) Military and political career opportunities provided rural residents who traditionally had no such prospects for upward mobility.

6) Protection of youths from military conscription by Nationalist armies or from abduction by Japanese labor gangs. 7) The "hit and run" military strategy of meeting the Japanese or Nationalists in the field only when or where Communist forces were strong enough to have the advantage.

Few analysts dispute the centrality of organization and strategy in Communist success. Yet they differ considerably about which of these factors were crucial. For Chalmers Johnson, Communist organization was crucial because it articulated a national ideology and focused on strategic areas where as the sole Chinese organization, it could reap any benefit accruing from the upsurge of peasant nationalism. For Mark Selden (*The Yenan Way in Revolutionary China*), the policies that benefitted the peasantry as a class were crucial. For "rational choice" students of politics, such as Mancur Olsen, of overriding importance were the selective incentives [*See the essay on the "Comparative Revolution: The Case of Vietnam"*], and the public goods in the form of stable, non-corrupt village government as provided by the Communists. Institutional analysts such as Philip Selznick (*The Organizational Weapon*) and

Franz Schurmann (*Ideology and Organization in Communist China*), hold that the systematically articulated and inculcated Chinese Communist ideology provided a practical guide to action and a unified, simplified worldview that rendered Communist organization unusually resilient and disciplined. These different analytical perspectives on Chinese revolutionary organization enrich the study of "resource mobilization" as an explanation for revolution.

STATE-CENTERED EXPLANATIONS

In the 1980s, state-centered explanations of revolution—so-called because they emphasize the coherence of state structures, their internal politics, their relationship to the ruling classes, and the international pressures to which they are subject—have taken a central place among theories of revolution. According to this perspective, as articulated in Skocpol's *States and Social Revolutions*, in the major revolutions, mass movements from below, typically peasant rebellions, do not by themselves topple previously stable old regimes. Rather, they succeed only if they occur in the context of a split between the state and the ruling class occurring in conjunction with international economic or military challenges.

China figures prominently in Skocpol's analysis because it appears to illustrate the central features of a state-centered perspective. The Communist movement in China did not overthrow a unified and coherent state. Rather, it moved into a vacuum created by the Japanese invasion and the Nationalist retreat to far western China; and after the end of World War II it won, in a political contest, control from a corrupt Nationalist government that was beset by factionalism and the fragmentation of its military power, whose currency was collapsing under conditions of hyper-inflation, and that had irretrievably lost control over cities it had evacuated in ignominious retreat twelve years earlier.

In *Civil War in China* (1978), Suzanne Pepper analyzes the pivotal 1945–49 period, in which the Nationalists moved from a position of strength to defeat, and portrays a ruling party plagued by corruption, an incompetent military strategy, and economic mismanagement, and engaging in police-state terror campaigns against democrats among the intelligentsia and middle classes. Its miserable postwar performance alienated most urban citizens, leading them to view the little-known rural Communists, of whom many were suspicious, as the only viable Chinese government. Such a review of the historical record leads one legitimately to question whether the revolution should be laid more to Communist strategy and organization or to Nationalist bungling. That history is fascinating in its own right, but more importantly, it provokes basic questions about the underlying causes of revolution.

III. ISSUES FOR DISCUSSION

Instructors are referred to the questions at the conclusion of section I of the paper. These may be useful in prompting class discussion.

IV. SELECTED READINGS

Hinton, William. *Fanshen: Documentary of Revolution in a Chinese Village.* New York: Vintage, 1966 (student reading). Classic, readable account of how Communist guerrillas mobilized peasants and conducted revolution in the countryside during the late 1940s.

Johnson, Chalmers. *Peasant Nationalism and Communist Power.* Stanford: Stanford University Press, 1962 (faculty background). Argues that the Japanese invasion generated an intense nationalism among Chinese peasants, one which the Communists were able to harness and which was essential to their victory.

Pepper, Suzanne. *Civil War in China.* Berkeley: University of California Press, 1978 (faculty background). Argues that whatever the Communists may have done in the countryside before the defeat of Japan, the political contest of 1945–49, featuring a battle over public opinion and not guerrilla warfare, determined the Communist victory. Questions whether that outcome should be seen less as the result of Communist policy or mass support than as a result of the corruption, repression, and incompetence of the Nationalists.

Selden, Mark. *The Yenan Way in Revolutionary China.* Cambridge: Harvard University Press, 1971 (faculty background). Account of how the base area of Yenan was administered in the 1930s and 1940s; argues that an effective and fair government implemented policies that generated mass support for the Communists.

Skocpol, Theda. *States and Social Revolutions: A Comparative Analysis of France, Russia, and China.* New York: Cambridge University Press, 1979 (faculty background). Case study of China that provides an excellent overview of the secondary literature and stresses Nationalist weakness and the nature of Communist strategy. A good brief overview, useful for preparing lectures, of the entire period from the mid-nineteenth century to 1949.

OTHER BOOKS MENTIONED IN TEXT:

Friedman, Edward. *Backward toward Revolution; the Chinese Revolutionary Party.* Berkeley: University of California Press, 1974.

Moore, Barrington. *Social Origins of Dictatorship and Democracy; Lord and Peasant in the Making of the Modern World.* Boston: Beacon Press, 1966.

Schurmann, H. Franz. *Ideology and Organization in Communist China.* Berkeley: University of California Press, 1966.

Selzenic, Philip. *The Organizational Weapon; a Study of Bolshevik Strategy and Tactics.* Glencoe, IL: Free Press, 1960.

Thaxton, Ralph. *The World Turned Rightside Up: Revolutionary Legitimacy in the Peasant World.* New Haven: Yale University Press, 1983.

Wolf, Eric R. *Peasant Wars of the Twentieth Century.* New York: Harper & Row, 1973.

Sociology:
China

Marxist Social Thought: Maoism

Andrew G. Walder

I.   INTRODUCTION:
     CENTRAL POINTS

II. MAJOR TOPICS
     *MAOISM AS A DOCTRINE OF
     REVOLUTION IN THE
     THIRD WORLD*
     *MAOISM AS POST-1949
     POLITICAL DOCTRINE*

III. ISSUES FOR DISCUSSION

IV. SELECTED READINGS

I. INTRODUCTION: CENTRAL POINTS

There are two quite separate and distinct versions of Maoist ideology: the first is the theory of third world peasant revolution developed and put into practice in the decades leading up to China's liberation in 1949, and the second is the radical ideology that was given expression in the Chinese Cultural Revolution in the 1960s. Each version has raised considerable controversy about its position in the history of Marxist thought. Because these controversies bear upon the defining features of classical Marxism, Leninism, and Stalinism, a classroom examination of Maoism may help students to clarify their thinking about the Marxist tradition in general. And because Maoism provides a link between the Marxism-Leninism of the Russian Revolution and the ideologies of more recent rural-based national liberation movements, it has broad relevance to contemporary politics that few other varieties of Marxism enjoy. As a theory of peasant revolution Maoism embraces Lenin's argument that revolution against capitalism would begin in countries threatened by imperialist domination, and not, as orthodox Marxists argued, in advanced capitalist nations. Just as Lenin revised classical Marxism to make it applicable to economically underdeveloped Russia, Mao revised Leninism to make it applicable to third world peasant societies. In a further departure from Marxist orthodoxy, Mao emphasized will, discipline, and ideological enthusiasm as the major determinants of history, in contrast to Marx and Engels' strict materialist emphasis upon the development of modes of production and class structures.

The controversy surrounding this version of Maoism focuses on whether these changes represent a logical and coherent development of a theory which as originally formulated by Marx, was found repeatedly to be at odds with actual social and political developments, or whether they represent a distortion of that theory. Some have seen Maoism as a further distortion of Marxist doctrine that was begun by Lenin and Stalin; others have seen it as a logical extension of Marxist analytic principles.

The second version of Maoism is that of a unique and iconoclastic strain of Marxism-Leninism. During China's Cultural Revolution, Maoists declared virtually all other socialist regimes to be "revisionist," that is, to have departed from the main tenets of Marxism-Leninism and to have degenerated into bureaucracies ruled by a corrupt "new bourgeoisie." Maoists chastised the rebellion of youth and workers against the party and government apparatus, punished bureaucrats and "bourgeois academics" in kangaroo courts and secret prisons, and tore apart the country's administrative apparatus, replacing it with "revolutionary committees" that claimed to be the highest expression of proletarian democracy.

The main controversy surrounding this version of Maoism has to do with its relation to different versions of Soviet and east European Marxism. Was Maoism a subvariety of the repressive doctrine of Stalinism, which saw traitors and class enemies everywhere and which justified mass purges and executions to seek out these enemies? Or was Maoism a strand of the post-Stalin revisionism that emerged in eastern Europe and the Soviet Union in the mid-1950s, and which sought to soften the authoritarian and bureaucratic nature of Soviet-style regimes? The predominant interpretation of this version of Maoism in the 1970s held that it is a populist and egalitarian doctrine, concerned with essentially the same problems of bureaucratic power and corruption that were identified by east European revisionists. In the 1980s, as more became known about actual events during China's Cultural Revolution, a revised interpretation emerged, one that regarded Maoism as a violent, fundamentalist offshoot of Stalinism, with its suspicions of a ubiquitous conspiracy against socialism, pursuing the same intolerant and repressive policies, although employing means far more extreme than those resorted to by Stalin.

The study of Maoism may thus be expected to provoke a lively and heated debate in the classroom, and encourage students to apply their knowledge of Marxist social thought to the interpretive problems that Maoism presents.

• Is the Maoist theory of peasant revolution in the third world a logical extension of basic Marxist propositions, or does it represent a distortion of a doctrine that in its original form has repeatedly proved irrelevant to twentieth century realities?

• As a doctrine of liberation from imperialist hegemony is the Maoist theory of peasant revolution more nationalist than Marxist?

• Was post-1949 Maoism a liberating and egalitarian doctrine that accurately diagnosed and addressed problems of Soviet-style socialism, or was it itself a form of Stalinism, an intolerant and repressive ideology that diverted attention from systemic faults by launching campaigns against hidden enemies and traitors?

II. MAJOR TOPICS

MAOISM AS A DOCTRINE OF REVOLUTION IN THE THIRD WORLD

Chinese Communist party theoreticians, as well as many outside observers, trace the origins of Mao's theory of rural revolution to Marxism by way of Lenin's theories of imperialism and of revolutionary vanguard party. In the beginning of the twentieth century, Lenin redefined revolutionary Marxism by amending to the orthodox Marxist theory in two ways. First, Lenin noted that, with the advent of the age of imperialism, capitalism had become a worldwide phenomenon. With the profits gained in their exploitation of underdeveloped nations, capitalists from advanced nations were able to offer workers in their own countries higher wages than they had in the earlier stage of capitalism. Lenin theorized that revisionist leaders of labor movements succumb to the lure of higher wages, develop a mere "trade union mentality" and, forsaking revolutionary consciousness, adopt an essentially "bourgeois" and reformist strategy of winning greater political rights and economic concessions for workers within the framework of capitalist democracy. Lenin therefore looked for the revolutionary spark to be set off in third world nations, which became the functional equivalent of the proletariat on a global scale.

Second, and as a logical extension of the above reasoning, Lenin argued that workers were easily led into false consciousness by capitalist concessions and revisionist leadership. He insisted, therefore, that a revolutionary party's line of action should not be determined by workers' consciousness at any given time. If workers appear to lack revolutionary consciousness, it does not mean that objective economic conditions are not yet ripe, but that revolutionary leadership is lacking. Lenin's innovative vision was of a vanguard party, separate from the working class itself, which would be the true repository of revolutionary consciousness. This "party of a new type" would be charged with the task of instilling that consciousness in workers and any others who would submit to its rigid discipline in an effort to achieve not electoral success but political warfare.

Mao's doctrine of revolution in the third world extended these two ideas further. In essays written in the 1920s, he analyzed rural classes, arguing that rural wage laborers and poor tenant farmers were the backbone of revolution; that "middle peasants" would waver in their allegiances; and that rich peasants and landlords were conservative forces. A revolutionary movement could be built in rural areas among these social classes, but in order to win power they would have to develop an alliance with other classes: the small but radical urban proletariat, and the "patriotic" capitalist class (those who resented economic domination by foreign imperialists). Mao argued that such a coalition of classes, with peasants as the main revolutionary force, could succeed in liberating China from imperialist domination.

Mao adopted Lenin's notion of a vanguard party as the repository of true proletarian revolutionary consciousness and placed it at the head of a largely peasant army. Revolution would thus be won by armed struggle in the countryside. From Lenin's notions of ironclad discipline Mao developed his ideas regarding the strict ideological indoctrination of troops and mutual supervision and criticism in small groups, ideas that would be put into practice by the Red Army.

Some scholars have argued that these changes distort Marx's original analytical thought, which repudiated utopian efforts to create a socialist society before objective conditions were ripe. Marx insisted that capitalism would prepare the way for genuine socialism, and that revolution would break out first in advanced capitalist nations where a large working class had become conscious of its historical mission. These critics argue that Lenin had fundamentally altered this doctrine by effectively ignoring the original "scientific" emphasis on objective economic developments, replacing it with an emphasis on discipline, and sheer revolutionary will. Mao's revision of Leninism, so this argument goes, represents an even further distortion of Marxism: it totally ignored the restrictions of economic backwardness and focused its strategy on the poor peasantry of a precapitalist rural economy, not the urban proletariat of a capitalist and industrial economy. Furthermore, by emphasizing political indoctrination and military struggle, Maoism completed the distortion of orthodox Marxism into a utopian doctrine that stressed superior will power and proper consciousness—precisely the kind of doctrine that Marx himself derided.

In summary, then, the Maoist doctrine of revolution in the third world has been regarded by some as the logical culmination of a process begun by Lenin of adapting and creatively developing a Marxist intellectual doctrine found repeatedly to be wrong in its predictions. Others see Maoism as completing the distortion, turning a scientific and intellectually rigorous analysis into a doctrine of power seizure that was essentially about discipline, organization, and strategy. The tension between these two interpretations rarely fails to stimulate student interest and debate.

MAOISM AS A POST-1949 POLITICAL DOCTRINE

The post-1949 doctrine of the Cultural Revolution— the version of Maoism that represents a critique of Soviet style socialism— is subject to similarly conflicting interpretations. On the one hand, Maoism has been interpreted as an essentially anti-bureaucratic and populist doctrine designed to avoid the ills of the Stalinist legacy in the Soviet Union. On the other hand, Maoism has been interpreted, whatever its self-proclaimed attitudes toward bureaucracy and corruption, as a radical doctrine essentially Stalinist in its presuppositions and consequences: the most important of these being that the revolution is constantly threatened by subversive elements which must be rooted out and punished.

Those who subscribe to the first interpretation hold that Mao launched the Cultural Revolution out of concern over the effects of Soviet-style socialism. His criticism focused chiefly on the growing prevalence of the following phenomena:

- a privileged stratum of officials who lived in comfort, whose children were given preferential treatment in school admissions and job assignments, and who showed clear signs of becoming a self-sustaining oligarchy;
- inefficiency, sloth, incompetence, self-promotion, and corruption among officials;
- stratification at all levels of society; the reliance on graded bureaucratic ranks with their corresponding privileges; wage differentials within a place of work; growing differences in income

and life style between city and rural workers;

• interest in foreign "bourgeois" dress, literature, entertainment, and consumer goods;

• the predisposition among some officials and managers to engage in "capitalist" practices to subscribe to profit motives and to motivate managers and workers with monetary bonuses;

• a tendency among officials, intellectuals, and youth to de-emphasize revolutionary values and traditions and embrace material, practical, "bourgeois" preoccupations and work habits; and a tendency to set themselves apart from the masses in their life style, attitudes, and daily routines.

In objecting to these developments, Mao was reacting as much to the course taken by the Soviet Union since the mid-1950s as he was to the situation in China in the mid-1960s. Mao launched the Cultural Revolution in response to these trends, which he interpreted as evidence that the vitality of the Chinese Communist party was being threatened from within by the party members who exploited the privileges accorded them by China's state system. The increasingly practical and nonideological orientation of these officials was an especially alarming sign of this emerging class society, and the perceived decline of socialist ideals among the youth caused Mao to fear that the revolution would soon be dead.

The main remedies that Mao enforced during the Cultural Revolution were the following:

• adherence to revolutionary ideals and a renewed loyalty to Chairman Mao himself, who championed these ideals against a recalcitrant bureaucracy;

• mass criticism and self-examination of intellectuals and officials at all levels to identify and reform those who betrayed bourgeois tendencies in their attitudes and work habits;

• a criticism and investigation of officials by organized student and worker groups who would seize power and participate directly in administration of organizations to which they were attached;

• purges of all those in the bureaucracy and universities who were found to have opposed Chairman Mao's vision;

• "reeducation" of intellectuals and bureaucrats in labor farms or on shop floors, vast reductions in the staffing of organizations, and the appointment of "representatives of the people" to help staff administrative posts;

• repudiation of privilege; redistribution of housing space by splitting up the large homes and apartments of the privileged; freezing of salaries and wages.

Those who emphasize the liberating, anti-bureaucratic aspects of Maoism point to the populist and egalitarian motives behind these actions. It was, of course, unprecedented for a ruling Leninist dictator to foster a mass movement to attack and dismantle the party and bureaucracy. The anti-bureaucratic aspects of the Maoist message are indisputable. And the demand for material equality was just as uncompromising as the demand for ideological conformity. Many scholars have thus interpreted Maoism as an anti-bureaucratic, anti-Stalinist movement, not unlike those led by Djilas in Yugoslavia, Trotsky while in exile, and many East European dissidents. While recognizing that Maoists also continued steadfastly to revere Stalin's memory and protect it against the denigrations of Khrushchev and other "revisionists," they nonetheless argued that in its main emphases and practical content, Maoism was fundamentally anti-Stalinist and anti-bureaucratic.

In the first five years after Mao's death in late 1976 a wave of revelations brought the Cultural Revolution into a sharper, and much different focus. Many victims and horrified bystanders began to tell their stories of the Cultural Revolution, and the new party leadership, many of them victims of the period, began to make known the atrocities they had experienced. The Cultural Revolution, which to many outside China had appeared as a principled attack against bureaucratism, was now described as a violent and uncontrolled campaign of persecution, torture, and murder, in which perhaps more than a million people died and millions more saw their families torn asunder and their careers ruined.

These revelations have led to a reexamination of Maoist doctrine. If Maoism was the essentially liberating, principled movement that many of its interpreters had described, how is one to explain the Cultural Revolution? One possible explanation is that the actual events did not reflect Maoist doctrine, but were unintended excesses that occurred in the midst of turmoil.

This reexamination of Maoist ideas in the light of firsthand information, however, has prompted scholars to consider aspects of Maoist thought ignored in previous interpretations, and to question the validity of its characterization as a significant departure from Stalinism. **For unlike dissidents in Eastern Europe, Maoists did not attribute all of their problems to the principles and practices of Marxism-Leninism that they had inherited from the Soviet Union of the Stalin era.** Rather, they staunchly denied that there was any need for "reform" or that the basic system of party dictatorship, public ownership, and (bureaucratic) management was somehow inherently flawed. They criticized as "revisionist" any Communist leader who sought to weaken the dictatorship of the party or to dilute the centralized powers of the bureaucracy. Instead, Maoists argued that the basic institutions and practices borrowed from Stalin actually defined socialism, and that while there may be mistakes in implementation, errors by degenerate and corrupt officials, and short-sighted policies by some leaders, the system itself, though badly in need of reinvigoration and restoration, was sound and should not be tampered with.

If the problems identified by the Maoists were not inherent in the institutions and especially the doctrines borrowed from Stalin, then to what could they be attributed? In considering this question, scholars have found revived and magnified in Maoism a core element of the Marxism-Leninism of the Stalin era: the idea that the nation is beset by a widespread hidden conspiracy. Maoists believed that the problems did not demonstrate that corruption, privilege, and oppression were inherent in the concentration of political and economic power that is characteristic of Leninist regimes. Instead, they were due to the fact that the system was being quietly undermined from within by agents of the bourgeoisie and "newly arisen bourgeois elements" in the party who were engaged in a vast conspiracy to restore capitalism.

While Stalin certainly never sought to mobilize workers and students to destroy the system he had created, he suspected treachery and conspiracy at every turn, and in the 1930s unleashed his secret police in a campaign of terror against the Party leadership and the population with the goal of extirpating any incipient capitalism. It was precisely this paranoia that led Mao, in China, thirty years later, to call out the masses to hunt down hidden subversives and drag them from their offices and homes; search their residences and confiscate their books and possessions; beat, torture, and sometimes murder them during extended interrogations, and keep them in hundreds of thousands of secret detention cells throughout the country.

Scholars who view Maoism from this perspective regard it as an extreme form of all too familiar Stalinist mentality that saw the class struggle as being threatened by conspiracy and betrayal. The Cultural Revolution launched under the banner of Maoism did not alleviate the problems it set out to correct but rather made matters much worse than before. This is because Maoists called not for mass democracy, despite what the Red Guard movement seemed to outside observers to imply, but for an intensification of loyalty to Mao and to the "proletarian dictatorship." Although it was carried out not by the secret police but by informal paramilitary groups (Red Guards) and later by the armed forces, the Cultural Revolution's chief objective was a vast purge of those suspected of disloyalty. This interpretation suggests that the legacy of the Cultural Revolution is directly attributable to a Maoist doctrine that did not depart from Stalinist presuppositions to the extent previous interpreters have suggested—at least not in the ways that really mattered.

III. ISSUES FOR DISCUSSION

Instructors are referred to the questions at the conclusion of section I of the paper. These may be useful in prompting class discussion.

IV. SELECTED READING

Schram, Stuart R. *Mao Tse-tung.* Baltimore: Penguin, 1968 (faculty or student reading). The definitive biography, stresses revolutionary strategy in changing circumstances rather than Mao's thought per se.

Schram, Stuart R. *The Political Thought of Mao Tse-tung.* New York: Praeger, 1971 (faculty or student reading). An excellent interpretive introduction regarding Maoism as a revolutionary ideology, with well-chosen annotated selections from Mao's writings.

Schwartz, Benjamin. *Chinese Communism and the Rise of Mao.* Cambridge: Harvard University Press, 1951 (several subsequent editions) (faculty reading). A masterly political history and examination of the logic of Mao's theory of peasant revolution, stressing its evolution away from core Marxist propositions.

Starr, John Bryan. *Continuing the Revolution: The Political Thought of Mao.* Princeton: Princeton University Press, 1979 (faculty reading). An elegant and comprehensive examination of Mao's post-revolution positions on bureaucracy, class struggle, and other pivotal concepts; in the mold of Sheldon Wolin's *Politics and Vision.* Portrays Mao as an anti-Stalinist concerned with equality and socialist democracy.

Walder, Andrew G. "Cultural Revolution Radicalism: Innovations on a Stalinist Theme." In *New Perspectives on the Cultural Revolution,* ed. by David Zweig, William Josephs, and Christine Wong. Cambridge: Harvard Contemporary China Monographs, 1989 (faculty reading). Challenges the perspective presented by Starr, emphasizing the arbitrary and repressive Stalinist elements in Maoist doctrine, in both theory and practice.

Wang Xizhe. "Mao Zedong and the Cultural Revolution." In *On Socialist Democracy and the Chinese Legal System: The Li Yizhe Debates,* ed. by Anita Chan, Stanley Rosen, and Jonathan Unger. Armonk, NY: M.E. Sharpe, 1986 (faculty and student reading). Written by a famous Chinese dissident who was active during the 1978–79 "democracy wall" movement, this lengthy essay portrays Mao as a repressive Stalinist and enemy of genuine reform, whose Cultural Revolution created a system of privilege and hypocrisy that was even more repressive and arbitrary than the one it replaced.

Sociology:
China

Sociology of Work: The Case of China

Andrew G. Walder

The case of China, where conceptions of a job, a career, of the work place as an organization, and of the nature of management authority contrast so completely with most Western conceptions, merits inclusion in a course on labor practices because it would greatly enhance students' understanding of work life in the West **by showing that many things we take to be universals are in fact variables**. These differences, in turn, require explanations; and the search for explanations leads one back to the fundamental questions of industrial sociology. What are the origins of contemporary work institutions; to what extent do they reflect universal imperatives of modern industrial growth, and to what extent do they vary according to different demographic, labor market, political, and cultural factors?

I. INTRODUCTION: CENTRAL POINTS

Work places in the People's Republic of China since the 1950s have exhibited the following noteworthy features:
   • **Socialist Dualism.** A clearly differentiated, dualistic pattern of employment, in which pay, benefits, and working conditions vary greatly according to the size and administrative rank of the institution. This pattern results not from market processes, but from planning priorities.

448

• **Permanent Employment.** A pattern of permanent employment in which there is very little turnover or job choice for the vast majority of employees. By the same token, layoffs and disciplinary firings are extremely rare. This very weakly developed labor market means that most people can expect to remain in their current place of employment until they retire.

• **Collective Consumption.** Employers provide not only wages, insurance, and health benefits, but are the main supplier of new housing, meals, certain consumer goods and many other services, which they provide free or at highly subsidized rates.

• **Career Paths.** In addition to the usual management hierarchies in workshops and staff offices, there is, within the workshop a hierarchy of political offices in the Communist party, youth league, and union organizations. These provide employees with a separate "political" career path that does not generally exist in Western firms.

• **Small-group Management.** Small-group management in workshops, with ordinary workers providing basic-level supervision; regular group meetings; and loosely defined job specialization.

• **Factory Patronage.** Widespread patterns of workshop patronage stemming from the distribution of goods and services and the option of the political career.

• **Management Paternalism.** Despite the absence of independent unions with legally enforceable rights, management displays a kind of paternalism that reflects a pronounced sensitivity to workers' opinions and dissatisfactions.

• **Paradox of Poor Work Performance.** Despite the broad formal powers of party and management, the weakness of workers' representatives, and the considerable dependence of employees on the work place for the provision of benefits, work discipline is notoriously slack.

II. MAJOR TOPICS

SOCIALIST DUALISM

Dualistic labor markets in Western economies are often attributed to the workings of both labor and product markets and, according to some schools of thought, are an inevitable part of capitalist development. Despite a virtual absence of labor markets, the irrelevance of product markets in planning decisions, and the commitment of Chinese authorities to full employment and benefits for over three decades, China has long exhibited a marked pattern of industrial dualism.

Beginning in the late 1950s, there developed a clear hierarchy of employment sectors. State-owned plants were at the top, followed by urban, and then rural collectives. In addition, there were sizeable numbers of temporary workers from urban areas and contract workers from rural areas in most enterprises. Within these categories, firms differed according to their size and administrative rank. The larger the industrial enterprise, the more attractive the benefits. And the higher the rank of the level of government that "owned" the firm, the better the benefits: for example, national ministry firms outranked municipal firms, which outranked county and city district firms, which outranked neighborhood firms, and so forth. There was therefore a marked hierarchy among firms as well as within them.

Within firms, there were marked differences in wages and benefits. On average, the salaries of permanent state workers were about 30 percent higher than those in urban collectives, and until the 1980s there was a similar gap between urban and rural collectives. The broad retirement, sick leave, and medical benefits available to state workers were less attractive for those in urban collectives, and largely nonexistent in rural collectives. The broad range of services and distributions available at all but the smallest state firms (see below) were also less attractive in the urban collectives, and largely nonexistent in the rural. Until the late 1980s, temporary and contract workers earned salaries that were only a fraction of those of permanent counterparts, and were usually not eligible for the same benefits and services provided at the work place.

Moreover, this pattern of dualism was much more rigid than in most market systems because of the bureaucratic allocation of labor within cities, and the strict prohibitions against rural residents taking up permanent employment in cities. Once assigned a job, it was until recently virtually impossible to change jobs (see below). Moreover, a system of household registers and grain rationing helped urban neighborhood police strictly enforce a ban on the movement of rural residents into cities in search of jobs. Temporary workers from urban areas occasionally were hired on as permanent workers, but contract workers from the countryside had no such chance.

It is interesting to note that this marked dualism occurred despite the relative importance of labor and product markets in the determination of management strategy. These arrangements were the result of planning decisions that reflected a policy of restricting incomes and benefits in favor of investment, and a strict policy of controlling rural migration to urban areas.

Interestingly, in the 1980s, when private economic activity and market activity on the margins of the central government's economic plan were introduced in urban areas, and when de facto private enterprise was encouraged in the countryside, this pattern of dualism became somewhat less pronounced. Incomes rose rapidly for workers in rural collective enterprises and for temporary workers in many areas, and as enterprises of all sorts gained more control over the expenditure of their profits, work places of all sizes poured money into benefits, housing, and other services.

PERMANENT EMPLOYMENT

Except in a minority of sectors, such as construction, and in the smaller rural collective enterprises, jobs are considered permanent. With very few exceptions, the employee does not have the freedom to leave the job, nor does the manager have the ability to lay off or fire the employee. While this pattern is not absolute, and while the rigidity of job assignments has loosened slightly in recent years, there is probably no country in the world in which jobs are such long-term affairs. A recent survey of one large Chinese city showed that over 70 percent of those polled had held only one job in their lifetime.

This phenomenon provides an interesting contrast case both with a pattern of relatively high turnover common in the West and with permanent employment as practiced in Japan, [See the essay, "Sociology of Work: The Case of Japan"]. In the United States, of course, labor markets lead to high turnover; in Japan, labor markets lead to relative job security and "permanent" employment in the larger, primary sector enterprises. But in China, permanent employment is a function of bureaucratic regulation; it is less the result of managerial considerations at the work place or worker preferences (the former would prefer to be able to lay off and fire; the latter would prefer to be able to choose their jobs freely), than it is the side-product of the government's desire to control the population of cities. Added to this is that so many benefits, including housing, are provided primarily at the work place. Some have argued that the practice of permanent employment is primarily due to a desire to reduce administrative confusion.

COLLECTIVE CONSUMPTION AT THE WORKPLACE

While large Japanese enterprises are known for their tendency to provide housing and recreational activities for employees, most Chinese enterprises far surpass them in this respect. While this pattern has diminished somewhat due to China's economic reforms in the 1980s, generally the pattern of the 1950s through the 1970s still holds. Work places provide housing for about 40 percent of China's current urban population. In large enterprises located on the edge or outside of cities, it is very common for virtually all employees to live in company housing, which is often located in "residential districts" maintained by the enterprise nearby. Enterprises in the 1980s still built over half of all new housing, and since there is still basically no private housing market in urban areas, they are the most likely source of new housing.

The work place also commonly provides a broad array of services: both sit-down and take-out meals; nursing rooms; nursery schools; kindergartens, primary, middle, and in some cases junior high and high schools; clinics and hospitals; recreation centers and theaters. They also provide access to scarce consumer goods, either through ration coupons (more common in the past), or by obtaining coveted brands for distribution or sale to selected employees. At some work places an array of miscellaneous services and items are available: retail shops and food outlets; barber shops; loans and grants to see employees through times of financial hardship; consumer loans; money for the funeral of family members; matchmaking services; shower and bathing facilities; vacation travel; and recreational programs. Not surprisingly, the larger, more isolated factories and the better funded government institutions and offices constitute nearly self-contained communities.

CAREER PATHS

In addition to the usual hierarchy of management positions, within the work place is a hierarchy of political offices that is separate from management and under Communist party organization. This hierarchy comprises the party committee's full-time staff at each managerial level (at the top a full office staff; in workshops this is usually two or three full-time employees), and the staff of such factory departments as security, propaganda, personnel, and political organization. The union office and the youth league office of the factory, both of which have small full-time staffs, are also part of the hierarchy.

There are therefore two separate career paths for ordinary employees who have already completed their education: the first is the usual one of promotion up through the managerial hierarchy; and the second is the additional political career path. Opportunities for mobility are therefore enhanced for ordinary workers who are willing to put in the extra hours on political activities required to join the party, since there are a larger number of political offices in the Chinese factory for which no formal training or education is necessary. In past decades this political path has provided a very important path of career mobility for ordinary workers, enabling some to move out of production work into political positions.

This political path is made more important by the fact that there is virtually no opportunity for advancement within a work place or externally for ordinary employees. China's wage grade system is very simple— eight pay grades nationwide, with about 30 percent of wages coming from bonuses that are variable more in theory than in practice. **Chinese managers simply do not arrange defined jobs in a progression of seniority, skill, and pay, as is common in many Western firms. Therefore there is very little sense of career progression, except for the very occasional pay grade hikes, for the vast majority of employees who stay, at the same work place for most of their lives.**

SMALL-GROUP MANAGEMENT

Not only do managers not organize internal labor markets by ranking jobs; they do not even define jobs precisely. Workers tend to be assigned to jobs flexibly as needed, a practice that is limited only by custom and interpersonal understanding. There are no large pay differentials associated with different kinds of work, nor are workers hired according to their skills for specific jobs. Instead, state labor agencies simply assign people to work places, which place them as they see fit and train them as necessary.

This conception of job definition fits well with an orientation toward small-group management. Most enterprise workshops are subdivided into small groups of about ten to fifteen workers, one of whom will be appointed group leader and perhaps another his or her assistant. Group leaders are selected by and report directly to the shop director. They hold regular meetings in which they relay orders and allocate tasks, record output for bonuses, and enforce discipline. Appointment as group leader is the first step on a career path to a management or political post, and responsible conduct in that post may prepare one for party membership.

There have been periodic efforts, fewer recently, to revitalize small groups and make them a model of work place democracy. In the 1950s through the early 1970s, especially, in a largely unsuccessful effort to enhance work discipline and motivation in the absence of wage increases, managers and party officials sought to revitalize small-group structures and involve every member in some kind of group responsibility. Sometimes the groups would meet virtually every day for long periods, conducting political study, mutual supervision, and criticism. Periodic efforts have also been made to elect group leaders democratically in order to make them more acceptable to the workers. At present, these groups enjoy a relatively limited degree of autonomy; and workers are generally supervised by monitors appointed from their own ranks, rather than exclusively by specialized inspection and supervisory personnel who themselves do not hold production jobs. These groups also play a role in helping to resolve family problems, financial difficulties, and other matters in the "private" lives of their members.

FACTORY PATRONAGE

A number of the features described above make China's factories fertile ground for the growth of patronage relationships within workshops and the management of shops as political machines. First is the extraordinary stability of the work force which lends a quasi-community quality to the factory. Second is the role played by the work place in meeting a wide array of employee needs. Third is the existence of political career paths under party auspices, and the role of factory officials in allocating these career opportunities. Fourth is the weakness of independent workers' organizations, which has the effect of leaving considerable personal discretion in the hands of factory officials in allocating goods, services, and opportunities.

Shop managers and party officials routinely select and groom a few of the more cooperative employees for party membership and eventual promotion. This is not much different from factories anywhere. But the factors mentioned above tend to generate long-term personal loyalties, which are cemented by material interests. These workers being groomed for promotion spends long hours after work helping shop officials prepare records, statistics, production or political meetings, and other factory events. As these cooperative relationships develop, the worker gradually becomes identified as one of the party's people, and is ostracized, sometimes subtly, sometimes not, from the other workers. This serves further to cement his ties with officials, whom he comes to regard as his patrons and protectors. Officials readily use the discretion at their disposal to benefit their protégé's careers, expedite their applications for housing, and so forth. These vertical alliances mark a prominent division in the work force; without them, management would have little means to control events in the shop. These relationships are not purely personal, however, since they emerge from formal management policy and party leadership and recruitment practices. **One striking feature about these relationships is that the participants often use the same language to describe them that the peasants, workers, and merchants used to describe their own patronage relations before the revolution.**

MANAGEMENT PATERNALISM

Stuck in a "company town" setting, dependent upon officials who allocate a wide array of goods and services, subject to the constant supervision of party officials and their appointed clients, and denied independent organizations to represent them, Chinese workers would appear to be a powerless and thoroughly dominated group. One would be inclined to predict a rather harsh regime of managerial authority.

Such is not generally the case. **Some of the same factors that appear to make workers so dependent on management also serve to tie the hands of managers.** While workers cannot voluntarily leave the firm, neither can they be readily fired. **In economies with labor markets, workers dissatisfaction is reflected in high turnover rates; in China, dissatisfactions accumulate within the firm and can cause innumerable management problems.**

Since managers are responsible for meeting production targets with their existing work forces—and in recent years have become responsible for the firm's profitability as well—they are especially careful not to provoke their employees to sullen resistance and minor acts of sabotage. Far more than planning authorities find tolerable, managers across the board have been extremely hesitant to discipline workers, to place undue pressure on them to increase productivity, or to differentiate rewards sharply according to performance. Moreover, managers make every effort, both legal and illegal, to enhance workers' income and benefits—especially improved housing.

Managers who fail to follow this course of action will find their production plans subtly undermined by absenteeism, soldiering, and the breakdown of machinery. They will also find worker dissatisfaction expressed in protracted haggling within workshops over bonuses, and they may find themselves besieged with complaints about the lack of housing and other services and benefits. Managers are sensitive to these complaints for two important reasons. First, compared to firms in market economies, there are not many things for which factory managers can be held directly and solely responsible. Because many important decisions are made in tandem with higher officials in the planning system that responsibility becomes blurred. But two things for which the manager is held directly responsible are labor productivity and costs, both of which are directly affected by workers' cooperation or lack thereof. Second, a manager who alienates his permanent work force is not likely to be regarded as successful. A manager is virtually powerless to mask dissatisfaction among his workers, and his career may be jeopardized if the factory gains a reputation as a trouble spot in the local planning system. Chinese managers therefore seem preoccupied with harmonious relations in the enterprise.

THE PARADOX OF POOR WORK PERFORMANCE

Given the very broad authority of factory managers in China—they are often political officials, heads of residential communities, and enterprise managers simultaneously—and given the absence of independent worker organizations, the expectation of observers familiar with Western market economies is that managers would use this advantage ruthlessly to extract maximum work efficiency from workers. Somewhat paradoxically, Chinese managers are able to extract only very low levels of labor productivity from their work forces.

This paradox highlights a sharp contrast between the factory as an institution in China and in Western market economies. In the market economies, the enterprise is a specialized organization whose survival depends solely on the profitability of its products. The main benefits that it provides its workers are in the form of wage and some health and retirement provisions (though these are usually the province of the union). While some firms may seek to attract and keep highly skilled employees in sectors where labor is scarce, they are certainly not legally obliged to keep these employees on; nor are the workers' movements restricted.

In China, on the other hand, the enterprise is primarily a permanent social institution that produces according to a state industrial plan. It is also responsible for making a profit, but even if it fails to do so, it still plays a useful role in helping to make the state's full employment policy a reality and in delivering housing and many other urban services and benefits to its workers. The closure of a factory in China therefore has social implications that extend far beyond the simple desire for full employment. Only the smallest and most insignificant firms are allowed to close.

Just as the role of the factory institution is very broad, and not highly specialized as in the West; so is the authority of the manager very broad and diffuse. Managers can award career opportunities, housing, access to many goods and services. They are responsible for monitoring not only job performance, but also political order and workers' political thinking, for mediating family disputes, giving permission to divorce, and organizing recreational activities. They do not have the institutional incentive, or even the authority to focus single-mindedly on productivity and work discipline that managers of Western market firms enjoy. Thus the paradox, in view of broad managerial authority, of weak managers and lax work discipline demonstrates that our common assumptions about workers' rights, including the right to organize, and managerial authority, are invalid when applied to an institutional reality organized in ways fundamentally different from our own.

III. ISSUES FOR DISCUSSION

1. What are the ways in which the Chinese factory differs from the American as a social institution? What additional social roles does the Chinese factory play, and why?

2. What are the incentives that Chinese managers are able to offer to workers? In what areas of activity are these incentives effective, and why?

3. Why, if Chinese workers depend on their factories for such a wide range of goods and services, is labor discipline such a serious problem in China?

IV. SELECTED READINGS

Andors, Stephen. *China's Industrial Revolution.* New York: Pantheon, 1977 (faculty background). Chronological account of factory management as an issue in Chinese politics. Emphasizes theory and state policy; however, its largely uncritical acceptance of official Maoist reports badly dates the book.

Henderson, Gail, and Myron S. Cohen. *The Chinese Hospital: A Socialist*

Work Unit. New Haven: Yale University Press, 1985 (student reading). Vivid and readable description of social life in China's tightly-knit work unit communities.

Walder, Andrew G. *Communist Neo-Traditionalism: Work and Authority in Chinese Industry.* Berkeley: University of California Press, 1986 (student and faculty reading). Comprehensive account, both descriptive and comparative, of factory life, reward systems, work motivation, and political leadership in Chinese factories from the 1950s through the early 1980s.

Walder, Andrew G. "Wage Reform and the Web of Factory Interests." *China Quarterly* 109 (March 1987): 22–41 (faculty background). Analyzes the continuing difficulties in motivating China's workers by highlighting some of the institutional features of the factory and the way they foster implicit wage agreements between managers and workers.

Whyte, Martin K., and William L. Parish. *Urban Life in Contemporary China.* Chicago: University of Chicago Press, 1984 (faculty background). Chapters on political control, supplies and distribution, and work unit organization put the Chinese work place into broader institutional perspective.

Sociology:
Comparative/
Interarea

Problems of Rapid Modernization: China, Taiwan, Korea, and Japan

Thomas B. Gold

I. INTRODUCTION: CENTRAL POINTS

China, Taiwan, South Korea, and Japan provide excellent cases for the study of the problems of rapid modernization.

• Growing out of a shared Confucian tradition whose core values and social structure were once considered antithetical to economic development, they have astounded the rest of the world by overcoming the devastation of World War II and, in the case of China and Korea, civil war, to **achieve extremely rapid rates of economic development and structural change as well as a dramatically improved quality of life for their people.**

• These late modernizers of East Asia have experimented with different development strategies, and from the 1980s have begun to converge around a model of **market-conforming, state-led economic development that also involves substantial integra-**

tion into the global economy and calls into question labels of "socialism" and "capitalism."

• After achieving rapid economic growth, these societies embarked on a **transition from authoritarian regimes toward democracy.**

• The experiences of these four East Asian economies pose a **challenge to both the modernization and dependency-world systems paradigms** that have dominated the study of development.

II. MAJOR TOPICS

DEVASTATED BY WAR

At the end of World War II, the countries of East Asia were devastated. With its industrial base reduced to rubble and, having suffered two atomic bomb attacks, Japan was utterly defeated. China had been officially at war with Japan since 1937 but had been occupied by Japanese troops for many years before that, and had been the scene of warlord battles and Communist rebellion since the 1920s. The civil war between the Kuomintang (KMT) Nationalists and the Communists revived soon after the Japanese surrender. Losing to the Communists in 1949, the Nationalists under Generalissimo Chiang Kai-shek fled to the Chinese island of Taiwan, severely straining the already meager resources of the island which, as a Japanese colony, had been subjected to Allied bombing. Korea had not suffered greatly in World War II, but it was racked by civil war from 1950 to 1953, from which it emerged divided. If any part of the world appeared unlikely to catch up with the developed countries, it was East Asia. Japan, Taiwan, and South Korea were also densely populated and resource-poor, dependent on imports for many of their raw materials and foodstuffs.

A TRADITIONAL LEGACY ANTITHETICAL TO MODERNIZATION

East Asia's value system and the political, economic, and social structures buttressed by it made it seem an unlikely candidate for successful modernization. In the Confucian value system which originated in China and spread to Korea and Japan, **the merchant occupied the lowest rung in the social hierarchy**. At the top were scholar-officials; just below them were farmers and then artisans. It was assumed that those whose work was oriented to making a profit were immoral and untrustworthy. Successful merchants used their wealth to purchase titles and bureaucratic positions for themselves, and also to fund the education of their sons, who might then take the civil service examinations and become scholar-officials, and thereby raise the social standing of the entire family. In this way, the entire family would enjoy high social status. Bureaucrats supplemented their salaries by squeezing merchants. There were thus major disincentives to becoming a professional businessman.

Although recruitment to the civil service was based on examinations, these tested not administrative skills but how well one had memorized Confucian classics and rigidly formularized writing styles; **generalists enjoyed prominence over specialists**, who were denigrated as mere technicians. The education system emphasized rote memorization and imitation, not the cultivation of independent thinking or specialized skills.

Students of East Asia have noted that Confucianism also **emphasized the particularistic values of loyalty to family and friends**, values that did not encourage the trust in others that is necessary to building a national market, industry, and modern economy. It was argued that because **Confucians were dependent on the collective family**, they lacked the individuality and pioneering spirit vital to successful entrepreneurs. Confucian society was like the family writ large: based on hierarchies of age and gender, it emphasized unquestioning obedience to authority. Individual initiative in all spheres was stifled. In addition, Confucians believed that **history moved in cycles**; they did not have a concept of progress toward a brighter future. The goal of statecraft was to **bring about harmony between society and nature, not to conquer nature**.

FROM ECONOMIC RUIN TO ECONOMIC MIRACLES

Prior to World War II, only Japan had achieved a significant degree of industrialization. Beginning in the middle of the nineteenth century, a group of Japanese reformers had devoted themselves to the study of Western learning in order to protect their country from suffering dismemberment by Western imperialists, as they had seen happen to China, Japan's former model. By the mid-1930s, Japan had built up a strong enough industrial base that it felt confident enough to join the Nazis and Fascists in waging war on the Allies, including China. By war's end, that base was utterly destroyed.

By the late 1970s, Japan had rebuilt itself so successfully that some began to talk about Japan as Number One. Taiwan and South Korea, having likewise developed their economies rapidly, were referred to as "little Japans"; the terms "Pacific Century," and "East Asian Edge" also gained currency. As these newly industrialized countries (NICs; usually including the much smaller city-state entrepots of Hong Kong and Singapore as well) emerged from the ashes of war they first developed their agriculture, a process that was facilitated by land reform. Although they did not follow identical strategies, each developed labor-intensive small-scale light industries before moving on to capital-intensive, knowledge-intensive heavy and high-technology industries. Small family enterprises gave way to conglomerates, some of whose names (Mitsui, Mitsubishi, Hyundai, Samsung, Tatung) are now household words throughout the world.

All three economies successfully utilized generous American aid and also welcomed investment by multinational corporations. They began with highly protectionist import substitution strategies and then moved on to export-oriented industrialization, still supported by protectionist policies. Their exports literally flooded world markets. In addition, the extremely high savings rates of their people, together with their carefully managed foreign debt resulted in the accumulation of huge reserves of foreign exchange.

RELATIVELY LOW INCOME-INEQUALITY

Economic growth is only one aspect of modernization and development. While industrializing their economies and raising the levels of productivity and quality, Japan, Taiwan, and South Korea also avoided the extreme discrepancies between rich and poor so common in rapidly developing societies. Some reasons for this include: successful and thorough land reform; an economic take-off based initially on local capital rather than that of powerful multinational corporations; the strength of small and medium-sized enterprises; and an egalitarian strain in Confucianism. Taiwan achieved the best record of the group, in part a result of the official ideology of the ruling Kuomintang (KMT) Nationalist party which stressed equality and legitimized state action to prevent the excessive accumulation of wealth. (Indeed, one of the factors leading to the defeat of the KMT and its expulsion from the mainland was its tolerance for extreme disparities in the distribution of wealth; it had learned its lesson and was determined not to allow this sort of inequality to develop in Taiwan.) In these societies, rapid economic development resulted in a vastly improved standard of living for the masses which, in turn, contributed to general social and political stability.

Ironically, some scholars now **attribute the success of these economies to some of the same Confucian values** that were formerly thought to be obstacles. For instance, they see family-based enterprises as an efficient way to maximize scarce capital resources; tightly-knit webs of friends and relatives as excellent networks for the procurement of supplies and the distribution of products; obedience to authority as a quality that makes for disciplined and diligent workers; the education system as one whose graduates are able to memorize technologies and to imitate and then improve on the best the world has to offer. It is more accurate to say that, due to war and external pressures, **the old Confucian political and social structure gave way to a new system whose leaders recognized that economic development had to be accorded top priority in order for the nation just to survive**. Many of the traditional values were redirected toward the goal of development, while others were effectively stifled.

CHINA'S EXPERIMENTS

The People's Republic of China followed a much different path than that of its East Asian neighbors. After the Chinese Communist Party, led by Mao Zedong, took power in 1949, faced with a blockade by the United States, it received a generous amount of assistance from the Soviet Union and adopted the Soviet model of a planned, state-owned economy. In 1958, however, Mao Zedong and other radical opponents of this model, with its anti-rural, anti-agricultural bias and the dependence it fostered on the USSR, launched the Great Leap Forward campaign to introduce an even more extreme collectivist economy based on autarchic self-reliance, labor-intensive technology, total collectivization, a cult of poverty, and moral-political incentives. This was based on the party's successful experience during the anti-Japanese War in its base in the poverty-stricken area of Northwest China around the city Yenan. Economic, social, and cultural life were highly poiliticized.

In the aftermath of the devastating Cultural Revolution (1966–76) there was widespread disaffection with the Chinese Communist party, and its legitimacy to rule was called into question. In order to regain support and prestige, some leaders under Deng Xiaoping called for a thoroughgoing structural reform to shift the party's focus from political struggle to achievement of the "four modernizations": agriculture, industry, science and technology, and national defense. This involved reassessing both Chinese culture and the meaning of socialism in order to create a synthesis called "**socialism with Chinese characteristics**." It also involved borrowing some key elements of the experience of Japan, Taiwan, and South Korea. **The Chinese Communists are continuing to try to find a way to balance the state dominance they see as essential to socialism while tapping into the dynamism so prevalent elsewhere in East Asia**. They have decollectivized agriculture by reintroducing family farming and free markets, although not private ownership of land. They are separating ownership from management of state enterprises, granting autonomy to the managers. They are expanding the role of the market as they shrink the sphere of the planned economy. They are creating an environment for private enterprise, and allowing private businesses to compete in certain sectors with state and collective firms. They are also opening the economy to the outside world, soliciting direct foreign investment, foreign loans, and technology transfer while also encouraging exports of industrial goods. They depoliticized education and made major investments in human capital development. Since the reforms began in late 1978, China's economy, the industrial sector in particular, has grown by double digits. However, by the late 1980s, the contradictions between the planned and market systems began to spawn inflation, fueled by corruption, which threatened the reform program. General popular disaffection resulted in massive demonstrations in the spring of 1989, which the regime brutally repressed. To a certain degree, the initial rapid success of China's structural reforms inspired the "perestroika" of Mikhail Gorbachev in the Soviet Union and reforms elsewhere in the socialist world.

A COMMON CHARACTERISTIC: A STRONG STATE

China, Japan, Taiwan, and South Korea **all share an economic model with a central role for the state**. This is multi-faceted. The strong state role in socialist China is well-known, but many are unaware of the major place of the state in the market-economies of Japan, Taiwan, and South Korea. In each of these countries, the state periodically produces plans for economic development; government agencies collect data on the local and international economies and make predictions as to their evolution. They target certain domestic sectors for special incentives (tax breaks and rebates, low-interest loans, access to foreign exchange, reduced import tariffs, etc.) in order to motivate local businesses to invest in those target industries. The states have considerable control over the banking system (through ownership of major shares in a number of banks and administration of the postal savings systems), which facilitates implementation of fiscal policies. The states also own many enterprises in key sectors, often as monopolies, enabling them to direct certain materials to targeted companies. These are **indicative plans**, not the command-type plans of a Soviet-style economy as in pre-reform PRC. What is more, they are **market-conforming**, that is, they try to anticipate market developments and assist private businesses to take optimal advantage of future trends. In addition to these positive tactics, the states can use various sanctions to elicit the desired response. By withholding incentives and licenses, imposing punitive taxes, auditing books, and exercising various forms of political coercion, the states can motivate recalcitrant businesses to conform. These are economies attuned to the market and they have large vibrant private sectors, but they are not strictly free enterprise economies as is often argued, because the state, directly and indirectly, is a major actor. Its role has shrunk since the 1950s, but it nonetheless continues to be a determinant.

An additional important role of the state that has had positive economic consequences has been its **massive investment in education in order to develop human capital**. The literacy rate in Japan, Taiwan, and South Korea exceeds 90 percent. There is severe competition for advanced education, but the governments have also invested in vocational training in order to provide a highly qualified cadre of technicians and workers.

There are a number of reasons for the dominance of the state in East Asian economies. **In East Asian tradition, people expect the state to play a dominant role in their lives, helping to create prosperity and ensuring social harmony; failure to do so is considered grounds for rebellion.** There is the historical legacy of the Confucian bureaucracy placing constraints on the activities of merchants, although one of the revolutionary aspects of contemporary East Asia is the high social prestige given to private businessmen. Bureaucrats still enjoy high status and a certain degree of insulation from politics, enabling them to work according to objective criteria.

As part of the 1868 Meiji Reform in Japan, the central leadership took a forceful approach to developing the country's economy in order to make it wealthy and strong and thereby able to fend off

Western imperialists. Japan took Taiwan, Korea, and Manchuria as colonies and implemented similar statist policies for their economies, introducing a structure which subsequent postcolonial governments adopted and continued. As in many underdeveloped economies, only the state had the necessary capital to establish key enterprises and build the infrastructure required for industrialization. This legacy of state-owned enterprises in crucial sectors has continued to the present.

Also, the governments of Taiwan and South Korea see themselves as under continued threat from their Communist enemies. This garrison mentality stimulates their efforts for economic development and legitimizes policies which interfere in private business decisions and activities in the name of national security. These governments are highly militarized and have created vast internal security networks, which frequently serve, through intimidation, to ensure compliance with state policies. It has also resulted in severe labor repression and the maintenance of labor peace, at least as long as incomes keep ahead of inflation. In China, the Communist party controls labor unions tightly. Defining itself as the party of the proletariat, it legitimizes labor repression by claiming that strikes work against the workers' own interests.

MIXED ECONOMIES

Japan, Taiwan, South Korea, and now to a greater degree than ever, China, have mixed planned and market economies, and a powerful state sector alongside a vibrant private sector. **The old dichotomies of capitalism and socialism are breaking down**. Other developing economies of various political stripes are increasingly attempting to adopt aspects of the East Asian systems.

PROBLEMS OF RAPID MODERNIZATION
IN EAST ASIA

Overall, the record of economic development in East Asia has been extraordinary. Nonetheless, some problems need to be mentioned. Because of the critical importance of exports in the economies of Taiwan and South Korea, especially, but also Japan and increasingly China, these countries face constant challenges in anticipating global trends. Incorrect policy choices can have disastrous effects on the economy, and indeed, on domestic stability. Dependent on trade, the governments aggressively push exports but maintain high protectionist barriers, visible and invisible, around their domestic markets. This has provoked a tremendous and dangerous backlash in some of their major markets, the United States and the European Community in particular. A related problem is the over-concentration of their trade. All of these countries export overwhelmingly to the United States, fueling America's enormous trade deficit. At the same time, they are dependent on the import of Japanese components for many of their manufactured goods.

Finally, in the headlong rush to industrialize, they have caused grave harm to their environments. To some degree, the major polluters are multinational corporations (first American, then Japanese) whose investment was solicited in East Asia at a time when they were facing strict environmental regulations in their own countries. But local companies are also at fault, and through reckless deforestation and poor land management have likewise contributed to destruction of the environment.

POLITICAL AUTHORITARIANISM

Perhaps the major shortcoming of the East Asian development experience has been the strict and often brutal political authoritarianism that has accompanied rapid economic growth. It has been suggested that this authoritarianism facilitated, indeed, is indispensable to growth, and is a small price to pay for the tremendous economic reward it has brought. In order for the state to play a strong role in guiding the economy and channelling resources efficiently, the argument goes, it needs to have unquestioned authority and force. This reasoning runs counter to the assumption, popular in the 1950s, that economic development would be accompanied by political "modernization," meaning the introduction of Western-style democratic institutions and practices. Although postwar Japan has instituted a democratic electoral system, in the 1930s its industrialization was led by a militarized fascistic state.

The KMT brought to Taiwan a militarized state with a far-flung internal security network. Comprised of a small cohort of mainland émigrés, it monopolized political power over 85 percent of the population who, while also Chinese, had lived on the island prior to its retrocession in 1945 from Japanese to Chinese control. Similar in structure to a Leninist communist party it penetrated Taiwan's society to stifle dissent and mobilize the people. It did not permit other parties and maintained its rule by martial law, dealing ruthlessly with its enemies.

By the 1970s the KMT regime had become largely civilian. The successive governments of South Korea have been more openly militaristic throughout much of this period. Generals-turned-president were replaced only through violent coups, and popular dissent was not tolerated. As the government of a divided nation, it claimed, as did the government of Taiwan, that it had to enforce social control in order to counter the very real threat from the Communist side.

On the Chinese mainland, the Communist party monopolized political power and used terror to transform China's class structure, liquidating landlords and removing the capitalist class and officials of the old regime. During the decade of the Cultural Revolution, Communist party cadres controlled political, social, economic, and cultural affairs directly and arbitrarily, unimpeded by law or other objective restraints.

EASING OF AUTHORITARIAN RULE

In the 1970s, social change in Taiwan and South Korea began increasingly to have political consequences. This pressured the regimes to liberalize and democratize, and gradually come to resemble the one-party, multifaction system of Japan that evolved with American help in the wake of World War II. To a certain extent, the regimes in Taiwan and South Korea were victims of their own success. By the 1980s they had brought about economic miracles which improved the lives of their people beyond anything that could have been imagined two decades earlier. This was unprecedented in the postwar developing world. With incomes outpacing inflation; high levels of education; increased contact with the outside world through trade, investment, and foreign advisors and experts; and influenced by a constant barrage of American popular culture and local propaganda that contrasted these "free" systems with those of their Communist enemies, members of the rapidly expanding middle classes began to press for reforms. In addition to political organizations, groups sprang up around issues such as pollution and the use of nuclear energy; "society" began to assert itself against the "state." Social structures— a shrinking rural sector, an expanding blue-collar working class, a fast-growing middle class of professionals, businessmen, bureaucrats and intellectuals— began to resemble those of the developed West. Dissidents argued that the anachronistic political systems were actually becoming an obstacle to further economic development, and that liberalization would stimulate growth.

The year 1987 proved to be a watershed for both Taiwan and South Korea. On Taiwan, the KMT abolished martial law and tacitly recognized the legitimacy of the opposition party, which until then had been illegal. It also began to step up exchanges with the Communist mainland, a sign of renewed confidence in itself and in its people. In January of 1988, President and KMT Chairman Chiang Ching-kuo died and was succeeded by Lee Teng-hui, a Taiwanese technocrat without military experience. The succession was peaceful, and the process of democratization and opening to the mainland continued and even accelerated. In South Korea, President Chun Doo-hwan bowed to public pressure to permit a constitutional change allowing the direct election of his successor. After a campaign in which two leading opposition figures opposed each other as well as Chun's hand-picked candidate, Roh Tae-woo, it was Roh who emerged victorious. He proceeded to speed up political liberalization and in 1988 did not prevent the public censure of his predecessor. In both Taiwan and South Korea, street demonstrations have increased, and there is a very visible radical component among Korean students. But in both societies, the process of political democratization has definitely begun; political modernization is catching up with economic and social development.

In China as well, the Communist party began to retrench from its efforts to dominate all aspects of political as well as social, cultural, and economic life. From 1986, leaders talked about separating the party from the government, introducing fixed terms in office and instituting a rule of law rather than of men. However, these reforms face enormous opposition within the party itself, which refuses to tolerate public expressions of dissent. But prior to the brutal crackdown on student demonstrations in the spring of 1989, Chinese life had become noticeably depoliticized and freer.

A NEW PARADIGM FOR THE STUDY OF MODERNIZATION?

The modernization paradigm that dominated the study of development from the end of World War II into the 1970s identified traditional values and social structures as barriers to the modernization of underdeveloped societies. The importation of values and practices from the developed world was prescribed to overcome these indigenous obstacles. Since the early 1980s, however, the East Asian region's spectacular growth has called for a reevaluation of the role of tradition in the modernization process.

Marxist-Leninist-inspired dependency world-system theory replaced modernization theory in the 1970s as the dominant paradigm for development studies. Citing cases of failed development in Latin America and Africa, its proponents argued that tight integration into the world system had resulted in the underdevelopment of the Third World. It was not native traditions but rather ruthless exploitation which made the core rich while impoverishing the periphery. Only socialism and autonomy from the world system could turn things around.

The East Asian miracle economies are very closely tied into the world system: however, they are trade-oriented (being resource-poor made this inevitable), welcome direct foreign investment, borrow from private and public international lenders, and try to restructure their economies to occupy niches in the international division of labor. The East Asian experience thus calls into question the simplistic assertion that dependency results in underdevelopment and that incorporation into the world system spells doom. The now publicly admitted failure of socialist and isolationist countries to develop their economies and societies to anywhere near the level of the East Asian market nations further weakens the dependency model as an analytical tool or strategy for development.

The East Asian cases suggest that, under certain conditions—which are probably not duplicable by all nations—the state can manipulate the social and cultural relations in which the economy is embedded in order to bring about rapid growth. There can be no generalized model of development; rather, leaders in each society need to assess the capabilities, opportunities, and constraints they face and work to mobilize human and other resources to bring about development.

III. ISSUES FOR DISCUSSION

1. Are all "traditional" values and practices inherently antithetical to modernization? Based on the East Asian experience, under what conditions might these values facilitate modernization?

2. How do the East Asian cases demonstrate that such terms as "socialist" and "capitalist" are of limited utility in describing actual economic systems?

3. What is the relation between economic growth and political democratization? Do the East Asian cases provide any guidelines for answering this question?

IV. SELECTED READINGS

Amsden, Alice H. *Asia's Next Giant*. New York: Oxford University Press, 1989 (faculty background). Detailed study of South Korea's economic development, focusing on the role of the state.

Berger, Peter, and Hsiao, H. H. Michael, eds. *In Search of an East Asian Development Model*. New Brunswick: Berger & Hsiao, 1988 (faculty background). Essays emphasizing the cultural aspects of modernization in East Asia.

Deyo, Frederic C., ed. *The Political Economy of the New Asian Industrialism*. Ithaca: Cornell University Press, 1987 (faculty background). Essays exploring the political and economic underpinnings of East Asian development, including policies on labor. Useful for comparing East Asia with Latin America.

Gasster, Michael. *China's Struggle to Modernize*, 2nd ed. New York: Alfred Knopf, 1987 (student reading). Places China's recent reforms in historical context.

Gereffi, Gary, and Wyman, Donald, eds. *Manufacturing Miracles*. Princeton: Princeton University Press, 1990 (faculty background). In-depth essays comparing development strategies of Korea, Taiwan, Brazil, and Mexico.

Gold, Thomas B. *State and Society in the Taiwan Miracle*. Armonk, NY: M.E. Sharpe, 1986 (student reading). Sociological analysis of Taiwan's development, examining issues of modernization and dependency theories.

Harding, Harry. *China's Second Revolution: Reform After Mao*. Washington: Brookings Institution, 1987 (student reading). Comprehensive analysis of China's post-Mao reform program.

Hofheinz, Roy, Jr., and Calder, Kent E. *The Eastasia Edge*. New York: Basic Books, 1982 (student reading). Explores commonalities among the East Asian nations, emphasizing their challenge to the West.

Johnson, Chalmers. *MITI and the Japanese Miracle*. Stanford: Stanford University Press, 1982 (faculty background). Detailed study of the role of the Japanese state in providing administrative guidance to the economy. First and last chapters especially useful.

Kallgren, Joyce K., ed. *Building a Nation-State: China After Forty Years*. Berkeley: Institute of East Asian Studies, 1990 (student reading). Review essays on China's foreign policy, politics, economics, society, and intellectuals.

Mason, Edward S., and Kim, Mahn Je, ed. *Studies in the Modernization of the Republic of Korea, 1945–75*. Cambridge, MA: Harvard University Press, 1979–81 (faculty background). Summary and synthesis of the research reported in eight other volumes in a series on Korea.

Wade, Robert. *Governing the Market*. Princeton: Princeton University Press, 1990 (faculty background). Detailed study of the role of the state in East Asian economic development.

Winckler, Edwin A., and Greenhalgh, Susan, eds. *Contending Approaches to the Political Economy on Taiwan*. Armonk, NY: M.E. Sharpe, 1988 (faculty background).

**Sociology:
Comparative/
Interarea**

Comparative Demography: The Cases of China, Japan and India

Moni Nag

I. INTRODUCTION: CENTRAL POINTS

Demography may be defined as the study of the size and composition of population, changes therein, and the components of such changes, which may be identified as fertility, mortality, and territorial movement (including urbanization). Social scientists have been recently engaged in the investigation of linkages between demographic variables on the one hand and sociocultural and economic factors on the other. **The two demographic giants of the world—China and India, with their respective populations of 1.136 billion and 853 million in 1990—represent almost two-fifths of humanity. With a population of 123 million (1990), Japan ranks seventh in the world. These three countries provide an excellent case for considering the role of sociocultural and economic factors in demographic stability and change.**

• All three countries have patriarchal traditions and had high birth and death rates up to the mid-nineteenth century, but differ considerably in their current rates.

• China, categorized by the World Bank as a low-income economy (per capita GNP US $300 in 1986), has succeeded in reduc-

472

ing drastically its birth, death, and population growth rates since the early 1970s, thus challenging the basic theory of demographic transition that aggregate decline of death rate followed by decline of birth rate occurs with progress of industrialization and rise of income.

• India, also categorized as a low-income economy (per capita GNP US $290 in 1986), has considerably higher birth, death, and population growth rates than those of China and some other less developed countries despite the fact that it launched a national family planning program in 1952, the first country in the world to do so.

• Japan attained demographic transition later but at a much quicker pace than Western countries.

• An understanding of sociocultural and economic institutions in historical perspective is necessary for explaining demographic stability and change in the three countries.

The recent estimates of selected demographic and socioeconomic variables for the three countries, along with those for all of Asia and the Pacific, and for the total world, are presented in Table 1.

It may be observed from the table below that the annual population growth rate in 1985–90 was smaller (0.4 percent) in Japan than in China (1.3 percent) and India (2.1 percent). The differences were associated more with differences in birth rate than in death rate. The crude birth rates in 1985–90 Japan, China, and India were 12.1, 21.2, and 35.1 per 1000 population, respectively. It is obvious from the table that the differential growth, birth, and death rates of the three countries do not have any linear correlation with economic and social indices represented by per capita GNP, adult literacy, and status of women. All three countries have gone through unique demographic and socioeconomic changes in the past centuries. Despite the paucity of accurate data for these countries, demographers and social historians have pieced together a fairly good picture of the interaction between demographic and socioeconomic factors that helps us to understand the current demographic situation in these countries.

The profile presented below of each country is organized under the following demographic factors: population growth and composition; male/female ratio; rural/urban migration; fertility and mortality.

II. MAJOR TOPICS

CHINA

Population Growth and Composition. China has a long history of census-taking dating back at least to the eleventh century B.C.E.

Recent estimates of selected demographic and socioeconomic measures for China, India, and Japan

	Population size (mil) 1990	Annual population growth rate 1985–90	Crude birth rate 1985–90[1]	Crude death rate 1985–90[2]	Infant mortality rate 1985–[3]	Per capita GNP US$ 1988	Per. adults lit. m/f 1985	Status of women score 1988[4]
China	1,135	1.3	21.2	6.7	32	330	95/94	58.5
India	853	2.1	35.1	11.6	99	340	58/29	43.5
Japan	123	0.4	12.1	7.0	5	21,020	99/99	68.5
Total Asia	3,108	1.9	27.6	9.1	73			
Total World	5,292	27.1	9.9	7.1				

Sources: United Nations, World Bank, UNICEF, and Population Crisis Committee documents
Notes: 1. No. of births per 1000 population in one year
2. No. of deaths per 1000 population in one year
3. No. of children dying in per 1000 born in one year
4. Scores out of 100 based on several specific indices of women's status

The accuracy of the figures collected in early counts is questionable, but they have led scholars to estimate that until about 1000 C.E. China's population fluctuated between thirty-seven and sixty million, showing no consistent trend. They suggest that the first recorded instance of sustained population growth took place in the first half of the eleventh century C.E., but growth was checked in the next three centuries by a series of dynastic struggles, civil wars, Mongol invasions, plagues, and natural catastrophes.

China's population grew more or less continuously for six centuries beginning in the early years of the Ming dynasty in the late fourteenth century. During certain periods of the Ming (1368–1644) and Qing (1644–1912) dynasties, the population growth rate rose to almost one percent per year and population pressure on the land became a matter of official concern. This prompted dynastic efforts to increase food production by expanding irrigation works, importing high-yield rice seed and new food crops from abroad, and emphasizing grain storage. The century prior to the founding of the People's Republic of China in 1949 was a period of great political and social turmoil and fluctuating population growth. The recorded population grew from 430 million in 1851 to 583 million in 1953, representing a growth rate of only 0.3 percent per year.

China's Communist government has consistently recognized the usefulness of collecting population statistics through censuses, a population registration system, and occasional surveys. Censuses were conducted in 1953, 1964, and 1982. But since the population statistics radically contradicted Communist ideology, they were largely unreported between 1959 and 1979. The regime embraced the orthodox Marxist ideology (formulated as a denouncement of Thomas Malthus's writings on the harmful consequences of unchecked population growth) that rapid population growth would not be a hindrance to raising living standards under socialism.

The population count of 581 million obtained in the 1953 census exceeded by almost 100 million previous estimates and seems to have come as a surprise to the authorities. The count of 695 million obtained in the 1964 census confirmed rapid population growth. During the first few years of Communist rule fragmentary economic and demographic data showing a definite improvement in the situation compared with the prerevolutionary period were released. Then followed a decade of almost complete statistical blackout, since the data no longer documented success under socialism. Mortality rose sharply and food production declined sharply during the Great Leap Forward (1959–1961) crisis. Subsequently, with a decline in mortality the population growth rate rose, resulting in sluggish per capita economic growth. Out of necessity, the radical leaders came to regard favorably the concept of population control through family planning programs, but they were reluctant for a long time publicly to renounce the Marxist ideology. Any scholar or official who mentioned population growth as a problem was in danger of censure.

Until the death of Mao Zedong the Marxist viewpoint on population was promoted and defended, even though the government had already started a vigorous family planning program in order to reduce the population growth rate. This led to increasingly awkward official positions in the 1970s. Until mid-1979, official sources referred to China's population variously as 700 or 800 million, while the figures compiled from registration reports (but not published) were close to or over 900 million. Soon thereafter, as it became clear that the fertility and population growth rates were declining, the veil of secrecy was lifted. The 1982 census, estimating a population total of 1.008 billion, confirmed the trend of a declining growth rate. The annual growth rate is estimated to have declined from 2.6 percent in 1965–70 to 1.2 percent in 1975–80 with intermediate rates of 2.2 percent in 1970–75 and 1.4 percent in 1975–80.

The 1953 census recorded a sex ratio of 107.6 males per 100 females— a relatively high ratio of males compared to industrialized countries. There is evidence that this was not a reflection of undercounting of females, but of lower life expectancy for females than males. Females died at a higher rate than males in many age groups. The 1964 census reported a sex ratio of 105.5 which, according to some scholars, is an underestimate because the entire military population was excluded from that census. Age-sex distribution data in 1953 and 1964 suggest that female infanticide and severe neglect of little girls diminished during the early Communist period. However, among children in age group 0–2, there was a higher male ratio in 1982 than in 1953 and 1964. This shift may be due to the promotion of the one-child family in the early 1980s. The strong preference for a son among the Chinese might have led many couples to kill their infant daughters— either outright or by severe neglect— so that they could try again for a son.

China's Communist government has exercised much greater control over interprovincial and rural-urban migration than most developing countries. Without political and economic controls on migration China's urban population would have constituted a much higher proportion than the estimated twenty-one percent for 1985–90. During the Communist regime migration from rural to urban areas has been allowed or encouraged only for brief periods; sometimes it has been reversed.

A sense of optimism about the rapid spread of industrialization in the large cities and the consequent need for workers from rural areas led the government to allow rural-urban migration during 1949–51 and 1958–60 (Great Leap Forward). In addition, economic dislocations caused by the rural commune movement of the Great Leap Forward period pushed many peasants toward the cities. The proportion of the population living in urban areas increased from 13 percent in 1953 to 20 percent in 1960. Subsequently, however, efforts were undertaken to reduce the size of the urban population, including, for example, the mandatory transfer of urban youth to rural areas, sometimes to distant provinces on the western frontier. It was a policy that aroused resentment not only among the youths and their families, but also among the peasants in the areas to which the youths were sent. Hence some of them returned to their urban homes despite official orders. Since the beginning of the 1980s a number of them have been permitted to return home. As a result the largest cities, including Shanghai, are experiencing some growth again. Meanwhile, restrictions on migration to small and medium-sized cities, especially to those away from the already developed coastal areas, have been relaxed slightly, but workers are often forbidden to bring their families. China's restrictions on urban population growth have been based not only on practical considerations but also on the Maoist perception of city dwellers as people corrupted by material comforts and of peasants as hard-working, productive, and virtuous people.

Fertility. The only data available for assessing the fertility rate in pre-revolutionary China are those of the China Farm Survey conducted by John Lossing Buck in seven provinces during 1929–31. However this has not prevented various European scholars from recording their own impressions of Chinese fertility. Reports of a very large and growing population in China despite frequent epidemics, recurrent famines, and dynastic conflicts have often led to speculation of Chinese prolificness. The orthodox view of fertility in late traditional China is summed up in the following observation of R.H. Tawney in his book *Land and Labour in China* (1926, p. 104):

Sentiment, hallowed by immemorial tradition, makes it a duty to have sons, and the communism of the patriarchal family dissociates the production of children from the responsibility of their maintenance. Hence prudential restraints act with less force than elsewhere; and population, instead of being checked by the gradual tightening of economic pressure on individuals, plunges blindly forward, till whole communities go over the precipice.

Anthropologists with expertise in late traditional China and experience in analyzing genealogical data from Taiwan do not subscribe to the simplistic observations quoted above, although they differ among themselves about fertility levels, fertility motivations, and fertility differentials in various regions and social strata in late traditional China. There is also controversy about the conclusions that can be made from the 1929–32 survey data. The estimated total fertility rate and the total marital fertility rate (expected number of children born to a woman during her reproductive period) based on responses of married couples are 5.4 and 6.1 respectively. These figures contradict the view of a very high fertility level in late traditional China. There seems to be a consensus that women married early, that marriage was universal, and that there was an absence of any deliberate control of fertility through contraception or induced abortion. Explanations as to why the fertility level was significantly lower than the maximum biological potential include prolonged breastfeeding, temporary separation of husband and wife due to drought or seasonal migration, impairment of fecundity due to health-related factors, and lack of sexual interest in couples where the partners were raised together ("minor" marriages).

According to a survey conducted in 1982 by the State Family Commission, the Chinese fertility rate was high and relatively stable at about six births per woman between 1940 and 1970. During the 1970s it declined to a degree that has no documented parallel in demographic history, from 5.8 in 1970 to 2.6 in 1981. After a slight rise in 1981 and 1982 it started declining again but the trend in the late 1980s has been toward rising rates. The crude birth rate (number of births per 1000 population in one year) declined from 37 births per 1000 population in 1970 to only 18 in 1980 and has been fluctuating in a manner similar to the total fertility rate in the 1980s. The determination of the government to reduce fertility through its family planning program has perhaps contributed most significantly to the decline in fertility over the last two decades, but the program could not have been as effective without simultaneous efforts by the government to introduce societal changes.

Sociocultural Changes Affecting Fertility. The traditional household structure in China has always encouraged moderately high fertility. The system of patrilocal marriage combined with patrilineal descent was reflected in a strong preference for sons, which affected fertility: the desire of parents to have at least one son to care for them in their old age, coupled with uncertainty about infant and child survival tended to result in large families. **Inherent in the patrilineal system are other social features favoring high fertility but important changes have occurred during recent decades to reduce the pronatalist effects of the system.** A few of them are stated below:

1. The radical improvement in health services, particularly in rural areas, has increased the chances of infant and child survival.

2. Legislation and campaigns have succeeded in raising substantially the age at marriage of women so that daughters can contribute their household labor and earned income to their natal family for a longer period, and are therefore considered less of an economic liability than they were in the past.

3. Although officially discouraged, the custom of paying a bride price has been increasing, while the dowry has declined in importance, possibly because young women are now more valuable to a household.

4. The government has attempted to provide limited old-age support in order to reduce parents' dependence on sons in their old age.

In general, collectivization of land and other economic transformations introduced by the Communist government reduced the economic value of children and created local leadership that could exert strong community pressure to support government policies. The local cadres of the Communist party who had a strong hold on local economic and social matters were instrumental in implementing, often with a heavy hand, family planning programs. The rural decollectivization of land and the consequent reestablishment of the family farm, coupled with a decrease in the intensity of political control over the rural economy in the 1980s, are held by many scholars as factors contributing to the recent rise in fertility.

One of the most important social changes resulting in declining fertility is the change in women's status during the Communist regime. In the past, almost all decisions in a woman's life were made by men— in the household of her parents as well as of her husband. The Marriage Law promulgated in 1950 proclaimed equality between husbands and wives, accorded property and inheritance rights to females, and set minimum ages for marriage. The status of women has changed dramatically since the 1950s, although they have still not achieved equality. A greater degree of communication and greater sharing of decision-making between marriage partners have facilitated the practice of birth control. Also, women's changing economic role— for example, their employment in nonagricultural jobs— has likewise contributed to declining fertility.

With the expansion of education under the Communist regime, men and women have been more willing to challenge the traditional authority structure and to engage more effectively in family planning. The proportion of the Chinese population attending junior middle school increased from 5 percent in 1964 to 18 percent in 1982. The government claims that enrollment among primary school age children increased from 25 percent in 1941 to 85 percent in 1965. A survey conducted in 1982 demonstrated that in both urban and rural areas, the educational level of women was inversely correlated with fertility. The costs involved in educating a child are also a factor limiting the size of a family: tuition is charged for all levels of school, and a child attending school cannot contribute to the family's food production or income.

The dramatic decline in fertility witnessed in China would not have been possible without an effective family planning program. Although the government recognized the country's rapid population growth as a hindrance to its economic growth as early as the mid-1950s, when it began to make sporadic efforts to introduce family planning, a comprehensive family planning program was not developed until the 1970s. A strong element of social pressure— often considered by outside observers to be coercive— was incorporated into the program, thus setting it apart from programs in other developing countries. During 1969–78 the government tried to encourage couples to limit their children to two. By 1978 a majority of couples in China were practicing contraception— mostly with effective modern methods.

By the end of the 1970s the government realized that, in view of a huge bulge in the population at the young adult ages, the population would continue to grow at a rate unfavorable to the country's economic development. Thus it promoted the one-child family with a policy of publicly praising women who gave birth to one child only and imposing economics sanctions on those who gave birth to three or more. Implemented differently from province to province, the policy has been effective in spreading the use of contraceptives, although it has been widely criticized in international circles. Allegations of increased female infanticide as well as compulsory abortion and sterilization have also been made.

China's family planning program includes promoting late marriage. The Marriage Law of 1950 set the minimum legal marriage ages at eighteen for females and twenty for males, significantly later than the traditional pattern of early marriage. In the first half of the 1960s many areas promulgated administrative rules prohibiting marriage before the age of twenty-five for women and thirty for men. Urban units and factory complexes were likewise expected to encourage late marriage. According to the available data, the average age at marriage began to rise slowly in the 1930s; by 1950 the average age of women was 18.7 years, and by 1979 it had risen to 23.1. It rose sharply in the 1970s and had a strong negative effect on the crude birth rate. In 1980 a new law raised the minimum age at marriage to twenty for women and twenty-two for men.

Mortality. Reported death rates up to the 1970s are usually underestimates. Available data indicate that the crude death rate was high in pre-Communist China, on the order of 40 per 1000 population in the 1930s and 1940s. Active warfare between Japan and China as well as between the Communist and Nationalist armies during those decades was partly responsible for high mortality. The Chinese Farmers Survey data of 1929–31 indicate an infant mortality rate (number of deaths within the first year per 1000 live births) of about 300. In cities the rate was lower, but it is unlikely that China attained an infant mortality rate of below 200 before 1949. Around one-third of the total infant deaths in 1929–31 were reported to have been caused by infectious disease.

As in many other developing countries, there was a significant decline in mortality in China during the 1950s. The decline was steeper and more far-reaching in China partly because the mortality rate had been higher and more radical socioeconomic and public health measures were implemented in China than in other countries. The 1950 government estimate of 18 per 1000 population as a crude death rate may be assumed to be an underestimate. At that time a tumultuous land reform struggle was in progress, and public health efforts had barely started. Moreover, there were epidemics of typhus, measles, scarlet fever, and dysentery that contributed to high mortality. According to some demographers, the crude death rate of about 30 or above in 1950 was approximately halved by 1957. This extraordinary decline may be attributed to: (1) cessation of warfare and maintenance of public order; (2) reduction of economic inequity through the redistribution of land and the nationalization of business and commercial assets; (3) introduction of a system of state purchase, storage, and distribution of food grain; and (4) initiation of preventive public health measures on a mass scale.

After 1957 China undertook the Great Leap Forward which resulted in fewer public health services and in shortages of food that culminated in the famine of 1960. An estimated 30 million excess deaths occurred between 1958 and 1961. The country recovered fully from the famine in 1962 and since then mortality has remained relatively low. The rate of mortality declined dramatically again in the early 1970s with the massive deployment of barefoot doctors in rural areas. By 1980–81 China had reduced its crude death rate to 8 per 1000 population, and its infant mortality rate to 35 per 1000 births—a remarkable achievement for a low per capita income country. Excess deaths during the Cultural Revolution did not seem to have any significant effect on population growth rate, according to U.N. estimates.

INDIA

Population Growth and Composition. Located near the center of neolithic technology—including agriculture, domesticated animals, polished stone tools, and pottery—ancient India had the basis for a more thickly settled population than ancient Europe. Archeological evidence of city-building settlers in the Indus valley, represented by finds at Harappa and Mohen-jo-daro, and of the Aryan settlers in the Punjab and Gangetic plain, indicates that the peoples in these areas some three to seven thousand years ago possessed a technology sufficiently advanced to support a dense population. India also provided a favorable environment for the application of this technology. Archeological, literary, and historical evidence suggests that by ca. 300 B.C.E. the population stood at between 100 and 140 million. During the next two thousand years or so it remained at that level with periods of growth curtailed by catastrophe in the form of warfare, famine, or epidemic, that would shrink the population. This pattern continued up until the early part of this century. The annual growth rate was under two-thirds of 1 percent during 1891–1911 and negative during 1911–1921.

Since then the rate of population growth has accelerated, mainly due to a decline in mortality that has far outstripped the decline in fertility. Epidemics were controlled and DDT helped to check the impact of malaria. During the 1960s the annual growth rate rose up to 2.2 percent and remained at that level during the 1970s. It started declining in the 1980s. There are considerable variations in the growth rates among the Indian states.

There has been an excess of males over females in each census since census-taking began in the Indian subcontinent in the 1860s. The excess of males increased steadily from 1901 to 1971. This excess is due mainly to higher mortality of females from infancy through childbearing age—a reflection of discrimination against women in a patriarchal society. Kerala is the only state in which women outnumber men.

India has never experienced rapid rural-urban migration. The urban centers in pre-British India were few in number and did not rest primarily upon industrial and commercial development, but rather on political and religious functions. The growth of the city as a center of industry and trade is a recent phenomenon. Of the total population, those living in urban areas increased from about 11 percent in 1901 to 24 percent in 1981. Unlike the situation in many other countries, the excess of males among India's urban population is much greater than for the country as a whole. It has adverse consequences on women's economic and social status because infrastructure facilities are better in urban areas. The rural population, living in more than 500,000 villages (two-fifths with a population of less than 1000) is widely scattered, resulting in high per capita costs of providing a modern infrastructure, such as roads, schools, and health facilities.

Fertility. Hinduism, the religion of 83 percent of India's population, neither encourages high fertility nor prohibits contraception, but sociocultural institutions and beliefs associated with it (e.g., joint family system, patriarchy, performance by son of funeral rites of father, prepuberty marriage of girls) are favorable to high fertility. The institutions and beliefs associated with Islam (e.g., joint family system, patriarchy, and beliefs favorable to population growth and unfavorable to surgical sterilization), the religion of 11 percent of the population, are even more conducive to high fertility.

The crude birth rates, estimated from census data, varied between 45 and 50 per 1000 from 1881 to 1961: the average family comprised six to seven children, fewer than the theoretical biological maximum. The practices of prolonged breastfeeding and sexual abstinence after childbirth were perhaps the major mechanisms somewhat controlling fertility. There is evidence to suggest that even before the introduction of modern contraceptives, Hindus of higher castes had lower fertility than those of lower castes; and Hindus, generally, had lower fertility than Muslims and tribal groups. The explanation apparently does not lie in differential practices of traditional birth control methods (e.g., induced abortion, rhythm method, or withdrawal), but rather in the fact that customs like widow celibacy and prolonged sexual abstinence were practiced more rigorously by Hindus than others.

The birth rate has been declining since the mid-1960s, coinciding with a major expansion of the national family planning program that had been initiated in 1952 with the specific purpose of controlling population growth. The birth rate declined at a faster rate in the 1970s due mainly to the increased use of contraception and, to a lesser extent, the trend of higher age at marriage of women; for reasons not fully understood, the rate has remained relatively constant, between 32 and 34, throughout the 1980s.

The national family planning program provides contraceptive supplies, services, and information free of cost through its wide network of primary health centers and sub-centers. In 1986 about 41 percent of 133 million married couples of reproductive age participated in the program. Although various types of birth control methods are available, sterilization (mostly female) is the method of choice for two-fifths of couples practicing contraception. The reasons include (1) the desire of many couples to have at least two sons and one daughter before using any method; (2) fear of side effects of other methods and inadequate facilities for contraceptive counselling; (3) higher motivation to use contraception among women than men; and (4) belief that sterilization may have more harmful side effects on men than women.

The average age at marriage of women has always been quite low in India. The social institutions that favor early marriage of women include (1) the patrilocal system of newly-married couples living with the groom's parents for at least some years after marriage; (2) strong sanction against girls having premarital sexual relations; (3) higher amount of dowry necessary for marriage of older girls; and (4) the ideal of a wide age gap between bride and groom. Despite the existing law setting the minimum marriage age girls at eighteen, more than two-fifths of marriages involve girls under that age. However, the average age at marriage of women has been increasing steadily—from 13.7 in 1910–1919 to 18.7 in 1981.

Changes in the use of contraception and age at marriage reflect changes in sociocultural and economic conditions. Family planning programs have made it easier for couples so motivated to practice contraception, but the trend toward the small family during the last three decades is mainly due to perceived economic, social, and cultural changes in the value and costs of children to their parents. In a 1980 survey 56 percent of couples having one son and one daughter did not want any additional children. This represents a significant attitudinal change in a society where sons are highly valued and child mortality is still quite high.

Fertility rates vary considerably among different socioeconomic groups; better educated women tend to marry later and use contraceptives to a greater extent larger proportion than illiterate or less educated women. Fertility in urban areas is lower than in rural areas. Differences in married women's fertility rates according to education are greater in urban than in rural India. The higher fertility rate among Muslims than among Hindus is related in part to the relatively lower level of education, occupation, and income, to earlier age of marriage, and to the less prevalent use of contraceptives among Muslims. Muslim women give birth to an average of one more child than do Hindu women.

Interstate fertility differentials are quite high in India. For example, in 1984–86 the crude birth rate per 1000 population was 23 in Kerala compared to 38 in Uttar Pradesh, with a national average of 33. Kerala has attracted international attention for its relative success in lowering fertility despite its lower than the national average per capita income. Sociocultural factors favoring contraceptive use and delayed age at marriage of women in Kerala include: (1) relatively high literacy rate; (2) matriarchal tradition of various castes; (3) influence of Christian missionaries; (4) equity in social development due to radical social movements among some lower castes.

Mortality. Throughout the history of India, the changes in its population growth rate have reflected fluctuations not in the birth rate but rather in the mortality rate. The population grew when there was a relative absence of catastrophe— famine, epidemic, war— that sometimes took millions of lives. Statistics are available on three such catastrophes— the great famines of 1876–78 and 1898–1900, and the influenza epidemic of 1918 in which more than fifteen million people died.

There has been a sharper and steadier decline in the mortality rate in India since 1920 than at any previous time, although it had been declining very gradually over the course of the preceding century. The crude death rate is estimated to have declined from 47 per 1000 population in 1921 to 12 in 1984–86, attributable mostly to the control of epidemic diseases and famine. The gradual improvement of public health services significantly reduced the number of deaths due to diseases like smallpox, malaria, cholera, and plague.

The rate of mortality decline, however, has slowed since the mid-1960s, by which time the major benefits from low-cost public health measures like smallpox vaccination and DDT-spraying campaigns had already been derived. Diarrhea, dysentery, and respiratory diseases, particularly tuberculosis and pneumonia, in combination with chronic malnutrition have become the major causes of death. Any further lowering of the mortality rate will require massive public investment in the areas of nutrition, water supply, and primary health care.

In India the mortality rate has always been higher among female than among male children. The sex differential in infant mortality can be explained partly by female infanticide, but to a greater extent it is attributable to the preferential treatment of sons in terms of health care and food. In the patriarchal tradition of Indian society, boys are often considered as assets to the family, while girls are expected to leave the family at the time of marriage.

There is a large difference in mortality rates between urban and rural areas, due mainly to differences in health care services and educational attainment. For example, in 1978 the infant mortality rate was 136 per 1000 births in rural areas, compared to 71 in urban areas; only 24 percent of births in rural areas occurred in medical institutions or were attended by trained medical practitioners, compared to 66 percent in urban areas. Only 2 percent of the rural population had potable water in their homes, as compared to 64 percent of the urban population.

As in the case of fertility, interstate differentials in mortality are also significant. For example, in 1984–86 the crude death rate per 1000 population was 7 in Kerala, compared to 16 in Uttar Pradesh and 12 in India as a whole. Similarly, the infant mortality rate in Kerala was 27, compared to 132 in Uttar Pradesh and 96 nationally. One main factor underlying Kerala's unusual success in reducing mortality is its long tradition of providing good health care services. The sociocultural factors that have contributed to this tradition in Kerala are the same as those that have favored high contraceptive use and delayed age at marriage for women (mentioned above).

JAPAN

Population Growth and Composition. Demographers agree, on the basis of household registration data, that population growth accelerated in Japan during the first half of the Tokugawa period (1603–1867) but slowed almost to a standstill during the second half. From the early eighteenth to the middle nineteenth century, birth and death rates were high— as was the case in many regions in the pre-industrial era— and the population is estimated to have remained stable at a level of approximately thirty million.

Stagnant population growth at this time was due not only to natural catastrophes like famines and epidemics, but also to deliberate population control through abortion, infanticide, and delayed marriage. The following characteristics of the social organization in Tokugawa Japan allowed the shogunate, through village headman and council, to exercise a degree of control over a couple's fertility behavior: (1) relative cohesiveness and autonomy (e.g., in collecting land tax and maintaining local irrigation system) of the village; (2) use of social pressure to regulate individual behavior for the common good; and (3) authority of household head over marriage, divorce, setting up of branch house, outmigration of members. Toward the end of the Tokugawa period, however, the central shogunate and local feudal clans became concerned about the stagnant agricultural work force and took measures (e.g., birthsubsidies) to encourage high fertility and discourage rural-urban migration, but these were not effective.

After the Meiji Restoration in 1868 the population began to grow rapidly. The total population is estimated to have increased from 40 million in 1867 to 56 million in 1920 (beginning of census taking) and to 69 million by 1935. Rapid population growth became a matter of national concern following the "rice riots" in 1918, when the impoverished masses protested the high price of rice and rioted in many parts of the country. During the 1920s social scientists debated population growth policies, with some favoring Malthusian and others leaning toward Marxian doctrines. A government-sponsored commission produced eight reports between 1927 and 1930 on various aspects of population, including the desirability of birth control.

However, throughout the 1930s, when Japan was involved in minor wars and preparing for a major one, the political atmosphere was increasingly antagonistic to birth control. A shortage of manpower became the major concern and population policy was generally pronatalist. In 1940 the National Eugenic Law was promulgated with the objective of preventing the increase of "inferior" descendants and of protecting women for whom pregnancy would involve severe health hazards. An amended version of this law, called the Eugenic Protection Law, was passed by the Diet of Japan in 1948 and made effective in 1949. The stated justification for the law remained eugenic and medical but its following three provisions had a negative effect on fertility: (1) the performance of abortion by private physicians for reasons of maternal health, (2) the performance of sterilization for reasons of excessive childbearing as measured by health criteria, and (3) extension of contraceptive facilities. A national policy encouraging large families and early marriages was adopted in 1941 but the growth rate continued to decline because of a downward trend in fertility associated with socioeconomic progress and increase in birth control facilities. The annual growth rates have shown some fluctuations since 1950, ranging from a high of 1.4 percent in 1950–55 to 0.4 percent in 1985–90.

There is some evidence to suggest that male children outnumbered female children in Tokugawa villages indicating that most couples probably attained their desired family size by practicing female infanticide along with birth control through abortion and delayed marriage. The sex ratio in the total population continued to favor males until 1940. Since then it has always favored females, as in other industrialized countries. According to the 1980 census, males outnumber females at almost all age groups up to fifty years, but thereafter females outnumber males at a ratio that increases steadily with age.

Japan is among the world's most densely populated countries. The uneven distribution of its population has been observed since early times. Until the seventeenth century the area around Kyoto, the administrative and cultural center, and Osaka, the economic center, was the most densely populated part of the country. With the advent of the Tokugawa shogunate, the population shifted eastward to Edo (now Tokyo), the new capital. During the Meiji period the promotion of industrial development resulted in a more even distribution of the population, but since 1920 the distribution has been generally becoming more uneven, with the population becoming densely concentrated around Tokyo.

The urban population in Japan increased from 18 percent in 1920 to 76 percent in 1980. A recent significant aspect of urbanization is metropolitanization, the result of a government policy adopted in 1953, of promoting the annexation by large cities of small cities, towns, and villages. Urbanization in Japan is closely related to industrialization. The number of cities with a population of more than 100,000 increased from 16 in 1920 to 193 in 1970, and the proportion of total population in major metropolitan areas increased from 34 percent in 1960 to 46 percent in 1980. Metropolitanization has resulted in an outmigration of residents from city centers to outlying areas, with an increasing number of people commuting into the city for work, shopping, and school.

Fertility. Fertility data on premodern Japan, collected as a byproduct of the civil registration system *koseki*, are incomplete. For the period 1865–1920, crude birth rate estimates range from 31 to 38 per 1000 population, indicating a slight trend of increase beginning with the Meiji era. There was a more or less gradual trend of decline in the crude birth rate from 1920 to 1939, when it reached 27 per 1000 population. Severe fluctuations in the birth rate during the World War II years (1941–45) were followed by a postwar baby boom during 1947–49, when the birth rate varied between 33 and 35. Since 1950 the rate has been declining, more or less steadily. The rate plunged to 14 in 1966, the year of the "fiery horse"; according to Japanese folklore, ill luck befalls a child, particularly a girl, who is born in that year, which occurs once every six decades.

Modernization generally reduces fertility, but in the early years of economic development the birth rate often rises for reasons that vary according to sociocultural and economic situations. The trend of increasing birth rate in Japan from the late 1880s to the 1910s is attributed by some scholars to dramatic economic growth during the period due to industrialization. The decline of fertility since the 1920s (except the fluctuation related to World War II), especially since the 1950s, is clearly related to economic development, industrialization, and urbanization— processes that reduce the value of children to their parents and increase the costs of raising them. These processes, and the decline in fertility, occurred much faster in Japan than in Western countries.

By 1920 family planning was being promoted in Japan for population control as well as for personal and familial well-being. Birth control was also advocated in connection with the emancipation of women. Partly a consequence of Margaret Sanger's visit to Japan in 1922, birth control clinics were set up in some parts of the country, although on a small scale. Among the proponents of birth control were differences in attitude toward induced abortion; some regarded it as a necessary evil, others were bitterly opposed to it. The population control movement experienced a serious setback in 1935 when the government initiated policies favoring population expansion.

During the decade that Japan was at war, the birth control movement was virtually nonexistent; since 1945 family planning has become an accepted facet of Japanese life. In the years immediately following the war, growth, along with economic hardship for many families made birth control a subject of public debate. Newspapers launched extensive campaigns supporting family planning. Since contraceptive techniques available at the time were not sufficiently reliable, abortion was the most widely used fertility control method. Women in large number took advantage of liberalization of abortion, as provided in the 1948–49 amended version of the 1940 National Eugenic Law. The role played by induced abortion in the reduction of Japanese fertility has been significant, particularly during 1950–1960. Concerned over the high rate of induced abortion— over a million per year in the early 1950s— the government established a family planning program in 1952 to promote the use of contraceptives.

Contraceptive use among married couples of reproductive age increased from 20 percent in 1954 to 62 percent in 1979. The methods used by Japanese couples present certain unique features; there has been no significant change in the pattern of methods used during 1950–79. The most popular contraceptive method in Japan has always been the condom; Japan has the highest condom use rate in the world. In 1979, it was the method of choice for 81 percent of couples practicing contraception; the next in popularity was the rhythm method (23 percent), followed by contraceptive rings (8 percent). The reasons for the unusually high rate of condom use in Japan include: (1) low cost and convenience; (2) reluctance to use methods that involve surgery, insertion of foreign objects, intake of chemicals; (3) unavailability of other methods in a cultural context of embarrassment and passivity toward contraception; (4) strong motivation for family planning among males as well as females; and (5) high quality of Japanese-made condoms.

In contrast with China and India, early marriage for women was not always a social ideal in Japan during the preindustrial era. Household head often had the authority to delay the marriage of younger members of the household if he considered it necessary for the common good. The age at marriage of both women and men rose gradually with the advent of industrialization. By 1920 the average age at marriage (based on census data) was twenty-one for women and twenty-five for men; by 1960 it had risen to 25 and 28, respectively. Although the higher age of women at marriage had a negative effect on fertility, the increasing use of contraception was the most important factor in the decline of fertility in Japan.

As a consequence of substantially reduced fertility in Japan as in other industrialized countries, there has been for some time a trend toward an aging of the population. For example, the proportion of those aged 65 years and over has increased from 5.3 percent of the total population in 1920 to 9.1 percent in 1980. Since 1950, this trend has been primarily a result of declining fertility; improved mortality has played a smaller role. Population projections for the year 2025 suggest that Japan is likely to become the world's most aged population. The projected aging of the population (and the increasing proportion of elderly women) has raised a number of issues with regard to family structure, housing arrangements, and social security of the elderly.

Mortality. Although data prior to 1920 are incomplete, a gradual decline in mortality began in the second half of the nineteenth century. The crude death rate declined from about 23 per 1000 population in the early 1920s to 16 in the early 1940s. The death rate was higher during World War II, with a peak of 29 in 1945, but it declined rapidly to 15 in 1947. In spite of the postwar economic difficulties, the rate declined by about 48 percent between 1947 and 1960. By 1985–90 it had declined to 7 per 1000 population, but as a result of aging of the population the crude death rate is expected to stabilize in the coming decade. The estimated infant mortality rate of 5 per 1000 live births in Japan during 1985–90 is the lowest in the world.

In the decades before the war, respiratory diseases, gastroenteritis, and tuberculosis were the major causes of death in Japan, particularly among children under five years of age. With the introduction of antibiotics in the postwar period the major causes of death have been replaced by cerebro-vascular disease, cancer, and heart disease. Technology has enabled Japan to reduce its mortality level significantly but, at the same time, has increased the risk of mortality from causes related to modernization. For example, in 1979, accidents became the major cause of death among all males under twenty-five years of age and females under ten years; 82 percent of accidental deaths were due to motor vehicle accidents. In the same year, suicide, which had never been a major cause of death in the early 20th century, accounted for the highest proportion of deaths among males aged 25–34 years and females aged 15–34 years.

III. ISSUES FOR DISCUSSION

1. Identify the critical sociocultural and economic factors that have influenced the postwar demographic trends of China, India, and Japan.

2. Why is the fertility level of the United States or any other industrialized society significantly lower compared to that of contemporary India?

3. What are your policy recommendations for balanced population growth in the Third World?

IV. SELECTED READINGS

(The sources cited below do not require knowledge of analytical demography for comprehension and hence should not be difficult for students, but it is advisable to assign specific chapters of the books cited according to the specific interests of the students.)

Banister, Judith. *China's Changing Population.* Stanford: Stanford University Press, 1987.

Davis, Kinglsey. *The Population of India and Pakistan.* Princeton: Princeton University Press, 1951.

Nag, Moni. "Population in Asian Countries: Trends, Issues, and Strategies." *Economic and Political Weekly* 20(1985). Also published as "Population: An Overview." In *Encyclopedia of Asian History,* edited by Ainslie T. Embree, vol. 3, pp. 266–271. New York: Charles Scribner's Sons, 1988.

Taeuber, Irene B. *The Population of Japan.* Princeton: Princeton, University Press, 1958. United Nations. Economic and Social Commission for Asia and the Pacific.

Population of Japan. New York: United Nations, 1984.

Visaria, Pravin, and Leela Visaria. *India's Population: Second and Growing.* Washington: Population Reference Bureau, 1981.

Sociology: India

Education in India

Joseph W. Elder

I. INTRODUCTION: CENTRAL POINTS

Education in India has a history of some forty centuries, during which time it has been promoted with a variety of intentions, ranging from preserving the status of the elite to reducing the disparities among the different status groups. Both the content and form of education in India reveal a great deal about the many different groups in India and their differing ideologies and structures. These groups include religious communities, tribes (living in relative social and economic isolation), and castes [*Readers are referred to the discussion of the definition of caste in the essays on "Stratification, Inequality, Caste System: India," by Owen M. Lynch, and "Religion in a State Society: India," by Lawrence A. Babb*].

• Contemporary education in India is reflective of India's long and complex history. From the fifth century B.C.E. onward for nearly a millennium the two major forms of education in India were the Hindu mentor (guru)-disciple system and the Buddhist monastery-education system. The former system was exclusive, restricted almost entirely to the sons of elite families, and focused on the Sanskrit language and texts used by Brahman priests in performing their ceremonies. The Buddhist monastery-education system was open to boys and girls of all social classes, was con-

493

ducted in vernaculars, and focused on Buddhist doctrines on attaining release from the cycle of reincarnation. When Muslims appeared on the scene, they established neighborhood schools in which children were taught seventh-century Arabic so they could study the Qur'an in the language in which it was revealed. Centers of higher Islamic studies in India were linked to similar centers throughout the Muslim world.

• Beginning in the 1830s the British East India Company, after studying various alternatives, introduced in the sections of India under its control a system of education patterned after the British model with English as the medium of instruction (especially at the higher levels) and with courses and syllabi similar to those used in Britain. The goal was to produce a class of Indians who were "English in taste, in opinions, in morals, and in intellect." Within a century various prominent Indian citizens had launched alternative educational efforts designed to preserve and develop Indian, rather than British, languages and learning, and to prevent India's younger generations from becoming alienated from indigenous cultures.

• Following independence in 1947, the government of India decided to replace the English medium of instruction with local vernaculars. Even more radical was the government's system of "protective discrimination," which provided scholarships and financial assistance and reserved percentages of admissions into colleges, universities, and professional schools for the one-tenth to one-fifth of India's population belonging to the "scheduled castes and tribes" that for centuries had suffered widespread discrimination at the hands of higher castes.

• Despite these efforts, India is still a long way from providing the free compulsory education for all children through age fourteen, as envisaged in its Constitution. Considerable illiteracy still exists (particularly among girls and women); children not enrolled in schools today belong disproportionately to the scheduled castes and tribes. Surprisingly, English has emerged as a medium of instruction and as a link language throughout India, **despite** decisions made by India's leaders in the 1940s and 1950s to reduce the role of the English language.

II. MAJOR TOPICS

HISTORICAL OVERVIEW

A system of writing existed on the Indian subcontinent as early as 2500 B.C.E. Hundreds of small stone seals on which this writing was carved have been discovered in sites associated with the Harappan civilization settlements along the rivers and shorelines of northwestern India. The system of writing has never been deciphered, however, and nothing is known of the manner in which it was transmitted.

The earliest known educational system on the subcontinent, beginning about 1500 B.C.E., involved the transmission of **memorized**— rather than written— Hindu Vedas (sacred hymns) from a priest-teacher to his elite-class students. Special techniques were used to memorize and transmit the Vedas word for word (e.g., repeating each word independently, then with the preceding word, then with the following word). The language was Vedic, from which Sanskrit later evolved. Throughout this period, women and non-elite were generally discouraged (or actually prohibited) from learning the Vedic language or the Vedas. The knowledge being transmitted was of use primarily to Brahman priests in their performance of sacred rituals, which they increasingly monopolized.

Buddhism, founded around 500 B.C.E. by Siddhārtha Gautama, a prince in a north Indian ruling family, challenged the Brahman (Hindu) priests and their virtual monopoly of education and ritual performances. Buddhist teachers used the spoken languages (Prakrits) of the day and encouraged their followers to enter monasteries and convents where they could collectively receive an education in Buddhist texts written in Buddhist Sanskrit as well as in vernaculars.

For nearly fifteen centuries the two systems of education continued side by side. Elite Hindu boys studied Vedic and Sanskrit texts with their Brahman mentors (gurus) and applied their training to the preservation of written (as well as memorized) Hindu texts and the performance of Hindu rituals. The Hindu Brahman mentor-to-student education based on memorization of ancient texts has continued to the present.

Buddhist monasteries flourished all over India, teaching students from a variety of socioeconomic classes. In time, Buddhist monastic **universities** appeared, the most prominent of which was Nalanda University, founded in central North India in the fifth century C.E. Eventually it had an enrollment of some five thousand students, including foreign scholars, and offered instruction in the Vedas and Hindu philosophies as well as in the Buddhist texts. Libraries existed in private homes, monasteries, and royal courts; copying and preserving manuscripts became a profession. Although Buddhism had already been declining in

India for several centuries, the destruction of Nalanda University by Muslim armies in 1197 C.E. marked the end of widespread Buddhist monastic education in India.

Wherever they went, Muslims introduced neighborhood schools that featured instruction in the Arabic of the seventh century C.E., so that students could study the Qur'an (Koran) in its original language. Over time, seminaries were established in Muslim-dominated areas of India to train Islamic priests and scholars. Some of these scholars traveled for further training to such Muslim centers as Cairo and Mecca, thereby establishing links between Indian and worldwide Islamic scholarship.

EDUCATION UNDER
THE BRITISH RAJ

In the early 1500s, on the heels of Portuguese traders, Dominican and Jesuit missionaries arrived in South India; their evangelizing and educational activities continued in the Portuguese and French-controlled territories in India for the next four centuries. The British East India Company, however, prohibited any Christian missions or schools in the territories under its jurisdiction in an effort not to offend Hindu and Muslim sensibilities. With its charter revision in 1813 the Company changed this policy and committed itself to providing education in its territories, with the purpose of promoting the "extension, not the monopoly" of learning.

Company policymakers debated over the language and content of the education they should promote. The "Orientalists" argued that the Company-financed schools should teach vernacular languages, Sanskrit, and Oriental subject matter. The "Anglicists" argued that Western learning through the English language should be taught. In 1835 Thomas B. Macaulay's famous Minute on Education successfully urged the Governor-General's Council to adopt the "Anglicist" position:

> The question now before us is simply whether . . . when we can patronize sound philosophy and true history, we shall countenance at the public expense, medical doctrines which would disgrace an English farrier, astronomy which would move laughter in girls at an English boarding school, history abounding with kings thirty feet high and reigns thirty thousand years long, and geography, made up of seas of treacle and seas of butter . . . .We must at present do our best to form a class who may be interpreters between us and the millions whom we govern; a

class of persons, Indian in blood and color, but English in taste, in opinions, in morals, and in intellect.

Initially the British forbade religious instruction in Company-supported schools, making India's one of the world's first secular public school systems. After 1854, government grants were given to schools that were sponsored by Hindu, Muslim, or Christian groups requiring religious instruction. The principle observed was one of impartial support for all religious schools rather than non-support for any. (This contrasts with the U.S. position of no state aid to religious schools.)

In 1857 the Company founded the first universities in Calcutta, Madras, and Bombay, patterned after the British model, with a system of examinations and certification, and instruction by affiliated colleges. In 1882 the British decided to leave higher education to private enterprise whenever possible. This stimulated a rapid growth of colleges sponsored by religious groups, castes, and sects—paralleling the proliferation of colleges in the United States during the nineteenth century sponsored by religious groups and denominations.

In time, some Indians began to suspect that the ultimate purpose of the British system of education was to produce clerks and bookkeepers to support the functioning of the British Raj. Furthermore, Hindu and Muslim intellectuals expressed concern that the Western subjects taught in the rapidly growing colleges were alienating young Indians from their own heritage. The year 1875 saw the establishment of Aligarh Muslim University for the study of Arabic, Persian, the Qur'an, and Islamic subjects. In 1916 critics of British higher education founded Banaras Hindu University which focused on the Sanskrit language and classical Hindu and Buddhist subjects. In 1921 Nobel Laureate Rabindranath Tagore started Shantiniketan, a rural educational center specializing in Indian art, literature, music, and dance. In 1937 Mahatma Gandhi launched his Wardha Scheme for mass education that was to involve "education of body, mind and soul through the handicraft that is taught to the children" (e.g., spinning, weaving, farming). Gandhi hoped that children, especially in the villages, would learn the dignity of labor, the limitation of aspiration, and the avoidance of false Western values. His school system was to be self-supporting, serving as a model for the self-reliant village and nation. Gandhi himself said, "I have given many things to India. But this system of education together with its technique is, I feel, the best of them. . . ."

EDUCATION FOLLOWING INDEPENDENCE IN 1947

Secular Education Policy. According to India's Constitution (promulgated on January 26, 1950), education is primarily under the purview of state governments rather than under local school boards (as in the United States) or the central government (as in many developing countries). Article 28(3) of the Constitution elaborates the principle of religious neutrality by declaring that no government-aided school can require students to participate in religious instruction or worship. This secular policy is in contrast to the sectarian educational policies of Buddhist Sri Lanka, Muslim Pakistan, and Hindu Nepal.

The Problem of an Official Language. The English language had been a major facilitator in India's struggle for independence. It was the one common language spoken by educated Indians from all sections of the subcontinent. From its inception in 1888 the Indian National Congress, ultimately the main agency in India's struggle for independence, conducted its activities and annual meetings in English. India's preindependence leaders were typically university graduates, lawyers, educators, and journalists, many of whom prided themselves on their use of English. The 1928 Motilal Nehru report arguing for India's complete self-government with dominion status within the British Empire was entirely in English, as were the final documents granting India its independence.

India's Constitution, however, declared Hindi as the country's official language, but provided that English could continue to be used for official purposes for fifteen years (i.e., until 1965). Consequently, Hindi language instruction was introduced into schools throughout the land. But political agitation by the two-thirds of Indians who did not speak the language and feared "Hindi imperialism" led in 1967 to the Official Languages (Amendment) Bill extending indefinitely the use of English for official purposes. That same bill recommended that education in all states and at all levels should be conducted in the local vernaculars. The problem remains one of balancing the local vernaculars (the languages in which children learn most rapidly) against Hindi or English (the all-India languages for official use).

Protective Discrimination. Perhaps the most radical policy introduced in postindependent India was that of "protective discrimination," which favored India's "scheduled castes and tribes."

Between one-tenth and one-fifth of India's population had for centuries been considered ritually contaminated ("polluted" or "untouchable"), and had been denied access to certain Hindu temples, barred from traveling on certain roads and using certain wells, refused religious services by Brahman priests, and prevented from attending school. In the late 1800s non-Hindu missionaries and Hindu reformers became increasingly concerned about the plight of these "Untouchables." In 1921 Mahatma Gandhi linked the abolition of untouchability with the attainment of independence. By 1935 the British government had prepared a schedule listing the groups throughout India against whom discrimination had been especially severe. These came to be known as the "scheduled castes and tribes."

In 1950 the Constitution (drafted under the direction of Dr. Bimrao Ambedkar, a member of a scheduled caste) abolished "untouchability" and forbade discrimination in any form. Furthermore, it declared that members of all groups should have equal access to public facilities (similar to the U.S. civil rights legislation of 1964 and 1968), and provided for certain temporary policies of protective discrimination: for example, a certain proportion of seats in parliament and in state legislative assemblies and a number of jobs in the state and central civil services were reserved exclusively for members of the "scheduled castes and tribes." (India's proportional "quota system" for dealing with historical inequities would be considered unconstitutional in the United States, where "guidelines" are suggested instead.)

States, in turn, introduced their own protective discrimination policies, especially regarding education. Children from "scheduled castes and tribes" were sometimes provided with scholarships, book allowances, room and board in dormitories, and special admission quotas into universities and professional schools.

In addition to targeting the "scheduled castes and tribes" for special benefits, India's Constitution identified "backward classes" as also entitled to special attention, although it provided no clear criteria for determining which groups constituted so-called backward classes (unlike the lists of "scheduled castes and tribes" that are relatively unambiguous). As a result, political candidates have sometimes promised that, if elected, they would place certain groups on the backward classes list, thereby entitling their members to special benefits. This has engendered considerable tensions and, occasionally, outbursts of violence among different groups. The 1985 riots in Ahmedabad that left scores dead and hundreds injured were sparked by political candidates proposing changes in the ratios of castes admitted as backward classes into local engineering, agricultural, veterinary, and polytechnic institutions.

CONTEMPORARY PATTERNS OF EDUCATION IN INDIA

Literacy. Following independence, the literacy rate in India rose from 17 percent in 1951 to 36 percent in 1981; during that same period, however, the actual number of illiterates in India rose from 300 million to 437 million. Sharp differences exist between female and male literacy rates: using arbitrary definitions of what is meant by "literacy," according to some estimates in 1981 only 25 percent of women were literate, compared with 47 percent of men [*For slightly different estimates of literary rates, see Doranne Jacobson, p. 57*]. The gap between female and male literacy rates was wider in rural areas (18 percent and 41 percent) than in urban areas (48 percent and 66 percent). According to World Bank estimates, by the year 2000 India may have the largest illiterate population in the world (about 55 percent of the world's illiterate population between the ages of fifteen and nineteen).

Universal Education. Article 45 of the Indian Constitution established as a national goal, to be achieved by 1960, the provision of free, compulsory education to all children through age fourteen. As the following table shows, in 1986, twenty five years after the target date, that goal had not been realized. Most of the children not in school belong either to the lower status groups, including those from families of rural landless laborers or urban slum dwellers or to the "scheduled castes and tribes"; more than two-thirds of those not in school are girls.

SCHOOL ENROLLMENTS IN INDIA, 1986

School Level	% School-age Population	Millions
grades I–V	95%	89 million
grades VI–VIII	56%	29 million
High School	26%	14 million
College & University	4%	4 million

In 1984 India was spending only about 3.1 percent of its gross national product on education (contrasted with an average of 3.7

percent in other developing countries, 5.0 percent in the United States, 5.1 percent in Japan, and 6.4 percent in Sweden).

Enduring Importance of English. One unanticipated consequence of India's education policies has been the enduring prevalence of the English language. When India became independent, virtually every national leader, including Nehru, Gandhi, the mayors of its largest cities, and the vice-chancellors of its major universities declared themselves committed to reducing the prominence of the English language and its associated subjects in India's educational system. They generally subscribed to the view that for too many years the Western educational system had attracted the young elite away from their ancient heritage, and had converted them into pale imitations of Westerners, with false, foreign values and a deeply ingrained sense of inferiority to the West. Only the tiniest fraction of India's population spoke English as their mother tongue, and with the colonial masters gone and with no indigenous base of support, the English language would wither away, to be replaced by the vernaculars spoken by the vast majority.

Today far more Indians have facility in English than was the case when India became independent in 1947. A network of six hundred central schools throughout India educate in English the children of central government employees who are subject to be transferred to any area of the country. The best private schools in India either teach entirely in English or have bilingual English and vernacular programs. In addition, a vast network of tutorial institutes, intensive language programs, and private tutors have developed to meet the demand for English-language training. How could this be?

As indicated earlier, Hindi was unacceptable in much of India as a replacement for English. Because of their confinement to limited sectors of India, vernaculars could not replace English. So English continued to be used because it was needed— as the language of higher education and technical training, of legislation and legal codes, of parliamentary debate and national party dialogue, and of national-circulation newspapers and magazines. English was the language that enabled Indian citizens to move from the local to the national base, and from the national to international base. India's radio and television do much of their broadcasting in English. India's growing numbers of five-star hotels require employees (from waiters to top-level administrators) to be fluent in English. Today English is, in effect, the link language of the 100 million members of India's middle class; as their numbers grow, India's educational institutions will be increasingly required to produce graduates who are fluent in English. From the socio-logical perspective, the postindependence survival and growth of English in India reflects an interesting setting in which the social and economic advantages of knowing English are so strong that policies enunciated by even the most powerful political figures at the highest levels could not prevent more and more millions of Indians from studying and using English.

III. ISSUES FOR DISCUSSION

1. In certain societies (Hindu India two millennia ago) an ac-knowledged goal of the educational system was to preserve the status of the elite by restricting access to education. In certain other societies (e.g., the contemporary United States) an acknowl-edged goal of the educational system has been to "level the play-ing field" by broadening access to education. Describe the different strategies (e.g., language of instruction, funding for edu-cation, admission requirements) societies have adopted to achieve these two different goals. Over time, how successful have different societies been in achieving these two different goals?

2. The British East India Company's imposition of English-me-dium instruction, the British school system, and British univer-sity syllabi on India have been labeled "cultural imperialism" and has been seen as an effort by the British to "alienate" young Indians from their own culture and to convert them into function-aries of the British Raj. However, the Indian nationalist movement that fought for—and eventually won—India's independence from the British was founded and led by men and women who were products of this "cultural imperialism." Instead of being "alien-ated" from India, they championed India's freedom. How can one explain such a paradox?

3. When India became independent in 1947, virtually every national leader advocated the termination of English as the me-dium of instruction, and India's constitution declared that after fifteen years English would no longer be an official language of India. Yet today English continues to be one of India's official languages, and the popularity of English-language instruction is at an all-time high. How can one explain an historical event such as this, where, despite near-unanimity among those in power and near total control of the nation's educational system by those in power, the policies they advocated were, from the beginning, widely ignored and eventually were overruled by popular demand? Can one think of similar instances where popular demand over-

ruled policy decisions made by powerful ruling elites? What sociological variables seem to come into play in such instances?

IV. SELECTED READINGS

Chauhan, B.R.; Desai, I.P.; and Chitnis, S. *Scheduled Castes and Education*, Meerut: Anu Publications, 1975 (faculty background). A review of the Indian government's efforts to improve the socioeconomic position of the scheduled castes through preferential educational admissions and support.

Elder, Joseph. "Society." In *India Briefing*, 1987, edited by Marshall M. Bouton. Boulder, CO: Westview Press, 1987 (student reading). A brief survey of India's society in the 1980s, including information on population, education, and literacy.

Saini, S.K. *Development of Education in India: Socio-economic and Political Perspectives*. New Delhi: Cosmo, 1980 (faculty background). A survey of education in India, seen within the broader contexts of Indian society and governmental policies.

Singh, Amrik, and Altbach, Philip G. (eds.). *The Higher Learning in India.* Delhi: Vikas, 1974 (faculty background). A wide-ranging collection of articles by specialists on many topics related to higher education in India.

Sopher, David E. "Sex Disparity in Indian Literacy." In *An Exploration of India: Geographical Perspectives on Society and Culture*, edited by David E. Sopher. Ithaca: Cornell University Press, 1980 (faculty background). An examination of the uneven distribution of literacy throughout India.

Sociology: India

Industrial Sociology: The Indian Case

Joseph W. Elder

I. INTRODUCTION

The processes of industrialization in any country are shaped by sociological as well as economic factors specific to that country. In India these processes reflect the country's colonial past as well as its postindependence experiments with a partially planned economy:

• European traders were initially attracted to India because of India's relatively advanced economy and the possibilities of lucrative trade in its luxury items.

• Britain's economic relationship with India determined the introduction of industrialization into India and shaped its subsequent development. India's entrepreneurs emerged primarily from marginal groups within the Indian social fabric. Strong kinship ties played an important part in the early days of industrialization, and continue to do so.

• Following the achievement of independence from Britain,

India adopted a "socialist pattern of society" in which the government controlled the "commanding heights" of the economy (i.e., many of the heavy industries), but left large segments of the industrial sector (e.g., textiles, light industries) to be developed by private interests. Labor unions have become affiliates of political parties and function in different ways from their counterparts in the United States. The Indian industrial scene today encompasses a much wider variety of enterprises than exist now in the United States.

• India's industries reflect the wide range of economic conditions in contemporary India, a society where the most important social ties are still those with one's immediate and extended kinship groups.

II. MAJOR TOPICS

EUROPEAN ECONOMIC RELATIONSHIPS WITH INDIA

For several centuries prior to the arrival of the Europeans around 1500 C.E., India's external trade was conducted primarily by Arab carriers who visited Muslim port enclaves along the western coastline of India and carried small luxury items (e.g., jewels, silks, spices) back to the Arabian and European worlds to sell at high profits. Eventually European traders recognized that **they** too might make handsome profits in India's luxury trade if they could replace the Arabs.

The Portuguese were the first to settle in India, repeating the Arab pattern of buying spices and luxury items and making high profits through selling in Western markets. The British East India Company (founded by the Crown as a monopoly trading company in 1600), the Dutch East India Company (founded in 1602), and the French Compagnie des Indes Orientales (founded in 1664) all developed seaport bases in India and southeast Asia. Economic, political, and military competition eventually left the Dutch in control of what became known as the East Indies, the French of Indochina, and the British of India. English trade in India gradually shifted from spices and luxury items to cotton and other bulk textiles.

In the eighteenth century, Britain's relations with India underwent several significant changes. In 1765 the British East India Company, in the wake of successful military ventures, became the land-revenue collector of a large area in northeastern India. In subsequent decades it became increasingly involved in land-revenue collection, civil administration, and the maintenance of law and order, ultimately extending its influence to three-fifths of India's territory. In 1833 the Charter Act of India abolished the Company's trading activities entirely; in 1858 the Company was dissolved, and India came under the direct control of the British Crown through a resident viceroy. For the next ninety years, India's economy was closely tied to that of Britain.

INDUSTRIALIZATION IN INDIA BEFORE INDEPENDENCE

During the final decades of its existence, the East India Company encouraged the investment of British capital in India. For example, in 1853, when telegraph and railway services began, the company saw to it that British investors were guaranteed certain levels of financial return regardless of the actual profits or losses realized by those services. By 1900 India contained the third-largest railroad network in the world, one of the world's five largest cotton textile industries, and a well-developed coal industry. In the twentieth century, however, India's industrialization did not expand like that, for example, of Japan, which had began developing about the same time. A major reason was India's political subordination to Britain's economic interests, in contrast to Japan's political and economic independence. Britain's tariff policies, for example, implemented to support its investments in the West Indies and elsewhere, blocked the growth of India's sugar, tobacco, and silk industries. And India's cotton and textile industries were shaped to accommodate the needs of the textile industry in Britain. India was thus unable to encourage indigenous industrialization by establishing protective tariffs, purchasing its own governmental supplies from Indian manufacturers, or sending young Indians abroad to receive technical training necessary for building particular industries back home, as Japan did.

Although British capital launched many of the early industrial projects in India, indigenous Indian capital was not far behind. Indian capital and India's business leaders came disproportionately from particular groups:

The Parsis. When Muslims entered Persia in the seventh century and converted the population to Islam, many of the Parsis, who maintained their Zoroastrian religion, migrated to India, settling along its western coast. Over the centuries they married exclusively among themselves, maintained their own religion (as represented in their fire temples), and attained a high level of affluence. The absence of social taboos against eating and drinking with nonrelatives permitted the Parsis to mingle socially with the British. The Parsis today comprise about .03 percent of India's population. A number of outstanding Parsi business families—the Wadias, the Petits, and the Tatas, for example—have played significant roles in India's industrialization. The Tatas founded the Tata Iron and Steel Company in 1907 and built India's first steel plant and accompanying city (Jamshedpur) in Bihar. A Parsi scholar and businessman, Dadabhai Naoroji, traveled to England in 1855, where he was eventually elected to parliament and developed his "drain" theory, which held that any economic policies enunciated by Britain were ultimately for Britain's own benefit at India's expense. His arguments were adopted by Mahatma Gandhi and others who used them to undergird their own appeals for equal treatment of Indians as British subjects.

Trading Groups from Gujarat. These trading groups included the Jains, a religious group dating back to the time of their founder, Mahāvirā, around 500 B.C.E. The Jains, like the Parsis, maintained their own religious institutions. Their religion stresses noninjury to living creatures and, in effect, prohibits their engaging in agriculture (since plowing kills small creatures in the ground) or in crafts (since insects are destroyed by the open fires so often used in crafts). Many Jains had entered the fields of banking and finance. The Dalmias are a prominent Jain industrial family. The Gujarati trading groups also included Hindu merchant families, such as the Scindias, who founded the Scindia Steam Navigation Company.

The Marwaris. A drought in the Marwar area of Rajasthan in the 1800s drove the local Jain and Hindu merchant groups to Calcutta, where they served as intermediaries between the British and the local Bengali trading communities. J.D. Birla, a Marwari, was an especially close friend of Mahatma Gandhi (in fact, Gandhi was assassinated in Birla's backyard). Today Marwaris live in virtually every major city in India, providing each other with a remarkably successful all-India business network.

Parallels can be drawn between prominent U.S. families (e.g., the Carnegies, Duponts, Fords, Mellons, Morgans, and Rockefellers) and prominent Indian families (e.g., the Birlas, Dalmias, Scindias, and Tatas) spearheading (and exploiting) industrial growth in their respective countries. The fact that large, well-inte-

grated, religiously conservative families have served as major entrepreneurs in both the United States and India challenges the
sociological thesis that "traditional" attitudes and family structures must yield to "modern" attitudes and family structures before groups can engage in "modernizing" activities.

INDUSTRIALIZATION IN INDIA
AFTER INDEPENDENCE

The partition of the Indian subcontinent into the new nations of
India and Pakistan in 1947 displaced millions of people on both
sides of the new borders. Groups of Sindhis, Punjabis, and Sikhs
who entered India from Pakistan as refugees often survived by
becoming entrepreneurs in such fields as bus, taxi and trucking
services, and in construction. Those who had lost farms in Pakistan established milling, sugar, and other food processing plants.

For the first thirty years after independence, the government of
India adopted a "socialist pattern of society" in which, through a
series of five-year plans, it controlled the "commanding heights" of
the economy in the public sector (e.g., iron and steel, petroleum,
coal, railway, airline, defense, banking, and life insurance industries), leaving the major part of India's economy to operate according to market forces in the private sector. During this period the
national annual growth rate averaged an uninspiring 3 percent,
while the industrial growth rate declined from 7 percent in the
1950s to 6 percent in the 1960s and to 4.5 percent in the 1970s.
In the 1980s—particularly following the inauguration of Rajiv
Gandhi as prime minister—many government controls and restrictions were lifted, certain tax burdens were reduced, licensing was
streamlined or eliminated, the average national growth rate rose to 7
percent, and India's stock markets boomed. Where in 1980 there
had been only two million investors, by 1989 there were ten million.
During that same period, the amount of capital raised annually
through new share issues tripled, and the value of all shares in the
market increased eightfold. Tata Iron and Steel Company and Tata
Engineering and Locomotive Company remained India's top two
companies in terms of net sales. But a cluster of new entrepreneurs,
some with no business record, rose in the ranks of India's industrialists, producing and marketing products such as colored television
sets, pharmaceuticals, and computers. The decade also witnessed
several dramatic takeovers and takeover attempts.

Following independence in 1947 trade unions rapidly evolved to
become appendages of India's political parties. The same factory

might contain several unions, one affiliated with the Congress party, one linked to one of several Communist parties, and the third to a local or regional political party. The parties could depend on their union members to participate in political rallies, sit-ins, street marches, etc. In return, union members could turn to their political parties for assistance in wage-and-benefits negotiations, unfair labor-practice actions, and strikes. Factory workers sometimes paid dues to several unions to expand their own protection. This pattern differs considerably from patterns of unionization in the United States.

During the 1980s India's trade unions did not fare especially well. A 1982 textile strike ended unsuccessfully after losing one million workdays during sixteen months. And a long-awaited workers' agitation against the Tata Engineering and Locomotive Company was finally called off without any significant gains. The most marked advance for labor came when the nation's Board for Industrial and Financial Reconstruction ordered Kamani Tubes, a failing Bombay-based company, to be turned over to a workers' cooperative. Since then, workers in other ailing companies have been negotiating for similar arrangements.

Today, despite the fact that 71 percent of India's total work force continue to earn their livelihood from agriculture, India is one of the ten leading industrial countries in the world, with an industrial labor force of some twenty-five million. About two-thirds of these workers are employed in government-managed public-sector enterprises (e.g., railways, petroleum industry, coal mining, etc.), and the other one-third in private-sector enterprises (e.g., textiles, food processing, plastics, etc.).

Only laborers in the larger firms (e.g., those firms employing one hundred workers or more) are protected by certain legislative guarantees of minimum wages, safety requirements, and dispute-settlement procedures; sometimes these protections make it virtually impossible for a laborer to be fired. Nevertheless, no more than half the workers in larger firms are covered by any kind of social security benefits. Most of the industrial labor force must still depend on relatives for assistance when they are ill or laid off or after retirement. These patterns, too, differ markedly from those in the United States.

VARIETIES OF INDIA'S INDUSTRIES

A number of features characterize India's industries. Many of them are labor—rather than capital—intensive: throughout India the cost of labor is cheap, whereas machinery is expensive. Importing equipment from abroad (e.g., machines, spare parts) requires government permits, reserve-bank foreign currency clearances, servicing arrangements, etc. Cost efficiencies may actually dictate greater, rather than less, use of human labor in India. American visitors to Indian factories are frequently struck by: "surplus" employees in any given work situation (retained in order to compensate by hand labor for periodic mechanical breakdowns); the number of ancillary employees who wait on managers by bringing them tea, carrying messages, running errands, etc. (in a society where prestige is measured in part by the number of one's personal retainers); the lack of cleanliness in the work place (related to the fact that the job of "picking-up" is typically assigned to employees from the lowest castes who have nothing to gain by doing an exemplary job of "picking up"); "inefficiencies" in plant operations (engendered by pressures on production crews to fall behind in production schedules in order to justify hiring additional employees from the pool of employees' relatives looking for work); rigid hierarchies between categories of staff; the prevalence of nepotism; complex systems of bookkeeping that conceal as much as they reveal; and elaborate relationships with external inspectors, auditors, and government authorities. A firm may realize greater profits through "deals" than it could through the operation of strictly market forces. India's industrial organization today includes a wide variety of types:

High-tech, Capital-intensive Plants. These are usually run by high-caste, high-status members of India's industrial elite with the most advanced training. Many have been educated abroad, their managerial and marketing practices are patterned after Western models.

Large-scale, Assembly-line Plants. These are often run by members of an owning family. In such plants, the managerial staff is frequently drawn from the same caste, religious, linguistic, and ethnic groups as the owner. The caste and ethnic backgrounds of the managers and foremen are often reflected in the composition of their work crews, since those in a position to offer work are generally approached by relatives wanting jobs. Plant equipment may require greater inputs of labor and maintenance than would be considered acceptable in similar plants in the West. Since the preservation of jobs is so important, few pressures exist for streamlining industrial processes or introducing labor-saving devices. Plant hierarchies often reflect caste hierarchies, with the highest castes at the top, and the lowest at the bottom. [*Readers are referred to the discussion of the definition of caste in the essays on "Stratification Inequality, Caste System: India," by Owen M. Lynch, and "Religion in a State Society" by Lawrence Babb.*]

Small-scale Plants. These are often owned and operated by members of the same family or caste group, who therefore are able to maintain tight managerial control and low labor costs. Such enterprises may have evolved from some earlier form of activity such as dairying, weaving, brass-working, carpentry, oil-pressing, sugar-distilling, or the preparation of medicines.

Contract-labor Crews. Much actual construction work in India is performed by contractors, who bring crews of laborers into cities from tribal, rural or other economically depressed areas, often including women and children who also do construction work. These crews frequently live in squatter areas with minimal water and sanitation facilities. Sometimes their members cannot understand the local language. Since they usually work for lower wages than local residents, they are often resented for depressing the living standards of the neighborhood, and they can become easy targets for police and ethnic harassment. After their construction projects end, the crews sometimes stay on, forming a more permanent ethnic pocket of semiemployed and unemployed urban dwellers.

Putting-out System. In certain industries the raw materials are "put out" to individuals, who process the materials and then return with the finished product for payment on a piecework basis. Much of this work is done by women and children, who have few alternative ways to earn their livelihood. Workers under this system are subject to considerable exploitation (e.g., by receiving monetary advances, they often accrue long-term indebtedness). The putting-out system is used in the production of such products as rough textiles, *biḍi* (leaf cigarettes), incense sticks, and flower garlands.

Comparing any countries according to their industrial statistics poses some difficulties. Comparing any countries with India according to India's industrial statistics poses greater difficulties than most. Because of India's complicated industrial organization, among India's statistics-gatherers arbitrary decisions are constantly being made regarding what does— and does not— comprise an "industrial plant"; who is— and who is not— in the industrial labor force, and which men and women are permanent— and which ones are temporary—employees. Scholars attempting to make rigorous comparisons using Indian industrial data are advised to use considerable caution.

III. ISSUES FOR DISCUSSION

1. In the early decades of the twentieth century, sociological studies were carried out of industrialization and industrial labor in the United States. In what ways do the patterns of industrialization and industrial labor in the United States described in those early studies resemble the current patterns of industrialization and industrial labor in India? In what ways are they different?

2. "Socialism" and "socialist" are popular terms in India and have been adopted as platform planks by virtually every Indian political party. "Socialism" is an unpopular term in the United States and U.S. political parties and politicians go to considerable effort to avoid being called "socialist." Why do the terms "socialist" and "socialism" have such different connotations in the two countries?

3. "Modernization theory" has argued that "traditional" attitudes and social structures must be replaced by "modern" attitudes and structures before a country can undergo "modernization." Yet in both India and the United States some of the leading entrepreneurs who ushered in industrialization held "traditional" religious and political views and relied heavily on their "traditional" kinship networks to expand their enterprises. Can "modernization theory" be redefined to accommodate the India/U.S. findings? Can terms such as "modern" and "traditional" be defined and operationalized sufficiently clearly to be useful for research purposes?

IV. SELECTED READINGS

Ahluwalia, Isher J. *Industrial Growth in India: Stagnation Since the Mid-Sixties.* New Delhi: Oxford University Press, 1985 (faculty reading). An analysis of twenty years of slow industrial growth in India.

Buchanan, Daniel H. *The Development of Capitalistic Enterprise in India.* New York: Augustus M. Kelley, 1966 (originally published by The Macmillan Company, 1934) (faculty reading). A detailed historic survey of the rise of industrialism in India from pre-British times through the 1920s.

Gupta, Kulwant Rai. *A Profile of Indian Industry.* New Delhi: Atlantic Publishers and Distributors, 1980 (faculty reading). An overview of the industrial sector of India's economy.

Krishna, Raj. "The Economic Outlook for India." In *India 2000: The Next Fifteen Years*, edited by James R. Roach, pp. 169-178. Riverdale, MD: The Riverdale Company, 1986 (student reading). A focus on three dimensions of economic development (growth, investment, and poverty) as they relate to India's projected economy between 1985 and 2000.

Kurien, C.T. "Paradoxes of Planned Development: The Indian Experience." In *India 2000: The Next Fifteen Years*, edited by James R. Roach, pp. 180-192. Riverdale, MD: The Riverdale Company, 1986 (student reading). A focus on the fact that India's recent relatively rapid economic growth has been of almost no benefit to the bottom third of its population.

Sociology:
India

Urban Society and Urban Problems in India

Joseph W. Elder

I. INTRODUCTION: CENTRAL POINTS

A discussion of urban society and urban problems in India high-lights certain similarities and differences between the situations in India and the United States.

• India's earliest cities existed from approximately 2500 to 1500 B.C.E. along the Indus River and other rivers hundreds of miles to the south and east. Little is known about the inhabitants of these cities. Among India's modern cities a few, such as Banaras and Patna, have been inhabited continuously since the first millennium B.C.E.; others, such as Agra and Bangalore, date back to Muslim and Hindu kingdoms established ca. 1200 C.E.; still others, such as the port cities of Bombay, Madras, and Calcutta, were founded by the British East India Company. Relatively recent additions to the urban scene have been such planned cities as New Delhi and Chandigarh.

• India demonstrates a relatively slow rate of urbanization compared with both developing and developed countries. Only about one out of four of its citizens lives in a settlement with a population of over 5,000. India's cities are characterized by uneven population density, relatively distinct ethnic neighborhoods, an overrepresentation of males, and a concentration of the growing middle classes. Now, as in the past, India's cities are centers of ideological mobilization and dissent, represented today by both the environmental and the feminist movements.

• Market forces, rather than planning, have shaped the growth of most of India's cities. The results have included the emergence of cities such as Bombay and Delhi that contain some of the world's largest slums. In some of the most crowded sections of India's cities, contagious diseases are endemic, and infant mortality is high, as are unemployment and underemployment. Various forms of corruption flourish, and violence is a feature of India's urban scene, with the most serious incidents often occurring between "communal" (i.e., caste (*jāti*), linguistic, religious, and ethnic) groups, in much the same way that American cities were torn apart by race riots in the 1960s. Up to the present, India's periodic multiparty elections have provided urban residents with a vehicle for confirming or withdrawing their support for those in political power.

II. MAJOR TOPICS

URBAN CENTERS IN SOUTH ASIAN HISTORY

Beginning sometime around 2500 B.C.E. an urban civilization developed in South Asia primarily along the Indus River and its tributaries, but extending south to the Tapti and east to the Jamna rivers. It was characterized by city planning, street grids, drainage systems, and standardized weights, measures, and brick sizes. After the floods that recurred periodically, houses were rebuilt on the former ground plans. Excavators labeled this the Harappan civilization, after the site of Harappa where the earliest artifacts were discovered in 1872. These include small stone seals carved with figures and a system of still-undeciphered writing. These seals have been discovered as far away as Mesopotamia, suggesting ancient commercial or trading links between the Harappan and other contemporaneous civilizations. Little is known about the inhabitants of the Harappan sites. Their civilization declined sometime around 1500 B.C.E.

Some of India's next oldest cities are still urban centers today. Banaras (also known as Varanasi and Kashi) is arguably the oldest **continuously inhabited** city in the world, dating back to the beginning of the first millennium B.C.E. The city of Jerusalem, by contrast, existed as early as 1800 B.C.E., but was destroyed and its inhabitants were driven out on at least two occasions (in the sixth century B.C.E. and the first century C.E.). Still extant cities in China, Iraq, and Egypt were contemporaries of Banaras, but they, like Jerusalem, have not been continuously inhabited.

Other ancient North Indian cities that are still inhabited include Allahabad (once called Prayag), at the confluence of the Jamna and Ganges rivers; Bodh Gaya (the site where Buddha attained enlightenment); and Patna (called Pataliputra when it was the capital of the Mauryan empire). Ancient South Indian cities include Kanchipuram (Conjeeveram) and Madurai, both of which have become important Hindu pilgrimage centers.

India's ancient cities were the sites for the formalization and codification of elements of civilization as well as for the propagation of arts and learning. They were also centers for heresies and dissent movements and were the contact points of foreign travelers and ideas. Various seaports described in ancient texts can no longer be traced. This suggests that during the intervening centuries there was so little sea contact with other lands that the economies of the seaports declined and eventually the seaports were abandoned.

After 1200 C.E. various Muslim and Hindu rulers established their capital cities and administrative centers in different parts of India. North Indian cities whose prominence dates back to that period include Lahore, Delhi, Agra, Jaipur, Jodhpur, Udaipur, and Ajmer. South Indian cities include Hyderabad, Bijapur, Bangalore, Mysore, and Vijayanagar.

When Europeans arrived in South Asia, they developed a series of seaports that linked Europe to India. The Portuguese built up Goa. The French developed Pondicherry. The British founded Bombay, Madras, and Calcutta, which eventually grew to be three of contemporary India's four largest cities (the fourth is the Delhi/New Delhi urban complex located hundreds of miles inland).

The British, during the days of the Raj, built settlements, called cantonments, where they based their troops, and civil lines, where the colonial administrators lived, on the outskirts of many Indian cities. They also developed hill stations, such as the towns of Simla and Darjeeling in the Himalaya mountains, to where they and their families retreated during the hot season.

More recently India has witnessed the development of planned cities. New Delhi was laid out in imperial splendor, following the decision by the British in 1911 to shift their capital from the eastern seaport of Calcutta to north-central India, adjoining it to the old walled city of Delhi. Simultaneously the new industrial town of Jamshedpur was designed and built in the Bihar jungles following the principles of Fabian socialism and self-contained neighborhoods. After India achieved independence in 1947, the planned city of Chandigarh was built in the Punjab according to the designs of the Swiss architect LeCorbusier.

GROWTH AND CHARACTERISTICS
OF URBAN CENTERS IN INDIA

India has been viewed as a land of villages. As the Table below indicates, this view has been true for the past forty years and is still basically true today.

URBAN AND RURAL POPULATIONS IN INDIA, 1951–1991

	1951	1961	1971	1981	1991 (est.)
Rural Population	83%	83%	80%	77%	70%
Urban* Population	17%	17%	20%	23%	30%

*According to India's census, a settlement is defined as "urban" if its population is over 5,000.

Urbanization Rate. India's rate of urbanization has been relatively slow. According to the Washington-based Population Reference Bureau, in 1986 the urban share of total populations in selected world regions was 32 percent for China, 65 percent for Latin America, 70 percent for East Asia, and 74 percent for North America. Two reasons are often cited for India's slow rate of urbanization: (1) its relatively slow rate of industrialization, and (2) its relatively inhospitable and expensive urban environments. Rural migrants to cities are apt to find themselves crowded into slums or even living on sidewalks. Given the harsh realities of urban life, migrants often prefer to leave their wives and children in their villages while they themselves earn what they can in cities. When their sons become old enough to migrate to cities, fathers frequently "retire" back to their villages. In many Indian cities migrants from rural areas constitute more than half the population. As a result, in some of India's largest cities men outnumber women by as much as 175 to 100.

Uneven Density. One characteristic of India's cities is their uneven population densities. In Calcutta the ratio of highest-density neighborhoods to lowest-density neighborhoods is 100:1. In Banaras the ratio is 300:1. Density is typically highest in a city's oldest sections, where people live above or behind their shops, in squatter areas where new arrivals construct temporary shelters, in the "lines" or standardized housing that many of the larger factories provide for their employees, or in slums surrounding those "lines." Urban density is typically lowest in the British-built appendages (the cantonments and civil lines) or in the more recent suburban developments. Low-density areas are frequently separated from high-density areas by railroads, rivers, or other landmarks. Few Indian cities illustrate the concentric-zone land settlement patterns characteristic of many American cities (i.e., a central downtown business area, surrounded by a zone of deterioration, surrounded by a zone of low-cost housing, etc.).

Neighborhoods With Cities. Another feature of India's cities is their neighborhoods of relatively distinct regional, religious, ethnic, *jāti*, and trade groups. As was the case in New York, Boston, Philadelphia, and Chicago earlier in the century, new arrivals frequently move into neighborhoods already inhabited by relatives, former neighbors, or at least people speaking the same language, eating the same foods, and observing the same religious customs. India's cities thus tend to have identifiable Muslim, Bengali, Tamil, and Sikh neighborhoods, as well as areas in which foreign immigrants and refugees reside. Although the existence of these ethnic neighborhoods may ease the adjustment of new arrivals, they also tend to encourage communal violence. City administrators can usually identify the neighborhood "flash-points" in their cities, and can post police and ban public assemblies in specific neighborhoods when tensions rise.

Compared with rural areas, India's cities contain a disproportionate share of certain religious minority groups: Muslims, Christians, Jains, Jews, and Parsis. Temporary residents from foreign countries, e.g., Nepalis, tend to be attracted to cities, as are the more educated, high-caste Indians who comprise the majority of India's rising middle classes and depend for their livelihoods on government employment and the commercial enterprises that flourish in cities. Almost all of the 1.5 million foreign tourists who visit India each year stay in the more than five hundred urban hotels approved by India's Department of Tourism. In 1987–88 such tourists came largely from the United States, Canada, Britain, Western Europe, Australia, Southeast Asia, Japan, and West Asia and introduced into the economy approximately U.S. $1.2 billion in foreign exchange.

URBAN SOCIETY IN INDIA

As has been the case throughout history, India's cities today remain the contact points for foreigners and foreign ideas. Western film and TV stars have their followings in India's cities, as do Western singers, musical groups, and athletes. Those Indians who speak English, and who enjoy enough surplus income and leisure time to attend the Western films, concerts, and athletic events are members of India's new middle class. They are estimated to number about 100 million (or about 12 percent of India's population). Earning an estimated one-third of India's household income, their demand for consumer items is nearly insatiable. Sales of motorcycles, scooters, and mopeds increased by a factor of five during the decade following 1975; the sale of refrigerators quadrupled, and that of synthetic clothing tripled. And the sale of even such expensive items as automobiles more than doubled. India is now one of the world's largest markets for television sets (two million sets—including 800,000 color sets—were sold in 1985 to a population that then numbered about 750 million). And the demand for expensive VCRs exceeds the supply. A U.S. $100 million cosmetics industry caters to the fancies of the middle class. Home-appliance stores in India's cities offer wide selections of washing machines, vacuum cleaners, mixer-grinders, electric cookers, hot water heaters and air conditioners, urban supermarkets exhibit shelves full of processed foods, detergents, and bathroom supplies. A spate of high-quality magazines, complete with glossy photographs and English-language articles, have appeared, financed in large part by India's growing advertising industry.

Members of India's new middle class want to build homes and buy apartments. In Delhi alone 2,000 cooperative societies wait to be assigned land by the Delhi Development Authority so that they can start building residence units. In any large city in India one sees lavish homes and architecturally planned housing colonies rising amidst the squalor of urban slums. In the largest cities, five-star hotels, built ostensibly for foreign tourists, have become settings for the lavish wedding receptions of India's new middle class. And the middle class investors have moved into the stock market. During the decade between 1975 and 1985, private holdings of company stocks increased tenfold, and the number of investors rose from 1.5 million to 7 million.

One of the highest priorities of these middle classes is a quality education for their children. In most Indian cities this has encouraged educational entrepreneurship from nurseries and preschools to private and convent elementary schools, high schools, and colleges. Between 1975 and 1985 the number of engineering colleges in India doubled, and universities and colleges added evening classes and correspondence courses in an effort to meet the rising demand. Today, especially in non-Hindi speaking sections of India, middle-class parents typically believe that fluency in English will ensure their children greater employment and advancement opportunities anywhere in India—or perhaps even in Britain, Canada, or the United States. As a matter of fact, in any given year in the late 1980s approximately 16,000 Indian students were studying in U.S. colleges and universities. And in the decades following the 1965 rewriting of U.S. immigration laws, an estimated 700,000 Indians have emigrated to the United States, where many of them have joined the ranks of the American middle class. Today most middle class Indian families have relatives living in the United States, Canada, or Great Britain. These overseas relatives can provide key contacts for further upward social and economic mobility.

Cities as Loci of Mobilization. As has been the case throughout history, India's cities today remain the centers for ideological mobilization and dissent. Radical political parties establish their headquarters in cities, as do conservative, fundamentalist, and religious-separatist groups. News agencies are concentrated in cities. During the 1970s India's environmental movement was dramatized by women in hill areas hugging trees to prevent commercial foresters from cutting them down and by a crowd of rural folk in Kerala preventing a dam from being built. During the 1980s the environmental movement found urban bases of support. Two environmental reports were released in New Delhi, assessing the havoc being wrought on India's environment by developers, industrialists, and government planners. The 1984 industrial disaster in the city of Bhopal, when a cloud of poisonous gas released by the Union Carbide factory killed 3,000 people and left another 50,000 with physical disabilities, further fueled India's environmental movement.

Cities have also witnessed the development of India's feminist movement. Toward the end of the 1970s women from radical and progressive backgrounds formed autonomous women's groups such as Stree Sangarsh (in Delhi), Forum against Rape, later renamed Forum against Oppression of Women (in Bombay), and Pennuramai Iyakkam (in Madras). And feminist publications such as the bimonthly *Manushi* (in Hindi and English) have attracted a wide readership in the major cities. The agendas of these groups and publications include criticizing patriarchy, ending the sexual and economic exploitation of women, and promoting women's equal access to education, improved divorce laws, women's property rights, and opportunities for women writers and for women in the political arena. Until recently, autonomous women's groups were found almost exclusively in India's major cities like Bombay, Madras, Calcutta, and Delhi. Now they are beginning to appear in smaller cities and towns all over India.

Urban Problems in India. In 1947, the drafters of India's Constitution shared no clear-cut urban policies. Gandhi, for one, strongly mistrusted cities, seeing them to be centers of accumulated political power, wealth, and exploitation. He advocated the return of city-dwellers to their ancestral villages, where they could live as farmers and craftspersons, enjoying a spiritual closeness to the land and participating in the simple activities of rural communities. Nehru, in contrast, was more willing to endorse cities. As a socialist and "modernist," he hoped that the growth of urban industries would provide jobs for surplus farm workers in India, just as urban employment had provided jobs for workers in Europe and the United States.

Because of these differences of opinion among India's leaders, its Constitution made no pronouncements regarding urban migration or rural-urban development. Market forces, presumably, would take care of industrial development, urban growth, and labor migration. Not until the late 1950s did planners begin to develop strategies for dealing with India's increasing urban problems, some of which, by then, seemed almost hopeless.

Urban Overcrowding. Today some have begun to question whether India's largest cities, like Calcutta and Bombay, are still habitable. Bombay is one of the most congested cities in the world, with a population density of approximately 385,000 people per square kilometer, four times that of New York City. Bombay averages 650 new arrivals every day. Nearly 4.5 million of Bombay's 8.2 million people live in slums or on the street. Dharavi, which covers 80 hectares and is inhabited by half a million people, has been called the largest slum in Asia. In 1981 the chief minister of the state of Maharashtra, A.R. Antulay, ordered the demolition of some of Bombay's slums, the deportation of 100,000 slum-dwellers beyond the city limits, and the eviction from the state of any slum-dwellers who were not Maharashtrian. Antulay's actions aroused such outrage that the People's Union for Civil Liberties filed a writ petition. The Supreme Court ultimately issued an interim order staying all large-scale demolitions. Bombay's slums continue to grow.

Calcutta is little better. About two-thirds of Calcutta's population of 9.2 million live in makeshift or mud and thatch-roofed buildings. One-third of the approximately 3.3 million people living in Calcutta's core area are jammed into dwellings with less than thirty square feet per person. Its streets are choked with lorries, cars, buses, handcarts, and 20,000 rickshaws. Until the 1990s, only one bridge spanned the Hooghly River between Calcutta and Howrah, which hundreds of thousands of vehicles and pedestrians crossed every day. Calcutta's urban decay reached the point where in 1985 the city's telephone authorities announced that 55,000 telephone lines were dead and could not possibly be restored in less than two years. Despite the fact that then-Prime Minister Rajiv Gandhi referred to Calcutta as a dying city, Calcutta maintains traditions of creativity seldom found elsewhere in India. Over 700 magazines devoted to pure literature are published in Calcutta every year. Bengali films made in Calcutta regularly win the president's annual Gold Medal. And the citizens of Calcutta continue to flock to evening discourses, concerts, and theater performances.

The doubling of India's population since independence has meant extraordinary crowding everywhere, but particularly in the slum sections of its cities. The lack of potable water in the slums, and the virtual nonexistence of adequate sewage-removal and treatment facilities have contributed to serious health problems in the cities. Endemic gastrointestinal disorders and the resulting dehydration account for unusually high infant– and early– childhood mortality (the infant mortality rate is 116 per 1,000 in India, compared with 11 per 1,000 in the United States). Medical facilities– some maintaining high standards– do exist in India's cities, but there is no effective health-insurance system for most of India's population, and quality health care is available only to those who can afford it. India's public-health programs, including the provision of safe drinking water, garbage and sewage removal, and mass immunization against diseases such as polio, typhoid, and diphtheria, generally remain inadequate. Unemployment and underemployment continue to beset India's urban population at all social levels. The sons and daughters of the urban middle classes can often not find jobs upon graduation. The landless or the rural unemployed migrate to the cities in search of work, moving into squatter areas or camping along the sidewalks, hoping to find jobs as day laborers, construction workers, or servants. If they can find no other employment, they may rent a cycle rickshaw and try to earn enough money each day to pay its rental costs and still buy food for their families. Their wives and children may earn supplementary incomes by rolling cheap cigarettes (*bidi*), collecting and selling wastepaper, stitching rags into quilts, milking cows and water buffaloes, peddling fruits and vegetables, making bricks, pushing handcarts, or, as a last resort, begging. The margin of survival is slim. A single illness or accident can drop a family below the subsistence level, with inadequate nutrition and attendant threats to health. In India's unique population pyramid, in which men outnumber women in every age category, it is the women and children who suffer the most.

Urban Corruption. Corruption is a problem in most large urban centers in the world, and India is no exception. Federal, state, and municipal agencies pass ordinances regarding everything from tax rates, to safety and quality standards, to prices, licenses, and quotas. Agents are hired to enforce the ordinances, and inspectors are hired to check on the agents. Individuals at all levels are susceptible to bribes and payoffs. One hears such statements as, "In former times, one bribed to obtain extraordinary services. Today one bribes to receive even the offered services." Harassment and extortion by police and other officials are not unusual, nor are payoffs in court cases, kickbacks by firms seeking contracts, and under-the-table payments for hirings and promotions. Nepotism is endemic. A number of top political leaders, including Prime Minister Indira Gandhi and Prime Minister Morarji Desai, each paid a heavy political price for extending special favors to their sons.

Urban Violence. Urban violence is a sociological phenomenon throughout the world; again, India is no exception. In the United States urban violence tends to occur between individuals. In India it tends to occur between "communal" (i.e., caste, linguistic, religious, or ethnic) groups. In form and ferocity, India's communal riots parallel the race riots that erupted in U.S. cities in the 1960s. Often, an incident will spark a violent explosion between two groups that, at least on the surface, had appeared to coexist relatively peacefully for years. Each side then launches indiscriminant attacks upon the members and property of the other. Reprisals are met with counter-reprisals. As the numbers of injured and dead mount, police and sometimes military units move in, using baton charges or firing tear gas to disperse the crowds. Accusations of police brutality are often made. By the time a communal riot ends, the toll of dead and injured may run into scores or even hundreds. And although on the surface life appears to return to normal with the groups once again living side by side, they now harbor fresh resentments against each other as well as against the police and government authorities. Particularly severe riots occurred in Delhi in 1984, Ahmedabad in 1986, and Meerut in 1987. Altogether the decade from 1980 to 1990 witnessed some 4,500 communal incidents involving an estimated 7,000 deaths. Most of the incidents occurred in urban settings. The demarcation of communal neighborhoods in Indian cities (as with black and Hispanic neighborhoods in U.S. cities) can contribute to tensions and violence between groups.

Political Mobilization. India's political system, with its periodic multiparty elections, has served to convey important messages from the governed to the those who govern. Those municipal, state, and central governments that have been **insufficiently** responsive to citizens' needs have been voted out of office. Those that have been **sufficiently** responsive have been voted back into office. For example, during the past two decades the Communist Party of India (Marxist) has been repeatedly returned to office in the state of West Bengal, which is where the sprawling metropolis of Calcutta is located. In contrast, during the same time political parties that have ruled in the states of Maharashtra (where Bombay is located), Tamilnadu (where Madras is located), and in the Union Territory of Delhi have been voted out of office, in some instances several times.

India's urban centers have generally been India's political centers, with party headquarters and party printing presses typically being located in India's larger cities. When India's political parties have had to choose between the interests of urban voters (e.g., lower food costs) and the interests of rural voters, (e.g., higher farm prices), the political parties have tended to favor the urban voters, recognizing the capacities of urban voters to mobilize rapidly and even to take to the streets. In recent years this has begun to change somewhat in northern India, as middle-income farmers have pressed their demands. But on the whole India's major political parties still tend to spend a disproportionate amount of effort trying to attract and retain urban voters in a country where more than two-thirds of the population still live in villages.

III. ISSUES FOR DISCUSSION

1. India's ancient Harappan civilization was characterized by cities that were rebuilt according to almost-identical street and house plans each time the cities were destroyed by floods. These ancient cities were also characterized by standardized weights, measures and brick sizes. What, if anything can one infer about the political and social dynamics of Harappan civilization?

2. The "urban concentric-zone hypothesis" has served American sociologists moderately well as a description of, and an explanation for, the ecological patterning of typical American cities. However, hardly any city in India demonstrates such a concentric-zone ecological pattern. How might one explain such marked differences between urban ecology in the United States and urban ecology in India?

3. During the past several decades, a number of major U.S. cities have been wracked by "race riots" involving Whites, Blacks, Hispanics and other ethnic groups. During the past several decades a number of major Indian cities have experienced "communal riots," involving Hindus, Muslims, Sikhs, and various caste groups. In what ways are they different? What strategies, if any, have been adapted in either country to prevent— or at least to limit the intensity and violence of— such urban riots?

IV. SELECTED READINGS

Bhattacharya, Bimalendu. *Urban Development in India, Since Pre-Historic Times.* Delhi: Shree Publishing House, 1979 (faculty background). A survey of the appearance, rise, decline, and disappearance of cities throughout India's history.

Bose, Ananda M. *India's Urbanization, 1901-2001.* New Delhi: Tata McGraw Hill, 1978 (faculty background). A view of India's urban growth during the twentieth century, with some extrapolations regarding possible future developments.

De Souza, Alfred (ed.) *The Indian City: Poverty, Ecology, and Urban Development.* New Delhi: Manohar, 1978 (faculty background). A collection of chapters describing some of India's urban problems, with suggestions for what might be done about them.

Fox, Richard G. (ed.) *Urban India: Society, Space and Image.* Durham, NC: Duke University Program in Comparative Studies on South Asia, Monograph Number Ten, 1970 (student reading). A collection of papers presented in a symposium at Duke University, dealing with a wide variety of topics associated with urbanization and urban growth.

Noble, Allen G., and Ashok K. Dutt. *Indian Urbanization and Planning: Vehicles of Modernization.* New Delhi: Tata McGraw-Hill, 1977 (faculty background). A discussion of India's efforts to deal with the processes and goals of urban planning.

Sociology:
Japan

The New Religions of Japan

Helen Hardacre

I. INTRODUCTION: CENTRAL POINTS

The new religions of Japan provide an excellent case study of religion's role in modern society, offering important qualifications to popular images of Japan and reflecting important issues in Japanese society.

• The phenomenon of new religions in Japan contradicts the dominant Weberian theory which holds that the importance of religion should decline as a society modernizes.

• The new religions demonstrate both a continuity with traditional religions as well as significant innovations in adapting doctrine and practice to modern circumstances; they thus offer an important corrective to the notion of modern religions as "crisis cults."

• A study of the new religions provides insights into women's social roles in voluntary associations beyond the domestic sphere, and more generally into the construction of gender in Japanese society.

• This case also offers important qualifications to the popular image of Japan as a thoroughly secular society.

II. MAJOR TOPICS

The new religions of Japan currently number over three thousand organizations, large and small, to which between one-fourth and one-third of the population, that is, between thirty and forty million people, belong. A single organization, Sōka Gakkai, has a membership of twelve million. While perhaps fifteen of these organizations are truly massive and powerful, with memberships of three million or more, the majority are much smaller in size.

The term *new religion* refers to any of the those religious associations founded since roughly the beginning of the nineteenth century down to the present which exist outside the ecclesiastical structures of temple Buddhism and shrine Shintō. In terms of their doctrine, the new religions include Buddhist, Shintō, Christian, and completely novel elements. They typically feature a number of elements found also in more primitive forms of religious association, such as the worship of ancestors, healing, and shamanic practices. Their novelty thus lies not in the body of their various practices and beliefs, but in the way they develop a perspective on human problems, a common orientation that may be described as a shared world view. In their incorporation of traditional practices there is continuity with past religious history, at the same time the new religions, whatever their doctrine, have developed a distinctive approach to the religious life and have adapted traditional beliefs and practices to modern circumstances.

THE FOUNDING OF NEW RELIGIONS

The new religions were founded in three distinct waves, each in the context of particular social and historical conditions. The first wave occurred during the period 1800 to the Meiji Restoration (1868). Of the organizations established during that time, three are most significant: Kurozumikyō (f.1814), Tenrikyō (f.1838), and Konkōkyō (f.1859). All were founded in the relatively prosperous area of western Japan: Tenrikyō in what is now Nara Prefecture, and Kurozumikyō and Konkōkyō in Okayama Prefecture. Contrary to the widely held notion of new religions being founded by the poor and oppressed, the founders of these three organizations came from stable, even prosperous, economic circumstances. Each experienced revelations or religious insights after severe illness or a series of disastrous yet inexplicable misfortunes.

While none of the founders of these organizations intended to establish a Shintō sect, by the early twentieth century all of them had adopted doctrine similar to those of Shintō. From the Restoration (1868) until 1945, the state sponsored the Shintō mythology and its emphasis upon such state-centered values as loyalty and national service.

The second wave of new religions came in the early twentieth century, with the establishment of Sōka Gakkai (1930), Seichō no Ie (1929), and Reiyūkai Kyōdan (1919–1925). Both Sōka Gakkai and Reiyūkai were Buddhist, while Seichō no Ie expounded the unity of all religious creeds. Sōka Gakkai remained relatively small until 1945, but its growth thereafter was stimulated by the martyrdom of its founder, Makiguchi Tsunesaburō (1871–1944), who was arrested in 1943, along with twenty other members for violating the Peace Preservation Law (1925, revised 1941), for advising followers not to observe Shintō rites and customs, and for opposition to the war. Seichō no Ie's founder, Taniguchi Masaharu, was an eclectic thinker and prolific writer who incorporated such diverse elements as psychoanalysis, spiritualism, and meditation in the thought and practice of his religion. Reiyūkai attracted its earliest following from among the very poor stratum of the society—recent migrants to Tokyo from rural areas—largely through the evangelism of its female founder Kotani Kimi (1900–1971); its male founder, Kubo Kakutarō (1892–1944), concentrated on developing doctrine. Until 1945 it preached a doctrine of ancestor worship by the laity combined with frank anti-clericalism; it also was a strong supporter of the prewar regime, as was Seichō no Ie. Reiyūkai spawned a number of schisms, which nevertheless have retained intact many of the parent organization's doctrines and practices—especially the emphasis on ancestor worship—suggesting that it has captured a religious impulse which a broad spectrum of adherents to the new religions regard as central to the religious life.

The third wave came in the postwar era, when hundreds of new religions were founded. Many of them would doubtless have been established earlier, had it not been for the repressive prewar state, and many of the organizations formed at this time in fact represented the reconstitution of religions suppressed before 1945. Thus, the appearance of so many new religions immediately after the war, "like bamboo shoots after the rain," to quote an often repeated phrase in the Japanese media, is somewhat misleading. It is not that they simply emerged in response to the crisis precipitated by defeat in war, although no one would deny that the defeat, by any definition, was a "crisis"; rather, with the lifting of wartime restrictions, many persons who sought earnestly to adapt their vision of the truth to the urgent circumstances Japan faced after 1945 were given the opportunity for the first time to establish religious groups.

Of the many new religions founded since 1945, the following stand out. Perfect Liberty Kyōdan (f.1946), which represented the reconstitution of an organization severely persecuted before the war. P.L. Kyōdan, as it is commonly called, adopted the slogan "religion is art" and fosters the practice of the arts in daily life. Sekai Kyūsei Kyō, which had also been suppressed during the war, practices faith healing and, somewhat more unusually, espouses the virtue of natural farming without the use of chemical fertilizers. Tenshōkōtai Jingūkyō, informally known as "the dancing religion" because of the "dance of no ego" which its members engage in, was founded in 1945 by the highly charismatic Kitamura Sayo (1900–1967), who even before the war's end had castigated the emperor as a puppet and civil servants as his "maggot beggars."

PATTERNS IN THE LIVES OF FOUNDERS OF NEW RELIGIONS

The life of the founder of Tenrikyō, Nakayama Miki (1798–1887) illustrates many of the features common to founders of the new religions. As were many of the new religions, Tenrikyō was founded by a woman, and its message, while purporting to have universal relevance, is especially attuned to the special concerns of women and invests the family with religious significance. The daughter of a village headman, Nakayama enjoyed, even as a child, a reputation for virtue and diligence. Her husband, while of the same social stratum, was a wastrel and irresponsible in his professional duties, leaving her to maintain the family's stability as best she could. Her son was afflicted with a chronic foot infection, and in those days medical treatment was quite limited, not only in its technical efficacy, but in that biomedical physicians generally limited their practice to those of the samurai class and above, leaving the rest of society in the care of herbalists and spiritual healers. Nakayama Miki had her son treated by such a healer. His method of treatment was to induce a trance in his female assistant for whom he then tried to elicit the identity of the spirits responsible for his clients' afflictions.

On one occasion, when the healer's medium was unavailable for the usual seance, Miki took her place, and quite unexpectedly she began to utter oracles entirely unrelated to her son's foot ailment. She announced that a spirit she called the Heavenly Shogun had taken up residence in her body and was the one true god of the universe. Henceforth Miki was to act as his mouthpiece and be freed from all social obligations which she had previously fulfilled, including those of wife and mother. This possession lasted more than a week, and in spite of various attempts by her family to restore her normal state of mind, she persisted in uttering revelations which made it clear that she would henceforth act not according to the expectations of her familial or gender roles but to the dictates of her religious mission.

Specifically, she rejected the notion of inherited wealth— perhaps a reflection of her experience with her husband, who had conspicuously squandered his own inheritance— and said instead that the religious life began when one had eschewed virtually all private possessions. Accordingly, she ordered her husband to pull down and destroy the family dwelling, which he reluctantly did.

For Nakayama and many other women founders deprived of access to secular education or the formal training given Buddhist and Shintō priests, ecstatic religious experience provided a mode of obtaining knowledge of the supernatural world. Such experience functioned also as a basis of authority, justifying the modification or rejection of women's prescribed social roles as wives and mothers.

Nakayama for a time entertained a rather limited conception of her mission: it would be principally directed to women and would feature charms for safe childbirth. She thus attracted a core of female followers and acquired a reputation as a healer. At a time when medical treatment was inadequate, the promise to women of safe delivery had a strong appeal and soon took on the aura of the miraculous. Nakayama developed her skills as a religious leader and began to systematize her doctrine, initially in the supportive environment of her predominantly female followers, a common pattern seen in the lives of female religious founders worldwide. Also typical of founders of the new religions, Nakayama soon came to be regarded as a living deity. Healing and other charismatic practices were understood as evidence of her close link with divinity.

Eventually Nakayama's conception of her mission broadened into a universal message which held that the universe was ruled by a single parent deity. Humanity may know the deity's will and live in harmony with it by practicing a life of service and charity, and one in which communal worship and labor are emphasized. Ecstatic dance is an important aspect of Tenrikyō ritual, and labor contributed to the organization is considered a significant group activity. Tenrikyō now has a membership of approximately 2,3 million persons, with chapters in every area of Japan. Its headquarters, Tenri City (Nara Prefecture), is a center of pilgrimage, comparable as a religious center to Salt Lake City, Utah, in the life of the Church of the Latter Day Saints.

THE COMMON WORLD VIEW OF THE NEW RELIGIONS

From the foregoing discussion it will readily be appreciated that there is great variety in the doctrines of the new religions. While some, such as Reiyūkai, derive from Buddhism and represent significant innovations upon traditional Buddhist doctrine and rites, others are more eclectic; still others have at one time or another in their histories acquired a Shintō identity to escape persecution but without necessarily originating in Shintō doctrine or having institutional connections to Shintō. That being the case, where, then, lies the unity of the new religions, and what do they have in common?

The new religions embrace a common perspective on human problems. Typically, they present themselves to potential converts as specializing in solving problems of illness, economic instability, and interpersonal relations. The new religions, whatever their doctrine, believe human beings are able to gain control over their circumstances through self-cultivation in certain core values embraced by Japanese culture, especially sincerity, harmony, loyalty, filial piety, modesty, and diligence. In contrast to such Western religions as Christianity, they reject the idea that human affairs are determined by the unknowable will of a single creator deity.

The new religions teach that when a problem arises it is because the self has not been sufficiently cultivated in the values espoused; the problem can be solved through renewed effort in the practice of these virtues. The self exists in a matrix of relations with the body, other persons, society, nature, and the supernatural world. When it is perfected in virtue, the self will naturally enjoy harmonious relations at each level of the matrix.

This formulation is inverted in the following way in order to diagnose and solve a problem. For example, an adherent who consults a leader of a new religion regarding illness typically will be questioned about the quality of personal relations in the household and advised to look there for the origin of the problem; perhaps repentance for a lapse of personal self-cultivation will be recommended. It is assumed that illness arises because the self is not in harmony with the body or with other persons, and hence the solution is to restore harmony, a return to health will follow as a matter of course. Sometimes the diagnosis indicates that the sickness arose because the patient was not sufficiently attentive to ancestral spirits. This idea represents the adaptation of the ancient practice of ancestor worship to the contemporary world; the new religions typically advise members how to worship their ancestors in a way that they will maintain harmony with these most proximate representatives of the supernatural world.

It goes without saying that the world view of the new religions has limited applicability in treating such diseases as cancer, but thousands of adherents believe that they personally have experienced a healing of a major or minor ailment through the ministrations of their religion. Whatever the status of their therapies in purely medical terms (and it is by no means self-evident that medical institutions in all cases preserve a more "objective" viewpoint about illness than the religions themselves), the fact that thousands of adherents believe that they have been healed through a restoration of harmony, however conceived in terms of the doctrine of a particular group, is widespread and remarkably enduring, quite independent of the progress of medical science. Investigation of cases of faith healing often reveals a profound dissatisfaction with Japanese medical practice and the social conventions that shape one's dealing with doctors.

HOW THE NEW RELIGIONS CREATE MULTI-FUNCTIONAL LIFE WORLDS

The largest and most powerful of the Japanese new religions seek to responde to adherents' needs from the cradle to the grave. Many of them operate schools, from nursery through high school; Sōka Gakkai even maintains a university, Sōka University, with a branch campus in California. They offer social activities for both sexes and every age, as well as doctrinal study circles in which members can rise in rank and gain prestige. Such cultural activities as choral groups, orchestras, and circles for the practice of traditional arts complement a strong emphasis on proselytization and more directly religious activities. Sōka Gakkai maintains a national newspaper with the nation's third largest circulation. Followers of the new religions are frequently persons excluded from the more usual avenues to prestige in Japanese society. They tend to come from the ranks of the self-employed or are employees of small or family businesses rather than large corporations; women outnumber men. Unable to gain prestige in the dominant society, they devote their talents and energies to the religious organization, which rewards them for their efforts in proselytization or doctrinal study. That the new religions regularly provide such alternative prestige structures is unquestionably one of the greatest sources of their long-standing appeal to women, whose opportunities for advancement in secular society remain quite limited. Since the new religions typically treat proselytization by its female members as an extension of their mother role, implying that they are "spiritual parents" of their converts, women can participate without fear that this extra-domestic activity compromises their role in their family.

SIGNIFICANCE OF THE NEW RELIGIONS IN CONTEMPORARY RELIGIOUS LIFE

Prior to 1945, temple Buddhism and shrine Shintō were associated with the prewar state, acting as its advocate and mouthpiece whenever possible. For this reason, they were morally discredited by the defeat in 1945. In addition, while most temples and shrines were located in the countryside, by 1955 the majority of the population resided in urban areas, undermining the economic base of Buddhism and Shintō. Although many temples and shrines have been built (or rebuilt) in cities since 1945, their parish organizations, always conservative and tending to accord prestige only to long-time members, have not readily incorporated new members. Thus, both Buddhism and Shintō have declined significantly since 1945.

The new religions have been more successful than Buddhism and Shintō in responding to changing social conditions. The larger ones maintain national networks of churches and a concentration of activities in urban areas. New arrivals to an area are easily incorporated into a new church and its activities. Members maintain extensive networks of contacts all over the country and can be assured of a welcome in any new locale. Furthermore, the new religions endeavor to make their doctrines and practices relevant to modern life; in contrast, temple and shrine life seems increasingly incomprehensible and irrelevant. Most significant of all, the new religions have proved able to address the concerns of women and to provide them with meaningful outlets for their talents and energies. Until Buddhism and Shintō can similarly respond to the needs of this majority of the population, their decline will probably continue.

THE NEW RELIGIONS AND POLITICS

In general, the membership of the new religions is politically conservative, an outlook it shares with Japanese society as a whole. The new religions have seldom sought to put forward political agendas, although the single greatest exception to this generalization has become an important force in Japanese political life. In 1964, Sōka Gakkai created Kōmeitō, or Clean Government party. At first the two were virtually duplicate organizations, with the membership of Sōka Gakkai voting as a block for Kōmeitō candidates. Over the years, however, Kōmeitō has broadened its base to become a party of the center with the third largest representation in the National Diet. As such, it exercises a critical swing vote. Most Kōmeitō Diet members are Sōka Gakkai candidates, but Kōmeitō also sponsors a number of non-Sōka Gakkai candidates, women and men known for their expertise on such matters as women in the labor force and environmental questions. The party favors an expansion of welfare measures and the preservation of the "peace" Constitution, and stresses ethics in government.

Other new religions have tended to become involved in politics only as sponsors of conservative candidates, to whom they extend financial support. As their rural population base continues to erode, conservative politicians look upon new religions as important sources of urban support. The new religions, for their part, see some protective value in patronizing politicians, should they require an influential person to hush up minor scandal or promote their interests in other ways.

In the 1980s, however, there has been a departure from this generally passive form of political involvement. The Buddhist group Risshōkōseikai (f. 1938, as a schism of Reiyūkai) is the second largest of the new religions, with a membership of roughly five million. Until recently, it routinely supported conservative politicians without placing conditions on that support, but now it applies a litmus test, which many politicians it formerly supported have failed. It withholds support, for example, from politicians found guilty of ethical wrongdoing, from those who favor state support for the Yasukuni Shrine (the former national shrine for the war dead and to some a symbol of the prewar state's suppression of religious freedom), and from those who would expand the role of the military. As head of the Union of New Religions, which includes more than three hundred organizations, Risshōkōseikai is in a position to influence the political practices of many other new religions.

FUTURE PROSPECTS

The new religions of Japan now have a history of nearly two centuries. Their appeal remains strong, and new organizations continue to be founded. Their combined membership, at one-fourth to one-third of the entire national population, represents a significant force in Japanese society. The concentration of membership among women, those engaged in small or family-run businesses and self-employed persons indicates significant strains within the Japanese social fabric and suggests that religious life remains a vital means for addressing those strains. The new religions remain a strong force in Japanese society at the end of the twentieth century, even as the prestige of science and technology increases, and when the outlook of much of the society is overwhelmingly secular.

III. ISSUES FOR DISCUSSION

1. Discuss the role of women as founders, leaders, and members of the new religions. What conclusions can be drawn about the position of women in Japanese society.
2. What needs are addressed by the new religions? What is the basis of their widespread appeal?
3. Compare the role of the new religions in Japan today with religion's role in the United States.

IV. SELECTED READINGS

Davis, Winston B, *Dojo: Exorcism and Miracles in Modern Japan.* Stanford: Stanford University Press, 1980 (student reading). A very readable account of one new religion, its founding, organization, and activities.
Hardacre, Helen, *The New Religions of Japan and Kurozumikyō.* Princeton: Princeton University Press, 1986 (student reading). A study of the Shintō group Kurozumikyō as illustrative of the common world view of the new religions and their social significance.

Hardacre, Helen, *Lay Buddhism in Contemporary Japan: Reiyūkai Kyōdan*. Princeton: Princeton University Press, 1984 (faculty background). A detailed study of the history, doctrine, rites, activities, and organization of this Buddhist group. Includes survey information, translations of testimonies, and chapters on women's roles.

McFarland, H. Neil, *The Rush Hour of the Gods: A Study of New Religious Movements in Japan*. New York: The Macmillan Company, 1967 (faculty background). A survey of various new religions; not theoretically sophisticated but provides much general information on many groups.

Sociology: Japan

Stratification and Mobility: The Case of Japan

Hiroshi Ishida

I. INTRODUCTION: CENTRAL POINTS

Japan represents a critical case for current theories of industrial society because it is the first nation outside the European cultural sphere to reach a "mature" level of industrial society. Theories of industrial society suggest that an industrial technology has determinant consequences for social structure and processes, so that a great extent of similarity is expected in these respects across all industrial nations. The examination of the Japanese case would provide an excellent opportunity for the students to enhance their understanding of systems of stratification prevalent in the West and to evaluate common features of social inequality and social mobility patterns among industrial nations. Characteristics of social stratification and mobility in Japan may be summarized as follows:

• Despite the prevalence of a "middle-class consciousness" among Japanese people, various resources (such as income and home and land ownership) are unequally distributed in contemporary Japan, as in other industrial nations.

• Although Japanese compulsory education is based on egalitarian principles, a highly stratified system of education is found in post-compulsory schooling.

• Gender is an important variable in the structure of inequality

in contemporary Japan. Japanese women occupy disadvantaged position in the educational hierarchy and in the labor market.
• Minority groups exist in Japan. The two largest groups are the *burakumin* (descendants of those identified as the outcasts in the pre-modern Tokugawa period) and the Koreans living in Japan.
• Japan exhibits both distinctive and similar patterns of intergenerational mobility, compared with other industrialized nations, depending upon the type of mobility in question. With regard to absolute rates of mobility, Japan seems to differ from European industrial nations in that the extent of the intergenerational stability and self-recruitment among the Japanese working class is low while generally high in European nations. However, the relative rates of mobility in Japan are very similar to those found in European nations.
• Although a low degree of career mobility may be found among employees of large firms, this is not the dominant feature of the Japanese labor market.

II. MAJOR TOPICS

UNEQUAL DISTRIBUTION OF RESOURCES

According to social attitude surveys conducted in contemporary Japan, over ninety percent of the people consider their standard of living to be in the middle level. Some scholars claim, based upon these attitude surveys, that Japanese society is characterized by a huge middle stratum belonging neither to the lower nor to the upper class and whose members are highly homogeneous with respect to their lifestyles and attitudes. This view, however, does not seem to be supported by empirical data. Income, occupational prestige, home ownership, land holding, and other resources are unequally distributed among different social classes (defined by employment status and occupation). These differences are too great to support the notion that their members are highly homogeneous and the boundaries between them are blurred. Cross-national evidence also indicates that the Japanese society does not show an unsually low degree of inequality, and that with regard to the distribution of these resources, Japan resembles those of other industrial nations. Although some theorists believe that income inequality in Japan is not as great as in other industrial nations, others claim that it is comparable to income distribution in West European nations.

The prevalence of a "middle class consciousness" among Japanese people probably comes from the increased standard of living achieved in the decades following the Second World War and the reduction in income inequality in the 1960s and early 1970s as a result of rapid economic growth. However, trends in the 1980s suggest an increasing tendency toward inequality in income and other resources. In particular, land ownership has become a critical factor in the stratification system. Due to a rapid increase in land prices in metropolitan areas, the gap in wealth between those who own land and those who do not has widened substantially.

What appears to be distinctive, however, in the stratification system in Japan is that size of firm in which Japanese workers are employed plays an important role in differentiating their life chances. "Permanent employment," the *nenko* (length of service) wage system, and a highly developed internal labor market are frequently cited as characteristics of large Japanese firms. On the other hand, workers in small- and medium-sized firms are generally expected to experience higher labor turnover, to be recruited from the external labor market, and to have lower wages and less favorable working conditions than those in larger firms. [*See the essay on "Sociology of Work: The Case of Japan."*]

It is also interesting to note that there is a relatively large sector of small-scale family enterprises (self-employed and family workers) in Japan compared with many other industrial nations. These tiny family enterprises are diverse and are found in retailing and manufacturing, as well as agriculture. The presence of small-scale firms in manufacturing is related to the practice of sub-contracting, where smaller firms supply components and parts to their parent firms. Although these family enterprises are on average less efficient than larger firms, they constitute a healthy and growing sector of the Japanese economy.

STRATIFICATION IN EDUCATION

An interesting opportunity to explore the ideas of equality and stratification is provided by the Japanese educational system, where these seemingly contradictory ideas coexist. Japanese compulsory education, which includes six years of elementary school and three years of junior high school, is characterized by a high degree of uniformity and equality. During these school years most Japanese students are enrolled in public schools based upon residential criteria. Schools are similar in physical facilities, academic standards, and quality of instruction. The academic curriculum and teaching materials are standardized and regulated by the Ministry of Education. Students throughout Japan learn basically the same subjects at approximately the same time and pace. Highly centralized and standardized feature of Japanese education provides an interesting comparison to more decentralized systems of the United States and Britain. [See the essay on "The United States and Japan in Comparative Perspective."]

The basic assumptions behind the Japanese compulsory education are that all students have equal potential and that differences in achievement are due largely to the matter of effort and self-discipline, not to differential ability. Tracking, ability grouping, and remedial programs are generally nonexistent; uniformity dominates the curriculum. These features seem to guarantee relatively equal opportunity for acquiring a basic education. However, it is important to note that because of the emphasis on uniformity, some students supplement their school work with private tutoring, which introduces unequal element into a basically egalitarian system.

Uniformity and equality quickly disappear in education beyond compulsory level. Students are sorted into different schools which have varying prestige, goals, and quality of instruction. The ranking of high schools in each district is very clear to the public. At the top of the hierarchy are college-preparatory schools which established reputations for placing their students to prestigious universities. Generally, public schools with long history, together with a small number of elite private schools, occupy the top of the hierarchy. At the bottom there are vocational and night schools, both public and private. Many in these schools are students who failed to gain entrance to public academic schools. A comparison of highly differentiated high school education in Japan with the American comprehensive model would be illuminating.

Postsecondary education is further stratified. Universities are at the summit of the hierarchical structure, followed by junior colleges which offer two- and three-year programs. Among some 460 universities, there is a clear and elaborate ranking, headed by national universities and a small number of private schools. The ranking of the university attended tends to be highly correlated with one's job prospects. For example, graduates of Tokyo University dominate high-ranking civil service jobs and top management positions in the private sector.

The sorting of students into one of differentiated high schools and universities is based upon the results of entrance examination. However, family background (such as family income, father's occupation and education) carries weight in this seemingly meritocratic selection process. Since there are restricted enrollment opportunities in public education after the compulsory level, a quarter of high school and over 70 percent of university and junior college students are obliged to enroll in private institutions. Further, private after-school tutoring programs and cram schools seem to influence success in entrance examination, and these charge tuition. A positive correlation is found, therefore, between the ranking of high schools and universities and family background: students of elite high schools and universities are more likely to come from wealthier families than students of the average high schools and universities. In conclusion, the egalitarian and unifying qualities of compulsory education is proceeded by a highly stratified system of high school and higher education. The co-existence of the principles of egalitarianism and inequality characterizes the Japanese educational system.

GENDER STRATIFICATION

Gender is an important variable in the structure of inequality in contemporary Japan. First, a notable disparity is found in educational attainment by gender. Although women are almost as likely as men to attend institutions of higher education, over 90 percent of junior college students, but only about a quarter of university students are female. Further, the proportion of women in elite universities is even smaller; for example, women account for less than 10 percent of the enrollment at Tokyo University. Women are more likely to major in home economics, the humanities, or the social sciences than the natural sciences or engineering. This inequality is not the result of overt discrimination against women in the selection process, but rather stems from societal expectations, traditional gender roles, and occupational opportunities for women. [See the essay on "Gender Roles: The Case of Japan."]

Second, the position of women in the labor market clearly distinguishes from that of men. Participation in the labor force among Japanese women is intermittent: the pattern of female labor force by age group shows an M-shape curve; with the first peak at ages 20–24 and the second peak at ages 40–45. Many Japanese women withdraw from the labor market at marriage and child birth and re-enter when they reach middle age. Greater opportunities for part-time employment recently are believed to be responsible for the increasing number of married women in the labor force. Gender is a factor in both types of occupation and employment status. Women are typically found in routine non-manual and production process work while men dominate the more prestigious professional and managerial positions. More than 80 percent of workers in family enterprises are women, while only about 30 percent of self-employed are women. Further, men are more likely to be placed in the internal labor market of a large firm than are women.

Classroom discussion of gender stratification in Japan is probably most informative when placed in a cross-national perspective. In so doing, it must be emphasized that the overall rate of female labor force participation rate is not much lower than that in other industrial nations. The image of Japanese women staying at home and taking care of the domestic duties is exaggerated. The intermittent nature of a woman's working life is not unique to Japan, either. An M-shape pattern is also reported in other industrial nations like Great Britain. However, cross-national comparisons of managerial status and wages suggest limited prospects of career advancement for Japanese women. Women hold fewer than 10 percent of managerial positions in Japan, compared with over 20 percent in Britain and the United States. The average monthly wage of Japanese female workers is less than 60 percent of that of male workers, a figure substantially lower than in other industrial nations. In short, many Japanese women work, but their prospects of career advancement appear to be rather limited.

MINORITY GROUPS

The study of minority groups in contemporary Japan is an important topic for several reasons. First, although the number of people in these groups is not large, the study will provide a balanced picture of Japan social structure. Despite the successful economic performance and rising standard of living in post-war Japan, minority groups continue to occupy unmistakable position in the social hierarchy. Second, the study will give comparative evidence to a discussion of minority groups in other nations. It is crucial in this respect to understand the historical background of Japanese minority groups. Third, the study can debunk the core of the persistent Japanese myth of racial and cultural homogeneity. The concept of "one nation, one culture, one people" is so strong that those who belong outside of the group are likely to face fierce exclusion.

Japan's largest minority group is the *burakumin*. Official government statistics put the *burakumin* population around one million, while the Buraku Liberation League, one of the organizations of the *burakumin*, estimates the population to be over three million. Although they are of the same racial, ethnic, cultural, and national origins as the rest of the Japanese population, when identified as *burakumin* (or *eta*, the derogatory term), they are likely to face prejudice and discrimination. Although the origins of the *burakumin* are not clear, discrimination against them was formalized during the Tokugawa period (1603–1868), when the rigid social hierarchy of samurai warrior, farmer, artisan, merchant, and two outcast groups of *eta* and *hinin* (pariah or, literally, non-humans) was established. Their residence was confined to designated hamlets and their occupations were limited to those thought to be polluting and undesirable, such as mortuary attendant, tomb guardian, butcher and tanner. As a result, they were easily identified by residence and occupation.

The Meiji government (1868–1912) abolished the outcast status and treated the descendants of the outcast group as "new common people." However, the identification as "new common people" in the household register system and their concentration in certain ghettos were clear indications of their social status. Although the household register is not available to the public any more without the permission of the family, the identity of a member of a minority group is frequently revealed in the course of investigations of prospective marriage partners (a common practice in Japan), and background checks of prospective employees.

Koreans are the largest ethnic minority in contemporary Japan. According to Japanese government statistics, about 690 thousand Koreans are living in Japan, approximately 80 percent of whom are second- and third-generation Koreans who were born in Japan. Many of them do not speak Korean language and are educated in the Japanese school system.

The presence of this large number of Koreans is largely a legacy of Japanese colonialism. When Korea was annexed in 1910, there were very few Koreans living in Japan. However, during the thirty-six-year colonial period, the number of Koreans in Japan increased sharply and by the end of World War II, 2.4 million Koreans were in Japan. Many of these were male workers of prime working age who had been brought to Japan as military and labor conscripts for work in mining, railroad construction, and stevedoring. Following Japan's surrender, 75 percent of the Koreans were repatriated. Those who decided to remain in Japan, however, continued to face legal and social disadvantages.

Because most Koreans do not hold Japanese citizenship, they

are denied certain basic rights. While they are obliged to taxes, they are denied the right to vote or some welfare services. Marriage to a Korean is often opposed by Japanese parents, and Koreans also face discrimination in employment opportunities.

It is important to note that the issue of second- and third-generation Koreans in Japan is partially the result, first, of the Japanese Nationality Law, which is based on the principle of *jus sanguinis*, holding that one's nationality is determined by parentage and not by the place of birth; and second, of the fact that, because until 1984 one's nationality was passed on through the father, children of Koreans were legally Korean even though they had been born in Japan and to a Japanese mother. Since these second- and third-generation Koreans are legally aliens, they are subject to mandatory fingerprinting and must carry a "certificate of alien registration" at all times. Although all foreign residents must be fingerprinted and registered, these requirements are particularly targeted at the Korean minority, who account for over 80 percent of resident aliens in Japan. Following the agreement between the Japanese and South Korean governments, beginning in 1992, Korean residents of Japan would be provided with registration cards with their photographs but no fingerprints.

In conclusion, the continuing discrimination against the *burakumin* and Koreans underlines the ideology of racial and cultural homogeneity to which many in Japan subscribe, resulting in a social system of in-group cohesion and out-group exclusion.

INTERGENERATIONAL MOBILITY

Some studies posit a theory of Japanese distinctiveness in intergenerational mobility patterns, while others stress the logic of industrial technology, suggesting a similarity in the pattern of intergenerational mobility among industrial nations. (The article by Ishida et al (1991) discusses these studies at length.) The Japanese experience shows both similar and distinctive patterns of mobility, depending upon whether absolute or relative mobility rates are examined. Absolute mobility rates refer to observed amount of mobility usually measured by inflow and outflow rates. Inflow rates show the pattern of intergenerational recruitment which is the indication of where the current members of the class came from. Outflow rates describe mobility chances of men from a certain class origin which is the indication of where the members of the class are found in the next generation.

In observing inflow and outflow rates, a distinctive feature of the Japanese working class—skilled and non-skilled manual workers—appears to emerge in comparison with European nations. There is a very low level of self-recruitment among the Japanese working class; that is, the proportion of industrial workers who were the sons of industrial workers is very small. A large proportion of industrial workers, instead, had a background in farming. The Japanese working class is also distinctive in its low level of intergenerational stability. A much smaller proportion of the sons of the working-class fathers stayed in the working class in Japan than in European nations.

Given its low self-recruitment and its low stability, the Japanese manual working class clearly lacks "demographic identity" which may be found in some European nations. This is directly related to the particular course of late but rapid industrial development followed by Japan. In countries that industrialized very early, such as England and Scotland, the decline of agricultural population took place a long time ago and a stable core of industrial working class has existed for some time over a few generations. Only at a later stage did the white-collar sector expand. In Japan, in contrast, the significant decline in agricultural population took place only after World War II and was accompanied first by the expansion of blue-collar employment and then followed almost immediately by the expansion of white-collar employment. Therefore, the uniqueness of Japan's economic history led to a distinctive pattern of absolute mobility.

When we shift to the examination of relative rates, however, it appears that rates among industrial nations, including Japan are similar. Relative rates of mobility are based on the comparison of mobility chances of workers of different class origins. These rates may be understood as the results of "competition" between men of different class origins to attain a certain class position. For example, a man of farm origin may have one to two odds on becoming a professional, rather than a farmer, while a man of professional origin may have two to one odds. Then a man of professional origin will have four times greater odds on becoming a professional, as opposed to a farmer, than a man of farm origin. Because these rates are based upon a comparison of mobility chances, they are independent of the shape of class structure. By examining relative rates, we may ask what the Japanese pattern of mobility would have been if Japan had not experienced such a dramatic course of industrialization. In other words, we may estimate the extent of mobility controlling for changes in the class structure.

Relative rates are conceptually different from absolute rates, which are heavily influenced by the shape of the class structure. We have already found that in Japan the white-collar sector expanded rapidly at almost the same time as the blue-collar sector. However, despite these structural changes, the principle of allocation of men of different class origins into the expanded sector may be assumed to be constant. For example, the lower chances in entering white-collar employment for the sons of farmers, compared with the sons of professionals, may remain the same even though a lot more sons of farmers are found in white-collar employment than a generation ago. It is possible for the principle of allocation or relative chances of mobility to be constant even though a society experienced a dramatic structural change. Conversely, it is also possible that mobility is the result of relative chances of mobility without any change in the class structure. Therefore, relative rates may be seen as measuring the extent of "fluidity" or "openness" in the society.

The comparison of relative mobility rates across industrial nations suggests a global similarity; Japan's distinctiveness in mobility patterns largely disappears and the pattern of relative mobility is basically similar to those of European nations. Therefore, it may be argued that features of mobility common among industrial nations are found in relative rates while absolute rates are influenced by socio-economic history of individual nations. The source of Japanese distinctiveness in absolute rates lies not in the underlying difference in the extent of fluidity but in the class structure which developed in the process of industrialization in a very different way in Japan than in European nations.

CAREER MOBILITY

The notion of a "permanent employment system" suggests a low degree of career mobility in the Japanese labor market: workers join a company following school graduation, are trained within the company, and remain in the same company throughout their entire working career. However, this type of employment practice appears to characterize only full-time male workers in large firms (probably at most a quarter of the labor force). Even among these workers in large firms the arrangement is not truly permanent because they face mandatory retirement at around age 55 or 60, when they move to smaller companies to begin second career.

A recent cross-national study by Koike (1988) also indicates that although the proportion of workers with less than two years' service is smaller in Japan than in West European nations, workers with more than twenty years of experience in the same company are not significantly more numerous in Japan than in Europe. Thus, the frequent claim that Japanese employees tend to stay with the same company for the entire working career is not entirely accurate.

III. ISSUES FOR DISCUSSIONS

1. Choose one dimension of stratification (e.g., gender inequality or hierarchy in the educational system) and compare with other nations.

2. How was the discrimination against the two largest minority groups institutionalized in Japan? Are these groups subject to similar forms of discrimination as minorities in other nations?

3. What are the effects of industrialization on the patterns of intergenerational mobility in Japan? Did the particular course of industrialization followed by Japan, namely late but rapid process of development, influence the patterns of mobility?

IV. SELECTED READINGS

Fukutake, Tadashi. *The Japanese Social Structure: Its Evolution in the Modern Century.* 2d ed. Tokyo: University of Tokyo Press, 1988 (student reading). A good introductory textbook. Includes chapters on stratification and class structure.

Rohlen, Thomas. *Japan's High Schools.* Berkeley: University of California Press, 1983 (faculty and student background). An excellent ethnographic account of stratification in Japanese high schools.

Lee, Changsoo, and DeVos, George. *Koreans in Japan.* Berkeley: University of California Press, 1981 (faculty background). A detailed study of history and present situation of Koreans in Japan.

Yoshino, I. Roger, and Murakoshi, Sueo. *The Invisible Visible Minority.* Osaka: Buraku Kaiho Kenkyusha, 1977. An introductory book on the *burakumin* minority.

Ishida, Hiroshi; Goldthorpe, John; and Erikson, Robert. "Intergenerational Class Mobility in Postwar Japan." *American Journal of Sociology* (January, 1991): 954–992 (faculty background). A reading on intergenerational mobility and industrialization.

Koike, Kazuo. *Understanding Industrial Relations in Modern Japan.* London: Macmillan, 1988 (faculty background). Includes a detailed discussion on workers' careers in large and small firms.

Sociology:
Japan

American Education in Comparative Perspective: What Can We Learn from Japan?

Robert C. Liebman

I. INTRODUCTION: CENTRAL POINTS

When studying the United States from a comparative perspective, Japan is a useful mirror.[1] With a free enterprise economy that is now the world's second largest, Japan is our peer. Yet, among the most industrialized democracies, Japan, as the only non-Western one, is unique. Looking at the United States in the mirror of Japan opens the way for two parallel inquiries: the first focusing on the similarities among all modern societies and the second focusing on differences which make America exceptional.

This essay examines the ideology and practice of education in the United States by first comparing differences in educational outcomes— that is, the skills, values, and knowledge acquired by members of the population—in the United States and Japan, and second, by asking how these societies have differently given shape to education as an institution.

My decision to examine educational outcomes is motivated by Japan's central place in debates over "the crisis in American education" and by the eagerness of American school reformers to remedy the situation by embracing Japanese practices. (I leave for others the question of whether there is really a crisis in American education.) The question of what **could** (and what **should**) be borrowed invites investigation of how schools "fit" with other institutions in BOTH Japan and the United States. The tolls of comparative analysis are right for the task. While my remarks draw on a number of reform reports, I focus on the widely read *A Nation at Risk* (1983) and the New York Stock Exchange's *People and Productivity* (1982).[2]

The task breaks into two parts. First, I demonstrate that the goals and patterns of schooling in two societies are structurally similar. Substantial investment in schooling and the production of human capital is a hallmark of all modern societies. Indeed, the United States and Japan are **alike** in terms of shared commitments to universal primary and secondary education, mass access to higher education, and meritocratic selection. These similarities suggest that the structure of schooling is not the chief determinant of cross-national differences in educational outcomes. How then can these differences be explained?

Second, I demonstrate that **differences** in the relationship between schooling and other institutions such as the examination system, the family, and the firm in the United States and Japan are the crucial determinants of their different educational outcomes. Schools are incorporated within society in strikingly different ways in the two countries; parents, educators, employers, and, above all, students have different expectations about the provision of education and their respective roles in the enterprise of schooling. These expectations arise out of historically different paths of educational expansion. In the United states, an early and politicized pattern of educational expansion made education a public entitlement. Initially through local governance and later through assimilation, schooling was a way of incorporating citizens into the polity. In contrast, Japanese educational expansion was a process of building a mass school system around the skeleton of an elite system. Japanese schooling is consequently more state centered, less responsive to special interests, and importantly, more avowedly meritocratic.

II. MAJOR TOPICS

SCHOOLING AS A NATIONAL SYSTEM: SIMILARITIES AND DIFFERENCES IN PATTERNS OF EDUCATIONAL EXPANSION

National indicators show the U.S. schooling system to be more like that of Japan than the system of European countries. Both the United States and Japan have reached the "universal" stage of secondary education and the "mass" stage of higher education. In 1981, of those eligible to enroll in high school, 96 percent of U.S. students and 94 percent of Japanese did so; estimated college enrollments are 46 percent and 37 percent for the United States and Japan, respectively. In most European countries, both high school and college enrollment rates are considerably lower. The United States and Japan are also alike (and unlike European countries) in organizing schooling in a 6-3-3-4 pattern and having nonselective elementary and junior high schools.[3]

However, their educational outcomes differ. Japan's rate of high school completion (roughly 90 percent vs. 75 percent for the U.S.) is the world's highest. In both countries males and females complete high school at about the same rate. However, while males and females attend college and earn the bachelor's degree at roughly the same rate in the United States, college enrollment rates in Japan continue a pattern of male predominance in four-year and female predominance in two-year institutions.[4] Perhaps the most striking difference in educational outcomes is observed in levels of functional illiteracy among the adults— roughly 13-20 percent in the United States compared with less than one per cent in Japan.[5]

Differences in national patterns of educational expansion set the context for explaining these differences. In the United States, educational expansion occurred **early**— coincident with the extension of the franchise in the first half of the 19th century.[6] Importantly, authority over schooling was **decentralized**. The Constitution made schooling the responsibility of states (not the federal government) and schools developed as community and neighborhood institutions. Consequently, schools played an ambivalent role in nation-building: they worked to assimilate waves of immigrants while at the same time, since they were decentralized, they encouraged ethnic and racial mobilization (and segregation) in politics. Though decisions are increasingly being made at higher levels of government as a consequence of federal and (more importantly) state funding and of the professionalization of education administration, public schooling is still primarily a local institution (e.g., the school board is comprised of residents of the community) and associated with local issues (e.g., the relationship between school quality and housing values).

In comparison, Japanese educational expansion was **late and more centralized**. In the Tokugawa period (1600–1868), schools served, with impressive results, the children of merchants, samurai, and some farmers; by 1850, at least one-quarter of the population was literate. The regional feudal governments set up han (feudal clan) schools to educate the sons of samurai. Following the example of the Tokugawa shogun's own school, Confucian studies were central to the curriculum. The purpose of schooling was to produce skilled and ethical administrators whose conduct and example would bring order to society.[7] Among the modernization reforms undertaken in the wake of the 1868 Meiji Restoration were sweeping changes in the nation's education system. The 1872 Fundamental Code of Education created a universal primary system in which, by 1900, 98 percent of school-age children were enrolled. The expansion of secondary and tertiary enrollments was more recent: in 1950, 43 percent of those eligible attended high school; less than one-tenth attended institutions of higher education; by 1970, the figures were 82 percent and 24 percent.[8] Importantly, educational expansion was instituted at the national level, which meant that access to education was relatively equal in urban and rural areas.

Japan's education system also bears the imprint of the country's late **democratic** development. The first parliament sat in 1890, male suffrage was introduced in 1925, and universal suffrage in 1947. The American Occupation authorities, whose primary mission was to institutionalize democratic practices, saw education as the backbone of postwar social reform and as a route to individual development, social equality, and national economic advance. While their efforts to decentralize Japan's school system largely failed, those aimed at the democratization of the system were more successful: universal coeducation in public schools and compulsory schooling through grade nine were introduced, and the 6-3-3-4 system, parent-teacher associations, and the Japan Teachers' Union were established. Contemporary Japanese schooling thus incorporates the dual legacies of a meritocratic system aimed at selecting an administrative elite and the democratic ideal of bringing all members of society into the system.

Focusing on these different national patterns of educational expansion, rather than on real or imagined differences in culture or national character is useful in a comparative study, for it places in a historical context the development of a philosophy of education in the two cultures. For example, the importance of "cultural consensus" as an explanation for Japan's success reflects both the hold of a centralized system and the relative homogeneity of its population. On the other hand, in the United States, where nation-building involved waves of immigration and internal migration, schooling has always been a channel for incorporating groups into society and the polity. Cultural consensus is weak, both because authority is not centralized and because schooling serves the divergent purposes of competing mobilized constituencies. Because the United States is committed to schooling for all and for all sorts of interests, it is hard to reach consensus on its purposes or its performance. Schooling is more politicized in America than Japan.

SCHOOLS AS ORGANIZATIONS: HOW SCHOOLS PROCESS PEOPLE

In modern democratic societies, schools serve contradictory commitments to equality and meritocracy. While the principle of equal access to education for all is central to the provision of public schooling, in practice, schooling is organized under the principle of meritocratic selection. Schools socialize students, but they also **sort** them.[9] While both the United States and Japan are committed to both equality and meritocracy, they incorporate these principles into the organization of schooling differently, as suggested by the results of international tests.

Those who would reform American schools frequently point out that, on **average**, Japanese students outscore students of other countries on international mathematics and science tests.[10] However, these scores reveal another dimension of educational outcomes; the **coefficient of variation** is greater among American than Japanese students. Indeed, of the ten or twelve countries that administer the tests, the scores of American students show the widest or second widest variance. What is remarkable is not Japan's top ranking, but its impressive combination of excellence and relative equality indicated by a high mean and a low variance. In the United States, by contrast, the top and bottom ranks are wide apart.

The reform reports largely agree that Japan's success originates in its schools. From there, it is easy to conclude that the solution to America's educational ills lies in remaking its schools along

Japanese lines. The idea of changing the inputs to alter the outputs is attractive, but it is based more on myth than fact. Consider three of the favorite medicines of reformers: money, time, and tracking.

Finance and Authority Over Schooling. Those who believe that an educational Marshall Plan would solve America's woes are unaware that education accounts for roughly the same share of government expenditure in Japan and the United States— 19.7 percent vs. 19.9 percent in 1980.[11] Rather than budget share, it is perhaps the **distribution** of funds that matters more to educational outcomes. Interdistrict inequality is low in Japan (near-zero among prefectures) compared with the United States, where per student spending in Texas exceeds $7,000 in the hundred most affluent districts, compared with less than $3000 in the hundred poorest.[12] In the United States, where school funding is tied to local tax bases, differences in per student spending are largely due to unequal property values. While schools rely on local taxes in Japan as well, government subsidies to poorer districts reduce inequality. The subsidies reflect the policy of Mombusho, Japan's Ministry of Education, which has no equivalent in the United States.

A standardized curriculum, uniform teacher certification, and other forms of central direction account in part for low variance in educational outcomes in Japan. In contrast, schooling in the United States, is a crazyquilt of fifty different state curricular and teacher certification requirements which make it one of the least centralized among industrial nations.

Organization of Space and Time. American and Japanese schools differ in the ways that they organize space and time for instruction. For example, average class size is twenty-eight in the United States and forty-two in Japan. Larger classes in Japan challenge the belief of many educators that students learn more in smaller classes. In fact, the association is unconfirmed in cross-national research. For example, a 1989 six-nation study by the Educational Testing Service found that U.S. thirteen-year olds scored lowest in math and near last in science, despite relatively small average class sizes.

Differences in time at school provide a more plausible explanation for differing national test scores. Japanese students spend more time in school than their American counterparts, 240 days vs. 180 days (on average). The school year begins in April and ends in mid-March, interrupted by breaks at New Year (two weeks) and summer (six weeks). Students attend school five and one-half days a week. Japanese high school students spend more time commuting to school and more time doing homework than their American counterparts, who spend more time at part-time jobs (held by 50 percent of eleventh graders, 66 percent of seniors while 18 percent male and 11 percent female Japanese high school students work part-time) and socializing with the opposite sex (dating begins after high school graduation for most Japanese).[13]

Thus, over the three years in grades 10–12, Japanese students are at school 180 more days—roughly one full United States school year. The additional hours of homework (roughly 2:1 in favor of Japan) broaden the disparity. Although we lack evidence to confirm, Rohlen's assertion that "the average Japanese high school graduate has the equivalent basic knowledge of the average American college graduate," it is undeniable that the average Japanese high school graduate has done **more** schoolwork.[14]

Another way to evaluate the time in school is to look at how it is used. A Nation at Risk laments time allocation: of a total of thirty hours, the average U.S. high school devotes twenty-two to instruction. Much time is spent on transitions from activity to activity and from room to room whereas in Japanese high schools, all classes are taken with the same group and mostly in the same room. In Japan, **teachers** move and students stay put. Students eat lunch in their homeroom and are responsible for keeping it clean (reducing the school's custodial costs). The long "homeroom period" is the only block of time students have for discussing their school or personal problems. Consider, in contrast, the importance to American students of their lockers, which line high school hallways. A student's locker is "home" during the school day; posters and photographs are marks of ownership and individuality. In Japan, there are no lockers. A student's "place" is the shared space of the homeroom group.

Tracking and the Organization of Schools. How schools sort or track students shapes a nation's education outcomes. In this country, tracking starts early: elementary schools use standardized tests and teacher evaluations to group students by their abilities in reading and math. In many high schools, students are assigned to ability-graded sections of English, mathematics, and other required subjects. In Japan, tracking is absent and there is a fixed curriculum and evenly allocated resources (including a national scale for teachers' salaries) until grade nine. This practice of mixing student ability levels in each classroom is a postwar innovation. Before 1945, a highly developed tracking system organized public elementary and middle schools. Japanese teachers, represented by a union which is strongly committed to equalizing society, mix and balance abilities to encourage comradeship. There are no programs for gifted children and weaker students are almost never held back. The lack of remedial instruction is, as will be seen, a cause for complaint by many parents.[15]

The pattern of uniform instruction ends with high school entrance, a more crucial juncture than college entrance because virtually the entire youth population is involved. Consider the supply-demand imbalance faced by the 1975 cohort in Kobe, Japan: 6,000 openings in public academic high schools and 15,112 junior high graduates with roughly 95 percent (14,300) planning to attend high school; of whom 80 percent preferred tuition-free public schools.[16] The 5,000 or so who were denied admission had to choose between a public vocational school and a private high school, most of which offer a second-rate college preparatory program. Admission to public high schools depends on entrance exams and/or teachers' judgments based on rank in class and aptitude test scores. (Note: In some areas, there is an unofficial affirmative action scheme by which high school teachers set quotas for the best junior high schools to increase the chances for admitting students from the poorer sections.) Thus, nearly universal secondary education has not brought utopia, but a system in which many students aspire to a kind of high school which remains out of reach. "The education level of the entire generation has advanced, but elitism and social hierarchies have not been fundamentally altered by the rapid growth of secondary education."[17] Getting into the right high school determines career chances because (1) academic high schools prepare students for college entrance and (2) Japanese employers rank high schools and allocate desirable jobs to the top schools.[18] At high school, the Japanese system shifts from lumping to splitting. Tracking occurs **between** schools. The neighborhood organization of grade and junior high schools gives way to a "large district system" in which public high schools are open on a competitive basis to any resident (as are private high schools). In this country, tracking occurs **within** schools. While large cities often have selective schools, the comprehensive high school drawing from nearby neighborhoods and combining academic and vocational programs is the American ideal-type. Tracking operates in U.S. high schools "involuntarily" when classes in required subjects (English, History, etc.) are ranked according to ability (Honors, 1, 2, 3) and "voluntarily" as students select among various "diplomas" (college, vocational, general) and elect their courses accordingly.

Summary. We began by asking how the inputs of schooling—money, time, and tracking—might explain educational outcomes. Reformers promise that **more** of all three would improve outcomes. Comparing the United States and Japan, however, suggests that, with the exception of time in school, Japan's success cannot be explained by greater inputs. Rather, it is HOW schooling is organized. The Japanese national system distributes funds more evenly, sets a national curriculum, and oversees teacher selection. These factors homogenize schools and instruction. They contribute to what is most impressive about Japanese schooling: the evenness of educational outcomes.

LOOKING BEYOND SCHOOLS: RELATIONS BETWEEN SCHOOLS AND OTHER INSTITUTIONS

In looking to Japan for answers to the problems of America's schools, it is important to consider the network of resources and institutions that **collectively** affect educational outcomes. Indeed, looking one by one at the various pieces of Japanese schooling—coeducation, the 6-3-3-4 sequence, teachers lecturing students, and so on—one is struck by how much they are like our own. It is then not so much the individual pieces but the way these pieces fit into a system of schooling and the way that the system fits with other institutions which is distinctively Japanese. In Japan, three institutions—the exam system, the family, and the firm—are most important in structuring the effects of education on society. The United States is an especially good mirror for Japan given its very different way of setting boundaries between public and private allocation of education.

Exams and the Informal System of Schooling. Exams are the centerpiece of schooling in both the United States and Japan. Students earn grades by them, teachers (often with regret) teach to them, and a large industry has grown up to create them and to prepare students for them. In Japan, however, the size of the exam preparation industry and its embrace by parents and students suggest the greater importance of exam taking. Indeed, the weight of exam performance in lifetime success in Japan has led to the creation of an informal system of schooling which operates in a symbiotic and ambivalent relationship with public schooling.

Its major agencies are cram schools: *juku* for students in grades 1–9 and their cousins, *yobikō* for grades 10–12.[19] While cram schools exist in other Asian countries (South Korea, Taiwan, Hong Kong, Singapore), only in Japan do they serve as a kind of insurance policy in the "college entrance war." A 1976 national survey revealed that more than one-third of middle-school students and nearly one-fourth of students in grades 4–6 attended *juku*. In many cities, the proportion of middle school students in *juku* exceeds 50 percent. As the vice president of a Tokyo *juku* put it: "Americans go to the Boy Scouts. Japanese go to *jukus*."[20] The purpose of *juku* and *yobikō* is to prepare students for high school and college entrance exams. Whereas SAT prep schools teach test-taking techniques, *juku* "stress the mastery of scientific principles and facts, mathematical logic, mountains of social science data, the minutia of language skills, and the ability to remain poised under great pressure."[21] Exam prep schools in the United States teach shortcuts. *Juku* teaches endurance. Students typically attend a two-hour session two or three afternoons a week in year-long programs. The average *juku* is small, staffed by an experienced teacher. In the survey cited above, 43 percent reported that the level of *juku* instruction is "considerably higher" than that of public schools. Unlike public schools, about 30 percent of *juku* arranged classes by ability. Juku themselves are broadly differentiated between *shingaku juku*, which prepare better students for the competitive high school and college entrance exams, and *hoshū juku*, which tutor students who must catch up with their current schoolwork. The former use competitive exams to select the best students, and often cover material that is a year ahead of the standard curriculum.

Thus, while *juku* supplement schooling, they do not necessarily reflect the egalitarian ideals and practices of public primary schools. For example, males outnumber females (by as much as 10 percent–30 percent depending on grade-level). I have not found data on the association between parental income and *juku* attendance, but high enrollment rates suggest that *juku* are within the reach of most families. In a 1968 national survey, 80 percent of parents believed college was a possibility for their children; the percentage is probably higher today. *Juku* have sprouted up to serve every budget, although the best are accessible only to those who can afford the high tuition. Thus the *juku* system tends to reinforce a system of stratification.

In summary, the *juku* both supplements schooling and provides remedial education. As a supplement, the informal system serves parental aspirations for children's success in competitive entrance exams. Indeed, much of the purpose of *juku* is character-building. It is important to note that *hoshū juku* provide remedial instruction that is offered without cost by American schools. While *juku* contribute to the high scores of Japanese students on international tests, they represent a form of privatizing the costs of education which would be unacceptable to most Americans.

Schools and Families. A sample of mothers of first and fifth graders in Sendai (Japan) and Minneapolis were asked to rank four factors according to importance— effort, ability, task difficulty, and luck— in determining a child's school performance. Differences for luck and task difficulty were not statistically significant. The striking differences were for ability and effort. American mothers ranked effort slightly above ability; Japanese mothers rated effort as **twice** as important as ability. Stevenson (1983) associates the greater perceived importance of effort in Japan with parental beliefs in the value of hard work and more time spent on homework. Another interpretation associates these beliefs with mothering styles.[22] White suggests that **"The central human relationship in Japanese culture is between mother and child."** The Japanese mother feels that "her child possesses the potential for great success" which can be realized only through the encouragement of a devoted mother. Devotion encourages dependence (*amae*) in Japan where the most valued quality is "an ability to maintain harmony in human relationships." United States childrearing practices stress independence.[23]

Suzanne Vogel's (1978) ethnography of the Tokyo "professional housewife" married to the *sarariman* (salaried urban professional) illustrates how education has shaped and been shaped by the mothering role in postwar Japan. With few employment opportunities, after marriage (95 percent by age 35), women have traditionally been full-time housewives while their husbands worked long hours in a standard six-day workweek. Raising her children and ensuring their success in the exam competition became her primary responsibility. The ideal *kyoiku mama* ("education mother") sends her children off to school with a nutritious lunch, attends PTA meetings, enrolls in a *mama-juku* where she is taught how best to help her child study, meets the returning child with a snack, and assists in doing homework.

The *kyoiku mama* illustrates differing ideals of mothering in this country and Japan. These are reflected in the different beliefs that Japanese and U.S. mothers hold about how they can best help their children do well in school. In the Sendai-Minneapolis survey, the Japanese mothers believed helping the child (supervising homework or reading to him/her) was their most important task, while American mothers thought encouraging the child (to develop self-esteem) and becoming involved (being available, taking an interest in school) were their two most important roles. The Suzuki method of teaching violin in which mothers attend lessons to learn the piece and practice with the child between lessons is a noteworthy example of how Japanese mothers supplement formal instruction at home.

What then are the different conceptions of the school-family relationship? American parents place more faith in **public** schooling and demand more from it than Japanese parents. Japanese families mobilize more effort and invest more resources in supplementing public education.

It is fair to assume that parents in both countries want success for their children. For Americans, the downpayment on a child's success is often a mortgage on a house in the right school district. The realities of Japanese education are different: while public schools are not all the same, the range of variation is small and few parents move in order to change schools.[24] Place of residence does not confer an advantage in a largely uniform system.

Yet, the selective high school system pressures parents early on to give their children a competitive edge in gaining admittance to a good university. Indeed, the fundamental paradox of Japanese education is the contrast between the egalitarianism of grades 1–9 and the differentiation which marks life forever after. In a funnel-shaped system in which the demand for higher education exceeds supply, some will be left out. "It's not enough to rely on what you learn in school," reports an Osaka high school student in a discussion of college entrance.[25] The two countries differ in what is provided publicly and without cost and what must be obtained privately through family resources. U.S. and Japanese parents form strategies in response to these differences.

Schools and Firms. "Adopt-a-school programs" in which a corporation promises employment to graduates of a selected high school are an innovation in American education. Few Americans, however, are aware that many Japanese firms have for decades guaranteed jobs to a number of graduates of particular high schools. In the United States, the adopt-a-school program is intended to save failing urban schools. In Japan, firms only continue to offer jobs to schools whose graduates consistently demonstrate a high level of ability.

Comparing these differences gives a glimpse of the different ways that schools are linked to the labor market. In this country, job seeking operates through personal networks or an open market, while in Japan institutionalized linkages between schools and workplaces organize the matching of graduates to jobs. Consider first high schools. Fewer than 10 percent of U.S. students use high school (placement services, teachers or counselors) in their job search compared with 75 percent in Japan.[26] Many Japanese high schools and employers take part in a sixty-year old system of semiformal employment contracts (called *jisseki kankei*, literally "relationship based on past record"). The system, officially regulated by the Public Employment Security Office, shifts competition for jobs from the labor market into schools and among schools. Job opportunities are stratified by high school because company recruiters set quotas on the number and types of jobs that they offer to different schools. While the contract employers make up only a small fraction of all firms which recruit from high schools, they exercise considerable influence. Many are larger firms which offer the most desirable jobs. More importantly, they hire almost half the work-bound graduates of the average high school. Because schools and firms share a common interest in continuity, the system is self-reinforcing. Recruiters base their quotas on each school's track record. Teachers, for their part, send only students who meet the firm's standards.

Thus, schools must make meritocratic selections. Japanese employers insist that new hires have basic academic skills. Over 85 percent of employers use examinations to screen both high school and college graduates. Of these, nearly two-thirds test academic skills and knowledge. Consequently, teachers recommend students on the basis of rank in class. In a 1983 survey of teachers in high schools where more than half the graduates went to work, 47.5 percent reported that they do not recommend students with low school grades, even if the school's quota cannot be filled. The contract system reinforces the imperative of doing well. In sum, for the work-bound, school achievement matters in Japan. In this country, where schools and labor market are loosely related, pressures for school achievement are more relaxed.

However, practices for hiring college graduates in Japan resemble the open recruitment system of U.S. high schools and colleges. While some hiring is the result of the personal recommendation of a professor, most is done through ads and campus recruiting. The most prestigious employers, such as the Ministry of Finance, recruit from the most prestigious of Japan's 489 colleges and universities, and particularly from Tokyo University. Thus, for the college-bound, "the widely acknowledged importance of the university attended for determining later success concentrates life-long career ambitions on the entrance examinations."[27] The ranking of universities is a byproduct of job competition in Japan, while in the United States, the academic hierarchy is multidimensional, reflecting rankings for research, teaching quality, and professional studies. Jobs are more loosely allocated in this country where top-ranking graduates of less prestigious schools can compete with those of more prestigious institutions.

CONCLUSION: LINKING DEMOCRACY AND EDUCATION

The comparative analysis developed here suggests two conclusions: (1) while the structures of schooling in the United States and Japan are in many ways alike, their educational outcomes (notably test performance and rates of school completion and literacy) are quite different; and (2) these differences may be explained by the different relations among schooling and other institutions of society, namely, the examination system, the family, and the firm. Thus, comparative analysis reveals two chief weaknesses of most reform reports: (1) they exaggerate the contrast between schooling in the United States and Japan, and (2) they tend to ignore the context in which schooling takes place in the two societies.

The differences reflect and in part result from historically different patterns of educational expansion. While both are modern **democratic** societies, a comparative-historical approach qualifies the extent of commonality between the two countries. A consideration of the differences in their populations and in the way the boundaries between public and private have been set is revealing.

Consider first the extent of differentiation.[28] The Japanese population is racially, ethnically, and linguistically homogeneous. Non-Japanese, Koreans and *burakumin* (an indigenous "untouchable" group), comprise three percent of the population. As a result of restrictive entry requirements enacted after World War II, there are few foreign workers and virtually no immigrants. In contrast, roughly 10 percent of adults in the United States are foreign-born, and roughly 25 percent of public school students are black or Spanish-speaking. Also, income differentials are smaller in Japan than in the United States; the lowest fifth of the population in Japan receives a larger share of national income than its counterparts in Western nations. Finally, there is less diversity in parenting in Japan. Five percent of children are in single-parent families (more than half because of the death of a parent) compared with 20 percent of children in the United States, where the per capita divorce rate is five times greater than Japan's and where nearly 20 percent of children are born out of wedlock compared with 1 percent in Japan. Even if U.S. and Japanese patterns of schooling were identical, given such different inputs, it would be unreasonable to expect that their educational outcomes would be similar.

The second contrast between the United States and Japan relates to the different ways that the boundaries between public and private have been set in schooling. The public sector provides more of the nation's instruction in the United States than in Japan. As seen in the billion dollar *juku* industry, Japanese parents pay for remedial tutoring and supplementary schooling for exam preparation. U.S. schools are charged with both preparing children for college and offering remedial education to slow learners. Americans expect more from their schools and expect more schooling from government as a comparison of post-Sputnik higher education expansion demonstrates. In this country, between 1963 and 1980 the number of college students increased by a factor of 2.5; 87 percent of the increase was accommodated through the expansion of public institutions.[29] In Japan, where the number of students tripled from 1960–76, the pattern was reversed: private institutions accounted for 83.9 percent of the increase, and the number of public institutions remained roughly constant. However, the demand for a bachelor's degree continues to exceed the number of openings. In 1980, when there were 412,000 openings, 452,000 seniors and nearly 200,000 ronin (those who did not get into university in previous years) sat for the examinations. Of those trying for the first time, roughly one in three failed to get in.[30] The mismatch between supply and demand underlies "examination hell" (*juken jigoku*) and reinforces the *juku* system. Compare the United States, where supply matches or, to the dismay of college administrators, often exceeds demand.

Adult education offers another example of the differences in public-private provision of schooling. From workingmen's schools, through classes for immigrants to the GI Bill, American federal, state and local governments provided for delayed and interrupted educational careers. These practices have no public equivalent in Japan. The returning or non-traditional student, now prominent on U.S. campuses, is virtually unknown in Japan, where students march more or less in lockstep through the age-graded crossroads of an educational career.[31] Americans take pride in the abundance of educational second chances, in keeping with a national commitment to public schooling for all. In Japan, large corporations are perhaps the leading provider of continuing education, a fact which some credit with the underdevelopment of graduate studies.

In sum, differences in the structure of schooling in the United States and Japan reflect and, in part, result from the differing balance between public and private provision of education. Those who suggest that different outcomes can be explained chiefly through the contrast between a homogeneous and a heterogeneous society have overlooked the fact that schooling reflects the different democratic experiences of the two countries.

Rather, Japanese educational outcomes are in large part the result of the ways that **private** support supplements and reinforces schooling. Families, firms, and juku are partners of schools in the work of educating Japan. Public schooling itself bears the imprint of an elite system and of a long tradition of schooling in the service of the central state. These historical legacies help us make sense of the limits of public funding and the resulting mobilization of family resources in the postwar educational expansion. In the highly competitive search for national talent, "the whole educational system has become a sort of screening apparatus."[32]

Looking at the United States in the mirror of Japan, one sees the particular ways that the boundaries between public and private have been set in education. Commitments to universal access and to public voice in setting school policy which shape U.S. schooling reflect a founding principle of American democracy, namely, that education is both the entitlement of all individuals and the guarantor of collective participation in the polity. Americans adhere to the principle of schooling for all. Consequently, education is more a matter of public provision and is more openly politicized in the United States than in Japan. Cries of a crisis in American education must be seen in light of how this historical legacy frames our thinking about the relationship between schooling and society.

Schooling in the two societies differs most strikingly in the ways that it incorporates the differing democratic experiences of the two nations. By demonstrating that schooling serves multiple purposes and that historical legacies determine the priorities which societies set, comparative analysis can enhance our understanding of American education.

III. ISSUES FOR DISCUSSION

1. While Americans and Japanese both adhere to the principle of educational equality, they have different meanings of equality (equality of opportunity vs. uniform treatment). Compare one or two structures of schooling which reflect **differences** in American and Japanese concepts of equality.

2. How might differences in the attitudes of parents influence the school achievement of students in the two countries?

3. How has the trend toward "universal" college attendance shaped the structure of primary and secondary schools in the two countries?

4. What features of Japanese schooling might be introduced into our school system? What features of American schooling might be introduced into the Japanese school system?

Note: full bibliographic citations as well as an annotated bibliography appear in section IV. of this paper.

NOTES

1. I am grateful to colleagues and students at Portland State University and Princeton University who served as sources or sounding boards in the writing of this paper, especially Sarane Spence Boocock, Robert Everhart, Hiromi Kato, Ryoto Kato, Laurence Kominz, David Morgan, Takashi Okamura, Gilbert Rozman, Mizuho Saito, and Hideki Yoshikawa. Elaine S. Friedman's comments helped sharpen the argument. I am responsible for any errors.
2. See bibliography in Bastian, et. al., 1985.
3. Rosenbaum and Kariya, 1981: 1337.
4. Chronicle of Higher Education, September 20, 1989: A48.
5. White 1987: 2; low U.S. figure from National Assessment of Education Performance.
6. Katznelson and Wier, 1985.
7. Rohlen, 1983: 47.
8. Cummings et al., 1979: 68, 107.
9. Bowles and Gintis, 1976.
10. Rohlen, 1983: 4,5.
11. Cummings, et al., 1986: 104.
12. *New York Times*, October 3, 1989: A9.
13. See time, budgets, in Rohlen, 1983: 272 ff.
14. Ibid. 321.
14. Cummings 1979; Rohlen, 1978: 223.
16. Rohlen 1988: 121 ff.
17. Rohlen: 127.
18. Rosenbaum and Kariya, 1989: 1350–1352.

19. Rohlen, 1980.
20. Fiske, 1983: July 12.
21. Rohlen, 1980: 210.
22. White, 1987: 21 ff.
23. See Tobin, Wu, Davidson, 1989.
24. Rohlen, 1983: 117.
25. Fiske, 1983: July 12.
26. Rosenbaum and Kariya, 1989. While unstated, their data apply to commercial, general, and industrial high schools.
27. Vogel, 1980: 163.
28. Rohlen, 1983: 112–117.
29. U.S. Department of Education, 1988: 142.
30. Rohlen, 1983: 84.
31. Cummings, et al., 1979: 72.
32. Kitamura in Cummings, et al., 1979: 72.

IV. SELECTED READINGS

Cummings, William K. *Equality and Education in Japan.* Princeton: Princeton University Press, 1980 (faculty background). Argues that post WWII Japanese schooling transformed society by promoting equality in skills and creating commitment to the value of equality. This is the view of the national teachers' union which is profiled here. Primary schools (and especially primary teaching) provide the best evidence; the high school pattern is quite different.

Cummings, William K.; Beauchamp, E. R.; Ichikawa, S.; Kobayashi, V.N.; and Ushiogi, M. *Educational Policies in Crisis.* New York: Praeger, 1986 (faculty background). A collection of articles which describe curriculum, enrollment patterns, reform efforts, and other topics in Japan and the U.S., and through cross-national comparisons. A solid source book for nonspecialists.

Fiske, Edward B. "Education in Japan: Lessons for America." *New York Times* July 10–13, 1983 (student reading). A series of four articles which describe Japanese schooling and argue that little can be borrowed by the U.S. Perhaps the best short treatment for students, especially on curriculum, a topic excluded from the paper.

Rohlen, Thomas. *Japan's High Schools.* Berkeley and Los Angeles: University of California Press, 1983 (student reading). Based on fieldwork in five Kobe high schools (1974–1975), the book examines high schools as social systems linked to the worlds of higher education, family, and work. Comparisons to U.S. high schools and teen life enliven the text, but, in my view, the tilt toward readability often results in overdrawing **contrasts** between the societies. Nevertheless, the best starting place for studying high schools.

Rosenbaum, James E., and Kariya, Takehiko. "From High School to Work: Market and Institutional Mechanisms in Japan." *American Journal of Sociology* 94 (May, 1989): 1334–65 (faculty background). Describes the "contract" system between high schools and firms and compares with U.S. practices. An important supplement to Rohlen's High Schools which emphasizes college entrance.

ADDITIONAL REFERENCES

Bastian, Ann; Fruchter, Norm; Gittell, Marilyn; Greer, Colin; and Haskins, Kenneth. *Choosing Equality: The Case for Democratic Schooling.* New York: New World Foundation, 1985 (student reading).

Bowles, Samuel, and Gintis, Herbert. *Schooling in Capitalist America.* New York: Basic Books, 1976 (student reading).

Boyer, Ernest. *High School: A Report on Secondary Education in America.* Princeton: Carnegie Foundation for the Advancement of Teaching, 1983 (student reading).

Boyer, Ernest; Amano, Ikuo; and Kitamura, Kazuyuki. *Changes in the Japanese University: A Comparative Perspective.* New York: Praeger, 1979 (faculty background).

Goodland, John I. *A Place Called School.* New York: McGraw-Hill, 1984 (student reading).

Katznelson, Ira, and Weir, Margaret. *Schooling for All.* New York: Basic Books, 1985 (faculty background).

Meyer, John. "The Effects of Education .as an Institution." *American Journal of Sociology* 83 (1977): 55–77 (faculty background).

New York Stock Exchange. *People and Productivity.* 1982 (student reading).

Oakes, Jeannie. *Keeping Track: How Schools Structure Inequality.* New Haven: Yale University Press. 1985 (faculty background).

Rohlen, Thomas. *For Harmony and Strength.* Berkeley and Los Angeles: University of California Press, 1974 (student reading).

Rohlen, Thomas. "The Juku Phenomenon: An Exploratory Essay." *Journal of Japanese Studies* 6 (1980): 207–242 (faculty background).

Tobin, Joseph J.; Wu, David Y. H.; and Dividson, Dana H. *Preschool in Three Cultures.* New Haven: Yale University Press, 1989 (student reading).

U.S. Department of Education. *Digest of Educational Statistics.* Washington: Government Printing Office, 1988.

U.S. National Commission on Excellence in Education. *A Nation at Risk.* Washington: Government Printing Office, 1983 (student reading).

Vogel, Ezra F. *Japan as Number One.* New York: Harper Colophon, 1980 (student reading).

Vogel, Suzanne H. "Professional Housewife: The Career of Urban Middle Class Japanese Women." *The Japan Interpreter* (1978): 16–43 (student reading).

White, Merry. *The Japanese Educational Challenge.* New York: Free Press, 1987 (student reading).

Sociology:
Japan

Work in America in Comparative Perspective: What Can We Learn from Japan?

Robert C. Liebman

I. INTRODUCTION: CENTRAL POINTS

HOW CAN WE LEARN FROM JAPANESE SOCIETY?

A comparative approach is especially useful in studying work in America.[1] Given the hold that Japanese economic success now exercises on the American psyche (and on the American economy itself), the case for comparing work structures in the United States and Japan is compelling. Some reasons:

After Max Weber, the conviction that bureaucracy is the archetype of modern administrative and economic structure pervades Western thinking. But a U.S.-Japan comparison shows that bureaucracy wears different faces in different societies. An examination of the correspondence between Weber's ideal-type bureaucracy and actual organizational structures in the United

567

States and Japan reveals differences in structurally similar forms and invites consideration of theories which might explain them.

An understanding of these differences, their origins, and their consequences is useful in evaluating the suggestion that the United States might solve its economic woes by copying Japanese practices. The question of which practices should be borrowed impels us to reexamine American values and practices in order to understand how (if at all) Japanese work structures might "fit" with them. Through the examination of work structures in context, comparative analysis can lay bare the realities of work in America and also strip away many myths that Americans hold about Japan.

The transfer of work structures from the United States to Japan in the years following the Second World War and from Japan to the United States more recently provides a useful case for understanding just which elements lend themselves to transfer. Differences in diffusion and adoption are determined by differences in the social organization of societies. A look at specific instances of borrowing and implantation can offer insights into the complexities of American and Japanese organizational structures.

THE ECONOMIES OF AMERICA AND JAPAN: SIMILARITIES AND DIFFERENCES

Thoughtful and dispassionate comparisons of economic organization in the United States and Japan are too rarely heard in the often emotional debate that accompanies America's changing role in the world economy. Instead we have myths of Japan's unchallenged lead in productivity, false portraits of the Japanese economy as comprised primarily of large and well-managed firms, and the misleading claim that Japan's miraculous economic growth has brought benefits to workers, consumers, and citizens which ought to be the envy of all Americans.

Consider first the myth of Japan's unchallenged lead in productivity. Like many myths, it contains a kernel of truth. In manufacturing, Japan's productivity roughly matches that of the United States. The aggregate statistic, of course, lumps the figures for individual industries where Japan has some shining successes (machine tools) together with those where there are embarrassing shortfalls (wood products). But the United States leads in services, transport and communications, construction, and agriculture. Considering that manufacturing accounts for only 30 percent of Japan's GNP, its economic miracle of dramatic and sustained growth seems less impressive. Indeed, the remaining 70 percent of GNP derives from a broad residual category that includes many small, low productivity enterprises in retailing and farming. For example, in the United States, where large farms predominate, agricultural productivity is four times greater than in Japan.

Thus, the portrait of the Japanese economy as comprised primarily of extraordinarily successful large firms is false. A comparison of twentieth-century U.S. and Japanese labor force surveys indicates that there is a greater likelihood of employment in smaller establishments in **Japan**.[2] The proportion of manufacturing workers in establishments of fewer than 100 employees was about 50 percent for Japan vs. 25 percent for the United States. Recent data suggest that the Japanese tendency toward smaller work units applies to firms as well as establishments; 38.9 percent of the labor force work in firms with fewer than 30 employees, 56.4 percent with fewer than 100, and 78.2 percent with fewer than 1000.[3] Although the data suggest that in Japan manufacturing firms tend to be larger (28.2 percent have fewer than 30 employees, 47.3 percent fewer than 100, and 73.8 percent fewer than 1000), the prevalence of small firms, even in this sector, makes clear that the portrait of Japan as a land of Fortune 500-type firms is incorrect.[4]

Consider last the claim that the Japanese economic miracle has brought benefits to workers, consumers, and citizens which ought to be the envy of all Americans. To be sure, this is a complicated claim, the validity of which depends on whose standards one chooses. However, some facts are clear. First, in both Japan and the United States, as in all industrial economies, many jobs are monotonous, many are dangerous, and there are wide discrepancies in prestige and pay. We need therefore to look at worker rewards and satisfaction in context. Second, per capita income in Japan has steadily risen and living standards are far above what they were two decades ago. However, compared to the United States, rates of home ownership are lower, working hours are longer (paid leave is shorter), and food costs consume a larger share of the family budget (a reflection of inefficient agriculture) in Japan. Third, as one result of its policy of prioritizing investment in manufacturing, the ratio of social capital stock to national income dropped steeply in the 1950s and has not increased appreciably since. Social insurance is less comprehensive[5] and government spending on health, education, parks, and environmental protection accounts for a smaller percentage of GNP in Japan than in the United States. The inadequacy of social insurance is one of the chief reasons Japanese give for their high rate of personal savings (they also save for their children's education, for contingencies due to illness, and for the purchase of a home). The differing public-private balance is a major factor in explaining differences in the organization of work relations in the two countries.

In sum, thoughtful and dispassionate U.S.-Japan comparisons undo the caricatures of the Japanese economy offered up by uninformed observers. Indeed, these comparisons are helpful in disabusing Americans of the notion that the Japan and the United States are better described by their differences than their similarities. Some things are different, but there are striking similarities between the economic and work structures of the two countries. The economies in both countries serve mass markets, have high capital-labor ratios, use similar technologies in production, and enable the accumulation of profit and private property. In both countries, enterprises are organized hierarchically. Yet, despite these structural similarities, the concept of a job and the typical career path differ in the United States and Japan. These factors are related to differences in the structure of authority in the workplace and in the mobilization of worker commitment. The following sections examine these differences with the aim of shedding light on patterns of work in America.

II. MAJOR TOPICS

CAREERS

The concept of career is the best vantage point for understanding similarities and differences in the experience of work in Japan and the United States. From a **structural** perspective, jobs are organized in a system described by three rules: first, positions are arranged hierarchically; second, rewards—including authority, prestige, and income—are distributed vertically; and third, criteria for promotion/demotion are well known. From the **individual's** perspective, a career path is a set of moves between positions. At the **organizational/societal** level, moves between firms produce aggregate rates of interfirm mobility; moves between jobs yield aggregate rates of intrafirm mobility. The differing arrangements of jobs and mobility between jobs offer a window onto the workings of different societies. In comparing the course of careers in the United States and Japan, we shall first examine permanent employment practices, then discuss promotion and reward systems, and close by discussing rates of inter- and intrafirm mobility.

Permanent Employment Practices. The vaunted Japanese lifetime employment system refers to a firm's practice of selectively recruiting high school and college graduates and retaining them until retirement. Layoffs and mid-career recruiting, common practices at most U.S. firms, are rare in Japan. The consequence is low turnover and long job tenures.

The extent of lifetime employment in Japan has often been misunderstood, blinding observers to its similarity to practices at large American firms. However, a majority of Japanese stand outside the permanent employment system, which covers at most 30–40 percent of the work force.[6] Some workers are temporaries or subcontractors; others are hired as quasi-members of firms, for example, the janitors, cooks, and others who do not do banking in Rohlen's study of the "Uedagin Bank."[7] Women are by far the largest excluded category; those employed by large firms are expected to practice *kekkon taishoku*, that is, retirement upon marriage. The practice is in part responsible for the high rate of self-employment among women and for their greater representation in smaller firms.[8]

The existence of a labor market in Japan can be seen in light on the fact that large firms in growing industries are more able to abide by the norm of permanent employment than are small firms and firms in declining markets.[9] The U.S. pattern is similar, reflecting the dualism of capitalist economies where large firms have a more stable work force than small firms. The existence of dual labor markets helps us make sense of the fact that the permanent employment system is a relatively recent phenomenon in Japan. Rather than a culturally unique practice, it was institutionalized as part of the postwar labor settlement in large firms.[10]

Job Ladders, Promotions, and Rewards. In large firms in both the United States and Japan, a management career involves a series of moves on a job ladder. Some believe what is distinctive about Japan is who gets ahead and how. The *nenkō* system refers to promotion "according to the merit of years of service." *Nenkō* is a cohort system in which advancement depends on a combination of seniority and merit. Employees serve for a fixed period before they are eligible for promotion. Evaluations of job competence order the eligible into a queue. The first in line are the first promoted, but not everyone advances. The last are left behind, sometimes literally and figuratively shunted to the sidelines as *madogiwa-zoku* (window-sitters) and sometimes sent to subsidiary companies which are tied to the parent firm through subcontracting relationships.[11]

Is *nenkō* different from promotion policies in large U.S. firms? No and yes. As in Japan, experience counts, though the possibilities for early advancement and a rapid rise are greater in the United States. Merit is important in modern enterprises everywhere, but the counterweight of age is greater in Japan where wagesare more dependent on seniority.[12] Unlike U.S. firms, however, Japanese firms attend to worker needs by providing family and housing allowances. For example, a cross-national survey of wages of manufacturing workers showed that age, seniority, and marital status had greater impact in Japan, while job attributes and managerial rank mattered more in the United States.[13] These data suggest that though many large firms moved toward Western-style job-evaluation wage systems for blue-collar workers during the 1960s, the effects of the *nenkō* system linger in wage-setting.[14]

However, not all employees within a given firm are paid and promoted under the *nenkō* system. In his bank study, Rohlen reported 40 percent of personnel— most of them women— worked without possibility of promotion.[15] But in U.S. firms, too, non-exempt, or unsalaried, workers, mainly clericals and nearly all of them women, are rarely moved into management. Until recently, at the professional and managerial levels, most firms were single sex organizations.[16] The barriers to women's entry and advancement which have been dismantled to some extent as a result of the post-1960s rights revolution and women's educational attainments in the United States are still firmly in place in large Japanese firms.

A Comparison of Rates of Interfirm and Intrafirm Mobility: Differences in the Concept of Job. Cole's study of job-changing among workers in Detroit and Yokohama uncovered a paradox.[17] Consistent with Japanese permanent employment practices, among workers in Yokohama the rate of interfirm moves among workers was roughly half that of workers in Detroit; but the rate of intrafirm moves was also about half. Controls for age, education, firm size, and industry did not affect the results. The comparatively low rate of intrafirm job changes among Yokohama workers runs counter to the expectation of elaborate internal labor markets in large Japanese firms suggested by Western theories of industrial organization. Why?

A comparison of job descriptions in the United States and Japan makes clear that the concept of job differs, and consequently, the pattern of job changes which typify a career varies between the two countries. In U.S. firms, there tends to be a proliferation of job titles, and workers pursue careers in special-ties.[18] Japanese firms, in contrast, discourage jurisdictional defini-tions of jobs through job rotation and loose contracts, and mute the differentiation between workers and managers by assigning tasks to groups in which first-line foremen are also team members. Moreover, the management/worker wage differential is much smaller in Japan than in the United States. Thus, although large Japanese firms do have internal labor markets, the rights and responsibilities of their employees are not structured around explicit job classifications with standard wage rates to the extent they are in U.S. firms.

The relative weakness of Japanese **unions**, partly a conse-quence of labor's exclusion from national politics before World War II, contributes to a different pattern of wage-setting. Formal recognition of the right to organize, to bargain collectively, and to strike came through the imposition of the 1945 Trade Union Law (modelled after the U.S. Wagner Act) by the American Occupation. Unions then organized on a massive scale; membership increased from 7 percent in 1936 to 36 percent in 1955, and has since stabilized at about one-third of the work force. Union density is higher in Japan than in the United States. More important than union density, however, is the widespread pattern of enterprise unionism (88 percent of all unions in 1959) under which each company has one union and each union is organized within only one company.[19] Consequently, pressures for industry-wide bar-gaining are muted in Japan.

ON THE JOB: WHY DO WORKERS WORK SO HARD?

Consider the paradoxes which arise from surveys of U.S. and Japanese blue-collar workers.[20] Japanese workers report higher levels of identification with the company than do their American counterparts. In a mid-1960s cross-national survey, 10 percent of Japanese workers placed company life above personal life, 60 percent ranked them equally.[21] Indeed, many workers do not take all the vacation time accorded them by law and their rate of absenteeism is quite low. Yet on surveys, they report they would like more free time. Japanese workers score high on items index-ing need for fulfillment at work but indicate relatively low levels of job satisfaction in several cross-national comparisons. Cole's De-troit respondents were more likely than their counterparts in Yo-kohama to report they would take the same job again and would recommend it to a friend.

Cole addresses the paradox of low job satisfaction and high commitment by distinguishing between the commitment to one's firm, one's work team, and the specific tasks of one's job.[22] There is no reason to expect equal commitment in all three spheres; in fact, commitment to the firm or work group may be compatible with dissatisfaction with one's job. Japanese firms encourage commitment through structures and circumstances which create a sense of common fate among their employees. Consider the ways in which the firm does this. Permanent employment practices make exit costly by limiting the availability of alternatives. Substantial bonuses based on company profits tie personal rewards to the success of the firm. Many workers depend on their firm for packaged vacation offers, for housing (in the late 1970s, 6.9 percent of dwellings were company-owned versus 5.8 percent publicly-owned) or housing subsidies, and for pensions which supplement the shortfall of social insurance. In other words, the weakness of public sector spending increases the worker's dependence on the firm. A weak labor movement generally goes hand in hand with limited public assistance and enterprise unions reinforce firm loyalties whereas industrial unions reinforce class politics. Compare the situation in the United States, as observed by Clark Kerr, where strong occupational identity forces a looser relation to the employer, with the situation in Japan where we find that a worker's primary identity is as a member of the firm.[23]

Consider next work teams. In the United States, management assigns tasks to individuals who are held accountable for their completion. In Japan, where tasks are assigned to the work team, integrating the individual into the group in order to complete the tasks has special importance.[24] Japanese team chiefs are considered part of the group, enforcing a reciprocal relationship in which superiors look after the interests of subordinates who work for and with them. Enterprise union practices reinforce the relationship; all regular (blue- and white-collar) employees below the rank of assistant section manager (including first- and second-line supervisors) must join the union when they join the firm. Compared with U.S. unions, enterprise unions provide little opportunity for individual workers to voice grievances.

In short, the Japanese work ethic is not organized around satisfaction with work tasks, but is mobilized by attachments to the firm and to the work group. Workers see the company not just as a place to work but as a community to which they devote their entire lives. Personal identities crystallize within the framework offered by the organization.

The lesson should not be lost when we turn to the United States. For in all industrial economies, many work tasks are intrinsically unsatisfying. In auto assembly, whether in Detroit or Yokohama, most jobs are monotonous, some are dangerous. The contradiction between the imperatives of mass production and the quest for gratifying work plagues modern economies in the West[25] and the East.[26] There is no utopia in Japan or the United States. One reviewer of Cole put it aptly: "I do not think that I could stand working in Toyota Auto Body."[27]

Then why do Japanese workers stay? Because the costs of exit are very high. The gap in wages, benefits, and job security between the upper and lower tiers of Japan's dual labor market is much greater than exists in the United States. Because good jobs in large firms are almost exclusively reserved for young entrants, the worker who leaves faces an almost certain fall in living standard. (Information on the alternative path of self-employment in Japan was not available at the time of this writing.) The permanent employment system, enterprise unionism, and dual labor markets work in combination to put a premium on loyalty; opportunities for exit and for voicing grievances are limited.

BORROWING: QUALITY CIRCLES

A quality circle is a small group of workers (ten on average) within a particular work unit who are taught statistical methods for identifying problems in production (chiefly defects, scrap [amount of wasted materials], rework [reworking doors to fit snugly on cars, for instance], and down-time) and for experimenting with alternative processes.[28] Cost reduction and increased productivity are primary goals, but also important are improvement of working conditions and enhanced morale through opportunities for participation, training, leadership, and recognition of worker achievements. The varying degree to which quality circles (QCs) are prevalent in the United States and Japan is associated with differences in the ways that work is organized in the two societies.

An examination of the use of quality circles is enlightening for three reasons. First, Americans believe that the Japanese are more quality conscious. In a telling experiment, psychologist Srully Blotnik took two identical RCA components, put a Sanyo label on one and asked 900 people to compare them. Seventy-six percent said the "Sanyo" was superior.[29] While expectations sometimes frame false perceptions, they often square with reality, as in Garvin's comparison of makers of room air conditioners.[30] His study of eleven U.S. and seven Japanese plants (representing every Japanese and all but one U.S. manufacturer) showed that assembly-line defects were seventy times greater and warranty service calls seventeen times greater for the products of U.S. manufacturers. The worst Japanese company had a failure rate of less than half that of the best U.S. manufacturer. Second, differing defect rates are associated with cross-national differences in the organization of work, including, of course, reliance on QCs. Indeed, a key strategy in the quest for quality by U.S. manufacturers is to copy Japanese management by introducing QCs. Third, the differing national experiences of borrowing QCs are now well-documented in studies by sociologists and management specialists.[31] I focus on two of their findings: (1) the diffusion of QCs was more rapid and extensive in Japan than in the United States, and (2) QCs were more effectively institutionalized in Japan than in the United States.

Consider first patterns of diffusion. Before World War II, Japanese exports had a reputation for poor quality, quite the opposite of what Blotnik found four decades later. According to Cole, the QC was the most important innovation contributing to improved product quality. The concept originated with the methods of American statisticians, such as William Deming, who went to Japan under the sponsorship of American Occupation officials to teach U.S. industrial standards to Japanese engineers at a time when Japan was struggling to rebuild its industries. Reinforced by 1949 legislation adopting "Japanese Engineering Standards," the ideas of the American advisors were championed by the Japan Union of Scientists and Engineers (JUSE) (founded 1948) and quickly spread by publishers who served the growing demand for translations of books on American management. The Korean War also facilitated the spread of quality control methods; firms which sought military procurement orders had to meet quality standards imposed by the U.S. Department of Defense. By 1964, there were an estimated 6,000 quality circles and by 1978, an estimated half-million, representing one of every eight Japanese employees.[31] In Japan, high-level management groups (particularly the Japanese Federation of Employers' Associations) and the academic-engineering alliance under JUSE fostered the diffusion of QC techniques.

In the United States in contrast, QCs were late in coming and slow to take hold. In 1980, perhaps 100 firms had them, most of which were in aerospace, pharmaceuticals, and hi-tech industries in which high defect rates were not tolerable. The major agencies of diffusion were the American Society for Quality Control, an association of quality control specialists at firms, and the International Association of Quality Circles, which promoted national conferences and conducted training sessions. While well-funded and well-connected national organizations spread the word in Japan, in the United States, QCs were regarded as something of a fad. Introductions occurred quickly,[33] but the record of institutionalizing QCs is mixed. In fact, some firms (e.g., Lockheed Air Missile) discontinued their QCs. Although there is no census of QCs in the United States, it is likely that while their numbers have risen sharply in the past decade, the total is far lower than in Japan.

Cole explains U.S.-Japan differences in the institutionalization of QCs as the consequence of differing macropolitical circumstances.[34] First, in Japan, the combination of a tight labor market in the late 1960s and early 1970s and rising education levels among new entrants who sought white-collar jobs but were assigned monotonous and often demanding factory jobs brought high turnover rates which obliged managers to seek workplace innovations. In the United States, with its large pool of unemployed workers, managers tolerated high turnover rates and turned to industrial engineers to simplify job content. Second, union responses differed. Among U.S. unions (excepting the United Automobile Workers and the Communications Workers of America), there was little support for employee participation which some leaders tagged as a scheme to destroy job control and weaken unions by building ties to management. In Japan, where unions were weaker and did not exercise job control, QCs fit within the historic prerogatives of management and were consistent with the union goal of economic prosperity. Finally, in Japan, top managers acted collectively to ensure the success of QCs, while in the United States, a union-management stalemate and the (not surprising) reluctance of Federal agencies to follow the prescriptions in studies by the Ford Foundation and other advocates of "quality of work life" meant a lack of elite sponsorship. It should be noted that government agencies were not central actors in either country.

While these macropolitical differences help make sense of the differing patterns of diffusion, in my opinion, differences in patterns of industrial organization provide a more convincing explanation for Japan's more effective institutionalization of QCs. Large Japanese firms use subcontractors to a greater extent than United States firms. For example, value-added in production accounts for 46.3 percent of the total value of goods shipped by American manufacturers, compared with 36.2 percent for all Japanese and 29.2 percent for larger Japanese firms.[35] Moreover, the use of standardized and made-to-spec components differ in the two countries. Standardization is more widespread in the United States where many firms incorporate off-the-shelf components into their products at the design stage. Japanese firms, however, rely more on made-to-order goods produced by subcontractors which have close and long-lasting relations with a core firm 64.5 percent of firms doing subcontract work depend on a single core firm for the purchase of over half their output.[36] Many core firms have established cooperative associations made up of their key suppliers (in the case of Toyota Motor, for example, 174 of its 250 primary subcontractors belong to such an association) for the purpose of exchanging information on engineering, production, and quality control. These institutionalized linkages have served as channels for diffusing QCs; in the machine-tool industry, for example, smaller firms were introduced to quality-control techniques by large firms. After these techniques are adopted, subcontractors typically receive continuous guidance from the core firm, making possible regular quality improvements. In the United States, greater turnover among subcontractors and the lack of Japanese-style associations dominated by core firms may explain in part the fact that although QCs are frequently introduced on a trial basis, they are less often institutionalized.

Finally, labor-force policies contribute to differences in receptivity to QCs. Consider Garvin's comparison of air conditioner manufacturers, all of which used a simple assembly-line process and much the same equipment to make a fairly standardized product.[37] Training took about six months at Japanese firms where each assembler was taught to handle all jobs on the line. At American firms, workers were usually trained for one task over a period of from several hours to several days. Before a new model was introduced at Japanese firms, workers learned their new tasks through after-hours seminars and trial runs; American workers received much less information. Staffing patterns also differed. In U.S. firms, the turnover rate was twice and the absenteeism rate was more than triple that in Japanese firms. Several U.S. manufacturers suffered from "bumping," when a layoff in one section of the firm triggered a series of job switches required by union provisions guaranteeing seniority rights. As high-seniority workers who had experience with other products replaced experienced but low-seniority workers, defect rates rose sharply. To my knowledge, the practice of bumping is unknown in Japan. Finally, Japanese firms invested more in catching defective units coming off the line; they employed one inspector for every 7.1 assemblers, compared to one for every 9.5 in U.S. firms. Garvin's description of training and staffing policies in one industry is suggestive of larger national patterns which are related to how readily QCs are accommodated in the two societies.

In sum, international economic competition spurred the cross-national diffusion of quality control methods, including QCs. The different forms of diffusion—by elite business associations in Japan (not the central state) and by professional networks in the United States—are revealing, but they cannot explain why QCs are more effectively institutionalized in Japan. The explanation lies in different patterns of industrial organization. Japan's more effective institutionalization of QCs occurred in two steps: first, they were voluntarily adopted by core firms, which then compelled captive subcontractors likewise to adopt them. The pattern was different in the United States, where core firms are larger and suppliers are coupled to them by market conditions rather than long-standing relationships. Core firms face strong suspicions and/or resistance from unions. Anti-trust laws and the make-or-buy mentality of U.S. managers discourage the transfer of QCs from core firms to suppliers. The consequence for American manufacturers will, I think, be greater reliance on technical solutions to trim costs and reduce defects rather than on the organizational innovations favored by the Japanese.

CONCLUSION

A comparative analysis of industrial structures in the United States and Japan sheds light on what is distinctive about work in America, and at the same time, tempers any tendency to exaggerate their differences.

All modern capitalist societies have many common patterns of industrial organization. In the examples of careers, commitment, and quality circles, we confront time and again the ways that labor-management accords, international competitive pressures, and public entitlements determined organizational forms in Japan and the United States and often with similar results. In fact, these examples are fraught with irony for Americans. Occupation officials played major roles in setting up the structures in which permanent employment, enterprise unionism, and quality circles took shape. In sum, the ways in which the United States helped shape Japan's reindustrialization following World War II are major ingredients in what is distinctive about Japan today.

Americans need to understand Japan, not, as has often been suggested, so that they can borrow work patterns that will enable them to compete, but because Japan has altered world circumstances in ways that profoundly affect the United States. Comparisons with nations in Asia and elswhere are helpful to an understanding of the everchanging world order, which is to a considerable degree a consequence of the postwar policies of the United States.

III. ISSUES FOR DISCUSSION

1. The permanent employment system covers fewer than half of all Japanese workers. How does the exclusion of women from the permanent employment system affect their status and life-chances in Japan? Which U.S. firms practice virtual permanent employment? Is the fate of American women likely to be better under permanent employment practices?

2. Promotion in large Japanese firms depends on a combination of seniority (nenkō) and merit, while in American firms years of service are less important than merit. Which system is likely to be more beneficial to the employee? to the firm? Would it be **desirable** or even **possible** to use the nenkō system in American firms?

3. In industrial economies, many jobs are intrinsically unsatisfying. In Japanese industry, commitment arises through attachments to the work group and to the firm rather than from satisfaction with work tasks. How does this differ from attachments in American workplaces? What practices in the Japanese workplace might it be desirable to introduce in the American workplace?

4. Differences in industrial organization, labor markets, and industrial relations help explain differences in the spread of quality control circles in the United States and Japan. How might these factors influence the borrowing of other Japanese practices such as just-in-time inventory systems? How do differences in the educational systems of these countries influence the prospects for borrowing?

NOTES

1. I am grateful to colleagues and students at Portland State University and Princeton University who asked provocative questions and who shared their knowledge, especially Dai Fujikawa, Kevin Hartzell, Hisako

Matsuo, and John Sutton. I am responsible for any errors.

2. Granovetter, 1984: 330–331.

3. 1982 figures in Granovetter, 1986.

4. See comparative firm size statistics in McMillan, 1985:60.

5. Cole, 1980: 245–47.

6. See Cole, 1979: 60–61 on how to estimate.

7. Rohlen, 1974.

8. Granovetter, 1986.

9. Cole, 1971: 37–40.

10. Cole, 1979: ch. 1.

11. Clark, 1979.

12. See Rohlen, 162, for salary over the life-cycle; Clark, 122–125, on rapid promotion as way to reassert importance of merit.

13. Kalleberg and Lincoln, in press cited in Lincoln and McBride, 1987.

14. Cole, 1979: 130,133.

15. Rohlen, 1974: 136.

16. Kanter, 1979.

17. Cole, 1979.

18. Katherine Stone, in "The Origins of Job Structures in the Steel Industry," *Review of Radical Political Economics* (Summer 1974:113–173) explains specialization as a strategy practiced by U.S. managers to divide workers and fragment class solidarity. Michael Piore and Charles Sabel (*The Second Industrial Divide*, New York: Basic Books, 1984) argue that the elaboration of job titles in American firms is an outcome of union strategies to secure workers' rights and control task assignments. Other factors reinforce American occupational consciousness, especially the strength of professions (law, medicine, etc.), vocationalism in schooling, and the pattern of pursuing careers within occupations across firms and communities.

19. Cole, 1961: 17,225; Woronoff, 1979: 76.

20. Lincoln and McBride, 304–306; Cole, 1979: 230–237.

21. Rohlen, 1974: 16.

22. Cole, 1979: 237ff. 23. See Rohlen, 1974.

24. See account in Kamata, 1982, of his training by other Toyota workers.

25. See Goran Palm, *The Flight from Work*, Cambridge: Cambridge University Press, 1977, on Sweden.

26. See Miklos Haraszti, *A Worker in a Worker's State*, New York: Universe Books, 1978, on Hungary.

27. Stinchcombe, 1981: 1158.

28. See Cole, 1979: 141, 143–155, and cross-national differences in statistical methods in Holusha, 1988.

29. Ellenberger, 1982:7.

30. Garvin, 1983.

31. Cole, 1979: 135ff; 1980, 1985, 1989; Mohr and Mohr, 1983.

32. Cole, 1979: 137; other figures in Cole, 1985: 564.

33. See high rates of trials reported in New York Stock Exchange, 1982.

34. Cole, 1985.

35. Minato, 1989:90–91.

36. Minato, 1989.

37. Garvin, 1983.

IV. SELECTED READINGS

Cole, Robert E. *Work, Mobility, and Participation.* Berkeley: University of California Press, 1979 (faculty and student background). A landmark study of the origins and operations of Japanese internal and external labor markets which addresses the institutionalization of permanent employment, job redesign, and the work ethic using field studies and survey data from the Detroit-Yokohama Comparative Work History Project.

Cole, Robert E. *Strategies for Learning: Small-Group Activities in American, Japanese, and Swedish Industry.* Berkeley: University of California Press, 1989 (faculty background). Cross-national study of the diffusion and adoption of participatory work structures.

Kamata, Satoshi. *Japan in the Passing Lane.* New York: Pantheon, 1982 (student reading). The diary of a left-leaning journalist who spent six months in 1972–73 as a seasonal worker assembling transmissions for Toyota. Ronald Dore's introduction tries to give balance to the account of the policy of speed-up in a firm with a sweetheart union and where workers become comrades in the struggle to meet production targets. Though dated, the book should be read by those who accept uncritically the idea of the Japanese miracle.

Lincoln, James R., and McBride, Kerry. *"Japanese Industrial Organization in Comparative Perspective."* Annual Review of Sociology 13 (1987): 289–312 (faculty background). Useful review of labor markets, internal structure of firms, employee work attitudes, and industrial organization, provoking the question of whether differences can be explained as the result of Japanese exceptionalism.

Rohlen, Thomas P. *For Harmony and Strength: Japanese White-Collar Organization in Anthropological Perspective.* Berkeley: University of California Press, 1974 (student reading). Based on participant-observer study of a provincial bank in 1968–69, the book is dated but stands as a model ethnography of the social organization of Japanese business. Sections on recruitment, promotion, and pay are compelling. Graphs, photos, and figures make it a particularly valuable resource.

ADDITIONAL REFERENCES
(not cited in Selected Readings above)

Clark, Rodney. *The Japanese Company.* New Haven: Yale University Press, 1979.

Cole, Robert E. *Japanese Blue Collar.* Berkeley: University of California Press, 1971.

Cole, Robert E. "Learning from the Japanese: Prospects and Pitfalls." *Management Review,* September (1980): 22–28, 36–42.

Cole, Robert E. "The Macropolitics of Organizational Change: A Comparative Analysis of the Spread of Small-Group Activities." *Administrative Science Quarterly* 30 (1985): 560–585.

Ellenberger, James N. "Japanese Management: Myth or Magic." *American Federationist,* April–June (1982): 3–12.

Garvin, David A. "Quality on the Line." *Harvard Business Review*, September-October (1983): 65–75.

Granovetter, Mark. "Small is Bountiful: Labor Markets and Establishment Size." *American Sociological Review* 49 (1984): 323–324.

Granovetter, Mark. "Japanese Firm Size: A Small Note." *Sociology and Social Research* 71/1 (1986): 27–28.

Holusha, John. "Improving Quality, The Japanese Way." *New York Times*, 20 July 1988.

Kalleberg, Arne, and Lincoln, James R. "The Structure of Earnings Inequality in the US and Japan." *American Journal of Sociology* (1987).

Kanter, Rosabeth M. *Men and Women of the Corporation*. New York: Basic Books, 1979.

McMillan, Charles J. *The Japanese Industrial System*. 2d rev. ed. Berlin: Walter de Gruyter, 1985.

Minato, Tetsuo. "A Comparison of Japanese and American Interfirm Production Systems." In *The U.S. Japanese Economic Relationship: Can it be Improved?* edited by Kichiro Hayashi. New York: New York University Press, 1989.

Mohr, William, and Mohr, Harriet. *Quality Circles*. Addison-Wesley, 1983.

New York Stock Exchange. *People and Productivity*, 1982.

Stinchcombe, Arthur L. Review of Robert E. Cole, *Work, Mobility, and Participation. American Journal of Sociology*, 86 (1981):1155–58.

Woronoff, Jon. *Japan: The Coming Economic Crisis*. Tokyo: Lotus Press, 1979.

Sociology: Japan

Sociology of Work: The Case of Japan

Andrew G. Walder

I. INTRODUCTION: CENTRAL POINTS

After years of media attention, Japanese industrial relations are by now a familiar subject to most Americans. Japan's economic success, and the apparent discipline, skill, and commitment of its work force have become the envy of many industrialized countries. This success has spawned an entire genre of books about Japanese methods of management, many of them are superficial and prescriptive, treating Japanese labor relations as a set of techniques that can be learned and applied to other settings.

While there is considerable debate over the applicability of Japanese labor relations practices to the American context, it is hard to imagine a course today on the sociology of work that does not include a serious treatment of Japan. Japanese practices contrast sharply with those that representatives of American management and labor, as well as many students of labor relations, have long thought of as the natural results of industrial capitalism. Moreover, unlike those of China [*See the essay, "Sociology of Work: The Case of China"*], where the contrasts are even more extreme, Japanese practices are indisputably successful. There is a sizable body of excellent and widely accessible academic writing on Japanese labor relations, most of it completed before the media hype of the 1980s, suitable for a course treatment, that seeks to specify accurately what these practices are. More importantly, these scholarly works have looked behind the stereotypes to determine precisely in what ways Japanese practices differ from American or British practices.

The existing literature on Japan also provides ample material for sociological explanations of **why** Japanese labor relations have evolved in the way they have. Some argue that Japanese practices are due to inherited cultural traditions; some that they reflect Japan's experience as a late developer; others that they reflect rational management and labor strategies given Japan's trajectory of development and conditions prevailing in its labor market.

The case of Japan exhibits the following noteworthy features, which set it off in contrast with more familiar Western patterns:

• Unlike their American counterparts, large Japanese firms strive to protect the jobs of their workers, and tend to view their work forces more like fixed assets than variable complements that can be reduced or expanded with the business cycle.

• Large Japanese firms are able to implement a permanent employment policy because they maintain networks of subcontracting relationships in their supply and assembly processes. When demand contracts and production needs to be curtailed, the cuts take place among the small subcontractors, whose workers are not ensured permanent employment.

• Large Japanese firms rely heavily on internal labor markets in filling positions within the firm. New hires are largely restricted to young graduates who will be trained and gradually promoted within the firm. Firms will not generally go outside to fill the better paying or more senior positions. This means that there are strong incentives for an employee to stay with a firm, and, after spending some years with a company, few attractive opportunities elsewhere.

• The larger Japanese firms provide housing for many of their employees, and try to foster a community atmosphere among recruits by organizing extensive recreational events outside of working hours, especially for white-collar staff.

• Career organization is extensive in Japanese firms. Companies try to foster a sense of career advancement for virtually all of their permanent employees by awarding annual pay increments based on seniority and others based on skill acquisition and continued education and training.

• The system of permanent employment enables Japanese managers to employ various consultative and team management practices designed to foster a sense of cooperation and collective involvement in the business of the firm. These techniques have proved markedly successful, particularly in fostering a commitment to quality.

• In seeking an explanation for these practices scholars have moved from an initial focus on distinctive cultural traditions to a deeper appreciation of the institutional and labor market realities that generated these practices relatively late in the process of industrialization. **These explanations (see conclusion) all deal directly with the most fundamental comparative question in the sociology of work: what are the origins of national diversity in industrial relations?**

II. MAJOR TOPICS

PERMANENT EMPLOYMENT

In the late 1950s and early 1960s, as foreign scholars began to take notice of Japan's emerging postwar labor relations practices, the most noteworthy was permanent employment. The first such observers, for example, James Abegglen in his *Modernization and the Japanese Factory* (1958), saw permanent employment as a manifestation of Japanese cultural traditions. The familistic analogy seemed to suggest the importance of traditional cultural norms, creating a cultural lag due to Japan's relatively late and rapid industrialization.

Later studies, however, established that permanent employment was prevalent only in the larger enterprises, and did not exist in the smaller subcontracting firms. Moreover, historical research would indicate rather clearly that permanent employment did not exist until the postwar period. Prior to the current era, from the earliest stages of Japanese industrialization in the nineteenth century, high rates of turnover much like in the West were common. These observations tended to undermine the simpler cultural interpretations, because similar cultural values would presumably be held by the managers and workers of both small and large firms. Moreover, if traditional cultural norms were primarily responsible for these practices, then one would have expected that they were more, not less, prevalent in earlier stages of industrialization.

These observations did not mean that Japanese cultural values were irrelevant; but rather, that they came into play under conditions determined by labor markets and management and labor strategy. In research conducted during the 1960s and 1970s, additional considerations came to the fore. Shortages of skilled labor, for example, were found to be common among countries coming late to the modernization process, because they employ relatively modern technologies and large-scale operations at an earlier stage of development than did the countries that embarked on modernization earlier. The shortage of skilled labor in an overwhelmingly rural society led to a management strategy of training and retaining skilled labor.

Another factor that contributed to permanent employment was that since the war most important Japanese industrial sectors have been growth, not cyclical, sectors. Japan's trajectory of rapid growth through exports throughout the postwar period meant that few of its industries have had to cope with the cyclical downturns long characteristic of such established American industries as automobiles and steel which did not depend on exports. When growth is more or less continuous, managers can afford to guarantee permanent employment and careers to a core of the most important employees; in cyclical industries, this is not economically feasible. Critics argue that Japanese industry, given its phenomenal postwar export drive, has yet to face the kind of downturn that will keenly test its commitment to permanent employment.

Finally, labor relations in Japan and in the United States are historically different. In the overpopulated Japanese countryside, where there was a large reserve of unskilled labor, workers' movement stressed job security as their primary goal. In the United States, with its prior tradition of industrial craft production, the labor movement focused first on control of the labor process, and then on pay rates and the definition of newly specialized tasks. The historical interaction of management and labor strategies in each country has played a major role in shaping these different systems, as labor historian Andrew Gordon and others have shown.

INDUSTRIAL DUALISM

The practice of permanent employment is made possible, as suggested above, by a sharply dualistic pattern of employment and benefits. A primary sector of large companies employs workers on a generally permanent basis and supplies them with an array of benefits. They also employ temporary or part-time workers, who are distinct from the permanent employees and do not get the same benefits. A secondary sector of smaller firms which serve primarily as subcontractors for large manufacturers, provide permanent employment to a lesser degree, depending upon the current business situation of their firms. The practice of permanent employment is an expression of one of the important features of Japanese industrial organization— the tight web of associations and alliances among large and small firms alike. These interdependent but unequal subcontracting relationships entail a number of economic benefits for the large firm, the most important, in the context of this essay, being that they cushion its labor force from fluctuations in the demand for its product, and allow it to maintain its core of permanent employees even in times of difficulty.

INTERNAL LABOR MARKETS

An important counterpart to permanent employment in large firms is the prevalence of internal labor markets, which are probably more highly developed in Japan than in any other industrialized country in the world. To an extent that surpasses that of large unionized American firms, Japanese firms rely very heavily, and in some areas almost exclusively, upon the recruitment each year of cohorts of young graduates. Since exits from a company are rare, openings are filled by promotion from within the firm. In general, Japanese firms greatly prefer filling jobs with "their own people," and look with suspicion upon a person who would be willing to forsake his or her employer for another.

This has important consequences for employee commitment to the firm. First, those recruited each year go through a rather rigorous process of group socialization and training in which both job skills and identification with the company are stressed. Company retreats, competitions, banners and songs are some of the more obvious aspects of this process.

Second, these cohorts of recruits proceed up the ladder of promotion together. Managers generally try to avoid promoting members of one cohort to higher positions than members of more senior cohorts. Even blue-collar workers are given a sense of career progression in the seniority system.

Third, these practices, coupled with a firm's reluctance to hire from outside, means an employee with several years' work experience with one company will find few attractive alternatives in the job market. To an extent that is uncommon elsewhere, Japanese employees become dependent upon their companies for their future livelihood, and the commitment is cemented. While the lack of free choice amounts to a subtle form of economic coercion, these conditions have generated a striking degree of employee commitment to and identification with the firm.

PATERNALISM

Japanese managers tend to treat that permanent part of their labor force with a kind of industrial paternalism. More so than is common among their Western counterparts, the Japanese company satisfies a wide range of employee needs and becomes an important focus of the employee's life. In a country where housing is expensive, in short supply, cramped and of low quality by Western standards, the provision of housing is one of the more valued benefits of employment with a large firm. Companies also organize extensive after-hours recreational, travel, and sports activities for employees, and place great stress on high rates of participation. Especially for white-collar workers, informal pressures to socialize after-hours in bars with coworkers and immediate supervisors can be intense; the Japanese company man spends a considerable amount of time away from home at these obligatory social affairs.

Managers consciously cultivate the image of the company as a family. Meetings, speeches, even rallies are common ceremonial activities designed to create a sense of a collective community. Managers consult extensively with subordinates before coming to decisions. Whether the decisions are unilateral or not, the goal is to have them seem to be consensual so as to gain the commitment of the group as a whole.

CONSULTATIVE MANAGEMENT

Many of the employment practices in a Japanese company might seem to be largely ceremonial and perhaps superficial, but they have proven very effective in gaining the commitment of employees to management goals. The most famous example is that of quality control circles, which are established in firms in order to involve each employee in the company goal to produce a high quality product. This practice has been credited for much of the Japan's success in certain industrial sectors.

In a quality control circle, a group of employees will be assigned to solve a specific problem. They will meet repeatedly to study and discuss the problem, take up and try out suggestions; some members go back to basic textbooks and upgrade their knowledge and skills. Eventually a solution will be presented to management for possible adoption. The circles combine production, technical, and supervisory personnel in a cooperative effort to solve problems that face the firm as a whole and, indirectly, enhance the welfare of all of the members of the company.

This approach to small group management is made feasible by the position of the Japanese employee in the firm. The company's permanent commitment to the employee helps generate loyalty to the firm that is expressed to in active group participation. The relatively loose conception of an employee, who is seen not primarily as an occupant of a specialized production slot at a specified rate of pay, but as a member of the company with a certain level of experience and seniority, also contributes to the success of these practices. The strength of the internal labor market in Japanese companies gives their employees a sense of career progression, although it robs them of attractive job alternatives elsewhere. This latter point has prompted many academic observers to argue that popular calls to emulate Japanese management techniques are not likely to work in American industry without the underlying labor relations practices that appear to make them possible.

EXPLANATIONS FOR THE DIFFERENCES

There has been a tendency in popular and to some extent in scholarly writings to idealize Japanese labor relations. But Japanese practices are not monolithic; they vary considerably according to sector and to company. Moreover, they have been evolving continuously in the postwar period. Take, for example, the seniority system: no sooner had it been described as uniquely Japanese than companies began to modify the once exclusive stress on seniority by introducing job differentials and skill examinations. Nor are all the practices uniquely Japanese; some of them seem distinctive only when placed against stereotypes of American practices (indeed, internal labor markets are also prevalent in certain American firms and sectors). Scholars of Japan have had to sort through a range of stereotypes to come to an accurate comparative assessment of what is distinctively Japanese.

This effort has gone hand in hand with the task of providing explanations for the differences in the two systems that one has established as genuine. There are several schools of interpretation, presented here roughly in the chronological order in which they enjoyed popularity among scholars.

Culturalist Interpretations. This interpretation, first presented by James Abegglen and heavily influenced by structural- functionalism and related modernization theories, saw Japanese employment practices as a reflection of traditional cultural values. These values were presumed to persist in a society that had been isolated from the outside world for long periods, that had developed rapidly, and whose recently urbanized population was still affected by rural values. Implicit in this perspective is the notion that Japanese practices are not fully modern, and therefore will fade away as modernization proceeds.

Functional Alternatives of Development. In his early work, Robert Cole argued that Japanese practices were simply an alternative to those that evolved in the West and that they were just as functional in terms of modernization and industrial efficiency. He argued further that they represented a melding of Japanese traditions with the conditions of industrial growth, and cannot be expected to fade away as modernization proceeds.

The Late Developer Hypothesis. According to Ronald Dore, late development entailed a more rapid process of growth that placed a greater demand upon the supply of skilled labor earlier in the industrialization process, which in turn led to a managerial strategy that sought to train and retain workers, leading eventually to permanent employment. One interesting twist to this interpretation is his claim, in *British Factory–Japanese Factory*, that the Japanese practices are in fact more "modern," than those in the West. He observes some convergence in Great Britain toward the Japanese model.

The Labor Market Interpretation. As presented in the work of Japanese labor economists, represented in the United States by Koji Taira, and in the later work of Robert Cole, this viewpoint holds that Japanese labor relations practices are economically rational managerial strategies that evolved under different economic conditions from those in the United States. According to this point of view, the traditional familistic patina that managers attempt to place over these practices are simply part of the public relations effort to ensure their acceptance.

The Historical Interpretation. As sketched out in the later work of Robert Cole, and substantiated in such recent historiographical studies as Andrew Gordon's *The Evolution of Labor Relations in Japan* (1986), and Sheldon Garon's *State and Labor in Modern Japan* (1988), this perspective emphasizes the interaction of conditions in labor markets in different historical periods, the evolution of management strategy in tandem with state policy, and the aspirations of union strategy in the Japanese context, as the determinants of Japan's labor practices.

III. ISSUES FOR DISCUSSION

1. In what ways do the hiring and reward practices of Japanese firms differ from those of American firms? Are Japanese firms invariant in this regard?

2. Some people argue that Japanese labor relations are the product of traditional Japanese culture; others that they emerged out of the peculiar labor market conditions and corresponding management strategies of Japan's economic history. What is the evidence for either proposition?

3. In view of writing about Japan, what factors would you argue determine the main features of any country's pattern of labor relations?

IV. SELECTED READINGS

Cole, Robert E. *Japanese Blue-collar: The Changing Tradition.* Berkeley: University of California Press, 1970 (student and faculty reading). Readable and scholarly account of industrial dualism, permanent employment, and employee obligation that reexamines theories of convergence.

Cole, Robert E. *Work, Mobility, and Participation: A Comparative Study of American and Japanese Industry.* Berkeley: University of California Press, 1979 (faculty background). More systematic analytical and statistical examination of many of the themes raised in the above work; places the Japanese case in the center of discussions about segmented and internal labor markets, mobility, and careers.

Dore, Ronald. *British Factory–Japanese Factory: The Origins of National Diversity in Industrial Relations.* Berkeley: University of California Press, 1973 (faculty background). Lengthy comparison of two pairs of Japanese and British companies, matched for comparability in size and product. Clearly specifies the Japanese traits, and presents a "late developer" hypothesis, contending that Japanese practices are the result of Japan's late start in modernization.

Gordon, Andrew. *The Origins of Industrial Relations in Japan: Heavy Industry, 1870–1950.* Cambridge: Harvard East Asia Monographs,

1986 (student reading). Definitive historical work showing that contemporary Japanese management practices coalesced only in the postwar period, and are not the result of management and labor traditions that extend back to the beginnings of industrialization.

Marsh, Robert, and Hiroshi, Mannari. *Modernization and the Japanese Factory.* Princeton: Princeton University Press, 1978 (faculty background). Tests a number of common generalizations about work in Japanese factories, through sustained analysis of extensive survey data. Questions a number of assumptions about Japanese uniqueness, in part by noting significant variations within Japan, and argues that there has been considerable convergence with Western organization in a number of respects.

Rohlen, Thomas P. *For Harmony and Strength: Japanese White Collar Organization in Anthropological Perspective.* Berkeley: University of California Press, 1974 (student reading). Vivid and readable description of the life of Japanese bank employees.

Other books mentioned in text:

Abegglen, James. *The Japanese Factory: Aspects of Its Social Organization.* Glencoe, IL: Free Press, 1958.

Garon, Shelden. *The State and Labor in Modern Japan.* Berkeley: University of California Press, 1987.

Taira, Koji. *Economic Development & the Labor Market in Japan.* New York: Columbia University Press, 1970.

Sociology:
Vietnam

Comparative
Revolution:
The Case of
Vietnam

Andrew G. Walder

I. INTRODUCTION: CENTRAL POINTS

Vietnam's seven-year revolt against the French colonial regime
and later the North's struggle against the American-supported
regime of South Vietnam provide, as does the Chinese revolution,
a prototype of protracted guerrilla warfare. A small and poor
country with ill-equipped forces was able to engage two of the
world's greatest military powers and force them, morally and politically debilitated, into ignominious retreat. How could such a
small and poor nation ultimately defeat two vastly superior economic and military machines? In addressing this question, social
scientists have generally focused on two considerations. The first
has to do with the sources of the extraordinary will to fight and
endure sacrifice on the part of the Communist armies and the
populations under their administration. This has entailed a debate about the nature of the traditional peasant village, its transformation in the modern era, and the sources of mass support for
Communist guerrilla movements. The second deals with the organizational ability of the Communists in maintaining discipline
and deploying their forces against a technologically superior enemy.
Whether taught thematically or on a case-by-case basis a course on

revolution could be enriched by a consideration of Vietnam.

• What social processes in the rural Third World in the post-World War II era bred the kind of powerful peasant movements that culminated in Vietnam's revolution?

• What is the appeal of Communist parties to the peasantry, and why are the governments that communist movements challenge often unable to maintain popular support?

• What role does organization and strategy play in enabling a revolutionary movement to defeat a economically and militarily superior opponent? What are the specific features of effective organization and strategy, and why are they effective?

II. MAJOR TOPICS

CLASS ANALYSIS

One important explanation for revolution— in fact, the oldest in the social sciences— is that revolution gives form to the struggle of social classes. In Leninist terminology, the peasantry in the contemporary Third World represent the proletariat of a world imperialist system. As the working classes of the advanced capitalist countries enjoy higher wages and succumb to "bourgeois" reformism, the proletarians of the Third World become the revolutionary force that will overthrow world capitalism.

Leninist class analysis completes the circle of Marx's original predictions about the revolutionary potential of working classes in advanced capitalist countries. It also helps provide Third World socialists and nationalists who attach themselves to the Communist camp with a coherent world view and political identity. But Leninist class analysis is more a broad world view than a social science theory. Other than claiming that peasants rebel because they are the exploited poor of the world capitalist system, it says little about the specific social processes that lead them to rebel at some times and places but not others (aside from the oft-repeated argument for a revolutionary Leninist party and army).

Jeffery Paige's *Agrarian Revolution*, which includes a lengthy case study of Vietnam, elaborates a general theory of rural class conflict that is both precise and sophisticated. Paige argues that the significant rural social movements of the postwar period have emerged in the commodity exporting countries that have become so prevalent in the Third World. He notes that agricultural production is organized in many different ways in these countries, and that rural social classes and rural class conflicts are defined by the kind of agricultural enterprise that spawned them. Not all rural class conflicts have the potential to generate a socialist revolution of the Vietnamese type.

Paige argues that rural social classes may be distinguished according to the sources of their income: cultivators (peasants and agricultural wage laborers) derive their income predominantly from either land or wages; noncultivators (landlords and agrarian capitalists) from either land or capital. Different combinations of income sources for cultivators and noncultivators breed rural class conflicts of widely varying types, and with differing degrees of ferocity. Noncultivators who derive their income from capital can accommodate demands from below by investing to increase productivity; those who derive their income from land, a fixed asset, cannot afford to compromise.

When the cultivating class derives its income from rights to land, and when noncultivators derive theirs from capital, one has a **small-holding system** in which freeholding peasants must deal with creditors and merchants in rural towns; their struggles are likely to be over terms of credit and marketing arrangements. The characteristic rural political movement is a commodity reform movement in which peasants demand reforms in the banking and wholesale distribution systems.

When cultivators derive their income from wages and noncultivators from capital, one has a **plantation system**. Noncultivators run their holdings as a capitalist enterprise, investing in fixed capital improvements that can boost productivity. They can often afford to buy off workers' movements with increased profits. The characteristic political action here is a labor reform movement, in which rural wage laborers fight for improved wages and working conditions.

When both cultivators and noncultivators derive their income from land, the system is similar to that of the **haciendas** of Latin America. Here, noncultivators are not entrepreneurs; they earn fixed rents from fixed landholdings. They allocate marginal plots of land to cultivators in return for labor services on their estates. These rural upper classes, unable to compromise in economic conflicts, establish harshly repressive regimes in their localities. But under certain circumstances, and when local oligarchies are weakened, peasants rise up suddenly and massively to dismember large estates and redistribute the land. These land grabs, however, do not constitute revolutionary movements, for once the peasants have attained landownership, their political activity ceases, and if these new arrangements become permanent, they evolve into a small-holding system.

Agrarian revolution, either socialist or nationalist in nature, occurs only when rural cultivating classes derive their income from wages, and rural upper classes from land. One such prototypical form is the decentralized sharecropping system of rice agriculture in Southeast Asia. Here, rural upper classes derive their income from a fixed asset, land, which they turn over to cultivators to work. If they give in to the demands of peasants, their income is directly diminished. The cultivator's wage represents the difference between his income from the land and his rent to the landlord. The risk of bad harvests is borne by the cultivator, who in poor years often goes into debt to pay rent. Moreover, in decentralized sharecropping systems, tenant farmers are not directly under the supervision of landlords, and they are in close proximity to many others of their class who are in an identical position. Rice sharecropping is thus a kind of rural agricultural enterprise that can generate class conflicts that lead to powerful revolutionary movements.

Paige argues that the Mekong Delta of southern Vietnam, the heartland of Vietnam's rice exporting economy, was the seed bed for rural revolution in Vietnam (he also notes that the Chinese Communists' earliest successes were in the rice sharecropping regions of southern China). Rice sharecropping, he claims, generates the only kind of rural class conflict capable of sustaining a massive revolutionary effort. Rural upper classes and their government cannot afford to compromise; and the easily mobilized peasants are unwilling to do so. Paige attributes the revolution in Vietnam to the unusual motivation of these tenant farmers, who provided an inexhaustible supply of recruits for the Communist guerrillas.

THE MORAL ECONOMY OF PEASANT REVOLUTIONS

While Paige paints a static picture of post-World War II agricultural enterprise and the accompanying class conflicts, others have pointed to the disruptive effects that the transition from subsistence to export agriculture (or commodity production) reputedly has upon the nature of the rural community as the key to understanding revolutions such as Vietnam's. James Scott, in *The Moral Economy of the Peasant*, elaborates an explanation of rural social change and the origins of revolution based upon research into several Southeast Asian nations, including Vietnam.

Scott argues that the traditional village had a hardy subsistence ethic and was a relatively closed, corporate structure. This corporate village prepared for bad harvests by maintaining several kinds of insurance mechanisms: village granaries to which the wealthier citizens contributed; flexible rents that could be reduced in times of difficulty; kinship organizations that provided relief to the poor members of a lineage; and ties of mutual obligation between rich and poor, landlord and tenant, which were marked by rituals of deference in return for paternalistic largesse and understanding in times of trouble. Scott calls this a "moral economy" and observes that it is defined by norms regarding what is customary and proper, norms that limited exploitation to tolerable levels.

This corporate village, characteristic in the subsistence agricultural hinterlands of the developing world, is disrupted when penetrated by world markets, a phenomenon that became prevalent in the 1920s and 1930s. World markets stimulate a shift to commodity production. With commodity production comes greater risk for the peasant, who begins to grow non-food crops whose prices may fluctuate widely regardless of the local harvest. As a result, rather than producing his own food, he must purchase it in the local market where prices do fluctuate widely depending on harvests. Moreover, those who produce food crops for export markets find that in addition to the risk of bad weather, there is the new risk of world price fluctuations for their commodity. It was this situation, brought about by the world depression of the 1930s, that led to the first round of large-scale peasant uprisings in Asia, which resulted in rural soviet governments in Vietnam and China.

When world markets penetrate an agricultural production system, not only are the peasant's risks greatly multiplied, but traditional village institutions that formerly provided insurance against hard times and excessive exploitation are eroded. When entire areas shift to production of a single commodity crop, bad harvests or crashing world prices leave all in a situation of poverty. But even more importantly, the market turns land into a commodity, and encourages rural elites to view their property as a profitable asset whose income is to be maximized. Village common lands, important for forage and cooking fuel, are closed off and brought under cultivation by the elites. Upper classes begin to neglect their customary village obligations, allowing traditional relief and insurance to lapse, sometimes even leaving their village holdings in the hands of agents who run their financial interests in the countryside while they move to the towns.

The peasant views these changes, which expose him to greater risk and erode the traditional village institutions that not only help to insure him against risk, but also create mutual bonds of obligation and restraint between the rural rich and poor, as violations of the traditional moral economy. In conclusion, these new village realities tend to radicalize the peasantry, resulting in a politically explosive situation.

Through an ironic twist these newly radicalized peasants become prime targets for Communist mobilization. They turn to Communism not because it holds out a new vision of the future, but because it appears to conform to the moral economy of the past to which they seek to return. That is not, of course, the intention of Communist parties, nor is it the way that their subsequent rural policies generally proceed. But in the struggle for power, Communists, with their essentially anti-market and egalitarian message, can count upon the support of masses of peasants whose feelings of injustice are inflamed by the erosion of their traditional way of life through world capitalism.

THE POLITICAL ECONOMY OF PEASANT REVOLUTIONS

A major controversy has been engendered by Samuel Popkin's *The Rational Peasant*, a spirited attack on the moral economy explanation for rural social change and revolution. Popkin argues that the traditional village was not so closed a corporate entity as those who subscribe to the moral economy perspective believe; that its insurance mechanisms did not work with the predictability implied; and that peasants make their economic and political choices in a manner that is much more rational and calculating than implied in assertions about their traditional moral economy.

Popkin's study, focusing on Vietnam, is a broad argument for a "rational actor" view of society and politics, as opposed to an "oversocialized" conception of human beings as motivated by customary norms. In an argument that is too elaborate to reproduce here, he pits his conception of peasant rationality against Scott's notion of subsistence as the overriding peasant concern, claiming that peasants are ever mindful of opportunities to advance, just as they are careful in assessing risk, and that they make decisions regarding cropping patterns, contributions to collective village funds, and support for political movements in the same calculating, rational manner.

Popkin views the spread of world markets also very differently from Scott. In Popkin's interpretation, while world markets present potentially increased risks, they also create opportunities for the many who are willing to take those risks. Markets, in other words, are not disruptive forces in a harmonious peasant world, but present an opportunity to escape from paternalistic domination of the traditional village. Peasant unrest arises when their efforts to avail themselves of these new opportunities are hampered by the local elite who attempt to retain the system of paternalism and monopolize new opportunities for themselves by manipulating and corrupting local government.

Popkin argues that Communists succeed not because of the content of their ideology, but because they are good political entrepreneurs. They provide tax relief, rent reductions, create marketing cooperatives, redistribute land, and reward their adherents in liberated areas preferentially. Unlike the corrupt paternalism of their predecessors, initially they provide impartial, effective, and noncorrupt government. Popkin buttresses his argument by pointing out that by providing these same benefits, a Catholic-inspired religious movement, the Hoa Hao, was able to control large areas of Vietnamese territory and mobilize vast numbers of peasants during the same period of the Communists' initial success in the 1930s. He interprets peasant revolution not as a reaction against market capitalism and an effort to return to a traditional social order, but as a product of emerging political competence on the part of peasants who seek escape from the oppressive paternalism of the past.

ORGANIZATION AND STRATEGY

Popkin's emphasis on organization and political strategy as a key to Communist success is supported in Jeffrey Race's *War Comes to Long An*, a lucid and compelling case study of how the countryside was lost to the Communists in one South Vietnamese province. But where Popkin deals almost exclusively with the peasant village and underlying social conditions, Race focuses on Communist strategy and conduct of political struggle.

Race argues that the Communists won the war because they gained the support of the population right out from under the existing local government. They were able to do so because they had a carefully articulated strategy that saw the war as fundamentally a political, not a military contest, whereas the South Vietnamese regime pursued only a military strategy.

The Vietcong (Vietnamese Communists) fought the war by quietly building up political forces in the countryside, while avoiding direct military confrontation until the balance of political forces was so far in their favor as to almost guarantee success. The Vietcong did not declare areas liberated, but established underground village governments, all traces of which disappeared when authorities of official government arrived. They selectively offered an array of incentives to their supporters: rent relief, tax relief, land redistribution, protection from the draft; they selectively reduced benefits to those who did not actively support them; they assassinated collaborators and informers. Government troops and police could get the population to inform only by terrorizing them. This created sympathy for the enemy, into whose arms the people were driven for protection (the best protection for young men was to join the Vietcong army). The Vietcong's strategy, moreover, was "bottom-up". Its cadres were in or near the villages and were directly involved in village affairs. They actually carried out the reforms they promised. The regime in the South, on the other hand, employed a "top-down" strategy: its edicts were passed down through successive levels of government. Provincial officials visited villages in motorcades, and organized elaborate public displays of Confucian concern for the popular welfare. But once the rally was over, the implementation of such village policies as land reform was left to local leaders—those who owned the land that was to be redistributed. Moreover, South Vietnam's land reform required peasants to pay landlords for the land they were allocated, thereby creating instantly a class of debtors. The Communists, in contrast, gave them the same land outright.

The Communists won, according to Race, because they had a sophisticated political strategy and organization at the grass roots to carry it out. Their organization provided tangible benefits on a selective basis, and punished severely and swiftly those who betrayed it. The government in South Vietnam, in contrast, which was without a political strategy, without effective grass roots government, and offered a few incentives to peasantry, used military means that succeeded only in driving the rural population toward the Communists.

More recent revisionist interpretations of the war in Vietnam argue that while Race's analysis is certainly correct as applied to the situation in the early and mid-1960s, the Vietcong leadership miscalculated the balance of political forces and suffered disastrous losses in the Tet offensive of 1968. They point out that from that time forward the war against the South Vietnamese government and its American supporters was largely carried out by regular North Vietnamese troops who infiltrated the South. In this view, it was North Vietnamese political determination, and American loss of heart, that sealed the outcome. If one accepts Race's analysis, however, it is hard to understand what could have made the South Vietnamese regime a viable government at the local level.

This array of contrasting and lucid social science explanations provide rich material for a course on the causes of revolution. Some, like Paige's and Scott's, stress rural social conditions and peasant motivation to the virtual exclusion of political organization and strategy; others, like Race's, focus on political organization and strategy, while ignoring underlying social conditions and patterns of change. The richness and variety of ideas and historical material about for this momentous revolution, which is also such an important part of recent American history, provide an excellent subject for classroom discussion and debate.

III. ISSUES FOR DISCUSSION

Instructors are referred to the questions at the conclusion of section I of the paper. These may be useful in prompting class discussion.

IV. SELECTED READINGS

Paige, Jeffery M. *Agrarian Revolution: Export Agriculture and Political Movements in the Developing World*. New York: The Free Press, 1975 (faculty background). Analytically sophisticated class analysis of the causes of various kinds of rural social movements. One of the long case studies is Vietnam.

Popkin, Samuel L. *The Rational Peasant: The Political Economy of Rural Society in Vietnam*. Berkeley: University of California Press, 1979 (faculty background). Lively critique of the "moral economy" perspective. Argues that peasants rebel not because they seek to restore traditional community, but because they seek to escape oppression by traditional elites. Political entrepreneurship, organization, and incentives, however, are essential in allowing peasants to act.

Race, Jeffrey. *War Comes to Long An: Revolution in a Vietnamese Province*. Berkeley: University of California Press, 1974 (student reading). Historically focused, readable account of how the government of South Vietnam lost the war in one rural province long before its eventual military defeat. Vivid account of Vietcong strategy and organization that portrays rural revolution as a contingent political process, not as an outcome of underlying social variables.

Scott, James. *The Moral Economy of the Peasant: Subsistence and Rebellion in Southeast Asia*. New Haven: Yale University Press, 1977 (faculty background). Classic exposition of the "moral economy" perspective: modern peasants rebel because world markets penetrate the countryside, disrupting traditional community and subsistence guarantees, pushing peasants into mass poverty and revolutionary movements.

Truong Van Linh. *A Vietcong Memoir*. New York: Vintage, 1986 (student reading). A vivid and dramatic personal account of an underground revolutionary from Saigon. Presents convincing insights into revolutionary organization, the weaknesses of the South Vietnamese regime, motivations of participants, and North Vietnamese political strategy.

Index

Contributors

Benedict R. O'G. Anderson is Aaron L. Binenkorb Professor of International Studies at Cornell University and director of the Cornell Modern Indonesia Project. His published works include *Java in a Time of Revolution* (1972); *Imagined Communities: Reflections on the Origins and Spread of Nationalism* (1983); *In the Mirror: Literature and Politics in Siam in the American Era* (1985); and *Language and Power: Exploring Political Cultures in Indonesia* (1990).

Lawrence A. Babb is professor of anthropology at Amherst College. He is the author of *The Divine Hierarchy* (1975) and *Redemptive Encounters* (1986), books dealing with various aspects of the Hindu tradition. His current research is on popular Jainism.

Theodore C. Bestor is associate professor of anthropology and a member of the East Asian Institute at Columbia University. Before joining Columbia's faculty, he was the program director for Japanese and Korean studies at the Social Science Research Council. He has spent over seven years in Japan. His first book, *Neighborhood Tokyo* (1989), received the Arisawa Memorial Award for Japanese studies from the American Association of University Presses and the Robert E. Park Award for urban studies from the American Sociological Association. Bestor's second book *Tokyo's Marketplace*, focuses on the Tsukiji wholesale fish market as a case study in the social and cultural context of economic organization in contemporary Japan.

John R. Bowen received his Ph.D. in anthropology from the University of Chicago in 1984, after fieldwork in Sumatra and Sulawesi, Indonesia. He has taught at Harvard University and is now associate professor of anthropology and chair of Social Thought and Analysis at Washington University in St. Louis. Bowen is the author of *Sumatran Politics and Poetics: Gayo History, 1990–1989*, a forthcoming book on Sumatran forms in Islam, and articles on religion, social structure, poetic performance, and political discourse.

Paul R. Brass is professor of political science and South Asian studies at the University of Washington. His publications include *The Politics of India Since Independence* (1990), *Ethnic Groups and the State* (1985), and, with Francis Robinson, *The Indian National Congress and Indian Society, 1885–1985: Ideology, Social Structure, and Political Dominance* (1987).

Myron L. Cohen is professor of anthropology at Columbia University, where he is also affiliated with the East Asian Institute. He has done fieldwork in north, east and west China, and in Taiwan. He is author of *House United, House Divided: The Chinese Family in Taiwan* (1976) and articles on Chinese family organization, kinship and community relationships, religion, social change, and national identity.

Stephen Philip Cohen holds a joint appointment as professor in the departments of political science and history and in the program in South and West Asian studies at the University of Illinois. Co-founder of the university's program in arms control, he is the author or editor of six books dealing with South Asia, including *The Indian Army* (1971) and *The Pakistan Army* (1984). Professor Cohen was president of the Midwest Conference on Asian Affairs in 1989–90.

Joseph W. Elder is professor of sociology and South Asian studies at the University of Wisconsin-Madison. He has spent eight years in India studying, teaching, conducting research and producing documentary films. He is editor and part-author of *Lectures in Indian Civilization* (1970) and the two-volume *Chapters in Indian Civilization* (1970) and author of "Society" in *India Briefing*, Marshall M. Bouton, ed. (1987). He is currently president of the American Institute of Indian Studies, the major funding institution for American scholars doing research in India.

Thomas B. Gold is chair of the Center for Chinese Studies and associate professor of sociology at the University of California, Berkeley. He is the author of *State and Society in the Taiwan Miracle* (1986) and several articles on the revival of private business in the People's Republic of China.

Helen Hardacre, Reischauer Institute Professor of Japanese Religions and Society at Harvard University, specializes in the modern religions of Japan, especially the new religions. She is author of *Lay Buddhism in Contemporary Japan: Reiyūkai Kyōdan* (1984),

Kurosumikyô and the New Religions of Japan (1986), and *Shintô and the State: 1868-1988* (1989).

Robert W. Hefner is associate professor of anthropology and associate director of the Institute for the Study of Economic Culture at Boston University. He is the author of *Hindu Javanese: Tengger Tradition and Islam* (1985) and *The Political Economy of Mountain Java: An Interpretive History* (1990), as well as numerous articles on culture and politics in Indonesia.

Hiroshi Ishida is an associate professor of sociology and a member of the East Asian Institute, Columbia University. His recent research focuses on the structure of inequality in contemporary Japan and the linkage between the educational system and the labor market in Japan, the United States, and Europe. He is the author of *Social Mobility in Contemporary Japan* (1992).

Doranne Jacobson is an anthropologist who has conducted extensive research in India over the course of more than two decades. She received her Ph.D. from Columbia University and is the author of *Women in India: Two Perspectives* (1977) and more than two dozen articles focusing on the roles of women in South Asia. Her photographs have appeared in numerous publications and exhibits around the world. She is currently director of International Images in Springfield, Illinois.

William W. Kelly is professor of anthropology at Yale University. He has been doing fieldwork in a region in northern Japan since 1976, and is the author of several books and articles on Japanese local society and regional economy. He has recently contributed "Finding a Place in Metropolitan Japan: Postwar Transpositions of Everyday Life," to Andrew Gordon, ed., *Postwar Japan as History* (forthcoming).

Laurel Kendall, who holds a doctorate in anthropology from Columbia University, is associate curator in charge of Asian Ethnographic Collections at the American Museum of Natural History. She is the author of *Shamans, Housewives and Other Restless Spirits* (1985) and *The Life and Hard Times of a Korean Shaman* (1988) as well as co-editor of volumes on Korean women and on religion and ritual in Korean society. Her research interests include ritual, biography, gender, contemporary matrimony, medicine, and various combinations thereof. She first went to Korea in 1970 as a Peace Corps volunteer.

Han-Kyo Kim is professor of political science, University of Cincinnati, where he teaches courses in East Asian politics including

Korea. He co-authored *Korea and the Politics of Imperialism* (1967), edited *Studies on Korea: A Scholar's Guide* (1980), and has recently completed a book length manuscript including translations of significant source materials in the modern history of Korea.

Carl H. Lande is professor of political science and East Asian studies at the University of Kansas. Specializing in Philippine politics, he has published extensively on that topic over an extended period of years. He is managing editor of *Pilipinas: A Journal of Philippine Studies*.

Robert C. Liebman is associate professor of sociology and international studies at Portland State University. He has taught at the University of Michigan, where he earned his Ph.D. in sociology and history, and at Princeton University.

Owen M. Lynch is Charles F. Noyes Professor of Urban Anthropology at New York University. He is the author of *The Politics of Untouchability* (1969) and editor of *Divine Passions: The Social Construction of Emotion in India* (1990) and *Culture and Community in Europe* (1984), as well as author of numerous articles on Indian urban life, untouchability, pilgrimage and emotions.

Moni Nag is senior associate, The Population Council, and adjunct professor of anthropology, Columbia University. He worked for the Anthropological Survey of India, Calcutta, from 1948 to 1965 and taught in the department of anthropology and division of sociomedical sciences of Columbia University from 1966 until assuming his present position in 1976. His main interest is in the socioeconomic and cultural aspects of demographic and health behavior. Among his publications are "Factors Affecting Human Fertility in Nonindustrial Societies" (*Yale University Publications in Anthropology No. 66*, 1962) and the collection *Population and Social Organization* (1965).

Andrew J. Nathan is professor of political science and director of the East Asian Institute at Columbia University and author of *Chinese Democracy* (1986) and *China's Crisis* (1990).

Clark D. Neher is professor of political science and associate of the Center for Southeast Asian Studies at Northern Illinois University. He has written extensively on politics in Southeast Asia, particularly regarding Thailand and the Philippines. His books include *Politics in Southeast Asia* (1987), *Modern Thai Politics* (1979), and *Southeast Asia in the New International Era* (1991).

Jean C. Oi is associate professor of government, Harvard University. She is author of *State and Peasant in Contemporary China:*

The Political Economy of Village Government (1989) and various articles on rural politics.

T.J. Pempel is professor of political science, adjunct professor of business, and director of the Center for Comparative Politics at the University of Colorado, Boulder. He was on the faculty at Cornell University, 1972–1991, where, from 1980 to 1985, he was director of the East Asian program. He has received research grants from the Fulbright Commission, the National Endowment for the Humanities, the Japan Foundation, and the National Science Foundation, among others, for research concentrated primarily on Japanese politics and economics. He is author of eight books and several dozen articles, including "Corporatism Without Labor: The Japanese Anomaly?" in Philippe C. Scmitter and Gerhard Lehmbruch, eds., *Trends Towards Corporatist Intermediation* (1979), "The Unbundling of 'Japan, Inc.' " in the *Journal of Japanese Studies* 13, no. 2 (1987), and *Policy and Politics in Japan: Creative Conservatism* (1982). Most recently he was editor of *Uncommon Democracies: The One Party Dominant Regimes* (1990).

Thomas G. Rawski ia a professor of economics and history at the University of Pittsburgh, where he teaches courses on the economies of China and Japan. His recent publications include "Japan as Number One, but for How Long?" *Nihon no teiryū Undercurrent* 1 (1983):1–12; "Productivity Change in Chinese Industry, 1953–1985," *Journal of Comparative Economics* 12 (1988):570–591 (with four co-authors); *Economic Growth in Prewar China* (1989). He is contributor and co-editor of *Chinese History in Economic Perspective* (1991).

Nancy Rosenberger is an assistant professor, department of anthropology, at Oregon State University specializing in the study of gender and concepts of self in Japan as they relate to the state, medical institutions, and the media. Her articles have appeared in journals such as *Ethos, Anthropological Quarterly,* and *Social Sciences and Medicine,* and in edited volumes, including *Japanese Sense of Self,* Nancy Rosenberger, ed. (1992).

Stephen R. Smith is a graduate of Columbia University, where he received a Ph.D. in anthropology and a Certificate of East Asian Studies from the East Asian Institute. His doctoral research was on alcohol use and abuse in Japan. He is assistant professor of anthropology in the department of sociology at Wittenberg University, Springfield, Ohio.

Andrew G. Walder is professor of sociology at Harvard University.

He is the author of *Communist Neo-Traditionalism: Work and Authority in Chinese Industry* (1986).

Edwin A. Winckler is a research associate at the East Asian Institute of Columbia University in New York City. He studies East Asian development in comparative and theoretical perspective. His publications include *Contending Approaches to the Political Economy of Taiwan* (1988), co-edited with his wife Susan Greenhalgh. He is currently completing a sequel analyzing the interaction of political-economic and socio-cultural processes in Taiwan's postwar development.